Reporting Made Easy

Commonly Used Reports

Illustrations and Perspectives

Release 4.0B

SAP Labs, Inc.
Palo Alto, California

Copyright

© 1999 by SAP AG. All rights reserved.

Neither this documentation nor any part of it may be copied or reproduced in any form or by any means or translated into another language, without the prior consent of SAP AG.

SAP AG makes no warranties or representations with respect to the content hereof and specifically disclaims any implied warranties of merchantability or fitness for any particular purpose. SAP AG assumes no responsibility for any errors that may appear in this document. The information contained in this document is subject to change without notice. SAP AG reserves the right to make any such changes without obligation to notify any person of such revision or changes. SAP AG makes no commitment to keep the information contained herein up to date.

Trademarks

SAP, the SAP logo, R/2, R/3, ABAP, and other SAP related products mentioned herein are registered or unregistered trademarks of SAP AG. All other products mentioned in this document are registered or unregistered trademarks of their respective companies.

R/3 Simplification Group
SAP Labs, Inc.
3475 Deer Creek Road
Palo Alto, CA 94304

www.saplabs.com/simple
simplify-r3@sap-ag.de

Printed in the United States of America.
ISBN 1-893570-62-2

This book uses EcoFLEX™ lay-flat binding. With this lay-flat feature—developed by and exclusively available at Johnson Printing Service (JPS)—you can open this book and keep it open without it snapping shut on you. You need not worry about breaking the spine. EcoFLEX makes books like this one easier to use.

Contents at a Glance

About This Guide ix

Financial Accounting—General Ledger Reports 1–1

Financial Accounting—Accounts Receivable Reports.................................... 2–1

Financial Accounting—Accounts Payable Reports 3–1

Controlling—Cost Center Reports.. 4–1

Controlling—Internal Order Reports 5–1

Controlling—Profitability Analysis Reports 6–1

Controlling—Reconciliation Reports.. 7–1

Human Resources Reports.. 8–1

Sales and Distribution Reports 9–1

Materials Management Reports.. 10–1

Plant Maintenance Reports.. 11–1

Production Planning Reports 12–1

Project System Reports 13–1

Quality Management Reports.. 14–1

Warehouse Management Reports... 15–1

Appendix A: Report Documentation Template A–1

Appendix B: List of Sample Reports in this Guide B–1

Appendix C: Glossary C–1

Appendix D: Index D–1

Acknowledgments

The publisher thanks the following individuals who provided time, expertise, and resources to help make the *Reporting Made Easy* series possible.

Julie Beehler and John Huck (Anheuser-Busch, Inc.)

Ron Greenfield, David Jones, and Ben Matteson (Anthro Corporation)

Ann Zediker and Chuck Marx (Arthur Andersen, LLP)

Bruce Scott (BrightStar Information Technology Group, Inc.)

Amy Vorbeck (CCAi, Inc.)

Nancy White (Chevron Corporation)

Tom Eisenhart (Lucent Technologies, Inc.)

Hans Hess (Metamor Enterprise Solutions)

Igor Smelansky and Winnie Chang (Network Associates)

Erin Andrews (PricewaterhouseCoopers LLP)

Mohamad Hakim (Softline, Inc.)

Clare Carver (The Pair Group)

Margie Coolidge, Ron Giovannelli, and Patrick Zalamea (Ziatech Corporation)

Pamela Anderson and Robert Smith (publishing consultants)

Werner Aigner, Simone Baeumer, Tami Becker, Randi Bethel, Sylvia Chaudoir, Muge Das, Elisa Davis, Ray Fan, Sampath Gomatam, Maria Gregg, Darrin Griggy, Reiner Herde, Michael Hielbrink, James Hill, Reiner Hoeltke, Claus Horn, Beverly Kennedy, Ruediger Kretschmer, Michael LaStella, Sylvia Lehnen, Robert Loughran, Bob Mackenzie, Rhondda Macleod, Natascha Marienfeld, Steffen Mock, Heinrich Mueller, Rolf Neuhaus, Doug O'Brian, Mary Odabashian, Wolfgang Otter, Brian Potter, Lori Ritzert, L.Kay Roberts, Thomas Rumbach, Sabine Scheppat-Hinze, Stefan Sigg, Donald Silva, Birgit Starmanns, Gerald Steele, Henri Stein, Peter Tillert, Cindy Vineberg, Wolfgang Weiss, Daniela Weckesser, April Wu, Daniel-Benjamin Zaidspiner, Peter Zimmerer, and Theo Zimmermann (SAP)

Detailed Table of Contents

About This Guide ix
    Why This Guide xi
    How This Guide is Organized xi
    Who This Guide is For xii
    What This Guide Covers xii
    How to Use This Guide xiii
    Navigating the System xiv
    Special Icons xv
    Typographical Conventions xvi

Financial Accounting—General Ledger Reports 1–1
    General Ledger Accounts List 1–2
    General Ledger Line Items 1–7
    General Ledger Account Balances 1–12
    General Ledger Balance Sheet/P+L 1–16

Financial Accounting—Accounts Receivable Reports 2–1
    Customer Open Item Analysis (A/R Aging) 2–2
    Accounts Receivable Information System 2–8
    List of Customer Open Items 2–14
    Customer Balances in Local Currency 2–19

Financial Accounting—Accounts Payable Reports 3–1
    List of Vendor Open Items 3–2
    Vendor Balances in Local Currency 3–6

Controlling—Cost Center Reports 4–1
    Cost Center Summary: Planned Costs, Actual Costs, and Variances 4–2
    Display Actual Line Items for Cost Centers 4–18
    Cost Center Summary: Plan/Actual Costs by Period and Year-to-Date 4–31
    Cost Center Summary: Target Costs, Actual Costs, and Variances 4–37

Controlling—Internal Order Reports 5–1
    Internal Order Summary: Planned Costs, Actual Costs, and Variances 5–2
    Display Actual Line Items for Internal Orders 5–17
    Internal Order List: Balance Displays 5–33

Detailed Table of Contents

Controlling—Profitability Analysis Reports 6–1
Profitability Analysis: Plan/Actual Comparison 6–2
Profitability Analysis: SBU/Product/Customer Analysis 6–14
Profitability Analysis: Sales Plan/Contribution Margin 6–27

Controlling—Reconciliation Reports 7–1
FI/CO Reconciliation in Company Code Currency 7–2
CO/FI Reconciliation in Group Currency 7–13
Cross-Company Code Reconciliation 7–27

Human Resources Reports 8–1
Staffing Level Development Report (or Headcount Report) 8–2
Payroll Journal 8–6
New Hire Report 8–11
EEO-1 Report 8–16
Entries and Withdrawals Report 8–21

Sales and Distribution Reports 9–1
List of Sales Orders 9–2
Blocked Sales Orders 9–7
Backorders 9–13
Incoming Order Report (SIS Statistical Analysis) 9–22
Incoming Orders for Customers and Materials (Document or Statistical Analysis) 9–29
Incomplete Sales Documents 9–34
List of All or Open Billings (Document Analysis) 9–38
Invoiced Sales Report (Statistical Analysis) 9–43
List of All or Open Deliveries (Document Analysis) 9–50
Shipping Report (SIS Statistical Analysis) 9–56

Materials Management Reports 10–1
Stock Overview 10–2
List Displays of PO—Material or Vendor 10–6
Material Documents for Material 10–13
List Display of Purchase Requisitions 10–20

Plant Maintenance Reports 11–1
List of Notification Tasks 11–2
Order Cost Element Display 11–6

Production Planning Reports 12–1
Stock/Requirements List 12–2
Production Order Overview 12–12
MRP List—Collective Display 12–22
Shop Floor Info System 12–27

Multi-Level BOMs 12–39
Missing Parts Info System 12–44
Backorder Processing 12–51
Capacity Planning—Evaluation 12–56

Project System Reports 13–1
Project Cost Reporting—Planned/Actual/Variance 13–2
Cost Element Reporting—Plan vs. Actual 13–5
Budget Reporting—Budget vs. Plan/Actual/Commitments 13–9

Quality Management Reports 14–1
Inspection Lots Without Completion 14–2
Inspection Lots Without Usage Decision 14–6
Inspection Lot Selection 14–9

Warehouse Management Reports 15–1
Stock Overview 15–2
Material Stock List 15–7
List of Posting Change Notices 15–11
Empty Storage Bins 15–18

Appendix A: Report Documentation Template A–1
Why Use a Template? A–2
How to Use this Template A–2
Application Area: Report Title A–3

Appendix B: List of Sample Reports in this Guide B–1
Sample Reports Organized by Application Area B–2

Appendix C: Glossary C–1

Appendix D: Index D–1

About This Guide

Contents

Why This Guide xi
How This Guide is Organized xi
Who This Guide is For xii
What This Guide Covers xii
How to Use This Guide xiii
Navigating the System xiv
Special Icons xv
Typographical Conventions xvi

About This Guide
Why This Guide

Welcome to *Commonly Used Reports: Illustrations and Perspectives*, the third book in the three-volume *Reporting Made Easy* guidebook series.

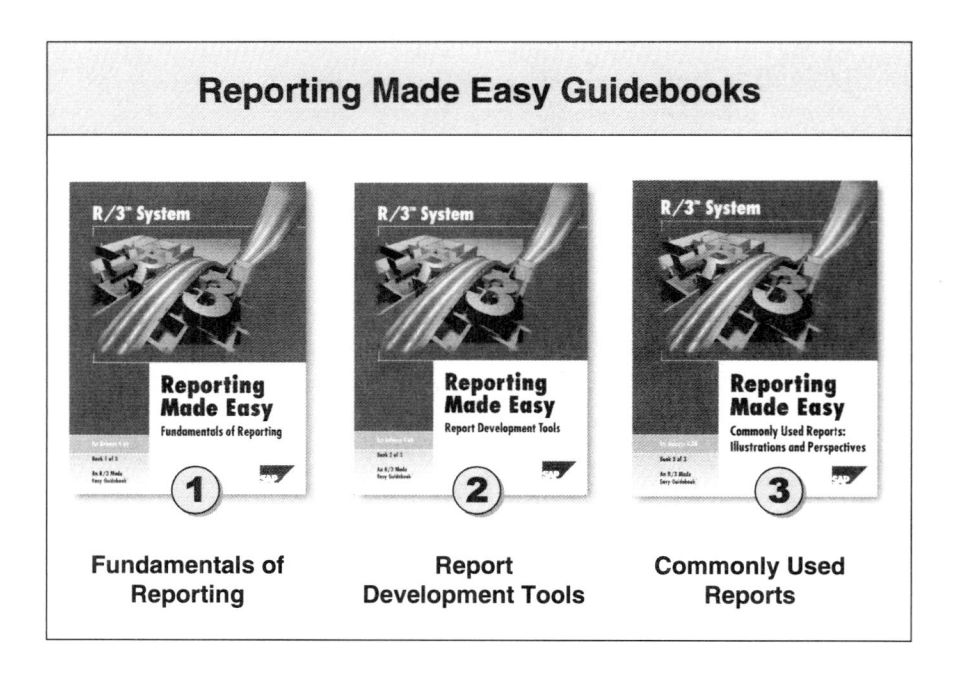

The R/3 System offers powerful and flexible reporting capabilities: You can choose from a library of over 3,000 standard business reports or build custom reports using a suite of report development tools.

With screenshots and step-by-step instructions, this guidebook introduces you to some of the most commonly requested business reports. It is intended to help new users better understand how to extract typical business data from the R/3 System. This collection of commonly used reports spans key application areas in the R/3 System. The sample reports you will find here are based on real-life business scenarios and are organized in a way that is easy to understand and use.

Other guides in the Reporting Made Easy series

The other two guidebooks in the *Reporting Made Easy* series are:
- *Book 1: Fundamentals of Reporting*
- *Book 2: Report Development Tools*

From a balance sheet report that meets external reporting requirements to a cost center report that meets internal reporting needs, every enterprise faces its own set of reporting challenges. Clearly, the ability to find, understand, and use standard R/3 System reports is paramount to R/3 System users.

These guidebooks are intended to bridge the gap in R/3 reporting knowledge and training. The guidebook set is geared toward users, implementation teams, and consultants who need a deeper understanding of how reporting works in the R/3 System.

For availability and ordering information, refer to the order form included with the guidebooks or visit our web site: *http://www.saplabs.com/rme*.

Why This Guide

The goal of this guide is to help new users:

- Make the transition from legacy system reports to the way reporting is approached in the R/3 System
- Explore sample reports that meet typical information needs in an enterprise
- Learn how to find, run, and use common business reports

How This Guide is Organized

The sample reports documented in this guide follow the same organization:

- Report elements (see table below)
- Business examples

Each report introduces you to the following key elements:

Report Element	Questions it Answers
Quick Access	What is the report name (or technical name)? What is the menu path to access the report? What is the transaction code to run the report?
Purpose	What is the business purpose of the report?
Prerequisites	What steps must be taken before running the report?
Integration	How is the report integrated with other functional modules in the R/3 System?
Features	What are the main features of the report?
Next Steps	Are there any activities that can be initiated after running the report?

You will then see some business examples of the report. These examples, with supporting screenshots, lead you through the steps needed to run the report.

Who This Guide is For

The target audience for this guide includes end-users, consultants, and implementation teams. This publication is intended to benefit a wide range of users—with varying levels of familiarity with the R/3 System.

The audience for this guidebook can be grouped as follows:

- **New users:** The sample business reports provided in this guidebook should help new users become familiar with the R/3 reporting environment. Users migrating from legacy system reporting should find this guidebook particularly useful.
- **Managers:** Managers in a company could use this guide to survey the wide range of standard reports available within the R/3 System.
- **New consultants:** New consultants or individuals seeking to better understand reporting topics could use this guidebook to learn about commonly used reports.

Assumptions

This guide assumes that you are:

- Familiar with R/3 System logon procedure, menu-tree program selection, and general navigation
- Familiar with basic Windows® or Macintosh® system operations
- Familiar with Microsoft®-based applications which may be needed, such as Word and Excel

What This Guide Covers

Since there are over 3,000 standard reports in the R/3 System, the reports selected for this guidebook only cover some of the most commonly used reports in the R/3 System.

In this guidebook, you will find reports from the following R/3 applications:

- Financial Accounting Reports
    - General Ledger Reports
    - Accounts Receivable Reports
    - Accounts Payable Reports
- Controlling Reports
    - Cost Center Reports
    - Profitability Analysis Reports
    - Internal Order Reports
    - Reconciliation Reports
- Human Resources Reports
- Sales and Distribution Reports

- Production Planning Reports
- Materials Management Reports
- Plant Maintenance Reports
- Quality Management Reports
- Project System Reports
- Warehouse Management Reports

> **Note:** This guidebook does not cover the basics of reporting; for more information on reporting basics, refer to the *Fundamentals of Reporting* guidebook.

How to Use This Guide

Depending on your experience, interest, or need, you may want to use this guidebook in any of the following ways:

- As a hands-on tutorial to learn about reports in the R/3 System
- As an introduction to the operational use of R/3 reports
- As a general guided tour of the R/3 System's reporting capabilities
- As a way to understand the differences among reports from various application areas

For best learning, you may want to start with the reports that are relevant to your particular business area.

Report Examples Use IDES Data

All report examples in this guide use sample data from SAP's International Demo and Education System (IDES) Release 4.0B. To use these report examples (with the specified data and results) as a tutorial, you will need access to an IDES system. If you are not sure how to access the model company data in IDES, ask your SAP system administrator for assistance. For more information about IDES and its current availability, visit the SAP web page at *http://www.sap.com*.

> **Note:** The reports documented in this guide were created according to standard reports available with R/3 Release 4.0B. Most reports should also be available in R/3 System Releases 3.x and 4.5x.

Caution: Although IDES Release 4.0B data was used to illustrate the sample reports, it is possible that you may not be able to replicate the same results on your system for all reports. If your results differ from those shown in this guide, a probable reason may be that necessary transaction data is not available on your system.

Build Your Own Report Documentation

To help users and implementation teams develop documentation for reports used in their particular business environment, a ready-to-use Microsoft® Word® template is supplied with this guidebook. The template should help you standardize the format of report documentation in your company.

For more information on the report documentation template, see appendix A.

Training and Documentation

This material may be reprinted or reused for user training or to develop internal company documentation. However, no part of this guide may be reproduced for commercial purposes without the written permission of SAP AG and the R/3 Simplification Group of SAP Labs, Inc.

Navigating the System

You may navigate the R/3 System using menu paths, transaction codes, or shortcut and function keys. If you use transaction codes, remember that you can enter the codes from the main *SAP R/3* screen.

But if you wish to jump from one transaction to another, you must precede the transaction with either **/n** or **/o**, as follows:

/n<trans code>	Example: /nVA01
	Use **/n** to exit the current transaction and start a new transaction. Your current transaction gets replaced by the new one.
/o<trans code>	Example: /oVA01
	Use **/o** to open a new session (window). Your current transaction is maintained, while a new window opens with the new transaction.

> **Caution:** Before you use **/n<transaction code>**, make sure you have saved all information. Otherwise, when you jump from one transaction to another, all unsaved information is lost. If you wish to review transactions side-by-side, you may want to start a new session by entering **/o<transaction code>** in the command filed.

Special Icons

Throughout this guide you will see special icons indicating important messages. Below are brief explanations of each icon:

Caution — Exercise caution when performing this task or step. An explanation of why you should be careful will be included.

TechTalk — This information helps you understand the topic in greater detail. It is not necessary to know this information to perform the task.

Tips & Tricks — This information provides helpful hints and shortcuts to make your work faster and easier.

Typographical Conventions

The table shown below lists all the typographical conventions and symbols, and icons used throughout this guide.

Word	What it Means
Click	Click the left mouse button to perform the action. The word "click" or "double-click" when the mouse is the *only* way to perform a certain function. "Choose" is always used for actions involving on-screen buttons or icons. Example: Click the node for *Production Planning*.
Choose	When you see the word "choose," you will either perform certain actions by choosing particular buttons on screen (using the mouse or a shortcut key, for example) or follow given menu paths. Examples: 1. Choose *File → Save* 2. Choose *Back.* 3. Choose *Enter.*
Select	Used with instructions for radio buttons and checkboxes. Example: Select *Generate Enterprise IMG*.

Typeface Style	What it Means
`User input`	Type in the text exactly as shown. Example: Enter `14287` in *Personnel Number*.
Object Style	Shown in italics, this word is usually an on-screen object, for example, button, field, screen title, book or chapter title, screen text or message. Example: In the *User Maintenance* screen, enter `SAP*` in *User*.

Section 1: Financial Accounting—General Ledger Reports

Contents

General Ledger Accounts List 1–2
General Ledger Line Items 1–7
General Ledger Account Balances 1–12
General Ledger Balance Sheet/P+L 1–16

General Ledger Accounts List

Quick Access To run this report, use one of the following access options:

Option 1: Menu Path

Information systems → Accounting → Financial accounting

General ledger → Periodic Processing → Info System → Report Selection

Lists → Account → Company code acct directory → G/L accounts list

Option 2: Program Name

Choose *System → Services → Reporting* and enter **RFSKVZ00** in the *Program* field. Then, choose *Execute* to run the report.

Purpose This report provides a listing of the General Ledger (G/L) accounts. The content can range from a simple description to more detailed information consisting of a G/L master record, such as document entry control and account management.

Depending on your specific needs, you can list the G/L accounts either as a simple range of accounts or as a combination of charts of accounts. You can base your selection on company codes, text, etc.

Prerequisites No prerequisites or selection criteria are required to run this report. However, most companies would have previously defined a range of G/L accounts, a chart of accounts, and one or more company codes. Thus, limiting the field list can restrict a listing of G/L accounts. For example, you can list only those G/L accounts that have been blocked for posting for a particular company code.

The *Output control* section of the first selection screen is useful for gathering information and determining the layout of this report. From this screen you can restrict the display to a single output criterion (for example, the document entry control for the G/L master record), view the entire master record, and sort the list results (for example, the output from the G/L account or the account group).

Integration You can use this report to obtain a wide range of information:

- Within the same chart of accounts, you can locate which G/L account is assigned to what company code.
- If the reference field (*Alternate account number*) has been entered in the G/L master, you can create a list that has both the current account number and the reference number for the legacy chart of accounts.
- Search with the output criteria of document entry control to determine which accounts are configured for automatic postings.

Section 1: Financial Accounting—General Ledger Reports

General Ledger Accounts List

Features   The selection screen of this report includes:
- Variants
- Dynamic selection options
- User variables
- Execution (and print) in background

The report list includes a listing of G/L accounts, grouped by account group.

Next Steps   This report contains data obtained from G/L account master records. As such, this data cannot be manipulated.

Guided Tour

Example 1: Using standard output criteria and restricted selection criteria, generate a simple list of G/L accounts for a company (Company code 3000) with a United States (U.S.) chart of accounts.

To access the first screen for this report, choose

Information systems → Accounting → Financial accounting

General ledger → Select report.

From the reporting tree, choose the following report:

Lists → Account → Company code acct directory → G/L accounts list.

1. Under *General selections*, enter CAUS in *Chart of accounts*.
2. Enter 3000 in *Company code*.
3. Choose *Execute*.

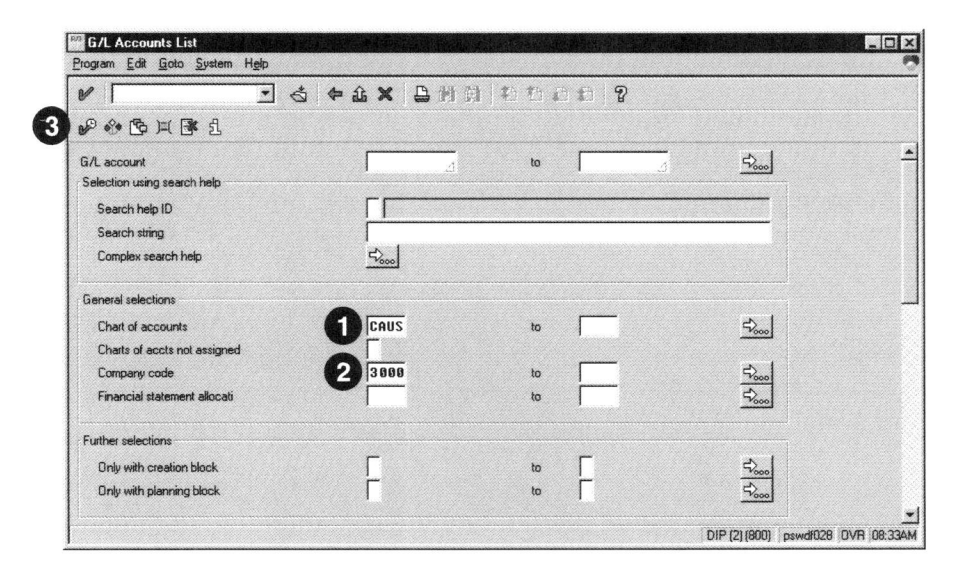

Commonly Used Reports: Illustrations and Perspectives

1–3

Section 1: Financial Accounting—General Ledger Reports
General Ledger Accounts List

A The report output shows that the G/L accounts are selected for the U.S. chart of accounts.

B The display is sorted first by the G/L account and then by the company code.

C The listing of each G/L account shows the name of the account and any specific information for the account. In this example:
- Account 1000 is for *Land*
- Company code is 3000
- Account belongs to the account group ANL and is maintained in U.S. dollars (USD)

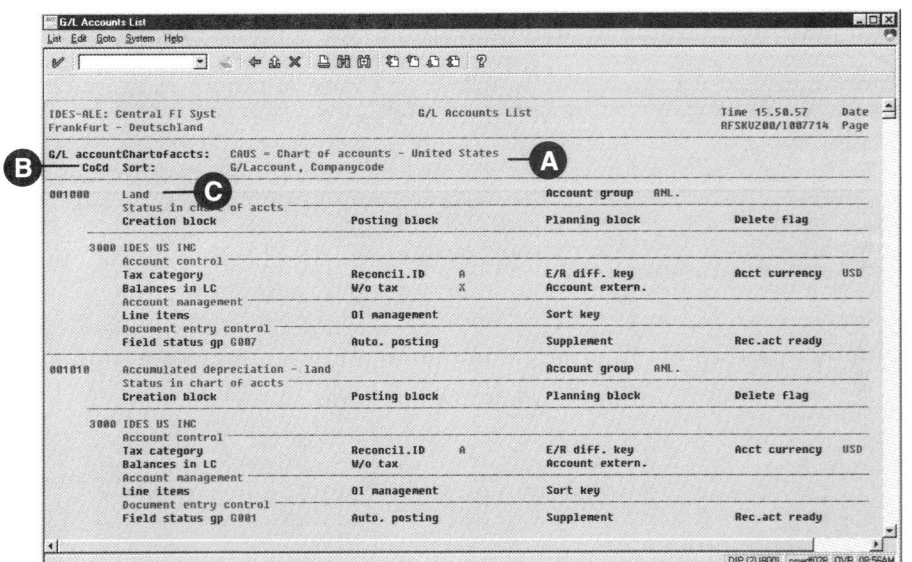

Example 2: Create a report for a range of accounts and company codes to determine which accounts are assigned to a certain company code.

---

1. Enter a range (for example, **200000** to **299999**) in *G/L account*.

2. Enter **CAUS** in *Chart of accounts* to limit your range of G/L accounts.

3. Enter a range of company codes (for example, **3000** to **4000**) in *Company code*.

4. Under *Output control*, select *Creation data for company code*.

5. Choose *Execute*.

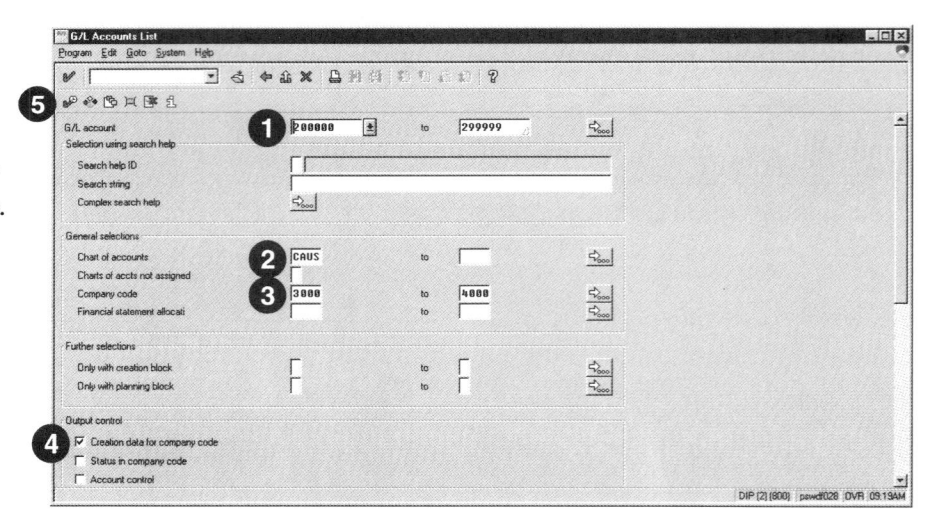

1–4 Reporting Made Easy

Section 1: Financial Accounting—General Ledger Reports

General Ledger Accounts List

A Company codes (listed for each G/L account)

B Creation date and name of person who created the account assignment

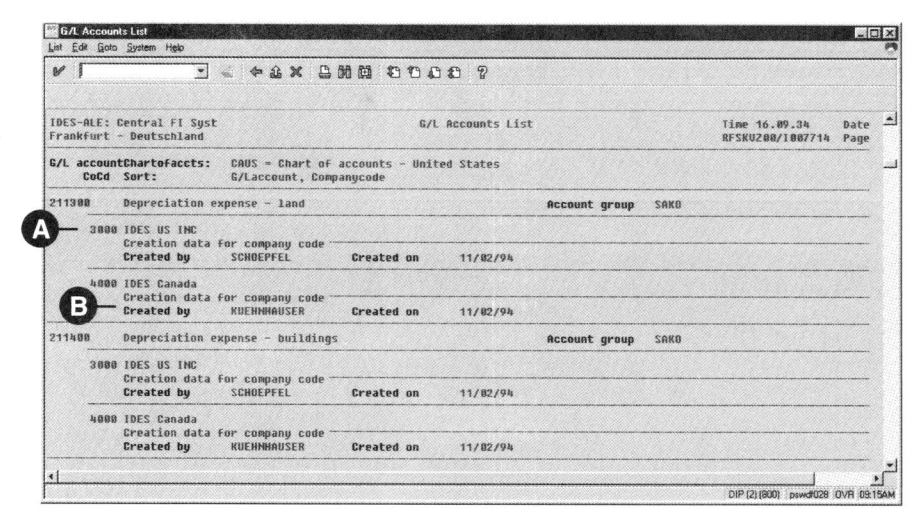

Example 3: Create a report to determine which accounts belong to which account group within a chart of accounts.

1. Enter **CAUS** in *Chart of accounts*.
2. Enter **3000** in *Company code*.
3. Scroll down the screen to the *Output control*.
4. Enter **2** in *Account sorting*. This option sorts the accounts first by account group, then by G/L account.
5. Choose *Execute*.

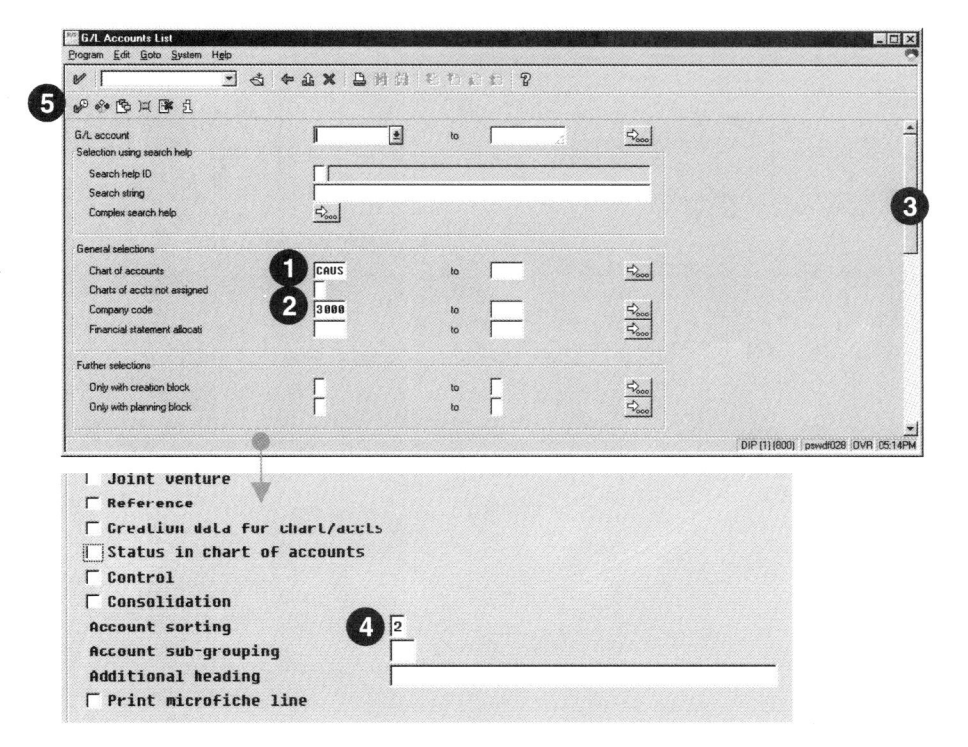

Commonly Used Reports: Illustrations and Perspectives

1–5

Section 1: Financial Accounting—General Ledger Reports

General Ledger Accounts List

A   Initial sort criteria, followed by the G/L account.

B   The first account group *ALL* is shown with four G/L accounts inside that group.

C   The account group *ANL* is shown with the G/L accounts belonging to that group.

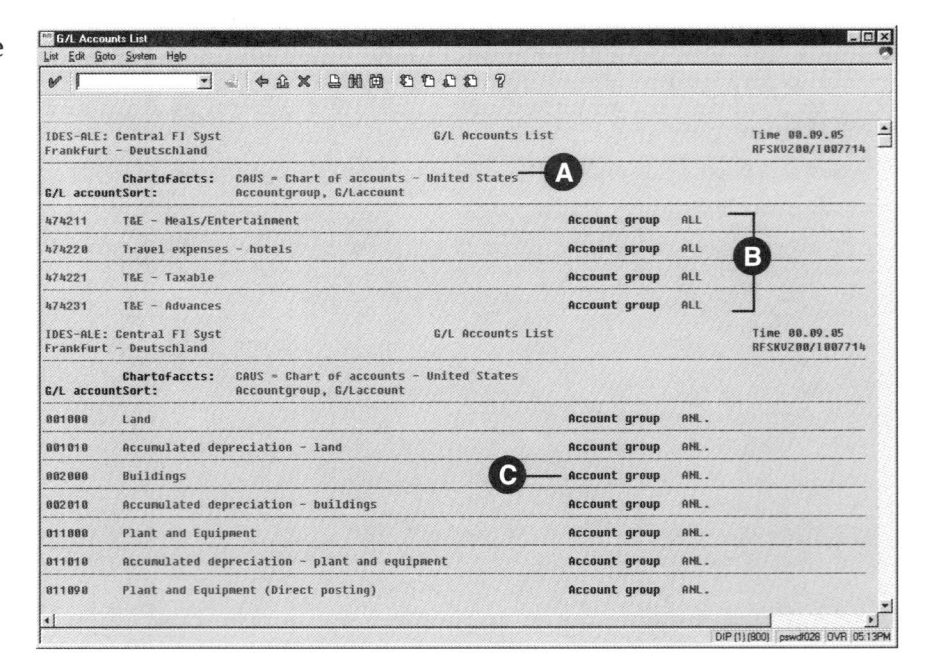

General Ledger Line Items

Quick Access To run this report, use one of the following access options:

Option 1: Menu Path

Information systems → *Accounting* → *Financial accounting*

General ledger → *Select report*

Information systems → *Account information* → *Line items* → *G/L line items*

Option 2: Program Name

Choose *System* → *Services* → *Reporting* and enter `RFSOPO00` in the *Program* field. Then, choose *Execute* to run the report.

Purpose This report lists open or cleared items. It is used for open-item managed accounts. You can use parked documents as selection criteria to capture both posted and preliminary posting documents in the same report.

Similar to many other standard reports, you can specify the key date which separates items posted before the key date and a range of dates for clearing.

Prerequisites You must select *Open items at key date* to run this report.

However, more selection criteria should be entered. Most companies using FI will already have a range of G/L accounts, a chart of accounts, and one or more company codes set up. Thus, limiting the selection fields can produce a more precise listing of the line items.

The *Output control* section of the initial selection screen allows for a separation of G/L accounts by company code as well as the ability to specify a unique printing option for each company code. An option also allows microfiche capabilities. The variable portion is comprised of company code (4 characters), G/L account (10 characters), business area (4 characters), and posting date (6 characters).

Integration Several types of information can be gained from this report. For example, you can research the line items of a particular G/L account for a specified time period, such as an accrual account and the subsequent reversals of those accruals. This report can also be used in an audit to review documents and line items posted to a company code for a specified period. This report is a good starting point before going to the *Display G/L Line Items* (FBL3) or *Displaying Documents* (FB03).

Section 1: Financial Accounting—General Ledger Reports
General Ledger Line Items

Features

The selection screen of this report includes:
- Variants
- Dynamic selection options
- User variables
- Execution (and print) in background

The report list includes:
- Separation of G/L line items and company codes
- Microfiche line

Next Steps

This report contains G/L account balance line items. As such, this data cannot be manipulated.

Section 1: Financial Accounting—General Ledger Reports
General Ledger Line Items

Guided Tour

Example 1: Using a U.S. chart of accounts and a company code, create a simple listing of G/L line items with a given *Open item at key date* (default is system date at time of entry) and restricted selection criteria.

To access the *G/L Line Items* screen, choose

Information systems → Accounting → Financial accounting

General ledger → Select report.

From the reporting tree, choose the following report:

Information systems → Account information → Line items → G/L line items.

1. Enter **CAUS** in *Chart of accounts*.
2. Enter **3000** in *Company code*.
3. *Open items at key date* defaults to the system date but you can change it to any desired date.

   The system selects all items that posted before the specified key date and are open for this period.

   The *Clearing date* (not shown) is usually the date of the paying document or the posting date of the invoice, whichever is the most recent.
4. Choose *Execute*.

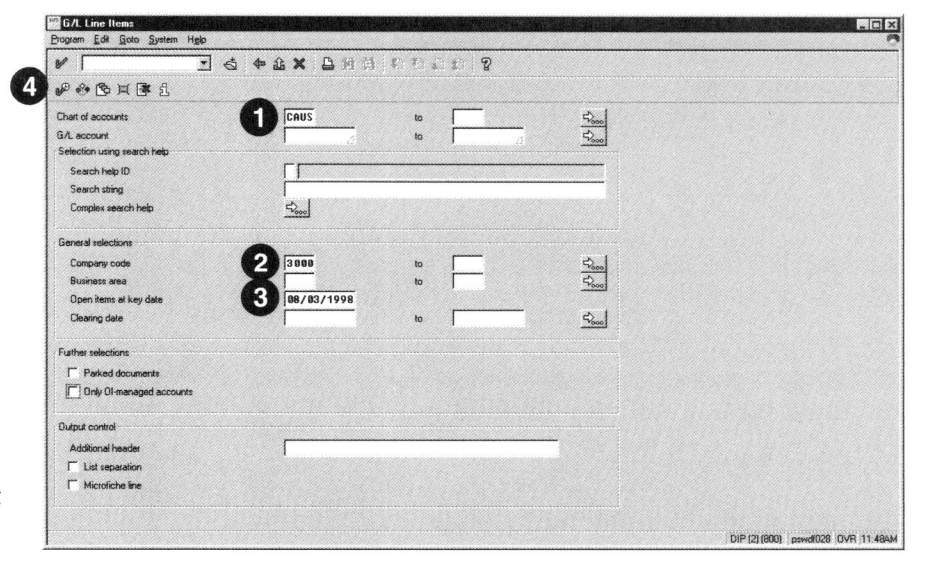

Commonly Used Reports: Illustrations and Perspectives

1-9

Section 1: Financial Accounting—General Ledger Reports

General Ledger Line Items

A   The screen header shows the order in which information appears in the report.

The report list is sorted by:
- Company code
- Account number
- Business area
- Posting date

B   For G/L account *099000*:
- Accruals were setup for the interest due on notes payable.
- Documents with type SA *100000299* and *100000300* cleared with documents type AB *100000625* and *100000626*.
- The clearing document is cross-referenced on the original document.

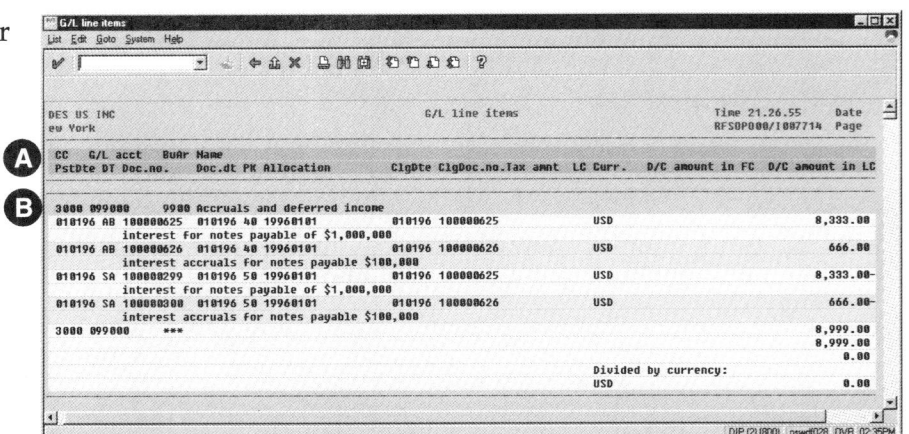

Example 2: Using the dynamic selection options, create a report to review line items set by a particular user. Limit the output to include only the particular user.

1. Enter **CAUS** in *Chart of accounts*.
2. Enter **3000** in *Company code*.
3. *Open items at key date* defaults to the system date but you can change it to any desired date.

   The system selects all items that posted before the specified key date and are open for this period.
4. Choose *Dynamic selection*.
5. Choose *Execute*.

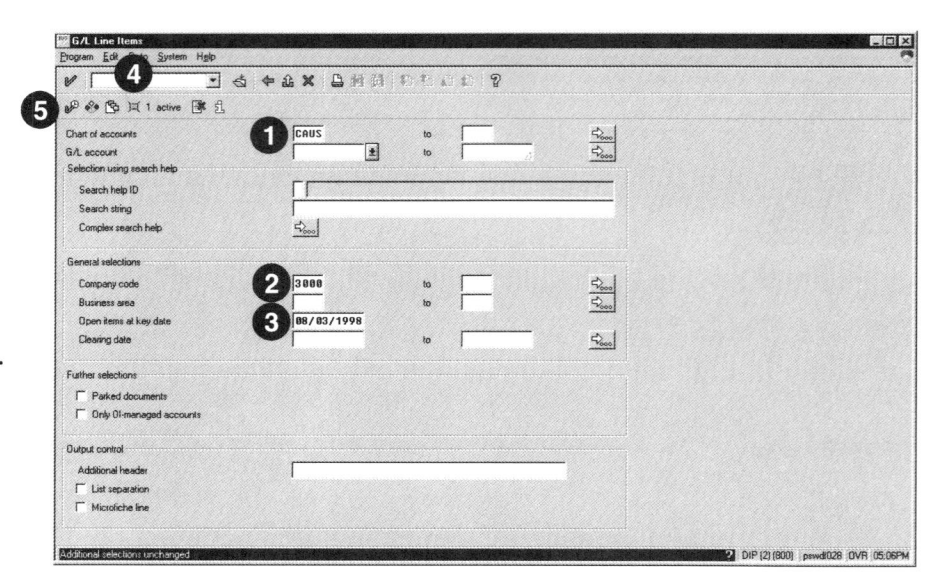

1–10   Reporting Made Easy

Section 1: Financial Accounting—General Ledger Reports
General Ledger Line Items

This screen shows a list of searchable *G/L Line Items*. By entering the user name (for example, **ODABASHIAN**), line items are restricted by this user.

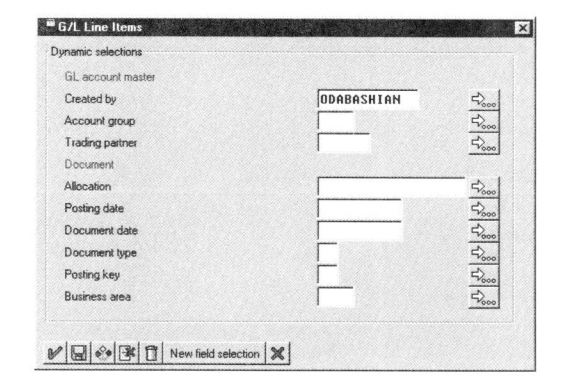

Line items appear for the specified user.

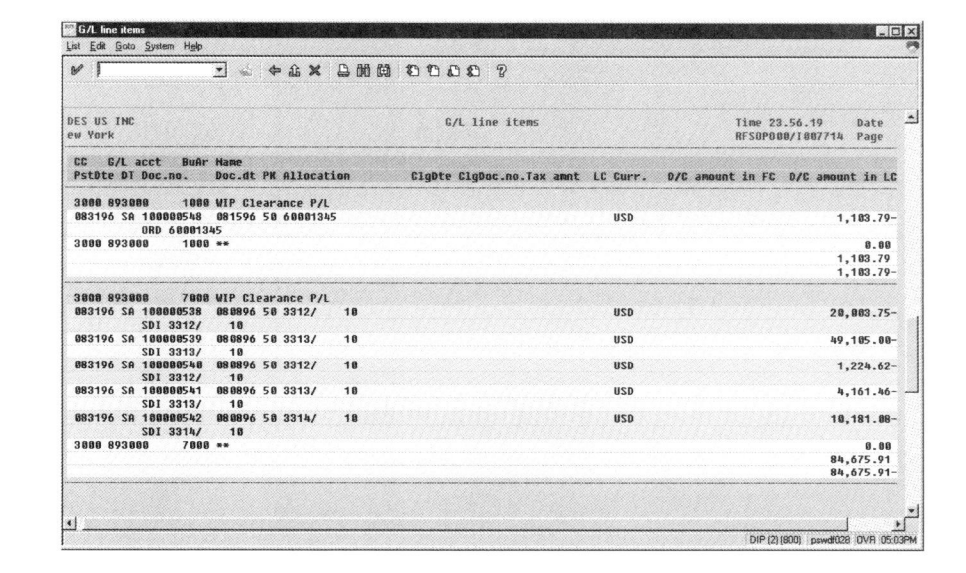

This screen shows a list generated without the dynamic selection criteria of user.

A Notice that additional entries of *$1,500.25* between both business areas *1000* and *7000* appear.

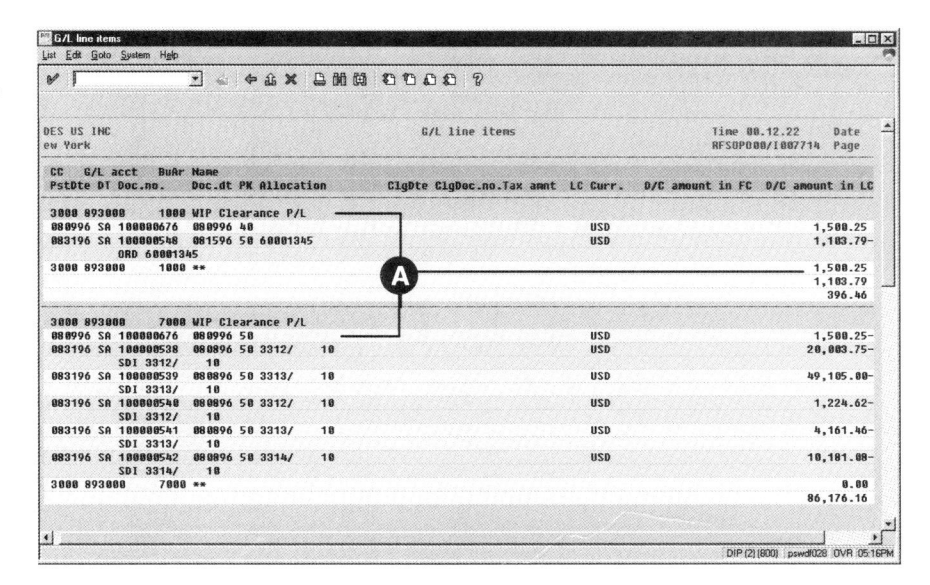

Commonly Used Reports: Illustrations and Perspectives

1–11

Section 1: Financial Accounting—General Ledger Reports
General Ledger Account Balances

General Ledger Account Balances

Quick Access To run this report, use one of the following access options:

Option 1: Menu Path

Information systems → *Accounting* → *Financial accounting*

General ledger → *Account balances*

Option 2: Program Name

Choose *System*→ *Services*→ *Reporting* and enter `RFSSLD00` in the *Program* field. Then, choose *Execute* to run the report.

Option 3: Transaction Code

In the *Command* field, enter transaction `F.08` and choose *Enter*.

Purpose This report lists the general ledger account balances.

Primary output includes:

- Balance carried forward at the beginning of the fiscal year
- Debit total of the reporting period
- Credit total of the reporting period
- Debit or credit balances at the close of the period

The output is normally shown for a given fiscal year, but you may use period selection fields to narrow the search to a particular period.

Prerequisites You must select *Fiscal year*, *Reporting periods*, and *Summarization levels* before running this report.

However, limiting the selection criteria will speed up searches and provide more focused results.

The output control section of the first selection screen allows for sorting based either on a standard or a corporate group version.

The sort sequence of the standard version is by:

1. Company code
2. Account number
3. Business area

Reporting Made Easy

The sort sequence for the corporate version is by:

1. Account number
2. Local currency of the company code
3. Company code
4. Business area

Summarization option 0 provides no summarization, and therefore is the most detailed. Additional output control is possible with the ability to separate the report by company code and print to a unique printer for each company code. There is also an option to microfilm the data. The variable portion has a layout that depends on the sort version.

The standard version is as follows:
- Company code (4 characters)
- G/L account (10 characters)
- Business area (4 characters)

The group version is as follows:
- G/L account (10 characters)
- Local currency of company code (5 characters)
- Company code (4 characters)
- Business area (4 characters)

Integration

With this report you can quickly identify the balance carried forward from the prior fiscal year and isolate the activity for the current periods. This report is often a good starting point for summarization of accounts at a high level. You can then use the *G/L account: Balance display* (FS10) to get in-depth information about the balances.

Features

The selection screen of this report includes:
- Variants
- Dynamic selection options
- User variables
- Execution (and print) in background

The output of this report includes a listing G/L account balances with a wide range of sorting options.

Next Steps

Data presented in this report is from G/L account balances. This report does not allow manipulation of data.

Section 1: Financial Accounting—General Ledger Reports
General Ledger Account Balances

Guided Tour

Example: Generate a simple list of G/L account balances for fiscal year 1996, including all sixteen posting periods in that year for 2 asset accounts. Use CAUS for the chart of accounts and 3000 for the company code. The summarization level has not been selected for this example.

To access the first screen for this report, choose

Information systems → *Accounting* → *Financial accounting*

General ledger → *Account balances*.

1. Enter **CAUS** in *Chart of Accounts*.

2. Enter **1000** in *G/L account*.

3. The *Multiple Selection for G/L account* appears. The desired G/L accounts can be entered individually or as a range. In this example, enter **1000** and **11000**.

   Note: The green arrow to the right of *G/L account* field (circled on the facing graphic) is highlighted indicating that additional accounts have been selected.

4. Enter **3000** in *Company code* and **1996** in *Fiscal year*.

5. Leave the *Output control* settings at standard values. In this example, use **0** for the *Summarization level*.

6. Choose *Execute*.

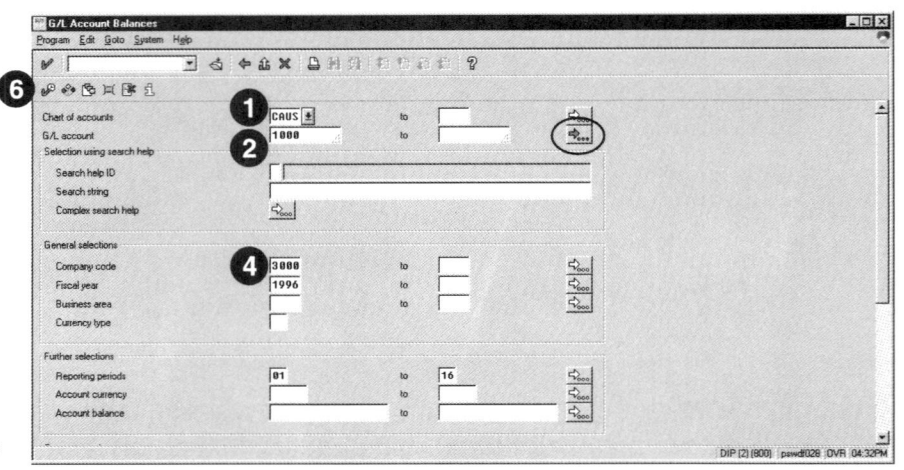

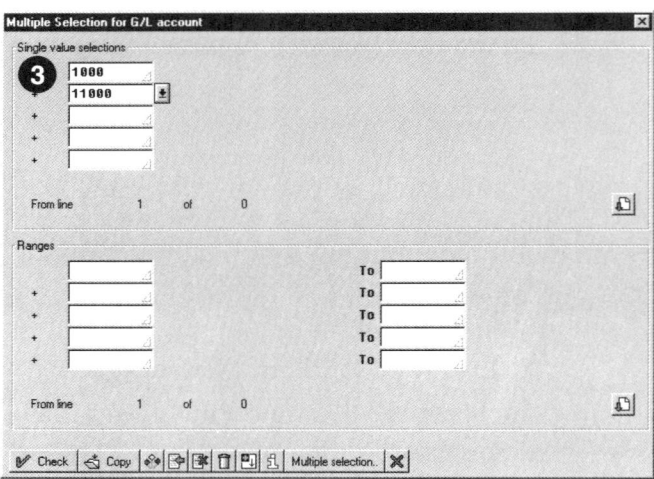

Reporting Made Easy

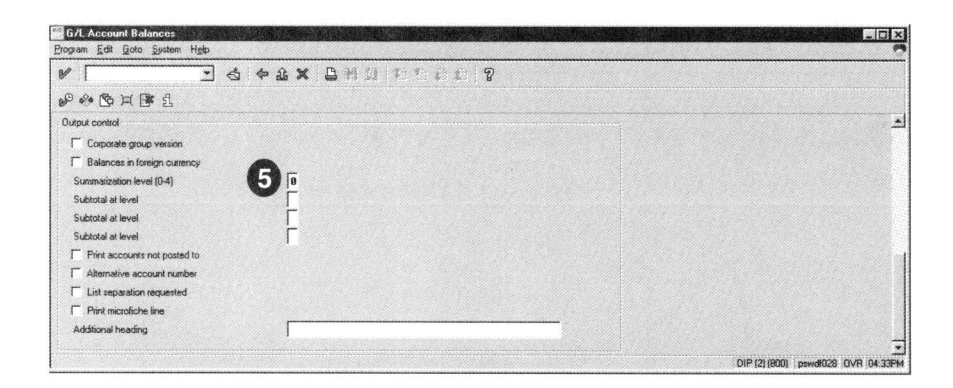

Section 1: Financial Accounting—General Ledger Reports

General Ledger Account Balances

A The report display shows the company codes, the reporting periods, the currency, and the order of the information.

B According to the standard version the balances are separated by business area. The carry-forward balance is listed for each business area.

C The reporting debit balance, reporting credit balance, and the total debit balance are listed.

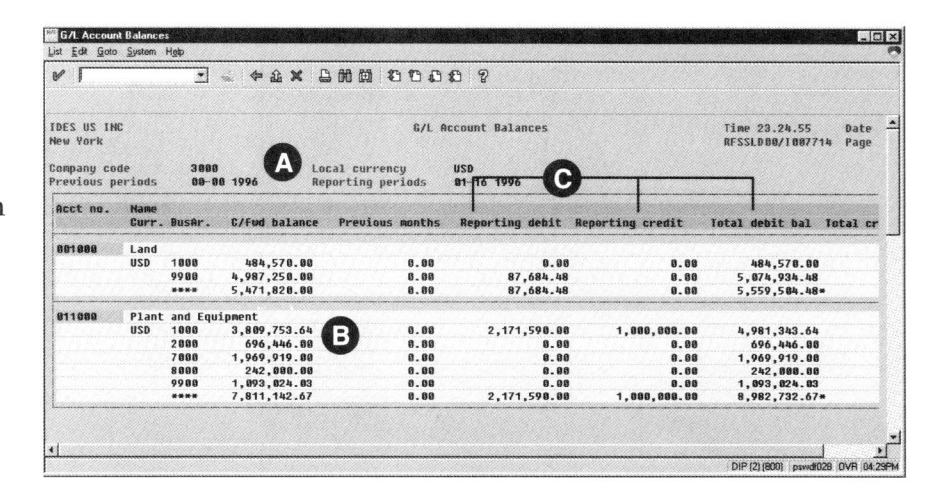

Commonly Used Reports: Illustrations and Perspectives

1–15

General Ledger Balance Sheet/P+L

Quick Access   To run this report, use one of the following access options:

Option 1: Menu Path

Information systems → *Accounting* → *Financial accounting*

General ledger → *Balance sheet*

Option 2: Program Name

Choose *System*→ *Services*→ *Reporting* and enter **RFBILA00** in the *Program* field. Then, click *Execute* to run the report.

Option 3: Transaction Code

In the *Command* field, enter **F.01** and choose *Enter*.

Purpose   This report creates the balance sheet and profit and loss statement for a user-defined reporting period and fiscal year. This balance sheet also uses *Financial Statement Versions* (FSV), which are defined during configuration. These FSVs reflect different views of the balance sheet, for example, the U.S. GAAP format, the British GAAP format, etc. The balance sheet and profit and loss statements can be viewed in comparison to prior periods or planned values.

Prerequisites   You can run the report with only the *Financial statement version*, *Fiscal year*, *Reporting periods*, and *Summarization levels* selected. However, it is practical to specify a chart of accounts, a company code, and a business area (4 characters).

The *Output control* section of the initial selection screen allows for various summarization levels: by company code, business area, and account level. It also allows you to separate the report based on the company code. An additional evaluation section allows for currency evaluation and the extrapolation of annual P/L figures from only a few periods.

Integration   With this report you can make quick comparisons of current and prior periods or fiscal years with relative ease. Performance evaluation on an actual-versus-plan basis is also relatively easy to do using the balance sheet and profit and loss statements. If a company has only partially completed its fiscal year, the balance sheet/P+L report has extrapolation capabilities to generate a P+L for the full year.

Section 1: Financial Accounting—General Ledger Reports
General Ledger Balance Sheet/P+L

Features

The selection screen of this report includes the following standard functionality:

- Variants
- Dynamic selection options
- User variables
- Execution (and print) in background

The output of this report includes a listing of the G/L account balances presented in a format defined by a financial statement version.

Next Steps

Data presented in this report is from *G/L account balances*. This report does not allow manipulation of data.

Guided Tour

Example: Generate a balance sheet for company 3000 using the financial statement version BAUS (the U.S. commercial balance sheet). The comparison years are 1996 and 1997.

To access the first screen for this report, choose

Information Systems → *Accounting* → *Financial accounting*

General ledger → *Balance sheet*.

1. Enter **CAUS** in *Chart of accounts*.
2. Enter **3000** in *Company code*.
3. Select **BAUS** from a pull down list for *Financial statement version*.
4. For the *Reporting year*, enter **1997**. Enter **1** to **16** as the comparison periods for both 1996 and 1997.

   Output control and parameters for special evaluations have been left with the default settings (not shown here).
5. Enter **1996** in *Fiscal year*.
6. Choose *Execute*.

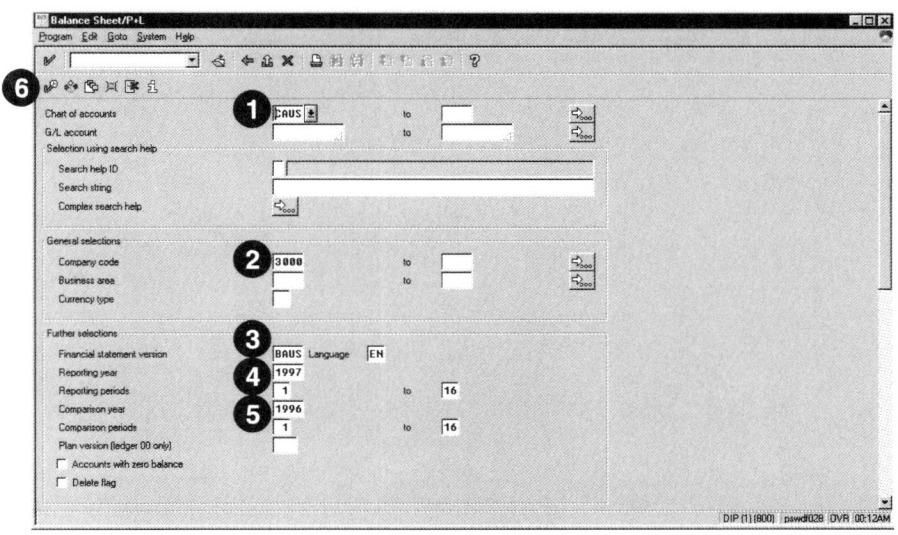

Section 1: Financial Accounting—General Ledger Reports

General Ledger Balance Sheet/P+L

A The display shows the commercial balance sheet for the USA with the current asset section shown in detail.

B The column headings list the financial statement version (not shown in screen shot), the company code, and the reporting periods under evaluation.

C Each section has a subtotal and foots down to a summation for each balance sheet category.

D Both absolute and relative differences between periods are calculated. In this example finished goods changed by USD 1,249,635.54 or 1.0%.

E The same report can be executed again with a slight change to the summarization level for accounts. In this case a **0** is selected for *Summary report* (account detail) to provide totals by asset classification only.

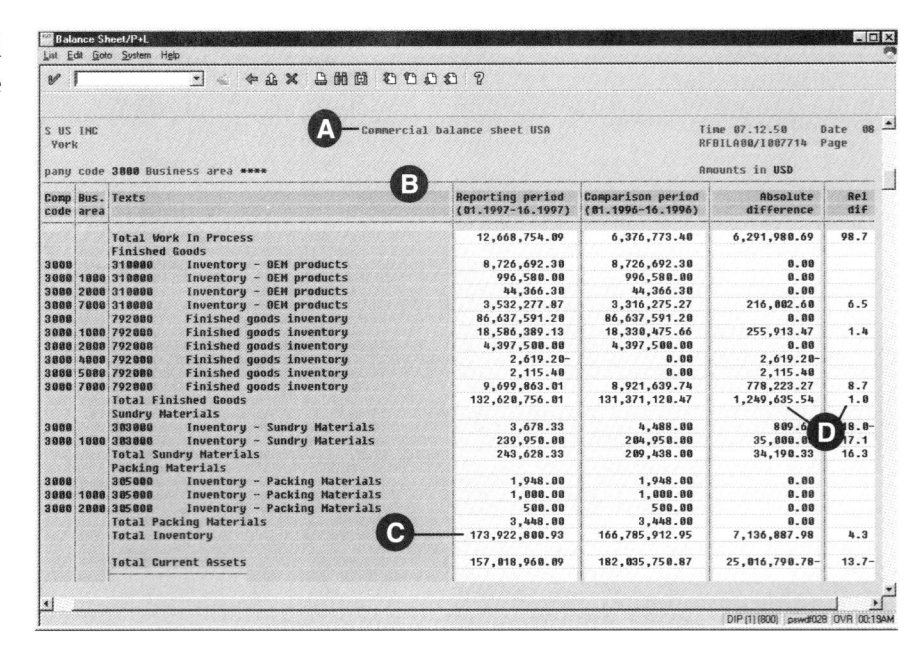

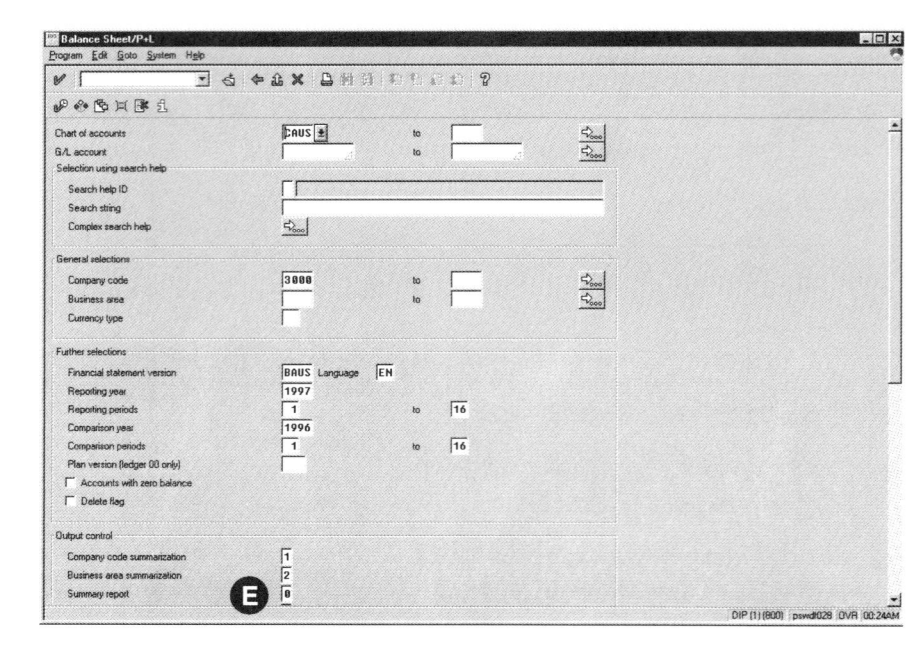

Section 1: Financial Accounting—General Ledger Reports

General Ledger Balance Sheet/P+L

F This is the same report, but it now hides the specific account detail. Current assets are at USD *157,018,960.09* as they were in the previous report. In this view of the balance sheet you can quickly see the composition of the current assets.

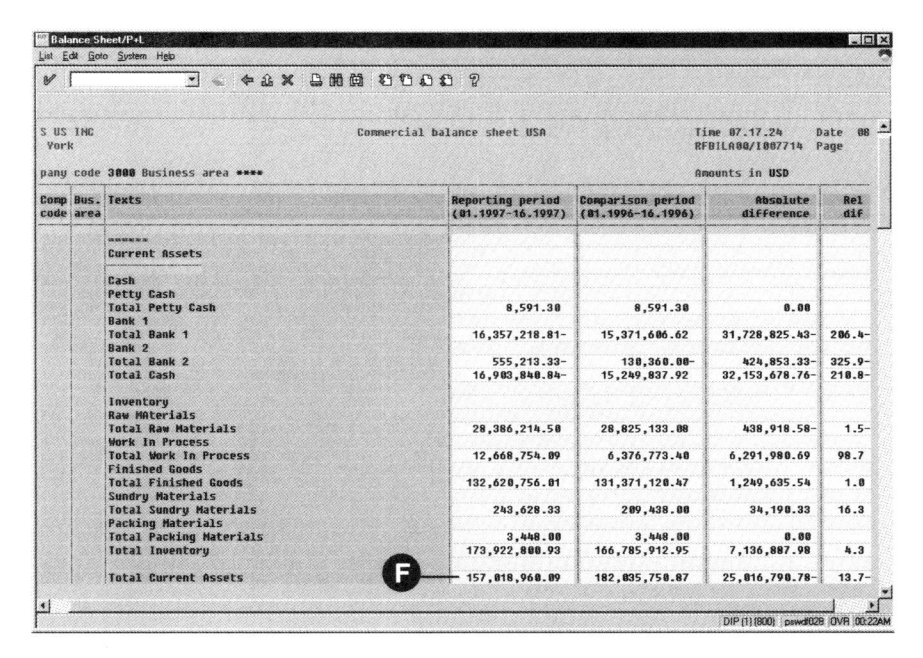

Texts	Reporting period (01.1997-16.1997)	Comparison period (01.1996-16.1996)	Absolute difference	Rel dif
Current Assets				
Cash				
Petty Cash				
Total Petty Cash	8,591.30	8,591.30	0.00	
Bank 1				
Total Bank 1	16,357,218.81-	15,371,606.62	31,728,825.43-	206.4-
Bank 2				
Total Bank 2	555,213.33-	130,360.00-	424,853.33-	325.9-
Total Cash	16,903,840.84-	15,249,837.92	32,153,678.76-	210.8-
Inventory				
Raw Materials				
Total Raw Materials	28,386,214.50	28,825,133.08	438,918.58-	1.5-
Work In Process				
Total Work In Process	12,668,754.09	6,376,773.40	6,291,980.69	98.7
Finished Goods				
Total Finished Goods	132,620,756.01	131,371,120.47	1,249,635.54	1.0
Sundry Materials				
Total Sundry Materials	243,628.33	209,438.00	34,190.33	16.3
Packing Materials				
Total Packing Materials	3,448.00	3,448.00	0.00	
Total Inventory	173,922,800.93	166,785,912.95	7,136,887.98	4.3
Total Current Assets	**157,018,960.09**	182,035,750.87	25,016,790.78-	13.7-

Commonly Used Reports: Illustrations and Perspectives

1–19

General Ledger Balance Sheet/P+L

Section 2: Financial Accounting—Accounts Receivable Reports

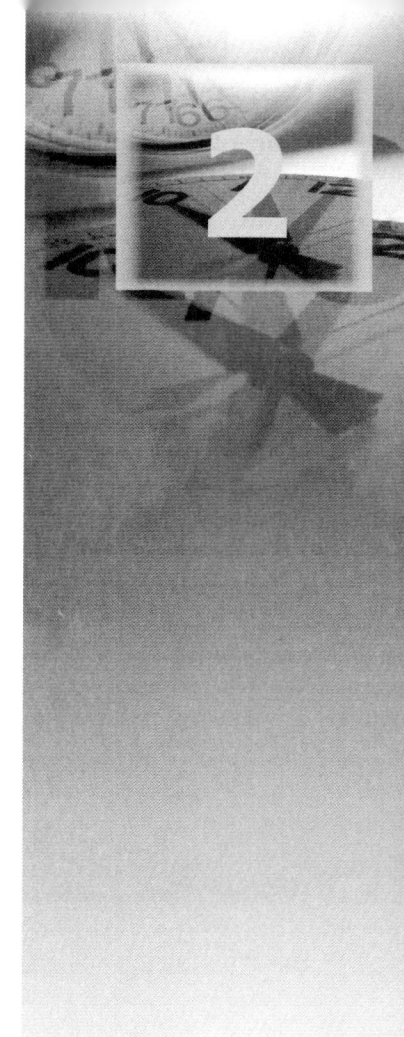

Contents

Customer Open Item Analysis (A/R Aging) 2–2

Accounts Receivable Information System 2–8

List of Customer Open Items 2–14

Customer Balances in Local Currency 2–19

Customer Open Item Analysis (A/R Aging)

Quick Access   To run this report, use one of the following access options:

Option 1: Menu Path

Information systems → *Accounting* → *Financial accounting*

Accounts receivable → *Select report*

Information system → *Account information* → *Days overdue analysis* → *Customer open item analysis*

Option 2: Program Name

Choose *System* → *Services* → *Reporting* and enter `RFDOPR10` in the *Program* field. Then, choose *Execute* to run the report.

Purpose   This report lets you select and analyze customer open items that are overdue and exceed a predefined amount. You can search by customer account number, company, deduction, and a specific level of balance. The report's dynamic options let you refine your search to allow for even greater levels of detail You can search by industry, country, accounting clerk, etc.

(If you do not want a selection with regard to the balance of the overdue items, you should check to see if you can use program name `RFDOPR00` for customer assessment with an open-item sorted list. It offers similar options and faster execution.)

Prerequisites   No prerequisites are required to run this report.

You can run the report with only the *Open items at key date* selected. However, we suggest a criteria-based search to produce a more targeted A/R aging analysis.

The *Output control* section of the first selection screen is used to gather information and to decide the report layout. There are two account sorting sequences:

- Option 1 (sorts by company code, accounting clerk, account number, and business area)
- Option 2 (adds currency to the sorting mix)

Summarization levels have six options, with option *0* offering the greatest level of detail. For the aging breakpoints, you can either accept the system defaults or use one of the five user-defined date ranges.

Section 2: Financial Accounting—Accounts Receivable Reports
Customer Open Item Analysis (A/R Aging)

Integration

Using the default settings in the first selection screen, you could select a particular company code and display a listing of all aged customer account balances for that company. The standard aging breakpoints currently set at *20, 40, 80,* and *100* may easily be adjusted to meet your individual analysis requirements. Using dynamic selections on the customer account field, you can create an analysis in which the selected accounting clerks or group key closely match a sales organization. The analysis can then approximate accounts receivables (or aging) by sales organization.

Features

The selection screen of this report includes:
- Variants
- Dynamic selection options
- User variables
- Execution (and print) in background

Next Steps

This report contains data obtained from A/R customer balances. As such, the data cannot be changed or manipulated from the report.

Section 2: Financial Accounting—Accounts Receivable Reports
Customer Open Item Analysis (A/R Aging)

Guided Tour

Example 1: Generate a report to analyze open items for a customer, with summarization levels set at *0* for the highest level of detail.

To access the first screen for this report, choose

Information systems → Accounting → Financial accounting

Accounts receivable → Select report

Information system → Account information → Days overdue analysis → Customer open item analysis.

1. Enter **AESC04D** in *Customer account*.
2. Enter **0001** in *Company code*.
3. Enter **08/07/1998** in *Open items at key date*.

   The system selects all items that posted before the specified key date and remain open for this period. The current date defaults to the system setting.

4. The *Due date sorted list* is set to a user-defined setting of **20, 50, 80, 100**, and **180** days.

5. Choose *Execute*.

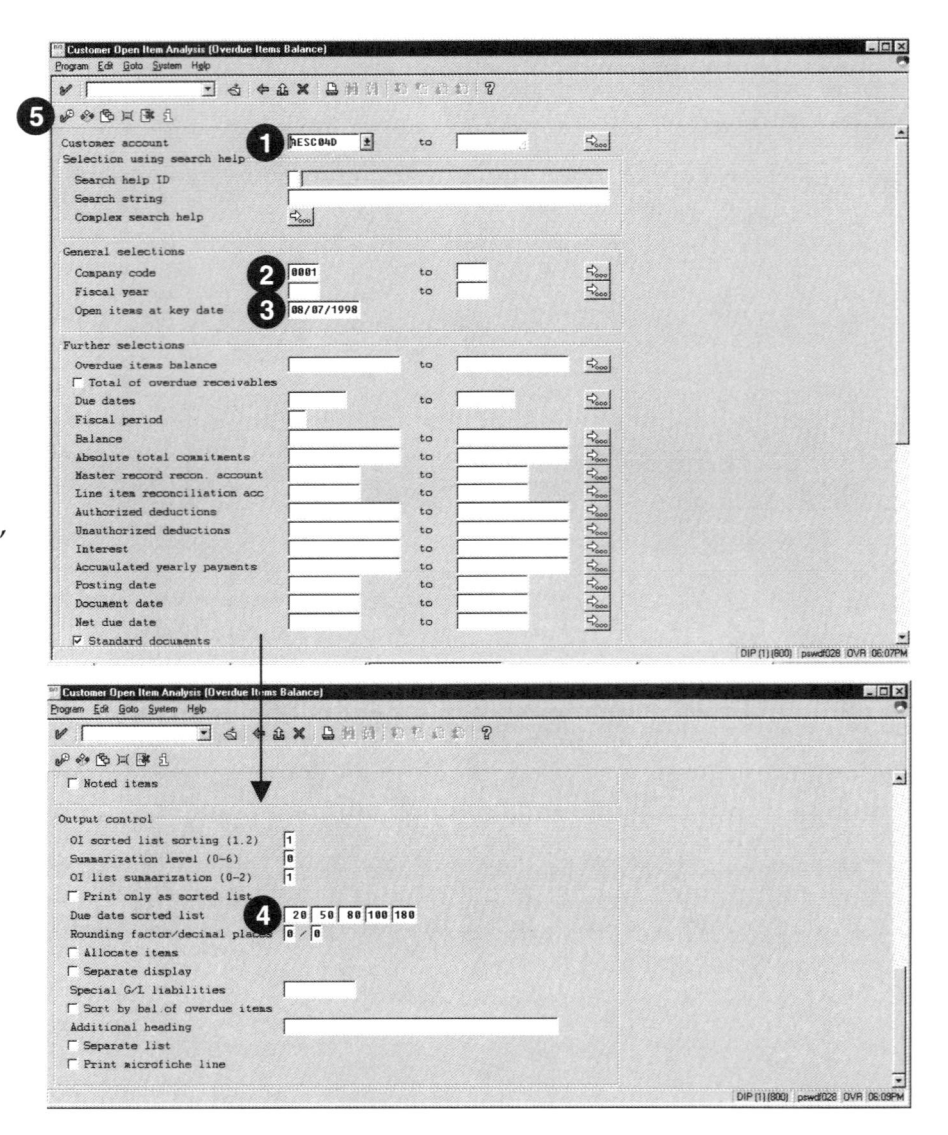

2–4

Reporting Made Easy

Section 2: Financial Accounting—Accounts Receivable Reports

Customer Open Item Analysis (A/R Aging)

The *Customer Open Item Analysis* screen provides several key pieces of information, including the customer's name and address.

A Total current liabilities for the customer (for example, USD 3,200)

B Annual purchases and deductions

C Terms of payment (for example, *ZB00* indicates that the payable is immediately due in full)

D Aging breakdown (for example, the open item total is *3,200*. At *20* days and less there is a credit of *1,000*.)

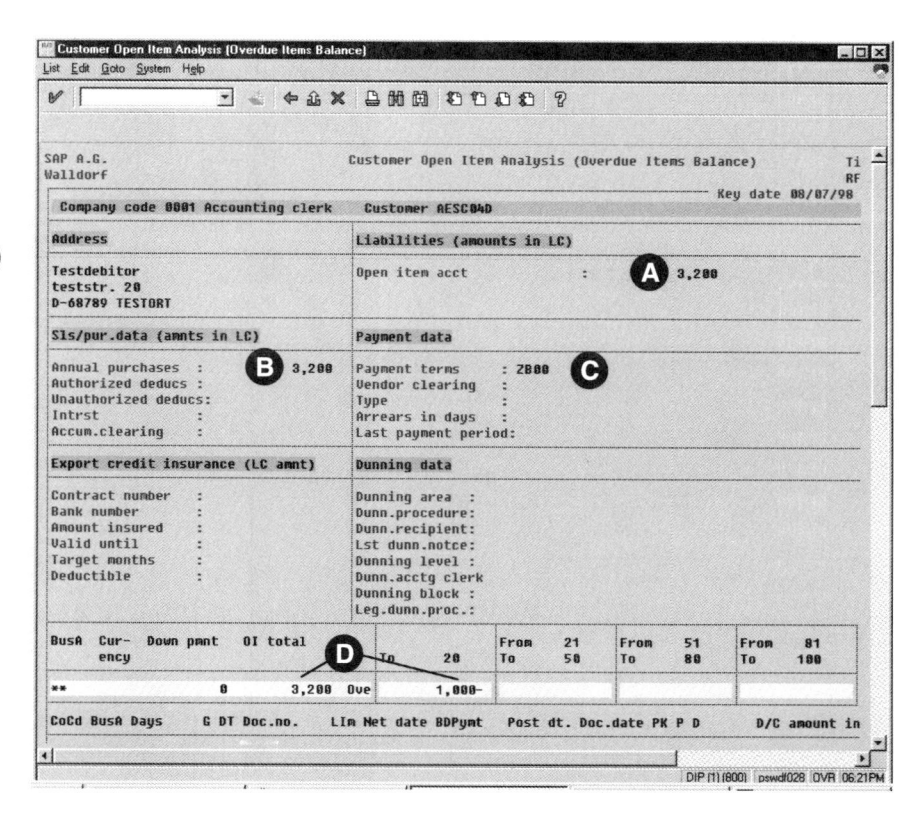

This screen shows the far right section of the report.

E Items aged *101* to *180* days are totaled at *2,200* and there are *2,000* worth of items aged at over *181* days.

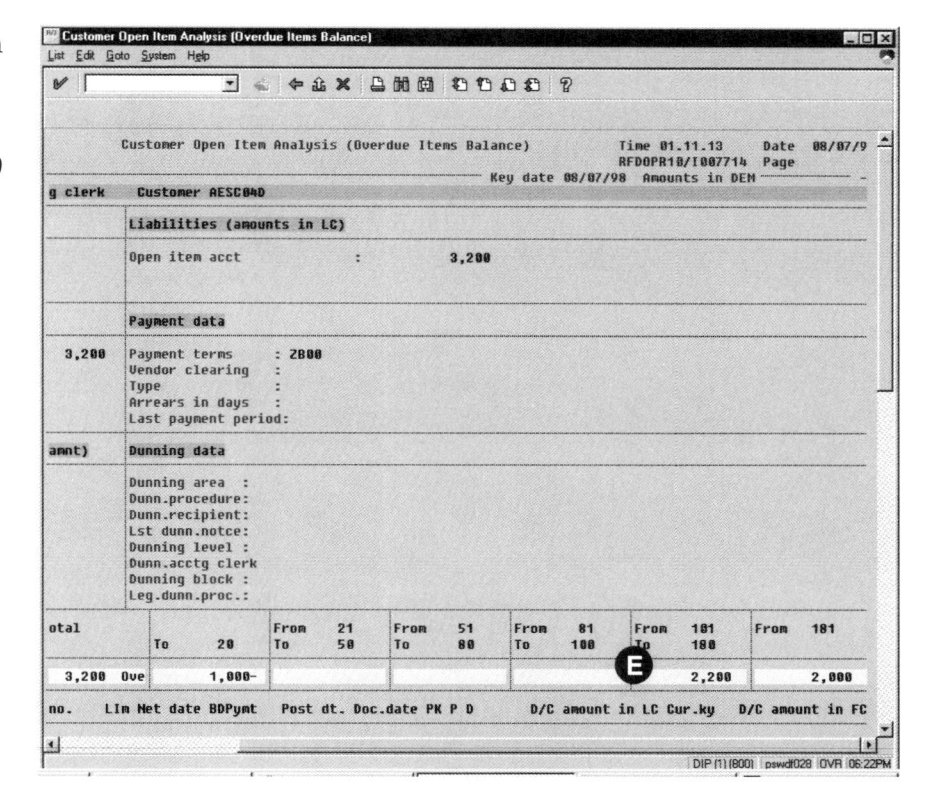

Commonly Used Reports: Illustrations and Perspectives

Section 2: Financial Accounting—Accounts Receivable Reports
Customer Open Item Analysis (A/R Aging)

This screen shows the middle section of the report.

F Detailed listing of open items with day count (for example, the second item has aged 127 days)

G The document number (for example, *1800000004*)

H Key dates (for example, *04/02/1998*)

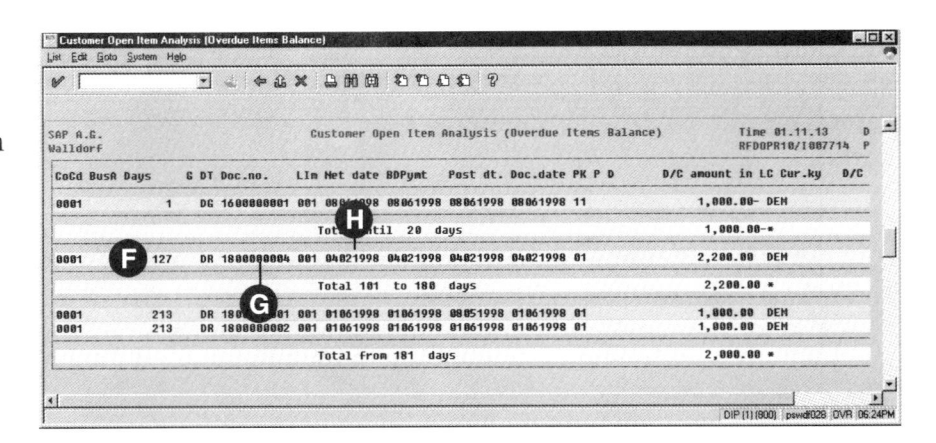

Example 2: Generate a summary of all customer accounts for a company as of a certain date, with the summarization level set at totals per clerk, company, and overall total.

1. Enter **1000** in *Company code*.
2. Enter **08/07/1998** in *Open items at key date*.

   The system selects all items that posted before this date and remain open for this period. The current date is the default setting.

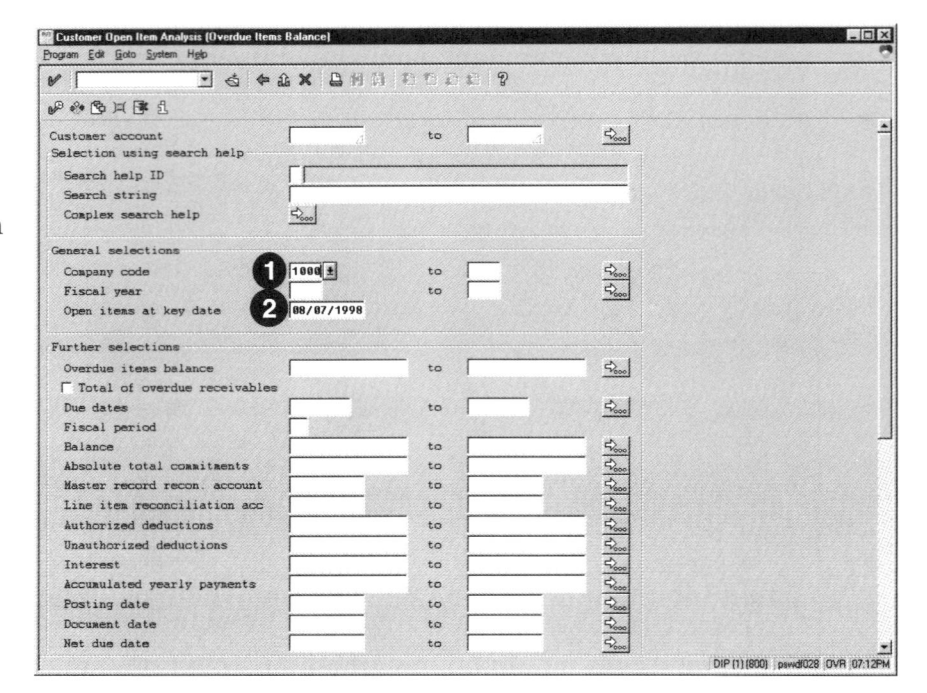

Section 2: Financial Accounting—Accounts Receivable Reports
Customer Open Item Analysis (A/R Aging)

3. Scroll down the screen to set the *Output control*.

4. Enter **6** in *Summarization level*. This will produce an open item list, totals per clerk, per company, and an overall total.

5. Accept the default of **20, 40, 80, 100** days in *Due date sorted list*.

6. Choose *Execute*.

A No detailed list appears since there are no open items at the key date.

B Total annual sales (listed by unassigned accounting clerk)

C Total annual sales (listed by accounting clerk, *D1 Claudia Forster*)

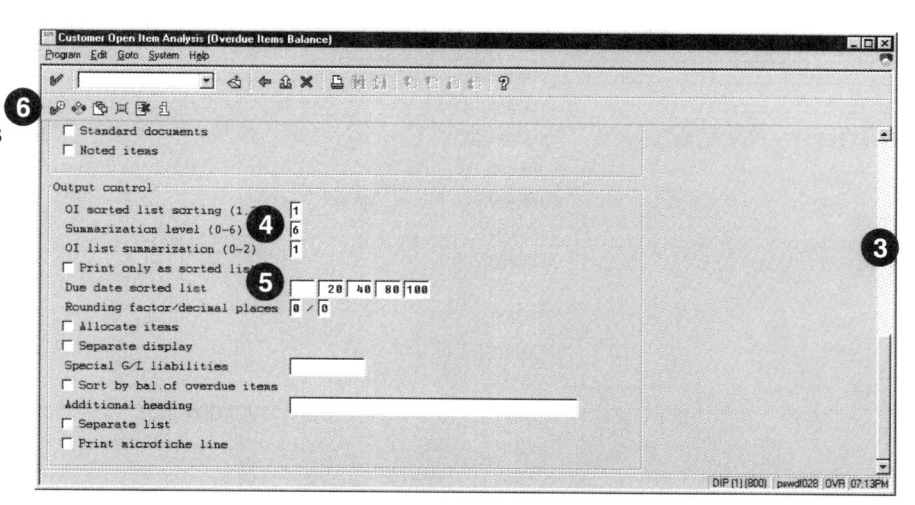

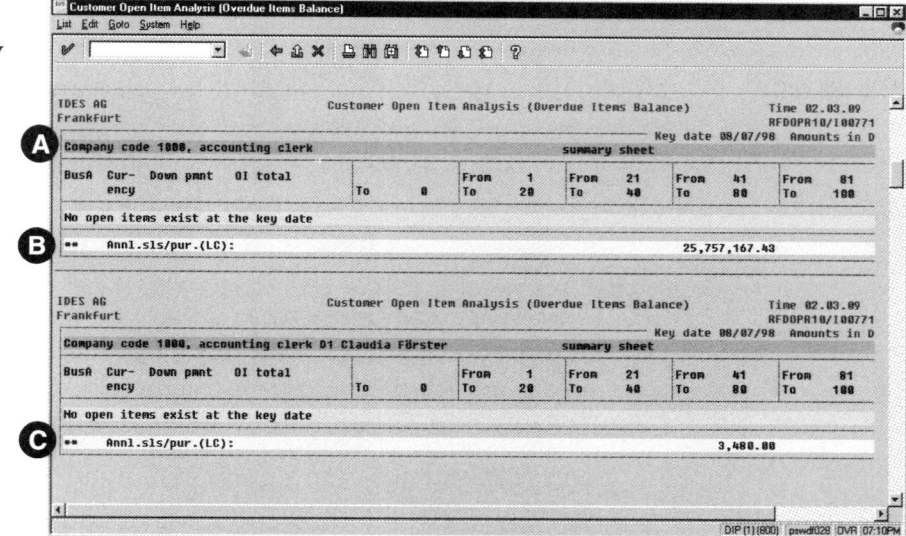

Commonly Used Reports: Illustrations and Perspectives

2–7

Accounts Receivable Information System

Quick Access To run this report, use one of the following access options:

Option 1: Menu Path

Information systems → Accounting → Financial accounting

Accounts receivable → Select report

Information system → Accounts receivable information system

Option 2: Program Name

Choose *System → Services → Reporting* and enter **RFDRRANZ** in the *Program* field. Then, choose *Enter*. Then, choose the desired evaluation view (for example, *Customer standard evaluations → Due date analysis*).

Purpose This report displays standard evaluations conducted in the following areas:

- Due date structure
- Payment history
- Currency risk
- Overdue items

You can further refine your choice of evaluation by company code, country, risk category, controlling area, dunning level, and so on. For example, the risk category evaluation node could be further exploded to lower levels to include group, credit control area, company code, or business area.

These evaluations are helpful as a high-level review tool, or as a research tool used to locate detail.

Prerequisites An evaluation must be created in advance of running this report. Do this by choosing *Accounting → Financial accounting → Accounts receivable → Periodic processing → Information system → Configure → Create evaluations*.

Integration

This report provides accounts receivable information analyzed by due date, payment history, currency, or over due items. For example, you can conduct a due date evaluation by dunning level for a company to check which customer accounts have reached a certain dunning level (such as level 3 or 30 days in arrears, assuming that dunning is configured in that manner.)

Extensive drilldown capabilities—with a host of sorting options for different levels of information—are available for the original accounting document.

You can generate graphics at certain levels of detail.

Additionally, some reports within the *Accounts Receivable Information System* can dynamically switch the format of the displayed output. For example, for the *Due Date Analysis* report, you can switch among total open items, an aging of open items due, and an aging display of open items not due, without ever having to regenerate the report.

Features

The output of this report includes :

- Dynamic sorting of output for a particular item (Shift+F5)
- Sorting capability (by column): Select a column, then choose *Edit → Sort in ascending/descending order* (Ctrl+shift+F5/F4)
- Summation by column: Select a column, then choose *Edit → Add up values* (Shift+F7)
- Additional field selection (Shift+F6)
- Graphics for displayed data (F5)

Next Steps

This report contains data obtained from customer account balances. As such, the data cannot be changed or manipulated from the report.

Section 2: Financial Accounting—Accounts Receivable Reports

Accounts Receivable Information System

Guided Tour

> **Example:** Generate a due-date analysis for all companies. Then, drill down by one company to a particular customer for items due. Finally, drill down to the line items and the original accounting document.

To access the first screen for this report, choose

Information systems → *Accounting* → *Financial accounting*

Accounts receivable → *Select report*

Information system → *Accounts Receivable Information System* → *Due date analysis*.

A partially exploded view of the *Accounts Receivable Information System's* standard evaluations displays with the following nodes:

- Due date analysis
- Payment history
- Currency analysis
- Overdue items

Each node has additional levels of evaluation at subnodes, or deeper levels of detail.

1. Click *Evaluation by Company code*.

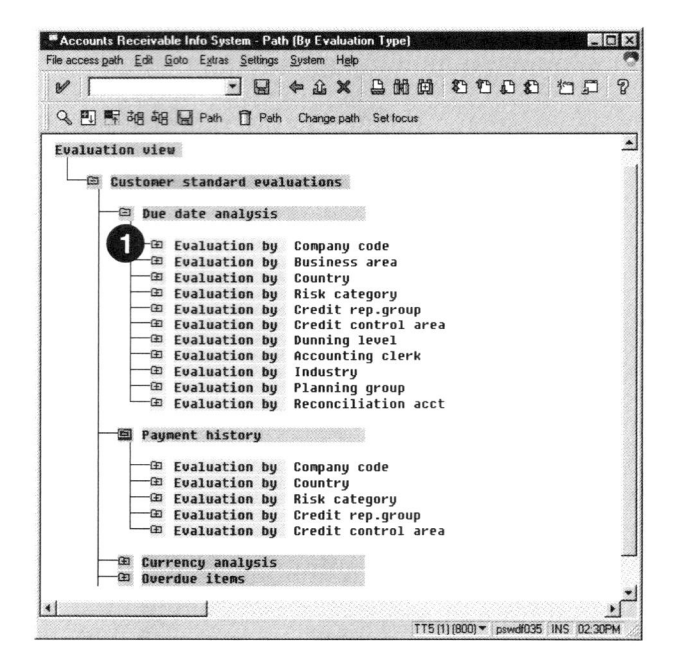

Reporting Made Easy

2–10

Section 2: Financial Accounting—Accounts Receivable Reports
Accounts Receivable Information System

Evaluation by company code has three subnodes:

- For group
- For credit controlling area
- For business area

2. Under *Evaluation by company code*, double-click on a subnode to execute its evaluation (for example, *800 IDES-ALE: Central FI Syst*).

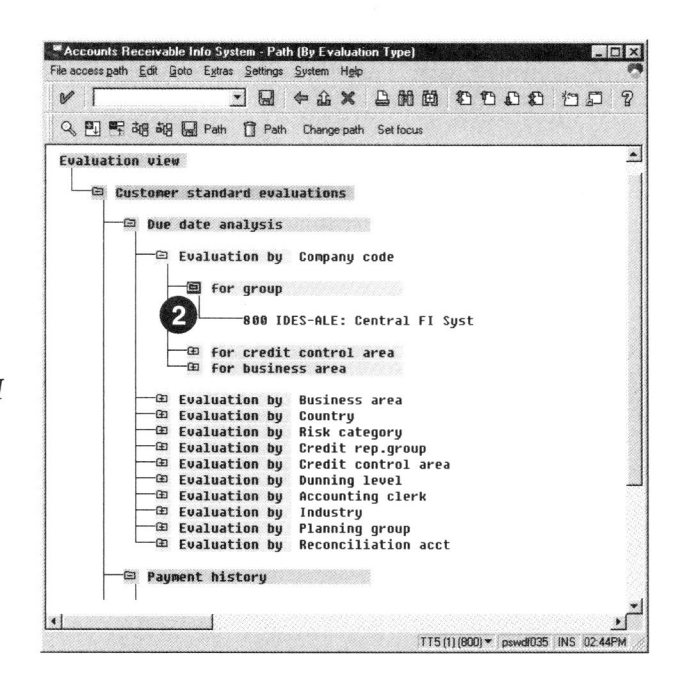

This screen shows the evaluation *800 IDES-ALE: Central FI Syst*. This is a high-level overview, comparing each company on a due and not due basis.

3. Double-click (drill down) on *IDES AG* to view the report for that company's open items.

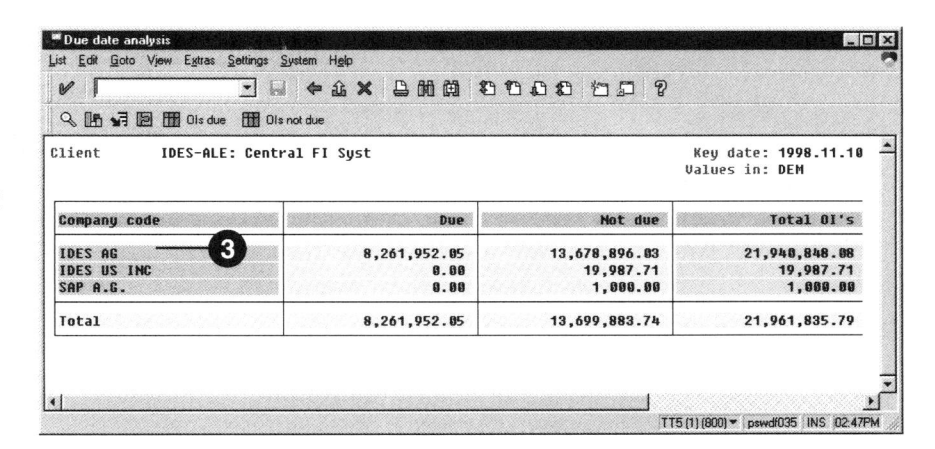

4. The two chart icons enable you to toggle between the total items format and the due items aging while showing the "order items not due.".

5. Drill down on the due balance of *468,986.85* for vendor *N.I.C. High Tech* to view a basic list of customer line items.

From this screen you can review the line list, or drill down to the original accounting document.

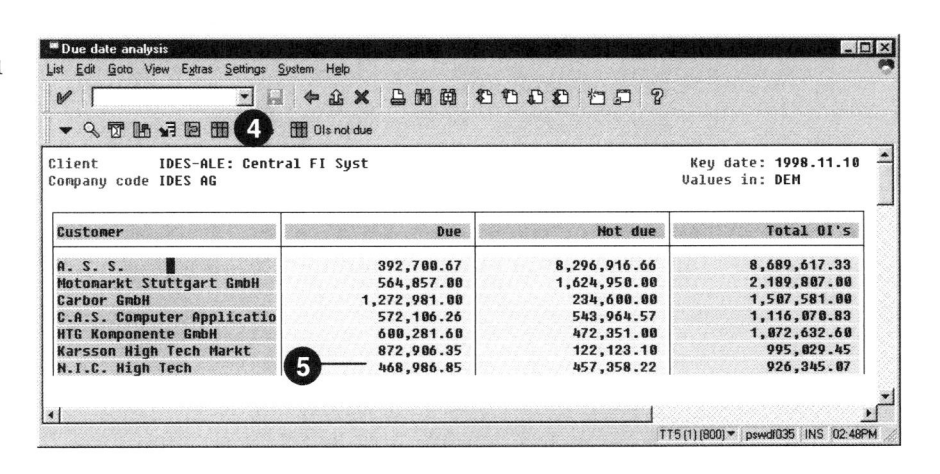

Commonly Used Reports: Illustrations and Perspectives

2–11

Section 2: Financial Accounting—Accounts Receivable Reports
Accounts Receivable Information System

The Customer line items: basic list for *N.I.C. High Tech* appears.

This list provides basic information (for example, amount, document date (*98.06.17*) and document number (*0100008125*)).

From this screen you can also review the line list or drill down to the original accounting document.

6. Double-click on the document number (for example, *0100008125*) to drill down to the accounting document.

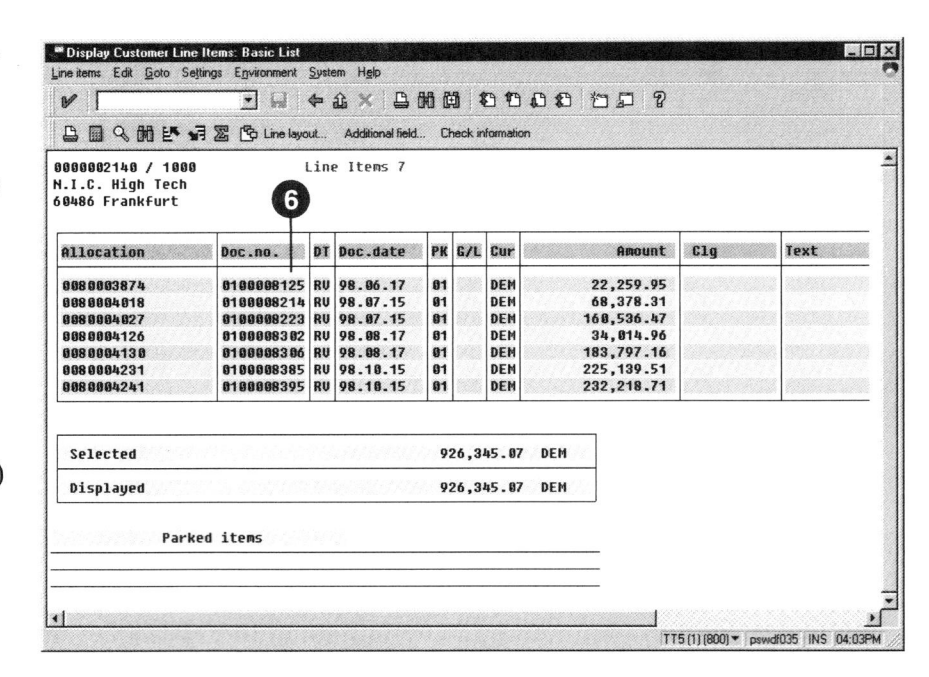

The accounting document shows:

A Payment terms (for example, *ZB01*)

B Business area (for example, *7000*)

C G/L account (for example, *140000*)

7. Choose *Overview* to view all the lines items.

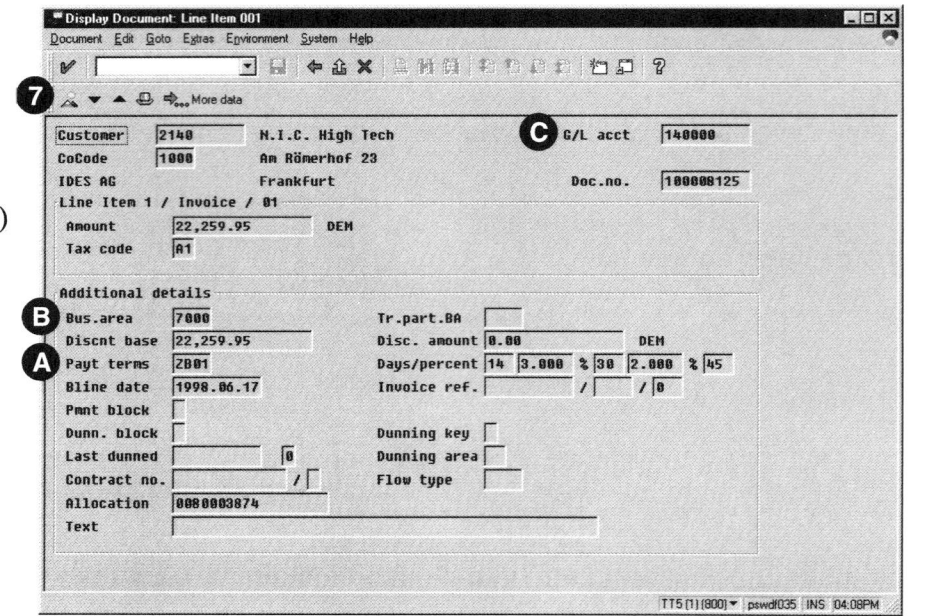

2–12 **Reporting Made Easy**

Section 2: Financial Accounting—Accounts Receivable Reports
Accounts Receivable Information System

D   Document line (for example, line item *001* is *DEM 22,259.95*)

E   Postings (for example, a quick review on the document line items reveals the posting of *22,259.95* to the customer *N.I.C. High Tech*, and the posting to the *Sales revenues* for *19,552.00*, *Sales deductions* for *195.52*, and the *Output taxt* portion of *2,903.47*)

F   To view the creation data for the document, choose *Document header*.

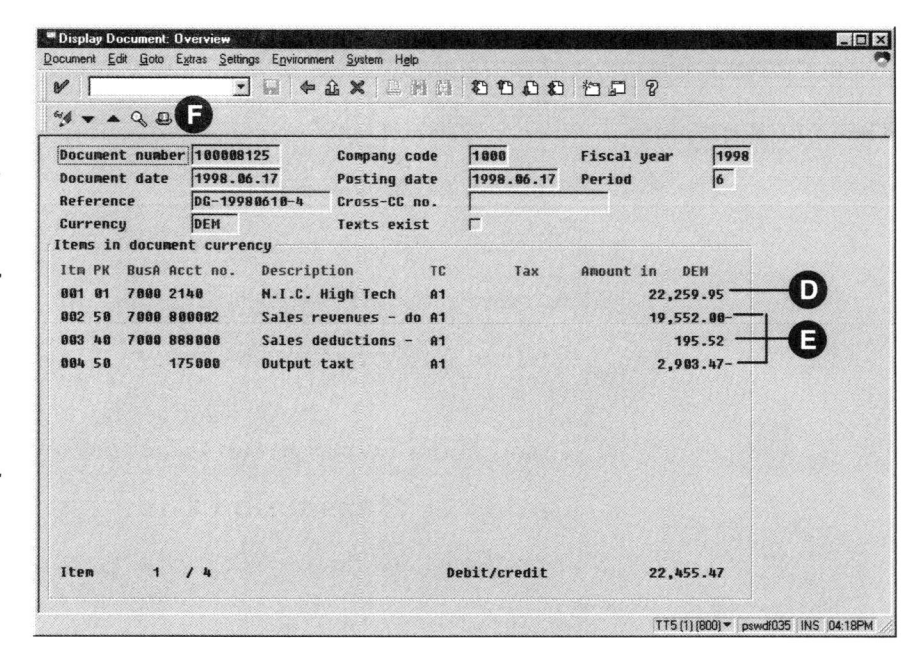

Commonly Used Reports: Illustrations and Perspectives

2–13

List of Customer Open Items

Quick Access To run this report, use one of the following access options:

Option 1: Menu Path

Information systems → *Accounting* → *Financial accounting*

Accounts receivable → *Open Items*

Option 2: Program Name

Choose *System* → *Services* → *Reporting* and enter `RFDOPO00` in the *Program* field. Then, choose *Execute* to run the report.

Option 3: Transaction Code

In the *Command* field, enter transaction `F.21` and choose *Enter*.

Purpose This report lists open customer receivables, sorted by key date. Line items may be suppressed to display only balances. Customer receivables can be analyzed based on a variety of selection parameters. The list of customer receivables offers dynamic sorting options that range from the A/R reconciliation account to the industry group of the customer to the accounting clerk who entered the item.

Prerequisites No prerequisites are required to run this report.

You can run the report with only the *Open items at key date* selected. However, we suggest a criteria-based search to produce a more targeted analysis. As a default, output is sorted by the reconciliation account.

For every account with selected postings, the following will be displayed:

CC	Company code
Recon. Acct	Reconciliation account
Acct No.	Customer account number
Account Name	Customer name
Key Date	Date used to calculate if items are open

The following information is displayed at the line item level:

Pstg Date	Posting date of line item
Do Ty	Document type
Document Number	Document number
Doc. Date	Document date
BusA	Business area
Lin	Line Item
PK	Posting key

DK	Dunning level
PK	Payment method
Cash Disc.Base	Cash discount base
PPBD	Baseline date
Dsc Dy 1	Days for first cash discount terms
Disc. Perc.1	Cash discount percentage for first discount terms
Net Due	Net due date
GL	Special ledger indicator
Currency	Same line lists transaction currency
	Second line lists local currency amount.
Amount Document Curr	Same line lists transaction currency amount; second line lists local currency amount.

The *Output control* section of the first selection screen is used to gather information and to decide the report layout.

The S-sort and P-sort indicators allow you many different types of groupings for customer open items.

Integration

You can view the debit and credits in document and local currency, net due date, reconciliation account, discount percentage, and so on of all customer open items for a given period. This, combined with the eight standard sorting criteria for master data (reconciliation account, country, group key, consolidated company, industry key, accounting clerk, account abbreviation, and account number) provides highly specialized ways of viewing customer open items.

Features

The selection screen of this report includes:
- Variants
- Dynamic selection options
- User variables
- Execution (and print) in background

The output includes a listing of the customer open items, sorted by various criteria.

Normal version sorting sequence: Company code, S-sort indicators (1-8), Account number, P-sort indicators (1-7), Allocation number, Posting date, Currency key, Sales indicator, Business area.

S-sort indicator for master data:

1. Sort by reconciliation account (default)
2. Sort by country
3. Sort by group key

Section 2: Financial Accounting—Accounts Receivable Reports
List of Customer Open Items

4. Sort by consolidated company
5. Sort by industry key
6. Sort by accounting clerk
7. Sort by account abbreviation (sort field)
8. Sort by account number

P-sort indicator for line item data:

1. Sorting by special G/L indicators (default)
2. Sorting by allocation number within the account number
3. Sorting by posting period/posting date
4. Sorting by due date
5. Sorting by document date
6. Sorting by business area
7. Sorting according to cash discount 1 due date (Cash discount 1 due date is issued in the list instead of the due date for the net payment)

Next Steps   This report contains data obtained from customer account balances. As such, the data cannot be changed or manipulated from the report.

Section 2: Financial Accounting—Accounts Receivable Reports

List of Customer Open Items

Guided Tour

Example: Generate a listing of all customer open items for company 1000.

To access the first screen for this report, choose

Information systems → Accounting → Financial accounting
Accounts receivable → Open Items.

1. Enter **1000** in *Company code*.

2. Enter **08/10/1998** in *Open items at key date*.

   The system selects all items that posted before this date and remain open for this period.

3. Select *Standard documents*. This excludes sample documents, recurring entries, and statistical documents.

4. Scroll down the screen to enter the default sort settings under the *Output control* section.

5. Enter **1** in *S-Sort indicator* to sort by reconciliation account and enter **1** in *P-Sort indicator* to sort by special G/L indicators.

6. Choose *Execute*.

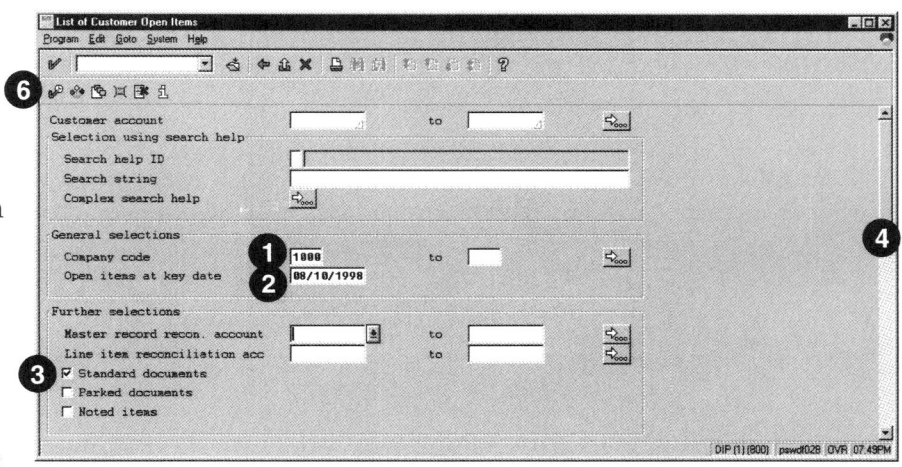

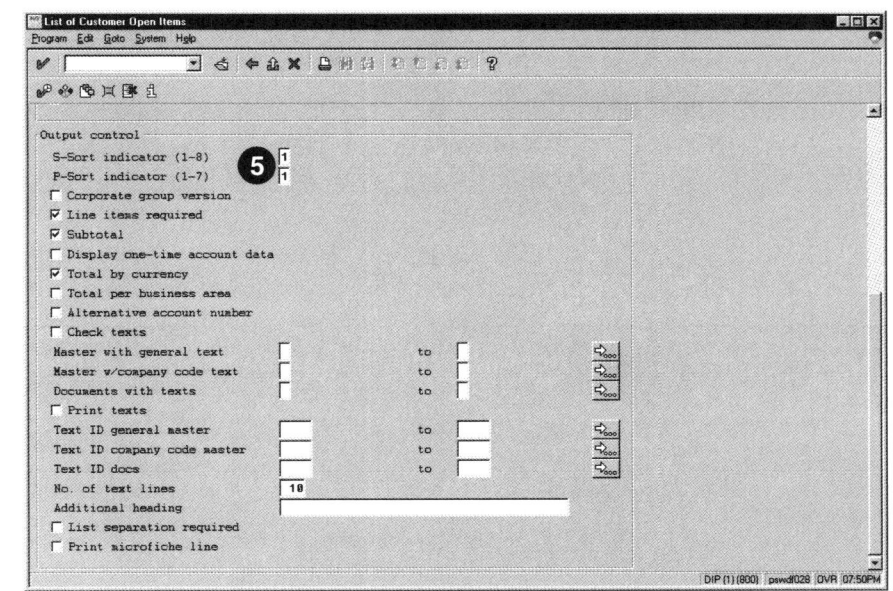

Commonly Used Reports: Illustrations and Perspectives

Section 2: Financial Accounting—Accounts Receivable Reports

List of Customer Open Items

This screen shows the list of customer open items for the selected company code.

A   Customer and address

B   Posting date (*063098*) and original document number (*100008156*)

C   Debit amount (*18391.05*)

D   Reconciliation account number (*140000*)

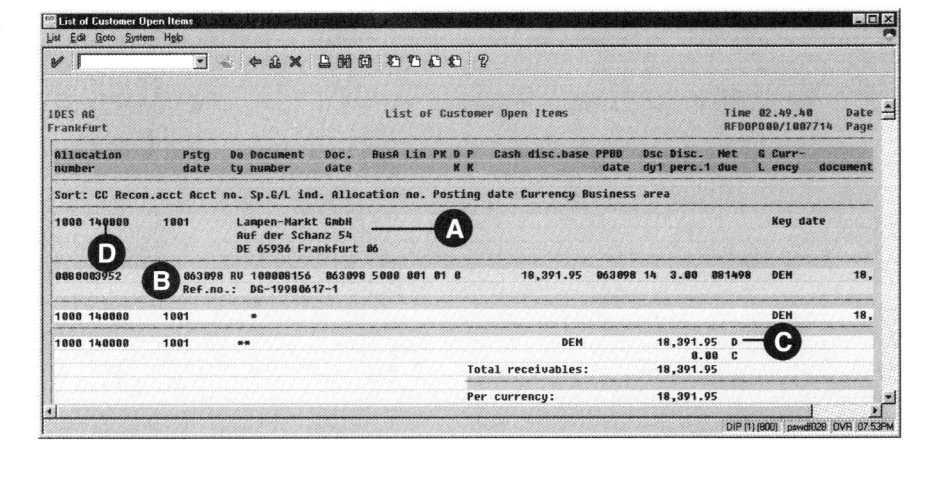

This screen shows the far right section of the report.

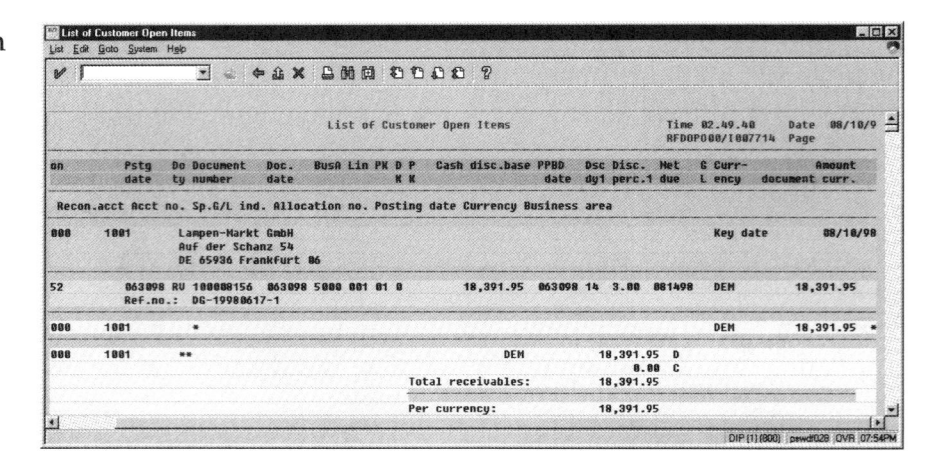

This screen shows the bottom section of the same report.

E   Total receivables for the company grouped by currency and special G/L

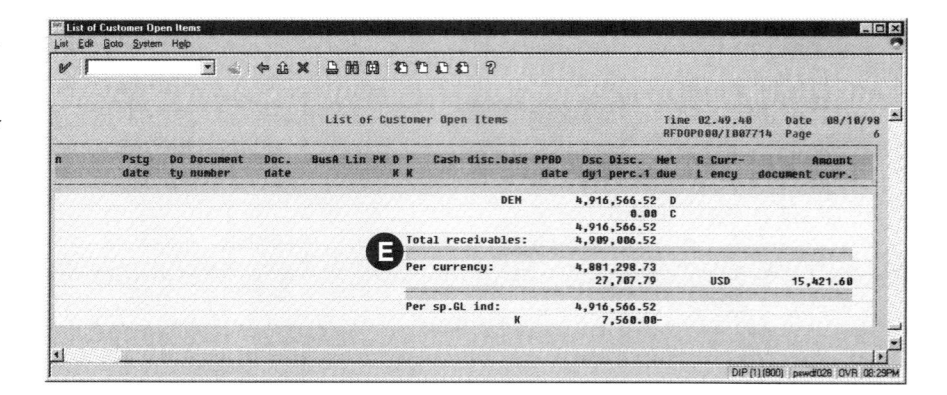

2–18   Reporting Made Easy

Customer Balances in Local Currency

Quick Access To run this report, use one of the following access options:

Option 1: Menu Path

Information systems → *Accounting* → *Financial accounting*

Accounts receivable → *Select report*

Customers → *Information system* → *Account information* → *Balances in local currency*

Option 2: Program Name

Choose *System* → *Services* → *Reporting* and enter **RFDSLD00** in the *Program* field. Then, choose *Execute* to run the report.

Purpose This report lists balances by customer account number and reconciliation account. It provides a high-level review of carry-forward balances, current debit, and credit balances for each customer in the local currency for the period selected.

The following data is issued at the end of the list for each local currency:
- Totals per company code
- Final total across all company codes

Prerequisites You must select a fiscal year and reporting period before running this report.

Output and sort sequence is flexible. As a default, output sorts by company code, reconciliation account, and then account number.

Accounting sorting sequences use option *1* which sorts by reconciliation account; option *2* sorts by account number. With both sort sequences, you can choose between a standard and a corporate version. In the standard version, the accounts are listed per company code. In the corporate version, the company codes are listed per account.

Account sort sequence 1 – standard version: The data is sorted by:

1. Company code
2. Reconciliation account
3. Account number

Summarization levels:

0 = No summarization (total per open item account)

1 = Summarization of the open item accounts (total per reconciliation account)

2 = Summarization of the reconciliation accounts (total per company code)

3 = End totals sheet only (totals across all company codes)

Account sort sequence 2 – standard version: The data is sorted by the company code followed by the account number.

Summarization levels:

0 = No summarization (total per open item account)

1 = Summarization of open item accounts (total per company code)

2 = End totals sheet only (totals across all company codes)

Recording data on microfiche: You can request information for recording on microfiche. The fixed part of the microfiche information is documented under its own parameter. The variable part (the report-specific part) has the following structure:

Standard version:
- Company code (4 characters)
- Reconciliation account (10 characters; only with sort sequence 1)
- Account number (10 characters)

Corporate group version:
- Reconciliation account (10 characters; only with sort sequence 1)
- Account number (10 characters)
- Currency key (5 characters)
- Company code (4 characters)

Section 2: Financial Accounting—Accounts Receivable Reports
Customer Balances in Local Currency

Integration In general, this report provides an overview of customer balances. The following key pieces of balance information with respect to a particular customer are viewable:

- **Balance at period start:** This consists of the carry-forward balance and any balances in the current year (for example, periods 1–4 if the reporting period selection was set at 5–12)
- **Debit or credit totals for the reporting period**: In the prior example this would be the periods 5–12
- **Debit or credit balance for the entire period**

Features The selection screen of this report includes:
- Variants
- Dynamic selection options
- User variables
- Execution (and print) in background

The output of this report includes a listing of the customer open items, sorted by various criteria.

Next Steps This report contains data obtained from customer account balances. As such, the data cannot be changed or manipulated from the report.

Section 2: Financial Accounting—Accounts Receivable Reports
Customer Balances in Local Currency

Guided Tour

Example: Generate a listing of all customer balances for company 3000 in the year 1996.

To access the first screen for this report, choose

Information systems → *Accounting* → *Financial accounting*

Accounts receivable → *Select report*

Customers → *Information system* → *Account information* → *Balances in local currency.*

1. Enter **3000** in *Company code*.

2. Enter the year for which customer balances are to be reviewed (for example, **1996**).

3. Enter a reporting period (for example, **01** to **16**) in *Reporting periods*.

   The period determines the reporting debit and credit balances. Any period that is excluded in this selection will be captured in the opening balance or the balance for the entire period.

4. Enter the standard setting of **1** in *Account sorting* to sort the report by company code, reconciliation account, and customer account.

5. Choose *Execute*.

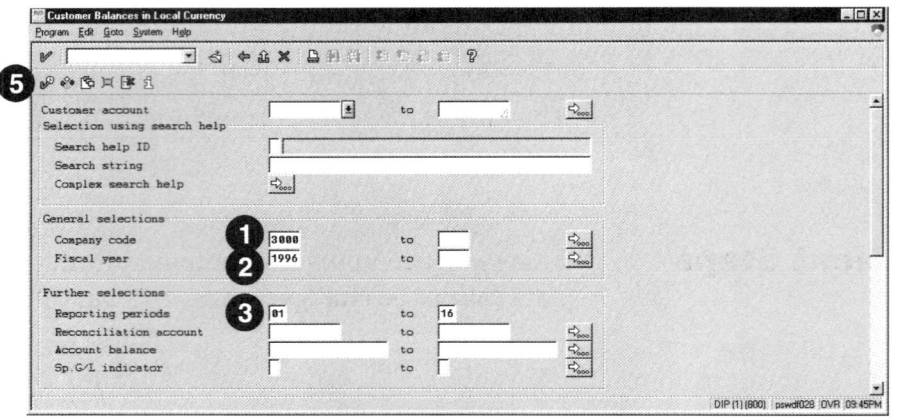

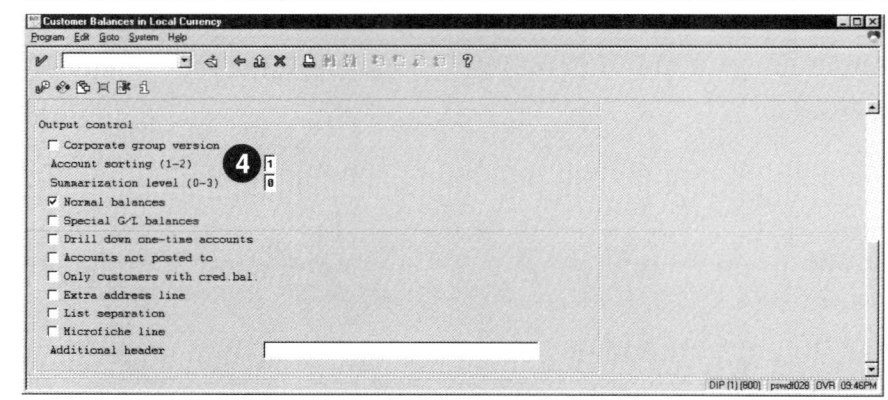

Section 2: Financial Accounting—Accounts Receivable Reports
Customer Balances in Local Currency

This screen shows the list of customer balances for the selected carry-forward period (*1-16 1996*).

A Company code (*3000*) and reconciliation account (*140000*), followed by the customer accounts

B Balances at the period start are listed for each customer (for example, customer *3000 BUSH* has an opening balance of *22,150.00*)

C Debit balance (*528,906.55*) for the period

D Credit balance (*551,056.55*) for the period

E Totals (provided by reconciliation account)

In this example, the carry-forward balance for the reconciliation account *140000* is *22,704.60*. The reporting debit and credit balances are listed as *14,580,582.41* and *14,603,287.01*.

F Total (for all reconciliation accounts in company code *3000*)

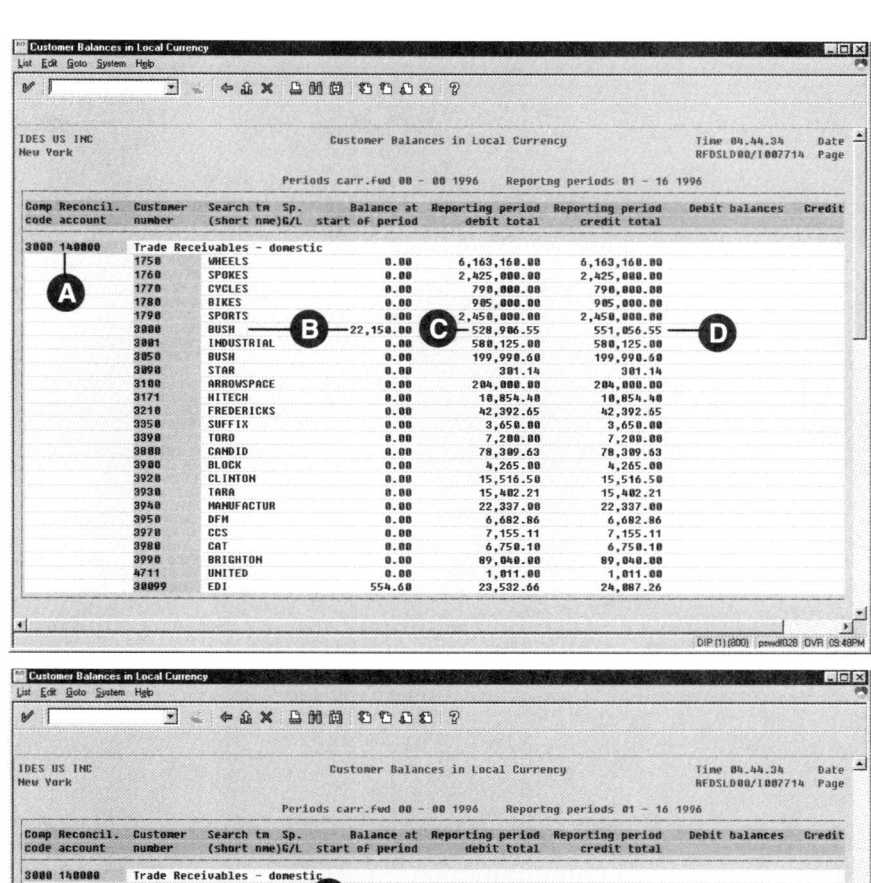

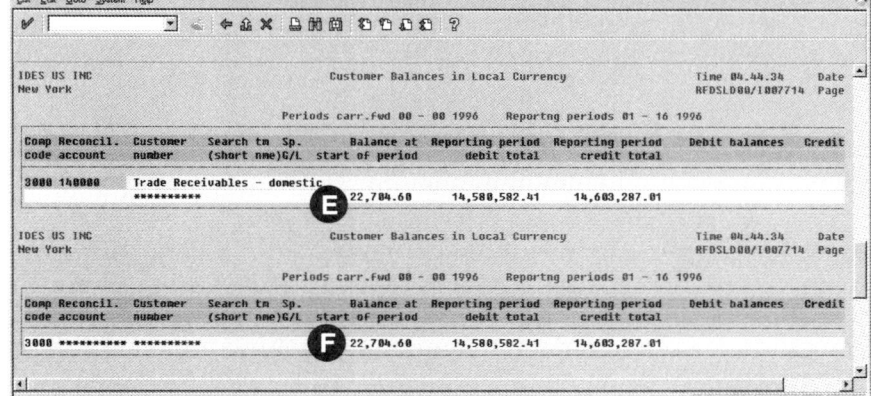

Commonly Used Reports: Illustrations and Perspectives

Section 3: Financial Accounting—Accounts Payable Reports

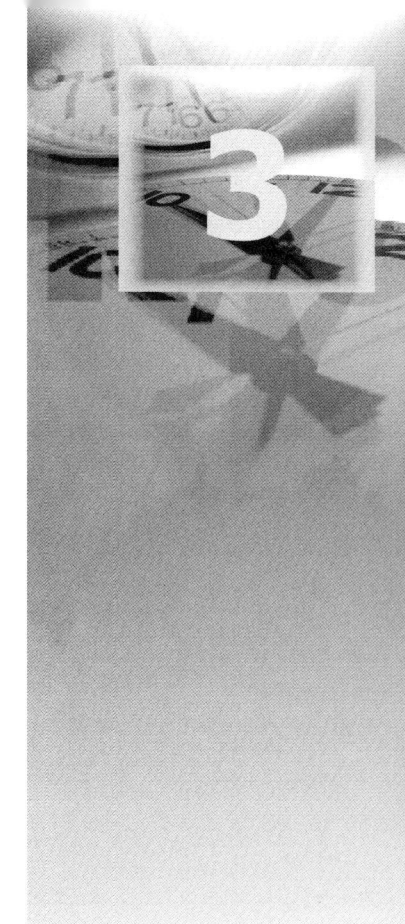

Contents

List of Vendor Open Items 3–2
Vendor Balances in Local Currency 3–6

List of Vendor Open Items

Quick Access To run this report, use one of the following access options:

Option 1: Menu Path

Information systems → Accounting → Financial accounting

Accounts payable → Open items

Option 2: Program Name

Choose *System → Services → Reporting* and enter `RFKOPO00` in the *Program* field. Then, choose *Execute* to run the report.

Option 3: Transaction Code

In the *Command* field, enter transaction `F.41` and choose *Enter*.

Purpose This report lists the open items by vendor for a given period. The list of vendor open items offers dynamic sorting options ranging from the A/P reconciliation account to the country of the vendor to the accounting clerk who entered the item.

Prerequisites You must make certain that *Open items at key date* (system date is the default) is selected before running this report.

You can plan the layout of the selected list from the output control section of the first screen. The S-sort and P-sort indicators allow you to group vendor open items by different criteria.

Output is sorted by default to the reconciliation account. Ideally, searches should be based on some criteria (for example, a company code). A practical approach would be to use the reconciliation account as a search criterion. Your company may have trade vendors assigned to one reconciliation account and employees to another reconciliation account. By using the reconciliation account as the selection criterion, for example, you could quickly view open items for trade vendors.

Integration When viewing vendor open items for a given period, you can show debits and credits (in local currency) of both the documents, the payment data (blocks, methods, and terms), the amount available for cash discount, the net due date, and the reason codes. When coupled with the eight standard sorting criteria for master data, this greatly increases the number of ways to both sort and view vendor open items.

Section 3: Financial Accounting—Accounts Payable Reports
List of Vendor Open Items

Features

The selection screen of this report includes:
- Variants
- Dynamic selection options
- User variables
- Execution (and print) in background

The output of this report includes a listing of vendor open items, sorted by various criteria.

S-sort indicators for master data enable you to sort by:
- Reconciliation account (default)
- Country
- Group key
- Consolidated company
- Industry key
- Accounting clerk
- Account abbreviation (sort field)
- Account number

P-sort indicators for line item data enable you to sort by:
- Special G/L indicators (default)
- Allocation number within the account number
- Posting period
- Posting date
- Due date
- Document date
- Business
- According to cash discount 1 due date (With this sorting method, the cash discount 1 due date is issued in the list instead of the due date for net payment.)

Next Steps

This report contains data obtained from vendor account balances. As such, the data cannot be changed or manipulated from the report.

Section 3: Financial Accounting—Accounts Payable Reports
List of Vendor Open Items

Guided Tour

Example: Create a listing of all vendor open items for company 3000.

To access the first screen for this report, choose

Information systems → Accounting → Financial accounting
Accounts payable → Open items.

1. Enter **3000** in *Company code*.

2. Enter **1998.11.12** in *Open items at key date*. The system selects all items that posted before the specified key date and are open for the given period.

3. Select *Standard documents*. This excludes sample documents, recurring entries, and statistical documents.

4. Under *Output control*, enter **1** in *S-Sort indicator* to sort by the reconciliation account. Enter **1** in *P-Sort indicator* to sort by special G/L indicators.

5. Choose *Execute*.

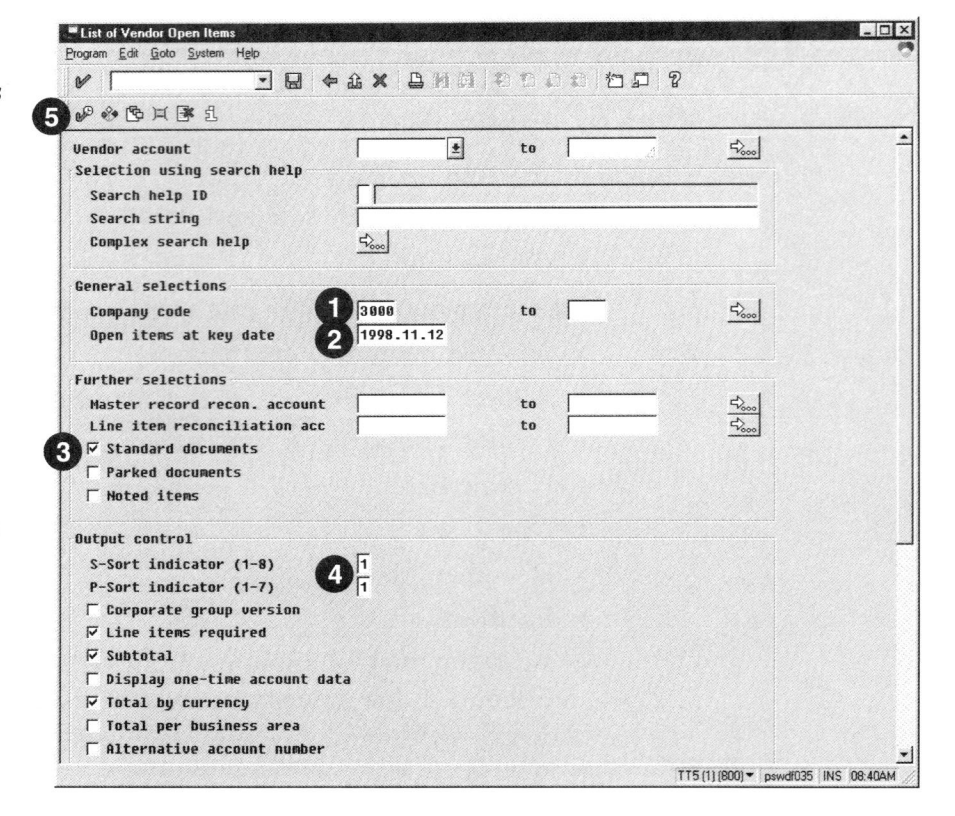

Section 3: Financial Accounting—Accounts Payable Reports
List of Vendor Open Items

A The list of vendor open items for the selected company code and the sort sequence for this report

B The vendor *C.E.B New York* and its address information

C The posting date of *08/31/98* and the original document number *5100000001*

D The credit amount of *9,750.00* displayed by currency

E The reconciliation account *160000*

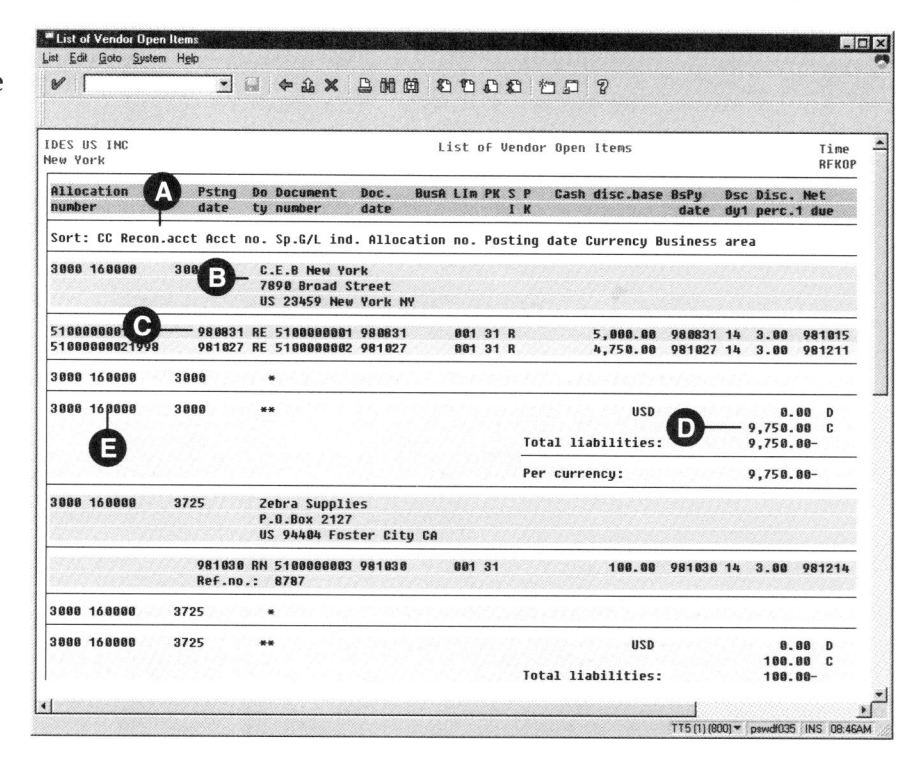

This screen shows the far right side of the *List of Vendor Open Items* report.

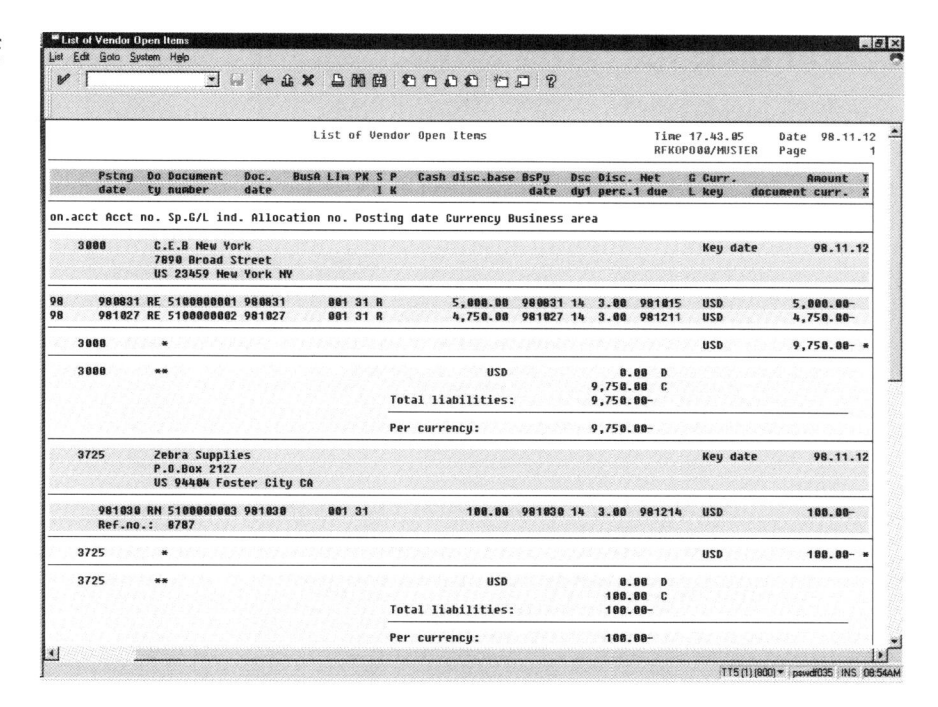

Commonly Used Reports: Illustrations and Perspectives

3–5

Vendor Balances in Local Currency

Quick Access To run this report, use one of the following access options:

Option 1: Menu Path

Information systems → Accounting → Financial accounting

Accounts payable → Account balances

Option 2: Program Name

Choose *System → Services → Reporting* and enter `RFKSLD00` in the *Program* field. Then, choose *Execute* to run the report.

Option 3: Transaction Code

In the *Command* field, enter transaction `F.42` and choose *Enter*.

Purpose This report lists the vendor balances by vendor account number and reconciliation account. Vendor balances in local currency provides a high-level review of carry-forward balances, current debit and credit balances for each vendor in the chosen period.

Prerequisites You must make certain that both the fiscal year and reporting period is selected before running this report.

The output defaults to account sorting by *1*, which means data sorts according to company code, then reconciliation account, and then the account number. Ideally, you should limit the report to criteria-based searches (for example, company code or a range of vendor accounts).

There are two account sorting sequences: *1* sorts by the reconciliation account, and *2* sorts by the account number. With both sort sequences you can choose between a standard and a corporate version. In the standard version, the accounts are listed by company code; in the corporate version the company codes are listed by account.

Account sort sequence 1—standard version: The data is sorted by:

1. Company code
2. Reconciliation account
3. Account number

Section 3: Financial Accounting—Accounts Payable Reports
Vendor Balances in Local Currency

Summarization levels:

0 = No summarization (total per open item account)

1 = Summarization of the open item accounts (total per reconciliation account)

2 = Summarization of the reconciliation accounts (total per company code)

3 = End totals sheet only (totals across all company codes)

Account sort sequence 2—standard version: The data is sorted by the company code followed by the account number.

Summarization levels:

0 = No summarization (total per open item account)

1 = Summarization of open item accounts (total per company code)

2 = End totals sheet only (totals across all company codes)

Recording data on microfiche: You can request information for recording on microfiche. The fixed part of the microfiche information is documented under its parameter. The variable part (that is, the report-specific part) has the following structure:

Standard version:
- Company code (4 characters)
- Reconciliation account (10 characters; only with sort sequence 1)
- Account number (10 characters)

Corporate group version:
- Reconciliation account (10 characters; only with sort sequence 1)
- Account number (10 characters)
- Currency key (5 characters)
- Company code (4 characters)

Vendor Balances in Local Currency

Integration In general, this report provides an overview of vendor balances in the local currency. The following information displays with respect to a particular vendor:

- **Balance at period start:** This consists of the carry-forward balance and any balances in the current year (for example, periods 1–4 if the reporting period range is set at 5–12).
- **Debit and credit totals for the reporting period:** In the previous example, this would be the periods 5–12.
- **Debit or credit balance for the entire period**

Features The selection screen of this report includes:

- Variants
- Dynamic selection options
- User variables
- Execution (and print) in background

Next Steps This report contains data obtained from vendor account balances. As such, the data cannot be changed or manipulated from the report.

Section 3: Financial Accounting—Accounts Payable Reports
Vendor Balances in Local Currency

Guided Tour

Example: Create a list of all vendor balances for company 3000 for the year 1996.

To access the first screen for this report, choose

Information systems → Accounting → Financial accounting
Accounts payable → Account balances.

1. Enter **3000** in *Company code*.

2. Enter **1996** in *Fiscal year*. Entering the year for which you want to review vendor balances is required to run this report.

3. Enter **01** to **16** in *Reporting periods*. This range determines the reporting debit and credit balances.

    Any periods that are excluded in this range capture in the opening balance or in the balance for the whole period.

4. Make certain *Account sorting* defaults to **1**.

    Sorting order is company code, then reconciliation account, and finally vendor account.

5. Choose *Execute*.

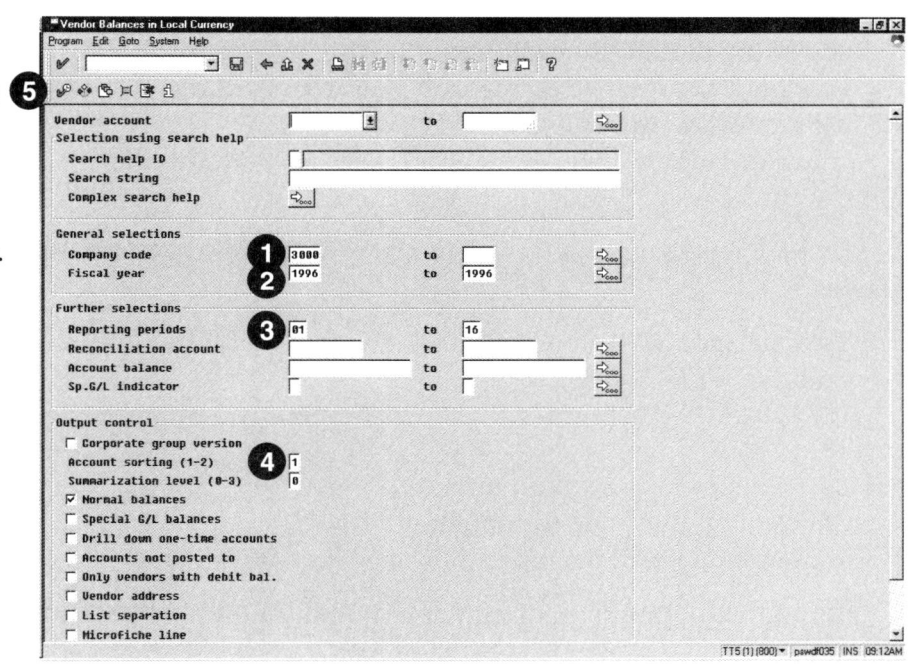

Commonly Used Reports: Illustrations and Perspectives

Section 3: Financial Accounting—Accounts Payable Reports
Vendor Balances in Local Currency

A List of vendor balances for the period (for example, *1-16 1996* indicates the carry-forward and reporting period selected)

B Company code (for example, *3000*), reconciliation account (for example, *160000*), and vendor accounts

C List of vendor balances at the start of the period (for example, vendor *3000 CEB* has an opening balance of *104,000.00*)

D Debit and credit balances at the end of the period (for example, vendor *3000 CEB* had a debit balance of *130,485.60* and a credit balance of *422,596.24*)

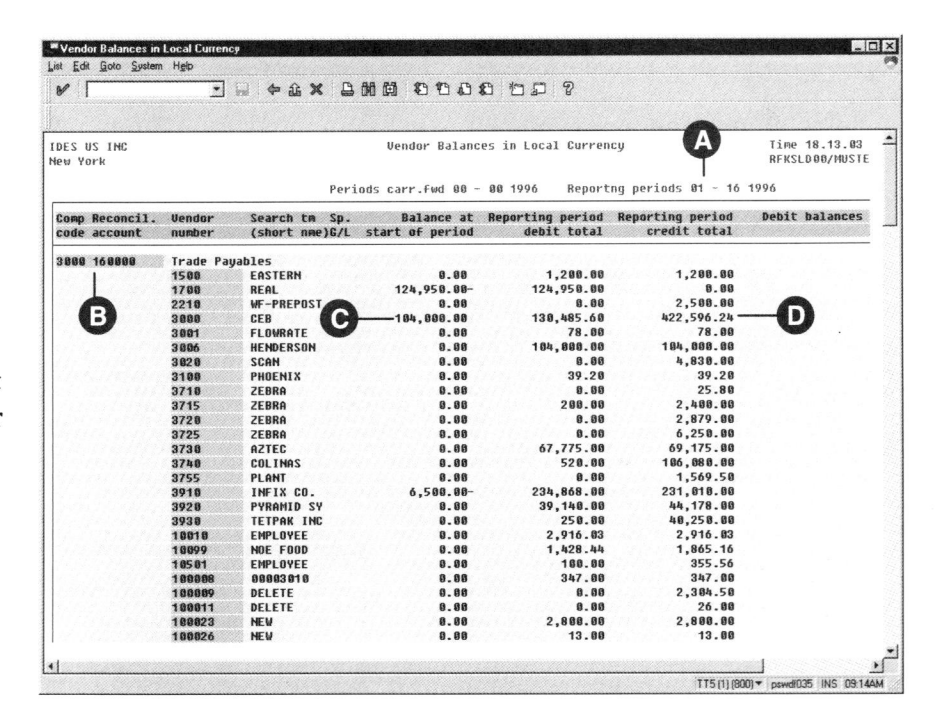

This is the far right side of the above screen.

E Total balance for the period (for example, *CEB* has a balance of *188,110.64*)

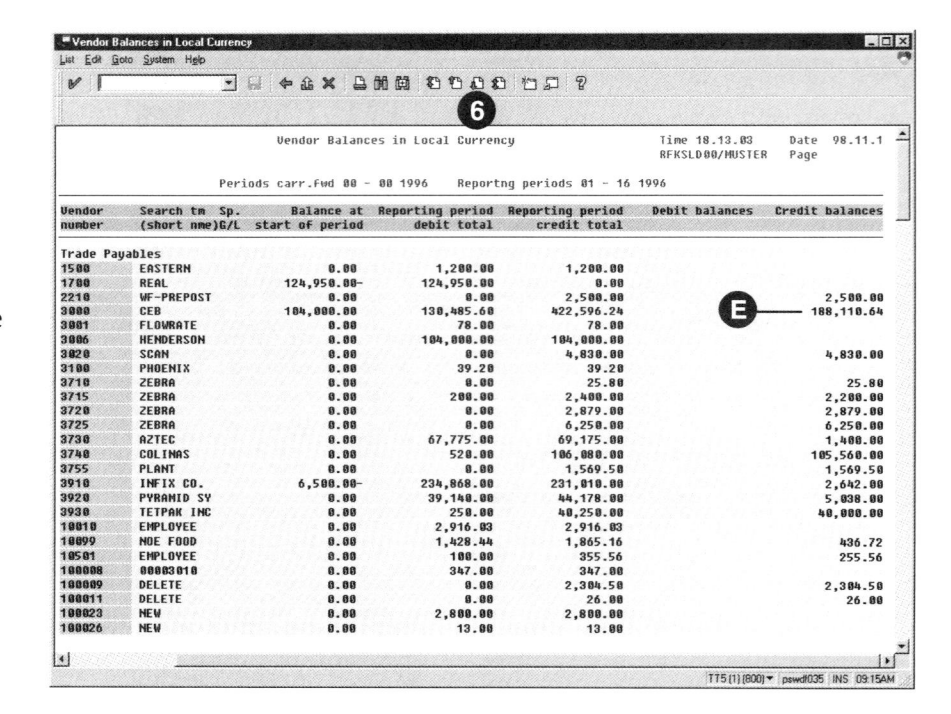

6. Choose *Page Down* to navigate to the next page of the report.

3–10

Reporting Made Easy

Section 3: Financial Accounting—Accounts Payable Reports
Vendor Balances in Local Currency

F The sorting breakpoint on the reconciliation account (for example, *160010*)

G Subtotals (at the end of each section or grouping by reconciliation accounts)

For example, *Trade Payables* had a balance carry-forward of *27,450.00*.

H The reconciliation account

For example, *160010* for *Trade Payables – Domestic one-time suppliers* shows and lists two non-recurring vendors *3010* and *3960*.

This is the far right side of the above screen.

I Credit balance for the period

For example, *Trade Payables* has a balance of *366,027.72*.

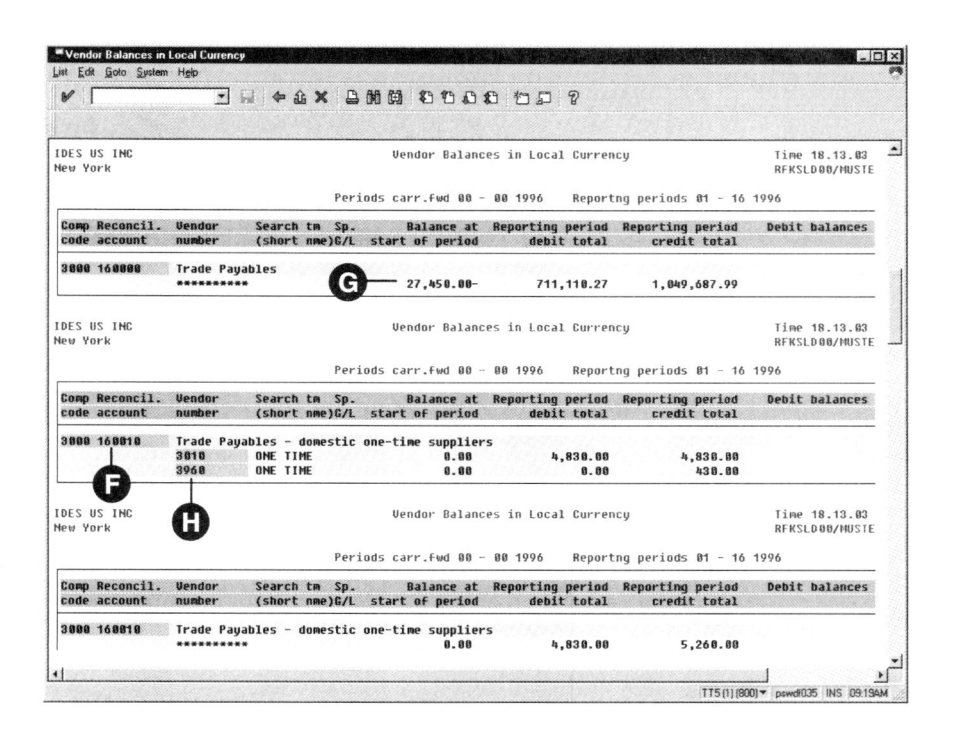

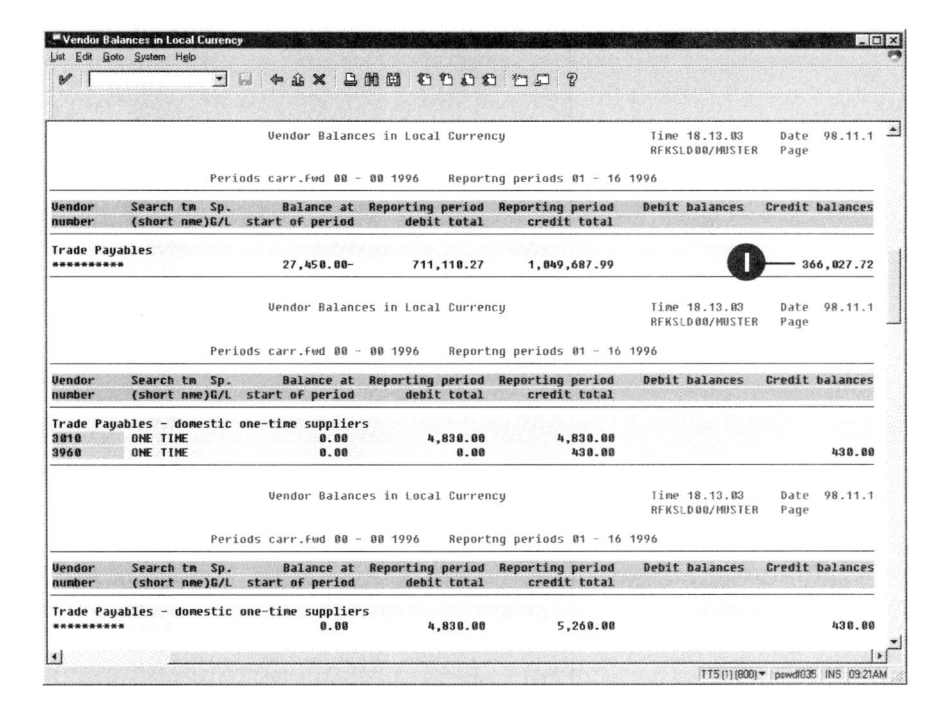

Commonly Used Reports: Illustrations and Perspectives

3–11

Section 4: Controlling—Cost Center Reports

Contents

Cost Center Summary: Planned Costs, Actual Costs, and Variances 4–2
Display Actual Line Items for Cost Centers 4–18
Cost Center Summary: Plan/Actual Costs by Period and Year-to-Date..........4–31
Cost Center Summary: Target Costs, Actual Costs, and Variances 4–37

Cost Center Summary: Planned Costs, Actual Costs, and Variances

Quick Access

To run this report, use one of the following access options:

Option 1: Menu Path

Information systems → Accounting → Overhead costs

Cost centers → Report selection

From the reporting tree, choose the following report:

Plan/Actual Comparison → CCtr: Actual/Plan/Variance → CCtr: Actual/Plan/Variance

Option 2: Program Name

Choose *System → Services → Reporting* and enter `J1SIPTEX` in the *Program* field. Then, choose *Execute* to run the report.

Purpose

This report provides a summarized view of the costs, activities, and statistical key figures that are posted to cost centers. The report includes both planned and actual postings, and calculates an absolute variance (difference), as well as a percentage of the variance.

A cost center manager would use this report to view planned costs and to monitor the progress of actual activity against the plan. The report allows for a consolidated view of multiple cost centers. The balance of the cost center is calculated from the debits and credits posted to the cost center. Any balance remaining in a cost center before month-end processing, either an over- or under-absorption of costs, is usually assessed to other cost centers or to profitability analysis.

Prerequisites

You must set the *Controlling Area* before running the report. Choose *Accounting → Controlling → Cost centers → Environment → Set controlling area*. For the examples in this section, the controlling area is set to *2000*.

You must enter a value in the selection fields before running the report. You may leave the cost center and cost element selection blank, and get a list that contains values for all cost centers and all cost elements in the selected controlling area. If you enter cost center groups and cost element groups, they must have already been set up. If they contain subtotals, hierarchy nodes should be created within the groups. Each hierarchy node then subtotals in this report.

Section 4: Controlling—Cost Center Reports
Cost Center Summary: Planned Costs, Actual Costs, and Variances

Integration You can run multiple context-sensitive reports from this cost center report. For example, when you position the cursor on a cell for planned costs, only the reports that contain planned costs list data. If you select a cell for planned costs and run a report that only contains actual data, no data lists.

The following reports run for a single cell or a range of cells:

- Actual line items for one or more cost centers
- Planned line items for one or more cost centers
- Planning overview for a single cost center
- Activity types, by period
- Statistical key figures, by period
- Cost center line items, by partner CO object (for example, partner cost center in a transaction, order, etc.)
- Cost center line items, by activity type

Two currencies are displayed for the cost center postings: the object (cost center) currency and the controlling area currency.

Section 4: Controlling—Cost Center Reports
Cost Center Summary: Planned Costs, Actual Costs, and Variances

Features

The selection screen of this report includes:

- Variants
- Dynamic selection options
- Background execution and printing
- Sorting capability (by column): Select a column, then *Edit → Sort in ascndng ordr* (Ctrl+Shift+F5), or *Edit → Sort in descending order* (Ctrl+Shift+F6)
- Adjusting the column width: *Settings → Column widths* (Ctrl+F12)
- Adjusting the numeric display, to set the number of decimals displayed and the scaling to hundredths, thousands, etc.: *Settings → Number format* (F5)
- Adjusting the summation-level for the entire report (F6)
- Mailing of the report (Ctrl+F9)
- Graphing portions of the report using SAP business graphics (F7)
- Exporting the report to a local file
- Increasing or reducing the detail displayed by double-clicking on subtotal lines. The double-click acts as a toggle switch. If the detail is displayed, double-clicking on the subtotal will hide it; if the detail is not displayed on a summary line (marked with one or more asterisks), double-clicking will display it.
- Displaying only threshold values, or values greater than or less than an entered criteria: *Edit → Threshold value* (Shift+F5).
- Creating an extract of reporting information (F5)
- Using variation to obtain multiple reports of cost center groups and hierarchy nodes (F6)
- Selecting from an extract or an archive: *Data source* (Ctrl+F1)

Next Steps

The system displays four columns for all sections of the report, including actual postings, planned data, and a calculation of the variance between the two, both as an absolute and as a percentage value (calculated by dividing the actual data by the planned).

By double-clicking on any subtotals in the report, the detail that makes up each subtotal can either be hidden or displayed. For example, double-clicking on the *Internal activities* line will hide the cost element detail. To display this detail again, double-click on this line.

This report contains data obtained from cost center postings. As such, the data cannot be changed or manipulated from the report.

This report contains five different blocks of data, as shown below. By navigating around these blocks, you can display different types of cost center data:

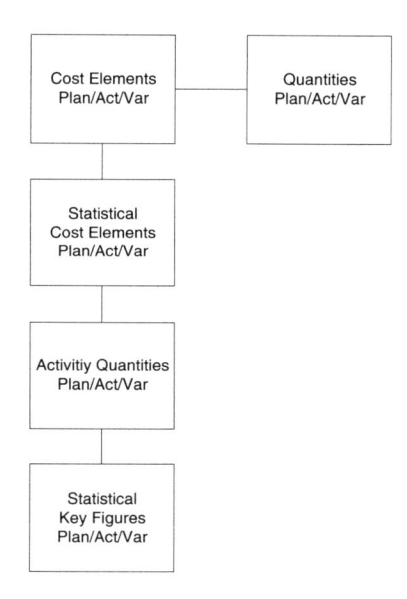

```
┌─────────────┐      ┌─────────────┐
│Cost Elements│──────│ Quantities  │
│ Plan/Act/Var│      │ Plan/Act/Var│
└──────┬──────┘      └─────────────┘
       │
┌──────┴──────┐
│ Statistical │
│Cost Elements│
│ Plan/Act/Var│
└──────┬──────┘
       │
┌──────┴──────┐
│Activitiy Quantities│
│ Plan/Act/Var│
└──────┬──────┘
       │
┌──────┴──────┐
│ Statistical │
│ Key Figures │
│ Plan/Act/Var│
└─────────────┘
```

Section 4: Controlling—Cost Center Reports
Cost Center Summary: Planned Costs, Actual Costs, and Variances

Guided Tour

Example 1: A cost center manager wants to analyze the detailed postings for a cost center, including all planned and actual costs, planned and actual activities, and planned and actual statistical key figures.

To access the first screen for this report, choose

Information systems → Accounting → Overhead costs

Cost centers → Report selection.

From the reporting tree, choose the following report:

Plan/Actual Comparison → CCtr: Actual/Plan/Variance → CCtr: Actual/Plan/Variance.

1. Under *Selection values*, enter **2000** in *Controlling area*.

2. Enter the year in *Fiscal year* (for example, **1997**). This report runs for only one fiscal year at a time.

3. Enter **1** in *From period* and enter **12** in *To period*. This range includes all periods in the fiscal year.

4. Enter **0** in *Plan version*.

5. Under *Selection sets*, enter **3200** in *Or value(s)*. You can also enter a range of cost centers or a cost center group.

6. Enter **OAS-TOTAL** in *Cost element group*. This is the name of the group which contains all cost elements.

7. Choose *Execute*.

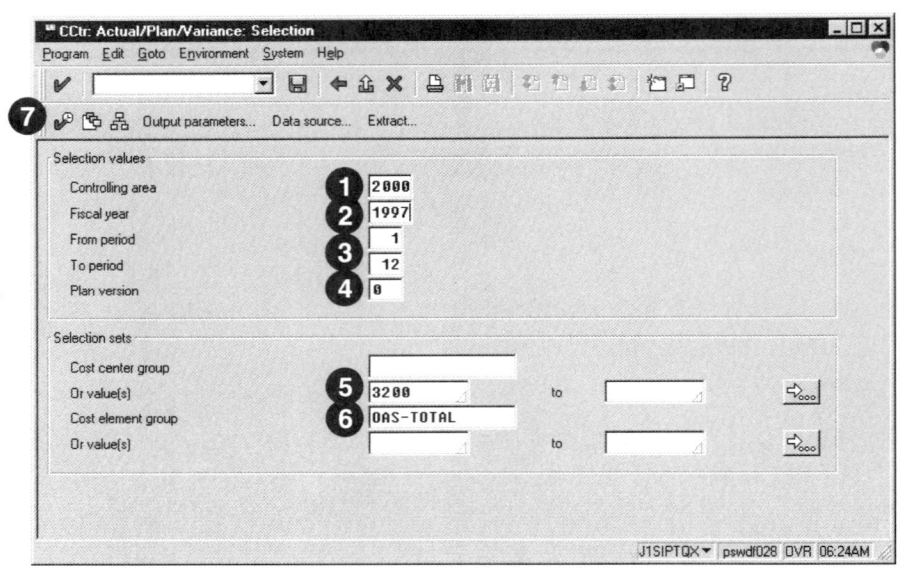

4–6

Reporting Made Easy

Section 4: Controlling—Cost Center Reports
Cost Center Summary: Planned Costs, Actual Costs, and Variances

The first screen of the report shows the cost elements, for which actual and planned costs are posted in the cost center.

Debits and credits are separated. If the cost element group contains hierarchy nodes, a subtotal is shown for each of these nodes. Absolute and percentage variances are also calculated.

Cost elements that are included in the cost element group, but for which no postings were made, are not shown.

8. Choose *Next columns*.

The next screen shows the cumulative costs posted to both primary and secondary cost elements, along with the absolute and percentage variances.

These costs are all the costs that posted to the order during the current fiscal year through the selected period.

9. Choose *Previous columns* to view the previous screen.

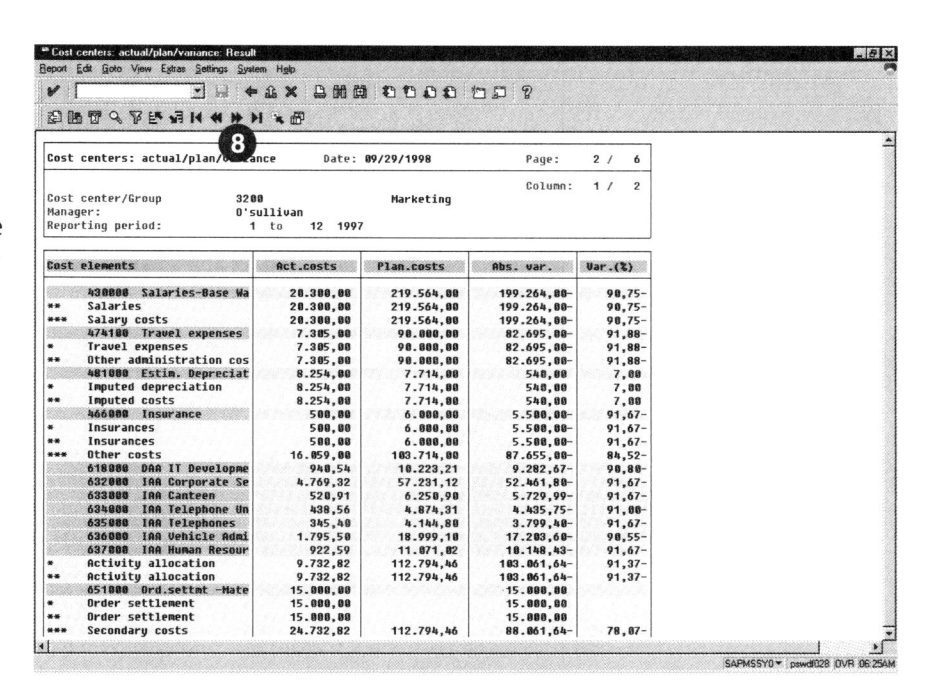

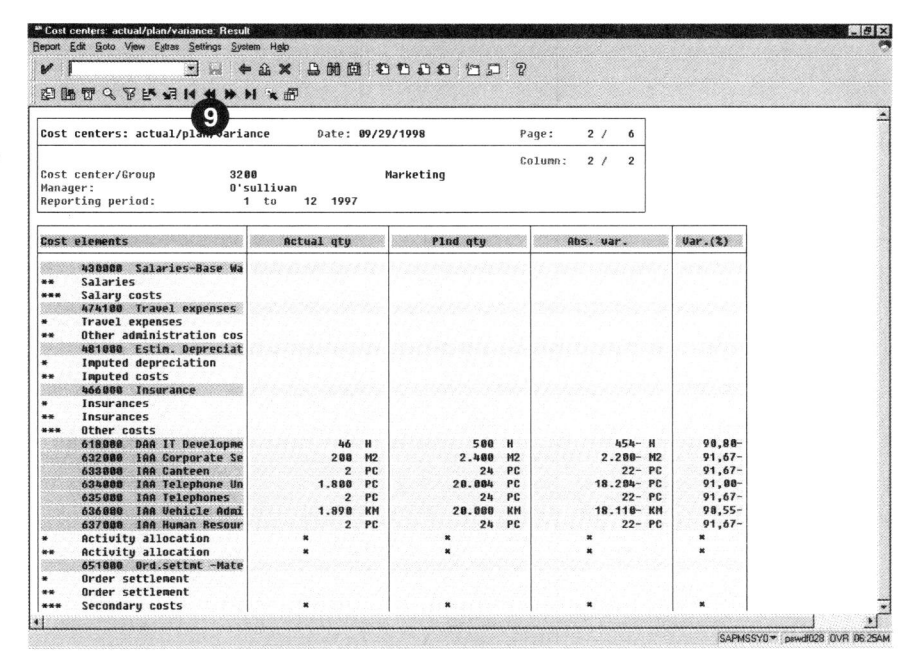

Commonly Used Reports: Illustrations and Perspectives

Section 4: Controlling—Cost Center Reports
Cost Center Summary: Planned Costs, Actual Costs, and Variances

The previous screen appears.

10. Choose *Page Down* to view the remaining cost element data.

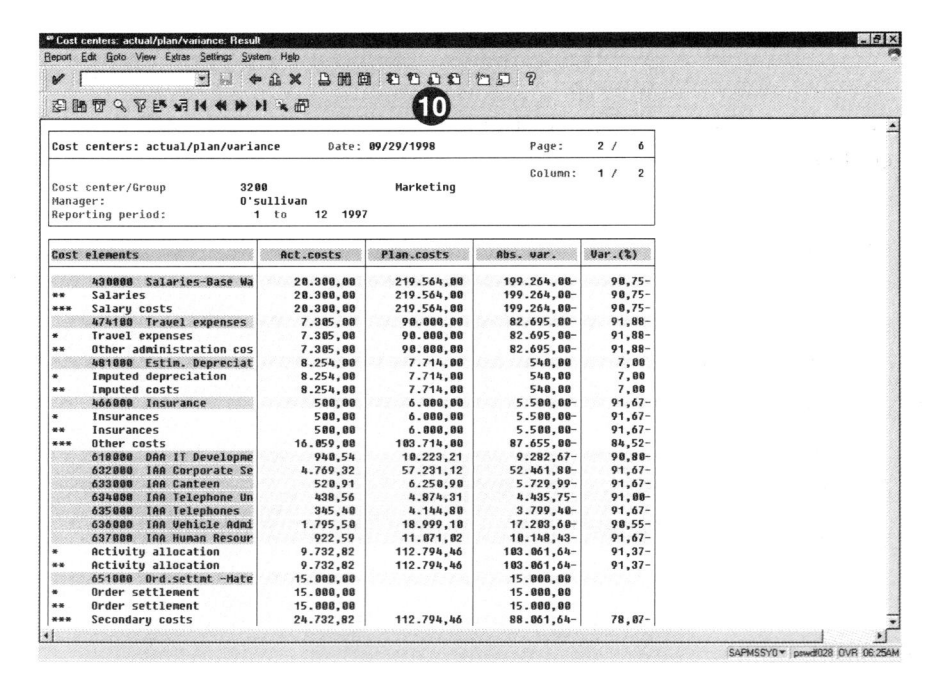

This section of the screen shows the remaining cost element data. For this example, all cost elements posted to the cost center did not fit on the previous screen.

11. Choose *Page Down* to navigate to the next block of data.

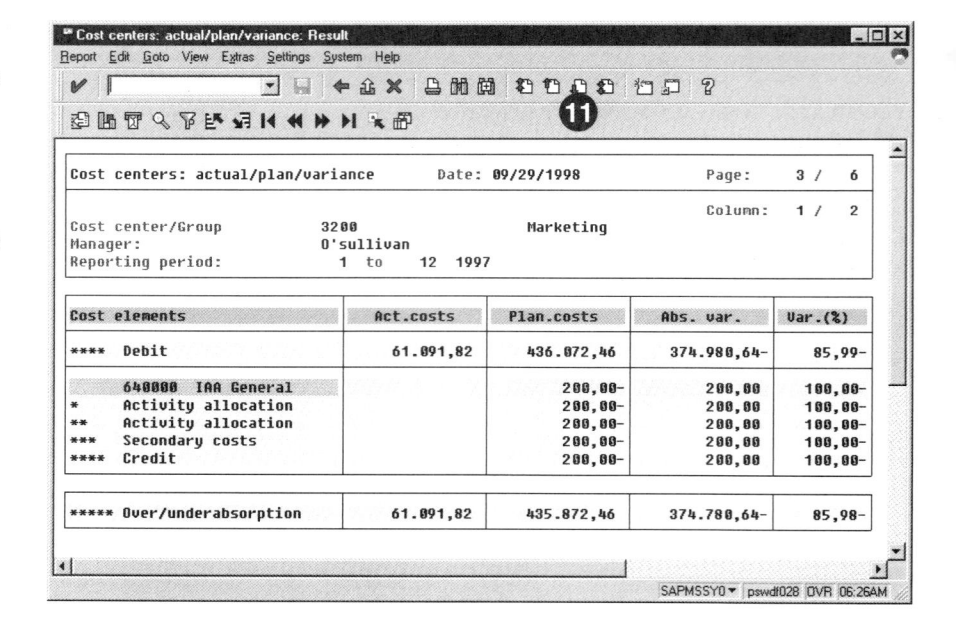

Section 4: Controlling—Cost Center Reports
Cost Center Summary: Planned Costs, Actual Costs, and Variances

These columns show the statistical postings made to the cost center. These cost elements were posted to another controlling object, such as an internal order—but with a statistical reference to this cost center. These postings are not reflected in the "real" postings shown in the previous section.

12. Choose *Page Down* to navigate to the next block of data.

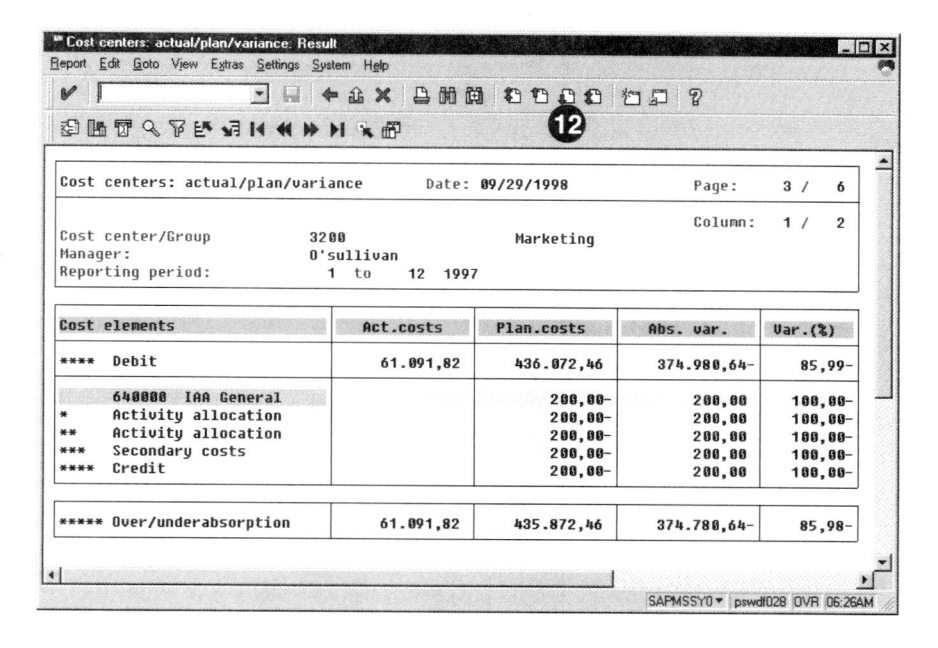

These columns show the activity quantities used in the postings, with the corresponding unit of measure. Absolute and percentage variances are also calculated.

13. Choose *Page Down* to navigate to the next block of data.

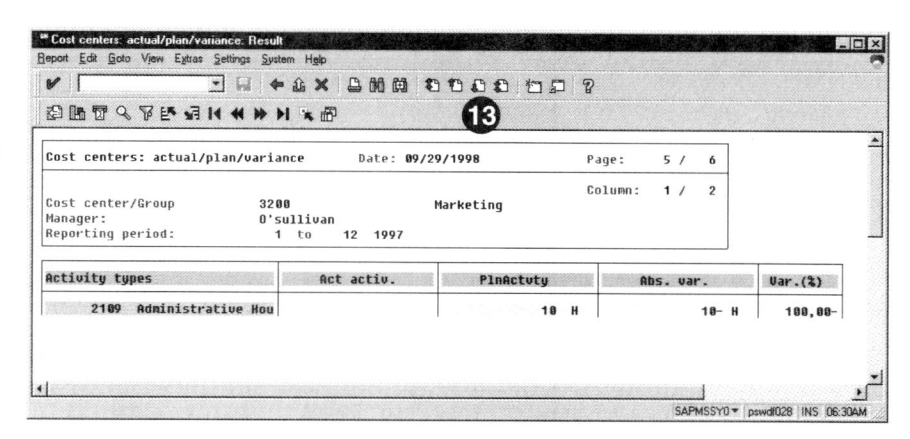

These columns show the postings to statistical key figures, with the corresponding unit of measure. Absolute and percentage variances are also calculated.

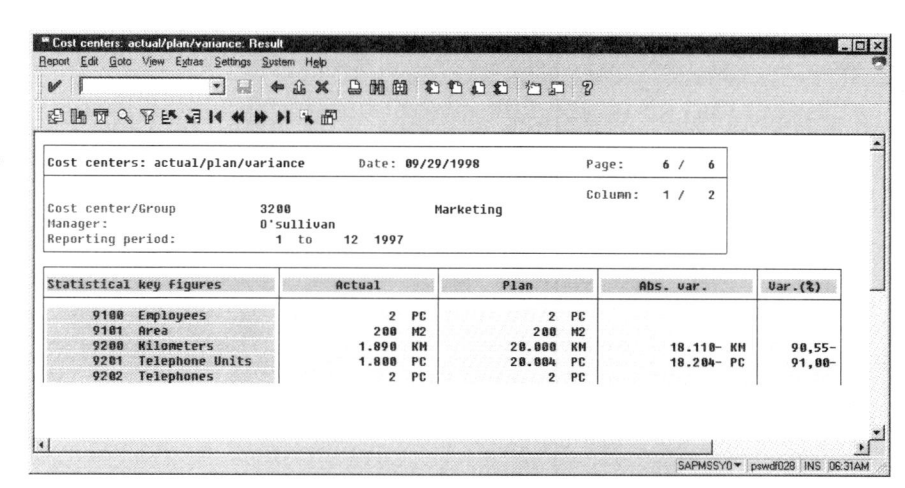

Commonly Used Reports: Illustrations and Perspectives

Section 4: Controlling—Cost Center Reports
Cost Center Summary: Planned Costs, Actual Costs, and Variances

Example 2: A manager of multiple cost centers wants to analyze only internal activity resources, or costs, that were incurred within a particular timeframe.

1. Under *Selection values*, enter **2000** in *Controlling area*.

2. Enter the year in *Fiscal year* (for example, **1997**). This report runs for only one fiscal year at a time.

3. Enter **1** in *From period* and enter **12** in *To period*. This range includes all periods in the fiscal year.

4. Enter **0** in *Plan version*.

5. Enter **H4400** in *Cost center group*. This contains all of the cost centers in the technical department.

6. Enter **OAS-IVERR** in *Cost element group*. This is the name of the group containing only cost elements that represent internal activities.

7. Choose *Variation*.

8. Make certain that the default, *Explode*, is selected. This results in data capture for hierarchy nodes, as well as for individual cost centers. Selecting the *SingleVal* option would only capture data for cost centers, with no totals for hierarchy nodes.

9. Choose *Enter*, then choose *Execute* (not shown).

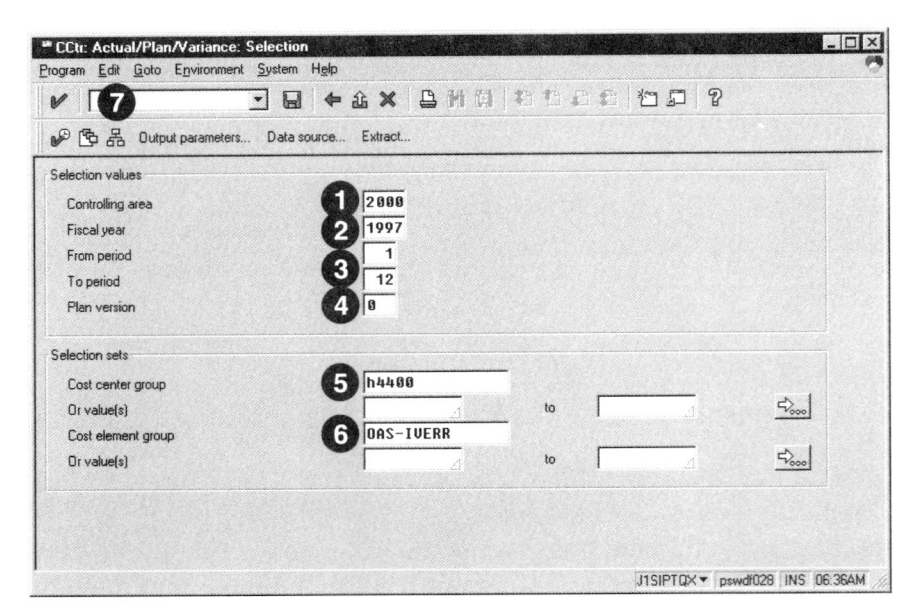

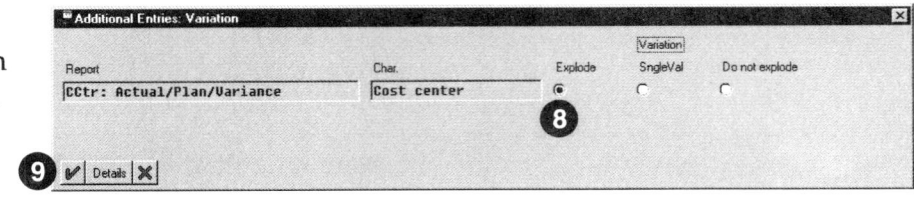

Reporting Made Easy

Section 4: Controlling—Cost Center Reports
Cost Center Summary: Planned Costs, Actual Costs, and Variances

The first screen of the report shows the cost elements, for which actual and planned costs are posted in the cost center.

Only those cost centers and cost elements that are included in the selected groups are listed. (This report does not show a complete picture of all the costs posted to these cost centers.)

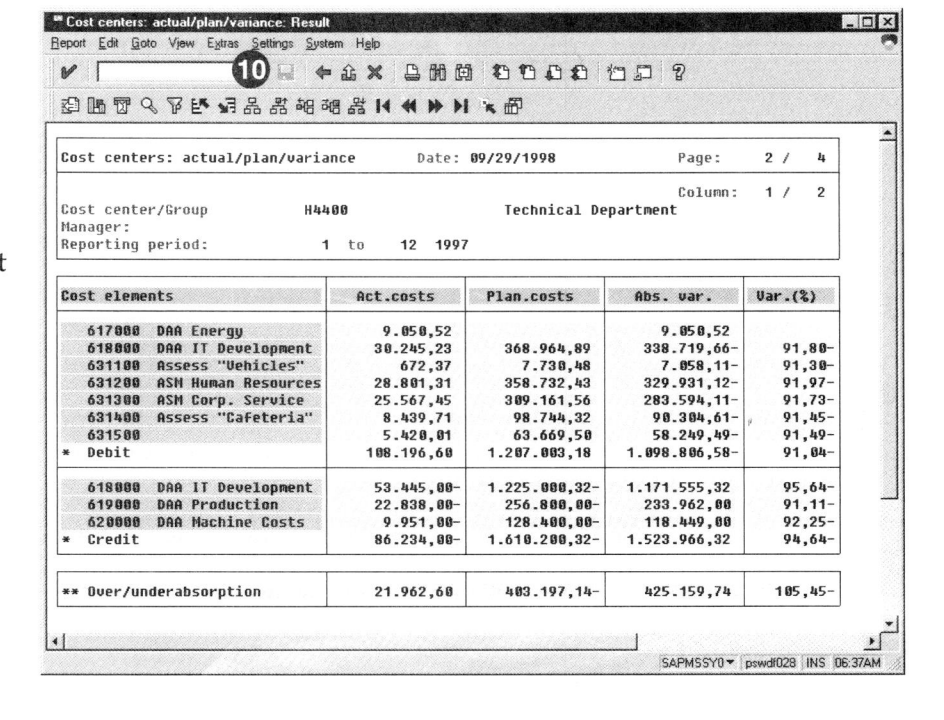

10. Choose *Variation*.

11. Choose *Field values on/off* to list the cost center numbers and hierarchy node codes, in addition to their descriptions.

12. Double-click on the *4-4200 Production PC-Parts* line to display only the values relevant to the cost center.

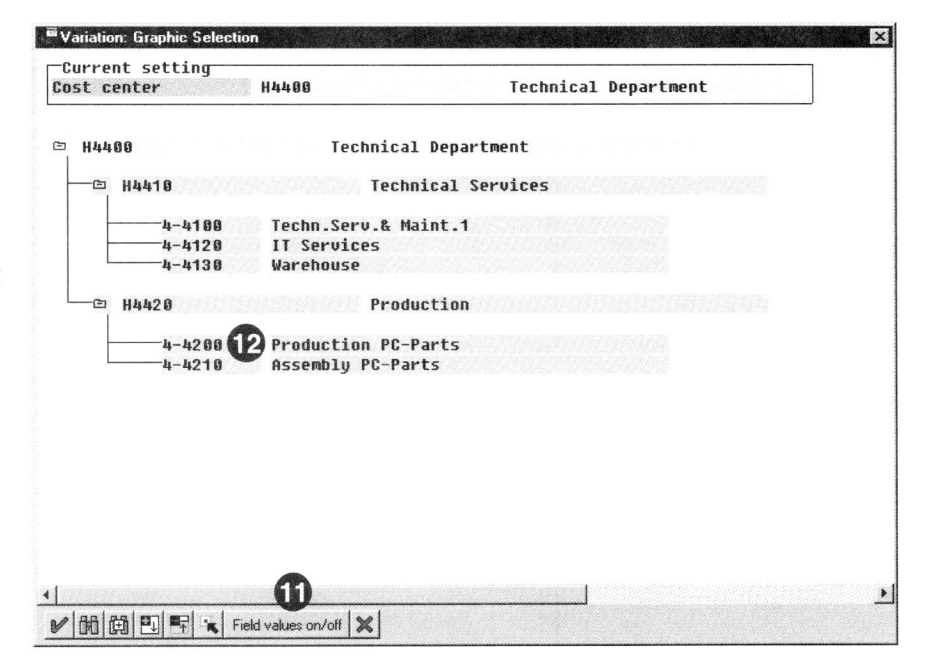

Commonly Used Reports: Illustrations and Perspectives

4–11

Section 4: Controlling—Cost Center Reports

Cost Center Summary: Planned Costs, Actual Costs, and Variances

The values change to reflect only the postings to the chosen cost center.

To scroll through the cost center group, its nodes, and its cost centers, use:

- Previous level/up
- Scroll left
- Scroll right
- Next level/down

All other sections of the report (units of measure, statistical postings, activity types, and statistical key figures) are also available.

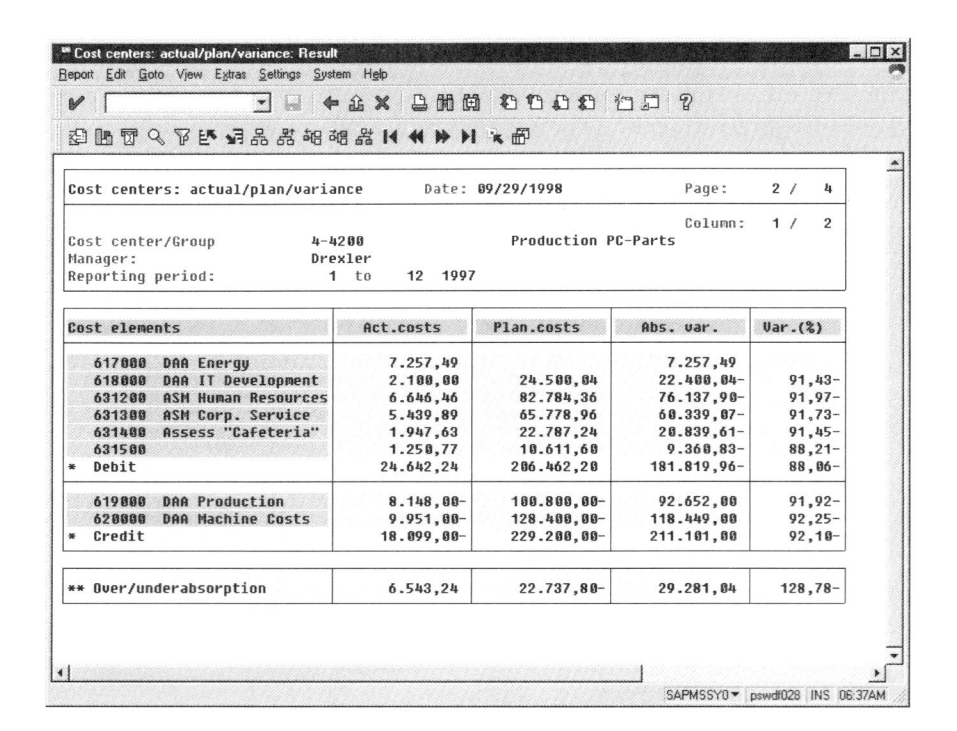

Example 3: If the run-time of a report is long due to the volume of cost centers and transactional data, or if the report needs to be saved for access by various people for an audit trail, you may want to generate an extract. An extract runs considerably faster and can be reviewed while the report is running in the background or overnight.

---

1. Under *Selection values*, enter **2000** in *Controlling area*.

2. Enter the year in *Fiscal year* (for example, **1997**). This report runs for only one fiscal year at a time.

3. Enter **1** in *From period* and enter **12** in *To period*. This range includes all periods in the fiscal year.

4. Enter **0** in *Plan version*.

5. Enter **H3** in *Cost center group*

6. Enter **OAS-TOTAL** in *Cost element group*. This is the name of the group which includes all cost centers in the controlling area.

7. Choose *Extract*.

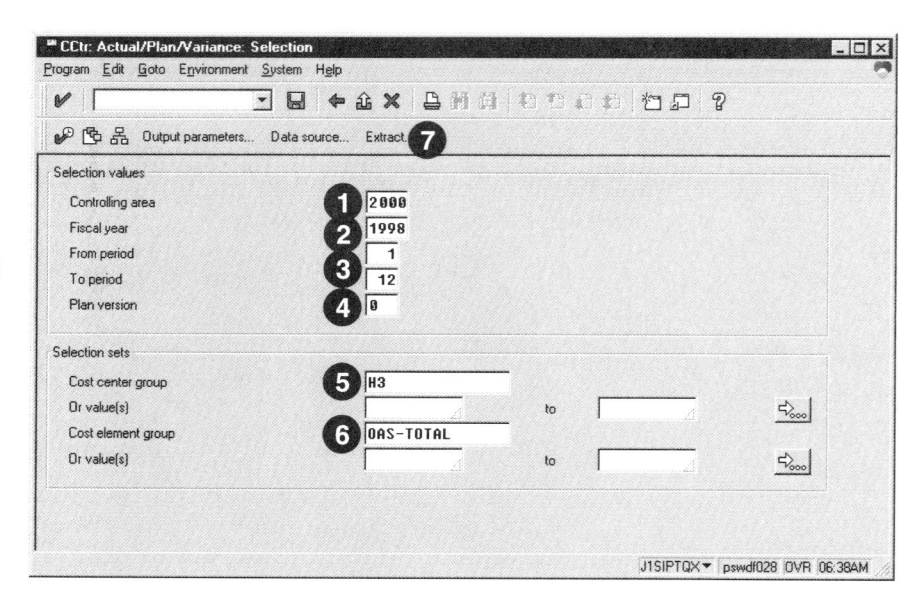

4–12   **Reporting Made Easy**

Section 4: Controlling—Cost Center Reports
Cost Center Summary: Planned Costs, Actual Costs, and Variances

8. Select *Create extract*.

9. Enter `H3 1-9, 1998` in *Description*.

10. Enter a password to protect the data. Then, enter the password again.

    A password is not required, but if one is not entered, unauthorized users may be able to access the data.

11. Enter `093098` in *Expires on*.

Assigning an expiration date:
- Ensures that the extract will not be viewed after this date
- Does not permit access to data by means of a historic audit trail
- Permits a periodic report to be run midmonth

12. Choose *Enter*.

    Selection values default for all values of cost centers.

13. Choose *Execute*.

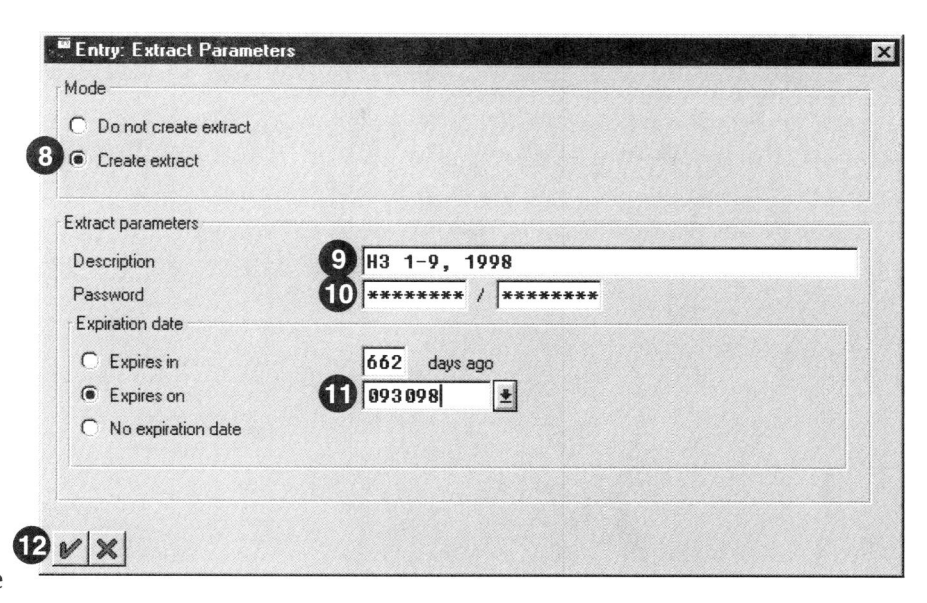

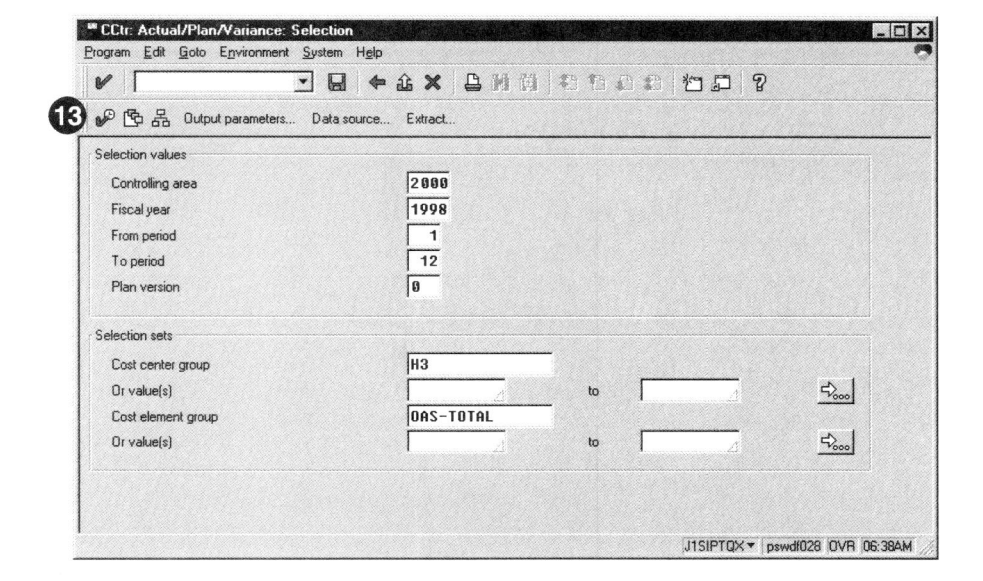

Commonly Used Reports: Illustrations and Perspectives

Section 4: Controlling—Cost Center Reports

Cost Center Summary: Planned Costs, Actual Costs, and Variances

This screen shows the report; the extract is automatically created and saved.

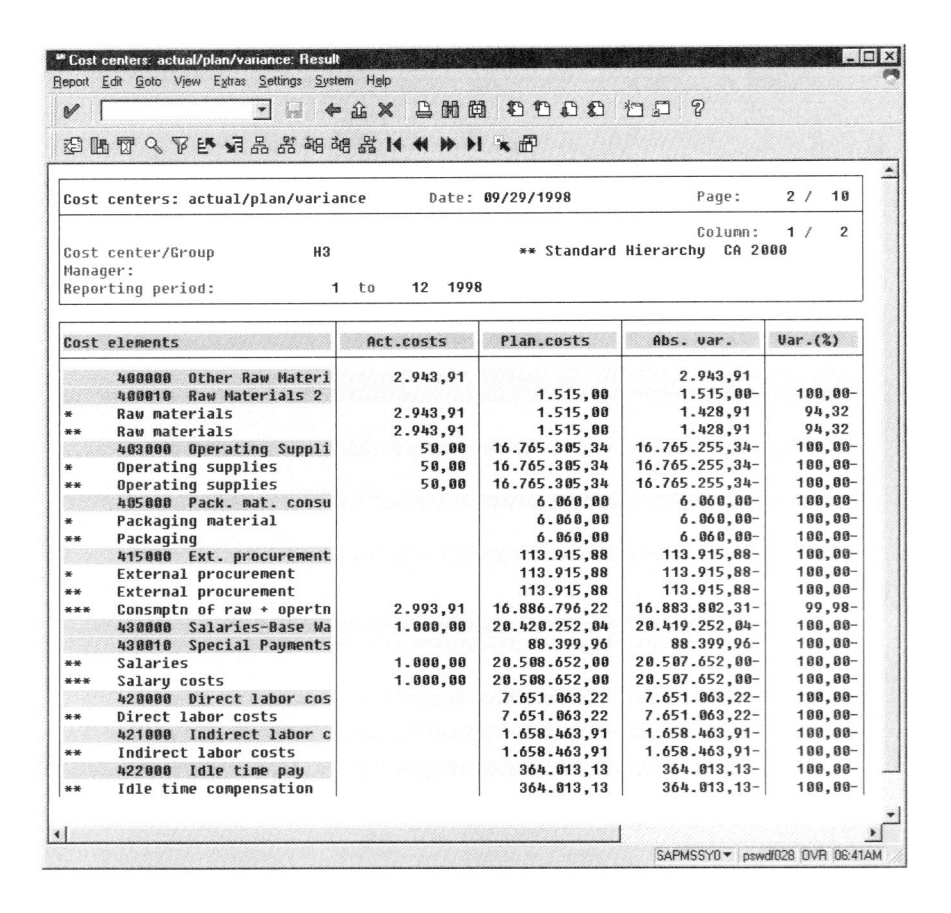

14. From the first selection screen of the report, choose *Environment* → *Find extract*.

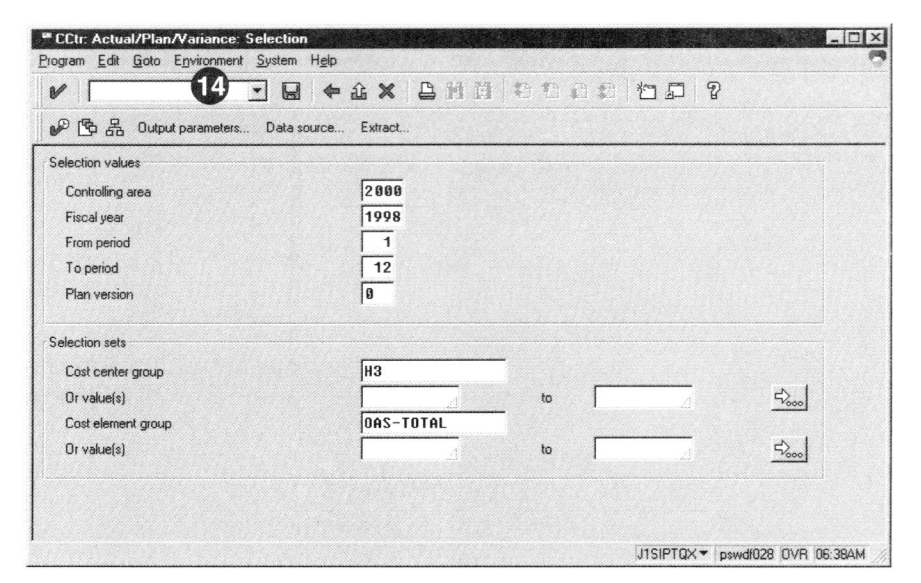

Reporting Made Easy

Section 4: Controlling—Cost Center Reports
Cost Center Summary: Planned Costs, Actual Costs, and Variances

A You can enter a description of the extract to search for the appropriate file.

B You can select the extract according to the ID of the user who created it.

C You can select the extract based on the creation date, or a range of dates.

15. Enter **1SIP** in *Report group*.

D You can enter additional selection criteria, such as a cost center group or individual cost center, to search for an extract.

16. Choose *Execute*.

This screen shows the selected extracts. Those with nodes were run using *Variation*.

17. Click the node next to **Extract: H3 1-9, 1998** to expand this extract.

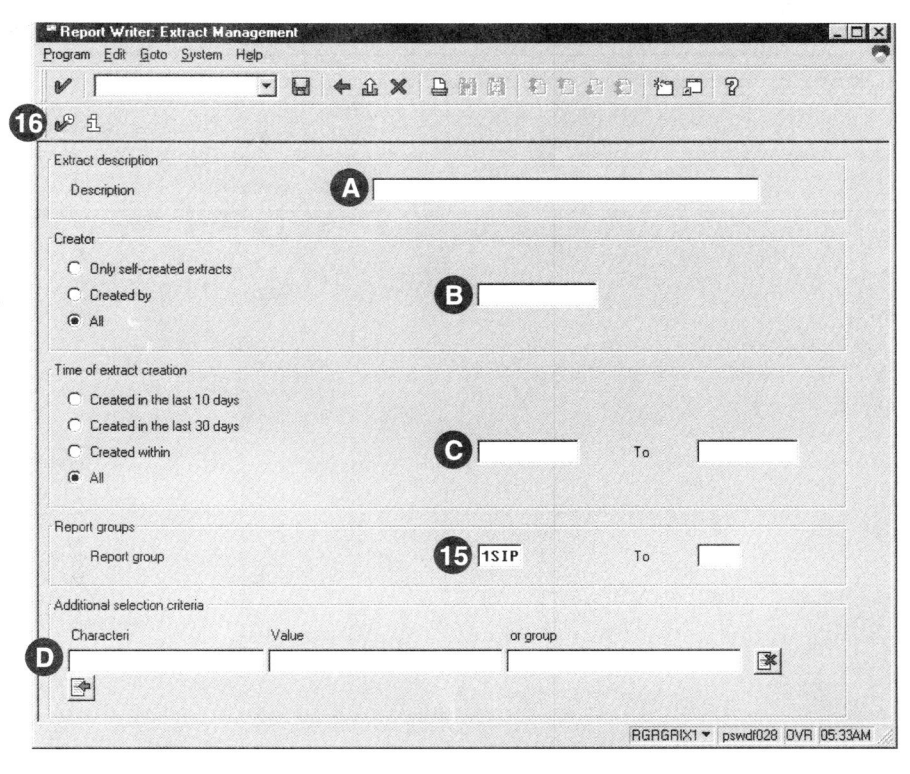

Commonly Used Reports: Illustrations and Perspectives

4–15

Section 4: Controlling—Cost Center Reports

Cost Center Summary: Planned Costs, Actual Costs, and Variances

For extracts created while using *Variation* on a report, a separate extract is created for each node and cost center.

18. Select *Cost center group H3*.

19. Choose *Display*.

20. If the extract was created with password protection, the password must be entered before the extract can be displayed.

21. Choose *Enter*.

Section 4: Controlling—Cost Center Reports
Cost Center Summary: Planned Costs, Actual Costs, and Variances

This screen shows the extract.

The normal functions are still available within the report including:

- Scroll left
- Scroll right
- Variation (to access corresponding extract)
- Drill down (to dynamically run another report)

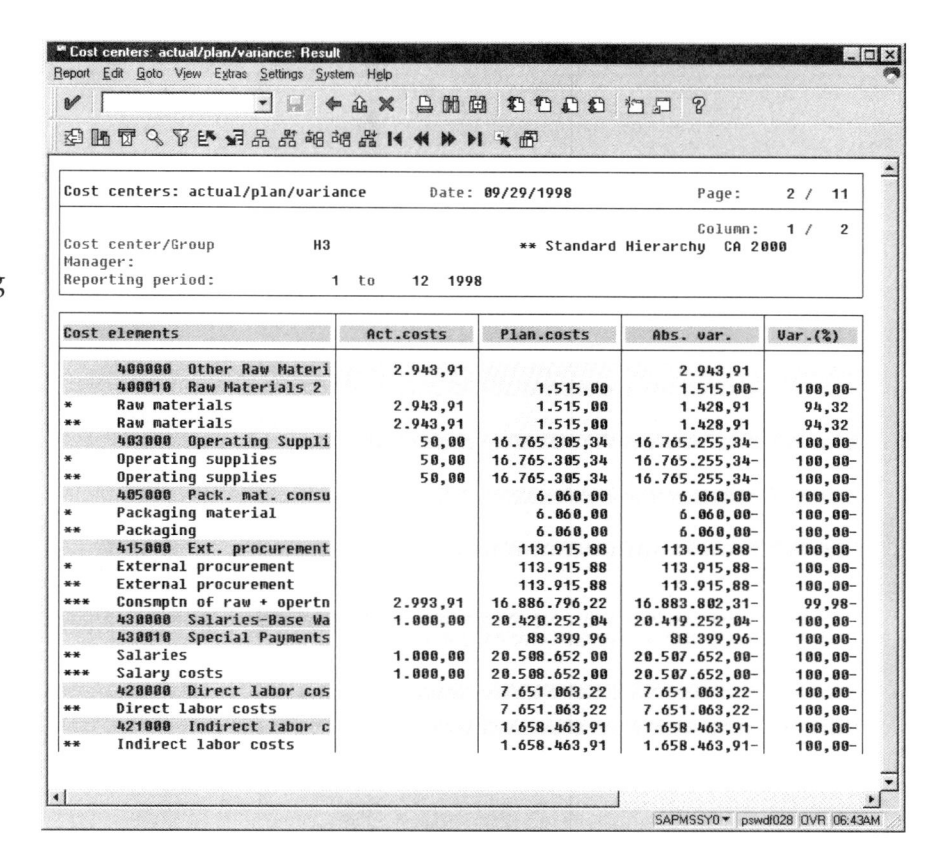

Display Actual Line Items for Cost Centers

Quick Access To run this report, use one of the following access options:

Option 1: Menu Path

Information systems → Accounting → Overhead costs

Cost centers → Line items → Actual

Option 2: Transaction Code

In the *Command* field, enter transaction **KSB1** and choose *Enter*.

Purpose This report lists individual line items that post to the selected cost center or cost center group. At the time the line items list, additional fields can be accessed to assist a cost center manager in monitoring the actual costs being posted to the cost center.

A cost center manager may often use this report to reconcile postings between the General Ledger (G/L) and cost centers, and to monitor the actual postings made to a particular cost center. This report may also assist a manager in searching for particular information, such as a specific material or purchase order posting.

Prerequisites You must set the Controlling area before running the report. Choose *Accounting → Controlling → Cost centers → Environment → Set controlling area*. For the examples in this section, the controlling area is set to *2000*.

You must enter a value in the selection fields before running the report. You may leave the cost center and cost element selection blank, so that all cost elements are selected. If you enter cost center groups and cost element groups, they must have already been set up. If they contain subtotals, hierarchy nodes should be created within the groups. Each hierarchy node then subtotals in this report.

Integration To display the original document, double-click on a line item in the actual line item report. For example, if a material posting was made to the cost center, drill down on a cost center line item to list actual costs contained in the original material document. If a direct financial journal entry was made, drill down on the cost center line item to display the original financial document.

Features

The selection screen of this report includes:

- Variants
- User variables
- Executing and printing in background
- Sorting capability (by column): select a column, then *Edit → Sort in ascndng ordr* (Ctrl+Shift+F5), or *Edit → Sort in descending order* (Ctrl+Shift+F6)
- Adjusting the column width to the widest setting per column: *Settings → Columns → Optimize width*
- Freezing a column in place to scroll right: *Settings → Columns → Freeze to column*
- Adjusting the numeric display, to set the number of decimals displayed and the scaling to hundredths, thousands, etc: *Settings → Number format* (F5)
- Saving the report to a local file
- Increasing or reducing the detail displayed, by double-clicking on subtotal lines. The double-click acts as a toggle switch. If detail is displayed, double-clicking on the subtotal will hide it. If detail is not displayed on a summary line (marked with one or more asterisks), double-clicking will display it.
- Changing the summarization, or subtotal, level (this is limited by the definition of the display variant being used): *Settings → Summation levels → Choose* and *Settings → Summation levels → Define breakdown*
- Displaying all accounting documents (financial, profitability analysis, special ledger, etc.) related to the original entry: *Environment → Accounting documents*
- Displaying the original document used to make the cost center entry (material document, purchase order, journal entry, settlement document, etc.) related to the original entry: *Environment → Source document*
- Selecting from an archive: *Extras → Data source*

Next Steps

The system displays the actual line items for the cost center according to the display variant chosen. Different display variants can be set up to display unique information. Subtotals are available for different columns, again as defined in the configuration of the display variant. By double-clicking on any subtotals in the report, you can hide or display the detail that makes up the subtotal. For example, double-clicking on a *Cost center* line will hide the cost element detail. To display this detail again, double-click on this line.

This report contains data obtained from cost center postings. As such, the data cannot be changed or manipulated from the report.

Section 4: Controlling—Cost Center Reports
Display Actual Line Items for Cost Centers

Guided Tour

Example 1: A reconciliation takes place at the end of the month to ensure that the postings in the different modules, such as the G/L and cost center accounting, are balanced. In this example, the postings are displayed for only one cost center.

To access the first screen for this report, choose

Information systems → Accounting → Overhead costs
Cost centers → Line items → Actual.

1. Enter **4277** in *Cost center*. You can also enter a range of cost centers, or a cost center group.

2. Enter **OAS-TOTAL** in *Cost element group*.

3. Enter a date range to limit the number of postings to the selected internal orders (for example, **01/01/1997** to **12/31/1997**). This report may also be run for dates that span fiscal years.

4. Enter **1SAP** in *Display variant*. This lists cost element detail for each line item.

5. Choose *Further settings*.

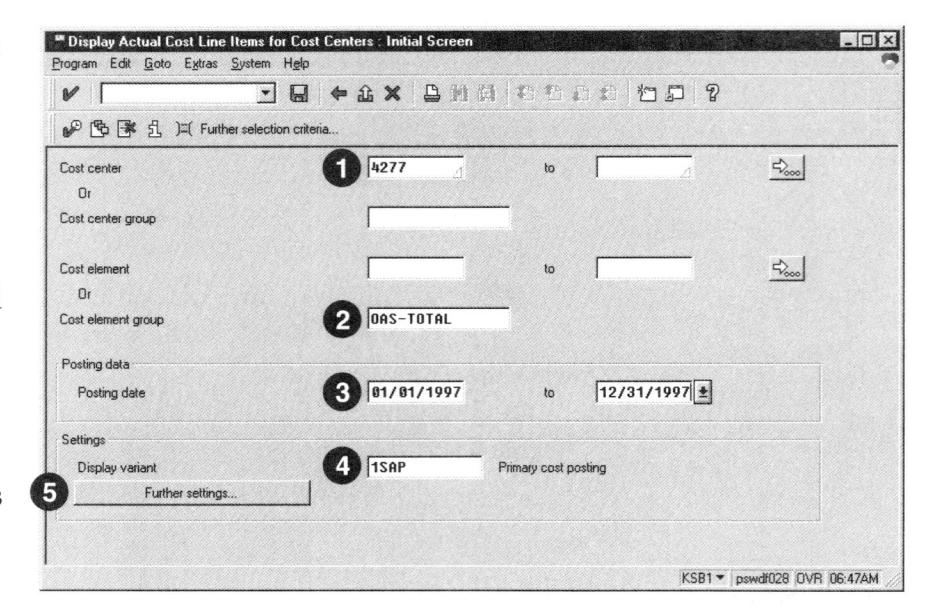

4–20 Reporting Made Easy

Section 4: Controlling—Cost Center Reports
Display Actual Line Items for Cost Centers

The *Variant fields only* checkbox should remain deselected for purposes of this example. This increases performance in selecting actual line items and also makes it possible for you to change the line item display after you make the database selection. If the *Variant fields only* checkbox is selected, only the fields relevant to the first display variant entered are selected from the database and made viewable.

6. Enter **5.000** in *Maximum no. of hits*. (Additional records—even if they fall within the date range—will not appear.)

7. Choose *Enter*, then *Execute* (not shown).

This screen shows the list of actual line items for the cost center.

8. Choose *Subtotal*.

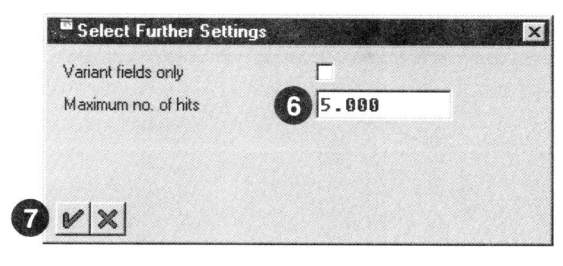

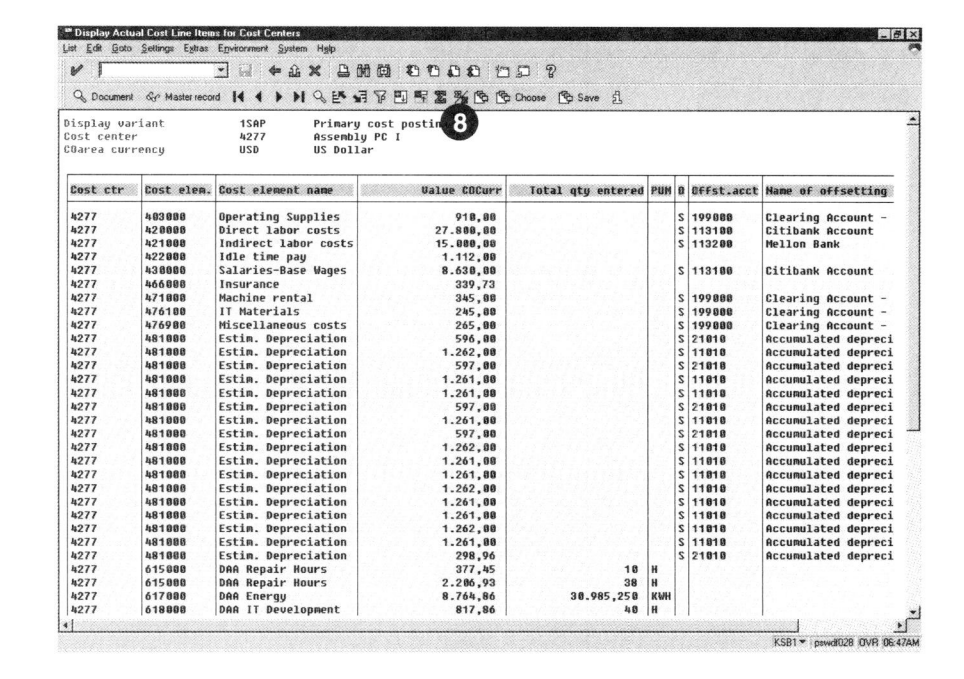

9. The current subtotals are based on the cost center field. Deselect the subtotal for the *Cost center*, and select the subtotal for the *Cost element*.

10. Choose *Copy*.

Commonly Used Reports: Illustrations and Perspectives

4–21

Section 4: Controlling—Cost Center Reports
Display Actual Line Items for Cost Centers

This screen shows the subtotals based on the cost elements within the cost center. (This allows for easier reconciliation of the General Ledger.)

11. Choose *Choose display variant*
    📇 Choose.

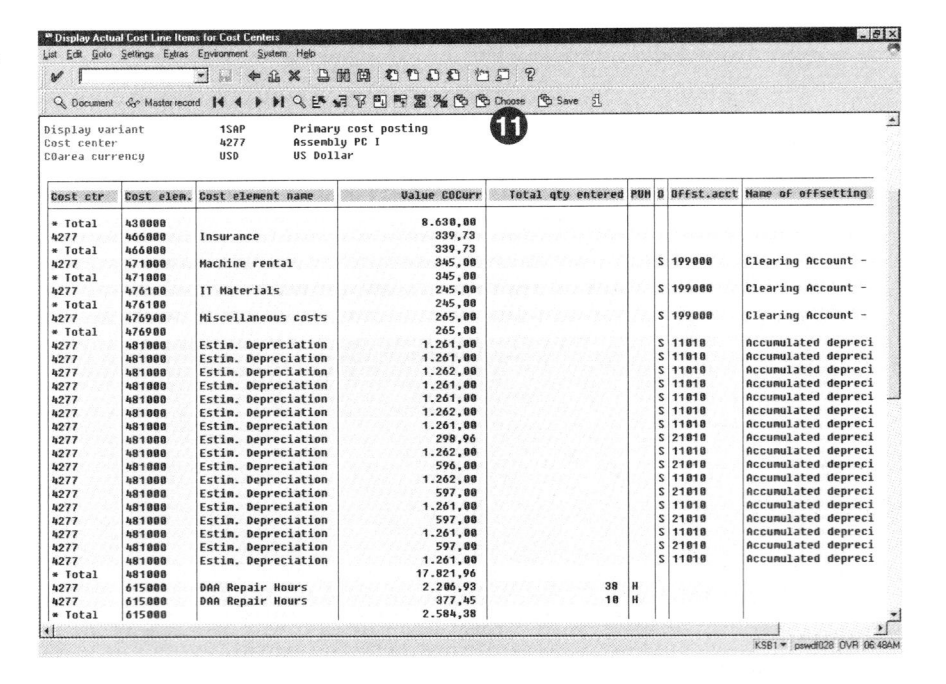

12. Select display variant (for example, *2SAP*) by clicking on it once. This creates a more detailed list of the actual line item posted to the cost center.

13. Choose *Copy*.

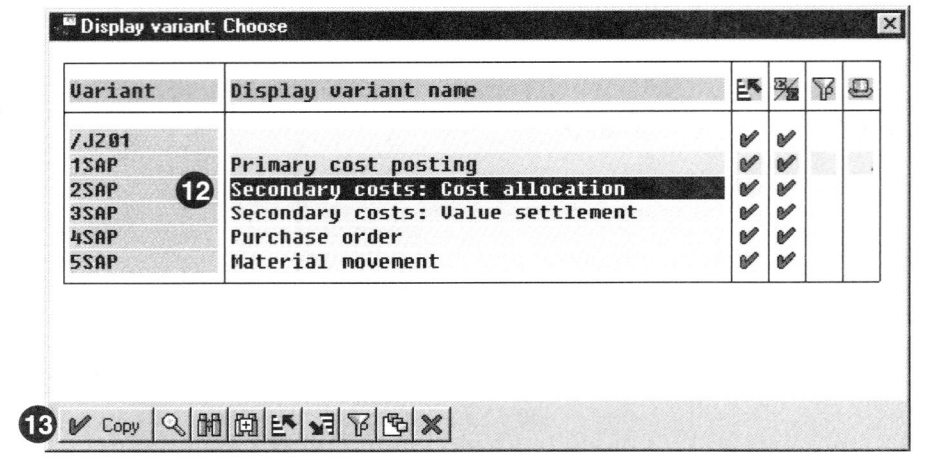

4–22

Reporting Made Easy

Section 4: Controlling—Cost Center Reports

Display Actual Line Items for Cost Centers

This screen shows the display variant and its *Partner object* involved in the cost center transaction.

If a column is blank, it indicates that the data was not relevant to the posting. The *Partner object* is generally an activity posting or an internal order settlement.

14. Position the cursor on the *Partner object* (for example, *800304*).

15. Choose *Display master record*
       Master record.

The master record of the internal order appears.

This function is context-sensitive; for example, if the cursor were placed on a cost center number on the previous screen, the cost center master would have been shown.

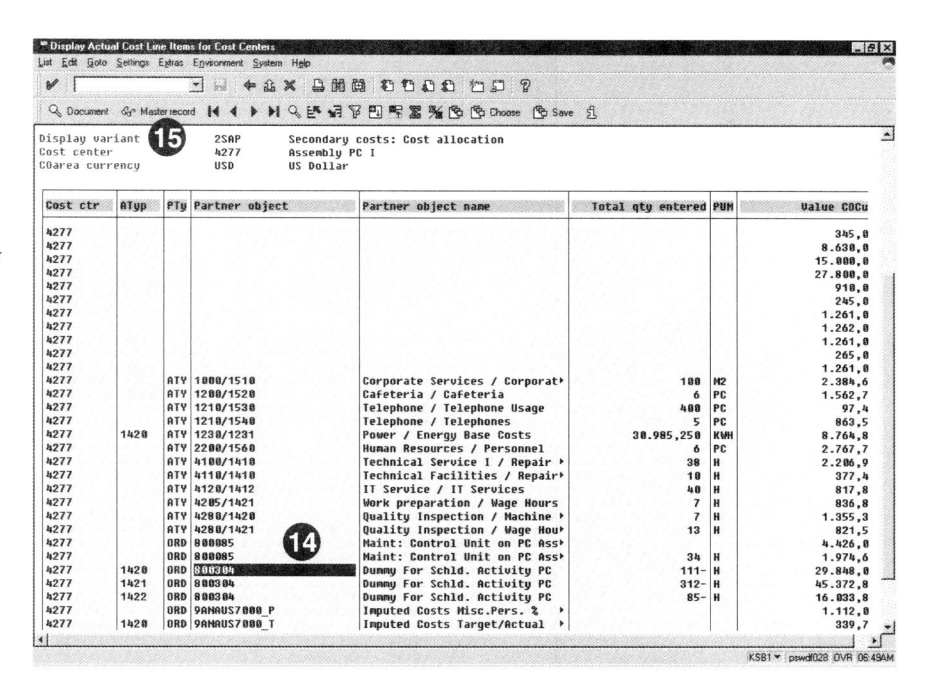

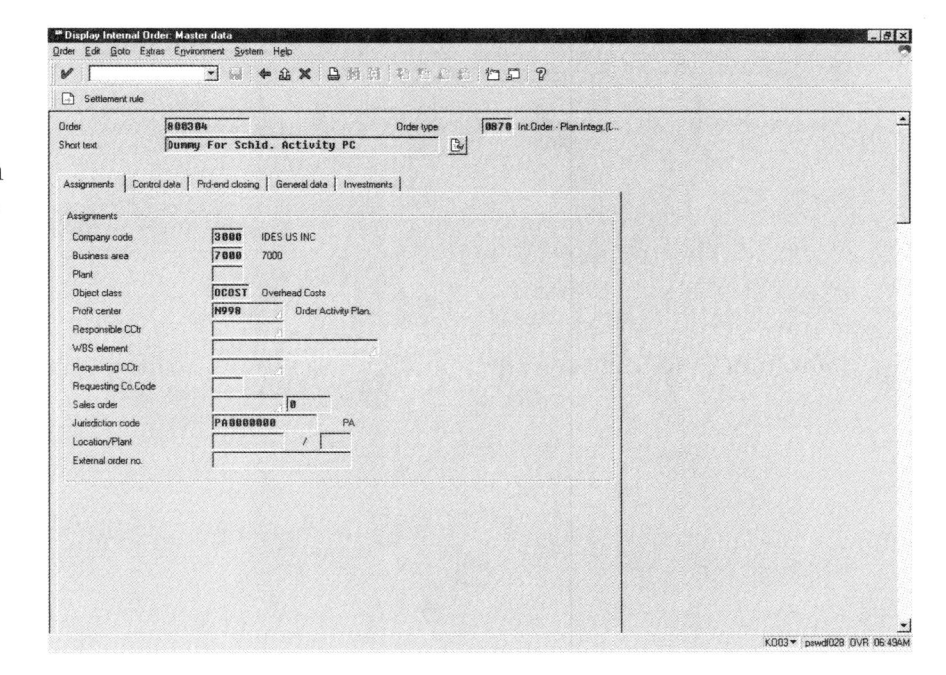

Commonly Used Reports: Illustrations and Perspectives

4–23

Section 4: Controlling—Cost Center Reports
Display Actual Line Items for Cost Centers

Example 2: A cost center manager wants to use a material number to report the postings to the cost center.

1. Enter **4100** in *Cost center*. You can also enter a range of cost centers, or a cost center group.

2. Enter **OAS-TOTAL** in *Cost element group*.

3. Enter a date range to limit the number of postings to the selected internal orders (for example, **01/01/1997** to **12/31/1997**). This report may also be run for dates that span fiscal years.

4. Enter **5SAP** in *Display variant*. This lists material number detail.

5. Choose *Extras → Select value type*.

6. Deselect the *Statistical actual value* checkbox. This delimits the report to reflect only actual material postings, not to statistical references to the cost center.

7. Choose *Copy*.

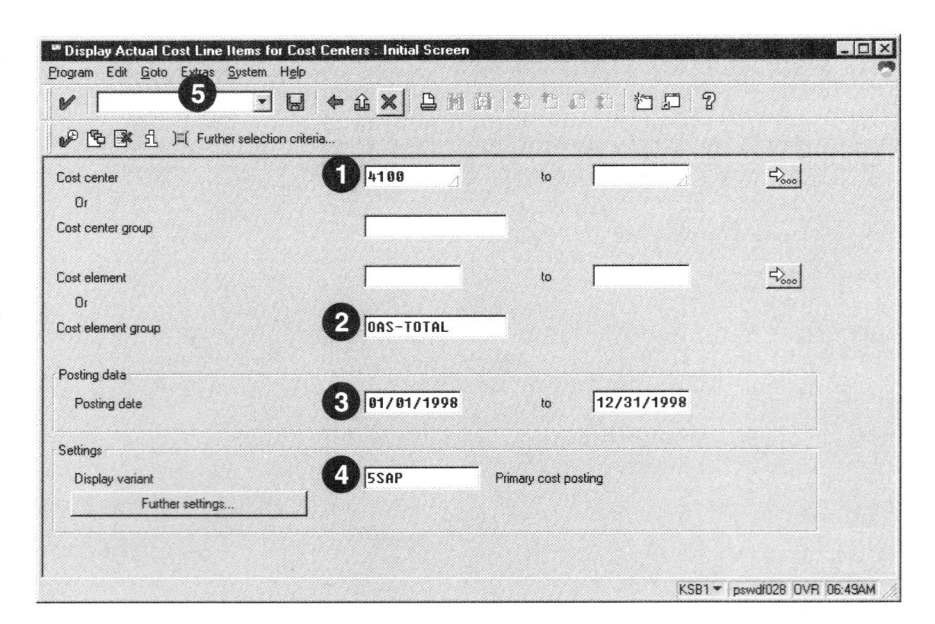

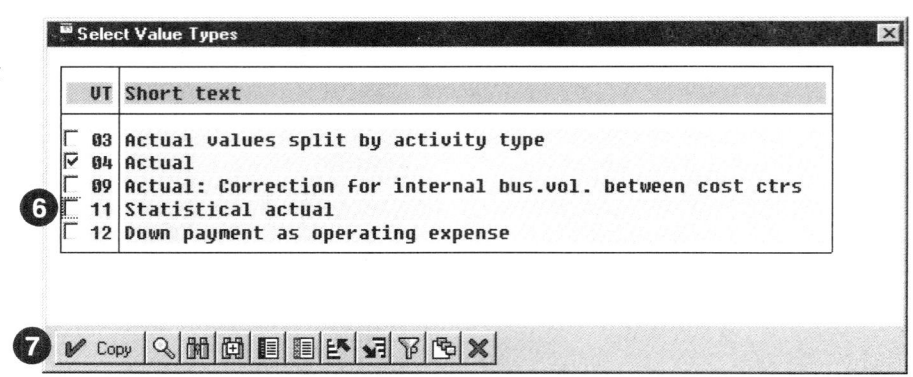

4–24

Reporting Made Easy

Section 4: Controlling—Cost Center Reports

Display Actual Line Items for Cost Centers

8. Choose *Execute*.

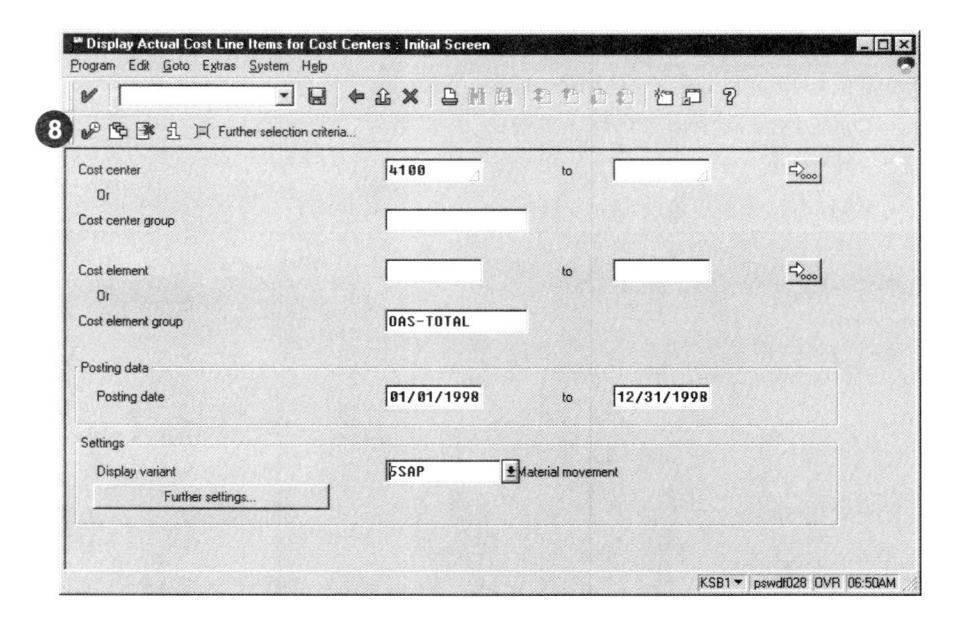

This screen shows the material number and description of the display variant. All other cost center line items where the material fields are blank were not material postings.

9. Choose *Current display variant*.

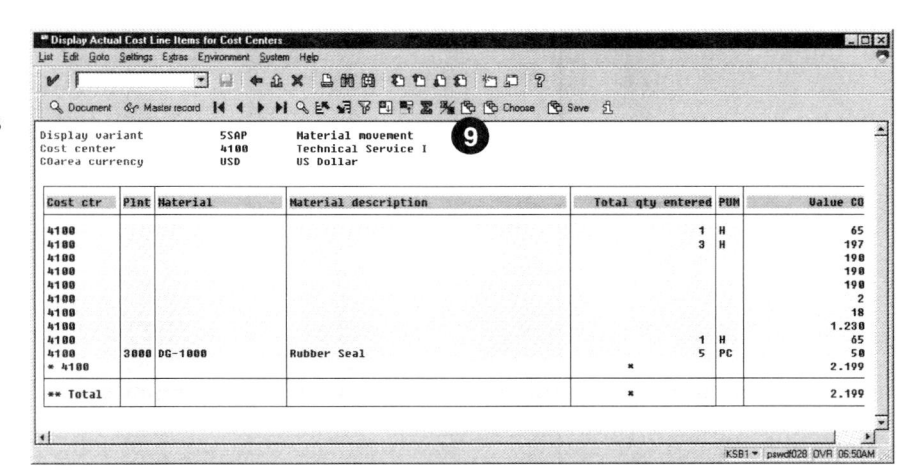

Section 4: Controlling—Cost Center Reports
Display Actual Line Items for Cost Centers

10. To display an additional field, you must first select it on the *hidden fields* area of the screen (for example, *Cost element*).

11. Select *Total qty entered*. (This is a reference point. *Cost element* will insert before this row.)

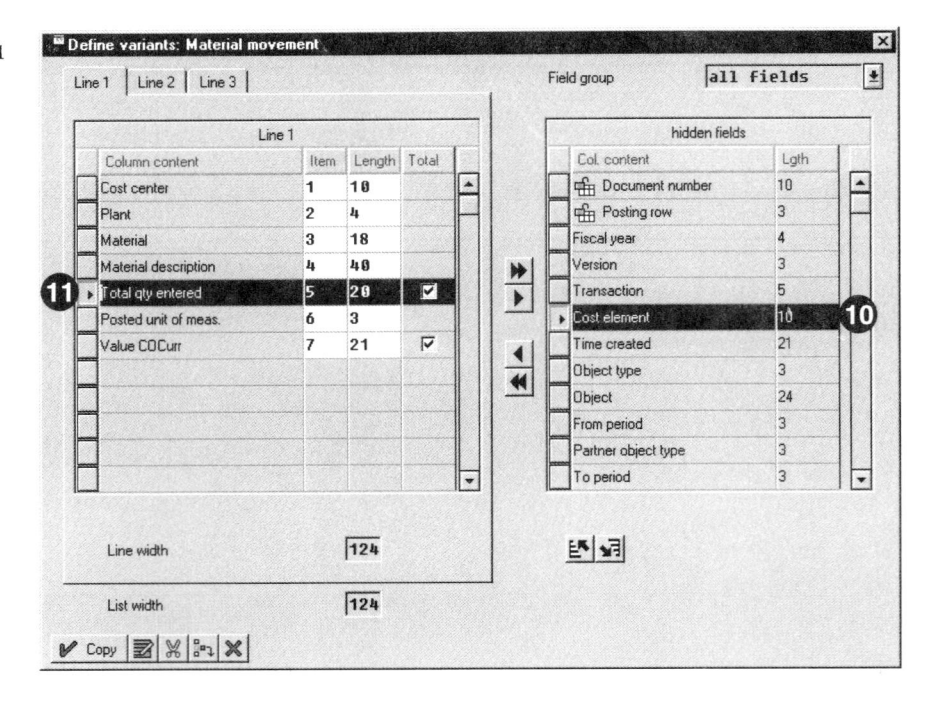

12. Choose *Show selected fields* to insert *Cost element*.

13. Choose *Copy* to accept changes in the display variant.

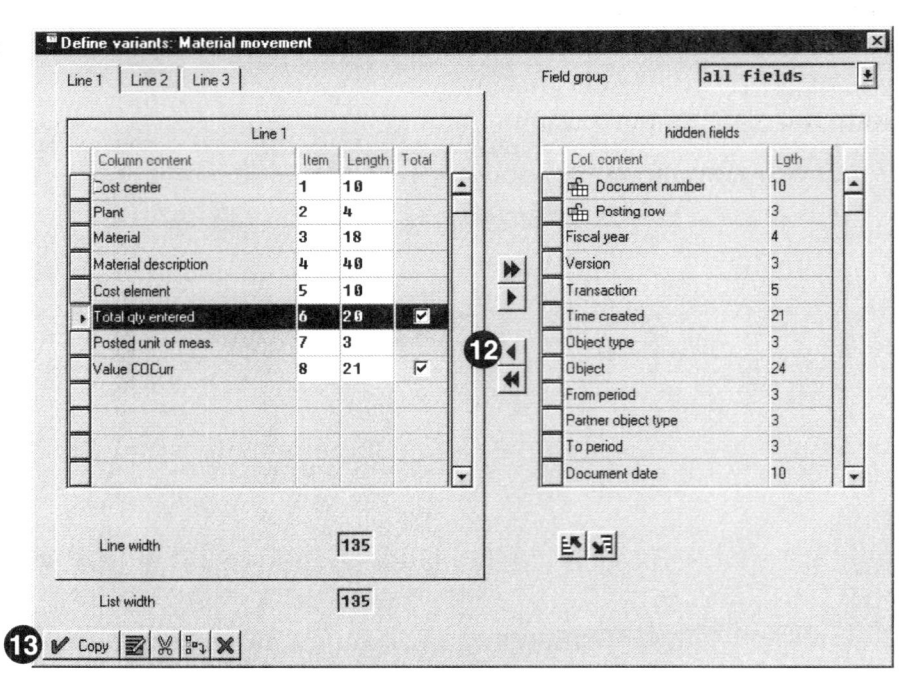

4–26

Reporting Made Easy

Section 4: Controlling—Cost Center Reports
Display Actual Line Items for Cost Centers

The cost element field appears.

14. Choose *Save display variant*.

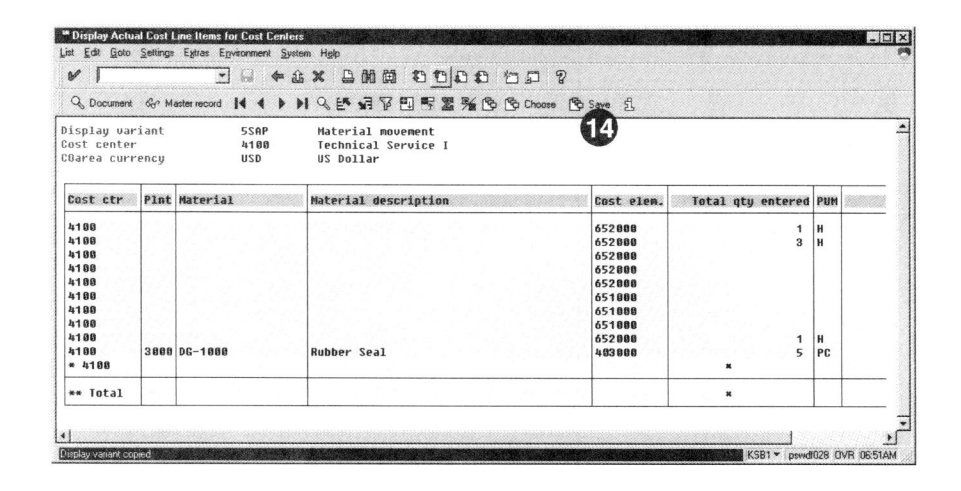

You can create and name a new display variant from this screen.

15. Enter **z5SAP** in *Display variant*.

16. Select *User-specific* to save the original display variant with the updated field for your user ID.

17. The additional parameters specify whether the active sorting and subtotaling settings should also be saved as part of the display variant.

18. Choose *Save*.

19. Position the cursor on the actual line item containing the material number (for example, *DG-1000*).

20. Choose *Display document*.

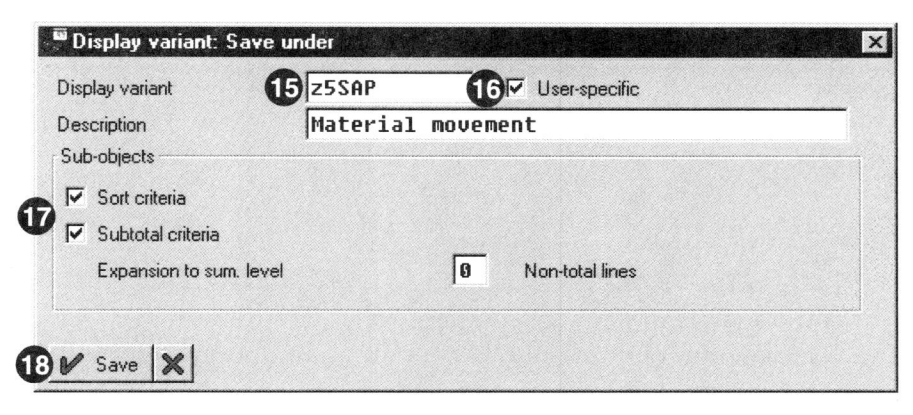

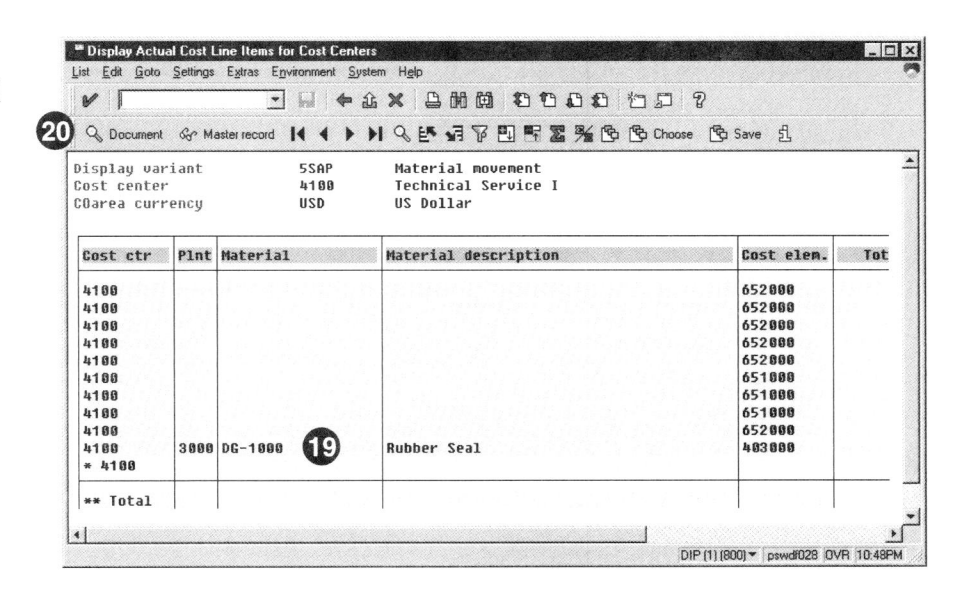

Commonly Used Reports: Illustrations and Perspectives

4–27

Section 4: Controlling—Cost Center Reports
Display Actual Line Items for Cost Centers

The original document that created the cost center posting appears. (In this example it is a *Material Document* that issued the material from inventory to the cost center.)

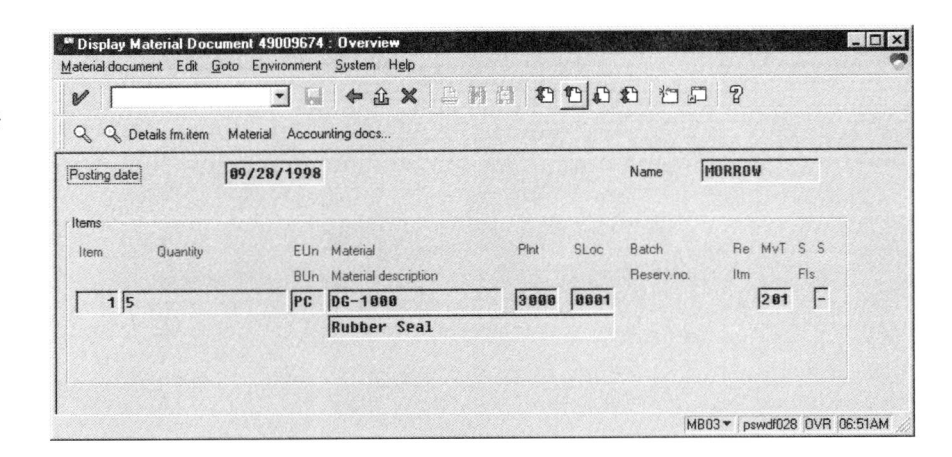

Example 3: To verify that the postings were made to the correct cost centers, search the cost centers for all postings that were made based on purchase orders. Line items will only be selected if they contain a purchase order number.

1. Enter **H3** in *Cost center group*. You can also enter a range of cost centers, or a cost center group.

2. Enter **OAS-TOTAL** in *Cost element group*.

3. Enter a date range to limit the number of postings to the selected internal orders (for example, **01/01/1997** to **12/31/1997**). This report may also be run for dates that span fiscal years.

4. Enter **4SAP** in *Display variant*. This creates purchase order numbers in the display variant.

5. Choose *Further selection criteria*.

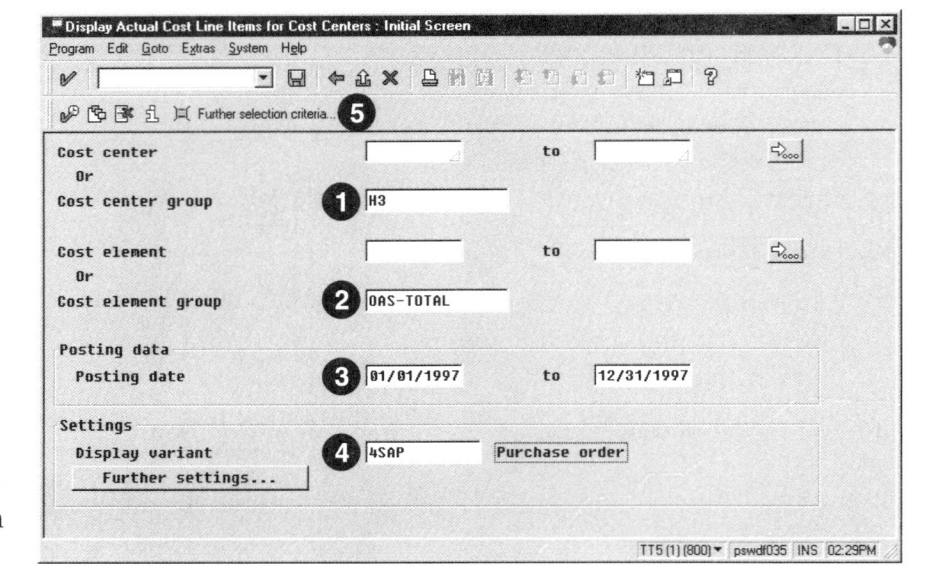

4–28 Reporting Made Easy

Section 4: Controlling—Cost Center Reports
Display Actual Line Items for Cost Centers

6. Select *Purchasing document number*. This allows for selection based on this data.

7. Choose *Copy*.

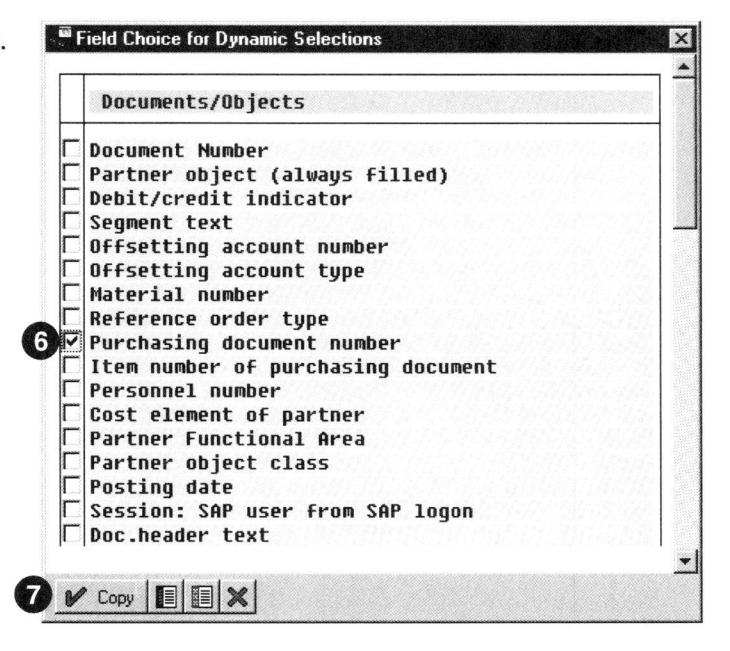

You can enter a purchasing document number range on this screen.

8. Choose *Selection options*.

9. Select the *Not equal to* line.
10. Choose *Enter*.

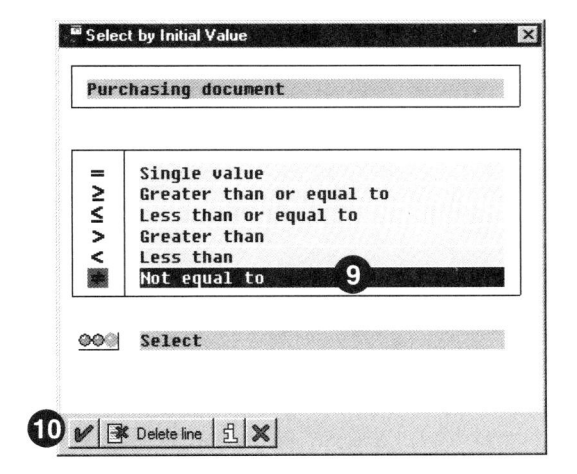

Section 4: Controlling—Cost Center Reports
Display Actual Line Items for Cost Centers

The selection option icon, *Not equal to* ≠ appears to the left of the *Purchasing document* field. For this example, since no purchase order number is entered, all line items where the purchasing document number is not blank will be selected.

11. Choose *Save*.
12. Choose *Execute*.

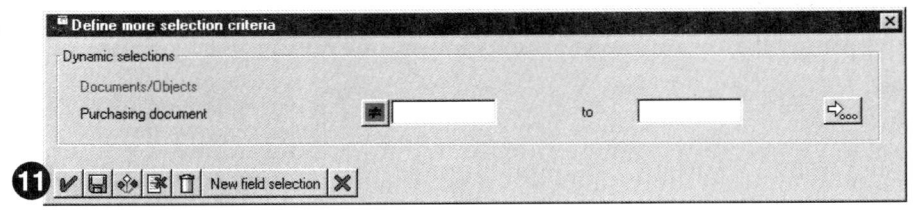

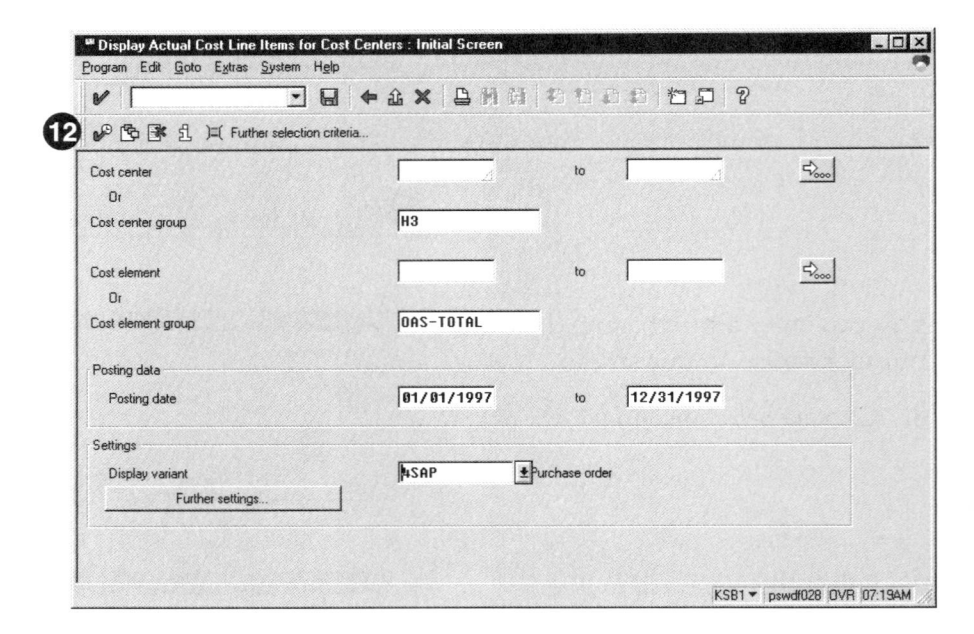

This screen shows only the actual line items that contain a purchase order document number. They are summarized by the cost center(s) to which they posted.

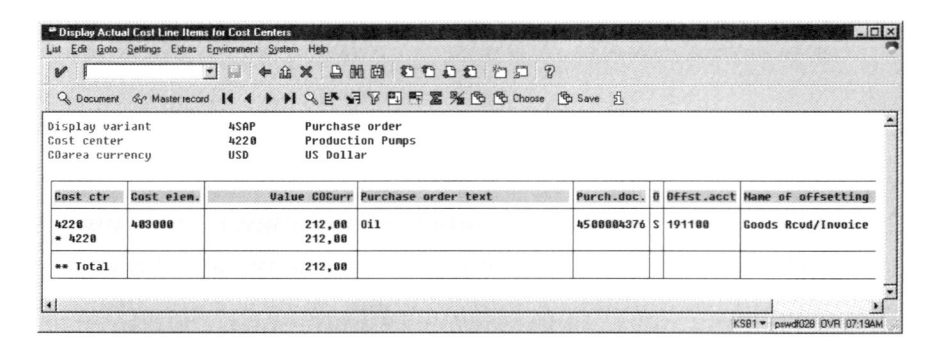

4–30

Reporting Made Easy

Cost Center Summary: Plan/Actual Costs by Period and Year-to-Date

Quick Access

To run this report, use one of the following access options:

Option 1: Menu Path

Information systems → *Accounting* → *Overhead costs*

Cost centers → *Report selection*

From the reporting tree, choose the following report:

Plan/Actual Comparison → *CCtr: Ongoing Period/Cumulated* → *CCtr: Current Period/Cumulated.*

Option 2: Program Name

Choose *System* → *Services* → *Reporting* and enter `J1SISTQX` in the *Program* field. Then, choose *Execute* to run the report.

Purpose

This report provides a summarized view of the costs, activities, and statistical key figures that posted to cost centers. It includes both planned and actual postings, and calculates an absolute and a percentage variance. In addition to a selected period, the report lists cumulative data from the beginning of the fiscal year through the selected period.

A cost center manager would use this report to monitor actual cost center performance against planned cost center performance, both on a periodic and cumulative basis. This report allows for a consolidated view of multiple cost centers and includes the balance of all cost center postings.

Prerequisites

You must set the Controlling area before running the report. Choose *Accounting* → *Controlling* → *Cost centers* → *Environment* → *Set controlling area*. For the examples in this section, the controlling area is set to *2000*.

You must enter a value in the selection fields before running the report. You may leave the cost center and cost element selection blank, so that all cost elements are selected. If you enter cost center groups and cost element groups, they must have already been set up. If they contain subtotals, hierarchy nodes should be created within the groups. Each hierarchy node then subtotals in this report.

Section 4: Controlling—Cost Center Reports
Cost Center Summary: Plan/Actual Costs by Period and Year-to-Date

Integration You can run multiple context-sensitive reports from this cost center report. For example, when you position the cursor on a cell for planned costs, only the reports that contain planned costs list data. If you select a cell for planned costs and run a report that only contains actual data, no data lists.

The following reports run for a single cell or a range of cells:

- Actual line items for one or more cost centers
- Planned line items for one or more cost centers

Features The selection screen of this report includes:

- Variants
- Dynamic selection options
- Executing and printing in the background
- Sorting capability (by column): select a column, then *Edit → Sort in ascndng ordr* (Ctrl+Shift+F5), or *Edit → Sort in descending order* (Ctrl+Shift+F6)
- Adjusting the column width: *Settings → Column width* (Ctrl+F12)
- Adjusting the numeric display, to set the number of decimals displayed and the scaling to hundredths, thousands, etc.: *Settings → Number format* (F5)
- Mailing of the report (Ctrl+F9)
- Graphing portions of the report using SAP business graphics
- Exporting the report to a local file
- Increasing or reducing the detail displayed, by double-clicking on subtotal lines. The double-click acts as a toggle switch. If detail is displayed, double-clicking on the subtotal will hide it. If detail is not displayed on a summary line (marked with one or more asterisks), double-clicking will display it.
- Displaying only threshold values, or values that greater than or less than an entered criteria: *Edit → Threshold value* (Shift+F5).
- Creating an extract of reporting information (F5)

Section 4: Controlling—Cost Center Reports
Cost Center Summary: Plan/Actual Costs by Period and Year-to-Date

Next Steps

The system displays four columns for all sections of the report, including actual postings, planned data, and a calculation of the variance between the two, both as an absolute value and as a percentage (calculated by dividing the actual data by the planned).

By double-clicking on any subtotals in the report, the detail that makes up each subtotal can either be hidden or displayed. For example, double-clicking on the *Internal activities* line will hide the cost element detail. To display this detail again, double-click on this line.

This report contains data obtained from cost center postings. As such, the data cannot be changed or manipulated from the report.

This report contains five different blocks of data, as shown below. By navigating around these blocks, you can display different types of cost center data:

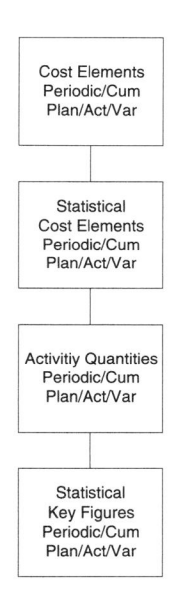

```
┌─────────────────┐
│  Cost Elements  │
│  Periodic/Cum   │
│  Plan/Act/Var   │
└────────┬────────┘
         │
┌────────┴────────┐
│   Statistical   │
│  Cost Elements  │
│  Periodic/Cum   │
│  Plan/Act/Var   │
└────────┬────────┘
         │
┌────────┴────────┐
│Activitiy Quantities│
│  Periodic/Cum   │
│  Plan/Act/Var   │
└────────┬────────┘
         │
┌────────┴────────┐
│   Statistical   │
│   Key Figures   │
│  Periodic/Cum   │
│  Plan/Act/Var   │
└─────────────────┘
```

Commonly Used Reports: Illustrations and Perspectives

Section 4: Controlling—Cost Center Reports
Cost Center Summary: Plan/Actual Costs by Period and Year-to-Date

Guided Tour

Example: A cost center manager wants to monitor the variances for the cost center for the current period, as well as for the year. This report shows detailed postings for a cost center, including all planned and actual costs, activities, and statistical key figures.

To access the first screen for this report, choose

Information systems → *Accounting* → *Overhead costs*

Cost centers → *Report selection*.

From the reporting tree, select the following report:

Plan/Actual Comparison → *CCtr: Ongoing Period/Cumulated* → *CCtr: Current Period/Cumulated*.

1. Under *Selection values*, enter **2000** in *Controlling area*.

2. Enter the year in *Fiscal year* (for example, **1997**). This report runs for only one fiscal year at a time.

3. Enter **9** in *Period*. This entry means that all values from period 1 through period 9 will be selected for analysis of cumulative planned versus actual postings.

4. Enter **0** in *Plan version*.

5. Enter **3200** in *Or value(s)*. You can also enter a range of cost centers, or a cost center group.

6. Enter **OAS-TOTAL** in *Cost element group*. This contains all cost elements.

7. Choose *Execute*.

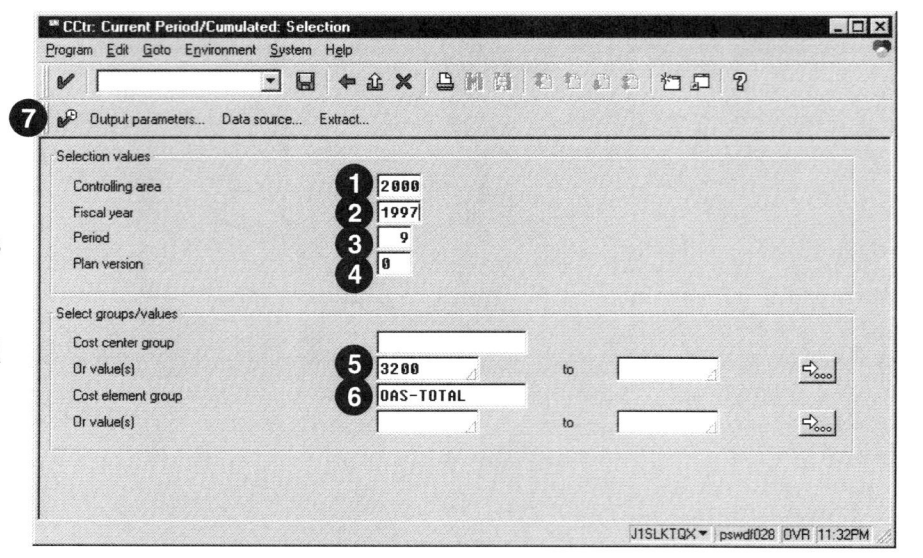

4–34   Reporting Made Easy

Section 4: Controlling—Cost Center Reports

Cost Center Summary: Plan/Actual Costs by Period and Year-to-Date

The first screen of the report shows the cost elements, for which actual and planned costs are posted in the cost center.

The columns to the left of the cost elements contain the data for the selected period.

The columns to the right of the cost elements contain the data for the cumulative fiscal year through the selected period.

Cost elements that are included in the cost element group, but for which no postings were made, are not shown.

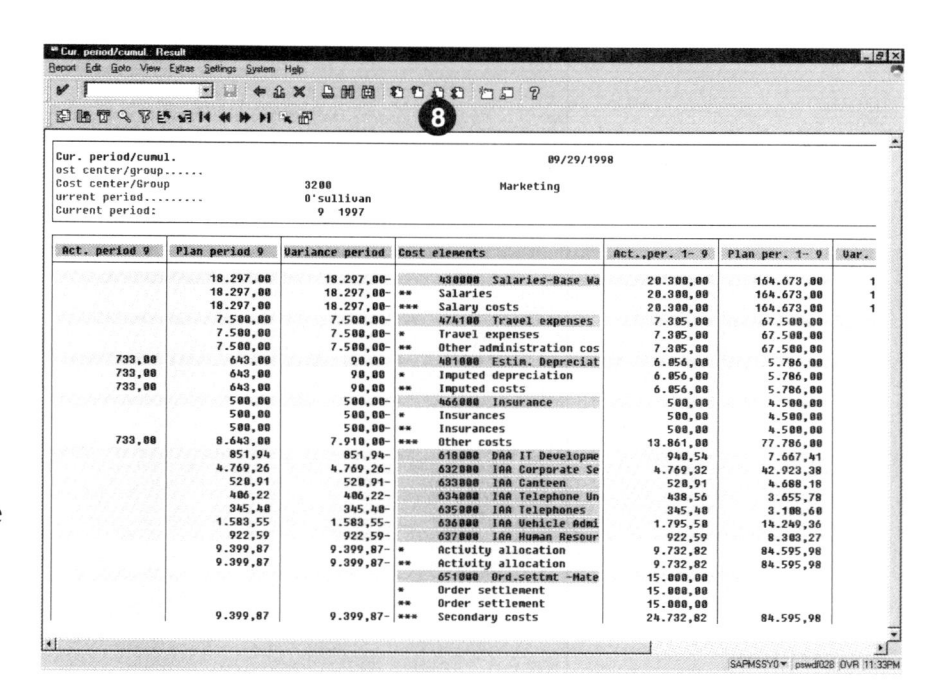

8. Choose *Page Down* to navigate to the next block of data.

This section of the screen shows the remaining cost element data. In this example, all cost elements posted to the cost center did not fit on the previous screen.

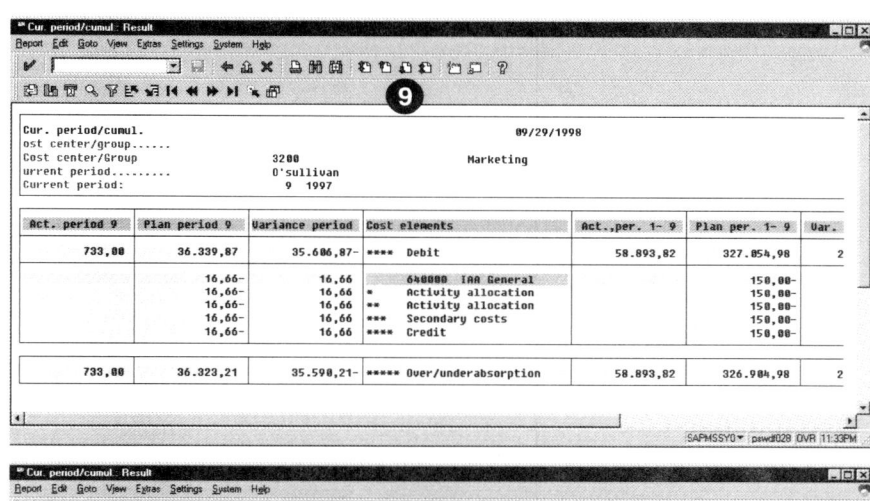

9. Choose *Page Down* to navigate to the next block of data.

These columns contain statistical postings made to the cost center. These cost elements posted to a controlling object, such as an internal order, but with a statistical reference to this cost center. These statistical postings are not reflected in the "real" postings seen in the previous section.

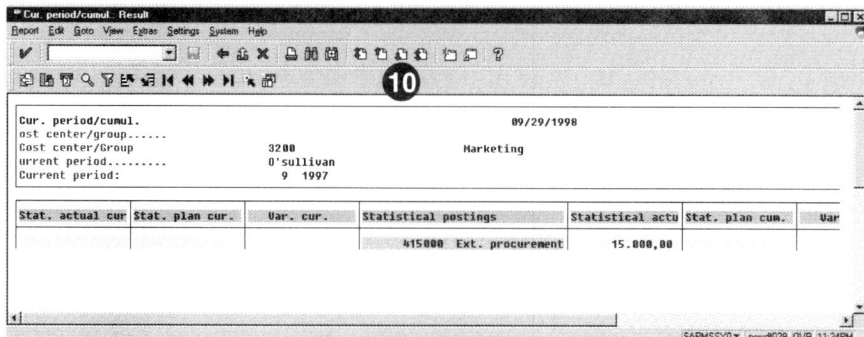

10. Choose *Page Down* to navigate to the next block of data.

Commonly Used Reports: Illustrations and Perspectives

Section 4: Controlling—Cost Center Reports

Cost Center Summary: Plan/Actual Costs by Period and Year-to-Date

These columns contain the activity quantities and corresponding unit of measure used in the postings, along with the absolute and percentage variances.

11. Choose *Page Down* to navigate to the next block of data.

The columns list the postings to statistical key figures, with the corresponding unit of measure. Absolute and percentage variances are calculated.

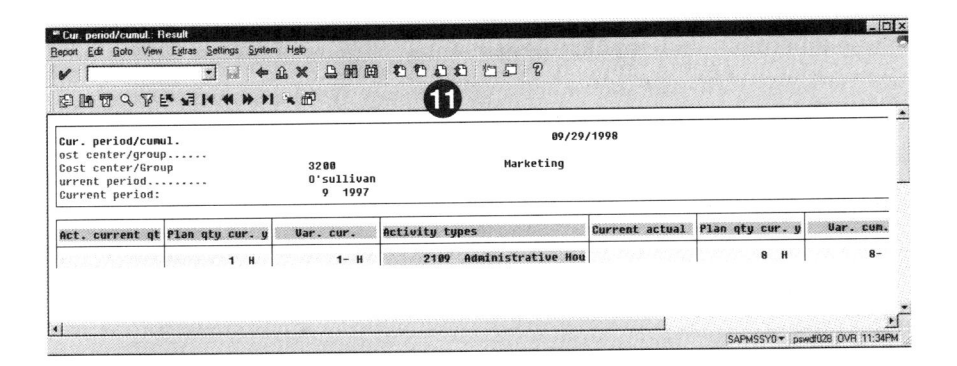

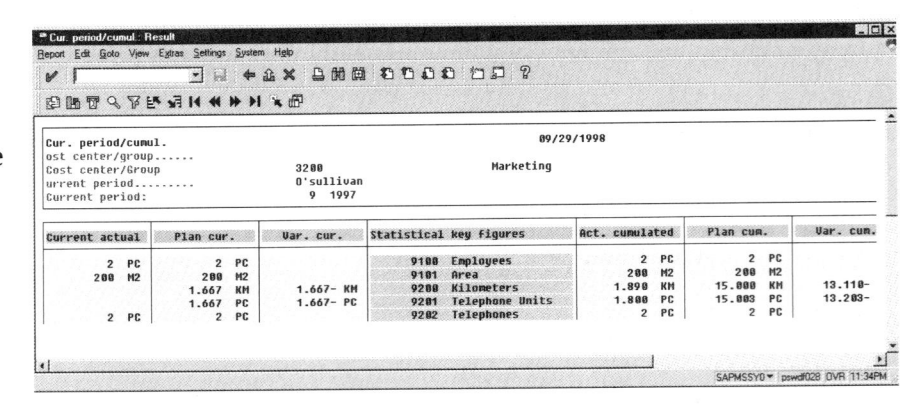

Reporting Made Easy

4–36

Cost Center Summary: Target Costs, Actual Costs, and Variances

Quick Access To run this report, use one of the following access options:

Option 1: Menu Path

Information systems → *Accounting* → *Overhead costs*

Cost centers → *Report selection*

From the reporting tree, select the following report:

Target/Actual Comparison → *CCtr: Actual/Target/Variance* → *Cost centers: Act/Targ/Variance.*

Option 2: Program Name

Choose *System* → *Services* → *Reporting* and enter `J1SISTQX` in the *Program* field. Then, choose *Execute* to run the report.

Purpose This report provides a summarized view of the costs, activities, and statistical key figures that posted to cost centers. This report lists calculations of target costs, which can be compared to actual costs and planned costs.

Target costs are used to calculate variance categories for cost centers. The planned costs are placed on the same basis of comparison, based on the operating rate of the cost center.

The operating rate is determined by dividing the actual activity by the planned activity, and multiplying the result by 100. The planned variable costs and planned variable quantities are then multiplied by the operating rate, to obtain the target costs and quantities. Fixed costs and quantities are not multiplied by the operating rate. The fixed and variable portions of the target costs and quantities are then added to obtain the total target cost.

$$\text{Operating Rate} = \frac{\text{Actual activity}}{\text{Planned activity}} \times 100$$

$$\text{Target Cost 1} = \text{Planned variable costs} \times \text{Operating rate}$$

$$\text{Target Cost 2} = \text{Planned variable quantities} \times \text{Operating rate}$$

$$\text{Total Target Cost} = \text{Target Cost 1} + \text{Target Cost 2}$$

The report is typically used by a cost center manager to compare the actual, planned, and target costs and quantities, and to analyze the source of the variance that may be calculated for the cost center.

Section 4: Controlling—Cost Center Reports
Cost Center Summary: Target Costs, Actual Costs, and Variances

Prerequisites

You must set the *Controlling Area* before running the report. Choose *Accounting → Controlling → Cost centers → Environment → Set controlling area.* For the examples in this section, the controlling area is set *to 2000*.

You must enter a value in the selection fields before running the report. You may leave the cost center and cost element selection blank, and get a list that contains values for all cost centers and all cost elements in the selected controlling area. If you enter cost center groups and cost element groups, they must have already been set up. If they contain subtotals, hierarchy nodes should be created within the groups. Each hierarchy node then subtotals in this report.

Additionally, since target costs are used in the splitting of activity-independent costs to activities, you should run this report at the end of the period, after all other period-end processes finish.

Integration

You can run multiple context-sensitive reports from this cost center report. For example, when you position the cursor on a cell for planned costs, only the reports that contain planned costs list data. If you select a cell for planned costs and run a report that only contains actual data, no data lists.

The following reports run for a single cell or a range of cells:
- Actual line items for one or more cost centers
- Planned line items for one or more cost centers
- Planning overview for a single cost center
- Activity types, by period
- Statistical key figures, by period
- Cost center line items, by partner CO object (that is, partner cost center in a transaction, order, etc.)
- Cost center line items, by activity type
- Two currencies displayed for the cost center postings, the object (cost center) currency and the controlling area currency

Section 4: Controlling—Cost Center Reports
Cost Center Summary: Target Costs, Actual Costs, and Variances

Features

The selection screen of this report includes:

- Variants
- Dynamic selection options
- Executing and printing in the background
- Sorting capability (by column): select a column, then *Edit → Sort in ascndng ordr* (Ctrl+Shift+F5), or *Edit → Sort in descending order* (Ctrl+Shift+F6)
- Adjusting the column width: *Settings → Column width* (Ctrl+F12)
- Adjusting the numeric display, to set the number of decimals displayed and the scaling to hundredths, thousands, etc.: *Settings → Number format* (F5)
- Mailing of the report (Ctrl+F9)
- Graphing portions of the report using SAP business graphics
- Exporting the report to a local file
- Increasing or reducing the detail displayed, by double-clicking on subtotal lines. The double-click acts as a toggle switch. If detail is displayed, double-clicking on the subtotal will hide it. If detail is not displayed on a summary line (marked with one or more asterisks), double-clicking will display it.
- Displaying only threshold values, or values that greater than or less than an entered criteria: *Edit → Threshold value* (Shift+F5).
- Creating an extract of reporting information (F5)

Section 4: Controlling—Cost Center Reports

Cost Center Summary: Target Costs, Actual Costs, and Variances

Next Steps

The system displays separate column blocks in this report, including actual, target, and planned costs, which are compared with each another. In several of the column blocks, fixed and variable costs are also identified for analysis. The system calculates the variance, or the difference, between each of the compared columns that list on the screen.

By double-clicking on any subtotals in the report, the amount of detail that makes up the subtotal can either be hidden or displayed. For example, double-clicking on the *Debit* line will hide the cost element detail. To display this detail again, double-click on this line.

This report contains data obtained from cost center postings. As such, the data cannot be changed or manipulated from the report.

The report contains nine different blocks of data, as shown below. By navigating around these blocks, you can display different types of cost center data.

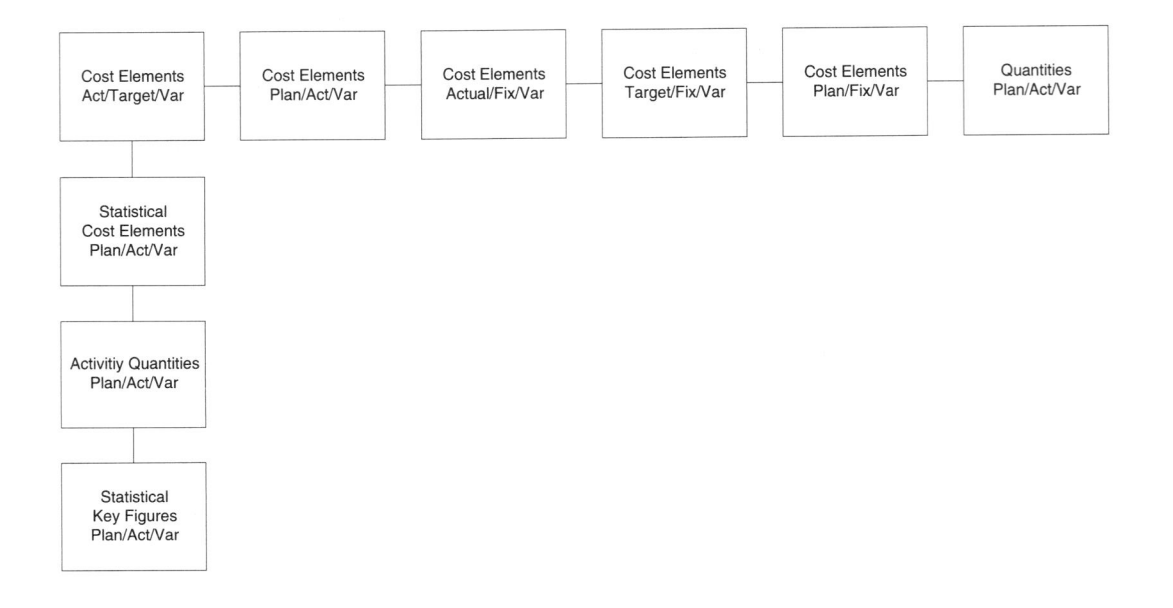

```
┌─────────────┐  ┌─────────────┐  ┌─────────────┐  ┌─────────────┐  ┌─────────────┐  ┌─────────────┐
│Cost Elements│──│Cost Elements│──│Cost Elements│──│Cost Elements│──│Cost Elements│──│ Quantities  │
│Act/Target/Var│  │ Plan/Act/Var│  │Actual/Fix/Var│ │Target/Fix/Var│ │Plan/Fix/Var │  │Plan/Act/Var │
└──────┬──────┘  └─────────────┘  └─────────────┘  └─────────────┘  └─────────────┘  └─────────────┘
       │
┌──────┴──────┐
│ Statistical │
│Cost Elements│
│ Plan/Act/Var│
└──────┬──────┘
       │
┌──────┴──────┐
│Activitiy Quantities│
│ Plan/Act/Var│
└──────┬──────┘
       │
┌──────┴──────┐
│ Statistical │
│ Key Figures │
│ Plan/Act/Var│
└─────────────┘
```

Reporting Made Easy

Section 4: Controlling—Cost Center Reports
Cost Center Summary: Target Costs, Actual Costs, and Variances

Guided Tour

Example: A cost center manager needs to analyze the target costs calculated for activity-dependent cost elements because these target costs are the basis for calculating cost center variance categories. The target costs for a cost center are based on the operating rate of the cost center.

To access the first screen for this report, choose

Information systems → Accounting → Overhead costs

Cost centers → Report selection.

From the reporting tree, choose the following report:

Target/Actual Comparison → CCtr: Actual/Target/Variance → Cost centers: Act/Targ/Variance.

1. Under *Selection values*, enter **2000** in *Controlling area*.

2. Enter the year in *Fiscal year* (for example, **1997**). This report runs for only one fiscal year at a time.

3. Enter **1** in *From period* and enter **12** in *To period*. This range includes all periods in the fiscal year.

4. Enter **0** in *Plan version*.

5. Enter **3200** in *Cost center*. You can also enter a range of cost centers, or a cost center group.

6. Enter **OAS-IVERR** in *Cost element group*. This creates a list of cost elements relevant to activities (for example, purchase orders, sales orders, and so on).

7. Choose *Execute*.

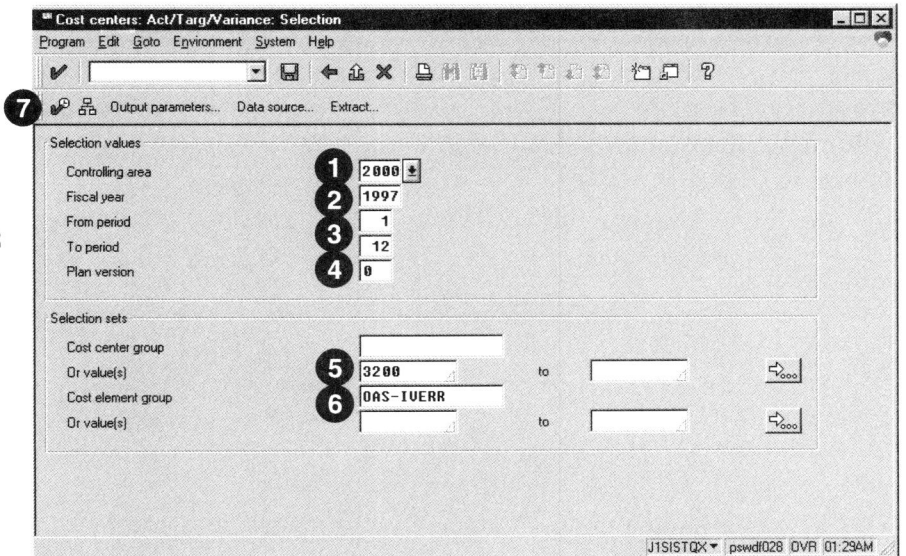

Commonly Used Reports: Illustrations and Perspectives

Section 4: Controlling—Cost Center Reports

Cost Center Summary: Target Costs, Actual Costs, and Variances

This screen shows the cost elements for which target, actual, and planned costs posted in the cost center.

Debits and credits are separated. If the cost element group contains hierarchy nodes, each node is subtotaled. Absolute and percentage variances are also calculated.

Cost elements that are included in the cost element group, but for which no postings were made, are not shown.

8. Choose *Next columns*.

These columns contain the actual costs, the planned costs, and the variance. (The planned costs in these columns are not multiplied by the operating rate.)

9. Choose *Next columns*.

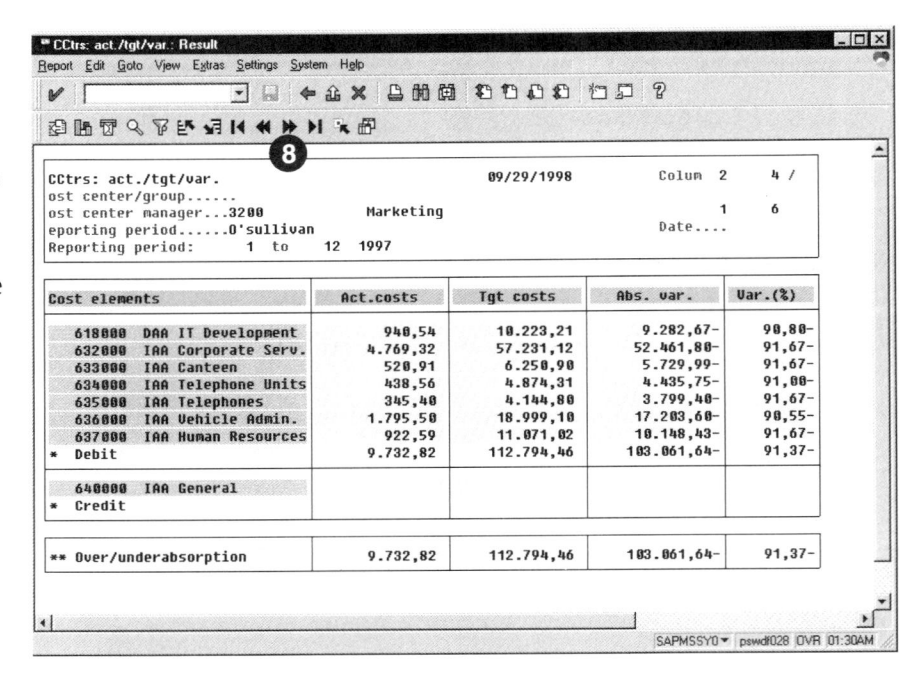

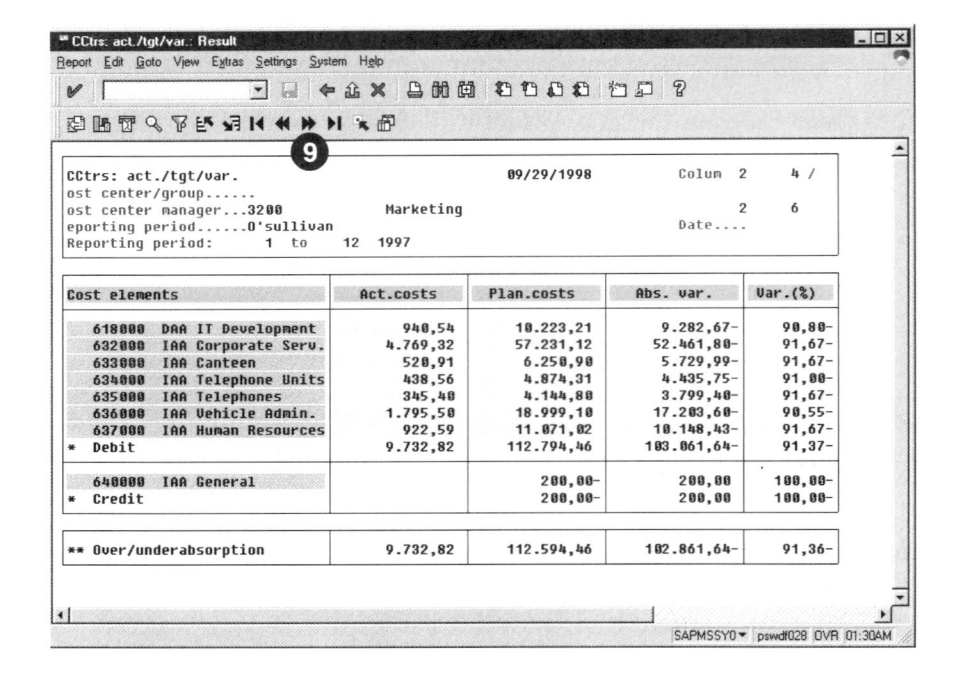

4–42

Reporting Made Easy

Section 4: Controlling—Cost Center Reports
Cost Center Summary: Target Costs, Actual Costs, and Variances

These columns show the fixed portion of the actual costs, the variable portion of the actual costs, and the percentage of the total costs represented by the fixed costs. (From a business perspective, fixed costs in a cost center can not usually be adjusted in the short term.)

10. Choose *Next columns*.

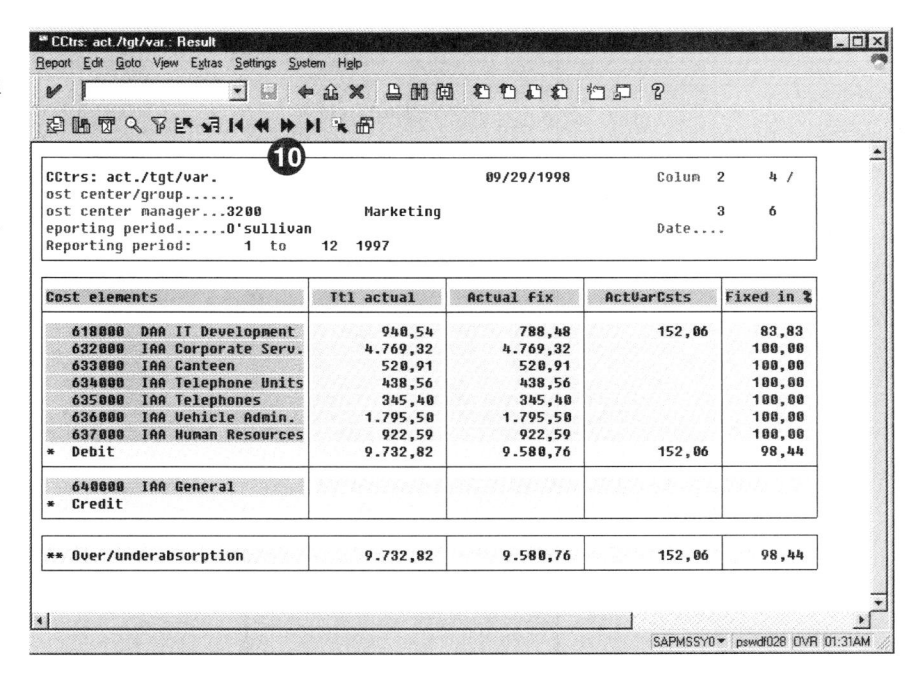

These columns show the total target costs, the fixed portion of the target costs, the variable portion of the target costs, and the percentage of the total costs represented by the fixed costs. (From a business perspective, fixed costs in a cost center can not usually be adjusted in the short term.)

11. Choose *Next columns*.

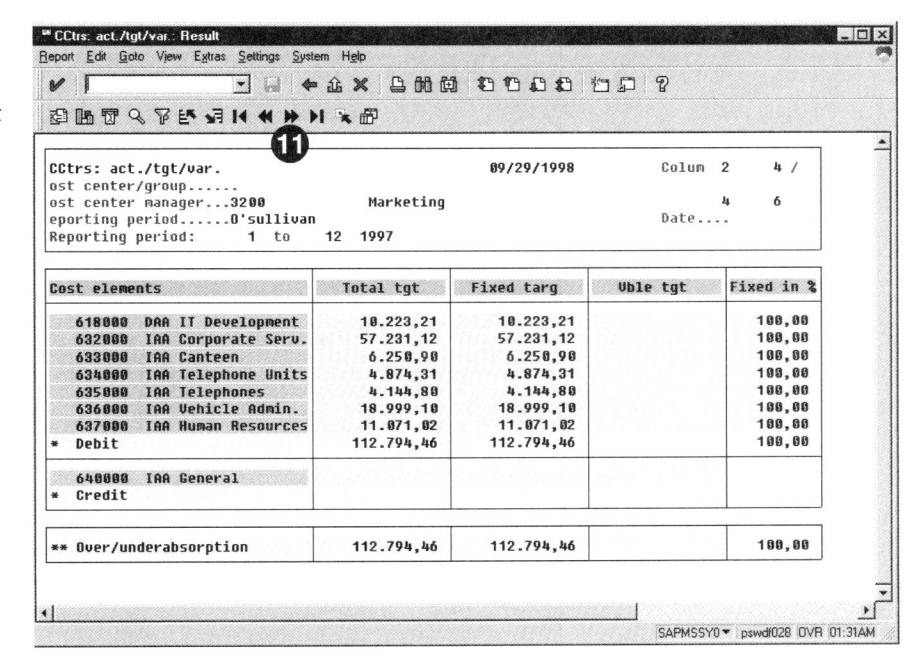

Commonly Used Reports: Illustrations and Perspectives

4–43

Section 4: Controlling—Cost Center Reports

Cost Center Summary: Target Costs, Actual Costs, and Variances

These columns contain the total planned costs, the fixed portion of the planned costs, the variable portion of the planned costs, and the percentage of the total costs represented by the fixed costs. (From a business perspective, fixed costs in a cost center can not usually be adjusted in the short term.)

12. Choose *Next columns*.

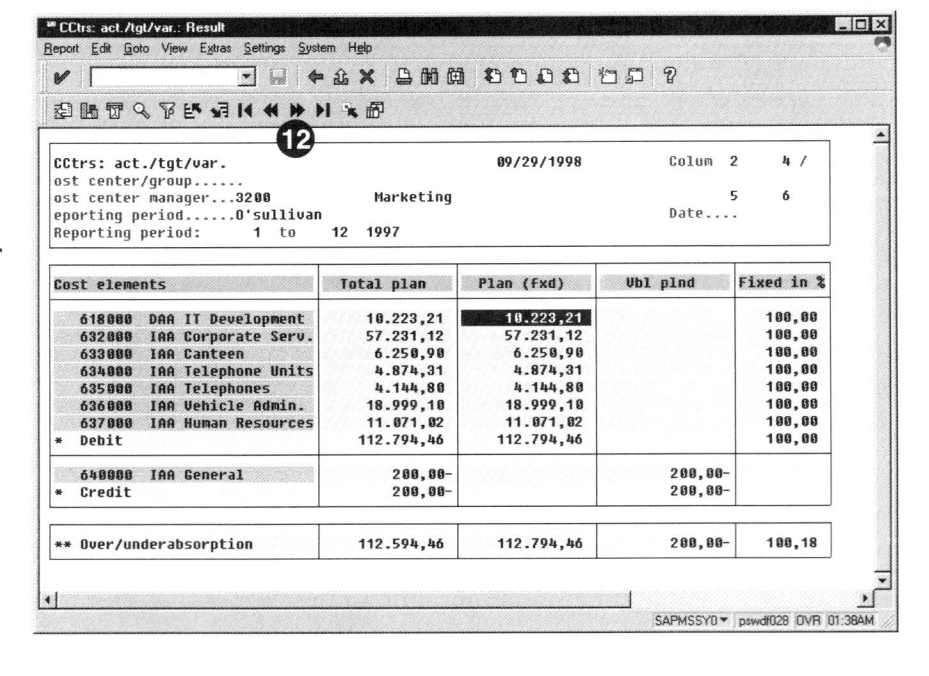

These columns contain the actual quantity, the planned quantity, and the difference.

13. Choose *First columns* to navigate to the first block of data in the report.

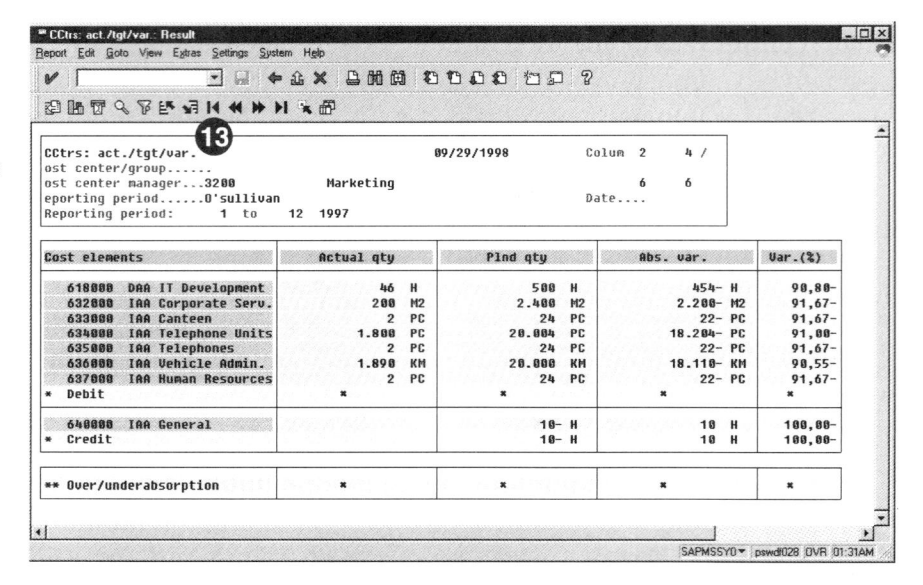

Section 4: Controlling—Cost Center Reports

Cost Center Summary: Target Costs, Actual Costs, and Variances

This screen shows the first block of data in the report.

14. Choose *Page Down* to navigate to the next block of data.

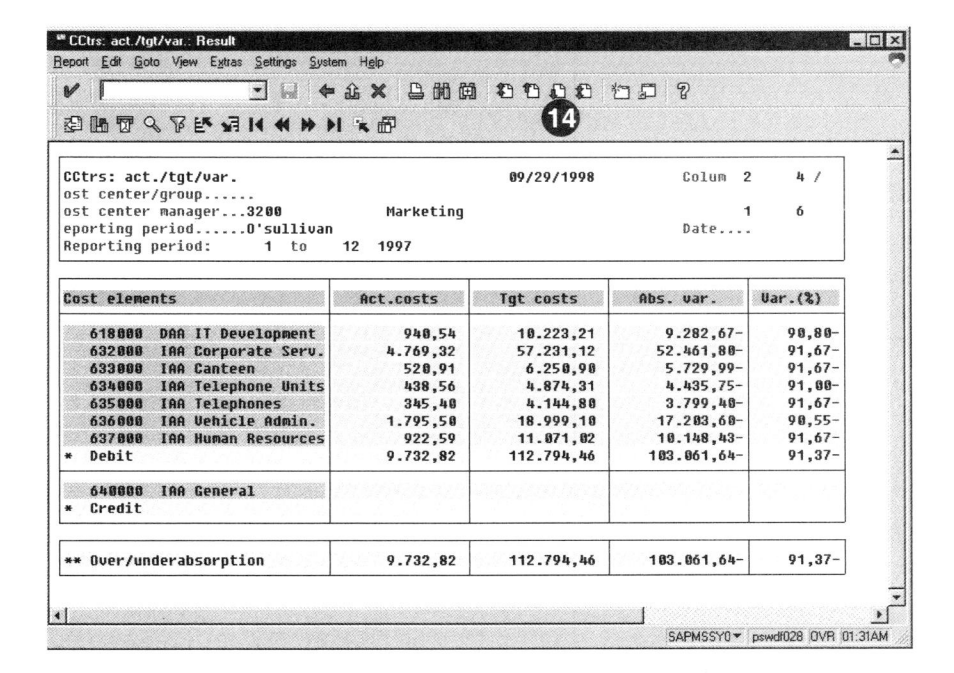

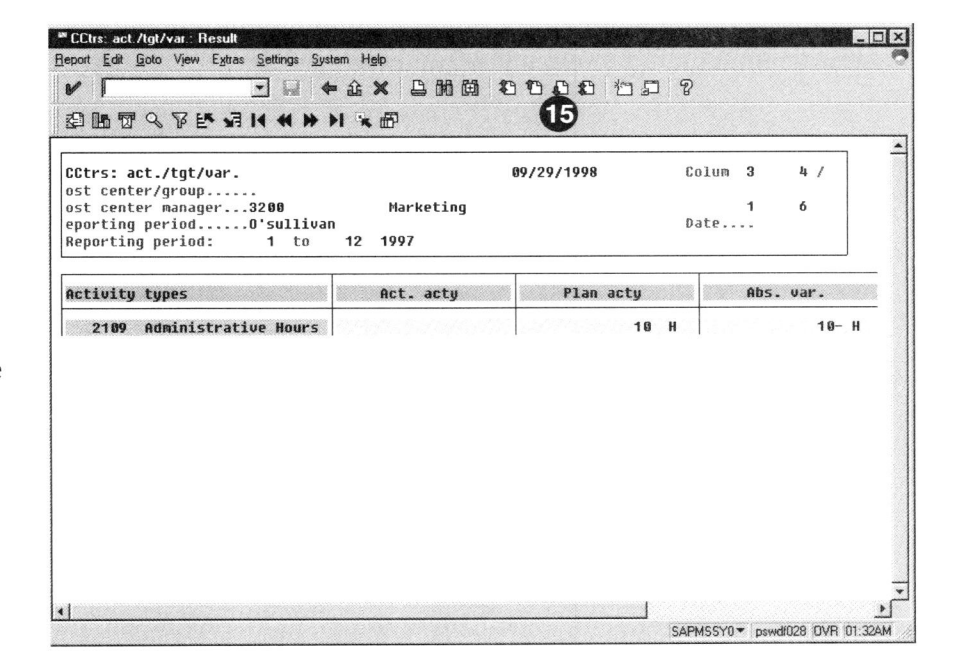

This screen shows activity quantities used in the postings, with the corresponding unit of measure.

If statistical postings existed for the cost center and cost elements, they would list on this screen. Since statistical postings were not made, this information is not included.

15. Choose *Page Down* to navigate to the next block of data.

Commonly Used Reports: Illustrations and Perspectives

Section 4: Controlling—Cost Center Reports

Cost Center Summary: Target Costs, Actual Costs, and Variances

This screen shows postings to statistical key figures, with the corresponding unit of measure. Absolute and percentage variances are also calculated.

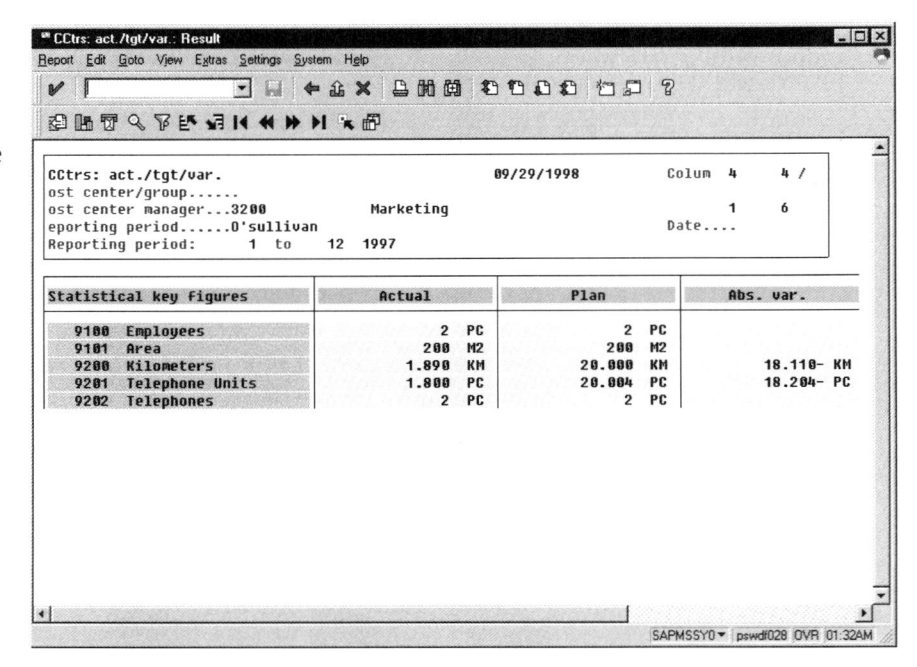

Statistical key figures	Actual	Plan	Abs. var.
9100 Employees	2 PC	2 PC	
9101 Area	200 M2	200 M2	
9200 Kilometers	1.890 KM	20.000 KM	18.110- KM
9201 Telephone Units	1.800 PC	20.004 PC	18.204- PC
9202 Telephones	2 PC	2 PC	

Section 5: Controlling—Internal Order Reports

Contents

Internal Order Summary: Planned Costs, Actual Costs, and Variances............5–2
Display Actual Line Items for Internal Orders...5–17
Internal Order List: Balance Displays 5–33

Internal Order Summary: Planned Costs, Actual Costs, and Variances

Quick Access
To run this report, use one of the following access options:

Option 1: Menu Path

Information systems → Accounting → Overhead costs

Orders → Report selection

From the reporting tree, choose the following report:

Plan/Actual Comparison → Order: Actual/Plan/Var. → Order: actual/plan/variance.

Option 2: Program Name

Choose *System → Services → Reporting* and enter **J6000TQX** in the *Program* field. Then, choose *Execute* to run the report.

Purpose
This report provides a summarized view of the costs, activities, and statistical key figures that posted to cost centers. The report includes both planned and actual postings, and calculates an absolute variance (difference), as well as a percentage of the variance. This report allows for a consolidated view of multiple internal orders at any given time. A balance of order postings is also calculated. Any balance left in the order, either an over- or under-absorption of costs, is usually settled to another receiver, typically a cost center.

A cost center manager who placed the order or a manager of a small project whose project work is performed by several different cost centers would use this report to plan costs and monitor progress against the plan.

Prerequisites
You must set the *Controlling Area* before running the report. Choose *Accounting → Controlling → Cost centers → Environment → Set controlling area*. For the examples in this section, the controlling area is set to *2000*.

You must enter a value in the selection fields before running the report. You may leave the cost center and cost element selection blank, and get a list that contains values for all cost centers and all cost elements in the selected controlling area. If you enter cost center groups and cost element groups, they must have already been set up. If they contain subtotals, hierarchy nodes should be created within the groups. Each hierarchy node then subtotals in this report.

Section 5: Controlling—Internal Order Reports
Internal Order Summary: Planned Costs, Actual Costs, and Variances

Integration

You can run multiple context-sensitive reports from this internal order report. For example, when you position the cursor on a cell for planned costs, only the reports that contain planned costs list data. If you select a cell for planned costs and run a report that only contains actual data, no data lists.

The following reports run for a single cell or a range of cells:
- Actual line items for one or more orders
- Planned line items for one or more orders
- Planning overview for a single order
- Actual values, by period (should be used for the cumulative views)
- Planned values, by period (should be used for the cumulative views)
- Internal order line items, by partner CO object (that is, partner cost center in a transaction, order, etc.)
- List of orders and balances
- Master data list of orders

Features

The selection screen of this report includes:
- Variants
- Dynamic selection options
- Executing and printing in the background
- Sorting capability (by column): Select a column, then *Edit → Sort in ascndng ordr* (Ctrl+Shift+F5), or *Edit → Sort in descending order* (Ctrl+Shift+F6)
- Adjusting the column width: *Settings → Column widths* (Ctrl+F12)
- Adjusting the numeric display, to set the number of decimals displayed and the scaling to hundredths, thousands, etc.: *Settings → Number format* (F5)
- Adjusting the summation level for the entire report (F6)
- Mailing of the report (Ctrl+F9)
- Graphing portions of the report using SAP business graphics (F7)
- Exporting the report to a local file
- Increasing or reducing the detail displayed, by double-clicking on subtotal lines. The double-click acts as a toggle switch. If detail is displayed, double-clicking on the subtotal will hide it. If detail is not displayed on a summary line (marked with one or more asterisks), double-clicking will display it.
- Displaying only threshold values, or values that are greater than or less than an entered criteria: *Edit → Threshold value* (Shift+F5).
- Creating an extract of reporting information (F5)
- Using variation to obtain multiple reports of internal order groups and hierarchy nodes (F6)
- Selecting from an extract or an archive: *Data source* (Ctrl+F1)

Next Steps

The system displays four columns for all sections of the report, including actual postings, planned data, and a calculation of the variance between the two, both as an absolute and as a percentage value (calculated by dividing the actual data by the planned).

By double-clicking on any subtotals in the report, the detail that makes up each subtotal can either be hidden or displayed. For example, double-clicking on the *Costs* line will hide the cost element detail. To display this detail again, double-click on this line.

This report contains data obtained from internal order postings. As such, the data cannot be changed or manipulated from the report.

This report contains five different blocks of data, as shown below. By navigating around these blocks, you can display different types of internal order data:

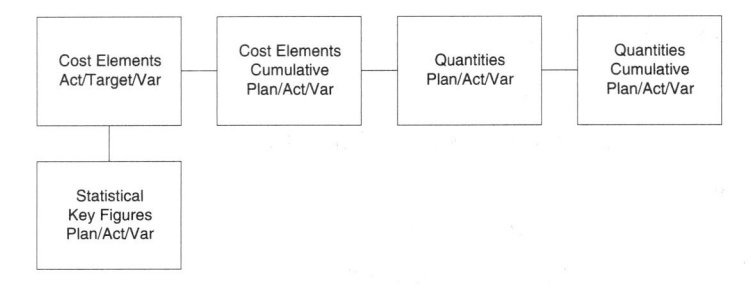

```
┌──────────────┐    ┌──────────────┐    ┌──────────────┐    ┌──────────────┐
│ Cost Elements│    │ Cost Elements│    │  Quantities  │    │  Quantities  │
│ Act/Target/Var│──│  Cumulative  │──│ Plan/Act/Var │──│  Cumulative  │
│              │    │ Plan/Act/Var │    │              │    │ Plan/Act/Var │
└──────┬───────┘    └──────────────┘    └──────────────┘    └──────────────┘
       │
┌──────┴───────┐
│  Statistical │
│  Key Figures │
│ Plan/Act/Var │
└──────────────┘
```

Section 5: Controlling—Internal Order Reports
Internal Order Summary: Planned Costs, Actual Costs, and Variances

Guided Tour

Example 1: A cost center manager, who placed an internal order, wants to analyze its performance. This report shows the detailed postings for the internal order, including all planned and actual costs, as well as planned and actual statistical key figures.

To access the first screen for this report, choose

Information systems → *Accounting* → *Overhead costs*

Orders → *Report selection*.

From the reporting tree, choose the following report:

Plan/Actual Comparison → *Order: Actual/Plan/Var.* → *Order: actual/plan/variance*.

1. Under *Selection values*, enter **2000** in *Controlling area*.
2. Enter the year in *Fiscal year* (for example, **1997**). This report runs for only one fiscal year at a time.
3. Enter **1** in *From period* and **12** in *To period*. This report will not provide a periodic breakdown of the costs, only totals for the period range list.
4. Enter **0** in *Plan version*.
5. Enter **800087** in *Or value(s)*. You can also enter a range of orders, or an order group.
6. Enter **OAS-TOTAL** in *Cost element*. This group contains all cost elements.
7. Choose *Execute*.

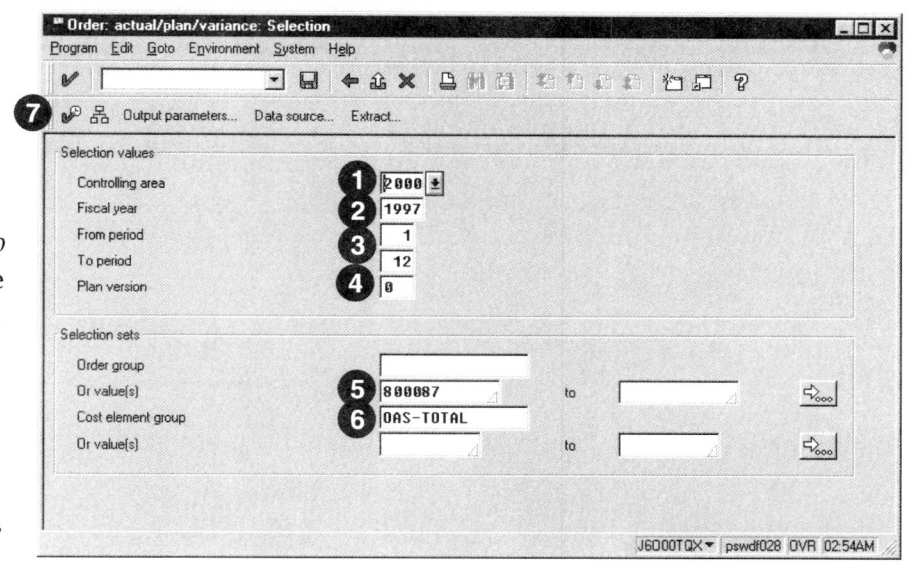

Commonly Used Reports: Illustrations and Perspectives

Section 5: Controlling—Internal Order Reports
Internal Order Summary: Planned Costs, Actual Costs, and Variances

The first screen of this report lists cost elements for which planned and actual costs posted in the internal order, along with the absolute and percentage variances.

Debits and credits are separated. If the cost element group contains hierarchy nodes, a subtotal is shown for each of these nodes.

8. Choose *Next columns*.

The next screen lists the cumulative costs posted to both primary and secondary cost elements, along with the absolute and percentage variances.

These costs are all the costs that have been posted to the order during the current fiscal year through the selected period.

9. Choose *Next columns*.

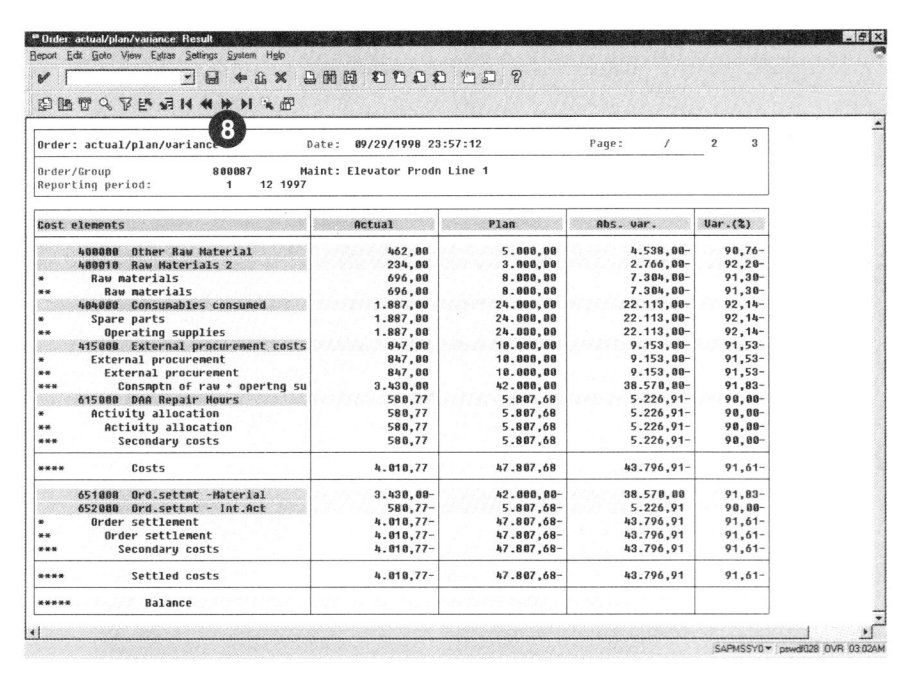

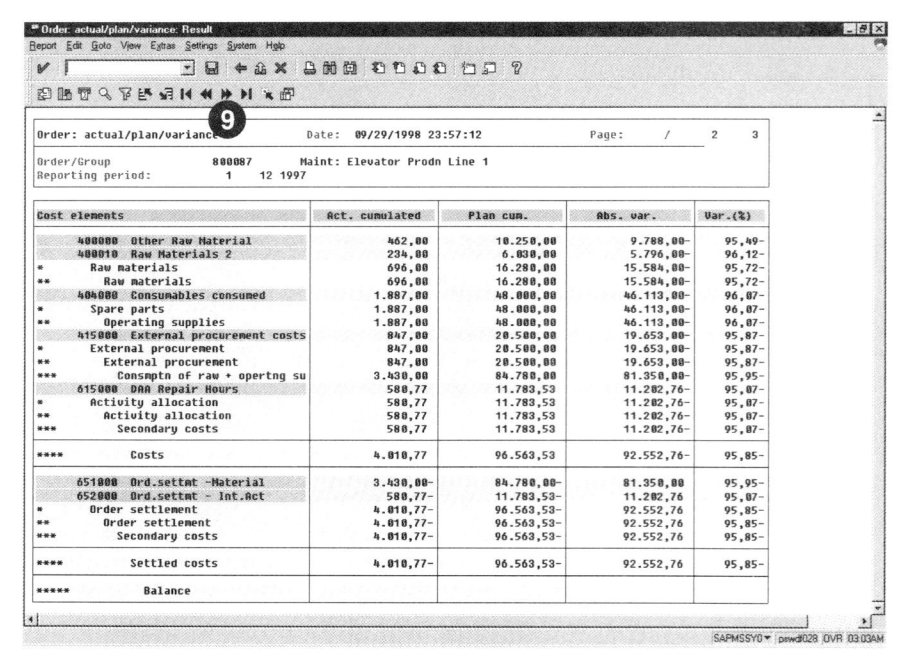

Reporting Made Easy

5–6

Section 5: Controlling—Internal Order Reports

Internal Order Summary: Planned Costs, Actual Costs, and Variances

This screen lists the quantities posted, provided the original document was posted with a unit of measure.

For cost element postings that do not involve a unit of measure, no value lists. Absolute and percentage variances are also calculated.

10. Choose *Next columns*.

These columns list the cumulative quantities posted to both primary and secondary cost elements, along with the absolute and percentage variances.

These costs are all the costs that posted to the order during the current fiscal year through the selected period.

11. Choose *First columns* to navigate to the first block of data in the report.

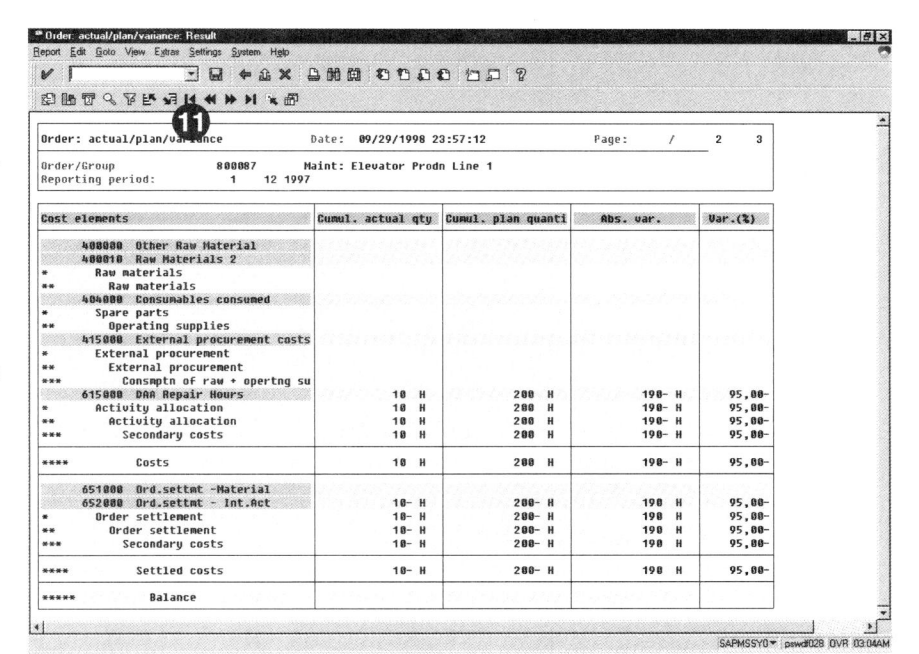

Commonly Used Reports: Illustrations and Perspectives

5–7

Section 5: Controlling—Internal Order Reports
Internal Order Summary: Planned Costs, Actual Costs, and Variances

This screen shows the first block of data listed for the report.

12. Choose *Page Down* to navigate to the next block of data.

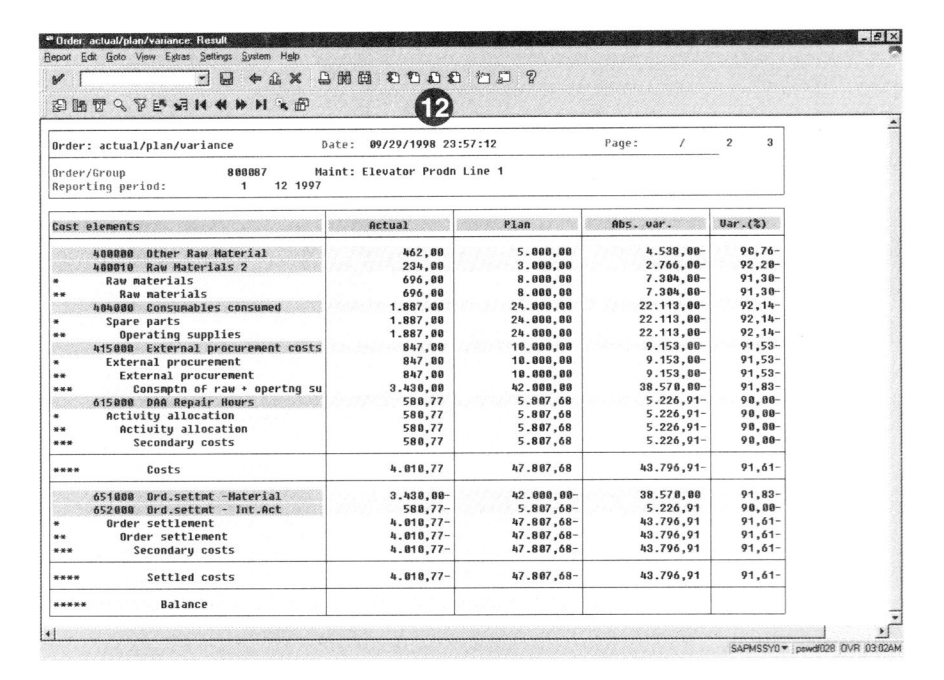

These columns show the postings to *Statistical key figures*, with the corresponding unit of measure. Absolute and percentage variances are also calculated.

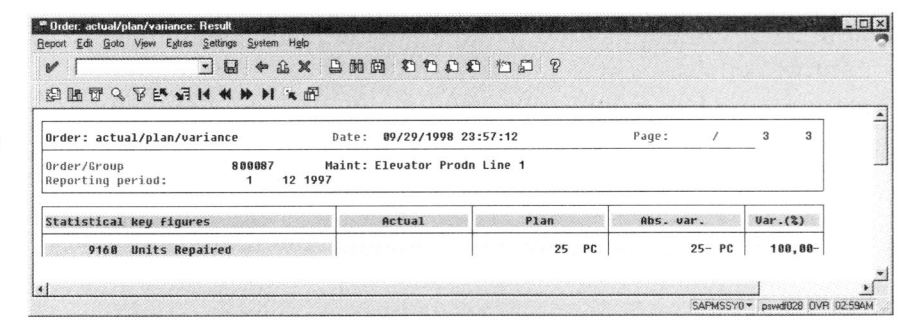

5–8　　　Reporting Made Easy

Section 5: Controlling—Internal Order Reports
Internal Order Summary: Planned Costs, Actual Costs, and Variances

Example 2: A cost center manager needs to set up multiple internal orders to track costs in more detail than is normally possible. The manager wants to analyze activities—or resources used—within a particular timeframe.

1. Under *Selection values*, enter **2000** in *Controlling area*.

2. Enter the year in *Fiscal year* (for example, **1997**). This report runs for only one fiscal year at a time.

3. Enter **1** in *From period* and **12** in *To period*. This report will not provide a periodic breakdown of the costs, only totals for this period range will be included.

4. Enter **0** in *Plan version*.

5. Enter **X0851** in *Order group*. This group represents all internal orders for maintenance work, based on the order type.

6. Enter **OAS-IVERR** in *Cost element group*. This group contains only cost elements that represent internal activities.

7. Choose *Variation*.

8. Make certain that the default *Explode* is selected. This results in data capture for hierarchy nodes, as well as for individual cost centers. Selecting the *SingleVal* option would only capture data for cost centers, with no totals for hierarchy nodes.

9. Choose *Enter*.

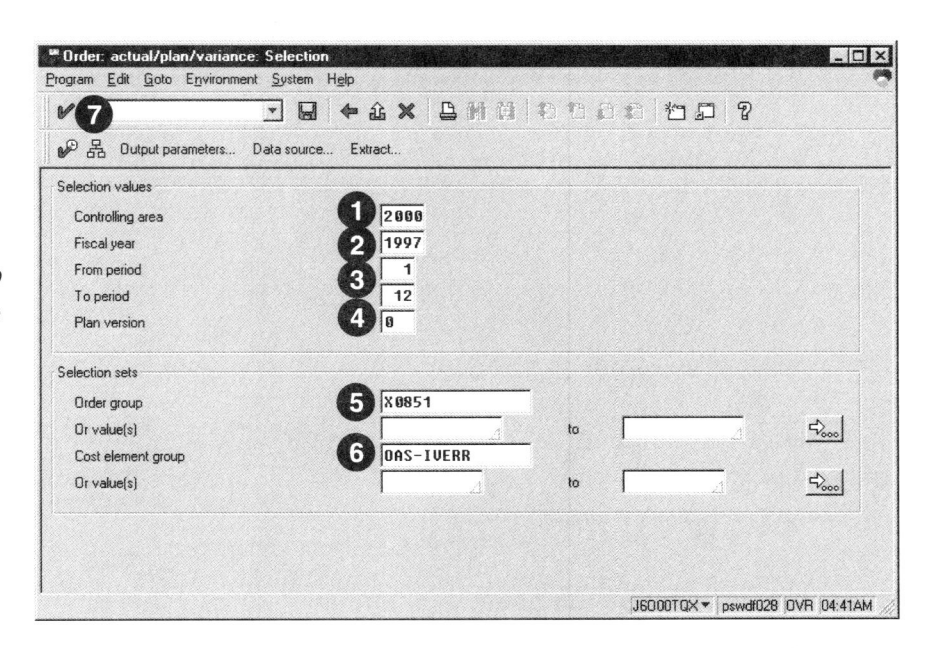

Commonly Used Reports: Illustrations and Perspectives

Section 5: Controlling—Internal Order Reports
Internal Order Summary: Planned Costs, Actual Costs, and Variances

10. Choose *Execute*.

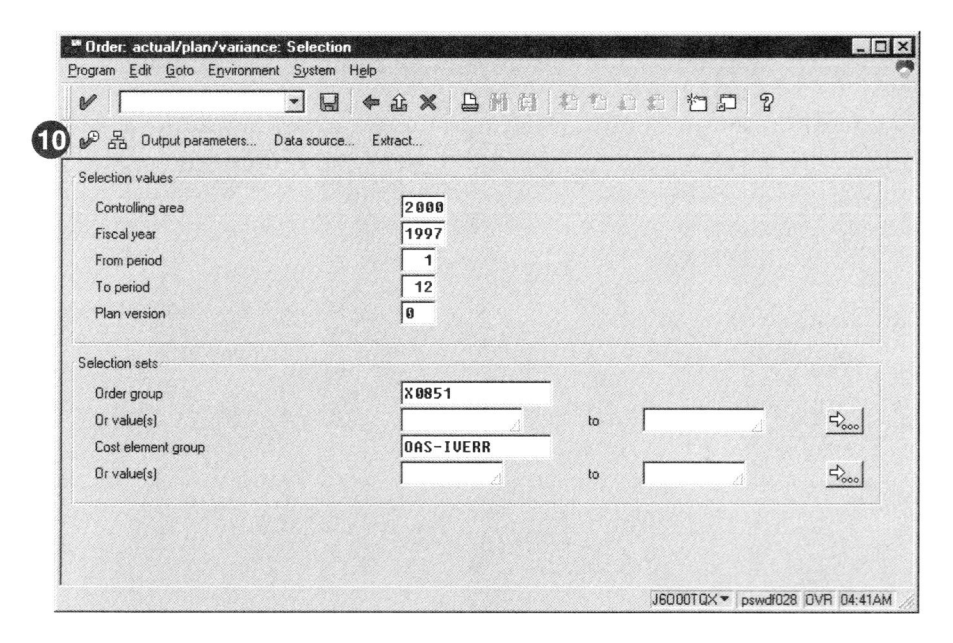

The first screen of the report shows the cost elements, for which actual and planned costs posted in the cost center.

Only those cost centers and cost elements that are included in the selected groups list. (This report does not show a complete picture of all the costs posted to these cost centers.)

11. Choose *Variation*.

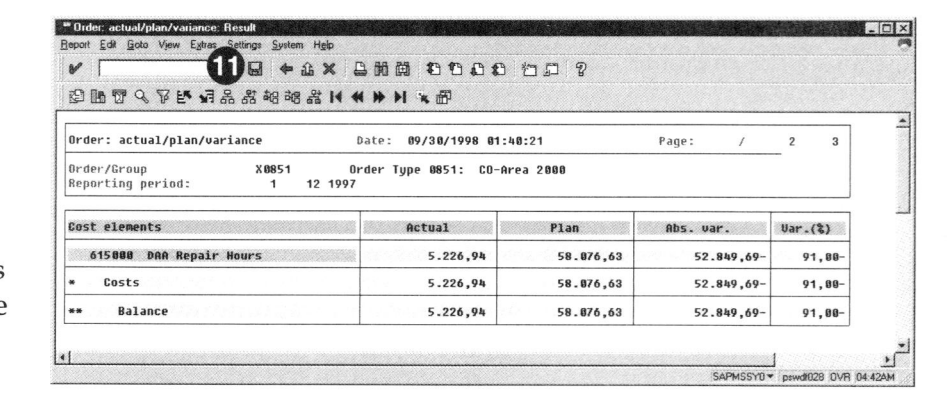

5–10

Reporting Made Easy

Section 5: Controlling—Internal Order Reports
Internal Order Summary: Planned Costs, Actual Costs, and Variances

12. Choose *Field values on/off* to list the cost center numbers and hierarchy node codes, in addition to their descriptions.

13. Double-click on the order number (for example, *800086*) to display only the values relevant to it.

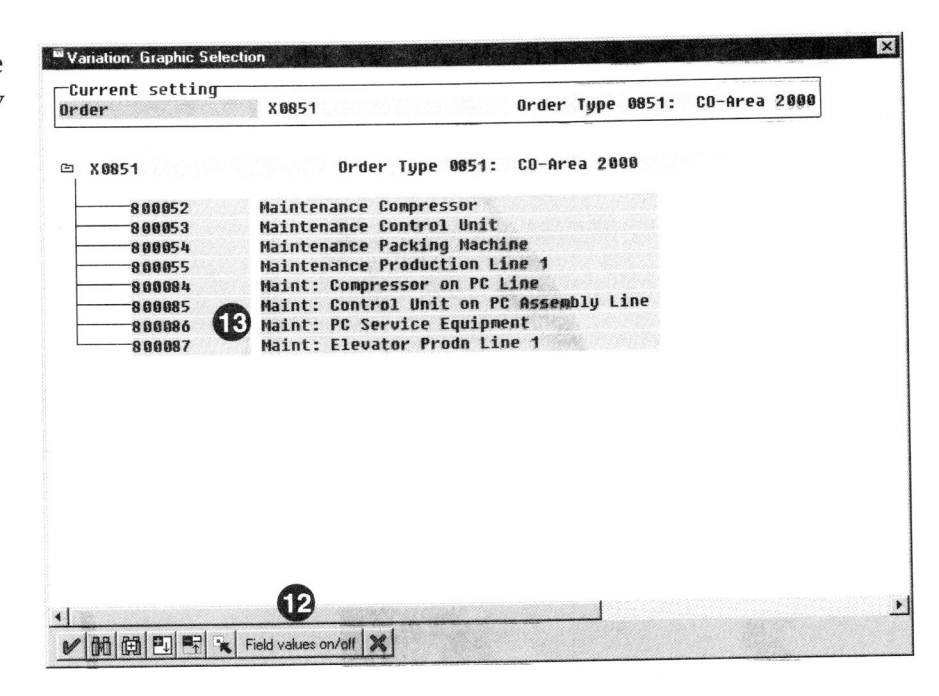

The values change to reflect only the postings to the chosen cost center.

To scroll through the cost center group, its nodes, and its cost centers, use:

- Previous level/up
- Scroll left
- Scroll right
- Next level/down

All other sections of the report (units of measure, statistical postings, activity types, and statistical key figures) are also available.

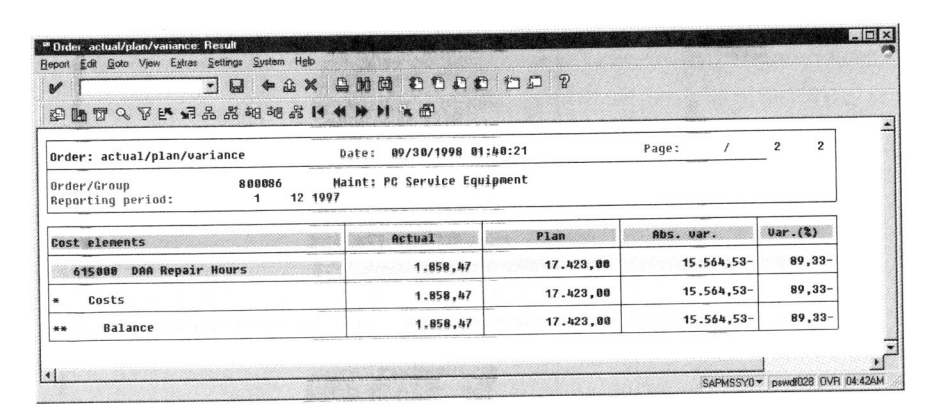

Commonly Used Reports: Illustrations and Perspectives

Section 5: Controlling—Internal Order Reports
Internal Order Summary: Planned Costs, Actual Costs, and Variances

Example 3: If a report has a long run time due to the volume of cost centers and transactional data, or if a report needs to be saved for access by various people for an audit trail, you may want to generate an extract. An extract runs considerably faster and can be reviewed while the report is running in the background or overnight.

1. Under *Selection values*, enter **2000** in Controlling area.

2. Enter the year in *Fiscal year* (for example, **1997**). This report runs for only one fiscal year at a time.

3. Enter **1** in *From period* and enter **12** in *To period*. This range includes all periods in the fiscal year.

4. Enter **0** in *Plan version*.

5. Enter **ALL-2000** in *Order group*. This group includes all internal orders in the controlling area.

6. Enter **OAS-TOTAL** in *Cost element group*. This group contains all cost elements.

7. Choose *Extract*.

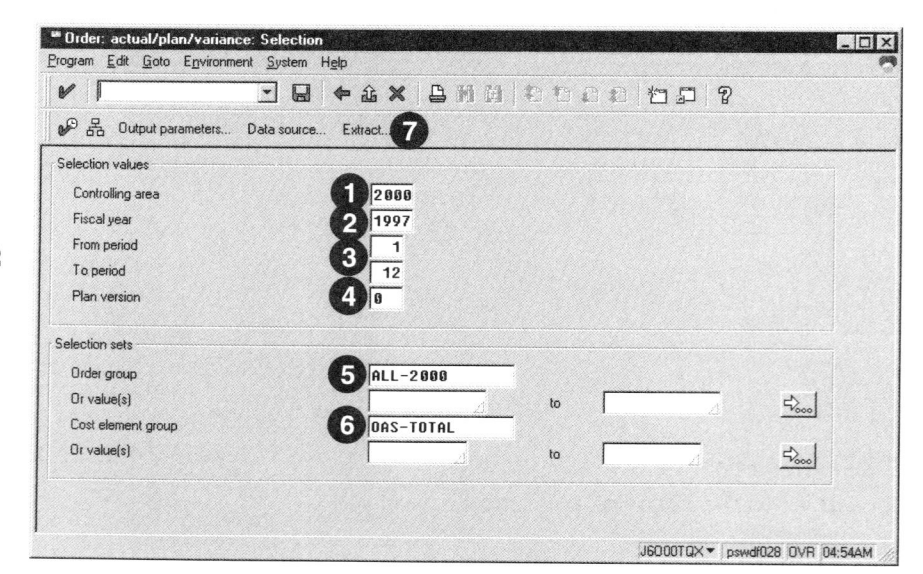

Section 5: Controlling—Internal Order Reports
Internal Order Summary: Planned Costs, Actual Costs, and Variances

8. Select *Create extract*.
9. Enter a *Description* (for example, `Controlling Area 2000, 1977`).
10. Enter a password to protect the data. Then, enter the password again.

    A password is not required, but if one is not entered, unauthorized users may be able to access the data.

11. Enter the number of days after which the extract will expire (for example, `30`.

Assigning an expiration date:

- Ensures that the extract will not be viewed after this date
- Does not permit access to data by means of a historic audit trail
- Permits a periodic report to be run midmonth

12. Choose *Enter*.

    Variation defaults for all values of internal orders.

13. Choose *Execute*.

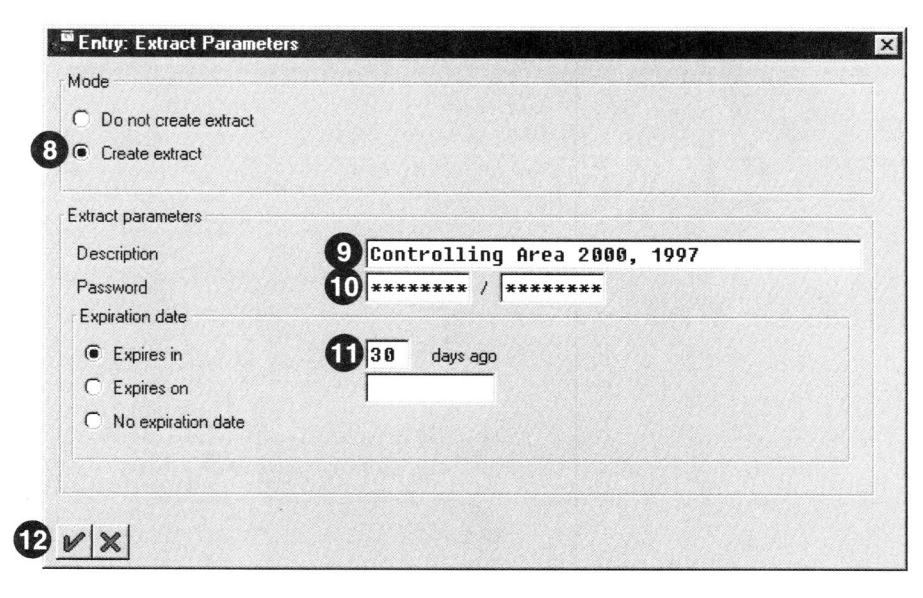

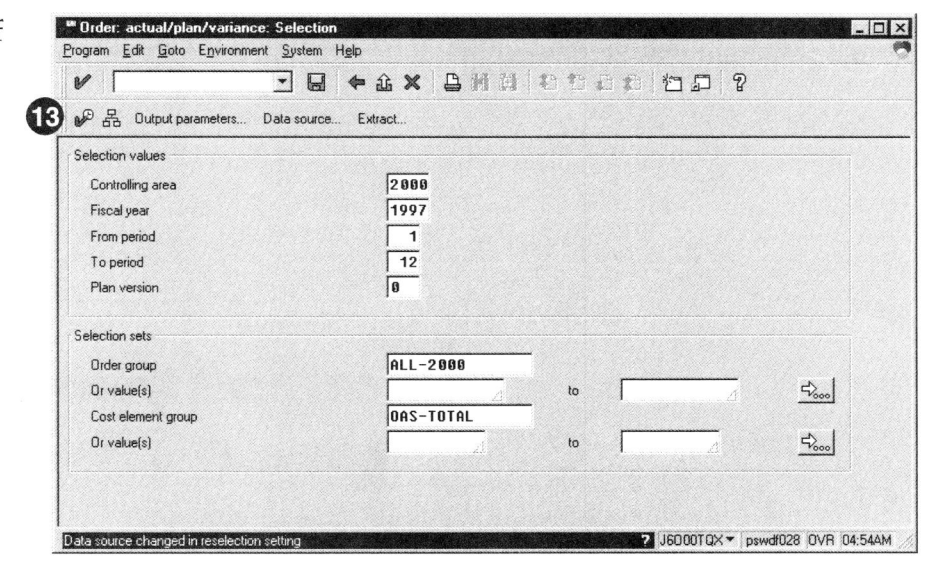

Commonly Used Reports: Illustrations and Perspectives

5–13

Section 5: Controlling—Internal Order Reports
Internal Order Summary: Planned Costs, Actual Costs, and Variances

This screen shows the report; the extract is automatically created and saved.

14. Choose *Back* ⇐.

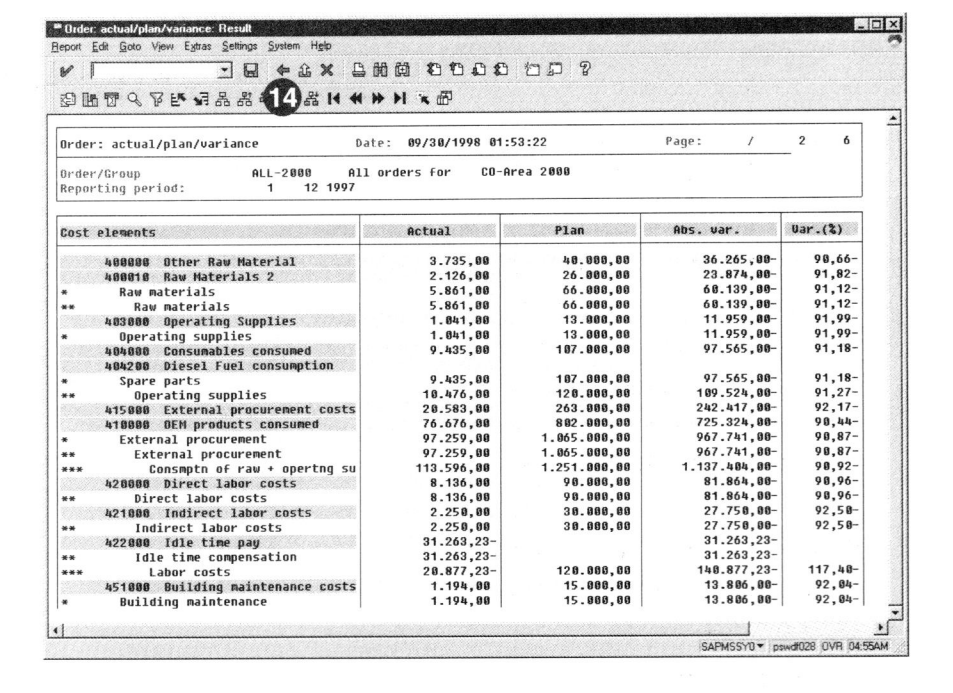

15. Choose *Data source* to view the extract.

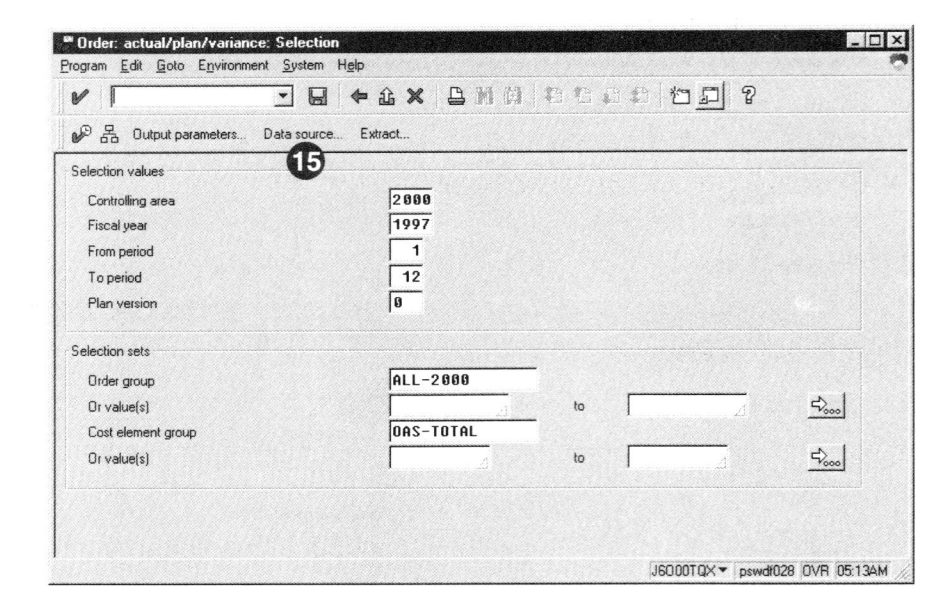

16. Select *Display extract*.
17. Choose *Enter*.

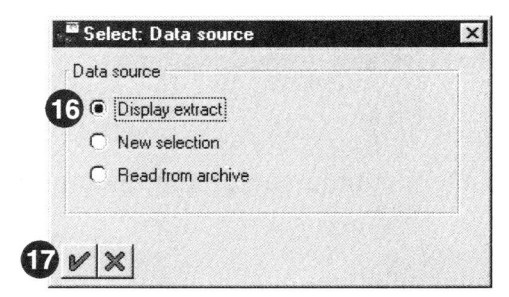

5–14 Reporting Made Easy

Section 5: Controlling—Internal Order Reports
Internal Order Summary: Planned Costs, Actual Costs, and Variances

This screen shows all extracts that match the selection criteria.

18. Position the cursor on the extract (for example, *DIPMUSTER*) to select it.

19. Choose *Enter*.

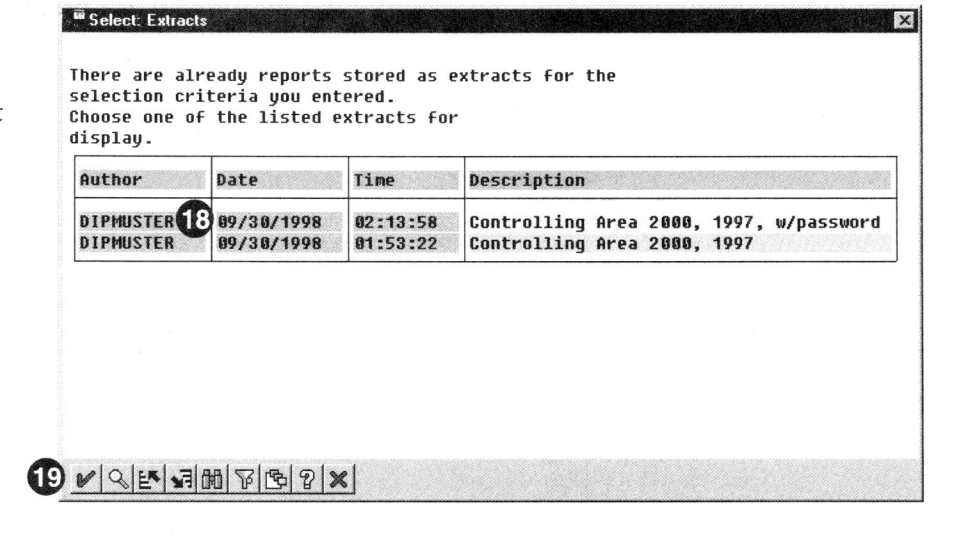

20. If the extract was created with password protection, the password must be entered before the extract can be displayed.

21. Choose *Enter*.

22. Choose *Execute*.

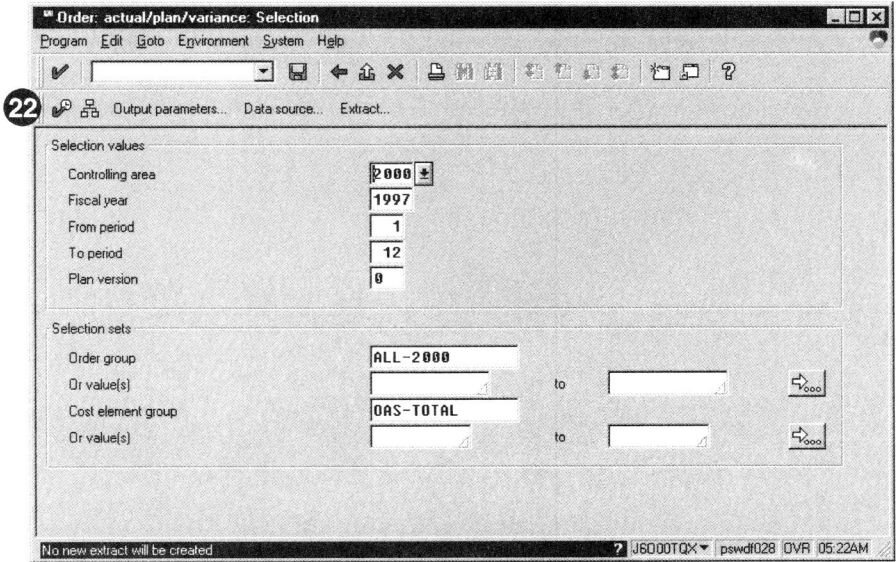

Commonly Used Reports: Illustrations and Perspectives

5–15

Section 5: Controlling—Internal Order Reports

Internal Order Summary: Planned Costs, Actual Costs, and Variances

This screen shows the extract.

The normal functions are still available within the report including:

- Scroll left
- Scroll right
- Variation (to access the corresponding extract)
- Drill down (to dynamically run another report)

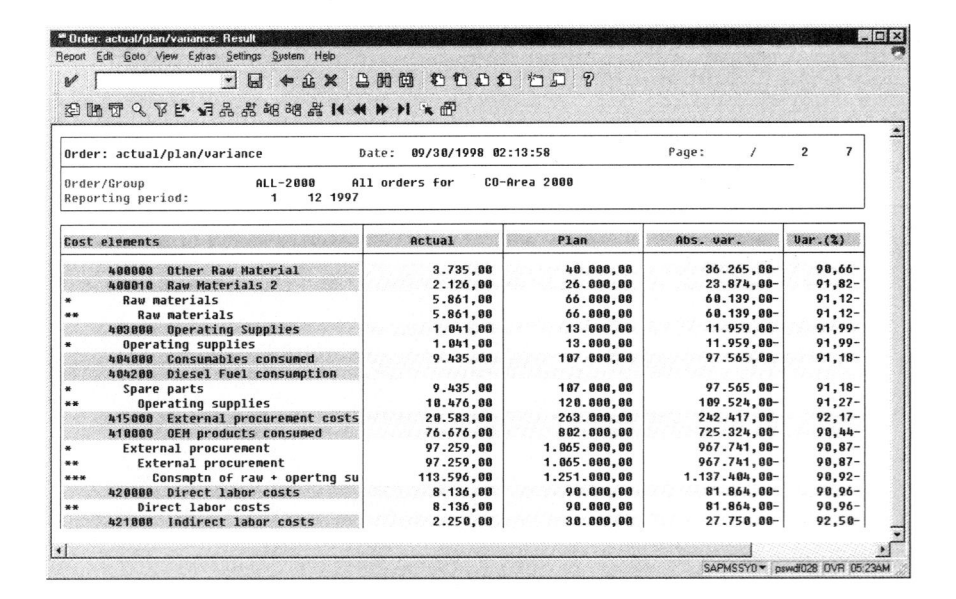

Reporting Made Easy

Display Actual Line Items for Internal Orders

Quick Access   To run this report, use one of the following access options:

Option 1: Menu Path

Information systems → *Accounting* → *Overhead costs*

Orders → *Line items* → *Actual*

Option 2: Transaction Code

In the command field, enter transaction **KOB1** and choose *Enter*.

Purpose   This report lists individual line items that post to the selected internal order or order group. At the time the line items list, additional fields can be accessed to assist a cost center manager in monitoring the actual costs being posted to the cost center.

A cost center manager may often use this report to reconcile postings between the General Ledger (G/L) and cost centers, and to monitor the actual postings made to a particular internal order. This report may also assist a manager in searching for particular information, such as a specific material or purchase order posting.

Prerequisites   You must set the Controlling area before running the report. Choose *Accounting* → *Controlling* → *Cost centers* → *Environment* → *Set controlling area*. For the examples in this section, the controlling area is set to *2000*.

You must enter a value in the selection fields before running the report. You may leave the cost center and cost element selection blank, so that all cost elements are selected. If you enter cost center groups and cost element groups, they must have already been set up. If they contain subtotals, hierarchy nodes should be created within the groups. Each hierarchy node then subtotals in this report.

Section 5: Controlling—Internal Order Reports
Display Actual Line Items for Internal Orders

Integration

You can run multiple context-sensitive reports from this internal order report. For example, when you position the cursor on a cell for planned costs, only the reports that contain planned costs list data. If you select a cell for planned costs and run a report that only contains actual data, no data lists.

The following reports run for a single cell or a range of cells:

- Actual line items for one or more orders
- Planned line items for one or more orders
- Planning overview for a single order
- Actual values, by period (should be used for the cumulative views)
- Planned values, by period (should be used for the cumulative views)
- Internal order line items, by partner CO object (that is, partner cost center in a transaction, order, etc.)
- List of orders and balances
- Master data list of orders

Features

The selection screen of this report includes:

- Variants
- Dynamic selection options
- Executing and printing in background
- Sorting capability (by column): select a column, then *Edit → Sort in ascndng ordr* (*Ctrl+Shift+F5*), or *Edit → Sort in descending order* (Ctrl+Shift+F6)
- Adjusting the column width: *Settings → Column widths* (Ctrl+F12)
- Adjusting the numeric display, to set the number of decimals displayed and the scaling to hundredths, thousands, etc.: *Settings → Number format* (F5)
- Mailing of the report (Ctrl+F9)
- Graphing portions of the report using SAP business graphics (F7)
- Exporting the report to a local file
- Increasing or reducing the detail displayed, by double-clicking on subtotal lines. The double-click acts as a toggle switch. If detail is displayed, double-clicking on the subtotal will hide it. If detail is not displayed on a summary line (marked with one or more asterisks), double-clicking will display it.
- Displaying only threshold values, or values greater than or less than an entered criteria: *Edit → Threshold value* (Shift+F5).
- Creating an extract of reporting information (F5)
- Using variation to obtain multiple reports of internal order groups and hierarchy nodes (F6)
- Selecting from an extract or an archive: *Data source* (Ctrl+F1)

Section 5: Controlling—Internal Order Reports
Display Actual Line Items for Internal Orders

Next Steps

The system displays the actual line items for the internal order according to the display variant chosen. Different display variants can be set up to display unique information. Subtotals are available for different columns, as defined in the configuration of the display variant.

By double-clicking on any subtotals in the report, the detail that makes up each subtotal can either be hidden or displayed. For example, double-clicking on the *Costs* line will hide the cost element detail. To display this detail again, double-click on this line.

This report contains data obtained from cost center postings. As such, the data cannot be changed or manipulated from the report.

Guided Tour

Example 1: A high-level manager wants to see what types of costs are the highest for internal orders or initiatives. In order to do this, the manager needs to list all internal orders and sort them by cost element.

To access the first screen for this report, choose

Information systems → Accounting → Overhead costs

Orders → Line items → Actual.

1. Enter `ALL-2000` in *Order group*. You can also enter a single order, or a range of orders.

2. Enter `OAS-TOTAL` in *Cost element group*. This group contains all cost elements.

3. Enter `1` in *From period* and `12` in *To period*. This report will not provide a periodic breakdown of the costs, only totals for this period range will be included.

4. Enter `1SAP` in *Display variant*.

5. Choose *Further settings*.

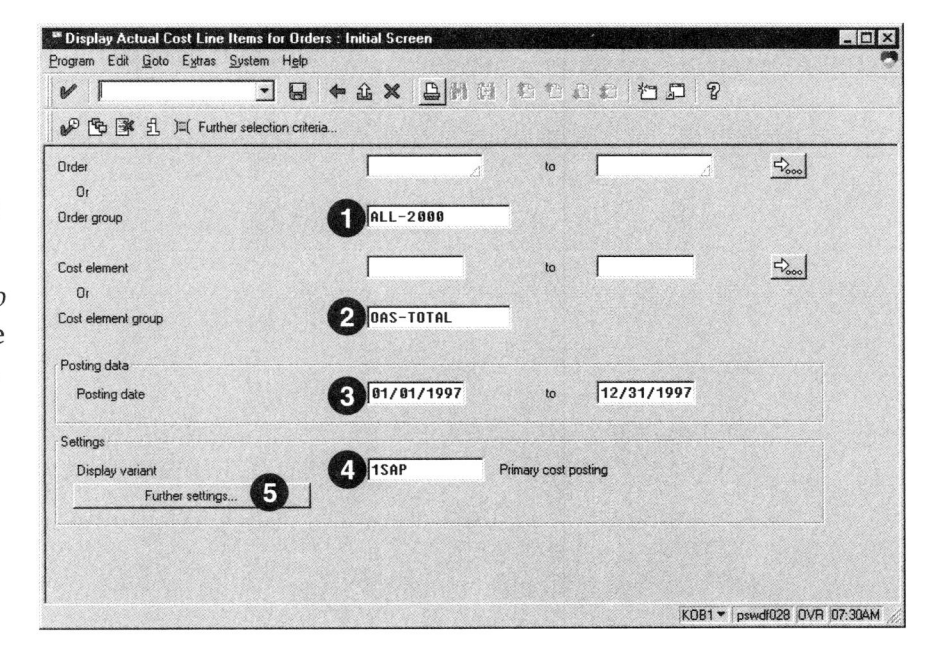

Commonly Used Reports: Illustrations and Perspectives

5–19

Section 5: Controlling—Internal Order Reports
Display Actual Line Items for Internal Orders

The *Variant fields only* checkbox should remain deselected for purposes of this example. This increases performance in selecting actual line items and also makes it possible for you to change the line item display after you make the database selection.

If the *Variant fields only* checkbox is selected, only the fields relevant to the first display variant entered are selected from the database. After the report runs, you cannot view additional fields.

6. Enter **5.000** (five thousand) in *Maximum no. of hits*. (Additional records—even if they fall within the date range—will not appear.)

7. Choose *Enter*.

This screen shows the list of actual line items for the cost center.

8. Choose *Subtotal*.

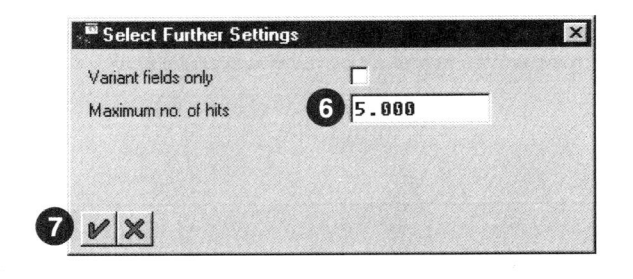

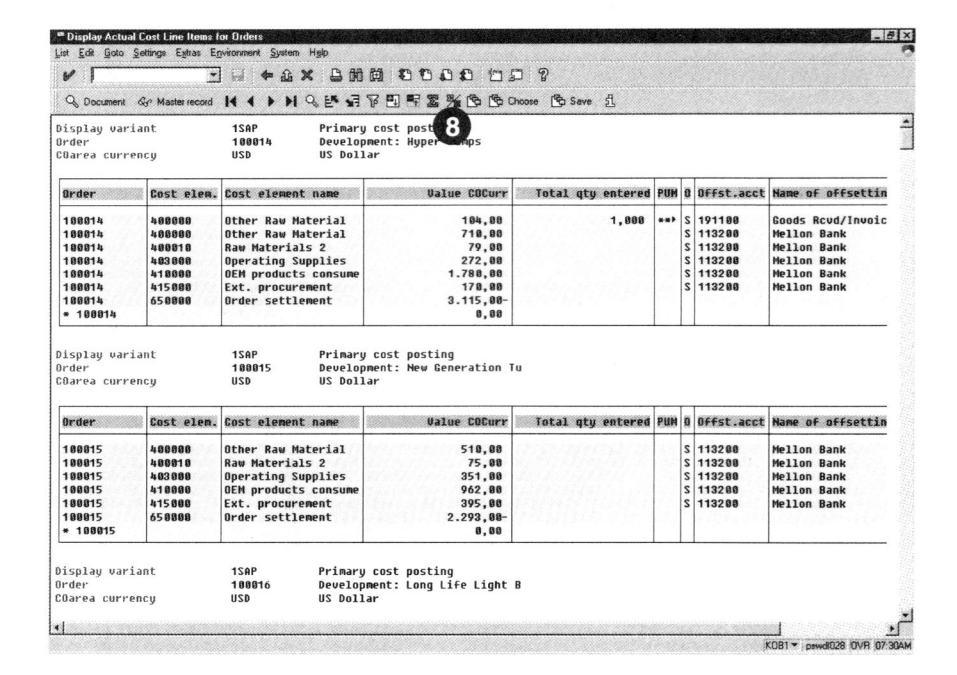

5–20

Reporting Made Easy

Section 5: Controlling—Internal Order Reports
Display Actual Line Items for Internal Orders

The current subtotals are based on the internal order field.

9. Deselect the subtotal checkbox for the *Order* and select the subtotal checkbox for the *Cost element*.

10. Change the sort sequence between *Order* and *Cost element* by overwriting the initial sequence.

11. Choose *Copy*.

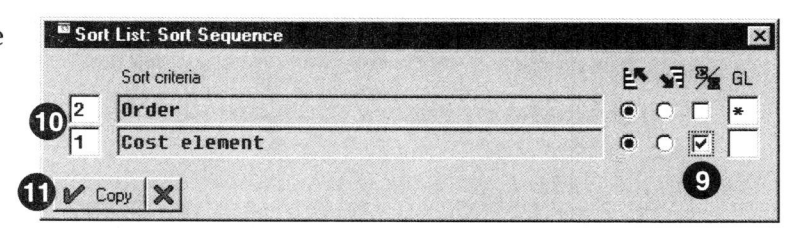

This screen shows the subtotals based on the cost elements within the orders.

12. Choose *Subtotal*.

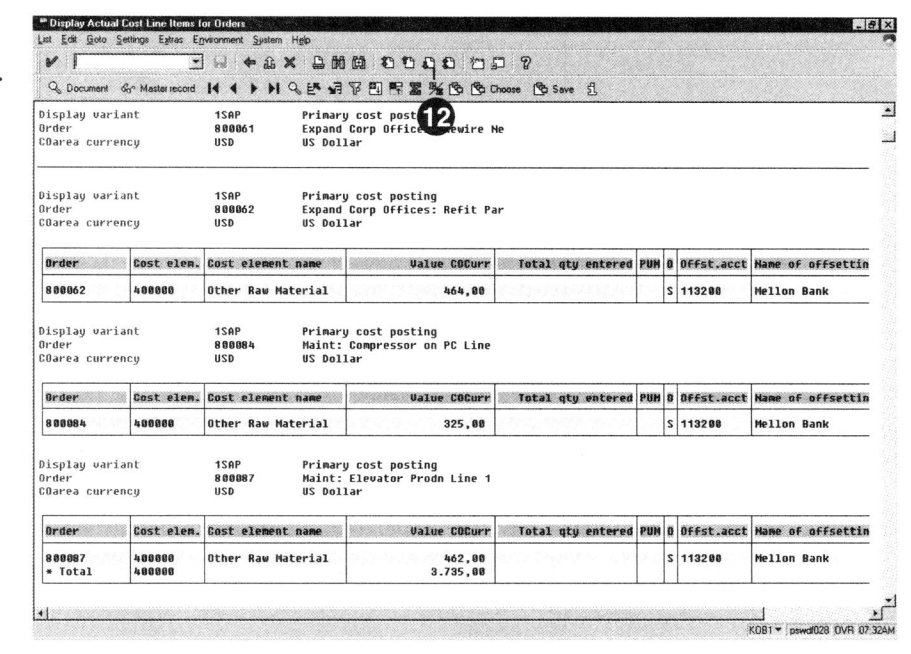

13. Delete the sort sequence for *Order*, so that a more consolidated view of the *Cost element* subtotal lists.

14. Choose *Copy*.

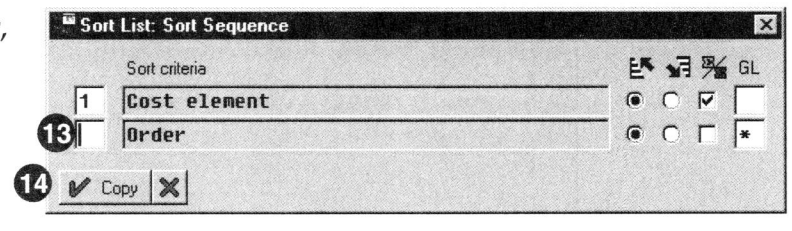

Commonly Used Reports: Illustrations and Perspectives

5–21

Section 5: Controlling—Internal Order Reports
Display Actual Line Items for Internal Orders

This screen shows the subtotals based on the cost elements within the internal order. (This allows for easier reconciliation of the General Ledger.)

15. Choose *Choose display variant*

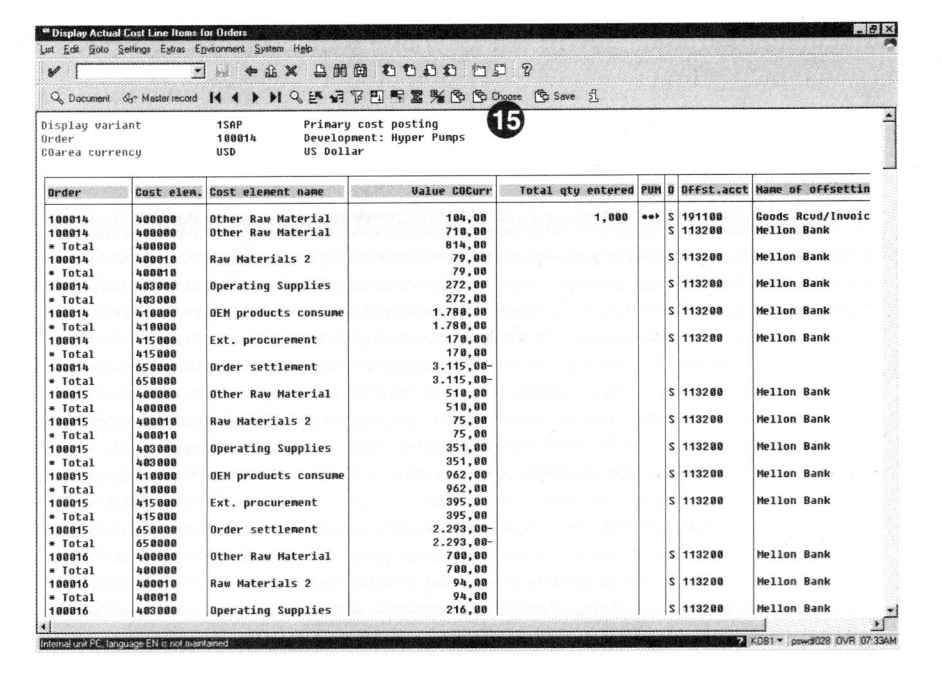

16. Select display variant *2SAP*, by clicking on it once. This creates a more detailed list of the actual line item posted to the internal order.

17. Choose *Copy*.

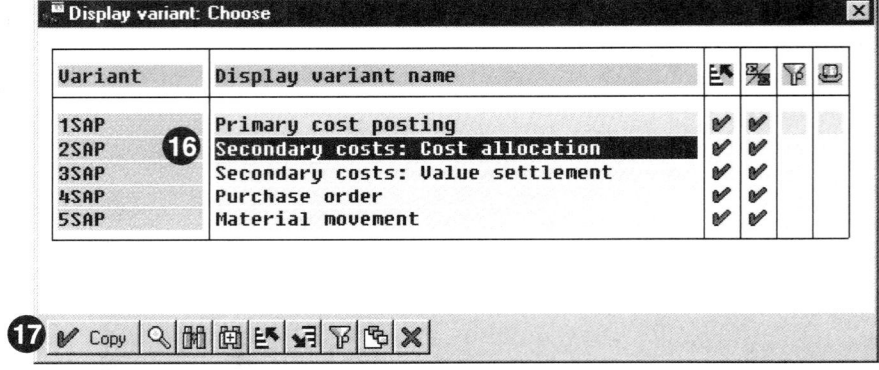

Section 5: Controlling—Internal Order Reports
Display Actual Line Items for Internal Orders

The variant displays the *Partner object* involved in the internal order transaction. If a column is blank, it was not relevant to the posting. The partner objects are, for the most part, activity postings from cost centers, order settlements, and overhead allocations.

18. Scroll down the report and position the cursor on an activity allocation, which includes both a cost center and an activity type reference (for example, *4100/1410*).

19. Choose *Master record*.

20. You can select one of two types of master records (for example, *Display activity type*).

21. Choose *Enter*.

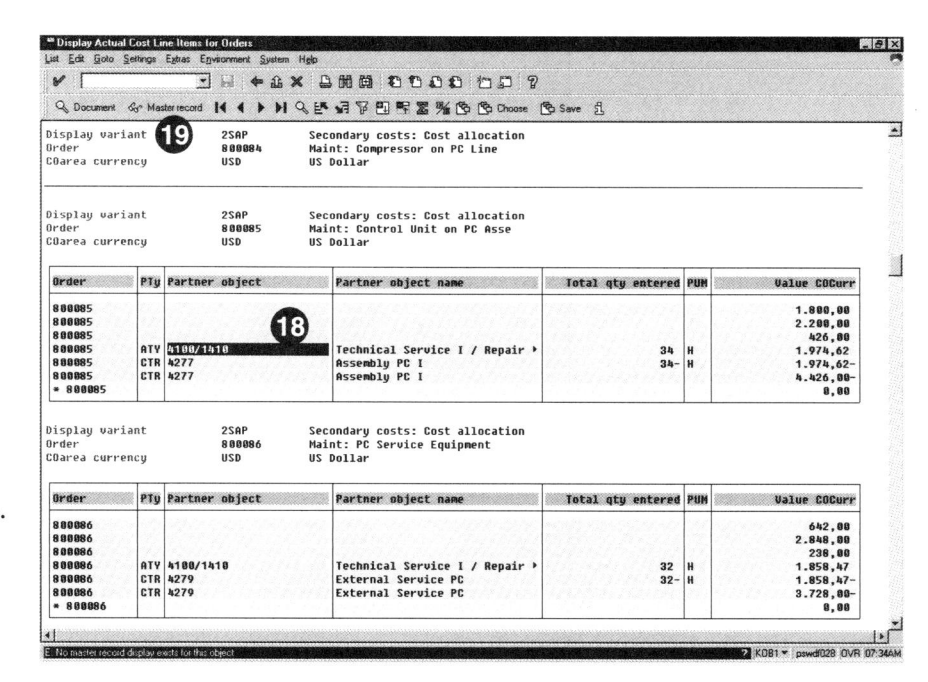

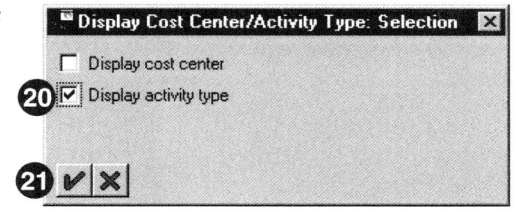

Commonly Used Reports: Illustrations and Perspectives

Section 5: Controlling—Internal Order Reports

Display Actual Line Items for Internal Orders

The master record of the activity type appears. This function is context-sensitive; for example, if the cursor was positioned on a profitability segment number on the selection screen, the characteristic values of the segment would have appeared.

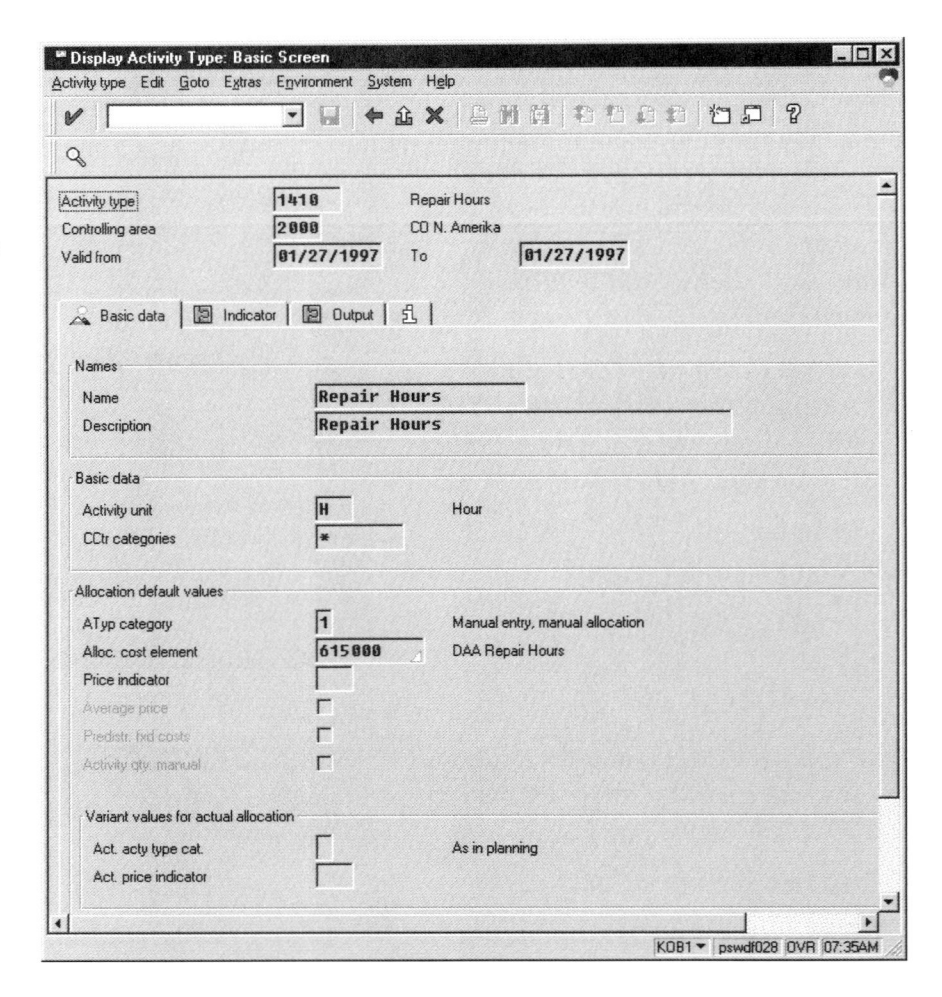

Section 5: Controlling—Internal Order Reports
Display Actual Line Items for Internal Orders

Example 2: A development manager needs to verify that all development orders were settled to profitability analysis as they closed.

1. Enter **X0101** in *Order group*. You can also enter a single order or a range of internal orders.

2. Enter **OAS-ORDER** in *Cost element group*. This contains all cost elements for internal order settlement.

3. Enter a date range to limit the number of postings to the selected internal orders (for example, **01/01/1997** to **12/31/1997**). This report may also be run for dates that span fiscal years.

4. Enter **3SAP** in *Display variant*. This provides settlement partner detail.

5. Choose *Extras → Select value type*.

6. Make certain that *Statistical actual value* is deselected, since you only want to list actual settlement postings.

7. Choose *Copy*.

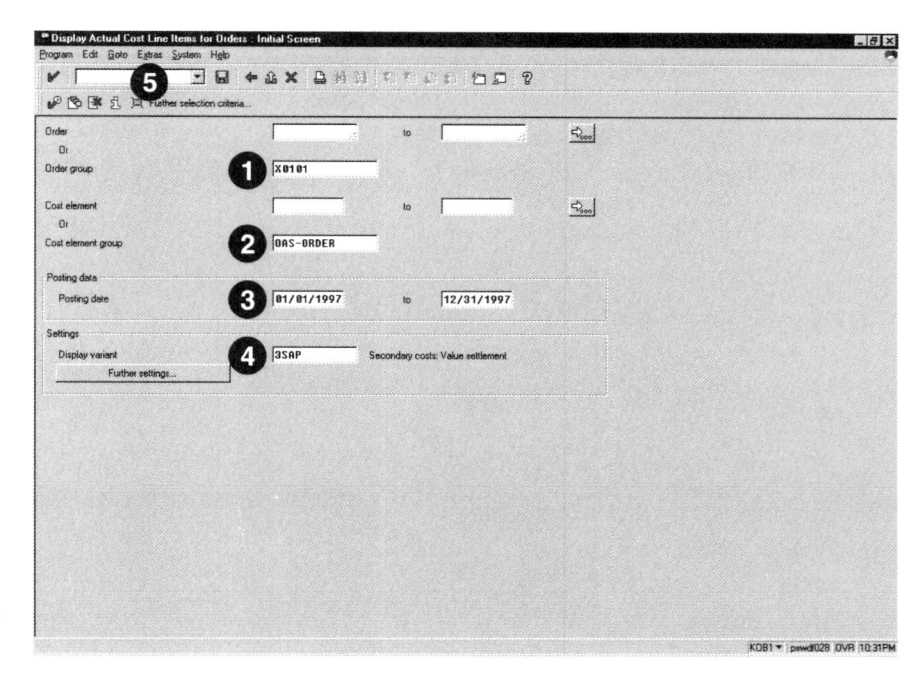

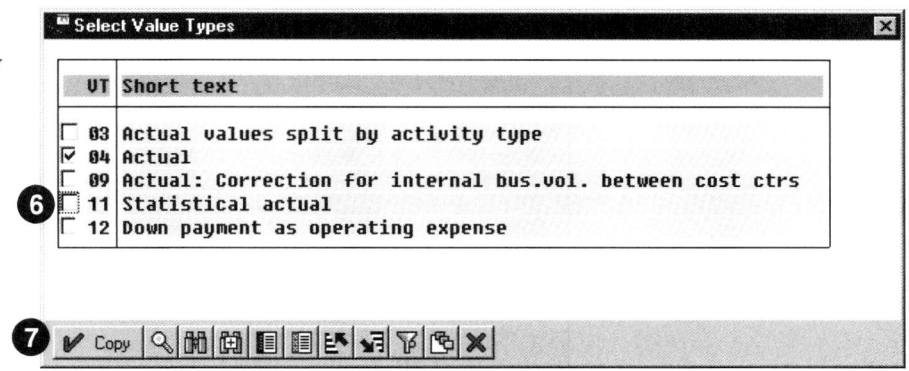

Commonly Used Reports: Illustrations and Perspectives

Section 5: Controlling—Internal Order Reports
Display Actual Line Items for Internal Orders

8. Choose *Execute*.

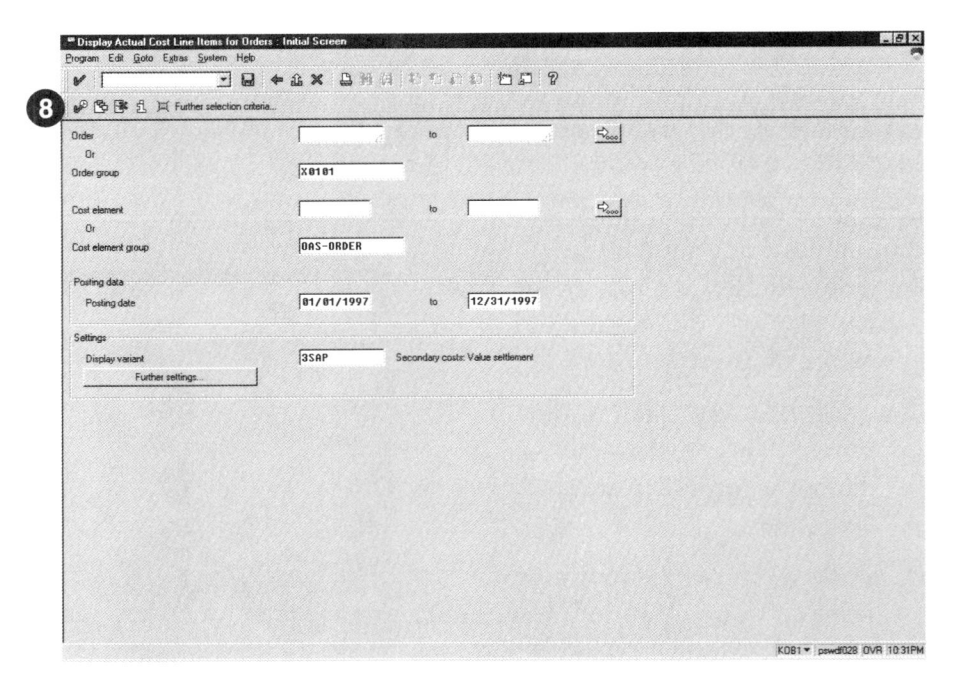

The display variant (for example, *3SAP*) shows the order, cost element, and type of object to which settlement occurred. *PSG* means that the settlement receiver is a profitability segment.

9. Choose *Current display variant*.

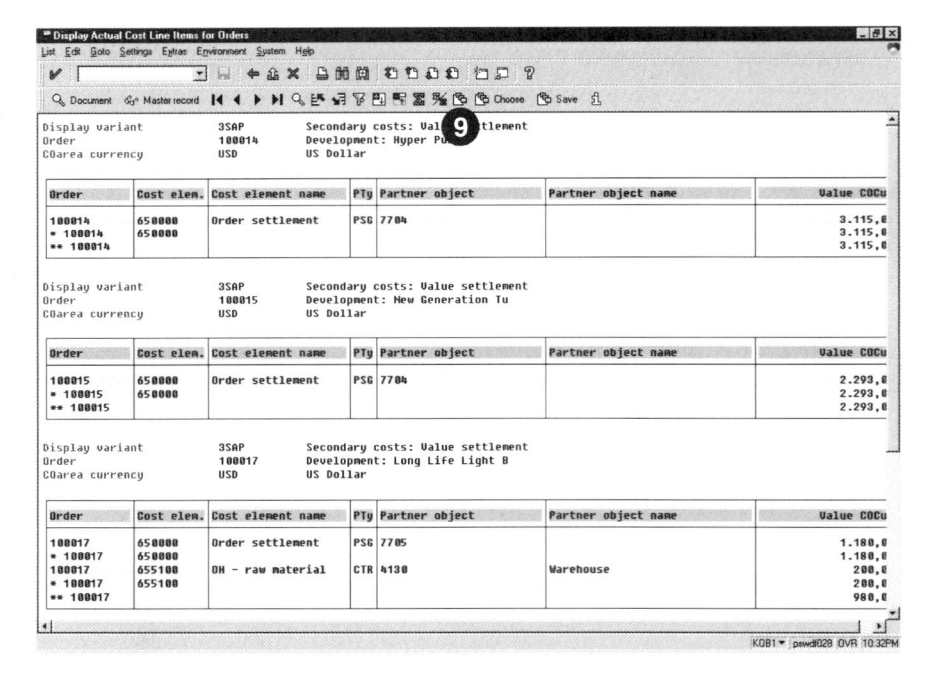

Section 5: Controlling—Internal Order Reports
Display Actual Line Items for Internal Orders

10. To delete a field from the display variant in the previous screen, you must first select it on the *Column content* area of this screen (for example, *CO partner object name*).

11. Choose *Hide selected fields* to remove the field from the display variant and this list.

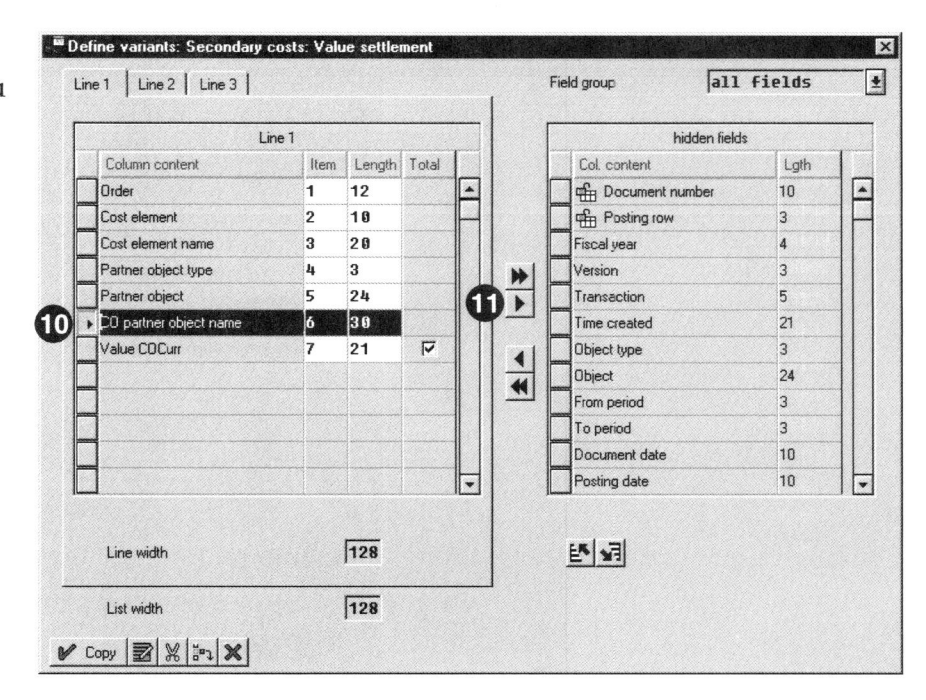

12. To add a field to the display variant, you must first select it on the *hidden fields* area of this screen (for example, *Posting date*).

13. Select *Value COCurr*. This is a reference point. *Posting date* will insert before this row.

    If no reference point is selected, the field will insert at the end of this list.

14. Choose *Show selected fields* to add the field to the display variant and this list.

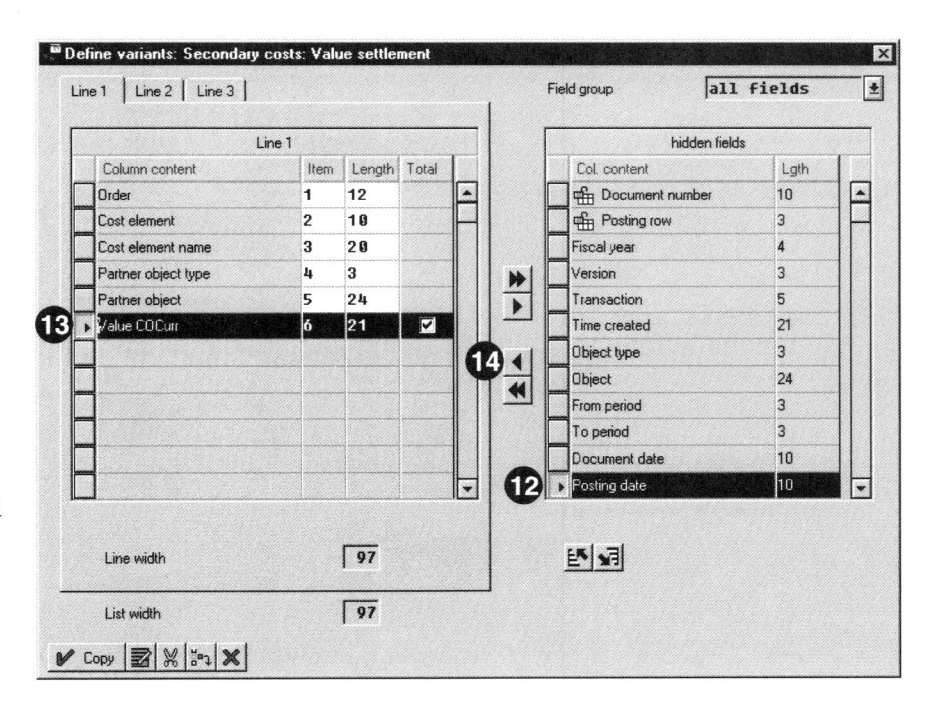

Commonly Used Reports: Illustrations and Perspectives

Section 5: Controlling—Internal Order Reports

Display Actual Line Items for Internal Orders

15. Choose *Copy* to accept the changes in the display variant.

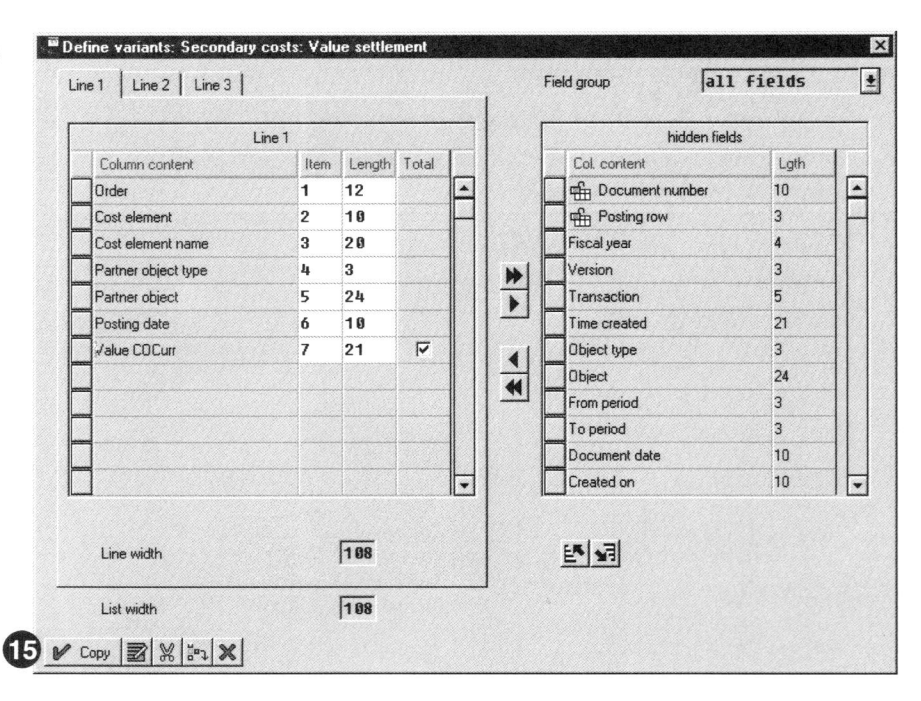

The screen now shows the *Posting date* field, and deletes the *CO partner object name* field.

16. Choose *Save display variant*.

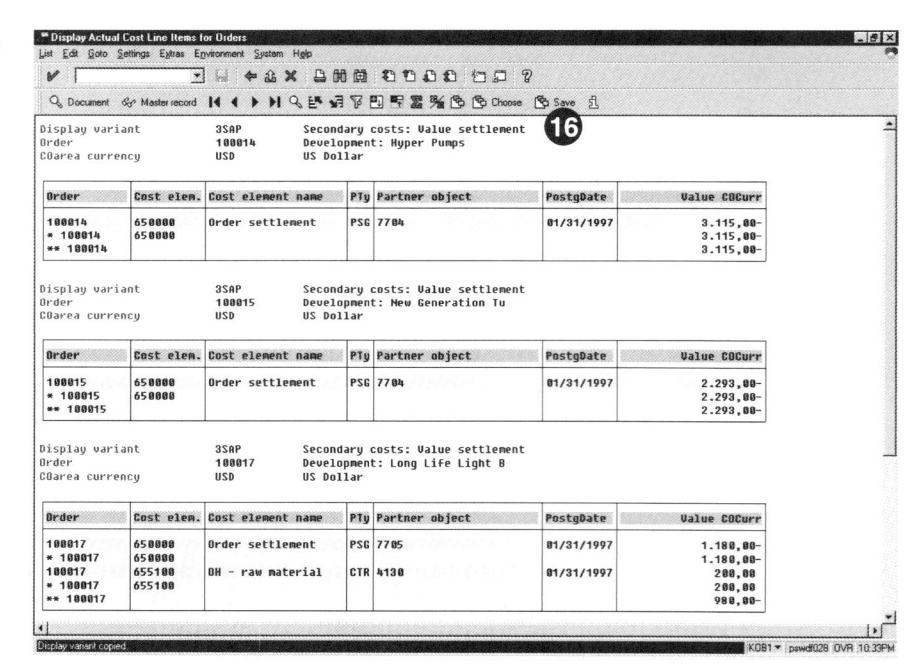

Section 5: Controlling—Internal Order Reports
Display Actual Line Items for Internal Orders

You can save a modified display variant from this screen.

17. Enter a new display variant code and description (for example, **Z3SAP** and **Secondary costs: Value settlement (PA)**).

18. Select *User-specific* to save the original display variant with the updated field for your user ID.

19. The additional parameters specify whether the active sorting and subtotaling settings should also be saved as part of the display variant.

20. Choose *Save*.

21. Position the cursor on the actual line item containing the profitability segment number (for example, *650000*).

22. Choose *Display document*.

The original document that created the cost center posting appears. For this example it is a settlement document that settled the costs from the order to a profitability analysis segment.

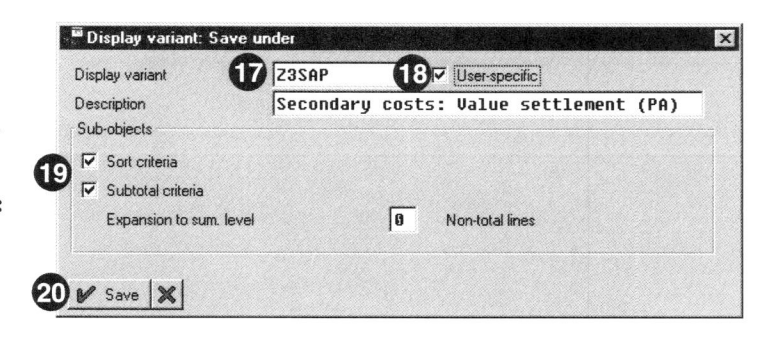

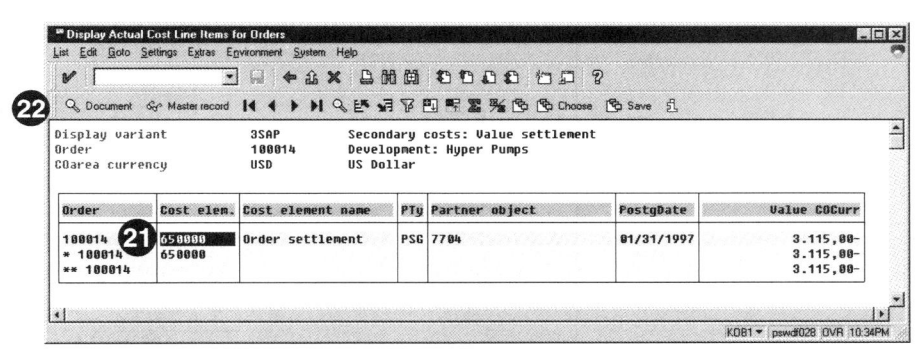

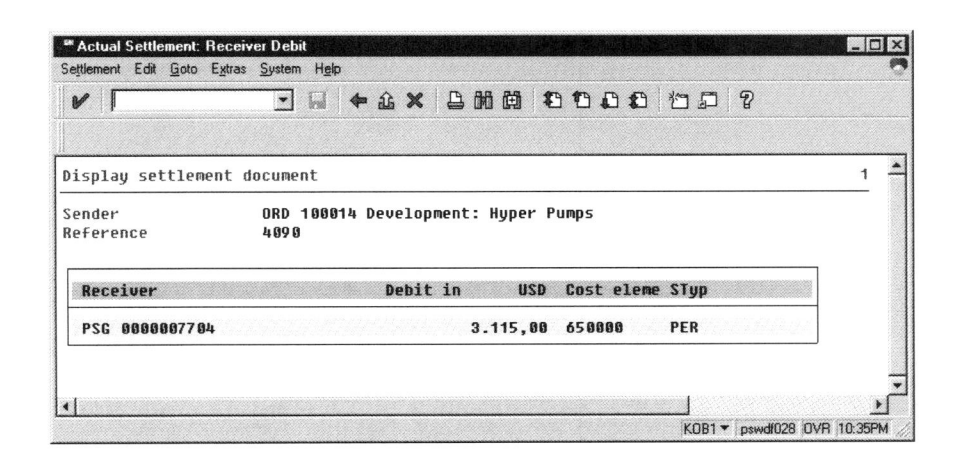

Section 5: Controlling—Internal Order Reports
Display Actual Line Items for Internal Orders

Example 3: For reconciliation purposes, the internal orders must be scanned for all postings that were offset to a particular bank account.

1. Enter internal order **ALL-2000** in *Order group*. You can also enter a range of orders or an individual internal order.
2. Enter **OAS-TOTAL** in *Cost element group*. This contains all cost elements.
3. Enter a date range to limit the number of postings to the selected internal orders (for example, **01/01/1997** to **12/31/1997**). This report may also be run for dates that span fiscal years.
4. Enter **1SAP** in *Display variant*. This creates purchase order numbers in the display variant.
5. Choose *Further selection criteria*.
6. Select *Offsetting account type*. This allows for selection based on this data.
7. Choose *Copy*.

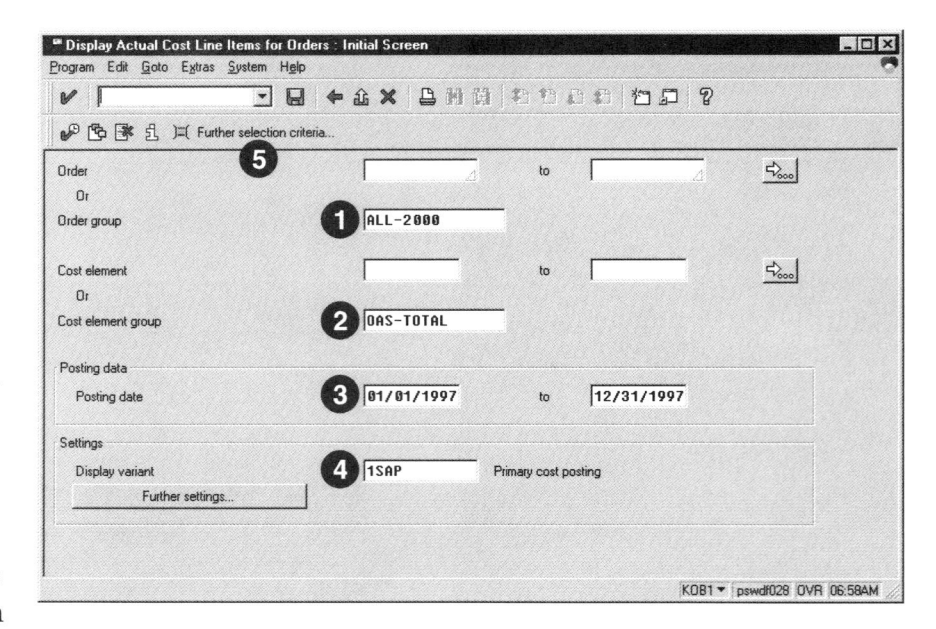

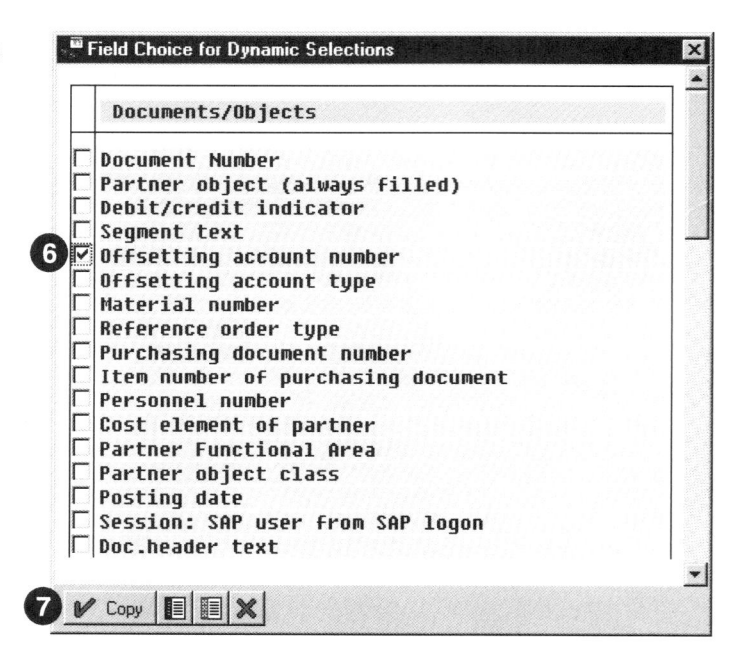

5–30   Reporting Made Easy

Section 5: Controlling—Internal Order Reports
Display Actual Line Items for Internal Orders

8. You can enter a G/L account range on this screen. Since only one account is desired, enter the account into the first field in the range (for example, 113200).

9. Choose *Save*.

10. Choose *Execute*.

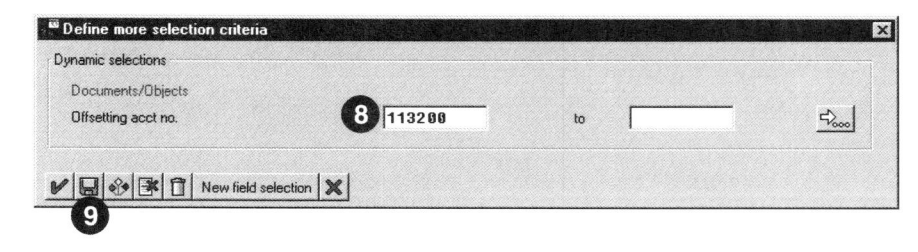

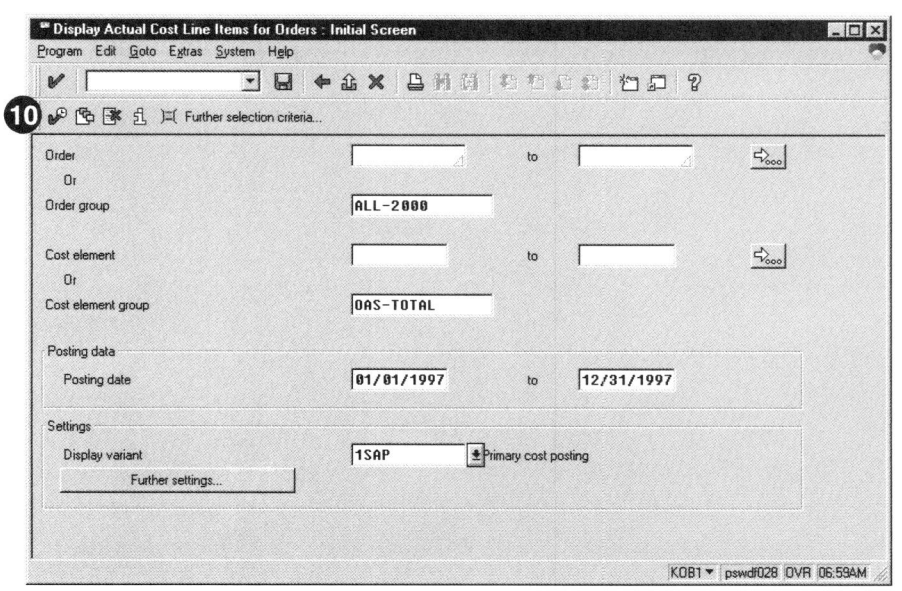

Only the actual line items that contain the requested offsetting G/L account number appear.

11. Choose *Next columns*.

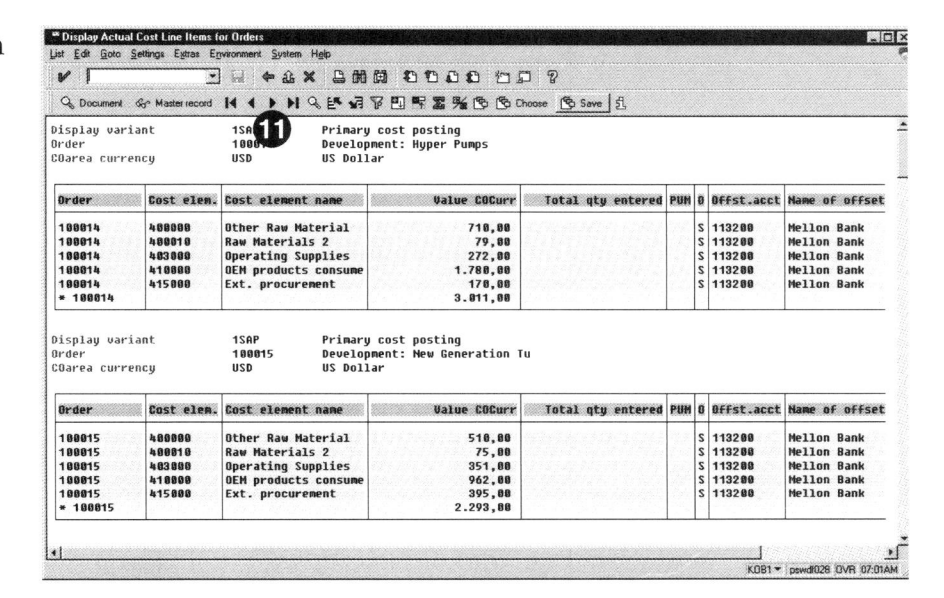

Commonly Used Reports: Illustrations and Perspectives

5–31

Section 5: Controlling—Internal Order Reports

Display Actual Line Items for Internal Orders

This screen shows the sum of all line items for the offsetting account.

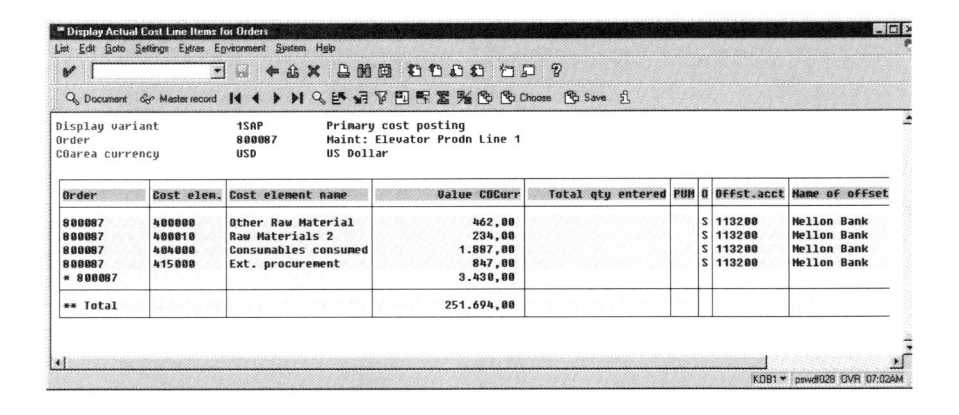

Internal Order List: Balance Displays

Quick Access   To run this report, use one of the following access options:

Option 1: Menu Path

Information systems → *Accounting* → *Overhead costs*

Orders → *Report selection*

From the reporting tree, select the following report:

Plan/Actual Comparison → *List: Orders* → *List: Orders.*

Option 2: Program Name

Choose *System* → *Services* → *Reporting* and enter `J6L00TQX` in the *Program* field. Then, choose *Execute* to run the report.

Purpose   This report provides a summarized view of the costs and quantities that have been posted to internal orders. The report includes both planned and actual postings, and calculates an absolute variance (difference), as well as a percentage of the variance.

This report provides an overview of internal orders and their postings so that you can quickly compare individual orders without needing to run separate reports or scroll through variation listings. This report is also an aid to reconciliation to the General Ledger (G/L), if it is run for particular primary cost elements.

Prerequisites   You must set the *Controlling Area* before running the report. Choose *Accounting* → *Controlling* → *Cost centers* → *Environment* → *Set controlling area*. For the examples in this section, the controlling area is set to *2000*.

You must enter a value in the selection fields before running the report. You may leave the cost center and cost element selection blank, and get a list that contains values for all cost centers and all cost elements in the selected controlling area. If you enter cost center groups and cost element groups, they must have already been set up. If they contain subtotals, hierarchy nodes should be created within the groups. Each hierarchy node then subtotals in this report.

Section 5: Controlling—Internal Order Reports
Internal Order List: Balance Displays

Integration

You can run multiple context-sensitive reports from this internal order report. For example, when you position the cursor on a cell for planned costs, only the reports that contain planned costs list data. If you select a cell for planned costs and run a report that only contains actual data, no data lists.

The following reports run for a single cell or a range of cells:
- Actual line items for one or more orders
- Planned line items for one or more orders
- Planning overview for a single order
- Actual values, by period (should be used for the cumulative views)
- Planned values, by period (should be used for the cumulative views)
- Internal order line items, by partner CO object (that is, partner cost center in a transaction, order, etc.)
- List of orders and balances
- Master data list of orders

Features

The selection screen of this report includes:
- Variants
- Dynamic selection options
- Executing and printing in background
- Sorting capability (by column): select a column, then *Edit → Sort in ascndng ordr* (*Ctrl+Shift+F5*), or *Edit → Sort in descending order* (Ctrl+Shift+F6)
- Adjusting the column width: *Settings → Column widths* (Ctrl+F12)
- Adjusting the numeric display, to set the number of decimals displayed and the scaling to hundredths, thousandths, etc.: *Settings → Number format* (F5)
- Mailing of the report (Ctrl+F9)
- Graphing portions of the report using SAP business graphics (F7)
- Exporting the report to a local file
- Increasing or reducing the detail displayed, by double-clicking on subtotal lines. The double-click acts as a toggle switch. If detail is displayed, double-clicking on the subtotal will hide it. If detail is not displayed on a summary line (marked with one or more asterisks), double-clicking will display it.
- Displaying only threshold values, or values that greater than or less than an entered criteria: *Edit → Threshold value* (Shift+F5).
- Creating an extract of reporting information (F5)
- Using variation to obtain multiple reports of internal order groups and hierarchy nodes (F6)
- Selection from an extract or an archive: *Data source* (Ctrl+F1)

Section 5: Controlling—Internal Order Reports
Internal Order List: Balance Displays

Next Steps

The system displays four columns for all sections of the report, including actual postings, planned data, and a calculation of the variance between the two, both as an absolute and as a percentage value (calculated by dividing the actual data by the planned).

By double-clicking on any subtotals in the report, the detail that makes up each subtotal can either be hidden or displayed. For example, double-clicking on the *Costs* line will hide the cost element detail. To display this detail again, double-click on this line.

This report contains data obtained from internal order postings. As such, the data cannot be changed or manipulated from the report.

This report contains five different blocks of data, as shown below. By navigating around these blocks, you can display different types of internal order data:

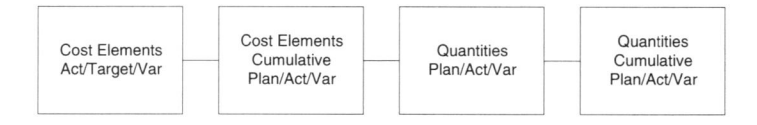

```
┌──────────────┐  ┌──────────────┐  ┌──────────────┐  ┌──────────────┐
│ Cost Elements│  │ Cost Elements│  │  Quantities  │  │  Quantities  │
│ Act/Target/Var│ │  Cumulative  │  │  Plan/Act/Var│  │  Cumulative  │
│              │  │ Plan/Act/Var │  │              │  │ Plan/Act/Var │
└──────────────┘  └──────────────┘  └──────────────┘  └──────────────┘
```

Section 5: Controlling—Internal Order Reports
Internal Order List: Balance Displays

Guided Tour

Example: List an overview of all internal orders so that costs of the orders can be quickly compared and summarized to ensure all period-end processing finished. If balances list, orders have not been settled and remain open.

To access the first screen for this report, choose

Information systems → Accounting → Overhead costs

Orders → Report selection.

From the reporting tree, select the following report:

Plan/Actual Comparison → List: Orders → List: Orders.

1. Under *Selection values*, enter **2000** in *Controlling area*.

2. Enter the year in *Fiscal year* (for example, **1997**). This report runs for only one fiscal year at a time.

3. Enter **1** in *From period* and **12** in *To period*. This report will not provide a periodic breakdown of the costs, only totals for this period range will be included.

4. Enter **0** in *Plan version*.

5. Enter **OAS-TOTAL** in *Cost element group*. This group contains all cost elements.

6. Enter internal order group **ALL-2000** in *Order group*. You can also enter a range of orders, or an individual order.

7. Choose *Execute*.

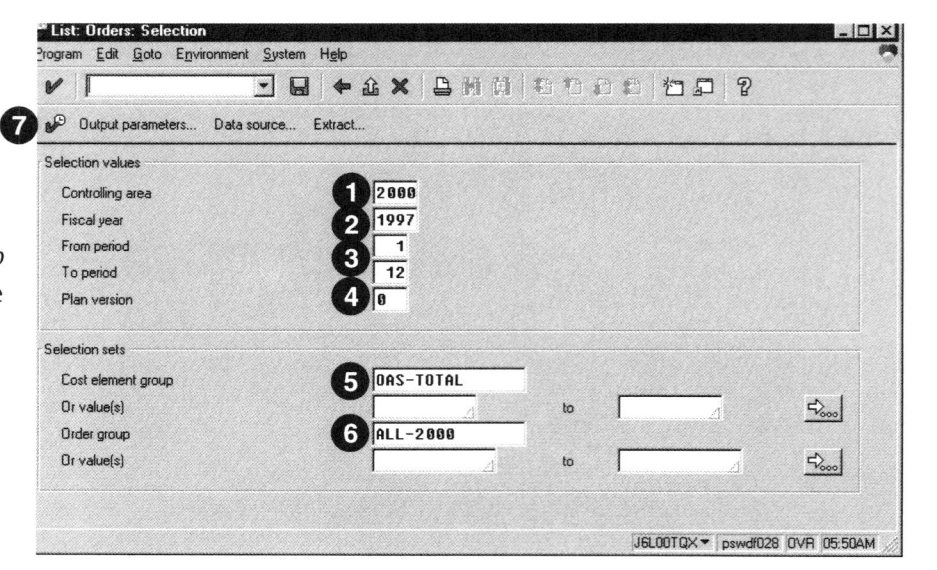

5–36 Reporting Made Easy

Section 5: Controlling—Internal Order Reports
Internal Order List: Balance Displays

This screen shows:
- Internal orders (summarized by group type)
- Subtotals
- Balance of all cost elements (selected from the cost element group lists)
- Actual and planned costs
- Absolute variance
- Percentage variance

8. Choose *Next columns*.

This screen shows:
- Internal orders (summarized by group type)
- Subtotals
- Balance of all cost elements (selected from the cost element group lists)
- Cumulative actual and planned costs
- Absolute variance
- Percentage variance

9. Choose *Next columns*.

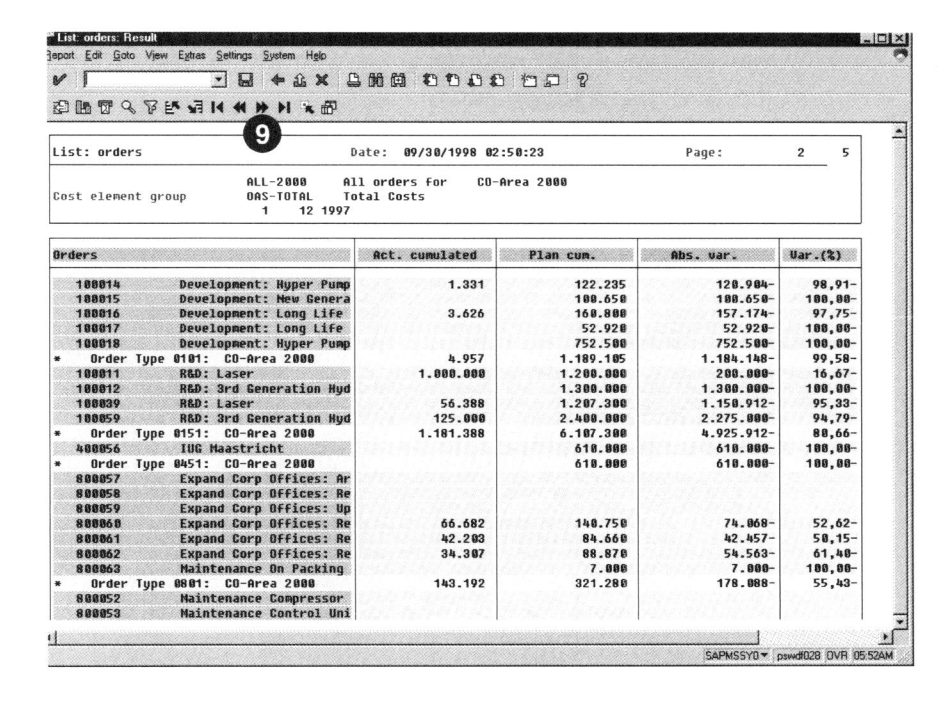

Section 5: Controlling—Internal Order Reports
Internal Order List: Balance Displays

This screen shows:
- Internal orders (summarized by group type)
- Subtotals
- Balance of all cost elements (selected from the cost element group lists)
- Actual and planned quantities (if original document had a unit of measure)
- Absolute variance
- Percentage variance

10. Choose *Next columns*.

This screen shows:
- Internal orders (summarized by group type)
- Subtotals
- Balance of all cost elements (selected from the cost element group lists)
- Cumulative actual and planned quantities (if original document had a unit of measure)
- Absolute variance
- Percentage variance

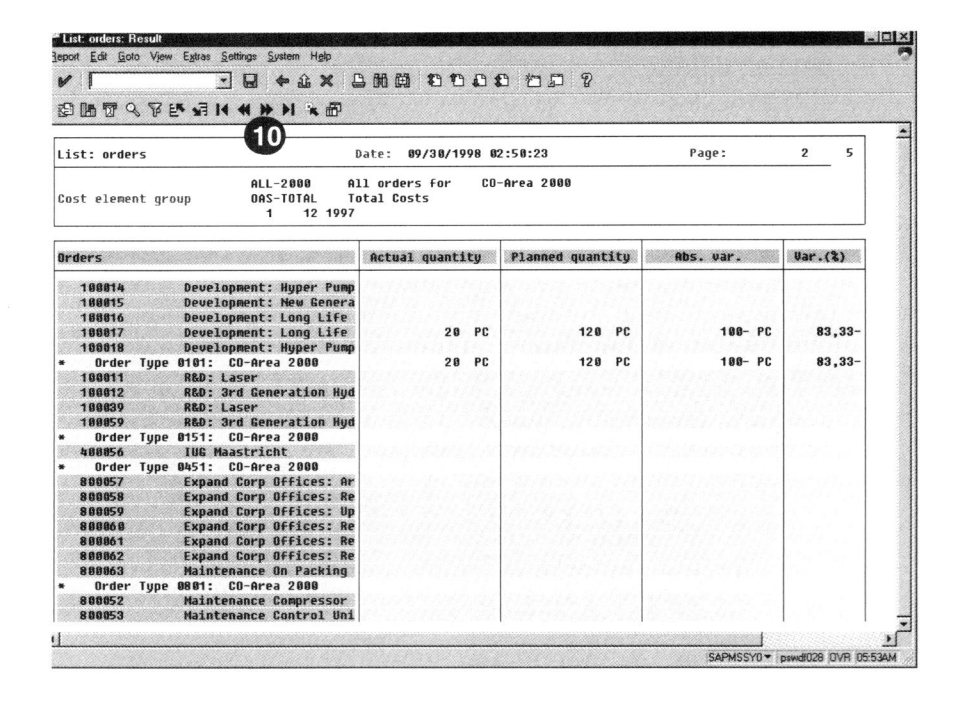

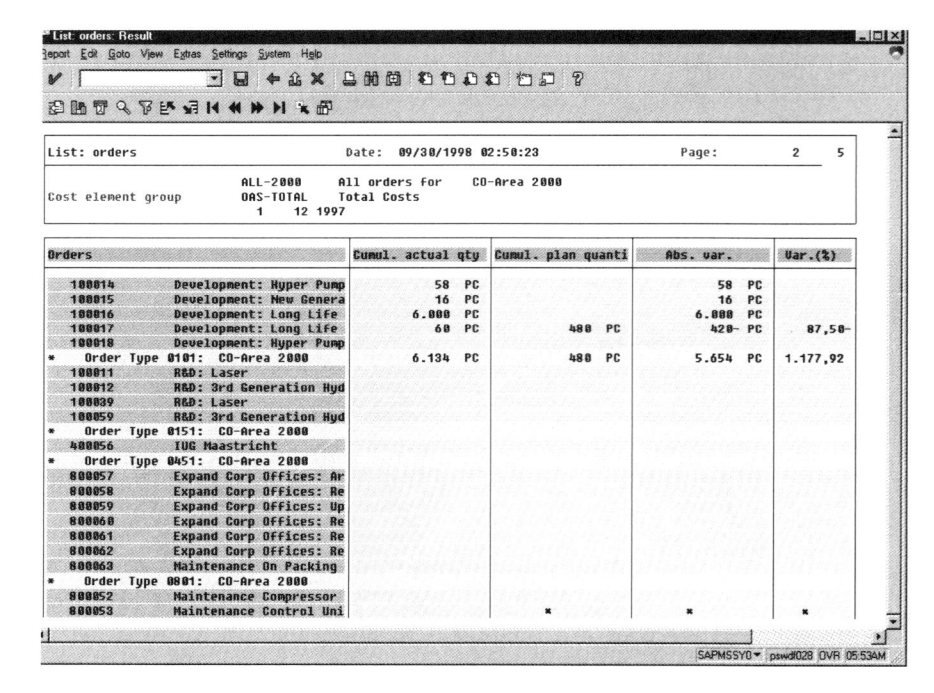

Section 6: Controlling—Profitability Analysis Reports

Contents

Profitability Analysis: Plan/Actual Comparison 6–2
Profitability Analysis: SBU/Product/Customer Analysis 6–14
Profitability Analysis: Sales Plan/Contribution Margin 6–27

Profitability Analysis: Plan/Actual Comparison

Quick Access To run this report, use the following:

Menu Path

Information systems → Accounting → Profitability analysis

Profitability report → Report selection

From the reporting tree, choose the following report:

Plan-/Ist Vergleich → Plan/Actual Comparison.

Purpose This report provides a contribution margin for divisions and products. Both actual and planned data list for the contribution margin, and a variance calculates for each value in it. This report summarizes revenues and contributions, and can do an in depth analysis of the margin for specific divisions or products.

A product line manager would use this report to monitor the performance of specific divisions and products and to identify the "bottom-line" impact of revenues and costs. Two features of this report, exception reporting and ranking, help to quickly identify both exceptional and marginal performers so that a product line manager can take immediate action to improve product performance.

Prerequisites You must set the *Operating concern* (but only when you first login). Choose *Accounting → Controlling → Profitability analysis → Environment → Set operating concern*. For the examples in this section, the operating concern is set to *IDEA* using cost-based profitability analysis.

All reports in profitability analysis are user-defined. This means you must configure and generate the operating concern before creating any reports and determine the rows, columns, variables, and general format by using drilldown reporting (forms and reports).

Due to the configuration of this report, you must enter all selection options (that is, period range and fiscal year).

Section 6: Controlling—Profitability Analysis Reports
Profitability Analysis: Plan/Actual Comparison

Integration

The profitability analysis line items which list are context sensitive. For example, when you position the cursor on a cell for a line item, only the reports that contain that line item show data. This improves performance of the report as a whole.

Once the original profitability analysis document appears, the original documents related to the line item may be retrieved. For example, from a sales document, a material master, customer master, billing document, and accounting document is available. From a direct financial entry, however, only the cost element and accounting documents are available. From settlement documents, the controlling object from which the settlement took place is generally available.

The integration data available from CO-PA includes:

- Material master
- Customer master
- Billing document (SD)
- Accounting documents (FI)
- All linked accounting documents (special ledger, consolidation, cost accounting, etc.)
- Sales order
- Cost element
- Cost center
- Internal order
- Project
- Selected costing reports, usually in product costing

Section 6: Controlling—Profitability Analysis Reports
Profitability Analysis: Plan/Actual Comparison

Features

The selection screen of this report includes:
- Variants
- Printing in background, after execution
- Ranking based on selected columns: *Edit → Ranking list → Top n/Top%/Last n/Last%*
- Creating a condition under which values are displayed, that is, higher or lower than a particular value: *Edit → Condition → Create/Change*
- Creating exceptions under which values are highlighted in different colors, i.e. higher or lower than a particular value: *Extras → Create exceptions/Change exceptions*
- Adjusting the numeric display, to set the number of decimals displayed and the scaling to hundredths, thousandths, etc.: *Settings → Number format* (Ctrl+F11)
- Hiding and displaying columns: *Edit → Columns → On/Off*
- Currency translation of the report: *Settings → Currency* (Ctrl+Shift+F4)
- Sorting capability (by column): select a column, then *Edit → Sort ascending* (Ctrl+F2), or *Edit → Sort descending* (Ctrl+F3)
- Determining how the characteristics are displayed, that is, using values, descriptions, or a combination: *Settings → Characteristic display*
- Determining whether and how a totals row is displayed: *Settings → Totals row*
- Exporting the report to a local file (Ctrl+Shift+F12)
- Mailing of the report (Ctrl+F6)
- Graphing portions of the report using SAP business graphics (Ctrl+Shift+F10)

Next Steps

Two different views are available in this report:
- Selected columns run across the report, while the characteristics (products, for example) run down the side
- All columns for a single selected product show as rows for a contribution analysis

You can analyze data using ranking lists, exception reporting, and sorting; list line items in the profitability analysis database; and access additional SAP data from this report.

This report contains data obtained from postings to cost-based CO-PA. As such, the data cannot be changed or manipulated from the report. Since cost-based—not account-based—CO-PA is used, value fields are used in the analysis instead of account numbers or cost elements.

Section 6: Controlling—Profitability Analysis Reports
Profitability Analysis: Plan/Actual Comparison

Guided Tour

Example: A product manager needs to analyze information from products with the highest revenue.

To access the first screen for this report, choose

Information systems → *Accounting* → *Profitability analysis*

Profitability report → *Report selection.*

From the reporting tree, choose the following report:

Plan-/Ist Vergleich → *Plan/Actual Comparison.*

1. Enter **1** in *From period* and **12** in *To period*. This report will not provide a periodic breakdown of the costs, only totals for the period range.
2. Enter **1998** in *From Fiscal Year*. This report runs for only one fiscal year at a time.
3. Choose *Execute*.

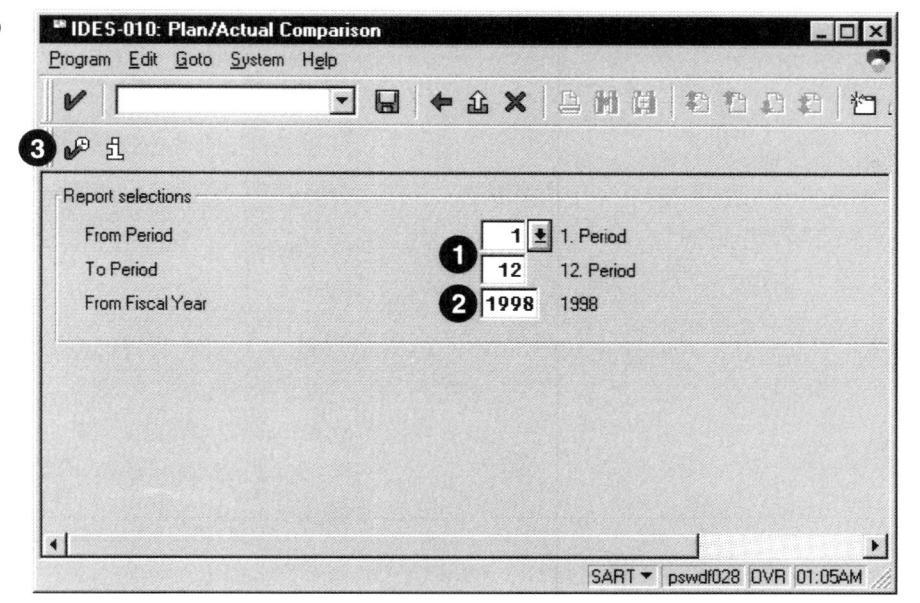

Commonly Used Reports: Illustrations and Perspectives

Section 6: Controlling—Profitability Analysis Reports
Profitability Analysis: Plan/Actual Comparison

The default sales organization number (for example, *1000*) cannot be changed.

Divisions show in rows. In this example, all postings were assigned to a division. If postings were not assigned to a division, *Not assigned* would appear in the last row.

Gross revenue and contribution margin data show in columns. For each of these values, planned and actual data appear, along with the absolute and percentage variances.

4. Double-click on the first division, *Pumps*.

This screen shows the products within the *Pumps* division. Notice the breakdown of the *Product* characteristic as compared to the previous screen.

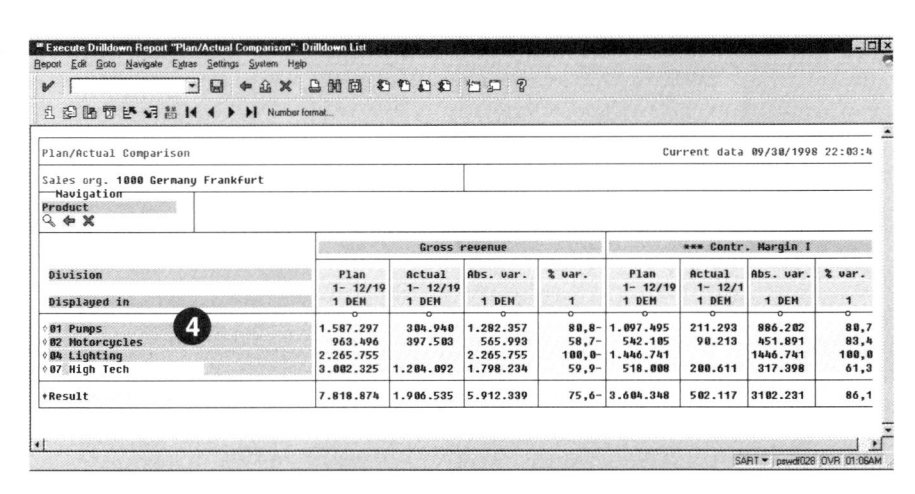

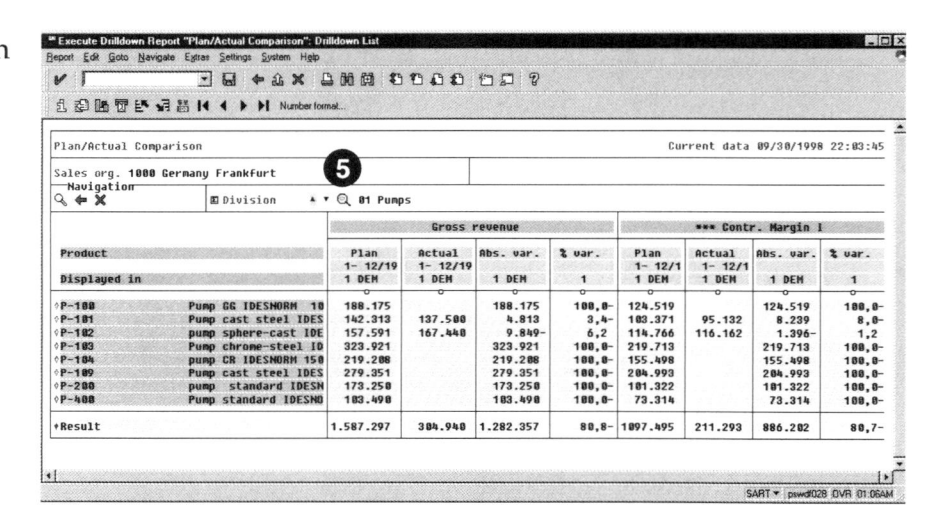

5. Choose *Display* to navigate to *Division* characteristic.

This screen shows all *Divisions*.

6. Select the *High Tech* line.

7. Choose *Enter*.

6–6 Reporting Made Easy

Section 6: Controlling—Profitability Analysis Reports

Profitability Analysis: Plan/Actual Comparison

The selection changes to *High Tech* division.

This screen shows 11 products within the *High Tech* division.

8. Choose *Division Summarization* ⊞ Division.

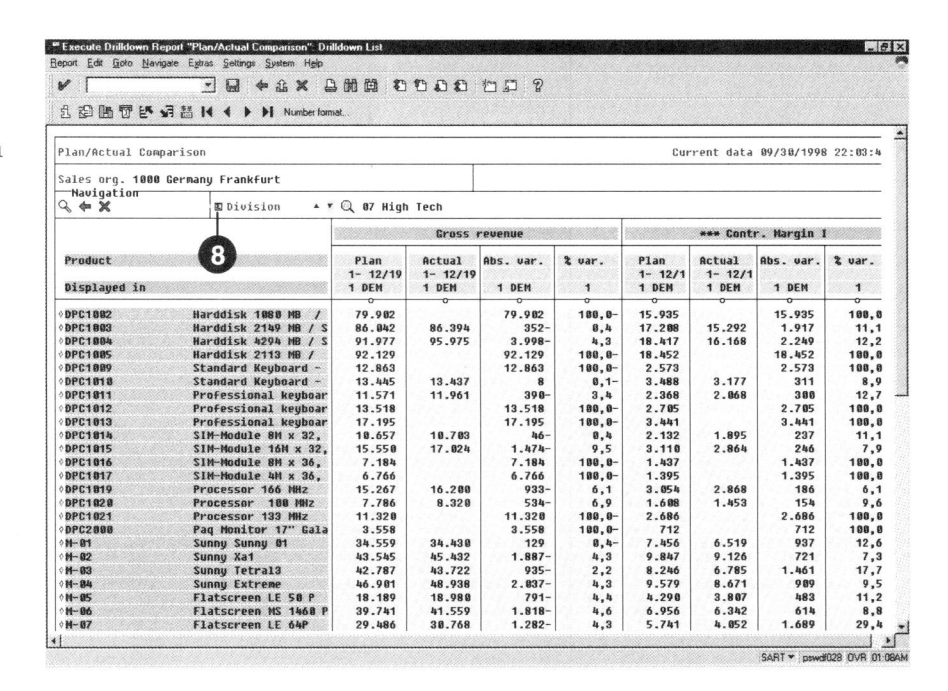

This screen shows all products, regardless of *Division*.

9. Click on *Actual* under *Gross revenue* to select the column.

10. Choose *Edit* → *Ranking list* → *Top 10%*.

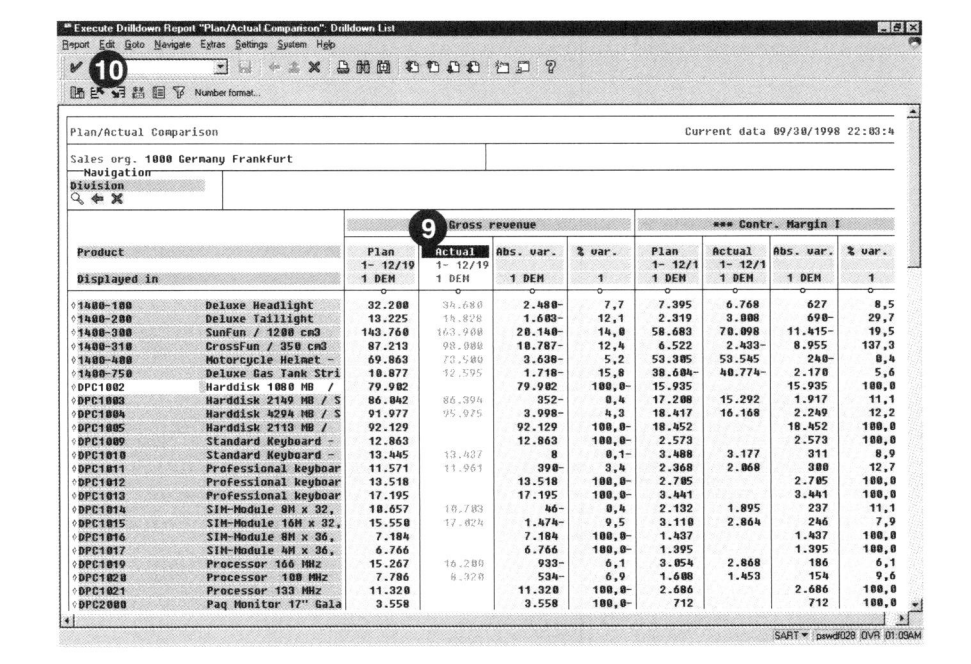

11. Change the percentage from the default of 80,00 to 10,00 (eighty down to ten).

12. Choose *Enter*.

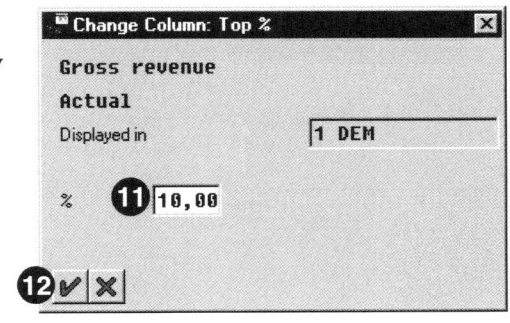

Commonly Used Reports: Illustrations and Perspectives

6–7

Section 6: Controlling—Profitability Analysis Reports

Profitability Analysis: Plan/Actual Comparison

Only the products that comprise the top 10% of actual gross revenue appear.

All other products summarize in the *remaining* row(s). In this example, since one product was less than 10%, and the two products exceeded 10%, the *remaining* row indicates that all other products comprise 76% of the actual gross revenue.

13. Click the diamond next to the first listed product, *P-102*.

    The diamond and navigation bars change color to indicate hot-spot activation.

14. Choose *Display*.

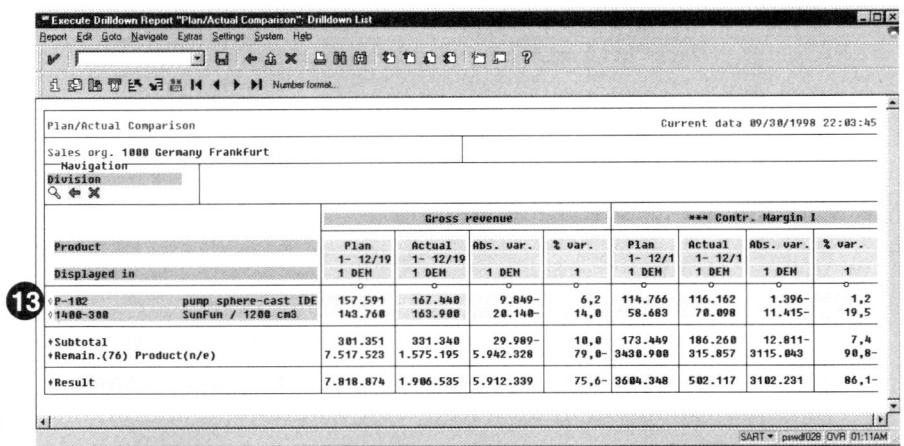

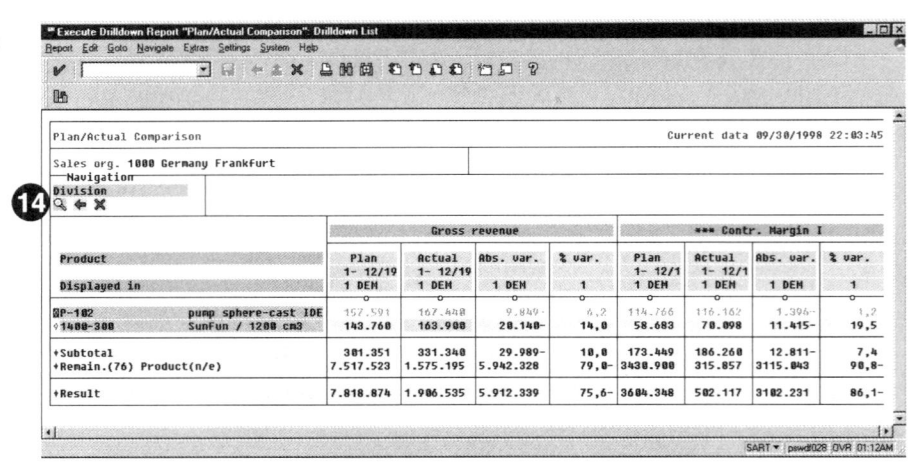

Section 6: Controlling—Profitability Analysis Reports

Profitability Analysis: Plan/Actual Comparison

The superimposed columns, *Gross Revenue* and *Contribution Margin*, appear as rows for the selected product.

Additional rows appear on this screen that were hidden in the alternative screen to provide a more complete picture of the contribution margin.

15. Choose *Page Down* to navigate to the remaining values in the contribution margin.

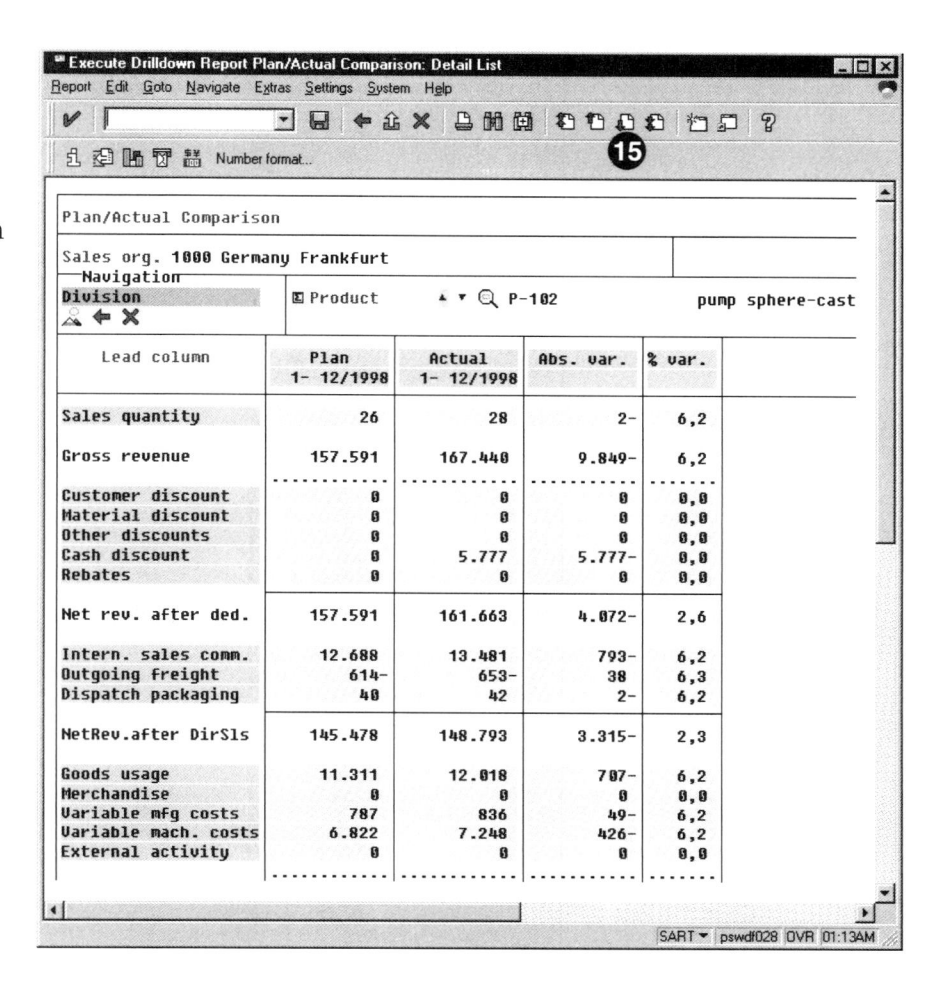

```
Plan/Actual Comparison
Sales org. 1000 Germany Frankfurt
Navigation
Division              Product      ▲ ▼ Q P-102        pump sphere-cast
```

Lead column	Plan 1- 12/1998	Actual 1- 12/1998	Abs. var.	% var.
Sales quantity	26	28	2-	6,2
Gross revenue	157.591	167.440	9.849-	6,2
Customer discount	0	0	0	0,0
Material discount	0	0	0	0,0
Other discounts	0	0	0	0,0
Cash discount	0	5.777	5.777-	0,0
Rebates	0	0	0	0,0
Net rev. after ded.	157.591	161.663	4.072-	2,6
Intern. sales comm.	12.688	13.481	793-	6,2
Outgoing freight	614-	653-	38	6,3
Dispatch packaging	40	42	2-	6,2
NetRev.after DirSls	145.478	148.793	3.315-	2,3
Goods usage	11.311	12.018	707-	6,2
Merchandise	0	0	0	0,0
Variable mfg costs	787	836	49-	6,2
Variable mach. costs	6.822	7.248	426-	6,2
External activity	0	0	0	0,0

Commonly Used Reports: Illustrations and Perspectives

Section 6: Controlling—Profitability Analysis Reports
Profitability Analysis: Plan/Actual Comparison

This screen shows the remainder of the contribution margin data.

16. Choose *Scroll Down* ▼.

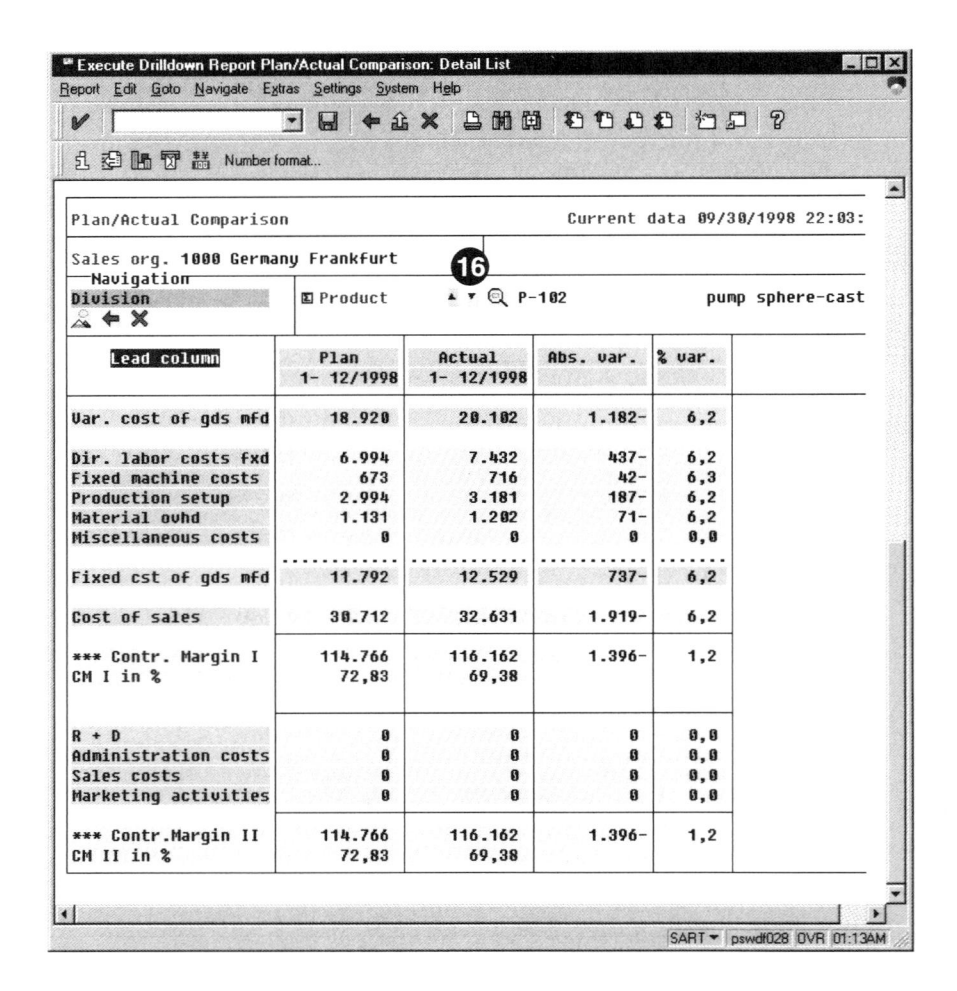

Lead column	Plan 1-12/1998	Actual 1-12/1998	Abs. var.	% var.
Var. cost of gds mfd	18.920	20.102	1.182-	6,2
Dir. labor costs fxd	6.994	7.432	437-	6,2
Fixed machine costs	673	716	42-	6,3
Production setup	2.994	3.181	187-	6,2
Material ovhd	1.131	1.202	71-	6,2
Miscellaneous costs	0	0	0	0,0
Fixed cst of gds mfd	11.792	12.529	737-	6,2
Cost of sales	30.712	32.631	1.919-	6,2
*** Contr. Margin I	114.766	116.162	1.396-	1,2
CM I in %	72,83	69,38		
R + D	0	0	0	0,0
Administration costs	0	0	0	0,0
Sales costs	0	0	0	0,0
Marketing activities	0	0	0	0,0
*** Contr.Margin II	114.766	116.162	1.396-	1,2
CM II in %	72,83	69,38		

Section 6: Controlling—Profitability Analysis Reports
Profitability Analysis: Plan/Actual Comparison

The contribution margin report appears for the next product.

17. Choose *Overview*.
18. Choose *Product*.

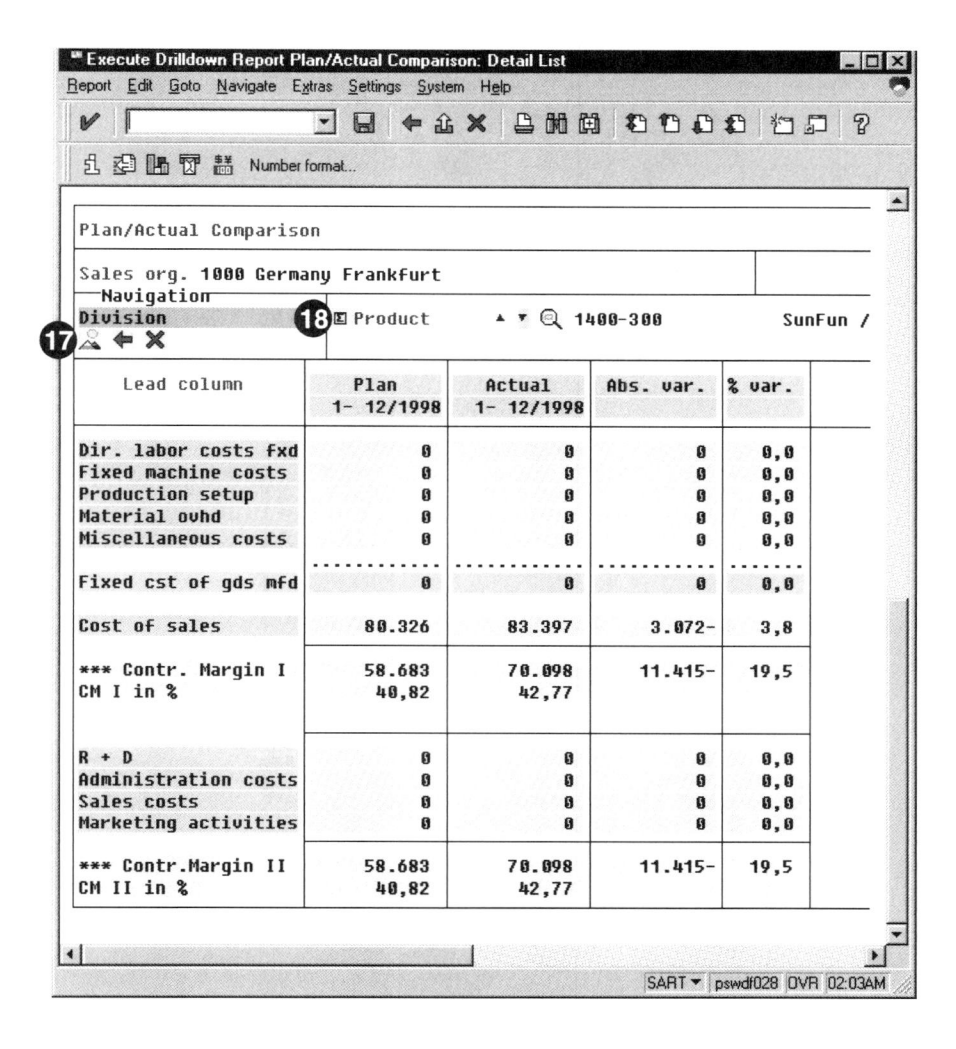

The previous report appears for the products.

19. Select the *167.440* line item in the *Actual* gross revenue column.
20. Choose *Goto → Line items*.

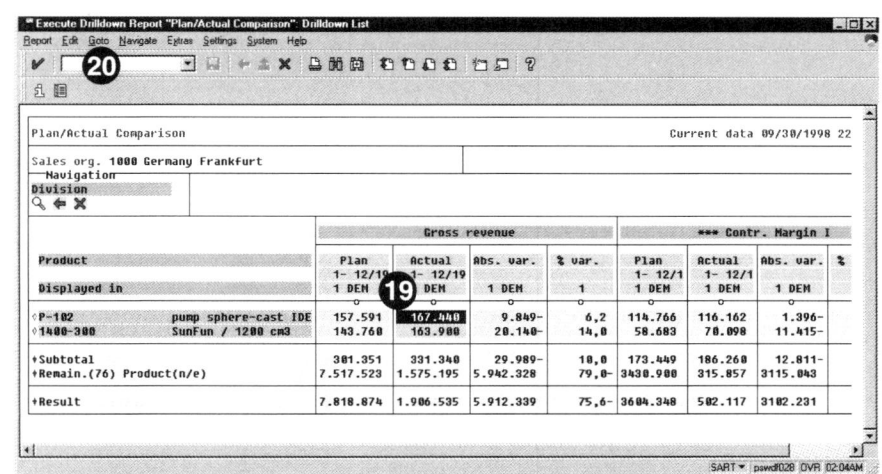

Commonly Used Reports: Illustrations and Perspectives

6–11

Section 6: Controlling—Profitability Analysis Reports
Profitability Analysis: Plan/Actual Comparison

This screen lists all CO-PA line items that comprise the selected cell.

21. Choose *FI/CO documents*.

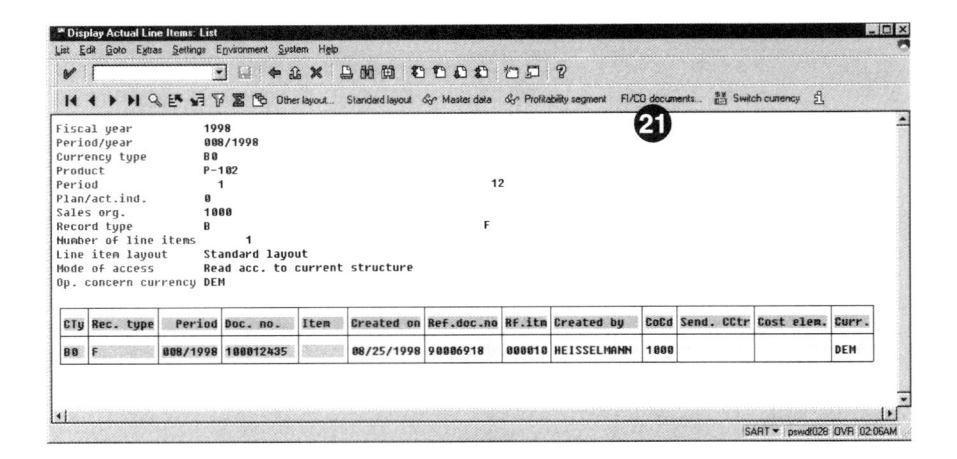

A list of all available financial and controlling documents linked to this entry can be shown by double-clicking on any line item.

22. Choose *Cancel*.

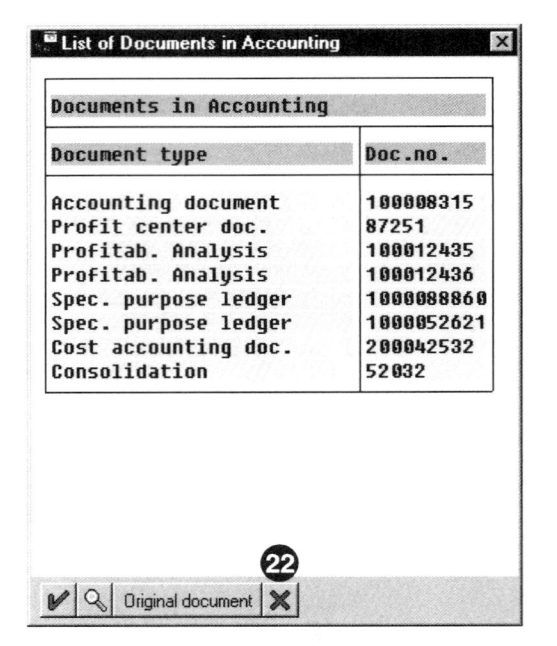

23. Position the cursor on the line item to select it.
24. Choose *Display*.

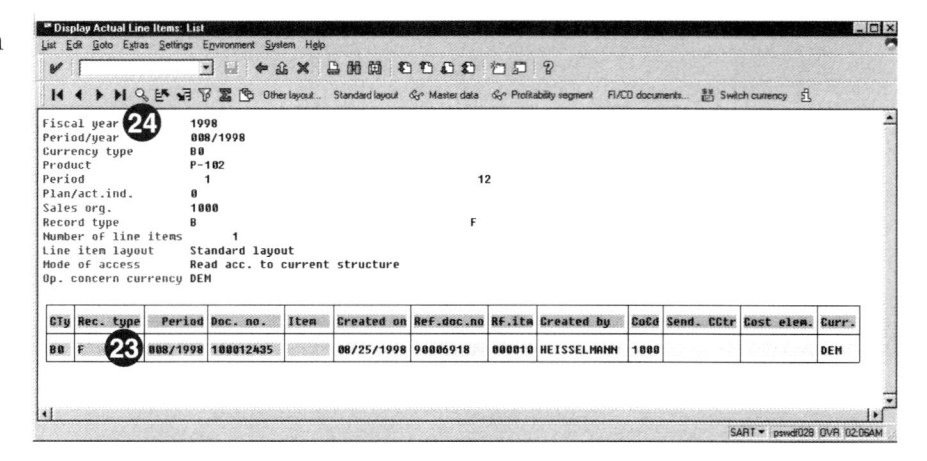

6–12 Reporting Made Easy

Section 6: Controlling—Profitability Analysis Reports

Profitability Analysis: Plan/Actual Comparison

This is the first screen of the profitability analysis document.

25. Choose *Environment → Integration*.

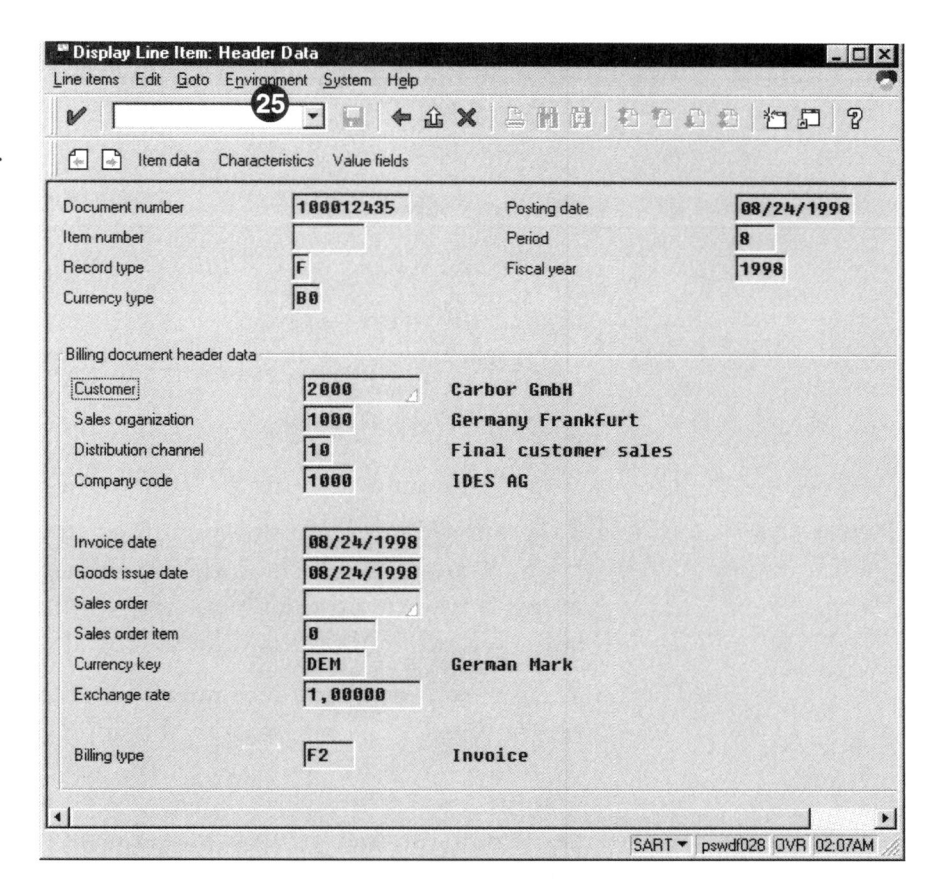

From this screen you can select/deselect all master data and transaction documents linked to the profitability analysis document.

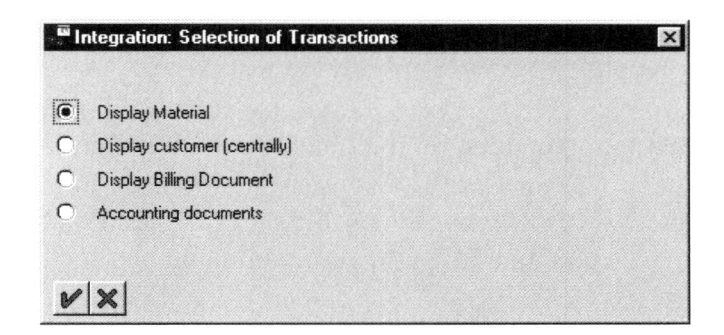

Commonly Used Reports: Illustrations and Perspectives

6–13

Profitability Analysis: SBU/Product/Customer Analysis

Quick Access To run this report, use the following:

Menu Path

Information systems → *Accounting* → *Profitability analysis*

Profitability report → *Report selection*

From the reporting tree, select the following report:

Istdaten → *SBU* → *Product* → *Cust. w/out Summ. Levels.*

Purpose This report compares sales quantities, gross revenues, and cost of sales for strategic business units, products, and customers. The characteristics available for product analysis include product hierarchies, industries, and divisions, which allow for a summarization of product lines for analysis.

A strategic business unit manager would use this report to monitor the performance of a portion of the business and to analyze which products and customers generate the most profits. Exception reporting and ranking allow quick identification of products that are exceptional performers, as well as poor performers, so that a unit manager can take steps to improve a product's performance. These features also allow an analysis of the largest customers and the products they purchase, which is useful in planning targeted marketing initiatives for those customers.

Prerequisites You must set the *Controlling Area* before running the report. Choose *Accounting* → *Controlling* → *Cost centers* → *Profitability analysis* → *Environment* → *Set operating concern.* For the examples in this section, the operating concern is set to *IDEA* using cost-based profitability analysis.

All reports in profitability analysis are user-defined. This means you must configure and generate the operating concern before creating any reports and determine the rows, columns, variables, and general format by using drilldown reporting (forms and reports).

Due to the configuration of this report, you must enter the date range and type of data. If planned data is run in this report, the version must also be specified. The record type is optional.

Integration

The profitability analysis line items which list are context sensitive. For example, when you position the cursor on a cell for a line item, only the reports that contain that line item show data. This improves performance of the report as a whole.

Once the original profitability analysis document appears, the original documents related to the line item can be retrieved. For example, from a sales document, a material master, customer master, billing document, and accounting document is available. From a direct financial entry, however, only the cost element and accounting documents are available. From settlement documents, the controlling object from which the settlement took place is generally available.

The integration data available from CO-PA includes:

- Material master
- Customer master
- Billing document (SD)
- Accounting documents (FI)
- All linked accounting documents (special ledger, consolidation, cost accounting, etc.)
- Sales order
- Cost element
- Cost center
- Internal order
- Project
- Selected costing reports, usually in product costing

Section 6: Controlling—Profitability Analysis Reports
Profitability Analysis: SBU/Product/Customer Analysis

Features

The selection screen of this report includes:
- Variants
- Printing in background, after execution
- Ranking based on selected columns: *Edit → Ranking list → Top n/Top%/Last n/Last%*
- Creating a condition under which values are displayed, that is, higher or lower than a particular value: *Edit → Condition → Create/Change*
- Creating exceptions under which values are highlighted in different colors, i.e. higher or lower than a particular value: *Extras → Create exceptions/Change exceptions*
- Adjusting the numeric display, to set the number of decimals displayed and the scaling to hundredths, thousands, etc.: *Settings → Number format* (Ctrl+F11)
- Hiding and displaying columns: *Edit → Columns → On/Off*
- Currency translation of the report: *Settings → Currency* (Ctrl+Shift+F4)
- Sorting capability (by column): select a column, then *Edit → Sort ascending* (Ctrl+F2), or *Edit → Sort descending* (Ctrl+F3)
- Determining how the characteristics are displayed, that is, using values, descriptions, or a combination: *Settings → Characteristic display*
- Determining whether and how a totals row is displayed: *Settings → Totals row*
- Exporting the report to a local file (Ctrl+Shift+F12)
- Mailing of the report (Ctrl+F6)
- Graphing portions of the report using SAP business graphics (Ctrl+Shift+F10)

Next Steps

Two different views are available in this report:
- Selected columns run across the report, while the characteristics (products, for example) run down the side
- All columns for a single selected product show as rows for a contribution analysis

You can analyze data using ranking lists, exception reporting, and sorting; list line items in the profitability analysis database; and access additional SAP data from this report.

This report contains data obtained from postings to cost-based CO-PA. As such, the data cannot be changed or manipulated from the report. Since cost-based—not account-based—CO-PA is used, value fields are used in the analysis instead of account numbers or cost elements.

Section 6: Controlling—Profitability Analysis Reports
Profitability Analysis: SBU/Product/Customer Analysis

Guided Tour

Example 1: A manager of a strategic business unit wants to analyze the products and customers in a single business unit.

To access the first screen for this report, choose

Information systems → *Accounting* → *Profitability analysis*

Profitability report → *Report selection.*

From the reporting tree, choose the following report:

Istdaten → *SBU* → *Product* → *Cust. w/out Summ. Levels.*

1. Enter **001/1998** in *Period from* and **012/1998** in *Period to*. This report includes all periods for a fiscal year and allows reporting across fiscal years.

2. Enter data type **0** in *Plan/act.ind.*

3. Leave *Version* blank because it is only required for planned data.

4. Leave *Record type* blank so that all posted records appear.

    Record type limits the source of viewable data (for example, data only from invoices, or direct journal entries).

5. Choose *Execute*.

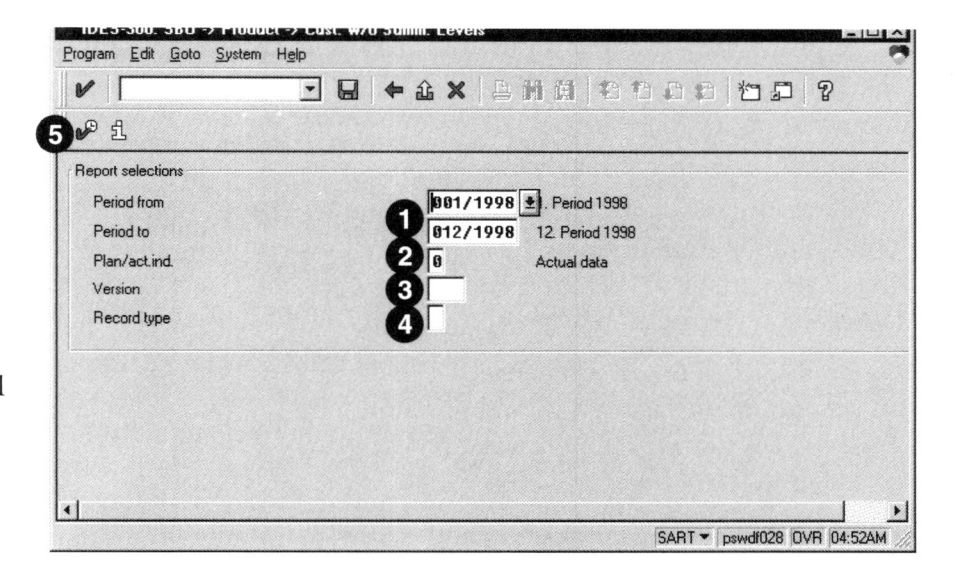

Commonly Used Reports: Illustrations and Perspectives

6–17

Section 6: Controlling—Profitability Analysis Reports
Profitability Analysis: SBU/Product/Customer Analysis

This screen shows data for the strategic business unit.

Columns separate the sales quantity, gross revenue, and cost of sales.

All postings not assigned to a division, appear in *Not assigned* in the last row.

6. Double-click on the *Wholesale* line to select it.

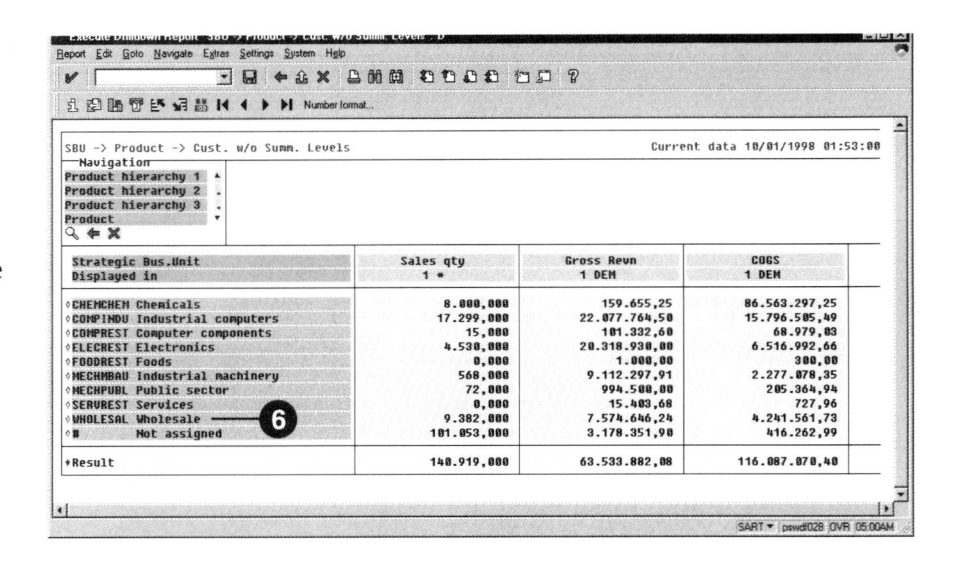

This screen shows the product hierarchy within *Wholesale*.

The *Strategic Business Unit* is now displayed above the columns, so that the current selection of data is easily visible.

Notice that *Product hierarchy 1 was* the first characteristic in the *Navigation* section (previous screen).

7. Double-click on *Vehicles*, the second *Product hierarchy 1* value, to show the top-most characteristic listed in the *Navigation* section.

8. Double-click on *Motorcycles*, the only *Product hierarchy 2* value.

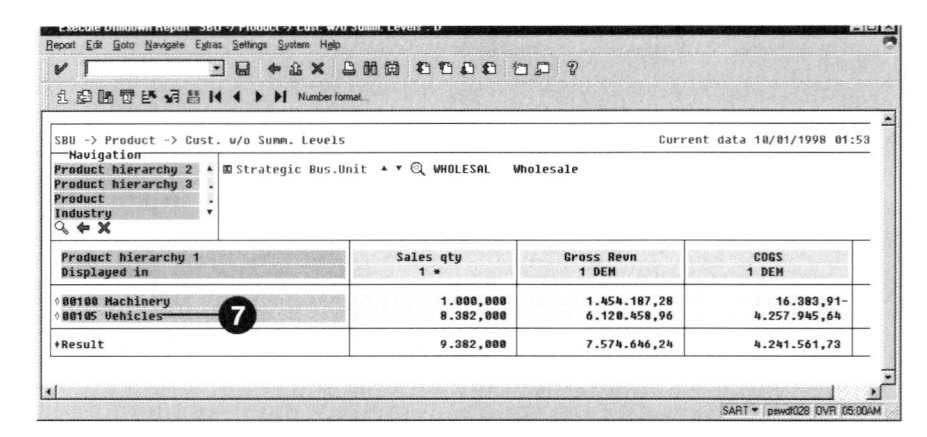

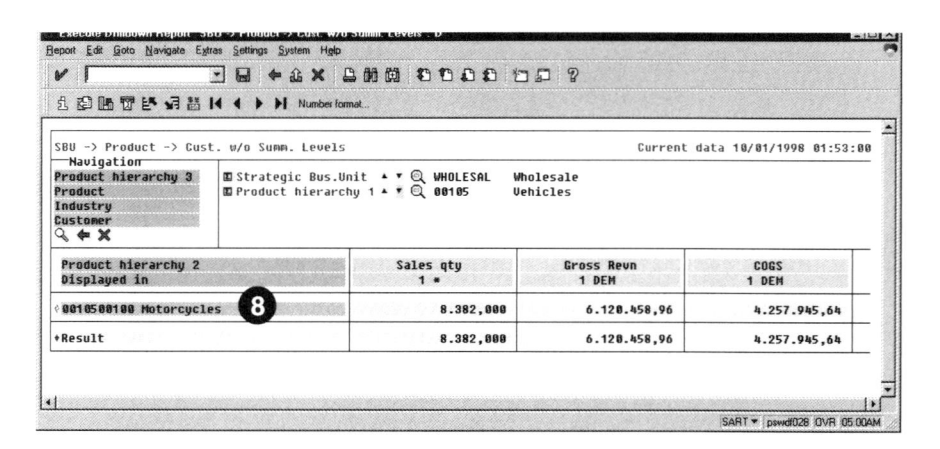

Section 6: Controlling—Profitability Analysis Reports
Profitability Analysis: SBU/Product/Customer Analysis

9. Double-click on *Components*, the second *Product hierarchy 3* value.

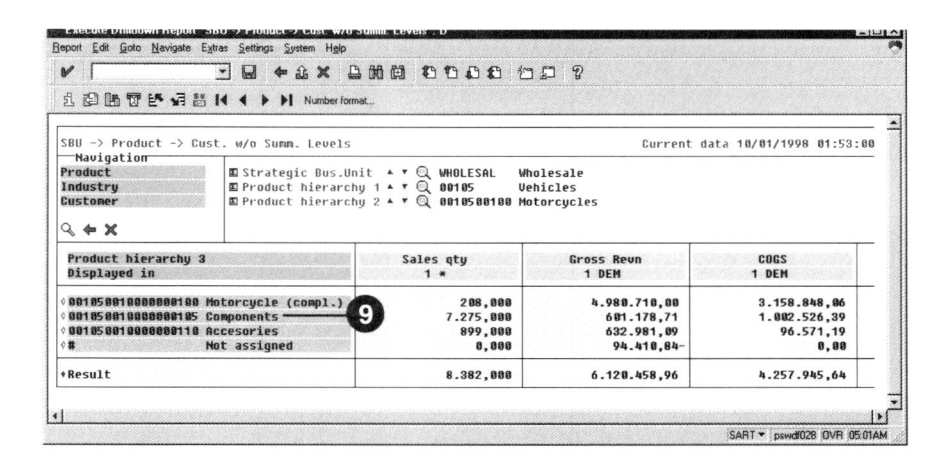

10. Double-click on the *Product* value, *Deluxe Taillight*.

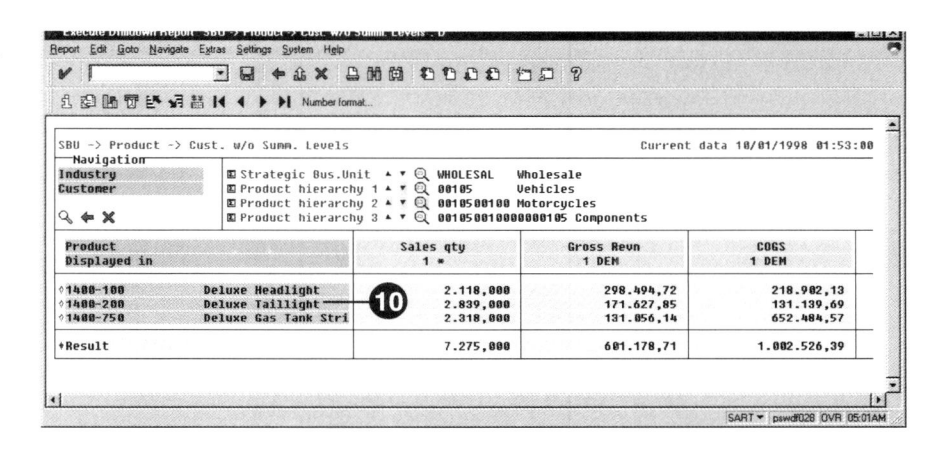

11. Double-click on *Trade*, the only *Industry* value.

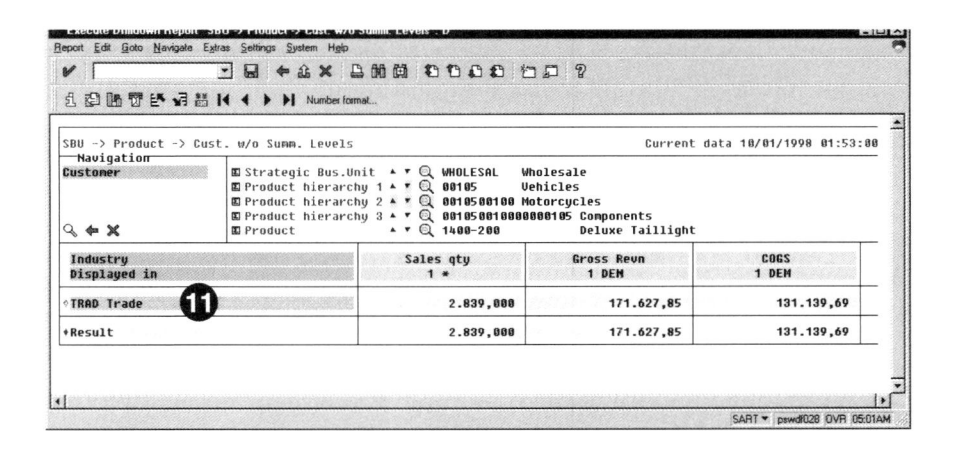

Commonly Used Reports: Illustrations and Perspectives

6–19

Section 6: Controlling—Profitability Analysis Reports
Profitability Analysis: SBU/Product/Customer Analysis

12. Click the diamond to the left of the the second customer.

13. Choose *Display*.

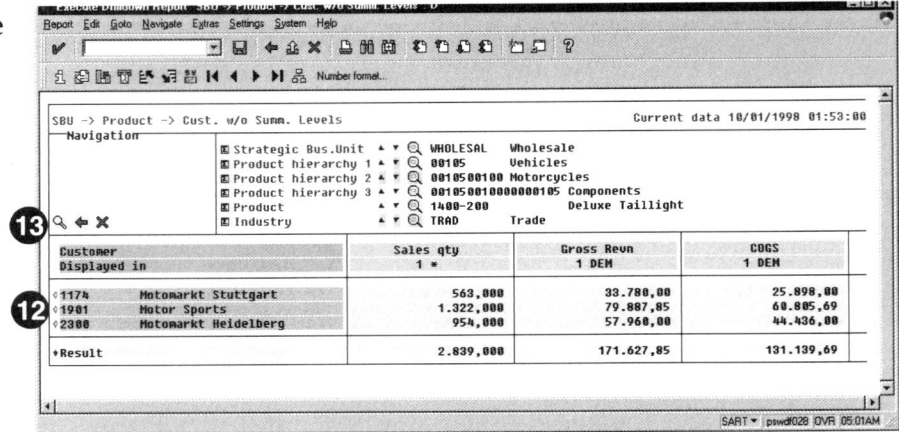

This screen shows the alternate view (columns). No hidden columns exist in this report.

14. Choose *Cancel*.

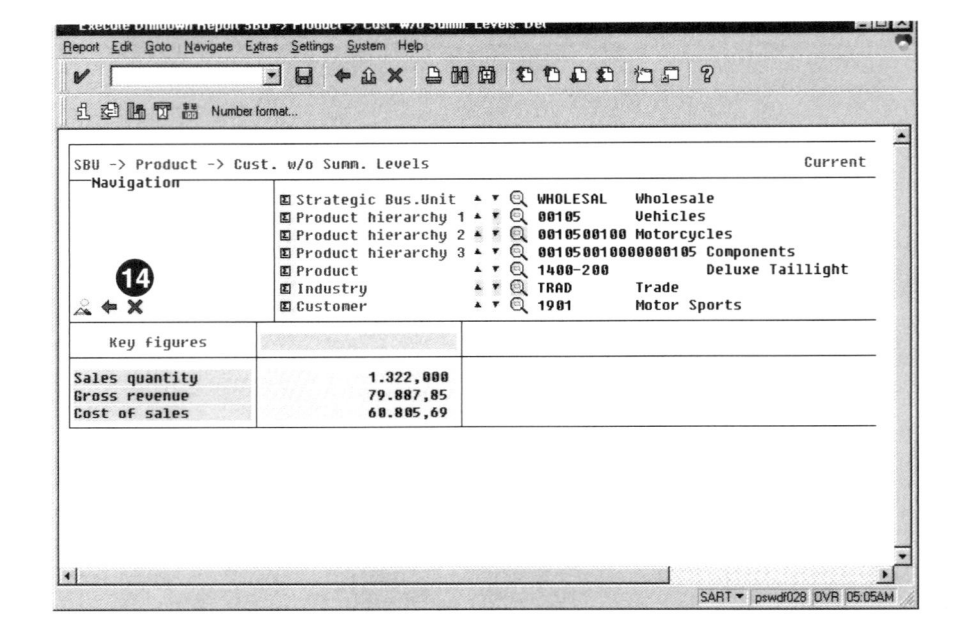

6–20

Reporting Made Easy

Section 6: Controlling—Profitability Analysis Reports
Profitability Analysis: SBU/Product/Customer Analysis

The first screen of the report reappears.

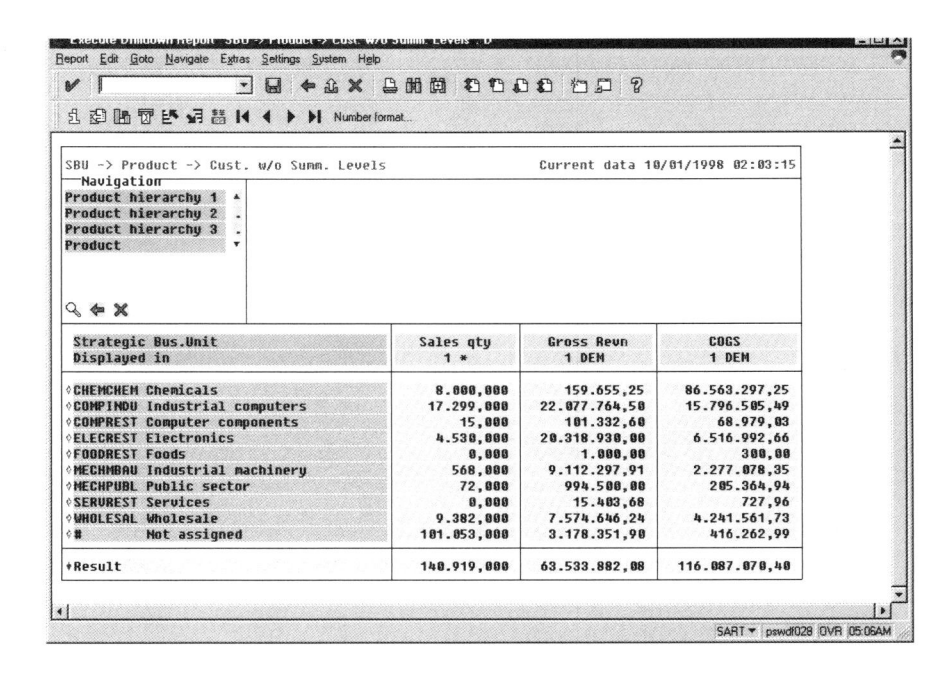

Example 2: Analyze customer data to identify customers who account for the highest revenue.

1. Enter **001/1998** in *Period from* and **012/1998** in *Period to*. This report includes all periods for a fiscal year and allows reporting across fiscal years.

2. Enter data type **0** in *Plan/act.ind*.

3. Leave *Version* blank, since it is only required for planned data.

4. Leave *Record type* blank, so that all posted records appear.

    Record type limits the source of viewable data (for example, data only from invoices, or direct journal entries).

5. Choose *Execute*.

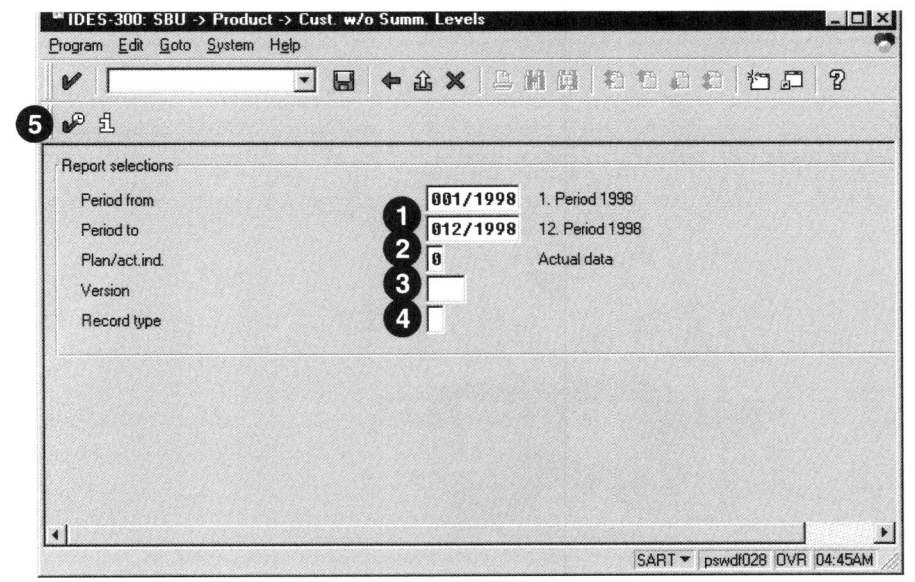

Commonly Used Reports: Illustrations and Perspectives

6–21

Section 6: Controlling—Profitability Analysis Reports

Profitability Analysis: SBU/Product/Customer Analysis

This screen shows data for the strategic business unit.

Columns separate the sales quantity, gross revenue, and cost of sales.

All postings not assigned to a division, appear in *Not assigned* in the last row.

6. Scroll down the list of characteristics in the *Navigation* section.

7. Click once on the header field, *Strategic Bus.Unit*.

8. Click once on the *Customer* characteristic in the *Navigation* section.

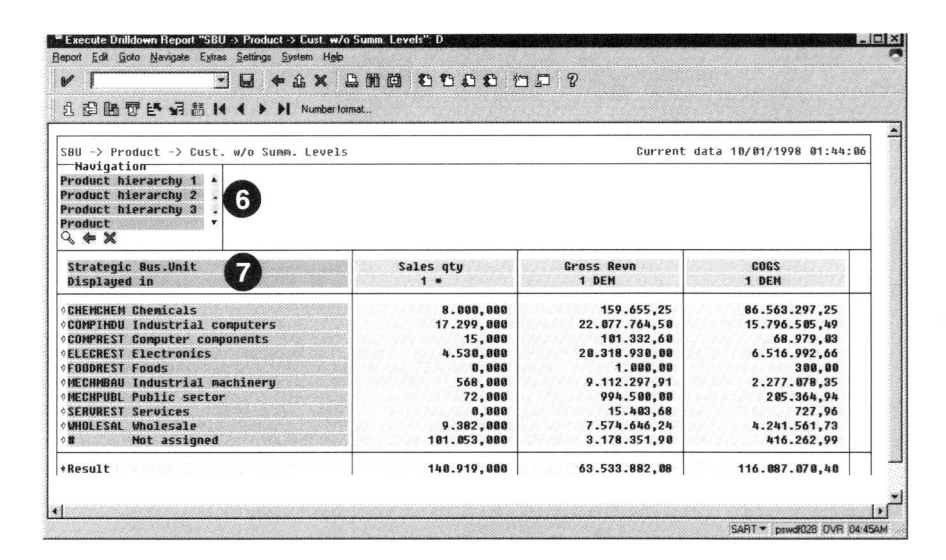

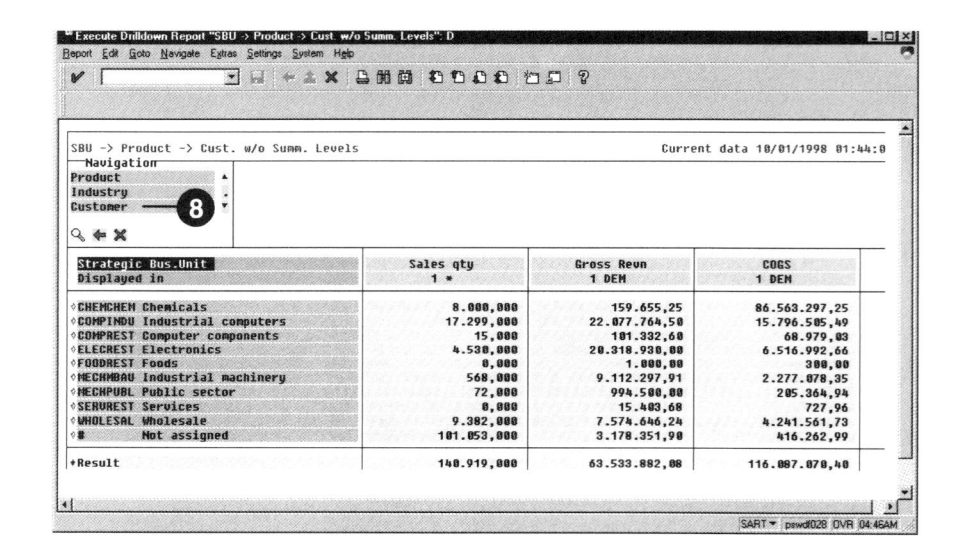

6–22

Reporting Made Easy

Section 6: Controlling—Profitability Analysis Reports
Profitability Analysis: SBU/Product/Customer Analysis

This screen displays customers in rows. The strategic business unit is an available characteristic, but it has not been selected. Therefore, all customers appear.

9. Choose the *Gross Revenue* column.
10. Choose *Extras → Create exception*.

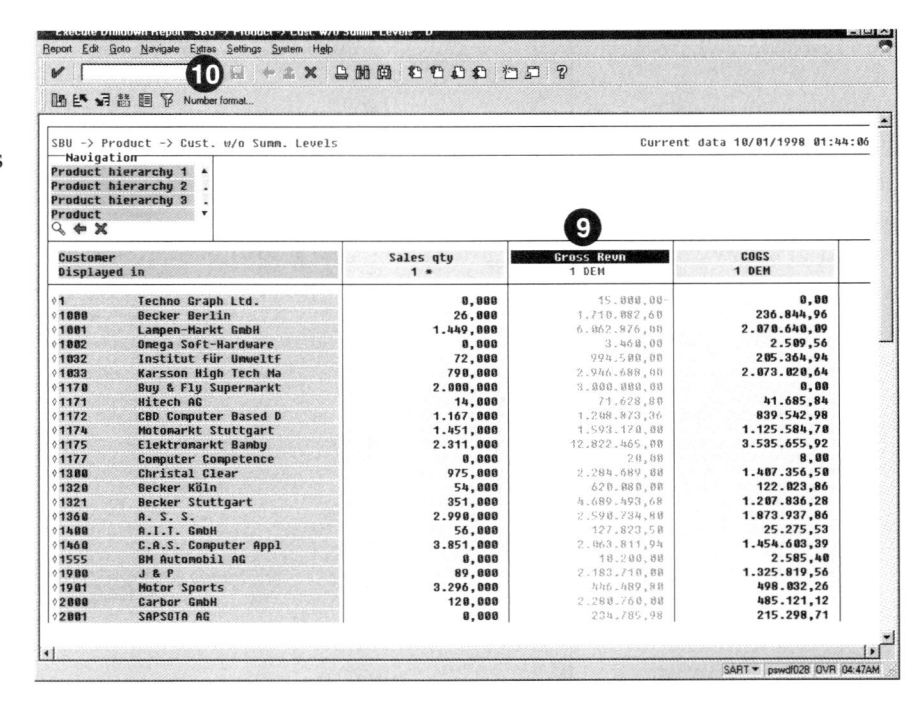

11. Select *Column* to create an exception rule for the entire gross revenue column.
12. Choose *Enter*.

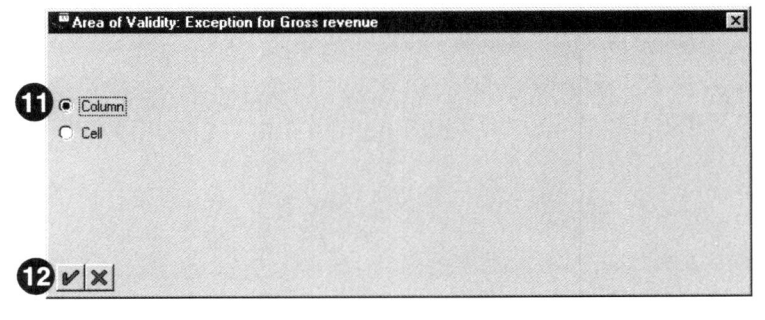

Commonly Used Reports: Illustrations and Perspectives

6–23

Section 6: Controlling—Profitability Analysis Reports
Profitability Analysis: SBU/Product/Customer Analysis

13. Enter a description for the exception (for example, **Customer Revenue**). Exceptions for the report are internally numbered.

14. Under *Lower threshold,* select *Active.*

15. Enter a threshold value (for example, **10.000,000**) This is the lowest allowable value before a customer's revenue flags in a different color.

16. Under *Color below threshold,* select a color to indicate all values meeting the lower threshold (for example, *Red*).

17. Under *Condition,* select *Less than or equal to.*

    In this example, because the latter is selected, all values less than or equal to the threshold amount are indicated in red.

18. Under *Upper threshold,* select *Active.*

    In this example, all values equal to or exceeding the threshold are indicated in green.

19. Choose *Enter.*

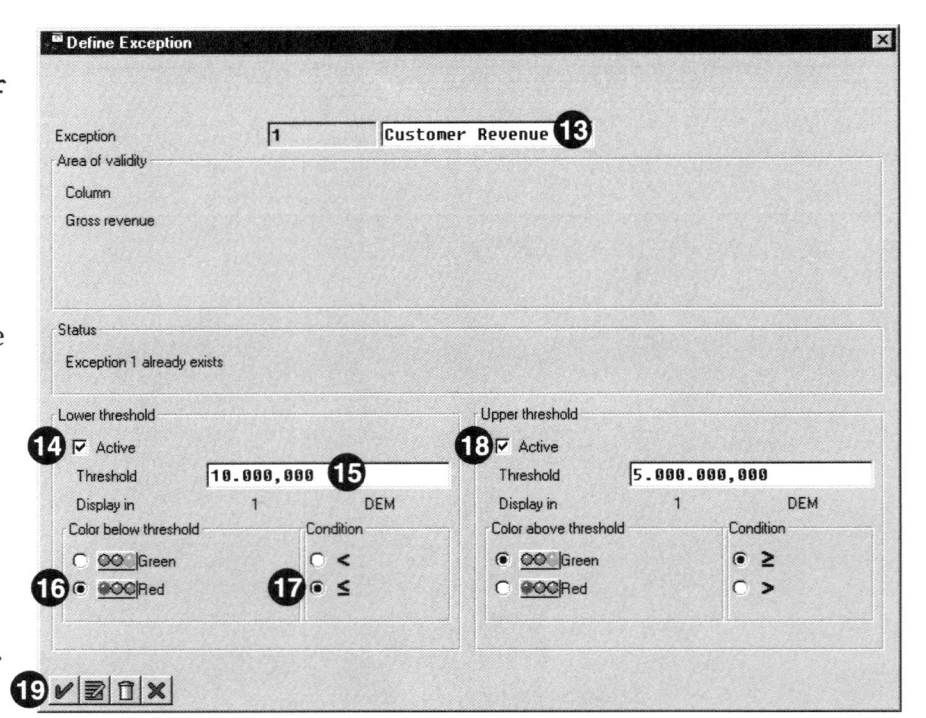

Section 6: Controlling—Profitability Analysis Reports
Profitability Analysis: SBU/Product/Customer Analysis

A The first customer's revenue is less than the lower threshold value, so the cell appears in red. You may need to take action toward better marketing to this customer.

B The third customer's revenue exceeds the higher threshold value, so the cell appears in green. You should treat this customer well!

In this scenario, the exceptions are created on an adhoc basis, so they should be deleted. If you do not delete the exceptions, they will remain active each time the report is run.

20. Choose *Extras* → *Delete exception*.

21. Choose *Yes*.

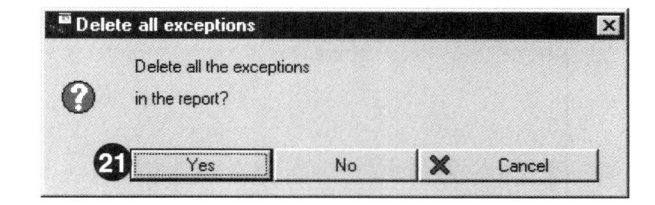

Threshold value flagging in red and green disappears.

22. Choose the *Gross revenue* column.

23. Choose *Edit* → *ranking list* → *top n*.

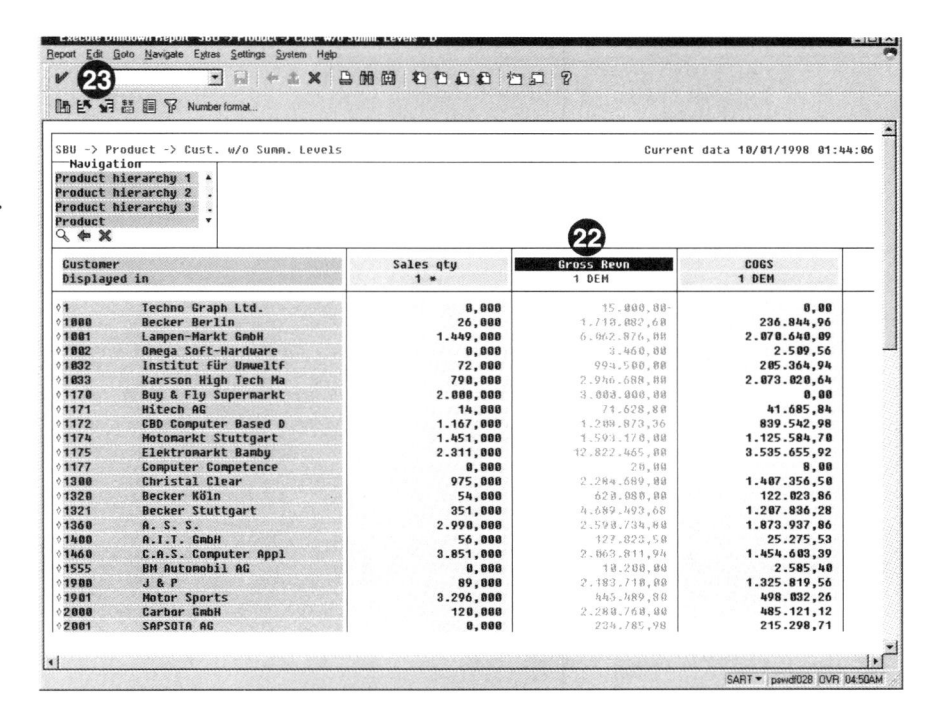

Commonly Used Reports: Illustrations and Perspectives

6–25

Section 6: Controlling—Profitability Analysis Reports

Profitability Analysis: SBU/Product/Customer Analysis

24. Change the customer ranking from the default of **15** to **5**.

25. Choose *Enter*.

The top five (5) customers appear, ranked according to their gross revenue.

The remaining 46 customers accounts summarize at the bottom of the report.

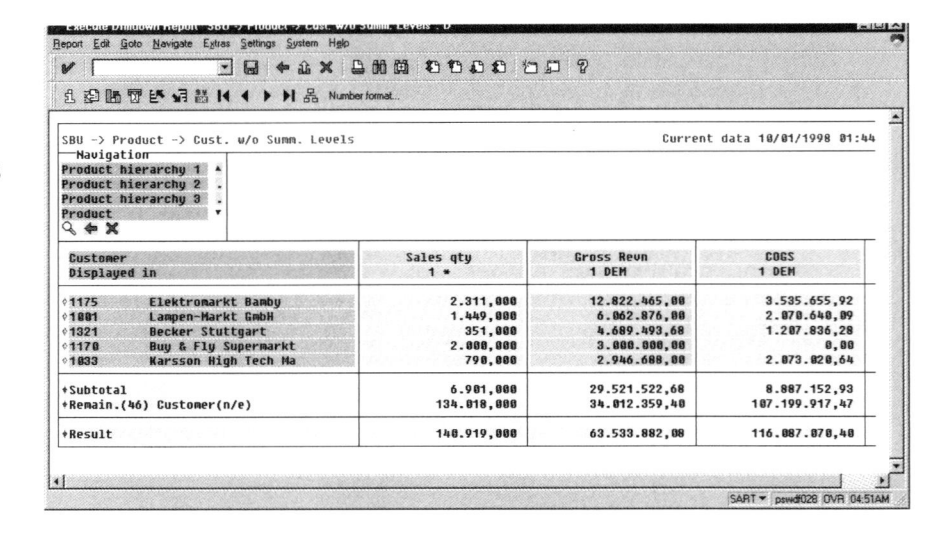

6–26

Reporting Made Easy

Profitability Analysis: Sales Plan/Contribution Margin

Quick Access To run this report, use the following:

Menu Path

Information systems → Accounting → Profitability analysis

Profitability report → Report selection

From the reporting tree, choose the following report:

Absatzplan → Sales Plan/1998.

Purpose This report provides a contribution margin for distribution channels, divisions, and products. Only planned data is displayed for the contribution margin. This plan can be used to provide forecasted data to marketing as well as to sales and operations planning.

A product line manager would use this report to project the anticipated performance of specific divisions and products and possibly to submit this budget to a vice-president. Actual data can be compared against plan data, and a plan can be developed using manual estimates, or formulas in which previous historical performance is taken into consideration.

Prerequisites You must set the *Controlling Area* before running the report. Choose *Accounting → Controlling → Cost centers → Profitability analysis→ Environment → Set operating concern*. For the examples in this section, the operating concern is set to *IDEA* using cost-based profitability analysis.

All reports in profitability analysis are user-defined. This means you must configure and generate the operating concern before creating any reports and determine the rows, columns, variables, and general format by using drilldown reporting (forms and reports).

You do not need to enter selection options for this report. All options are already hard-coded in the report. This means that only 1998 data is available. If you need to run a report for a different year, you must create a new report or define the period and fiscal year characteristics as variables within the report configuration.

Profitability Analysis: Sales Plan/Contribution Margin

Integration The profitability analysis line items which list are context-sensitive. For example, when you position the cursor on a cell for a line item, only the reports that contain that line item show data. This improves performance of the report as a whole.

Once the original profitability analysis document appears, the original documents related to the line item can be retrieved. For example, from a sales document, a material master, customer master, billing document, and accounting document is available. From a direct financial entry, however, only the cost element and accounting documents are available. From settlement documents, the controlling object from which the settlement took place is generally available.

The integration data available from CO-PA includes:
- Material master
- Customer master
- Billing document (SD)
- Accounting documents (FI)
- All linked accounting documents (special ledger, consolidation, cost accounting, etc.)
- Sales order
- Cost element
- Cost center
- Internal order
- Project
- Selected costing reports, usually in product costing

Section 6: Controlling—Profitability Analysis Reports
Profitability Analysis: Sales Plan/Contribution Margin

Features

The selection screen of this report includes:
- Variants
- Printing in background, after execution
- Ranking based on selected columns: *Edit → Ranking list → Top n/Top%/Last n/Last%*
- Creating a condition under which values are displayed, that is, higher or lower than a particular value: *Edit → Condition → Create/Change*
- Creating exceptions under which values are highlighted in different colors, i.e. higher or lower than a particular value: *Extras → Create exceptions/Change exceptions*
- Adjusting the numeric display, to set the number of decimals displayed and the scaling to hundredths, thousands, etc.: *Settings → Number format* (Ctrl+F11)
- Hiding and displaying columns: *Edit → Columns → On/Off*
- Currency translation of the report: *Settings → Currency* (Ctrl+Shift+F4)
- Sorting capability (by column): select a column, then *Edit → Sort ascending* (Ctrl+F2), or *Edit → Sort descending* (Ctrl+F3)
- Determining how the characteristics are displayed, that is, using values, descriptions, or a combination: *Settings → Characteristic display.*
- Determining whether and how a totals row is displayed: *Settings → Totals row*
- Exporting the report to a local file (Ctrl+Shift+F12)
- Mailing of the report (Ctrl+F6)
- Graphing portions of the report using SAP business graphics (Ctrl+Shift+F10)

Next Steps

Two different views are available in this report:
- Selected columns run across the report, while the characteristics (products, for example) run down the side
- All columns for a single selected product show as rows for a contribution analysis

You can analyze data using ranking lists, exception reporting, and sorting; list line items in the profitability analysis database; and access additional SAP data from this report.

This report contains data obtained from postings to cost-based CO-PA. As such, the data cannot be changed or manipulated from the report. Since cost-based—not account-based—CO-PA is used, value fields are used in the analysis instead of account numbers or cost elements.

Section 6: Controlling—Profitability Analysis Reports
Profitability Analysis: Sales Plan/Contribution Margin

Guided Tour

Example: A product manager wants to analyze the projected contribution margin of a particular product based on the anticipated distribution channel through which the products will be sold.

To access the first screen for this report, choose

Information systems → Accounting → Profitability analysis

Profitability report → Report selection.

From the reporting tree, choose the following report:

Absatzplan → Sales Plan/1998.

The default sales organization number (for example, *1000*) cannot be changed.

Divisions show in rows. In this example, all postings were assigned to a division. If postings were not assigned to a division, *Not assigned* would appear in the last row.

Planned data for fiscal year 1998 shows in columns.

1. Choose *Next columns*.

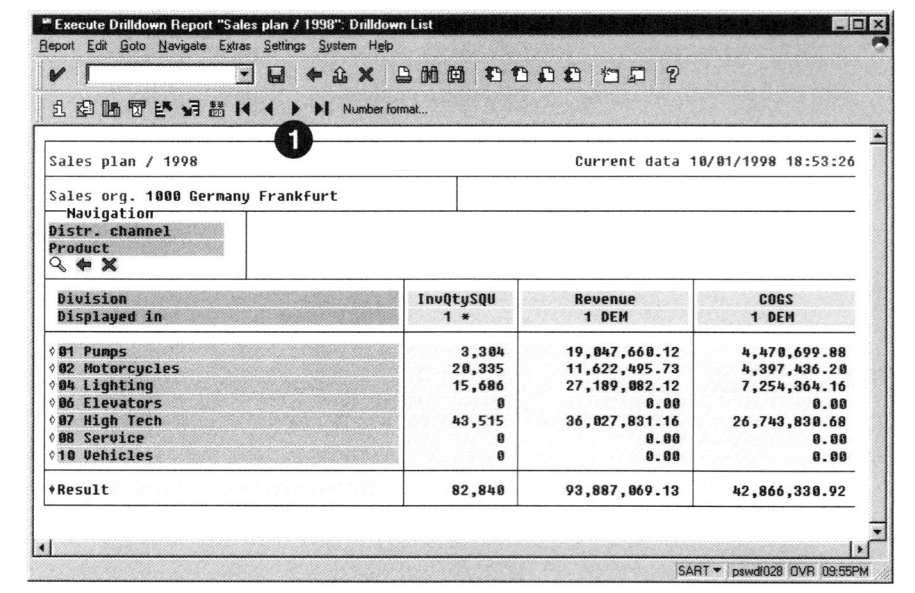

6–30

Reporting Made Easy

Section 6: Controlling—Profitability Analysis Reports
Profitability Analysis: Sales Plan/Contribution Margin

This screen shows additional planned data for fiscal year 1998.

2. Choose *Next columns*.

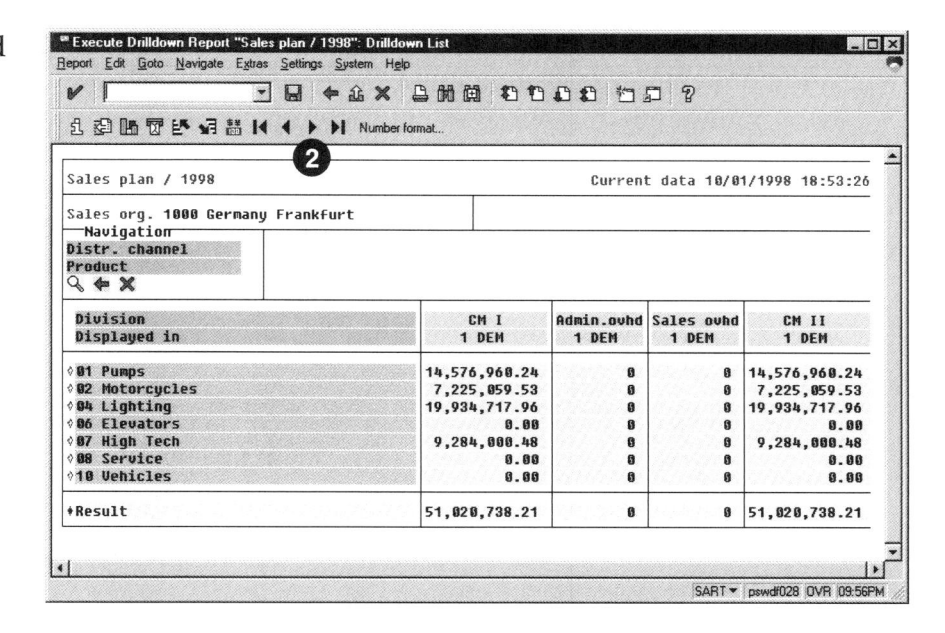

Division	CM I 1 DEM	Admin.ovhd 1 DEM	Sales ovhd 1 DEM	CM II 1 DEM
01 Pumps	14,576,960.24	0	0	14,576,960.24
02 Motorcycles	7,225,059.53	0	0	7,225,059.53
04 Lighting	19,934,717.96	0	0	19,934,717.96
06 Elevators	0.00	0	0	0.00
07 High Tech	9,284,000.48	0	0	9,284,000.48
08 Service	0.00	0	0	0.00
10 Vehicles	0.00	0	0	0.00
Result	51,020,738.21	0	0	51,020,738.21

This screen shows additional planned data for fiscal year 1998.

3. Click once on the header field, *Division*.

4. Click once on the *Distr. Channel* characteristic in the *Navigation* section.

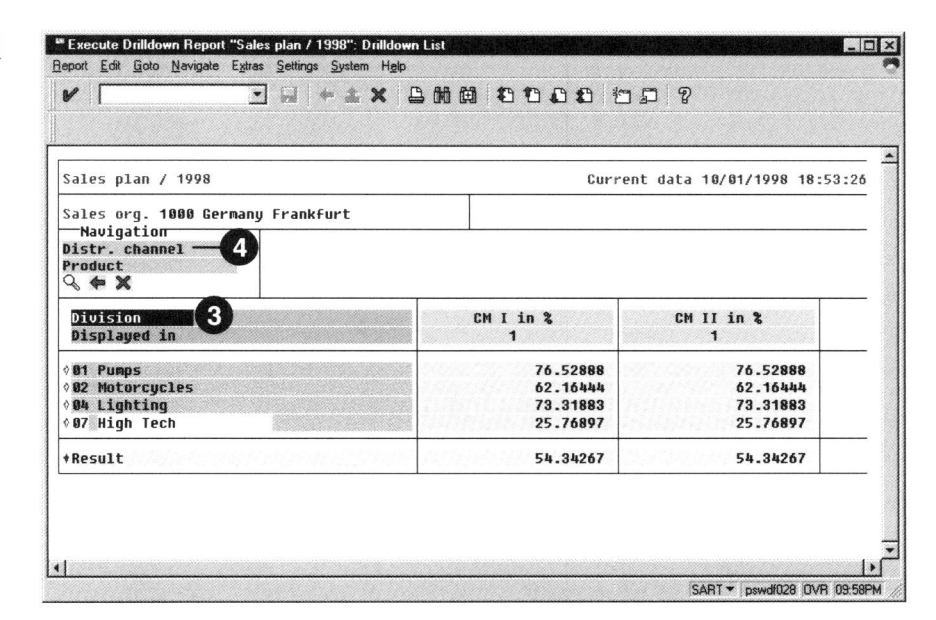

Division	CM I in % 1	CM II in % 1
01 Pumps	76.52888	76.52888
02 Motorcycles	62.16444	62.16444
04 Lighting	73.31883	73.31883
07 High Tech	25.76897	25.76897
Result	54.34267	54.34267

Commonly Used Reports: Illustrations and Perspectives

6–31

Section 6: Controlling—Profitability Analysis Reports
Profitability Analysis: Sales Plan/Contribution Margin

The distribution channels list in rows. The division is an available characteristic, but it has not been selected. Therefore, all distribution channels list.

5. Click the diamond next to the first listed distribution channel, *10*.

   The diamond and navigation bars change color to indicate hotspot activation.

6. Choose *Display*.

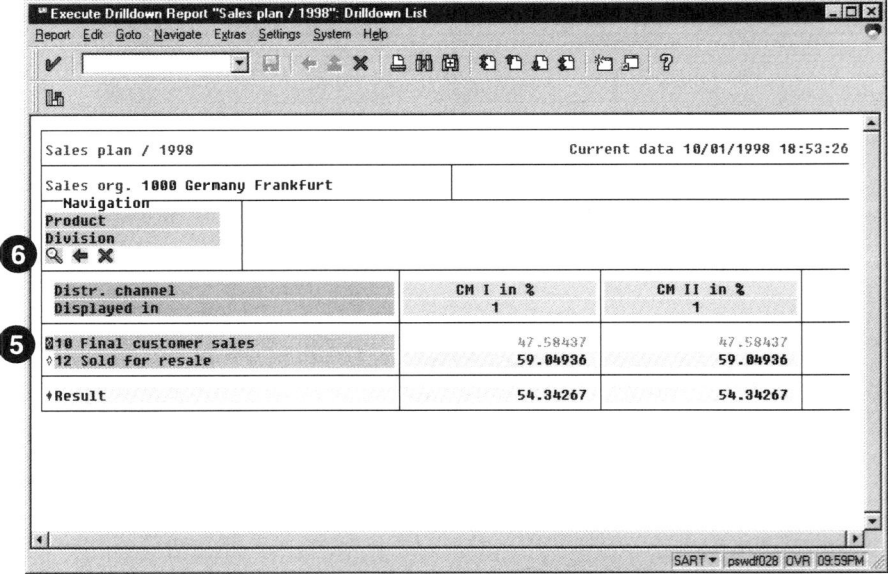

Columns show as rows for the selected distribution channel.

7. Choose *Scroll Down*.

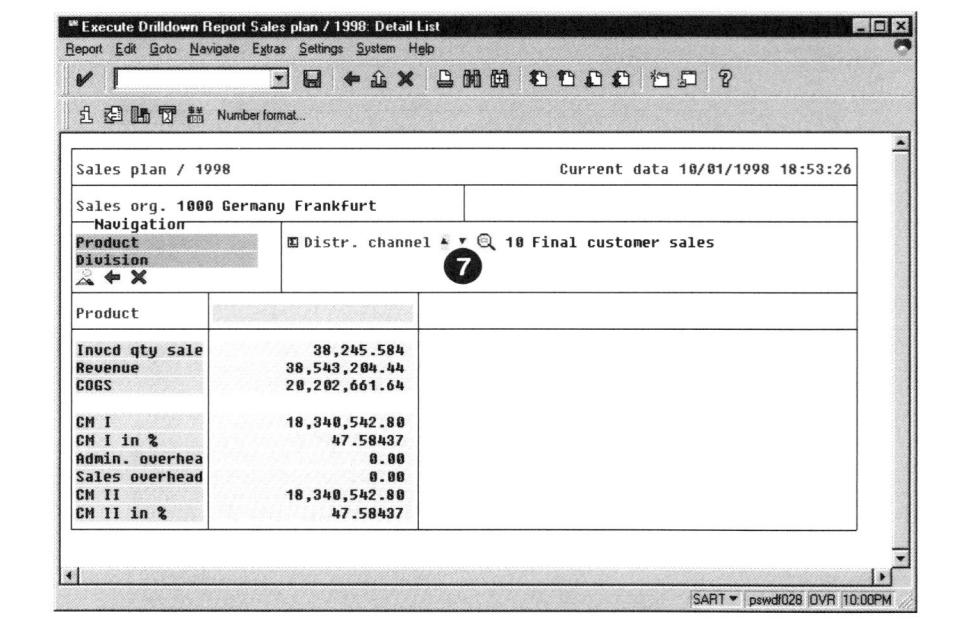

6–32

Reporting Made Easy

Section 6: Controlling—Profitability Analysis Reports
Profitability Analysis: Sales Plan/Contribution Margin

The projected contribution margin for the distribution channel can be analyzed from this section of the screen.

8. Select the *Product* characteristic in the *Navigation* section.

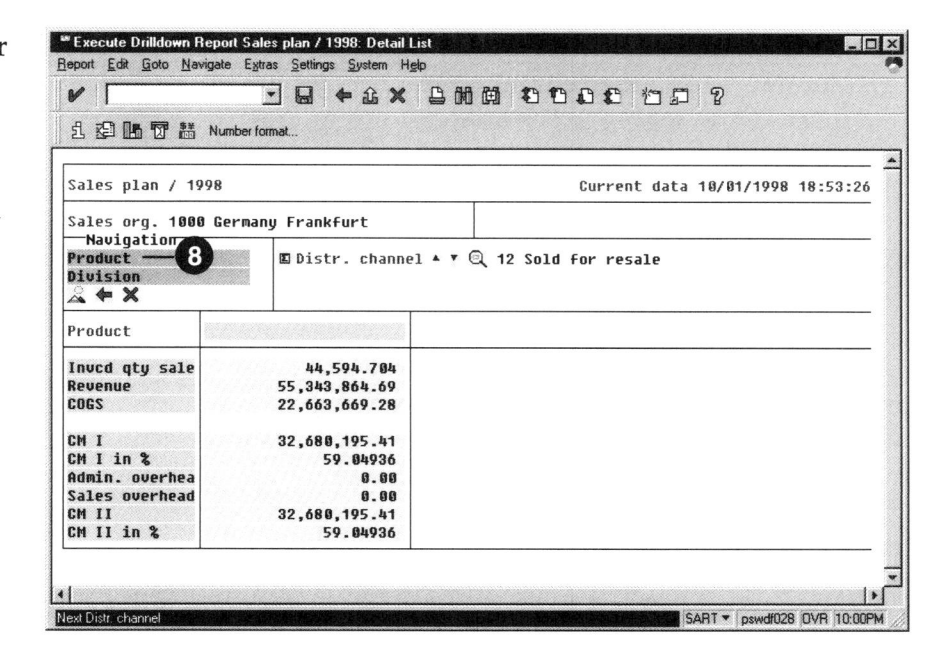

The contribution margin appears for an individual product.

9. Choose *Overview* in the *Navigation* section.

10. Click the *Product* characteristic to select it.

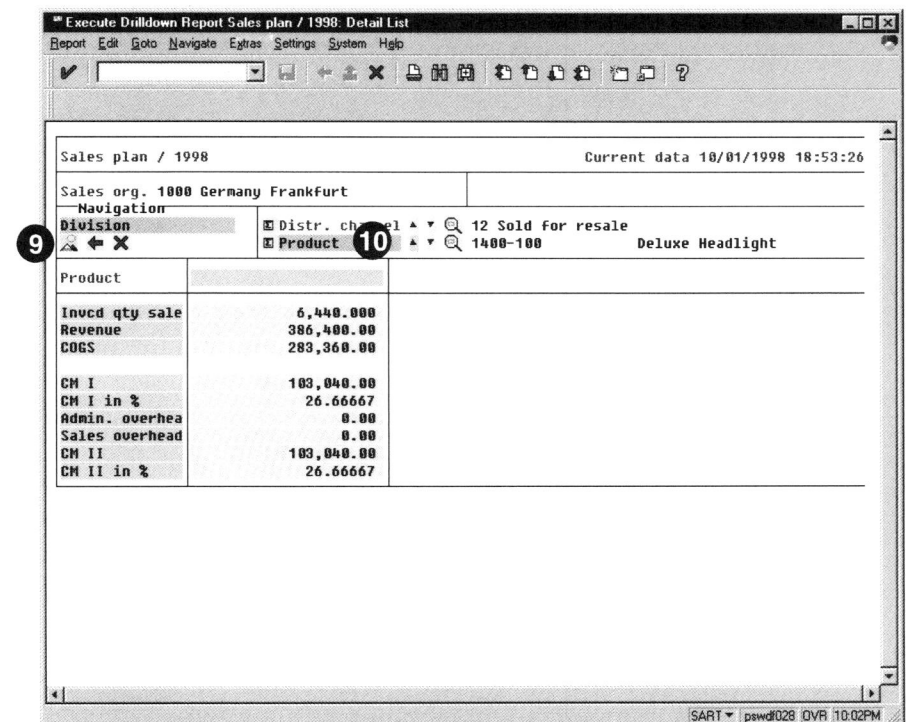

Commonly Used Reports: Illustrations and Perspectives

6–33

Section 6: Controlling—Profitability Analysis Reports
Profitability Analysis: Sales Plan/Contribution Margin

The original screen appears, distribution channel remains selected, and all products within the distribution channel show in rows.

11. Choose the *Contribution Margin I* column.

12. Choose *Edit → column(s) → On/off*.

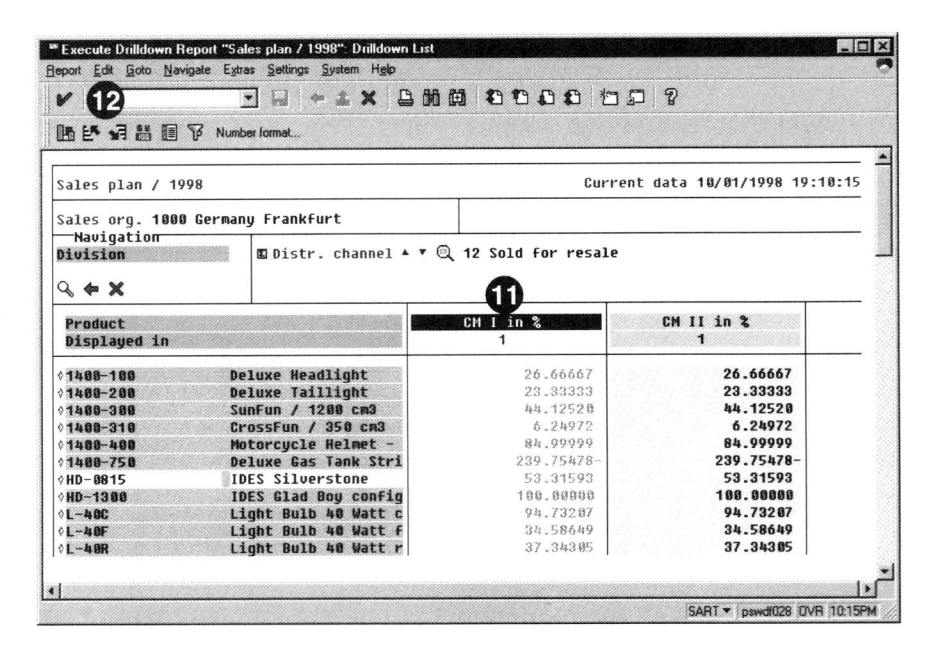

13. Deselect fields (for this example, as shown) that are not relevant to *Contribution Margin 1*.

    All fields are selected as the default.

14. Choose *Enter*.

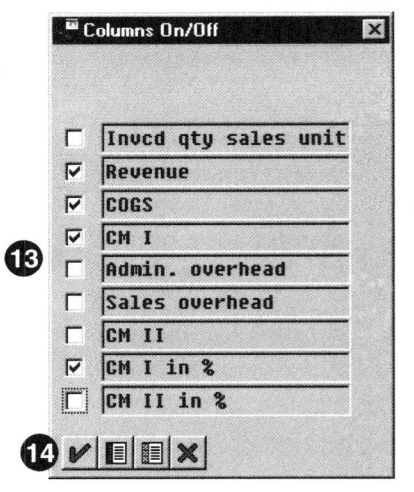

Reporting Made Easy

6–34

Section 6: Controlling—Profitability Analysis Reports
Profitability Analysis: Sales Plan/Contribution Margin

15. Select the *Revenue* column.
16. Choose *Sort descending*.

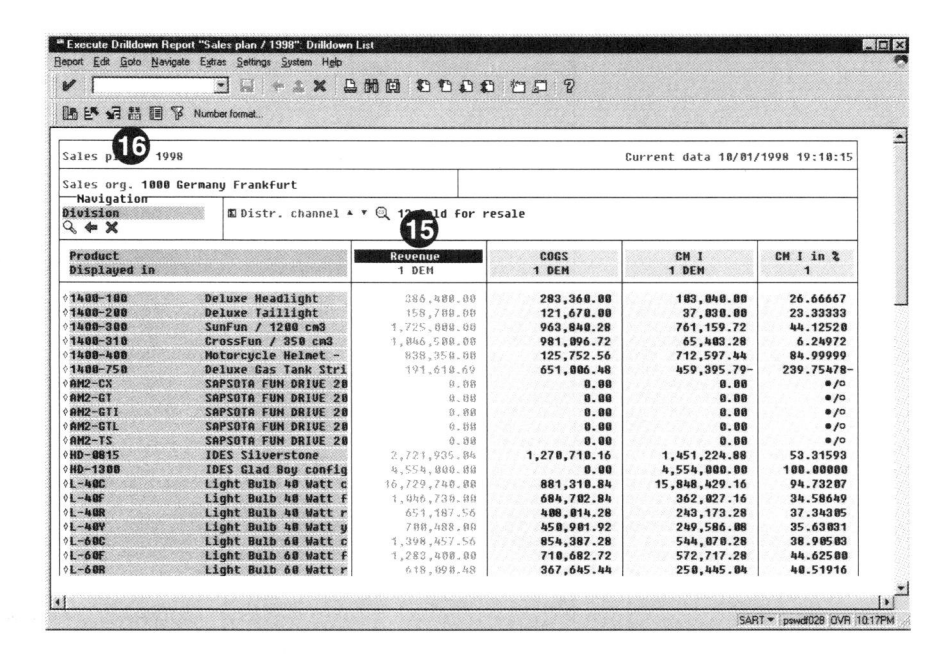

This screen shows the *Revenue* column sorted.

From this analysis, the contribution margin percentage does not always correspond to the revenue.

17. Choose *Display*.

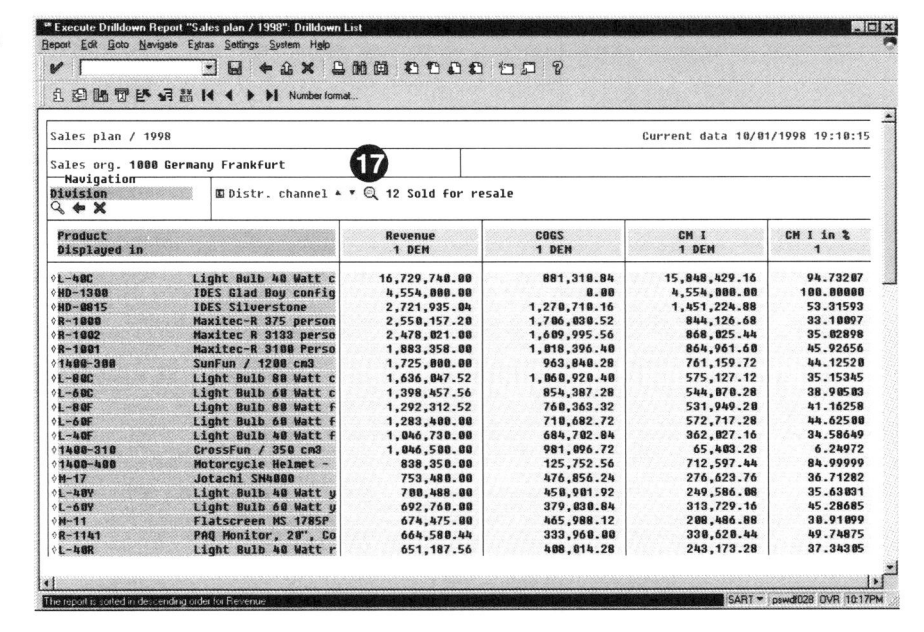

This screen shows all available values for the distribution channel.

18. Select the *Final customer sales* line.
19. Choose *Enter*.

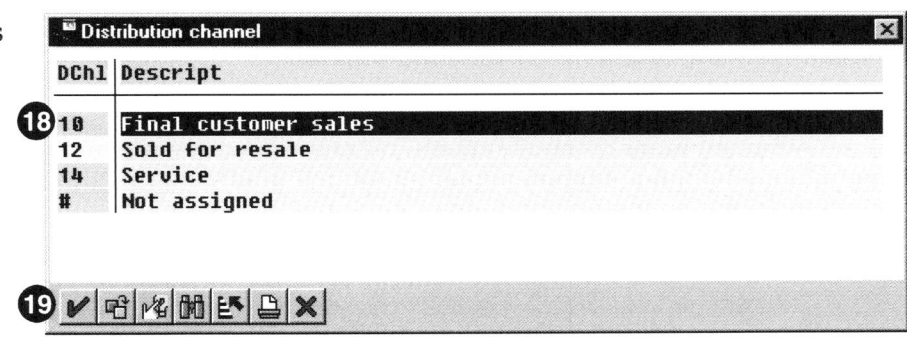

Commonly Used Reports: Illustrations and Perspectives

6–35

Section 6: Controlling—Profitability Analysis Reports

Profitability Analysis: Sales Plan/Contribution Margin

This screen shows a listing of products for the newly selected distribution channel.

The sort is still in place for the *Revenue* column.

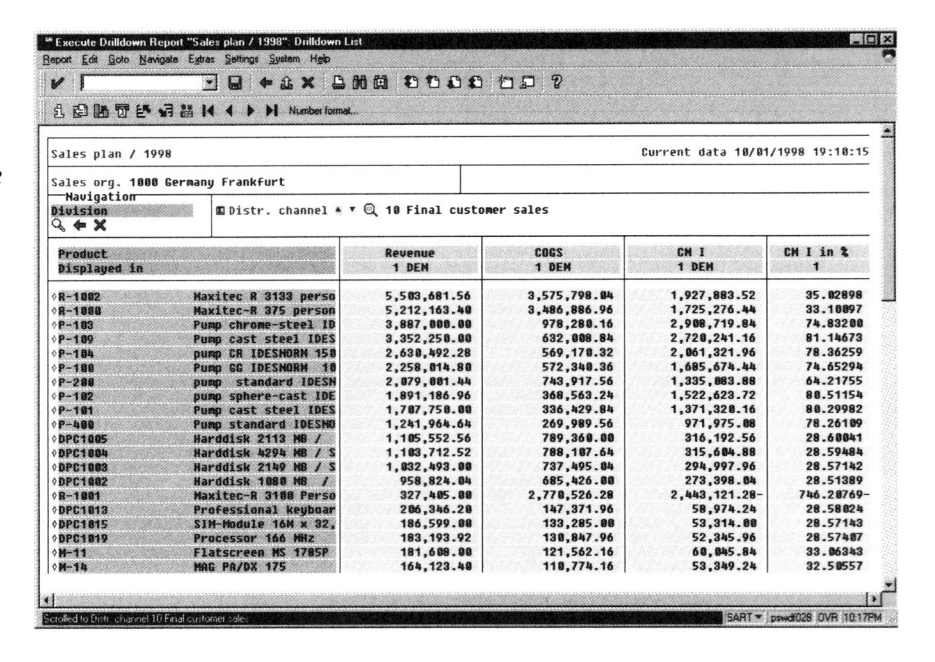

Section 7: Controlling—Reconciliation Reports

Contents

FI/CO Reconciliation in Company Code Currency 7–2

CO/FI Reconciliation in Group Currency 7–13

Cross-Company Code Reconciliation 7–27

FI/CO Reconciliation in Company Code Currency

Quick Access

To run this report, use one of the following access options:

Option 1: Menu Path

Information systems → Accounting → Overhead costs

Cost elements → Report selection

From the reporting tree, choose the following report:

Reconciliation CO/FI → In company code currency → CO/FI Reconciliation in CCde Crcy.

Option 2: Program Name

Choose *System → Services → Reporting* and enter `J5AF1TQX` in the *Program* field. Then, choose *Execute* to run the report.

Purpose

This report provides an overview of the reconciliation postings necessary to ensure that FI and CO postings made across company codes, business areas, and functional areas within the selected company code have been recorded to the General Ledger (G/L), both on a period and a fiscal year-to-date basis. The company code currency is used for this reconciliation.

The accounting department uses this report to ensure that financial and controlling transactions reconcile for CO postings that occur across company codes, business areas, and functional areas. Since cross-company code postings affect financial statements, this report monitors the expected reconciliation postings based on CO data, and the reconciliation postings made to FI.

Prerequisites

You must enter a value in the selection fields before running this report.

You may leave the company code selection blank, and obtain a list that contains values for all company codes for which reconciliation postings have been made. If you choose to use a group of company codes, you must first create a set that contains them in order to access Report Painter/Report Writer reports.

Integration

You can run a context-sensitive actual line item report from this reconciliation ledger report. For example, when positioning the cursor on a cell, only the line items that make up the cell total will appear. The actual line items for a reconciliation ledger report can be executed for either one cell, or a range of cells.

Section 7: Controlling—Reconciliation Reports
FI/CO Reconciliation in Company Code Currency

Features

The selection screen of this report includes:
- Variants
- Dynamic selection options
- Executing and printing in background
- Sorting capability (by column): Select a column, then *Edit → Sort in ascndng ordr* (Ctrl+Shift+F5), or *Edit → Sort in descending order* (Ctrl+Shift+F6)
- Adjusting the column width: *Settings → Column widths* (Ctrl+F12)
- Adjusting the numeric display, to set the number of decimals displayed and the scaling to hundredths, thousandths, etc.: *Settings → Number format* (F5)
- Adjusting the summation level for the entire report (F6)
- Mailing of the report (Ctrl+F9)
- Graphing portions of the report using SAP business graphics (F7)
- Exporting the report to a local file (F8)
- Increasing or reducing the detail displayed, by double-clicking on subtotal lines. The double-click acts as a toggle switch. If detail is displayed, double-clicking on the subtotal will hide it; if detail is not displayed on a summary line (marked with one or more asterisks), double-clicking displays it.
- Displaying only threshold values, or values that is greater than or less than an entered criteria: *Edit → Threshold value* (Shift+F5).
- Creating an extract of reporting information (F5)
- Using variation to obtain multiple reports of company code sets and subsets (F6)
- Selecting an extract or an archive: *Data source* (Ctrl+F1)

Section 7: Controlling—Reconciliation Reports
FI/CO Reconciliation in Company Code Currency

Next Steps The system displays four columns for all sections of the report, including:
- CO postings already made to the reconciliation ledger
- FI postings already made to the reconciliation ledger
- Variance between CO and FI postings
- Reconciliation values still to be posted

By double-clicking on any subtotals in the report, the amount of detail that makes up the subtotal can either be hidden or displayed. For example, double-clicking on a cost element summary line will hide the debit/credit detail. To display this detail again, double-click on this line again.

This report contains data obtained from postings to the reconciliation ledger. This is a fixed special ledger to which postings are made when CO transactions span company codes, business areas, and functional areas. As such, the data cannot be changed or manipulated from the report.

The report contains two different blocks of data, as shown below. By navigating around these blocks, different types of reconciliation ledger data can be viewed.

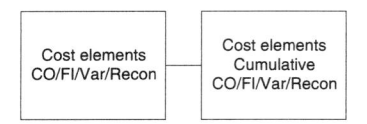

```
┌──────────────┐   ┌──────────────┐
│ Cost elements│   │ Cost elements│
│ CO/FI/Var/   │───│  Cumulative  │
│   Recon      │   │ CO/FI/Var/   │
│              │   │   Recon      │
└──────────────┘   └──────────────┘
```

Section 7: Controlling—Reconciliation Reports
FI/CO Reconciliation in Company Code Currency

Guided Tour

Example: An accounting manager needs to ensure that all month-end postings have been made, and then needs to analyze the postings in the company code currency.

To access the first screen for this report, choose

Information systems → Accounting → Overhead costs and then, *Cost elements → Report selection.*

From the reporting tree, choose the following report:

Reconciliation CO/FI → In company code currency → CO/FI Reconciliation in CCde Crcy.

1. Enter **1997** in *Fiscal year*. This report runs for only one fiscal year at a time.

2. Enter **1** in *Period*. This report shows the reconciliation postings for the company code in the selected period.

   In addition, the report shows a cumulative value of the reconciliation postings from period 1 through the selected period.

3. Enter **3000** in *Or value(s)*. You may also enter a range of company codes, or a company code group.

4. Choose *Execute*.

   As the report begins to run, a threshold value determines how detailed the output will be.

5. Choose *Enter*.

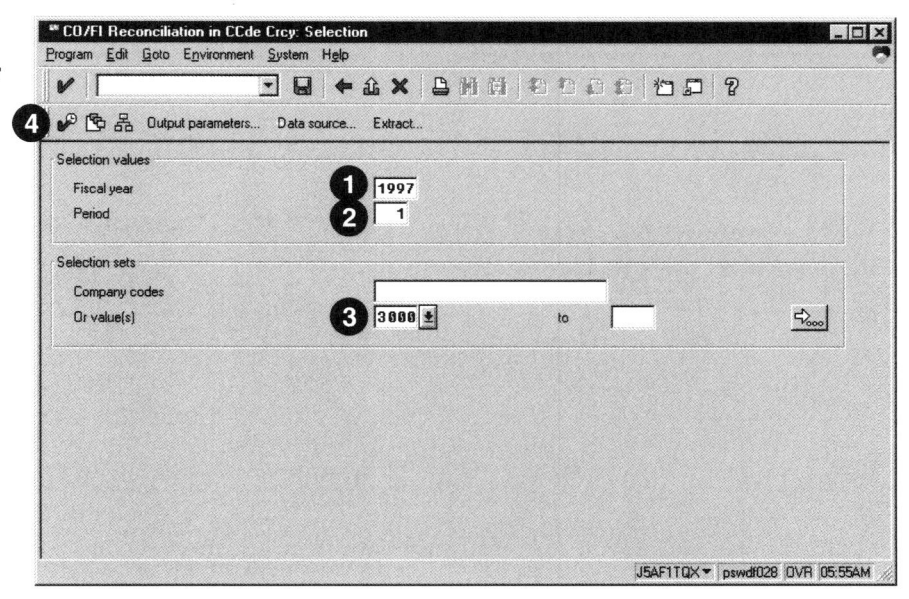

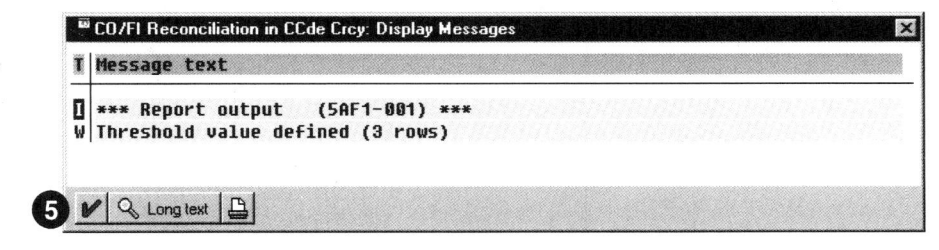

Commonly Used Reports: Illustrations and Perspectives

7–5

Section 7: Controlling—Reconciliation Reports
FI/CO Reconciliation in Company Code Currency

This screen shows the reconciliation accounts to which postings will be made from the reconciliation ledger. For primary cost elements, the system uses the same account. For secondary cost elements, the system determines the reconciliation account based on its configuration.

A CO postings to the reconciliation ledger

B FI postings to expense accounts

C Variance between the CO and FI postings

D Entries to the reconciliation ledger that have been made to FI (no values because the period-end process has not been executed)

6. Double-click on the reconciliation account to reveal its field text.

This screen shows the original data that generated the variance between CO and FI, and which posts to the G/L from the reconciliation ledger.

7. Choose *Next columns*.

This screen shows a cumulative view of the same data. Since the selected period is also period 1, the values are the same.

8. Choose *Previous columns* to navigate to the first block of data displayed in the report.

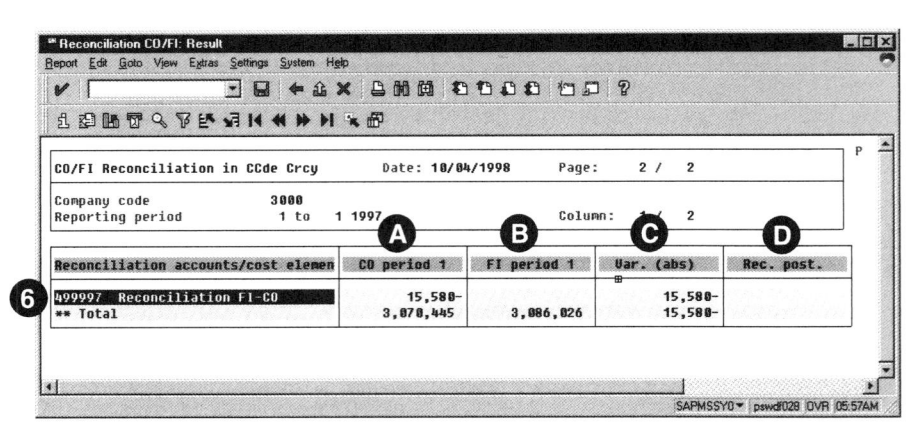

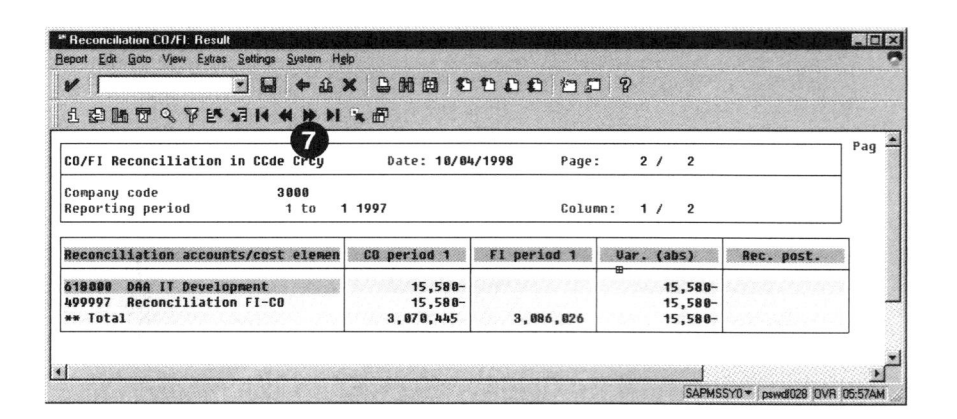

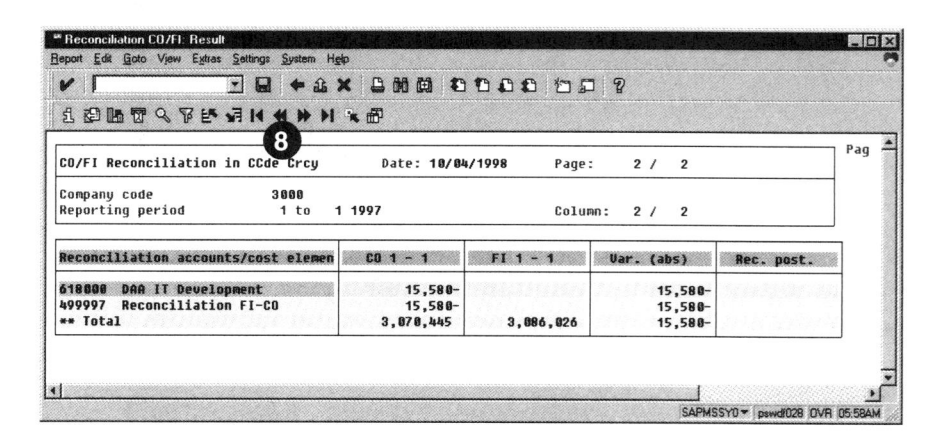

Reporting Made Easy

7–6

Section 7: Controlling—Reconciliation Reports

FI/CO Reconciliation in Company Code Currency

This screen shows the first block of data in the report.

9. Choose *Edit → Threshold value*.

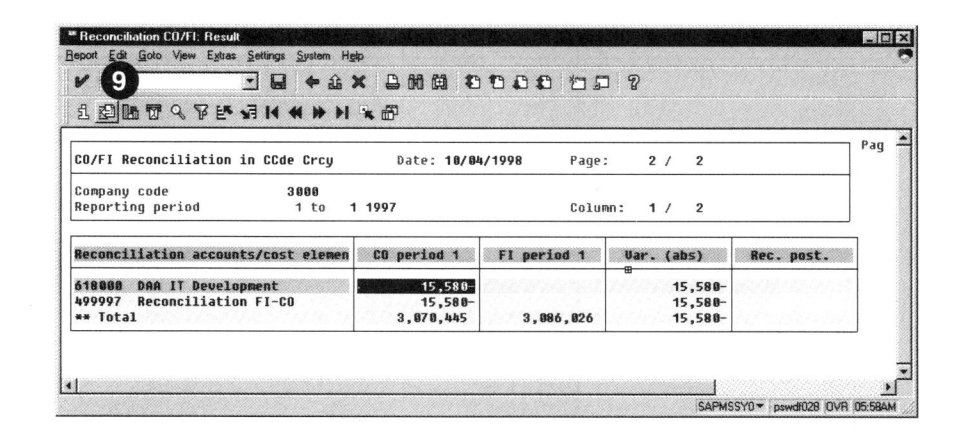

10. Make certain the threshold default *Active* is selected.

    This default specifies a row to appear only if the value in the variance column is greater than zero. If no row appears, there is no variance.

11. Choose *Display extras*.

12. Choose *Additional condition*.

Commonly Used Reports: Illustrations and Perspectives

7–7

Section 7: Controlling—Reconciliation Reports
FI/CO Reconciliation in Company Code Currency

13. Make certain the default *Ignore +/- sign* is selected.

    The *Condition* greater than (>) *Threshold value* (0) is determined from the absolute value of the column.

14. Make certain the default *Print selected rows only* is selected.

    This default specifies printing of only those rows which contain values (that is, which meet the threshold).

15. Make certain the additional default *Active* is selected.

    This default specifies a row not to print if the value of the CO column is zero.

16. Choose *Enter* to view the output.

17. Choose *Edit* → *Threshold value*. (not shown here)

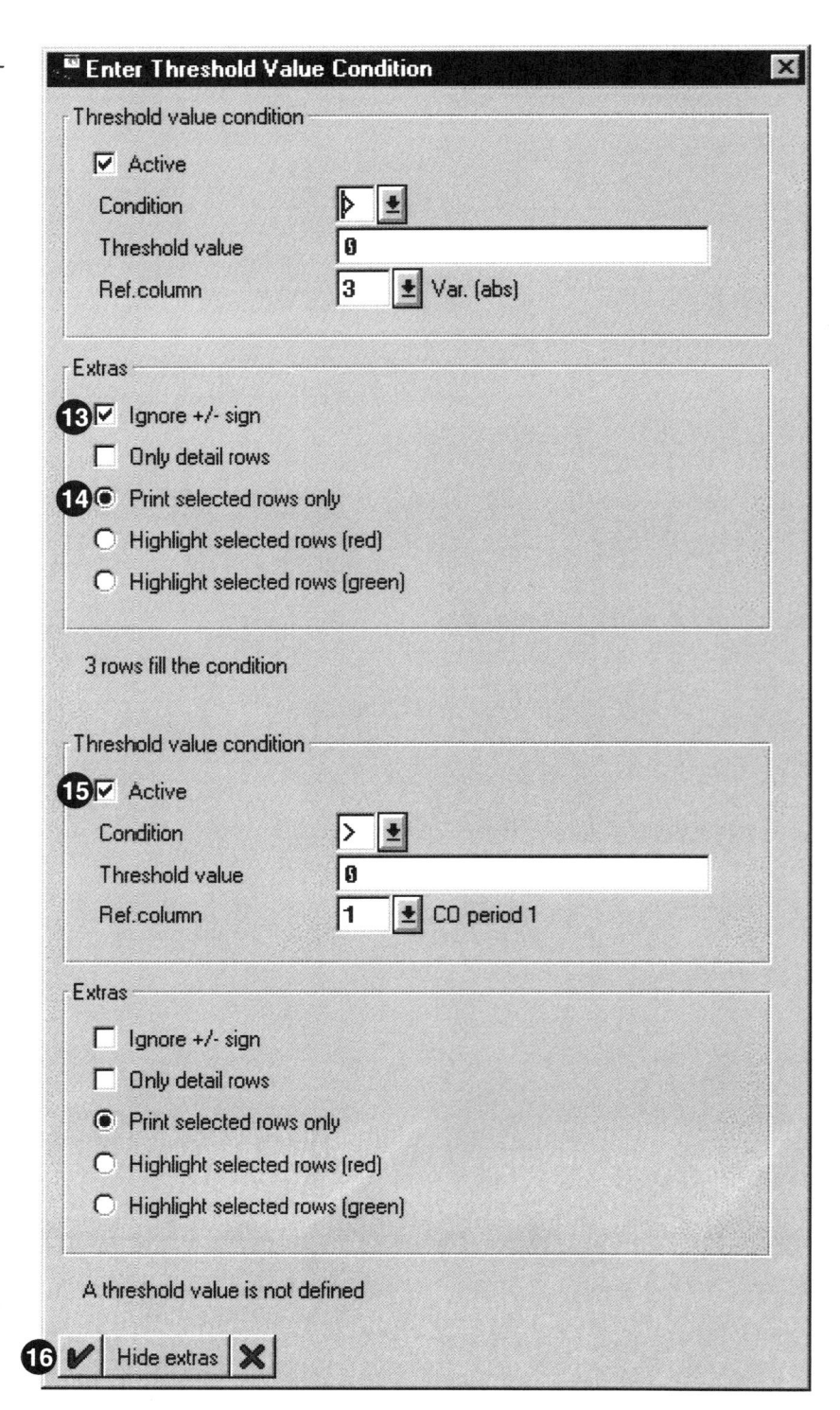

7–8

Reporting Made Easy

Section 7: Controlling—Reconciliation Reports
FI/CO Reconciliation in Company Code Currency

18. Under *Threshold value condition*, deselect *Active*.

    This selection references the variance column.

19. Further down the screen, under *Threshold value condition*, deselect *Active*.

    This selection references the CO value column.

20. Choose *Enter* to view the list.

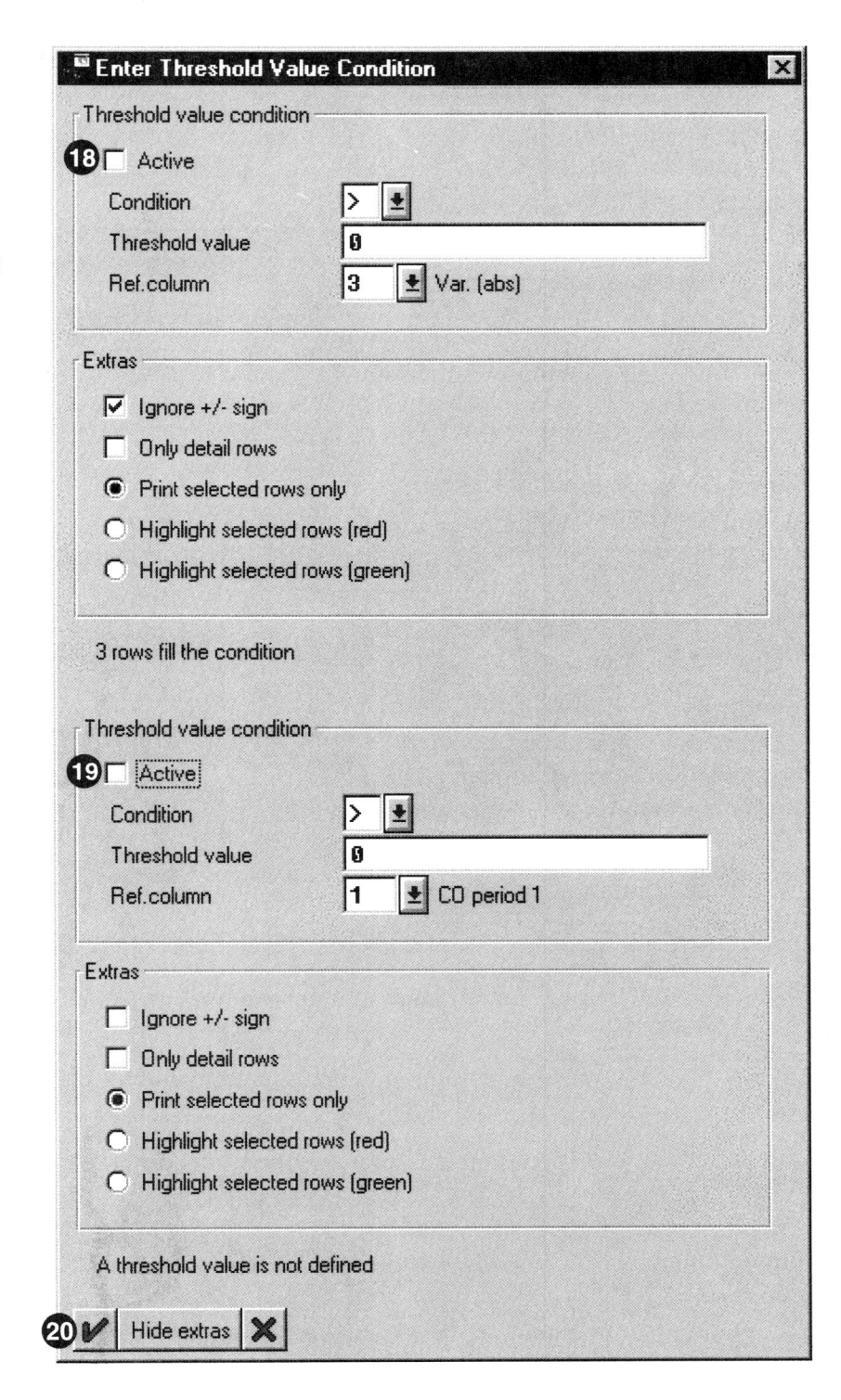

Section 7: Controlling—Reconciliation Reports
FI/CO Reconciliation in Company Code Currency

All values appear. Since there are no variances in the third column for the additional values, the CO and FI postings are in balance, and no reconciliation postings to FI need to be made.

21. Scroll down to display the report shown here.

22. Double-click on the only line with variances (for example, reconciliation account *499997*).

If reconcilation is required for primary accounts, the same account is used. This account is one of two used to capture reconciliation postings that are the result of secondary cost element postings.

The originating cost element detail of the reconciliation account appears. All of these cost elements are secondary cost elements.

23. Double-click on the line that requires a reconciliation posting (for example, *15,580-*).

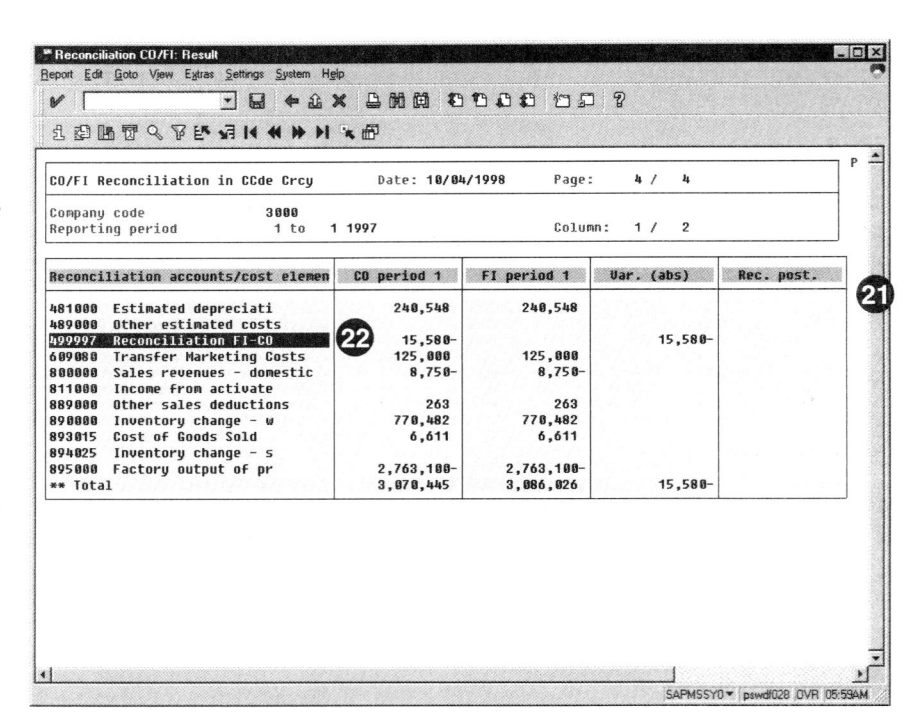

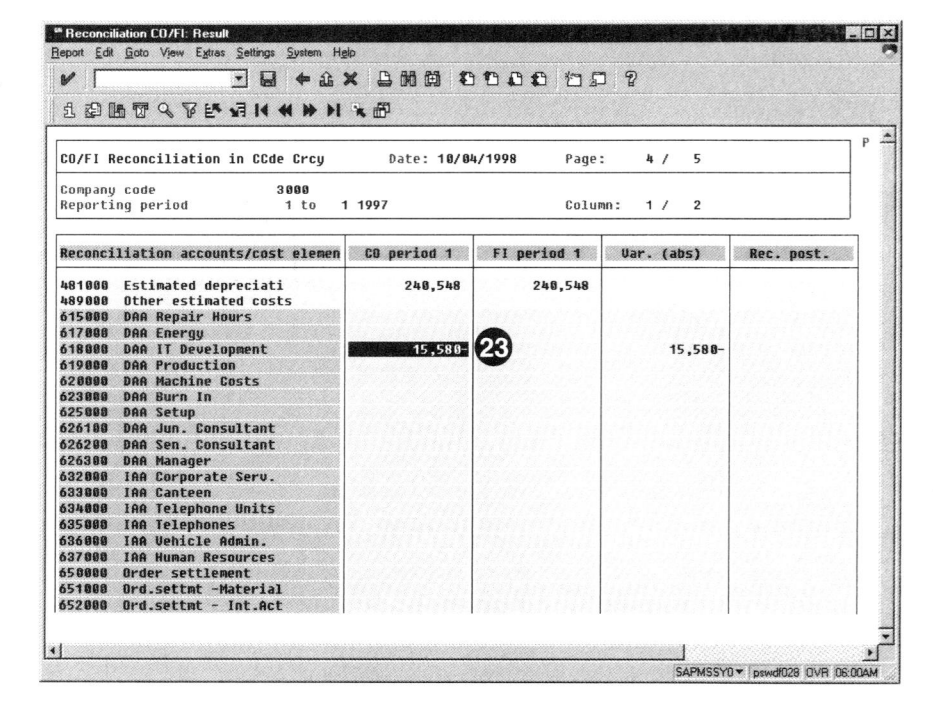

7–10

Reporting Made Easy

Section 7: Controlling—Reconciliation Reports

FI/CO Reconciliation in Company Code Currency

This screen shows a listing of line items from the reconciliation ledger using company code currency.

24. Choose *Choose display variant*.

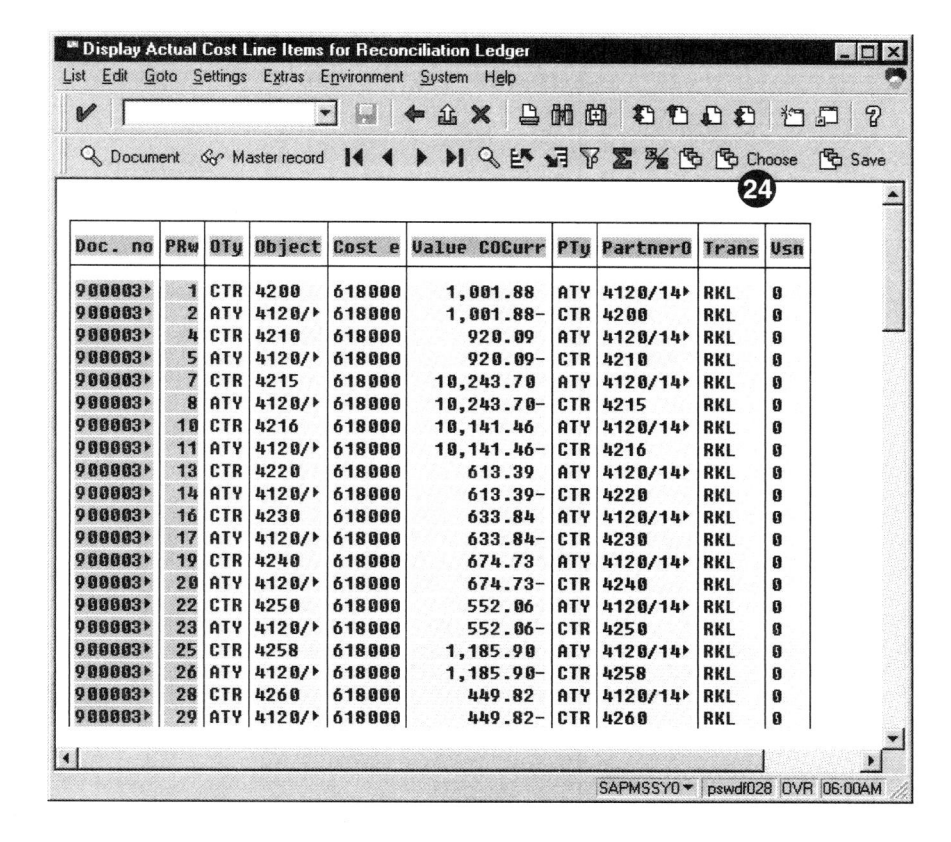

25. Double-click on the second variant, *2SAP*, to show the object currency. If the object is a cost center, cost center currency will be shown.

26. Choose *Copy*.

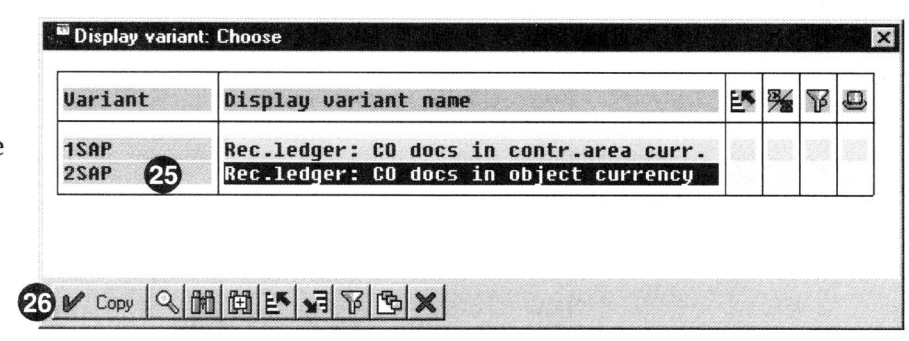

Commonly Used Reports: Illustrations and Perspectives

Section 7: Controlling—Reconciliation Reports
FI/CO Reconciliation in Company Code Currency

All line items appear with the object currency.

27. Double-click on the first line item.

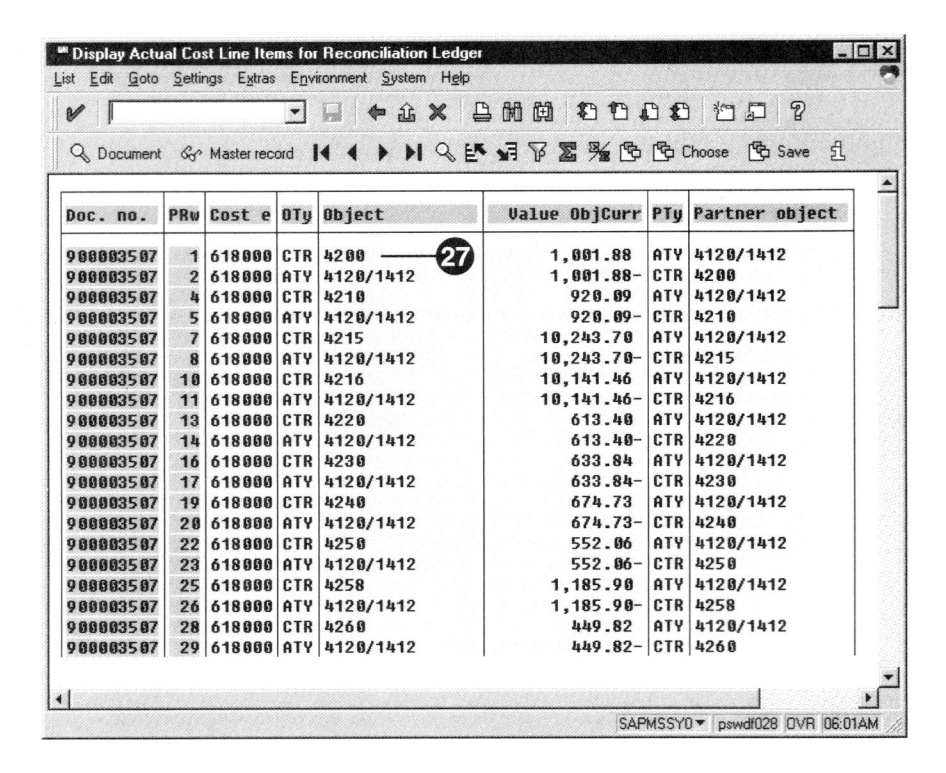

This screen shows the original document that caused the crossing of company code, business area, or functional area. In this example, it is an *Activity allocation* document.

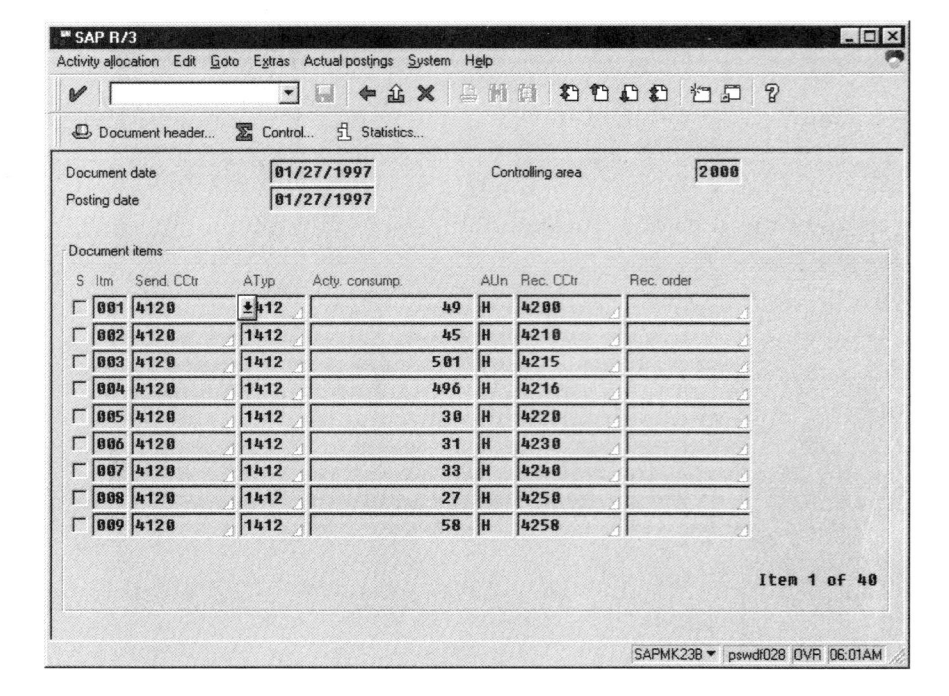

7–12

Reporting Made Easy

CO/FI Reconciliation in Group Currency

Quick Access   To run this report, use one of the following access options:

Option 1: Menu Path

Information systems → *Accounting* → *Overhead costs*

Cost elements → *Report selection*

From the reporting tree, choose the following report:

Reconciliation CO/FI → *In group currency* → *CO/FI reconciliation in group curr.*

Option 2: Program Name

Choose *System* → *Services* → *Reporting* and enter `J5AF2TQX` in the *Program* field. Then, choose *Execute* to run the report.

Purpose   This report provides an overview of the reconciliation postings necessary to ensure that FI and CO postings made across company codes, business areas, and functional areas within the selected company code have been recorded to the General Ledger (G/L), both on a period and a fiscal year-to-date basis. This report uses the group currency for the reconciliation, which in the example is the controlling area currency.

The accounting department uses this report to ensure that financial and controlling transactions reconcile for CO postings that occur across company codes, business areas, and functional areas. Since cross-company code postings affect financial statements, this report monitors the expected reconciliation postings based on CO data, and the reconciliation postings made to FI.

Prerequisites   You must enter a value in the selection fields before running this report.

You may leave the company code selection blank, and obtain a list that contains values for all company codes for which reconciliation postings have been made. If you choose to use a group of company codes, you must first create a set that contains them in order to access Report Painter/Report Writer reports.

Integration   You can run a context-sensitive actual line item report from this reconciliation ledger report. For example, when positioning the cursor on a cell, only the line items that make up the cell total will appear. The actual line items for a reconciliation ledger report can be executed for either one cell, or a range of cells.

Section 7: Controlling—Reconciliation Reports
CO/FI Reconciliation in Group Currency

Features

The selection screen of this report includes:

- Variants
- Dynamic selection options
- Executing and printing in background
- Sorting capability (by column): Select a column, then *Edit → Sort in ascndng ordr* (Ctrl+Shift+F5), or *Edit → Sort in descending order* (Ctrl+Shift+F6)
- Adjusting the column width: *Settings → Column widths* (Ctrl+F12)
- Adjusting the numeric display, to set the number of decimals displayed and the scaling to hundredths, thousandths, etc.: *Settings → Number format* (F5)
- Adjusting the summation level for the entire report (F6)
- Mailing of the report (Ctrl+F9)
- Graphing portions of the report using SAP business graphics (F7)
- Exporting the report to a local file (F8)
- Increasing or reducing the detail displayed, by double-clicking on subtotal lines. The double-click acts as a toggle switch. If detail is displayed, double-clicking on the subtotal will hide it; if detail is not displayed on a summary line (marked with one or more asterisks), double-clicking displays it.
- Displaying only threshold values, or values greater than or less than an entered criteria: *Edit → Threshold value* (Shift+F5).
- Creating an extract of reporting information (F5)
- Using variation to obtain multiple reports of company code sets and subsets (F6)
- Selecting an extract or an archive: *Data source* (Ctrl+F1)

Section 7: Controlling—Reconciliation Reports
CO/FI Reconciliation in Group Currency

Next Steps

The system displays four columns for all sections of the report, including:

- CO postings already made to the reconciliation ledger
- FI postings already made to the reconciliation ledger
- Variance between CO and FI postings
- Reconciliation values still to be posted

By double-clicking on any subtotals in the report, the amount of detail that makes up the subtotal can either be hidden or displayed. For example, double-clicking on a cost element summary line will hide the debit/credit detail. To display this detail again, double-click on this line again.

This report contains data obtained from postings to the reconciliation ledger. This is a fixed special ledger to which postings are made when CO transactions span company codes, business areas, and functional areas. As such, the data cannot be changed or manipulated from the report.

The report contains two different blocks of data, as shown below. By navigating around these blocks, different types of reconciliation ledger data can be viewed.

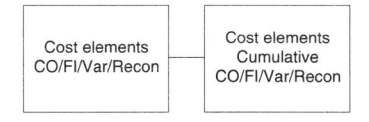

```
┌─────────────────┐   ┌─────────────────┐
│  Cost elements  │───│  Cost elements  │
│  CO/FI/Var/Recon│   │   Cumulative    │
│                 │   │  CO/FI/Var/Recon│
└─────────────────┘   └─────────────────┘
```

Section 7: Controlling—Reconciliation Reports
CO/FI Reconciliation in Group Currency

Guided Tour

Example: An accounting manager needs to ensure that all month-end postings have been made, and then needs to analyze the postings in the group (controlling area) currency.

To access the first screen for this report, choose

Information systems → *Accounting* → *Overhead costs* and then, *Cost elements* → *Report selection*.

From the reporting tree, choose the following report:

Reconciliation CO/FI → *In group currency* → *CO/FI reconciliation in group curr*.

1. Enter **1997** in *Fiscal year*. This report runs for one fiscal year at a time.

2. Enter **2000** in *Controlling area*. This controlling area uses the group currency that reflects in the reconciliation report.

3. Enter **001** in *Period*. The report will show reconciliation postings for the company code in the selected period.

   In addition, the report will show a cumulative value of reconciliation postings of period 1 through the selected period.

4. Enter **3000** to **4000** in *Or value(s)*. You may also enter a single company code, or a company code group.

5. Choose *Variation*.

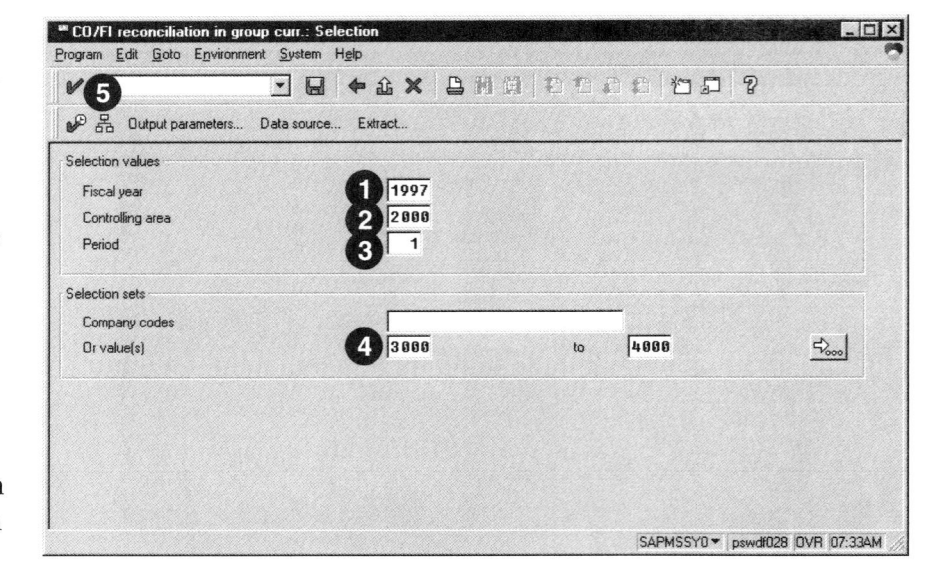

Section 7: Controlling—Reconciliation Reports
CO/FI Reconciliation in Group Currency

6. Make certain that the default *Explode* is selected. This results in data capture for hierarchy nodes, as well as for individual cost centers. Selecting the *SingleVal* option would only capture data for cost centers, with no totals for hierarchy nodes.

7. Choose *Enter*.

8. Choose *Execute*.

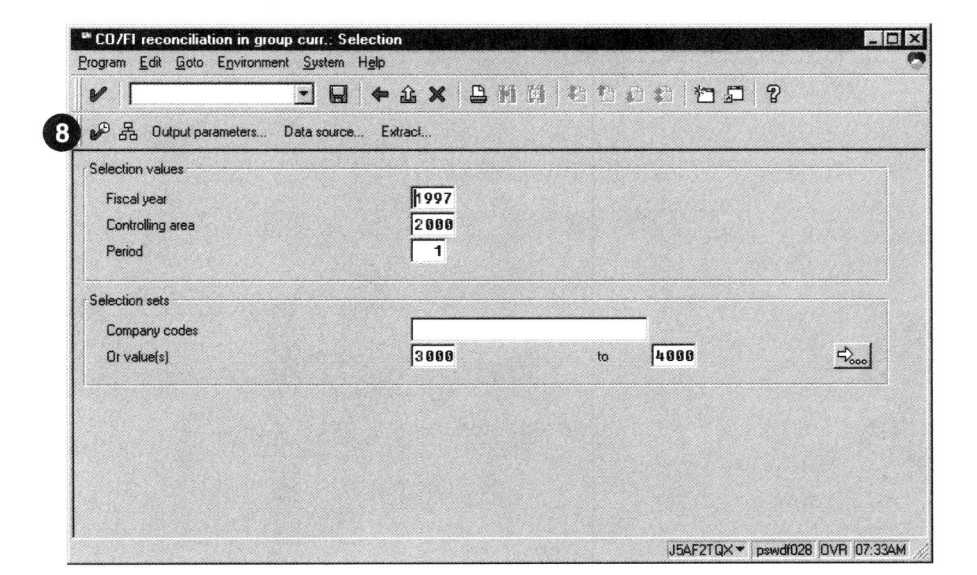

9. As the report runs, a threshold value determines the level of detail in the report output.

10. Choose *Enter*.

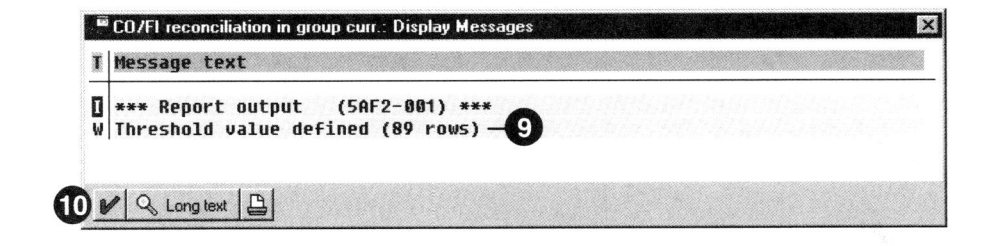

Commonly Used Reports: Illustrations and Perspectives

7–17

Section 7: Controlling—Reconciliation Reports
CO/FI Reconciliation in Group Currency

This screen shows the reconciliation accounts to which postings will be made from the reconciliation ledger. For primary cost elements, the system uses the same account. For secondary cost elements, the system determines the reconciliation account based on its configuration.

A CO postings to the reconciliation ledger

B FI postings to expense accounts

C Variance between the CO and FI postings

D Entries to the reconciliation ledger that have been made to FI (no values because the period-end process has not been executed)

11. Choose *Variation*.

12. Choose *Field values on/off* to list the company code and hierarchy node codes, in addition to their descriptions.

13. Double-click on the company code (for example, *3000*) to display only the values relevant to it.

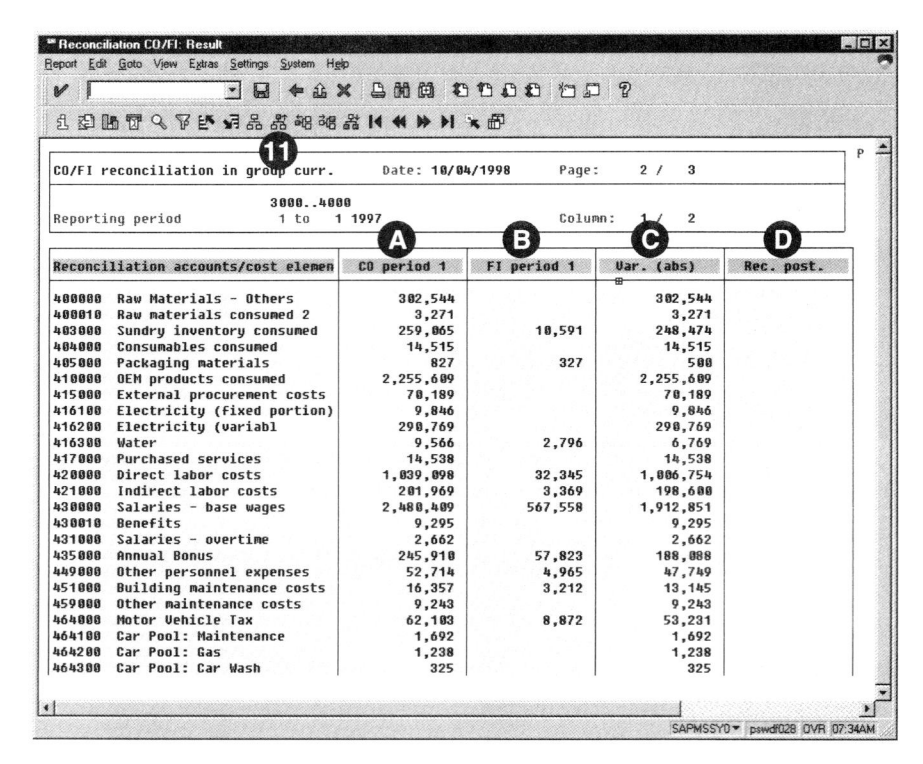

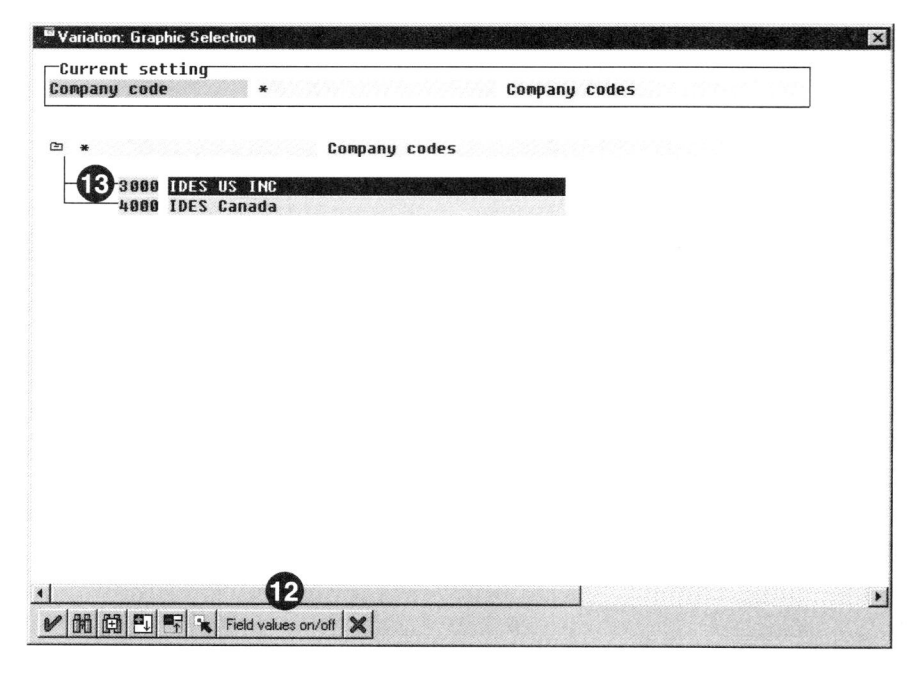

7–18   Reporting Made Easy

The values change to reflect only the chosen company code.

Additional variation icons are available to allow scrolling through the company code group, its nodes, and its company codes. These icons include:

- Scroll left
- Scroll right
- Previous level/up
- Next level/down

14. Choose *Page Down* to navigate to the remaining values in the reconciliation ledger.

15. Double-click on the line for the reconciliation account (for example, *499997*).

This G/L account is configured to be one of two reconciliation accounts for all secondary cost element postings to the reconciliation ledger.

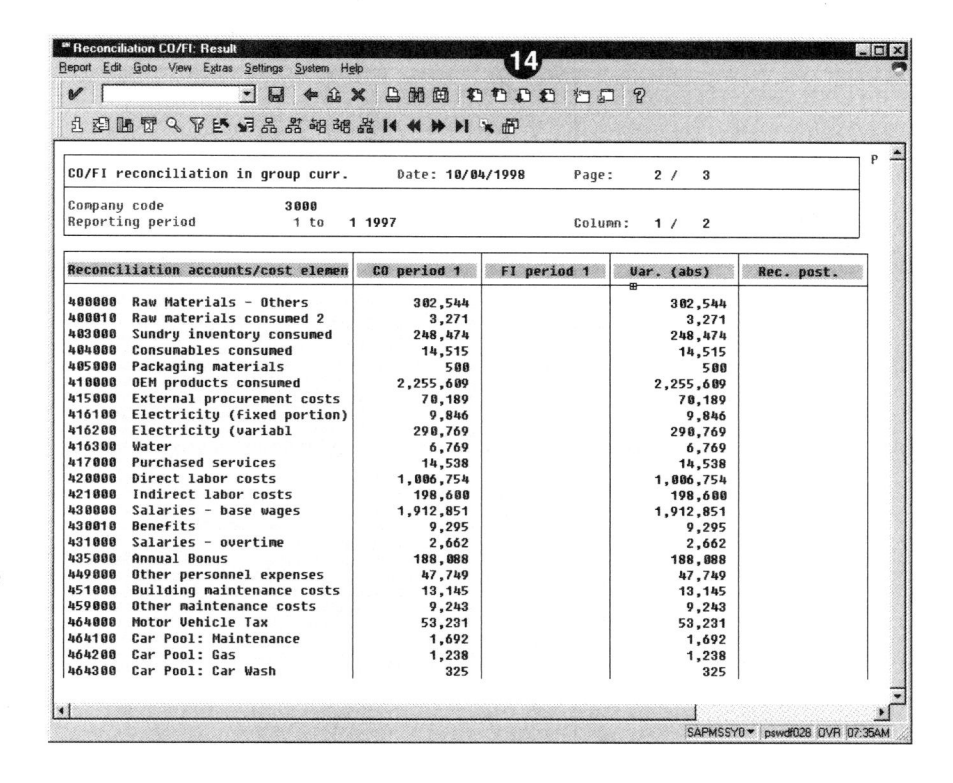

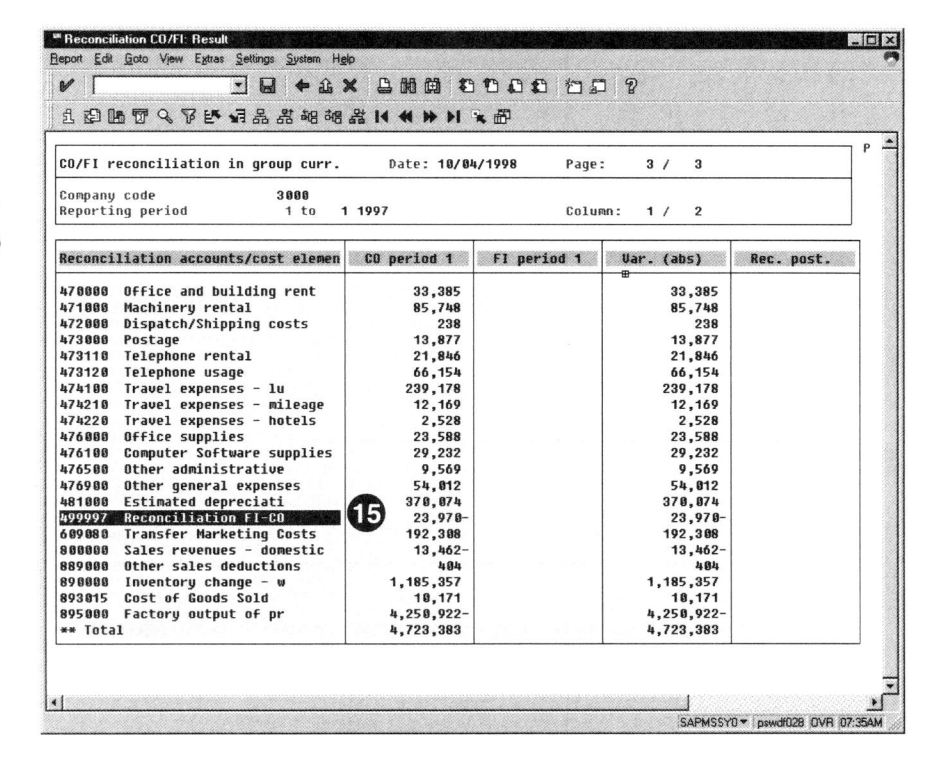

Section 7: Controlling—Reconciliation Reports
CO/FI Reconciliation in Group Currency

Notice that the field changes to show detail of the secondary cost elements as you position the cursor on the *CO period 1* line item.

16. Double-click on the line item (for example, *23,970-*).

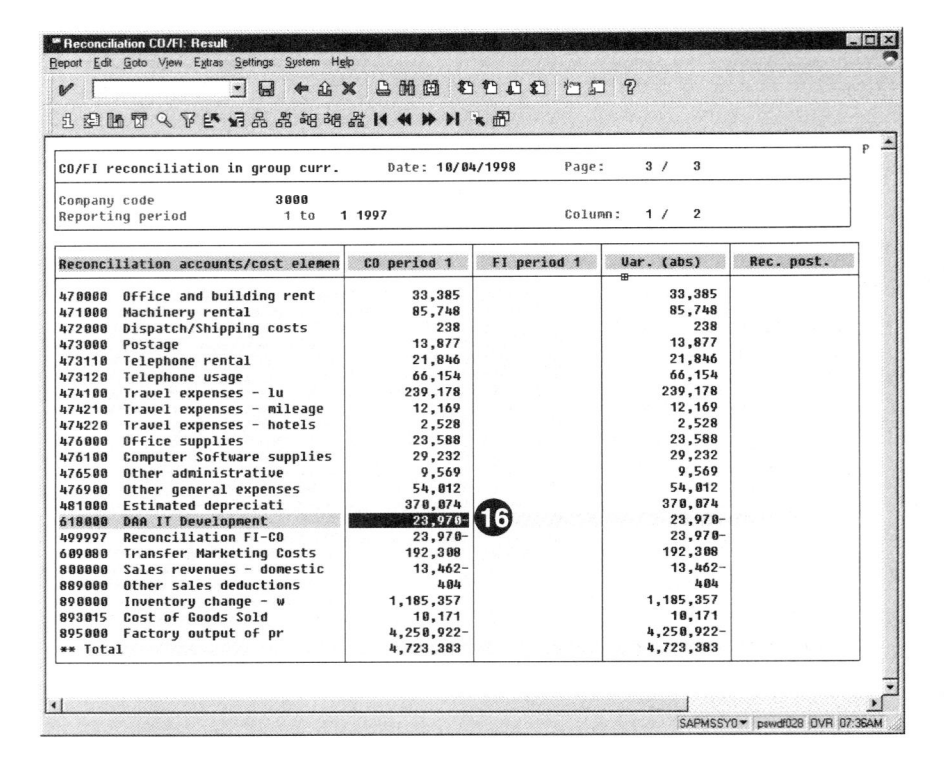

This screen lists the individual line items that comprise the total shown on the previous screen.

17. Choose *Current display variant*.

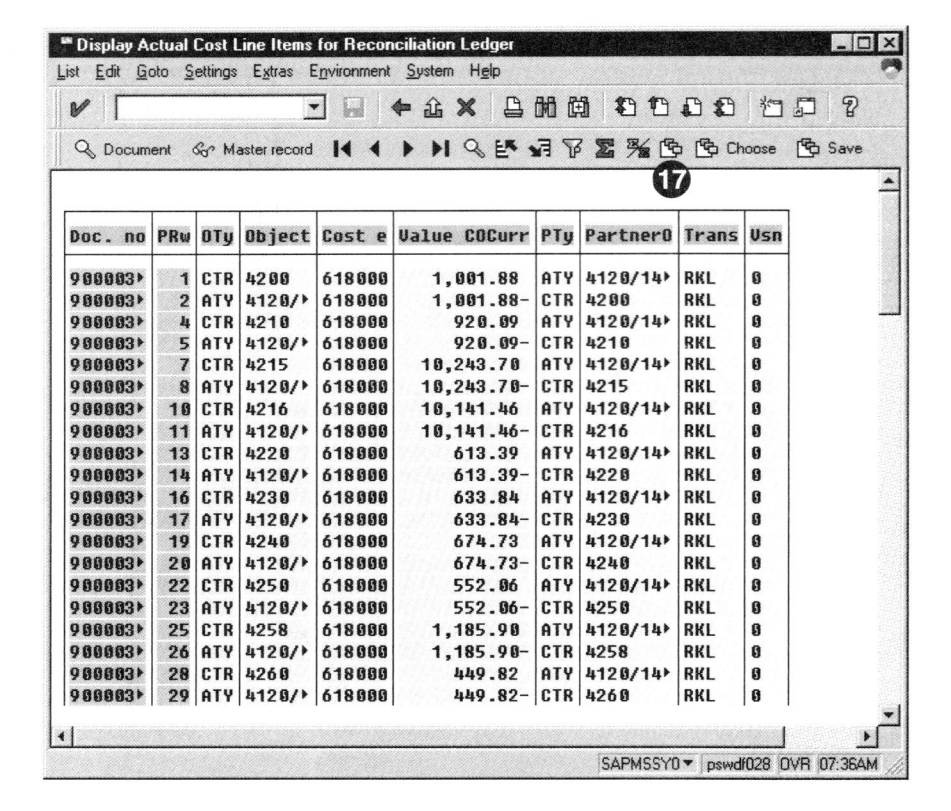

Reporting Made Easy

Section 7: Controlling—Reconciliation Reports
CO/FI Reconciliation in Group Currency

18. To delete fields from the display variant, you must first select them from the *Column content* area of this screen (for example, *Partner object type*, *Partner object*, and *Transaction*).

19. Choose *Hide selected fields* to remove the fields from the previous screen and this list.

   These fields will reappear in the *hidden fields* section of this screen.

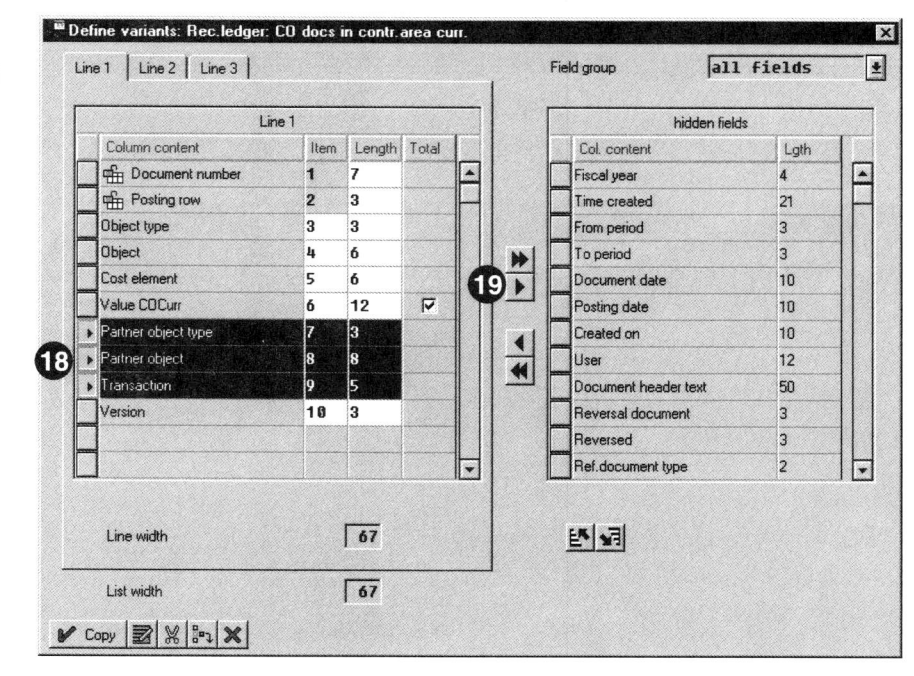

20. To add fields to the display variant, you must first select them on the *hidden fields* area of this screen (for example, *Company code* and *Partner compCde.*).

21. Select *Value COCurr*. This is a reference point. *Company code* and *Partner compCde.* will insert before this row.

   If no reference point is selected, the fields will insert at the end of the list.

22. Choose *Show selected fields* to add these fields to the display variant and to this list.

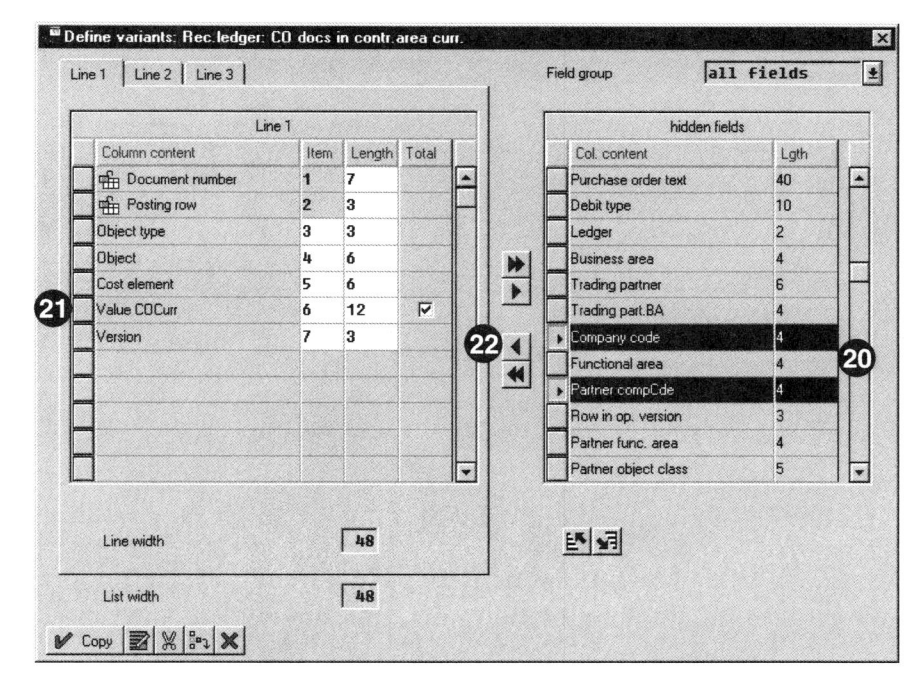

Commonly Used Reports: Illustrations and Perspectives

7–21

Section 7: Controlling—Reconciliation Reports

CO/FI Reconciliation in Group Currency

23. To add more fields to the display variant, as before, select them on the *hidden fields* area of this screen (for example, *Business area* and *Trading partBA.*).

    These were selected separately so that they would be sorted as desired.

24. Choose *Show selected fields* to add these fields to the display variant and to this list.

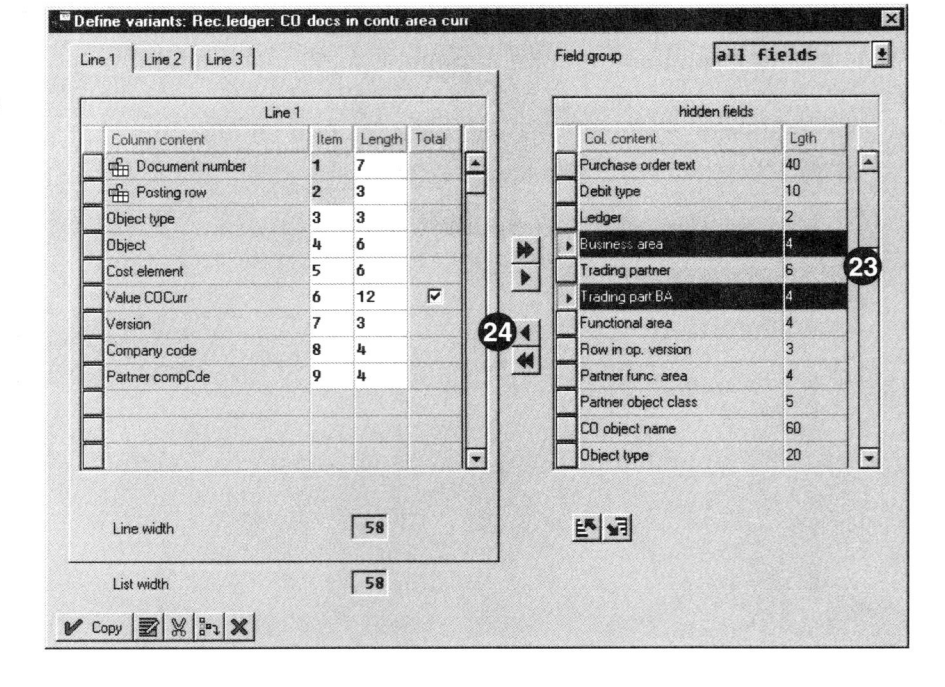

25. To add more fields to the display variant, as before, select them on the *hidden fields* area of this screen (for example, *Functional area* and *Partner func. area*).

    These were selected separately so that they would be sorted as desired.

26. Choose *Show selected fields* to add these fields to the display variant and to this list.

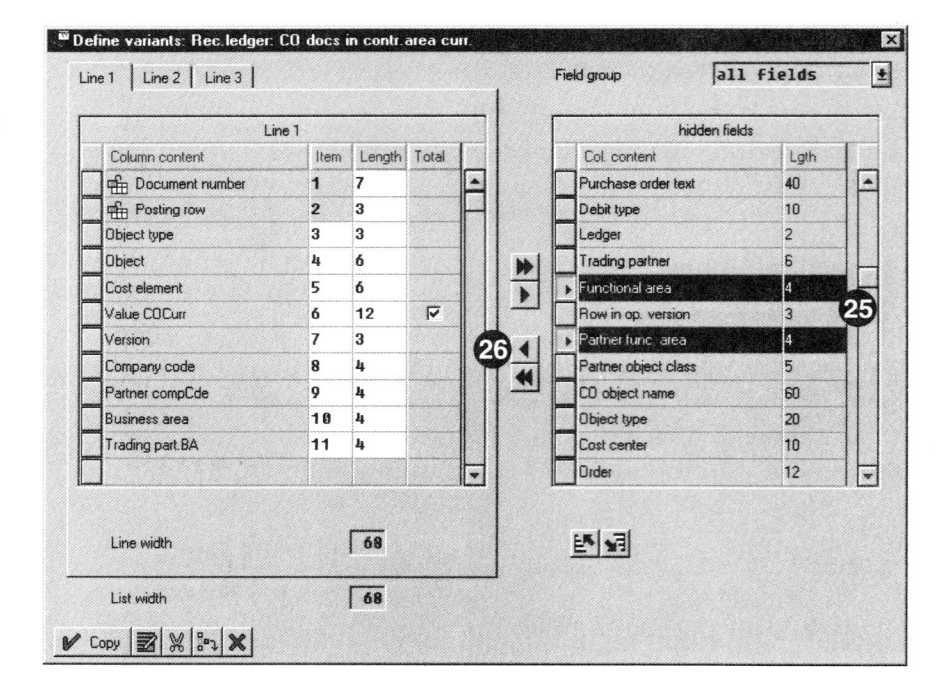

Section 7: Controlling—Reconciliation Reports

CO/FI Reconciliation in Group Currency

27. Choose *Copy* to accept the changes in the display variant.

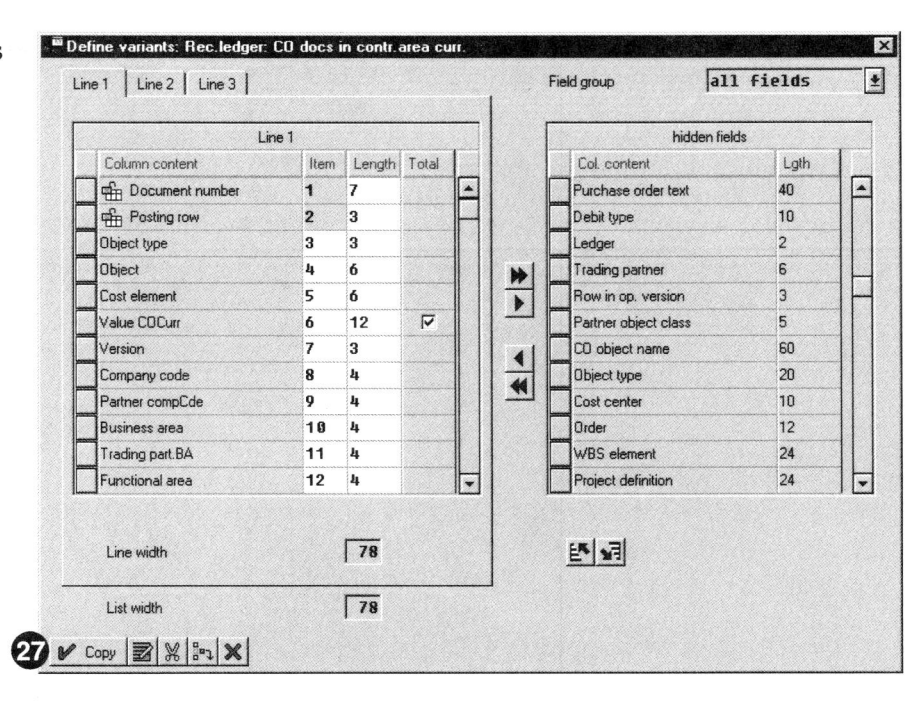

This screen shows the company code, partner company code, business area, partner business area, functional area, and partner functional area.

For postings to occur to the reconciliation ledger, at least one combination of the originating field and corresponding partner field must be different.

28. Choose *Page Down* to navigate to the next block of data.

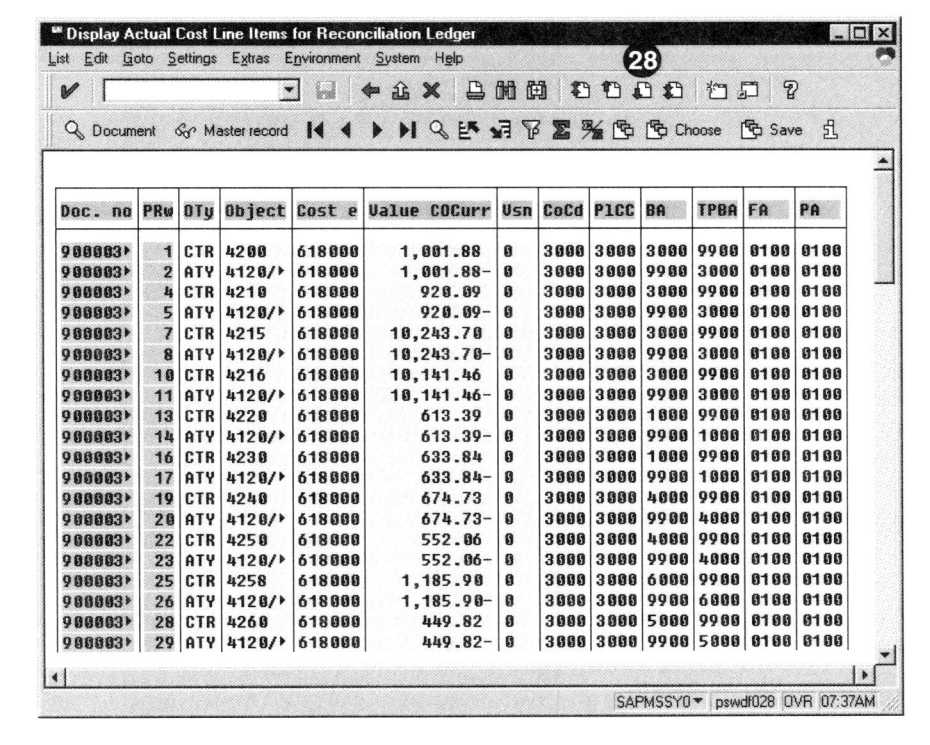

Commonly Used Reports: Illustrations and Perspectives

Section 7: Controlling—Reconciliation Reports
CO/FI Reconciliation in Group Currency

The remainder of the rows appear. Notice that a partner object can have a blank value.

29. Choose *Save display variant*.

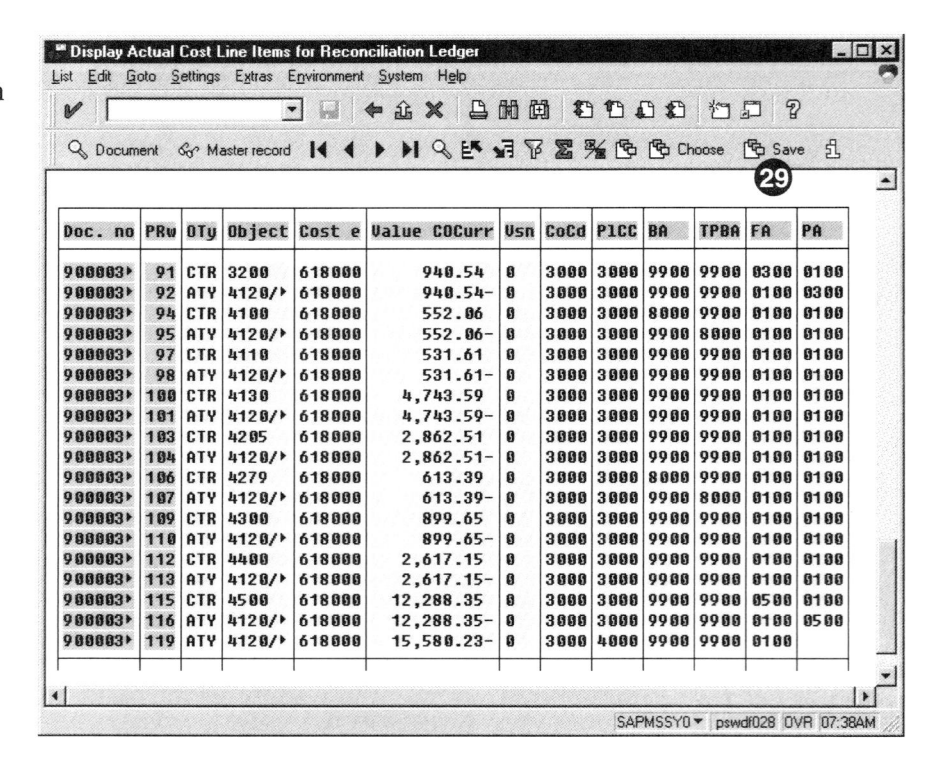

Doc. no	PRw	OTy	Object	Cost e	Value COCurr	Vsn	CoCd	PlCC	BA	TPBA	FA	PA
900003	91	CTR	3200	618000	940.54	0	3000	3000	9900	9900	0300	0100
900003	92	ATY	4120/	618000	940.54-	0	3000	3000	9900	9900	0100	0300
900003	94	CTR	4100	618000	552.06	0	3000	3000	8000	9900	0100	0100
900003	95	ATY	4120/	618000	552.06-	0	3000	3000	9900	8000	0100	0100
900003	97	CTR	4110	618000	531.61	0	3000	3000	9900	9900	0100	0100
900003	98	ATY	4120/	618000	531.61-	0	3000	3000	9900	9900	0100	0100
900003	100	CTR	4130	618000	4,743.59	0	3000	3000	9900	9900	0100	0100
900003	101	ATY	4120/	618000	4,743.59-	0	3000	3000	9900	9900	0100	0100
900003	103	CTR	4205	618000	2,862.51	0	3000	3000	9900	9900	0100	0100
900003	104	ATY	4120/	618000	2,862.51-	0	3000	3000	9900	9900	0100	0100
900003	106	CTR	4279	618000	613.39	0	3000	3000	8000	9900	0100	0100
900003	107	ATY	4120/	618000	613.39-	0	3000	3000	9900	8000	0100	0100
900003	109	CTR	4300	618000	899.65	0	3000	3000	9900	9900	0100	0100
900003	110	ATY	4120/	618000	899.65-	0	3000	3000	9900	9900	0100	0100
900003	112	CTR	4400	618000	2,617.15	0	3000	3000	9900	9900	0100	0100
900003	113	ATY	4120/	618000	2,617.15-	0	3000	3000	9900	9900	0100	0100
900003	115	CTR	4500	618000	12,288.35	0	3000	3000	9900	9900	0500	0100
900003	116	ATY	4120/	618000	12,288.35-	0	3000	3000	9900	9900	0100	0500
900003	119	ATY	4120/	618000	15,580.23-	0	3000	4000	9900	9900	0100	

Section 7: Controlling—Reconciliation Reports
CO/FI Reconciliation in Group Currency

You can save the modified display variant from this screen.

30. Enter a new display variant code and description (for example, `Z1SAP` and `Rec. ledger: CO docs w/Ccde, BA, FA`).

31. Select *User-specific* to save the original display variant with the updated field for your user ID.

32. Choose *Save*.

33. Choose *Back* to return to the main report.

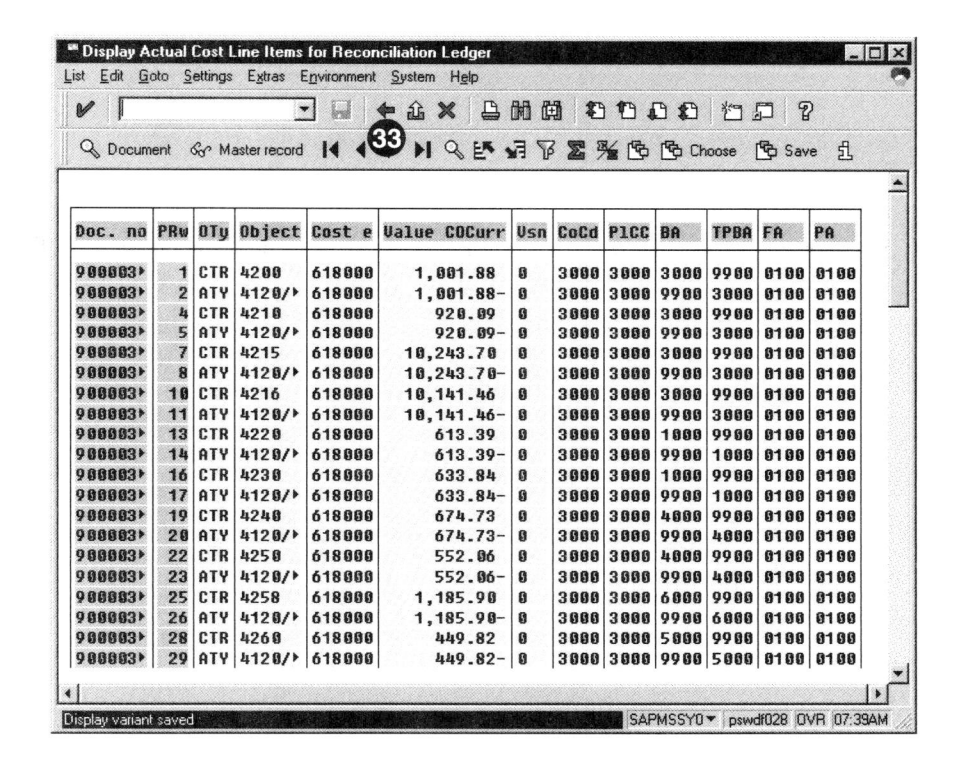

34. Choose *Yes*.

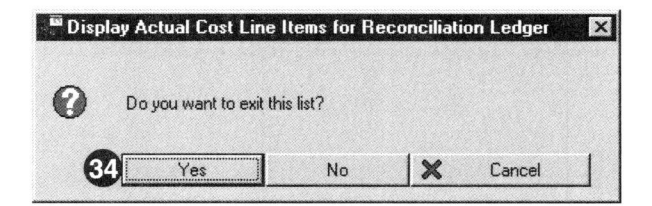

Commonly Used Reports: Illustrations and Perspectives

Section 7: Controlling—Reconciliation Reports
CO/FI Reconciliation in Group Currency

This screen shows the main report.

35. Choose *Next columns*.

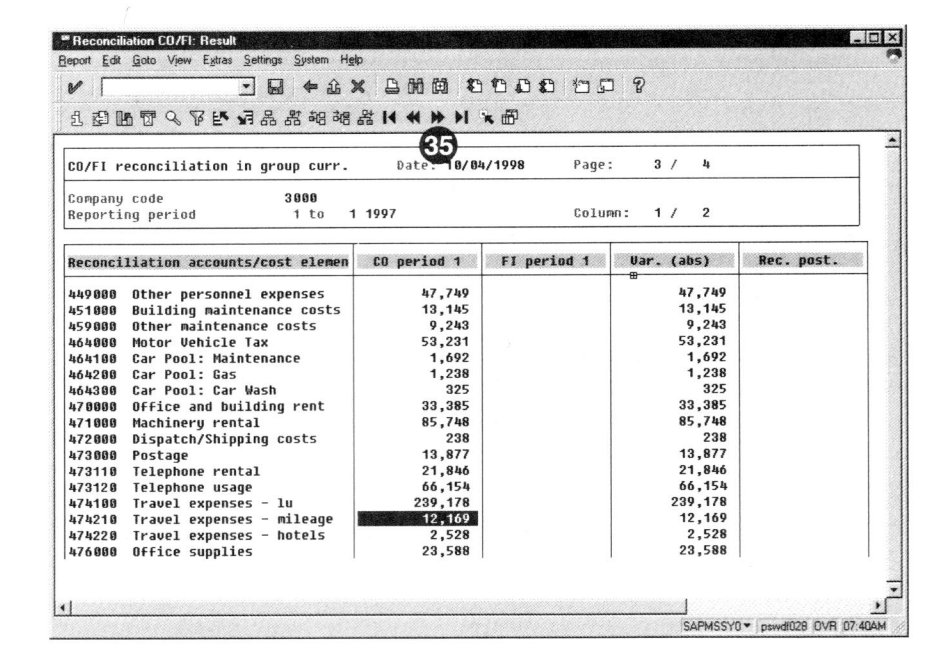

This screen shows a cumulative view of the same data. Since the selected period is also period 1, the values are the same.

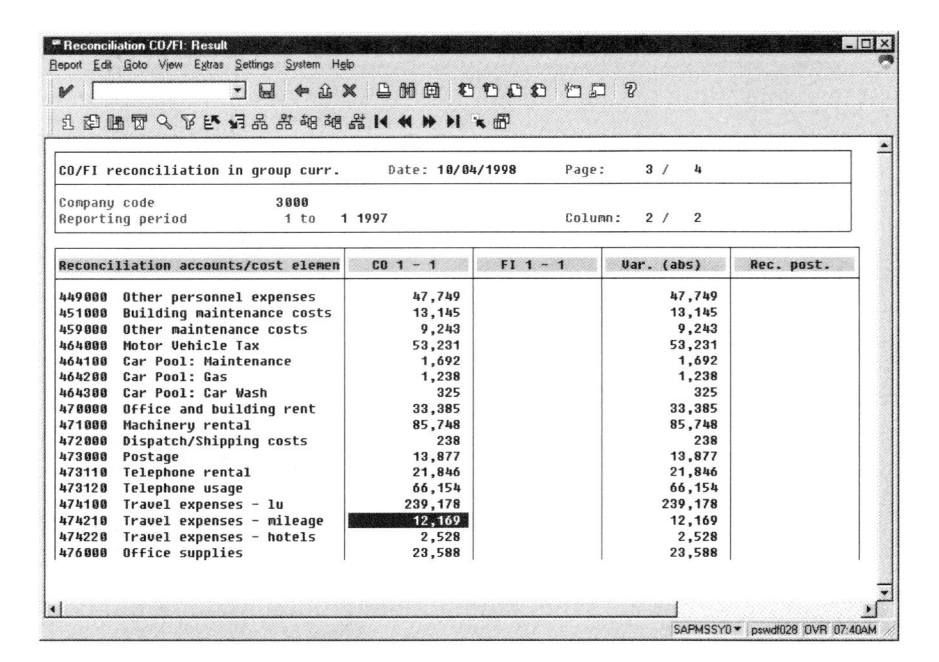

Cross-Company Code Reconciliation

Quick Access   To run this report, use one of the following access options:

Option 1: Menu Path

Information systems → Accounting → Overhead costs

Cost elements → Report selection

From the reporting tree, choose the following report:

Cost flow → Cross-company code → CElm: Company Code Allocations.

Option 2: Program Name

Choose *System → Services → Reporting* and enter `J5AB1TQX` in the *Program* field. Then, choose *Execute* to run the report.

Purpose   This report provides an overview of the reconciliation postings necessary to ensure that FI and CO postings made across company codes, business areas, and functional areas within the selected company code have been recorded to the General Ledger (G/L), both on a period and a fiscal year-to-date basis. This report is specifically coded to pick up only cross-company code postings, not cross-business area or cross-functional area postings.

The accounting department uses this report to ensure that financial and controlling transactions reconcile for CO postings that occur across company codes. Since cross-company code postings affect financial statements, this report monitors the expected reconciliation postings based on CO data, and the reconciliation postings made to FI.

Prerequisites   You must enter a value in the selection fields before running this report.

You may leave the company code selection blank, and obtain a list that contains values for all company codes for which reconciliation postings have been made. If you choose to use a group of company codes, you must first create a set that contains them in order to access Report Painter/Report Writer reports.

Integration   You can run a context-sensitive actual line item report from this reconciliation ledger report. For example, when positioning the cursor on a cell, only the line items that make up the cell total will appear. The actual line items for a reconciliation ledger report can be executed for either one cell, or a range of cells.

Cross-Company Code Reconciliation

Features

The selection screen of this report includes:
- Variants
- Dynamic selection options
- Executing and printing in background
- Sorting capability (by column): Select a column, then *Edit → Sort in ascndng ordr* (Ctrl+Shift+F5), or *Edit → Sort in descending order* (Ctrl+Shift+F6)
- Adjusting the column width: *Settings → Column widths* (Ctrl+F12)
- Adjusting the numeric display, to set the number of decimals displayed and the scaling to hundredths, thousandths, etc.: *Settings → Number format* (F5)
- Adjusting the summation level for the entire report (F6)
- Mailing of the report (Ctrl+F9)
- Graphing portions of the report using SAP business graphics (F7)
- Exporting the report to a local file (F8)
- Increasing or reducing the detail displayed, by double-clicking on subtotal lines. The double-click acts as a toggle switch. If detail is displayed, double-clicking on the subtotal will hide it; if detail is not displayed on a summary line (marked with one or more asterisks), double-clicking displays it.
- Displaying only threshold values, or values greater than or less than an entered criteria: *Edit → Threshold value* (Shift+F5).
- Creating an extract of reporting information (F5)
- Using variation to obtain multiple reports of company code sets and subsets (F6)
- Selecting an extract or an archive: *Data source* (Ctrl+F1)

Section 7: Controlling—Reconciliation Reports
Cross-Company Code Reconciliation

Next Steps

The system displays four columns for all sections of the report, including:

- CO postings already made to the reconciliation ledger
- FI postings already made to the reconciliation ledger
- Variance between CO and FI postings
- Reconciliation values still to be posted

By double-clicking on any subtotals in the report, the amount of detail that makes up the subtotal can either be hidden or displayed. For example, double-clicking on a cost element summary line will hide the debit/credit detail. To display this detail again, double-click on this line again.

This report contains data obtained from postings to the reconciliation ledger. This is a fixed special ledger to which postings are made when CO transactions span company codes, business areas, and functional areas. As such, the data cannot be changed or manipulated from the report.

The report contains two different blocks of data, as shown below. By navigating around these blocks, different types of reconciliation ledger data can be viewed.

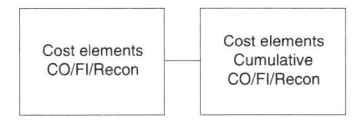

```
┌──────────────┐   ┌──────────────┐
│ Cost elements│───│ Cost elements│
│  CO/FI/Recon │   │  Cumulative  │
│              │   │  CO/FI/Recon │
└──────────────┘   └──────────────┘
```

Section 7: Controlling—Reconciliation Reports
Cross-Company Code Reconciliation

Guided Tour

Example: An accounting manager needs to ensure that all month-end postings across company codes have been made, and then needs to analyze the postings.

To access the first screen for this report, choose

Information systems → *Accounting* → *Overhead costs* and then, *Cost elements* → *Report selection*.

From the reporting tree, choose the following report:

Cost flow → *Cross-company code* → *CElm: Company Code Allocations*.

1. Enter **1997** in *Fiscal year*. This report runs for only one fiscal year at a time.

2. Enter **002** in *Period*. The report will show the reconciliation postings for the company code for the selected period.

   In addition, the report will show a cumulative value of period 1 through the selected period.

3. Enter **3000** in *Or value(s)*. You can also enter a range of company codes, or a company code group.

4. Choose *Execute*.

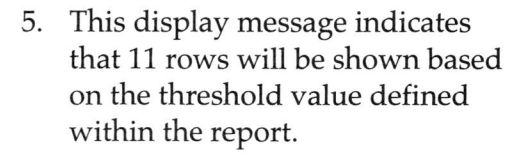

5. This display message indicates that 11 rows will be shown based on the threshold value defined within the report.

   Additional data may exist, but it will not be shown.

6. Choose *Enter*.

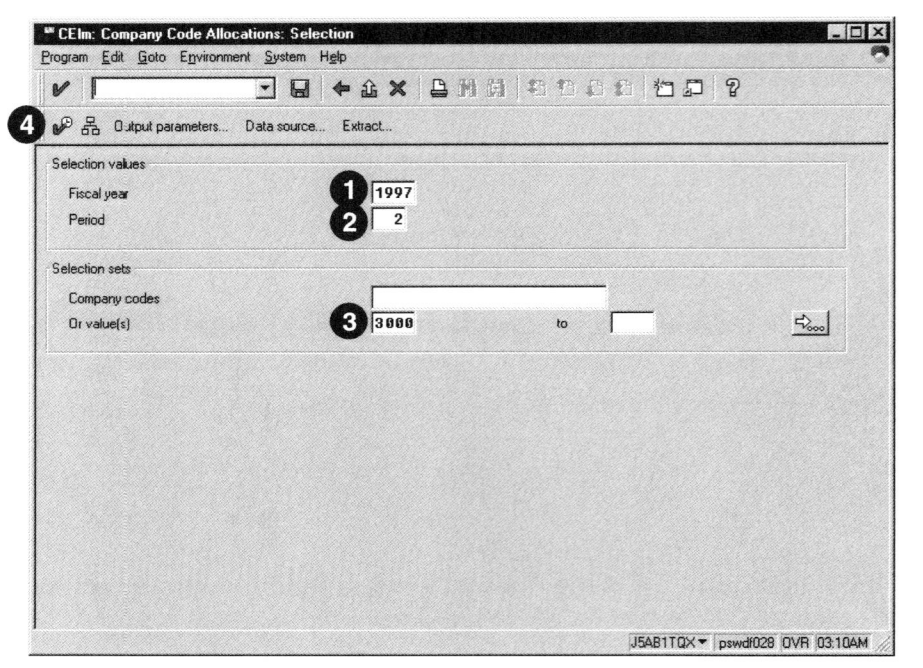

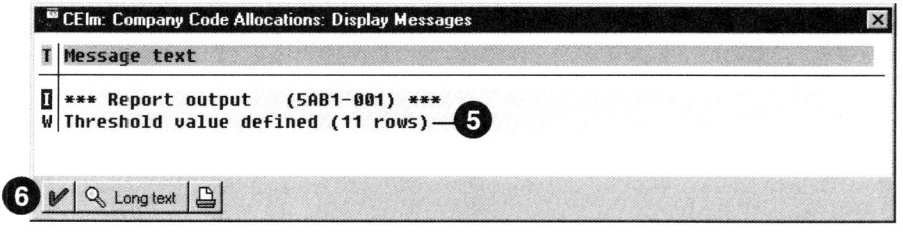

Section 7: Controlling—Reconciliation Reports

Cross-Company Code Reconciliation

These rows show the cost elements and the debit/credit indicators of all postings to the reconciliation ledger.

A The *CO period 2* column contains all CO postings made to the reconciliation ledger in period *002*, in which allocations were made into and out of company code *3000*.

B The *Reconciliation* column contains all postings to the reconciliation ledger made from FI.

C The *Reconcil.* column calculates the difference between the two columns. Non-zero values indicate values to be posted.

7. Choose *Edit → Threshold value*.

Section 7: Controlling—Reconciliation Reports
Cross-Company Code Reconciliation

8. Make certain the threshold default *Active* is selected.

   This default specifies a row to appear only if the value in the variance column is greater than zero. If no row appears, there is no variance.

   The lines that are suppressed are those in which there is no outstanding reconciliation posting to be made (a value of 0 in the *Reconcil.* column).

9. Choose *Display extras*.

10. Choose *Additional condition*.

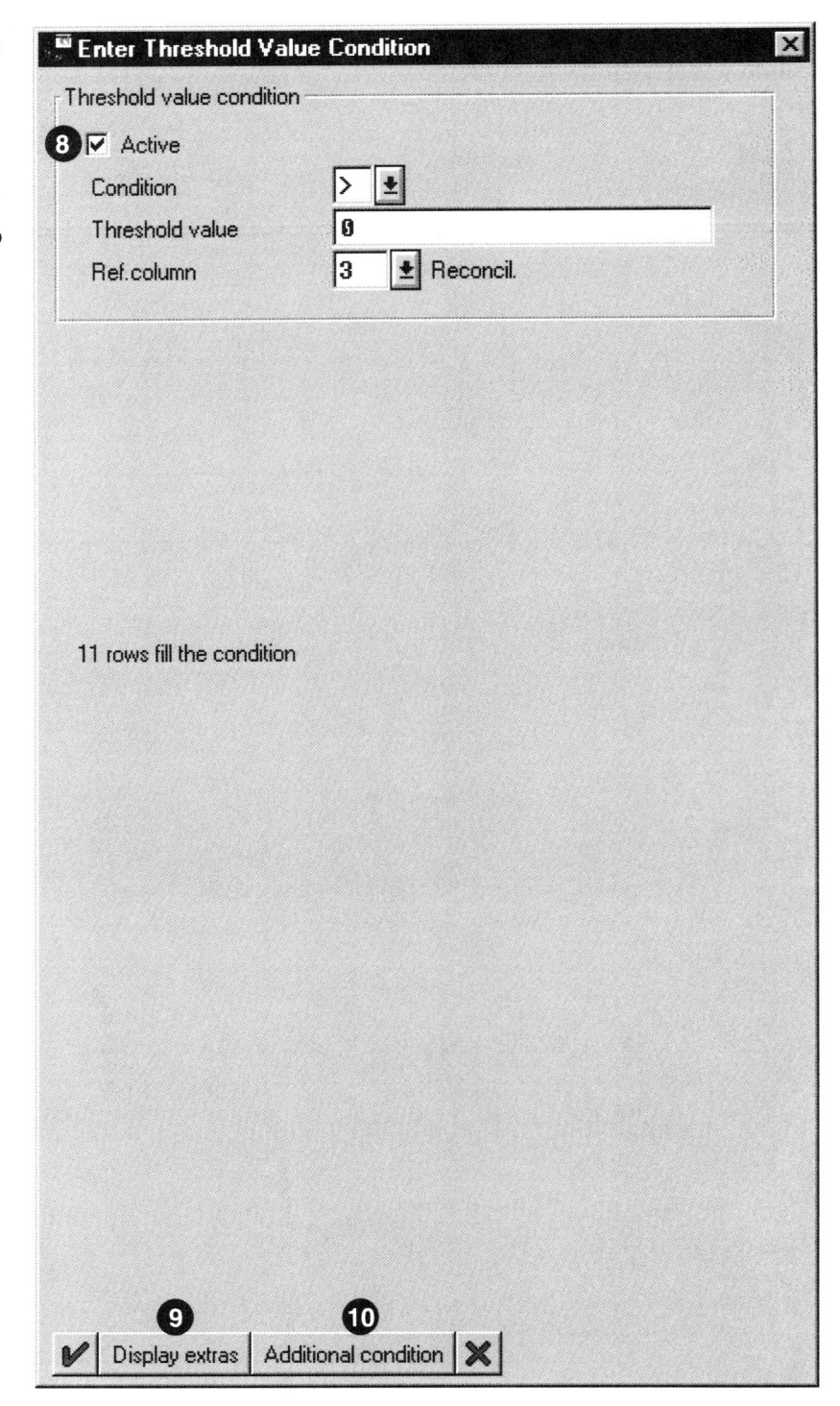

7–32

Reporting Made Easy

Section 7: Controlling—Reconciliation Reports
Cross-Company Code Reconciliation

11. Make certain the default *Ignore +/- sign* is selected.

    The *Condition* greater than (>) *Threshold value 0* is determined from the absolute value of the column.

12. Make certain the default *Print selected rows only* is selected.

    This default specifies printing of only those rows which contain values (that is, which meet the threshold).

13. Make certain the additional default *Active* is selected.

    This default specifies a row not to print if *Threshold value* is zero.

14. Choose *Enter*.

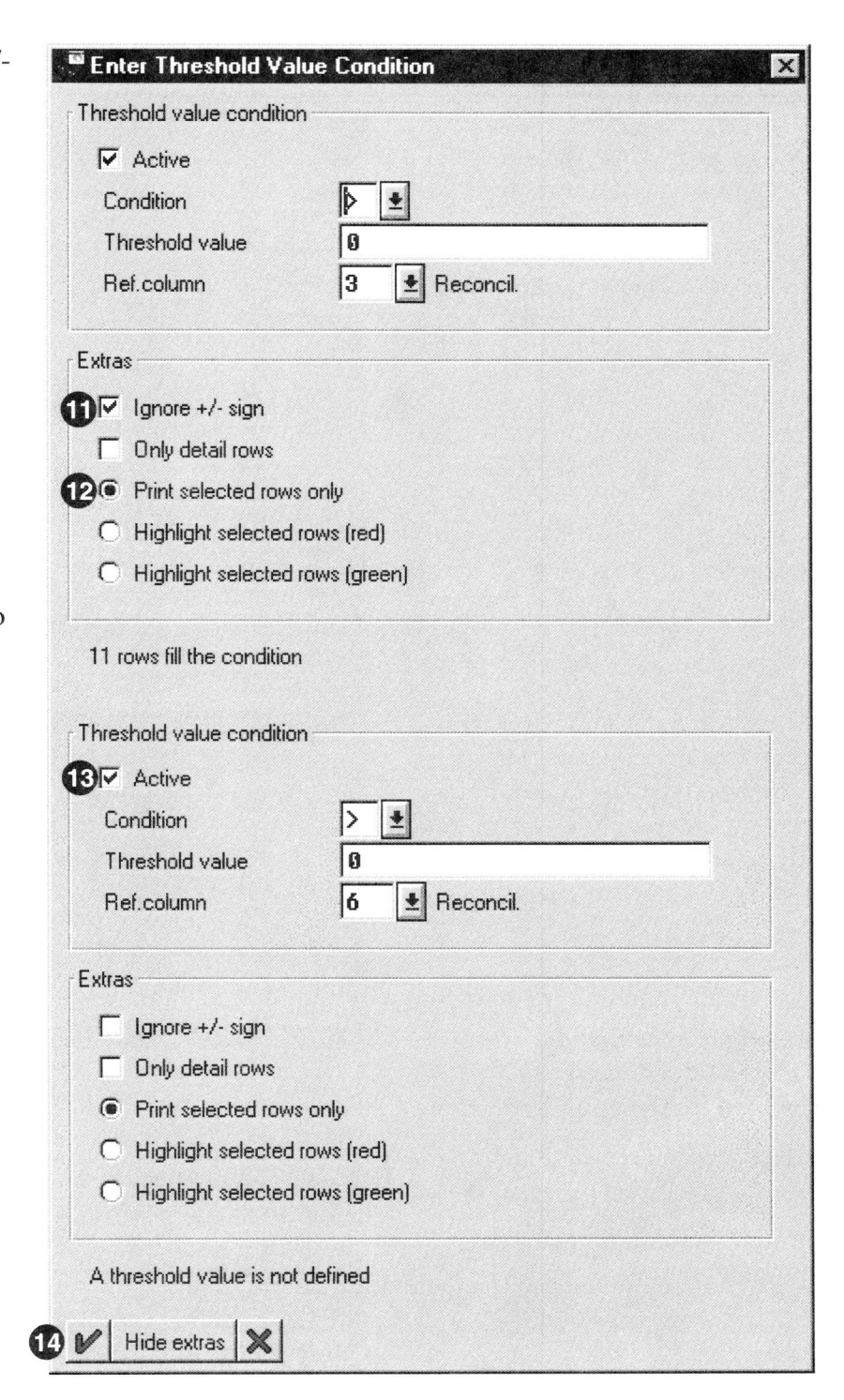

Commonly Used Reports: Illustrations and Perspectives

7–33

Section 7: Controlling—Reconciliation Reports
Cross-Company Code Reconciliation

15. Choose *View* → *Summarization level*.

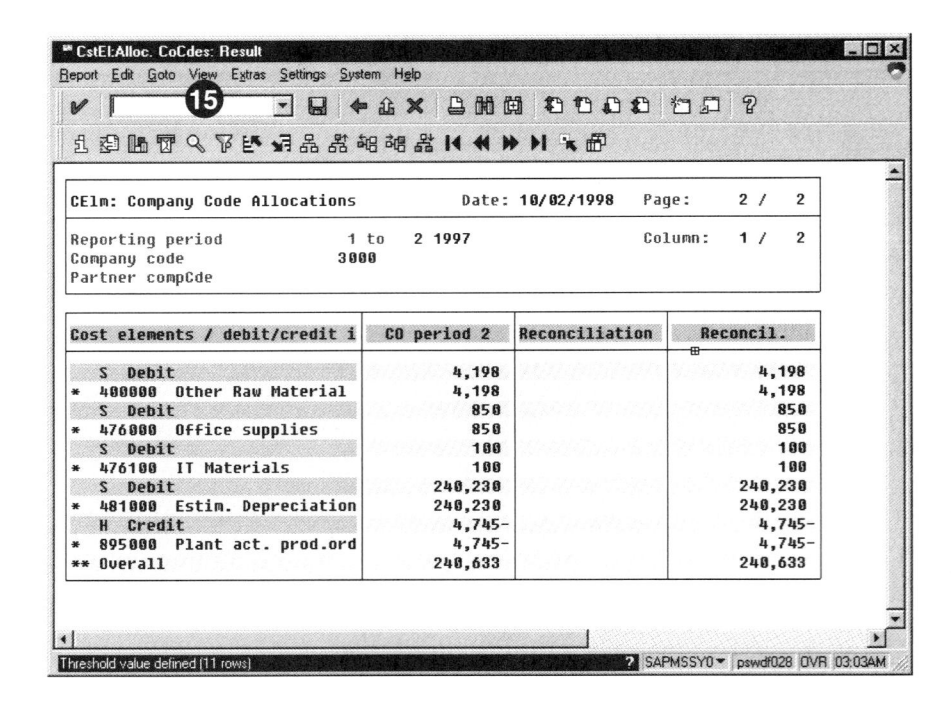

16. Enter *1* in *From level*. Up to this point, all detail (level 0) is scheduled for display in the report. Entering level 1 suppresses all detail less than the summary level marked with one asterisk (*).

17. Choose *Enter*.

This screen shows that the debit/credit detail has been suppressed for the entire report.

18. Choose *Next columns*.

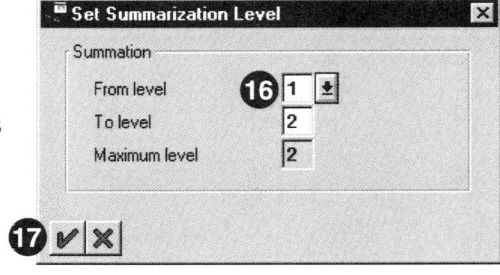

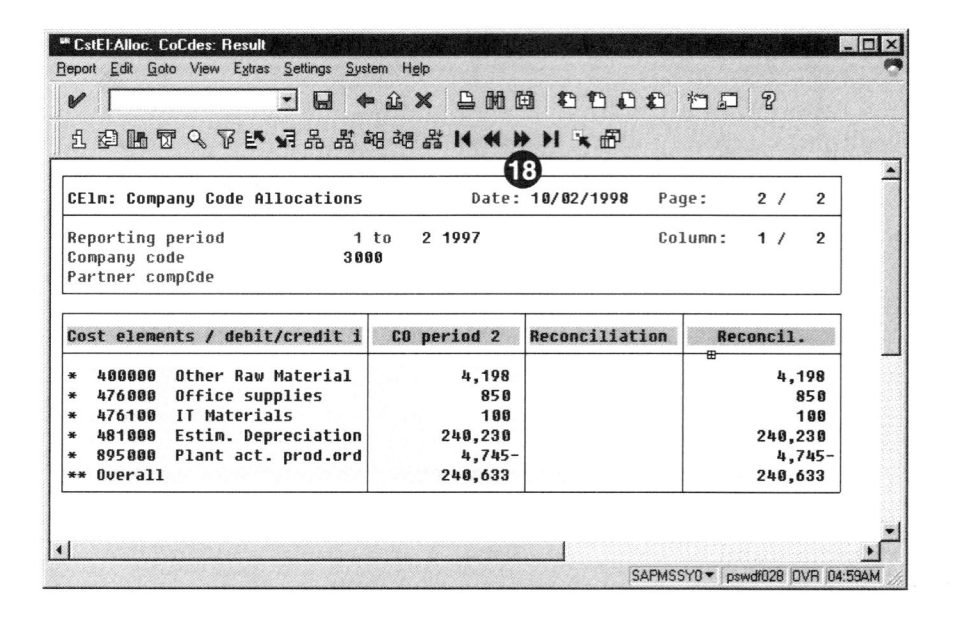

7–34

Reporting Made Easy

Section 7: Controlling—Reconciliation Reports

Cross-Company Code Reconciliation

This set of columns shows the cumulative reconciliation value within the fiscal year, from period 1 to the selected period, period 2.

19. Double-click on the line item (for example, *200,852*).

Cost elements / debit/credit i	CO 1 - 2	Reconciliation	Reconcil.
* 400000 Other Raw Material	200,852	⑲	200,852
* 476000 Office supplies	16,182		16,182
* 476100 IT Materials	19,101		19,101
* 481000 Estim. Depreciation	480,778		480,778
* 895000 Plant act. prod.ord	2,767,845-		2,767,845-
** Overall	3,326,659		3,326,659

CElm: Company Code Allocations Date: 10/02/1998 Page: 2 / 2
Reporting period 1 to 2 1997 Column: 2 / 2
Company code 3000
Partner compCde

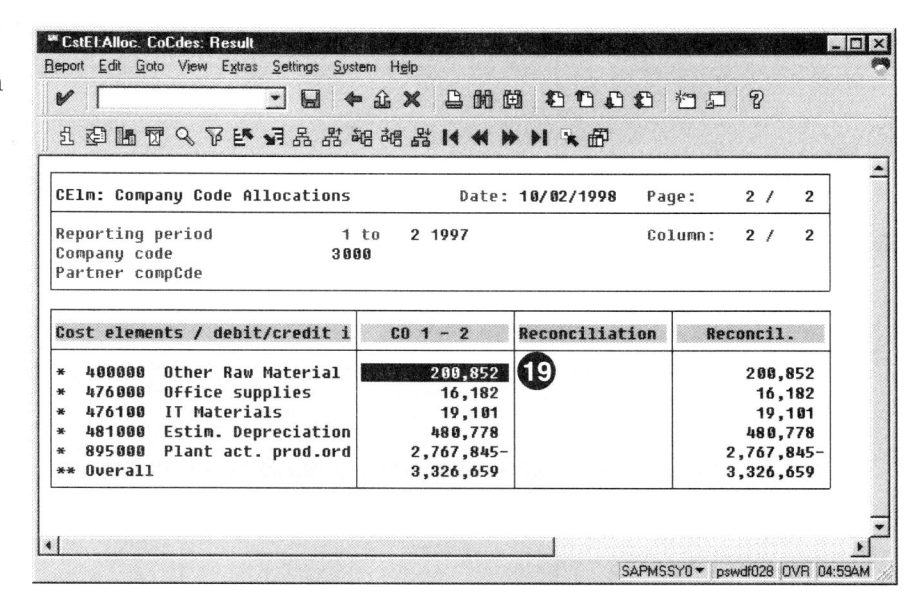

The debit/credit detail appears for the selected cell.

20. Double-click on the line item (for example, *200,852*).

Cost elements / debit/credit i	CO 1 - 2	Reconciliation	Reconcil.
S Debit	200,852	⑳	200,852
* 400000 Other Raw Material	200,852		200,852
* 476000 Office supplies	16,182		16,182
* 476100 IT Materials	19,101		19,101
* 481000 Estim. Depreciation	480,778		480,778
* 895000 Plant act. prod.ord	2,767,845-		2,767,845-

CElm: Company Code Allocations Date: 10/02/1998 Page: 2 / 3
Reporting period 1 to 2 1997 Column: 2 / 2
Company code 3000
Partner compCde

Commonly Used Reports: Illustrations and Perspectives

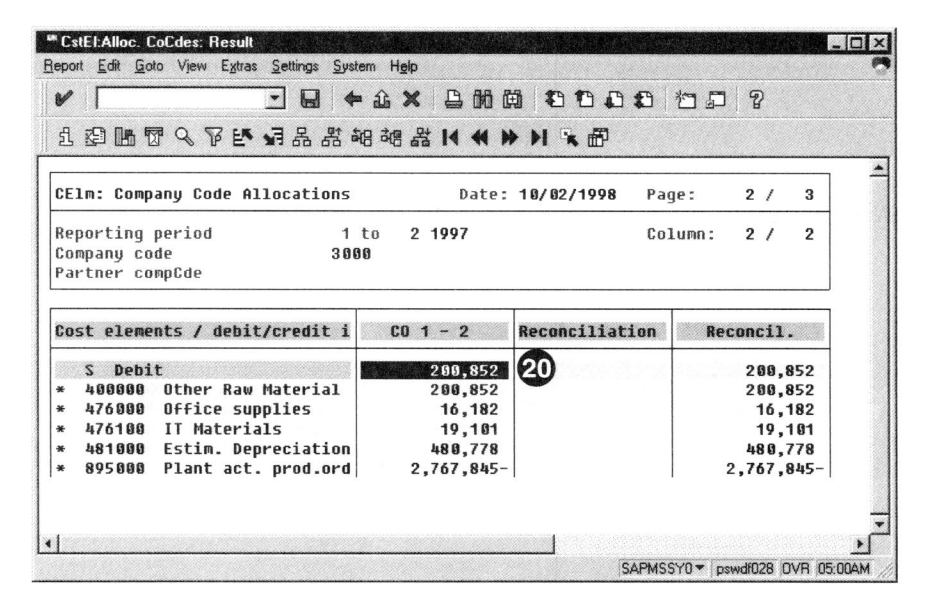

Section 7: Controlling—Reconciliation Reports
Cross-Company Code Reconciliation

The line item detail from the reconciliation ledger appears.

21. Double-click on the first line to view the original document that created the reconciliation posting.

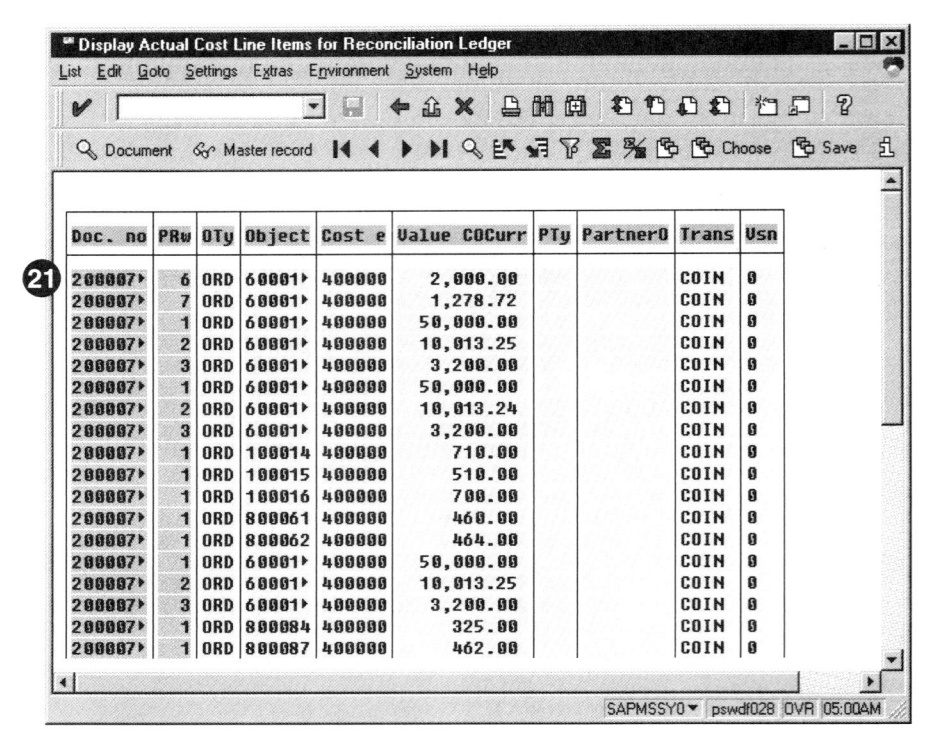

This screen shows the original document that caused the crossing of company code, business area, or functional area. In this example, the partner company code is due to a material issue.

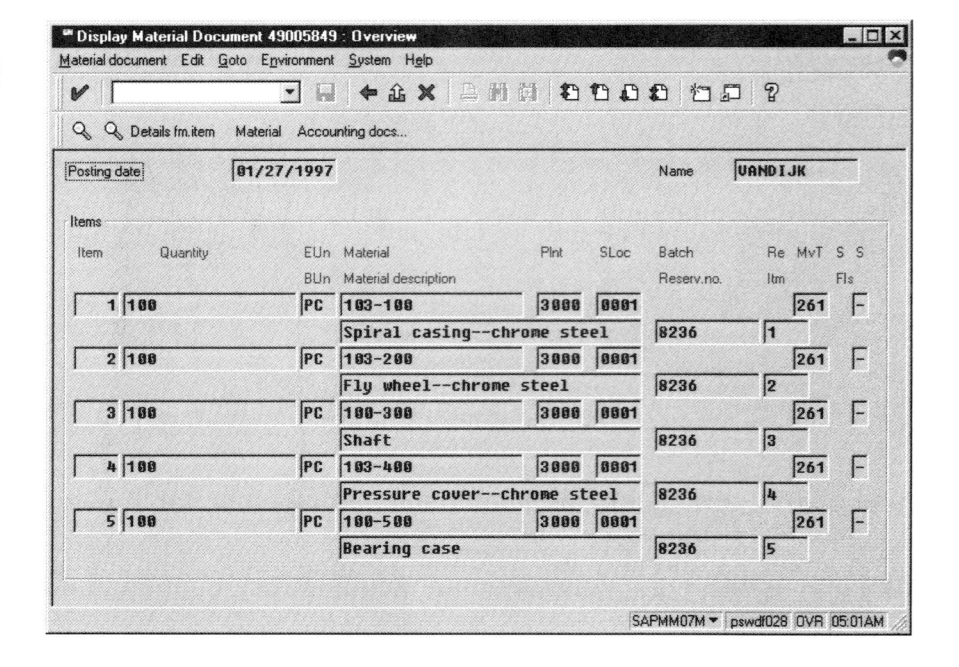

7–36

Reporting Made Easy

Section 8: Human Resources Reports

Contents

Staffing Level Development Report (or Headcount Report)..............................8–2
Payroll Journal 8–6
New Hire Report 8–11
EEO-1 Report..8–16
Entries and Withdrawals Report..8–21

Staffing Level Development Report (or Headcount Report)

Quick Access To run this report, use one of the following access options:

Option 1: Menu Path

Human resources → Personnel management → Administration → Reporting → Report selection → Organizational entity → Staff level development → Staffing level development

Option 2: Program Name

Choose *System → Services → Reporting* and enter `RPSDEV00` in the *Program* field. Then, choose *Execute* to run the report.

Purpose This report allows you to view detailed data at the personnel area (or subarea) and the employee group (or subgroup) levels. From this report, you can branch out into business graphics for a graphical representation of the data.

This report, commonly referred to as the headcount report, is a personnel administration report. It counts the persons assigned to a payroll area in a certain pay period.

Prerequisites You must enter a value in the *Payroll area* to run this report.

You may choose to use additional selection criteria to produce a more meaningful report. For example, you may want the report to list only those employees hired in a certain personnel area, employee group, and with a certain employment status, such as *1* for active employees.

Selection criteria for the *Payroll period* are used to gather data for this report. To specify the start and end date for the payroll period, use one of the following methods:

- **Explicit entry:** Enter the specific pay period from which employees are to be selected.
- **No entry in the period or additional data selection fields:** The period is determined from the payroll accounting area control record. Only data from the current accounting period is displayed.
- **Implicit entry:** Enter the additional data selection periods. These values are used for the person selection period.

Section 8: Human Resources Reports
Staffing Level Development Report (or Headcount Report)

In HR, payroll accounting periods can vary in length (for example, monthly, weekly, etc.). Use *Period modifier* to identify the accounting period. To choose a period-length for this report (RPSDEV00), enter a specific period modifier in the *Period modifier* field. If the *Period modifier* field is left blank, the period modifier of the selected payroll area is used. The system chooses a key date for each period you enter. The data is shown for the specified key date (for example, the last day in the pay period).

As a default, the report data is summarized for all payroll areas. However, you can specify that the data be summarized at the personnel area, personnel subarea, employee group, and employee subgroup level.

Integration

There are no other reports available from this report.

To automatically export the report data to Microsoft Excel®, Lotus 123®, or other spreadsheet tools, simply choose *SAP XXL list viewer* on the selection screen. To use this functionality, you must have the SAP-XXL component. Once the data is transferred you may determine control-breaks and form totals wherever required.

You may also transfer the displayed data to the SAP Business Graphics program.

The interface to SAP Business Graphics can only process 31 lines at a time; if the list is longer than 31 lines, you will be prompted to compress the data using one of the following options:

- **Compression of organizational assignment data** (removes unnecessary information)
- **ABC analysis** (the 30 organizational units with the most values display in the data table; the other organizational units summarize)
- **Combination of compression and ABC analysis**

Features

This report includes:

- Variants
- Execution (and print) in background
- Standard selection fields available
- Additional selection fields using *Further Selections* or *Matchcodes*
- Data output settings allowing for summary of data by personnel area, personnel subarea, employee group, and employee subgroup
- Chart functions using SAP Business Graphics: *Functions → Chart (F8)*

Next Steps

This report contains employee master data. As such, it cannot be changed or manipulated from the report.

Commonly Used Reports: Illustrations and Perspectives

Section 8: Human Resources Reports
Staffing Level Development Report (or Headcount Report)

Guided Tour

Example: Display the total number of active employees in a personnel area for a given pay period.

To access the first screen for this report, choose

Human resources → Personnel management → Administration → Reporting → Report selection → Organizational entity → Staff level development → Staffing level development.

1. Enter **US** in *Payroll area*. When you choose *Enter*, the current pay period information is filled in from the control record.

2. Under *Selection*, enter **3** in *Employment status*. This limits your selection to active employees.

3. Enter **300** in *Personnel area*.

4. Under *Additional data*, select *Pers. area*, *P. subarea*, *EE group*, and *EE subgr* in *List for*.

5. Choose *Execute*.

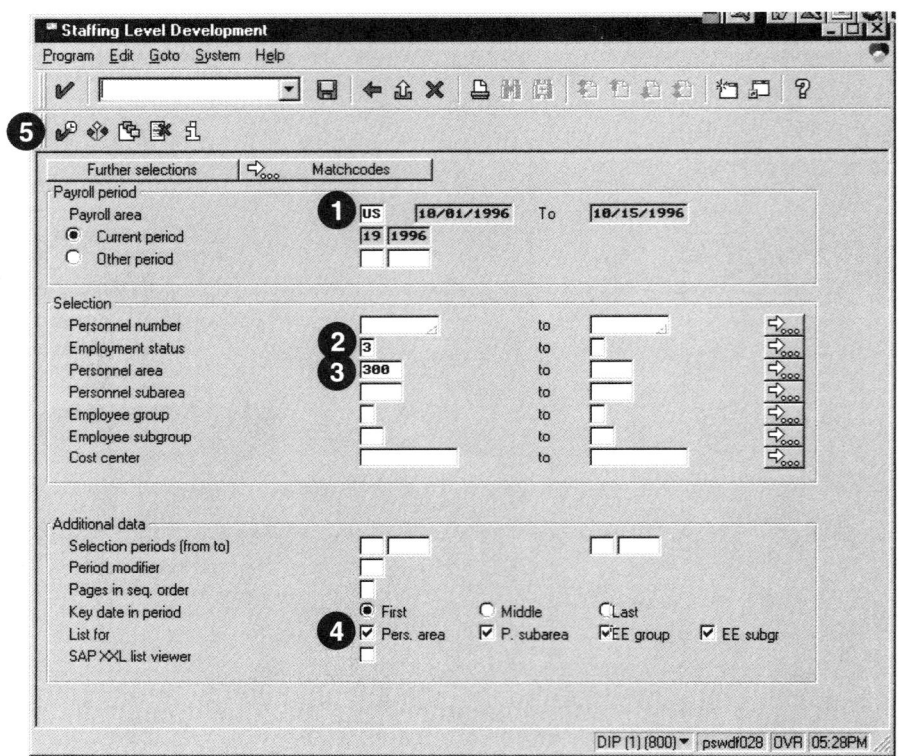

Section 8: Human Resources Reports

Staffing Level Development Report (or Headcount Report)

This screen shows:
- Selected personnel area
- Summaries of each personnel sub-area.
- Number of employees in each employee group
- Summaries of all subgroups

6. Choose *Chart*.

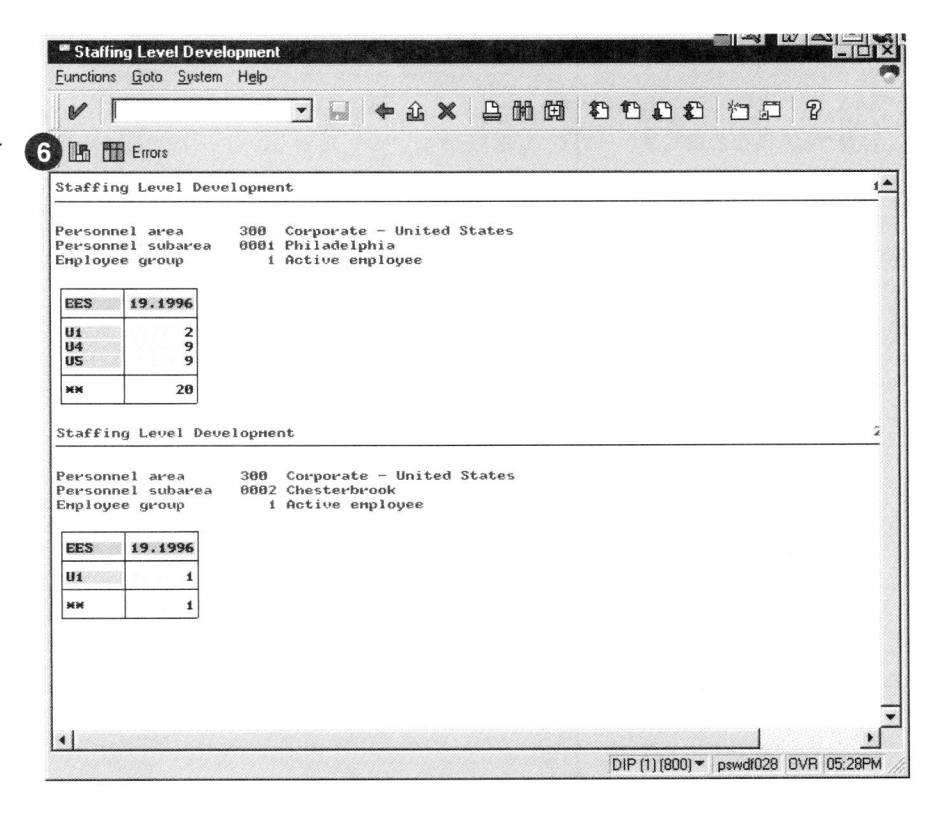

This screen shows a graphical display of the staffing level development with data groupings and a bar chart listing the exact numbers in each unit.

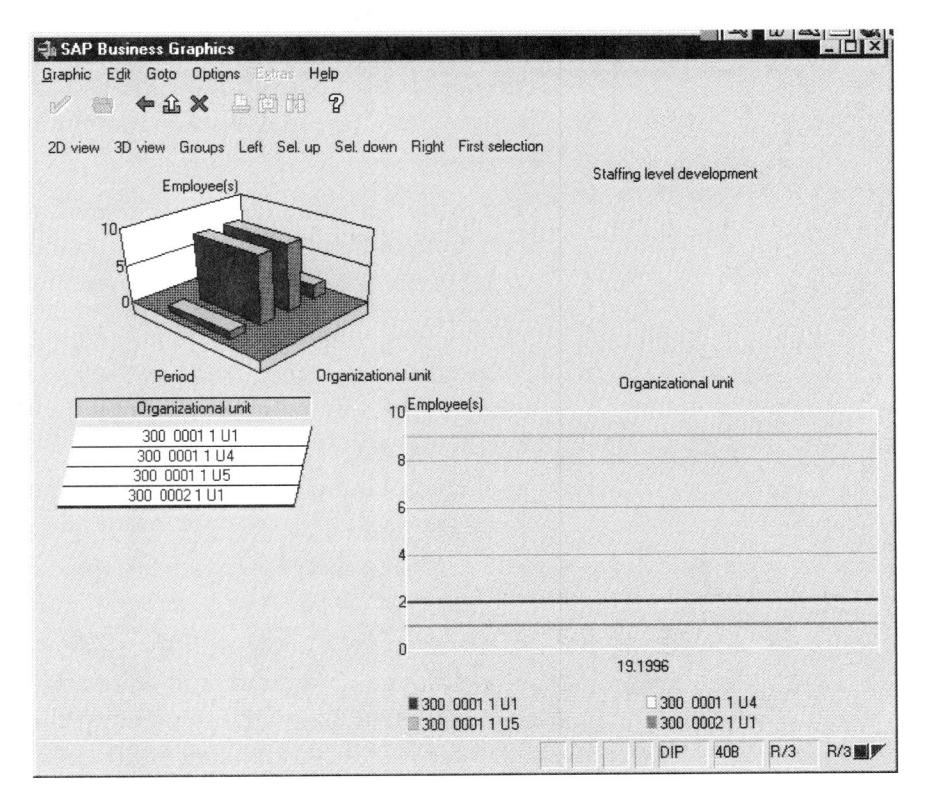

Commonly Used Reports: Illustrations and Perspectives

8–5

Section 8: Human Resources Reports
Payroll Journal

Payroll Journal

Quick Access To run this report, use one of the following access options:

Option 1: Menu Path

Human resources → Payroll → Subs. activities → Per payroll period → Lists/statistics → Payroll journal

Option 2: Transaction Code

In the *Command* field, enter transaction `PC1U`. Then, choose *Lists/statistics → Payroll journal* to run the report.

Purpose The flexibility of this report allows you to create earnings registers, deduction registers, or other miscellaneous payroll registers for a given payroll period.

Prerequisites This report only runs for employees with valid payroll results.

You must answer the following three questions on the selection screen before running the report:

1. **For which special run or period must the evaluation be started?**
   Pay period selection criteria are used for gathering data in this report. You must specify a payroll area and a specific pay period in which to select employees. You may also indicate if a special payroll run should be considered.

2. **For which employees must the evaluation be started?**
   Specific employee numbers may be entered to further limit the data selected. Additional selection fields may be made available using the *Further Selections* button.

3. **Which layout is required for the result of the evaluation?**
   The payroll journal consists of four individual forms which must be configured by the user:
   - Page header: The page header appears at the beginning of each printed page.
   - Employee data excerpt: Employee data excerpts appear on detail pages as a means of displaying individual employee's payroll results.
   - Continuation excerpt: If the system begins a new page when printing the employee data excerpt, it prints this form (a mini-header for the employee) on the new page before printing the remainder of the employee data excerpt. Additional control functions appear on the selection screen to provide special handling for retroactive payroll runs (for example, printing on separate versus the same page).

- Totals block: A totals block appears on the totals page below the page header. This form has the same function on the totals pages as the employee data excerpts on the detail pages.

You may select an alternate currency on the selection screen.

You may alter the output of the data by configuring the system's standard forms to produce a payroll register, earnings register, and deduction register.

Integration

No other reports are available from this report.

Features

This report includes :
- Variants
- Execution (and print) in background
- Standard selection fields
- Additional selections fields (use the *Further Selections* or *Matchcodes* buttons)
- Data output settings (provides a summary or detailed information using configurable forms)

Next Steps

This report contains employee payroll results. As such, it cannot be changed or manipulated from the report.

Section 8: Human Resources Reports
Payroll Journal

Guided Tour

Example: Display the payroll detail for all active employees in a personnel area for a given pay period.

To access the first screen for this report, choose

Human resources → *Payroll* → *Subs. activities* → *Per payroll period* → *Lists/statistics* → *Payroll journal.*

1. Enter US in *Payroll area*. When you choose *Enter*, the current pay period from the control record automatically appears.

2. Leave the *Special run* payroll type blank to indicate a regular payroll run.

3. Leave the *Only totaling required* field blank (as shown in this example) if you need employee detail.

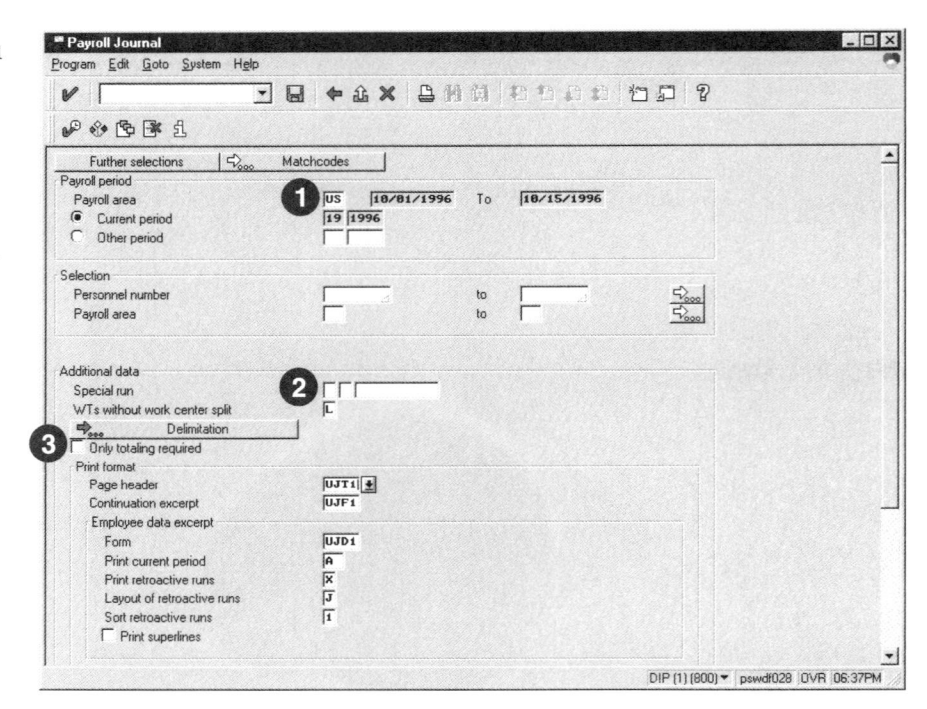

Reporting Made Easy

Section 8: Human Resources Reports
Payroll Journal

4. Under *Print format*, enter **UJT1** in *Page Header*.
5. Enter **UJF1** in *Continuation excerpt*.
6. Under *Employee data excerpt*, enter **UJD1** in *Form*.
7. Under *Totals display*, enter **UJS1** in *Form*.
8. Under *Output currency*, select *In-period*.
9. Choose *Execute*.

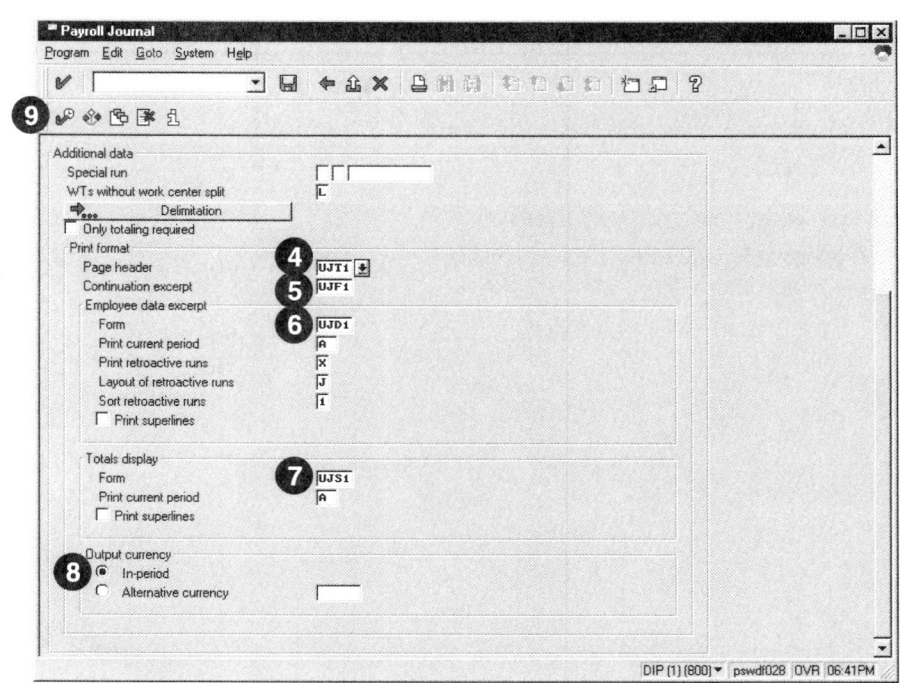

A The data output header (shown on each page)
B Employee data (as defined in the detail form)

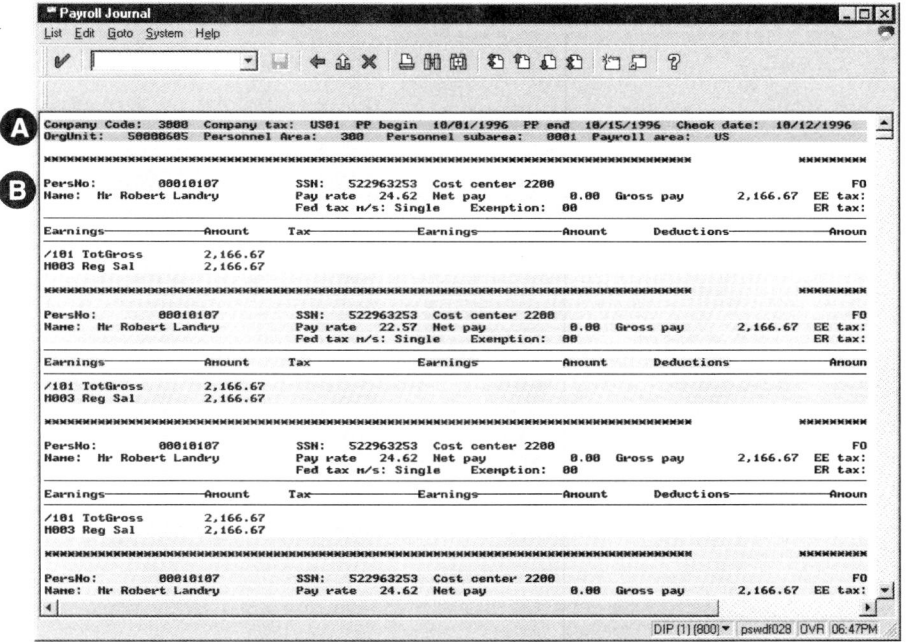

Commonly Used Reports: Illustrations and Perspectives

8–9

Section 8: Human Resources Reports
Payroll Journal

C All key fields of the header and data totals

D Summary level (indicated by an asterisk (*).

In this example, all personnel subareas are totalled for personnel area *3300*.

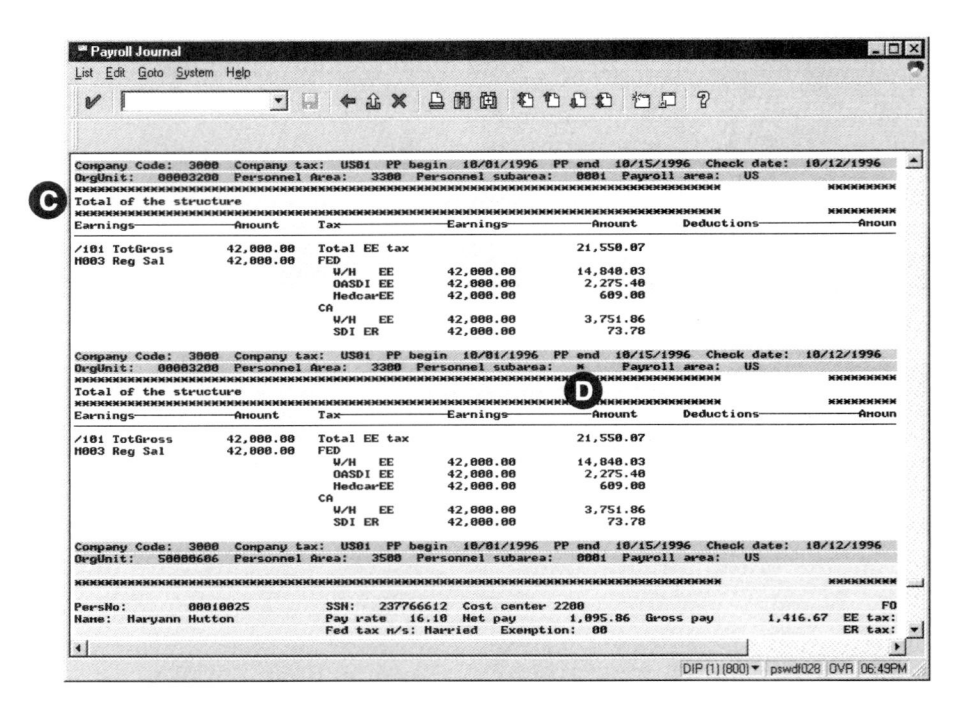

E All key fields of the header replace with an asterisk (*) to indicate final totalling.

F The count of the employees selected and processed.

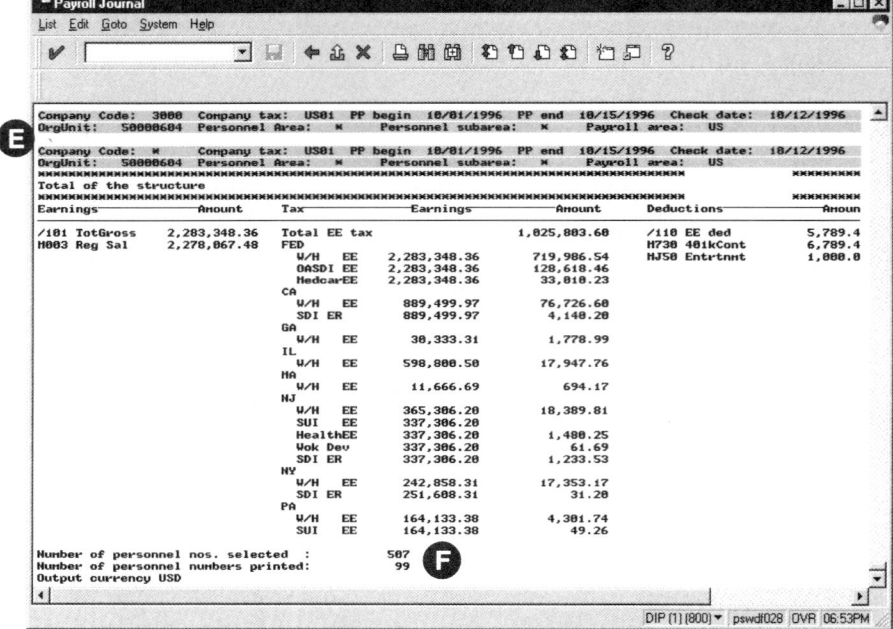

8–10   Reporting Made Easy

New Hire Report

Quick Access　To run this report, use the following:

Program Name

Choose *System → Services → Reporting* and enter `RPLNHRU0` in the *Program* field. Then, choose *Execute* to run the report.

Note: The standard menu path for this report is only available in R/3 System Releases 4.5A or higher.

Purpose　The purpose of this report is to provide regulatory reporting information on new hires within each state and tax company. For each state, the tax company to which the employees are assigned lists by the employer's address and Federal ID number. The employees hired during the reporting period list by their full name, social security number, and home address. This information may be used for federal reporting purposes.

Prerequisites　This report only runs for employees assigned to a valid personnel subarea. The personnel subarea must be assigned to a valid tax company. The tax company definition includes the official company address, as well as the assignment of the federal tax identification number.

Employees must also have a valid residence address in infotype *0006* addresses, and be assigned to a valid unemployment state (infotype *0209*).

Integration　No other reports are available from this report.

Features　This report includes:
- Variants
- Execution (and print) in background
- Standard selection fields available
- Additional selection fields via the *Further Selections* or *Matchcodes* buttons
- Detailed data output for further reporting

Next Steps　This report contains employee master data. As such, it cannot be changed or manipulated from the report.

Section 8: Human Resources Reports
New Hire Report

Guided Tour

Example: Display a list of newly hired employees in California for the current year.

In Release 4.0B, choose *System → Services → Reporting* and enter **RPLNHRU0** in the *Program* field. Then, choose *Execute* to run the report.

1. Under *Period*, select *Current year*.

2. Under *Selection*, enter **3** in *Employment status* to include only active employees.

3. Under *Report-specific selections*, enter **US01** in *Tax company* and **CA** in *State*.

4. Select the *Multiple selection* button for *Hire/rehire event type* to include multiple event types that represent hiring.

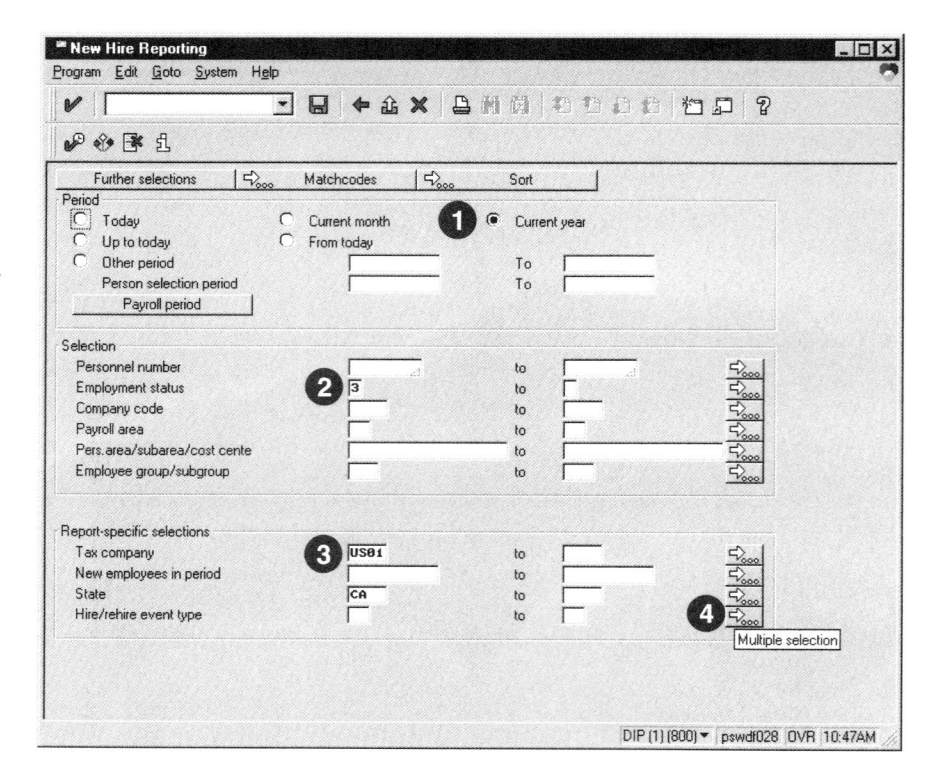

5. On the *Multiple Selection* screen, enter **01** and **12** to ensure inclusion of all hiring actions.

6. Choose *Copy*.

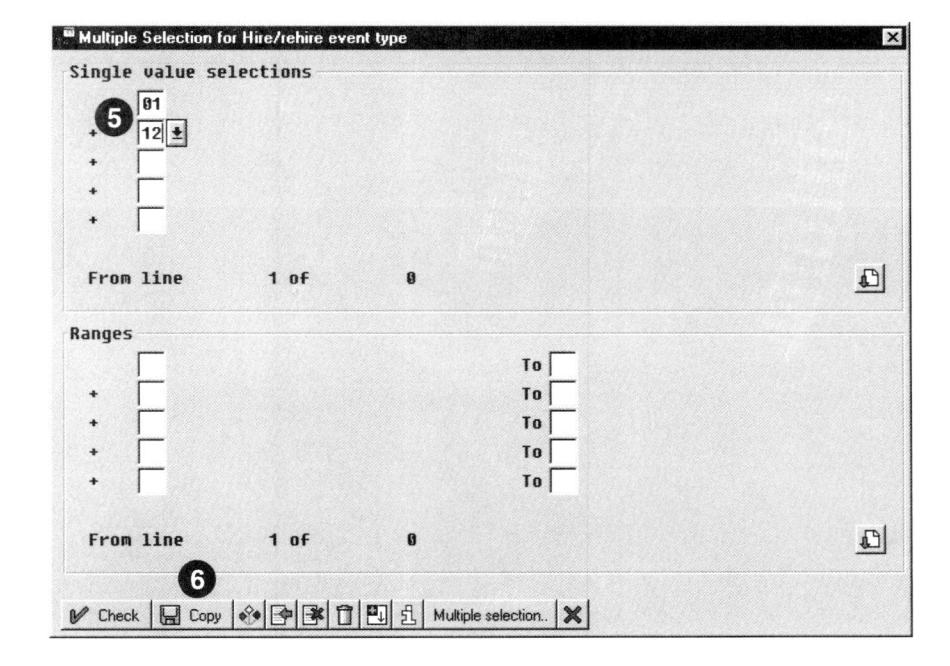

The event type selection now shows that multiple actions are being used.

7. Choose *Execute*.

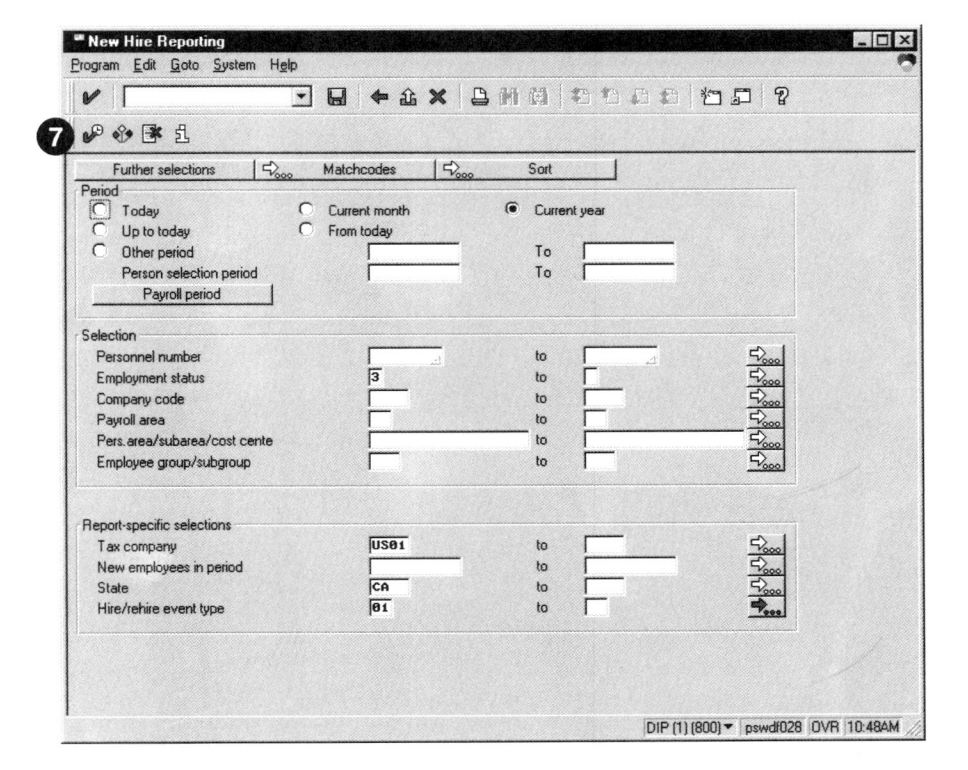

Section 8: Human Resources Reports
New Hire Report

A   The selected state with tax company information

B   Employee information (for each employee within the tax company)

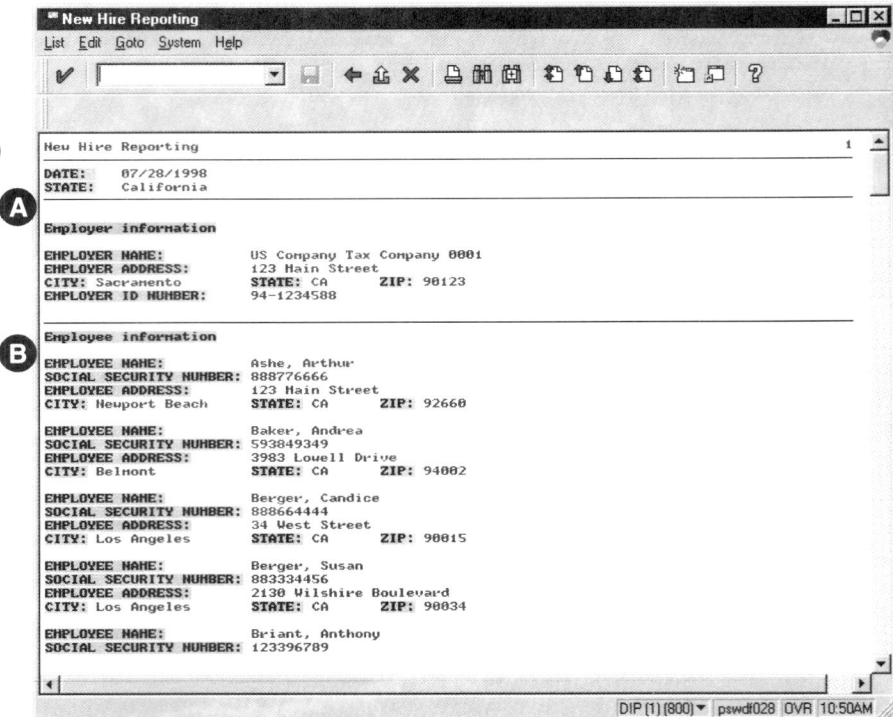

C   Summary of selection criteria (at end of employee information list)

D   Total number of new hires

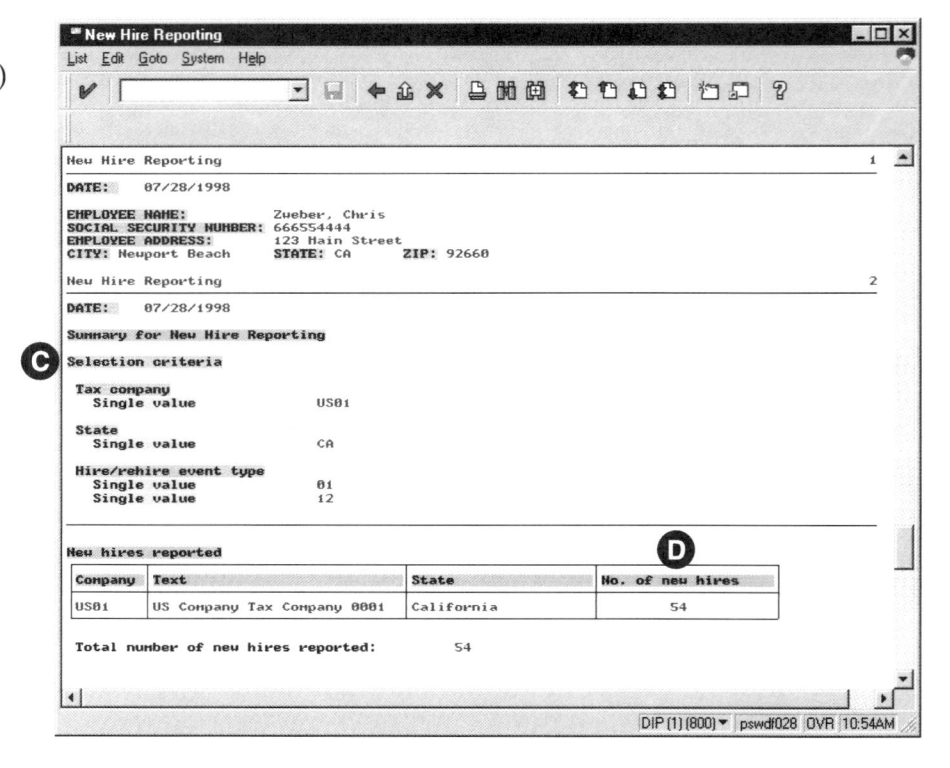

8–14

Reporting Made Easy

Section 8: Human Resources Reports

New Hire Report

E   List of employees included or excluded due to lack of information (located at the bottom of the screen)

Correct these records and rerun the report to ensure all relevant information is reported.

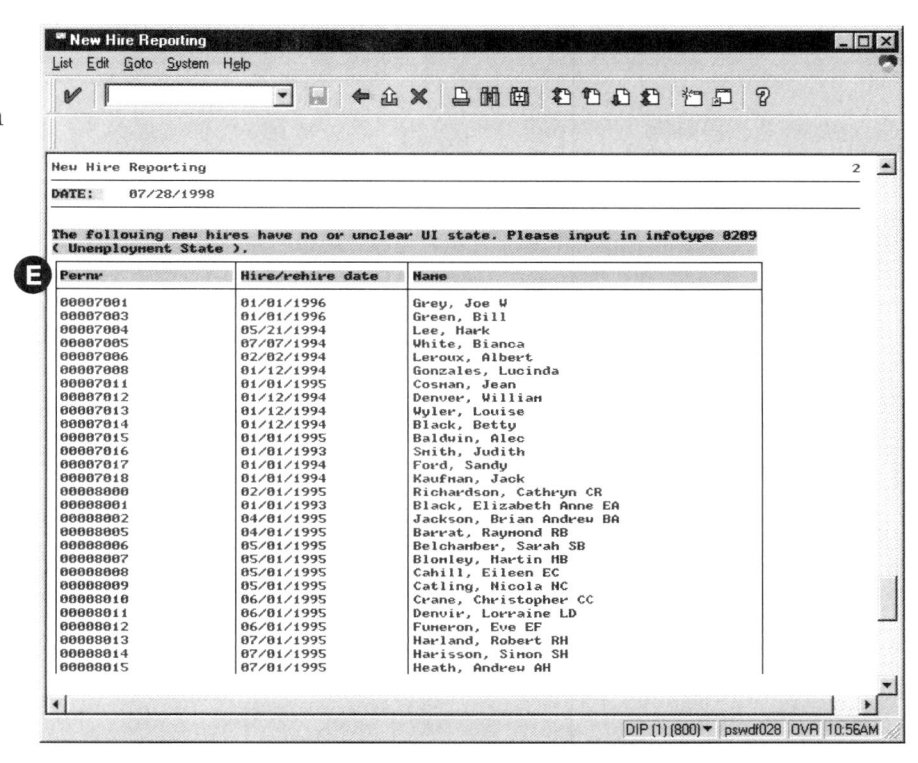

Commonly Used Reports: Illustrations and Perspectives

8–15

Section 8: Human Resources Reports
EEO-1 Report

EEO-1 Report

Quick Access To run this report, use the following:

Program Name

Choose *System* → *Services* → *Reporting* and enter **RPSEEOU1** in the *Program* field. Then, choose *Execute* to run the report.

Note: The standard menu path for this report is only available in R/3 System Releases 4.5A or higher.

Purpose The purpose of this report is to compile the EEO-1 data that US employers need to file every year with the Equal Employment Opportunity Commission (EEOC). The resulting statistic is formatted in accordance with the standards for computerized output prescribed by the EEOC. Section G (Certification) is omitted, since multi-establishment employers are required to file the certified consolidated report on the original EEO-1 form.

Prerequisites This report only runs for employees who have a valid organizational assignment infotype *0001*, including assignment to a personnel area/subarea and job.

Employees must also have a valid additional personal data infotype *0077*, including assignment of ethnic origin, and veteran status.

In addition, you must maintain the following system tables:

- T5U0P: Every personnel area subarea has to be maintained. The following country-specific fields—with country modifier *10* (US)—must be completed:
    - REPUN: Reporting organizational unit
    - COIND: Company ID
    - EEOHQ: Headquarters indicator (checkbox). Must be checked ONLY for headquarters unit.
    - SICNO: Standard industry code (T5USC)
    - EINUM: INS employer ID
    - DANDB: Dun & Bradstreet ID
- T5U13—Jobs: Country-specific field for country modifier *10* (US). For each job, the field EEOCT - EEO job category must be maintained. Standard EEO job categories are delivered.
- All EEO categories must be entered into feature EEOCT, which converts job categories to the row numbers (01 to 09) in the EEO-1 report. Features may be accessed using transaction **PE03**.
- T5UAD: For every reporting unit, an address should be created.
- T5URU - EEO unit number for each reporting unit should be then created. For each EEO unit number, an address has to be assigned.

- T5U0E - EEO Record: This report uses this table in several ways. The table provides:
  - Previously reported totals per reporting unit
  - Settings (that is, section C and E) for the current report
  - Totals for the current period (if needed)
- T505R - Ethnic origin: If table T505R is modified or extended to allow additional ethnic categories, feature EEOCL (transaction `PE03`) must be modified to reflect those changes. Feature EEOCL yields the EEO employee category based on ethnic origin and gender.

Depending on when you run the report, you will need to consider special requirements concerning totals previously reported to the government.

1. **Running the report for the first time:** For the period that provides the previous reported total, a record needs to be created for EACH reporting unit in *T5U0E*. This record should contain the totals per employee category and, preferably, the indicators for the questions in sections B and C reported for that period.

2. **Running the report in subsequent periods:** If the indicators for section B and C have not changed, it is not necessary to create the records for the current periods, since the report will read the indicators from the previous period. If the indicators have changed, a new record for the current period, containing the correct settings must be manually created. If desired, the report will update table *T5U0E* with the totals for the current period when the report is run. Choose *PA_UPDAT* to create or modify the entry per reporting unit in table *T5U0E* (see the selection screen below for further information).

EEOCT (Feature): Depending on the value used in table *T5U13* (field EEOCT), this feature must be modified to yield the correct row number for each EEO category.

The following parameters in the selection screen influence the report output:

Parameter	Function
Previous Period	Reads the period from previously reported totals.
Current Period	Determines the period from indicators for sections C and E.
	If the results are to be written into table *T5U0E*, the results will be written to this period.
Report Type	Changes the report headings to *SPECIAL REPORT*, and the report type (section A) to 5.
Write results	Writes the results per reporting unit and current period to table *T5U0E*.

Integration No other reports are available from this report.

Features This report includes:
- Variants
- Execution (and print) in background
- Standard selection fields available
- Additional selection fields via the *Further Selections* or *Matchcodes* buttons
- Data output formatted in accordance with the standards for computerized output prescribed by the EEOC

Next Steps This report contains employee master data. As such, it cannot be changed or manipulated from the report.

Section 8: Human Resources Reports
EEO-1 Report

Guided Tour

Example: Display a summary of employees in a reporting unit for the period 06 1998.

In Release 4.0B, choose *System* → *Services* → *Reporting* and enter **RPSEEOU1** in the *Program* field. Then, choose *Execute* to run the report.

1. Under *Period,* enter **06/01/1998** to **06/30/1998** in *Other period* and *Person selection period*.

2. Under *Selection,* enter **300** in *Personnel area* and **0001** in *Personnel subarea* to limit the selection of employees.

3. Enter **+3+** in *Status 1/status 2/status 3* (employment status) to include only active employees.

4. Under *Additional data,* enter **00 1996** in *Previous period*. This determines the period from which the previously reported totals are read.

5. Enter **06 1996** in *Current period*. This determines the period from which the indicators for sections C and E are read.

6. Choose *Execute*.

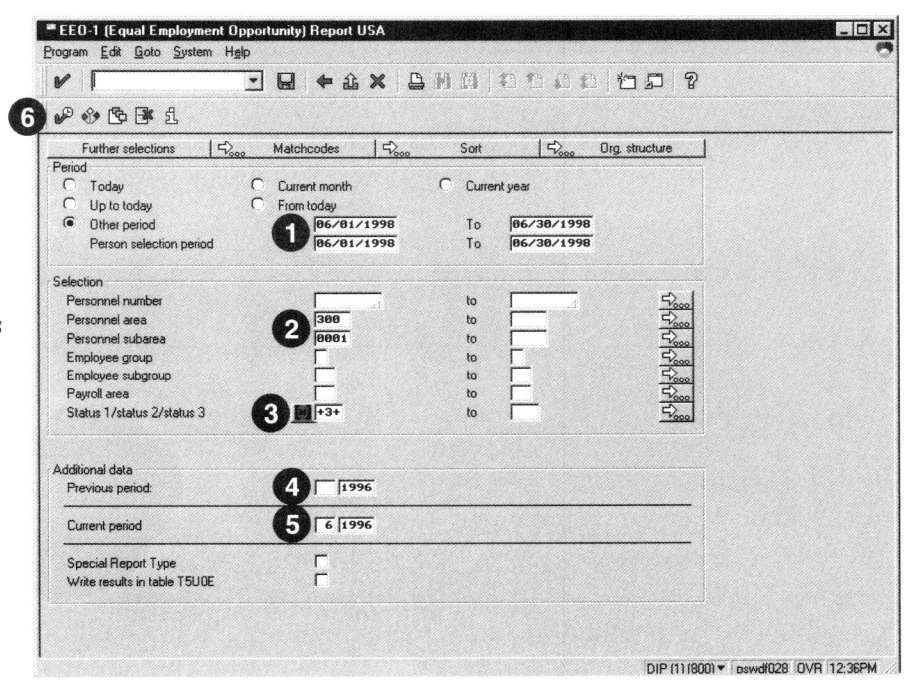

Commonly Used Reports: Illustrations and Perspectives

8–19

Section 8: Human Resources Reports

EEO-1 Report

A   The type of report, employer information, and filing data

B   Values for all EEO categories

The number of male and female employees found in each ethnic category appears to the left. Totals for all categories appear in the last row.

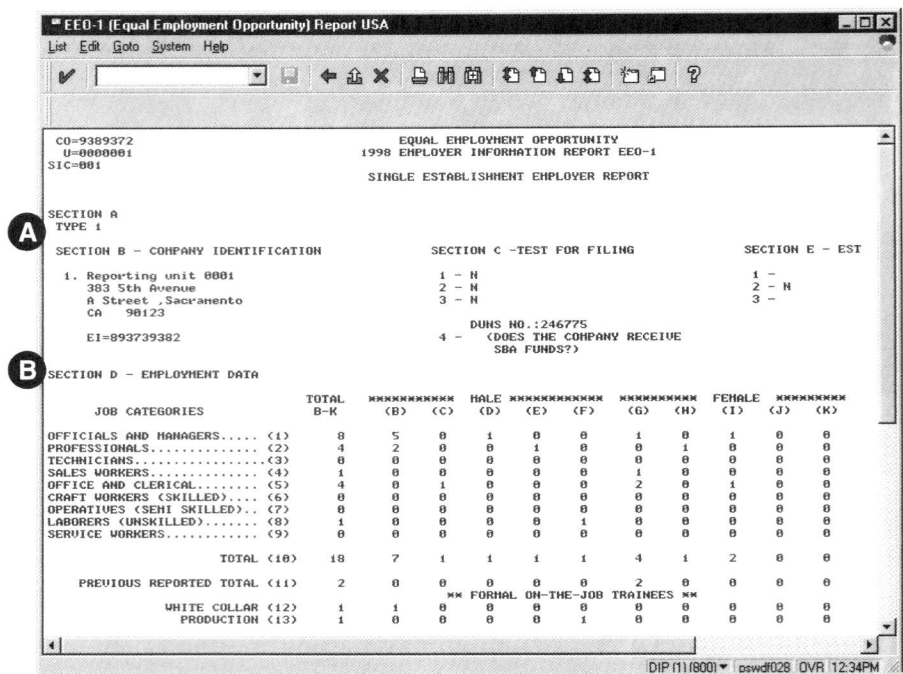

C   Error log with an explanation of the error (found at the bottom of the screen)

Errors should be corrected and the report rerun to ensure all relevant information is reported.

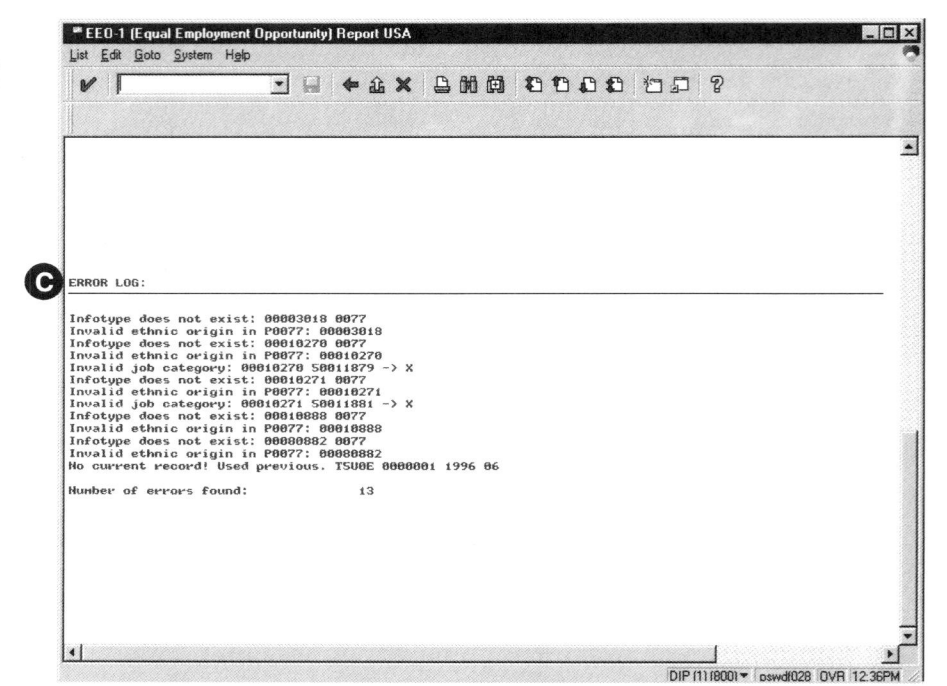

8–20

Reporting Made Easy

Entries and Withdrawals Report

Quick Access To run this report, use one of the following access options:

Option 1: Menu Path

Human resources → Personnel management → Administration → Reporting → Report selection → Employee → Entries/withdrawals → Employees who have Entered and/or Left the company

Option 2: Program Name

Choose *System → Services → Reporting* and enter **RPLEAT00** in the *Program* field. Then, choose *Execute* to run the report.

Purpose This report lists employees who have entered or left the company within a certain period. You can choose any period as a reference point for this report.

Prerequisites There are no prerequisites for this report. However, you may want use selection criteria to produce a more meaningful report.

Integration No other reports are available from this report.

The output is presented in tabular view. The screen may be changed to a formatted page layout view. Columns and rows may be hidden from the display with mouse or function key controls. The data may also be transferred to Microsoft Excel, Word, or HTML through pushbuttons or menu selections available on the output display. Furthermore, connection to SAP Office lets you send the report to another R/3 user as a mail attachment.

Features This report includes:

- Variants
- Execution (and print) in background
- Standard selection fields available
- Additional selection fields (use *Further Selections* or *Matchcodes* buttons)
- Selection of entries and/or withdrawals
- Sorting of data according to the user's preferences
- Data output to table or report, with links to Excel, Word, and HTML
- Ability to show/hide lines or columns of data

Section 8: Human Resources Reports
Entries and Withdrawals Report

Next Steps This report contains employee master data. As such, it cannot be changed or manipulated from the report, but it but does let you hide specific columns or rows of data.

Guided Tour

Example 1: Display a list of employees in one personnel area who entered or left the company in a specific year.

To access the first screen for this report, choose

Human resources → Personnel management → Administration → Reporting → Report selection → Employee → Entries/withdrawals → Employees who have Entered and/or Left the company.

1. Under *Period*, enter **01/01/1996** to **12/31/1996** in *Other period*.

2. Under *Selection*, enter **0** in *Employment status*. Select not equal to (≠) in order to exclude terminated employees.

3. Enter **300** in *Personnel area*.

4. Select *EEs entered/left* in order to include employees who have entered or left the company.

5. Choose *Execute*.

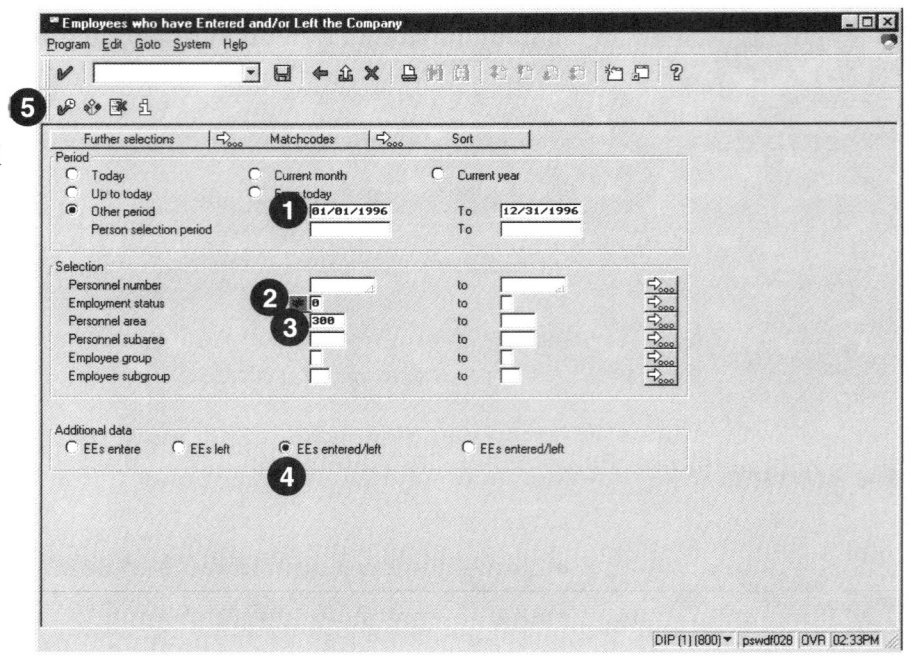

Section 8: Human Resources Reports
Entries and Withdrawals Report

This screen shows *Employees who have entered/left*. Entering employees have an *Entry* date, while departing employees have a *Leaving* date. Employees who have left and returned list in both columns (for example, Jonathan Benson left the company on June 1, but was rehired on June 2).

A   Total number of employees selected (for example, *26*)

B   Function used to transfer data to report layout, SAP Office, Excel, and Word

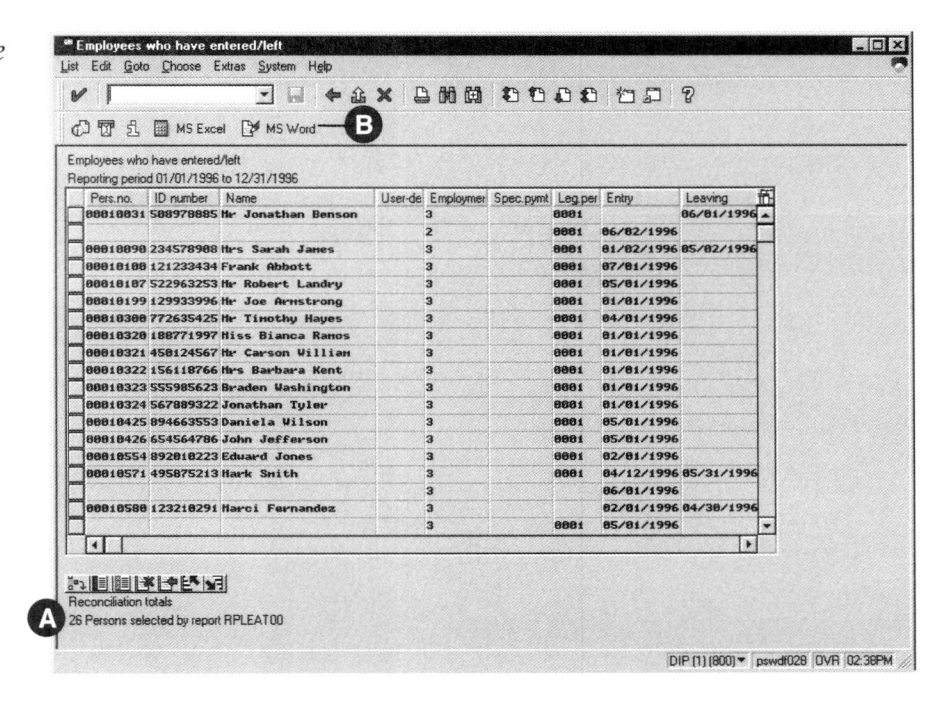

Example 2: Display a list of employees in one personnel area who have entered or left the company for a specific year. Hide columns that are not relevant and export the report to HTML.

1. Under *Period*, enter **01/01/1996** to **12/31/1996** in *Other period*.

2. Under *Selection*, enter **0** in *Employment status*. Select not equal to (≠) in order to exclude terminated employees.

3. Enter **300** in *Personnel area*.

4. Choose *EEs entered/left* in order to include employees who have entered or left the company.

5. Choose *Execute*.

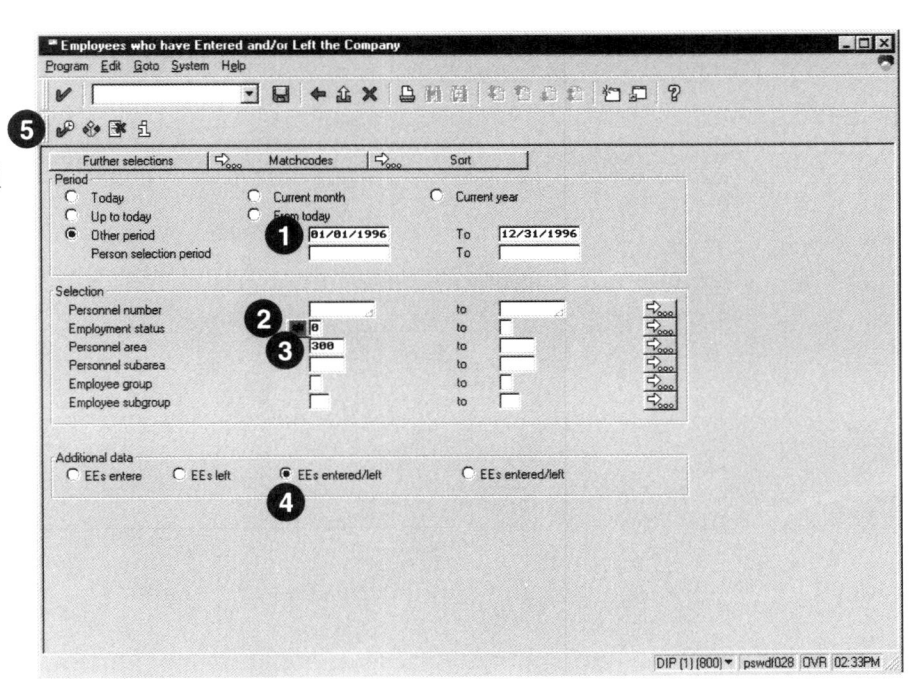

Commonly Used Reports: Illustrations and Perspectives   8–23

Section 8: Human Resources Reports
Entries and Withdrawals Report

This data is the same as that shown in example 1. Using CTRL and left mouse button, select columns *User-Def., Spec.payment* and *Leg.person*. Right-click the mouse to select *Hide lines/columns*.

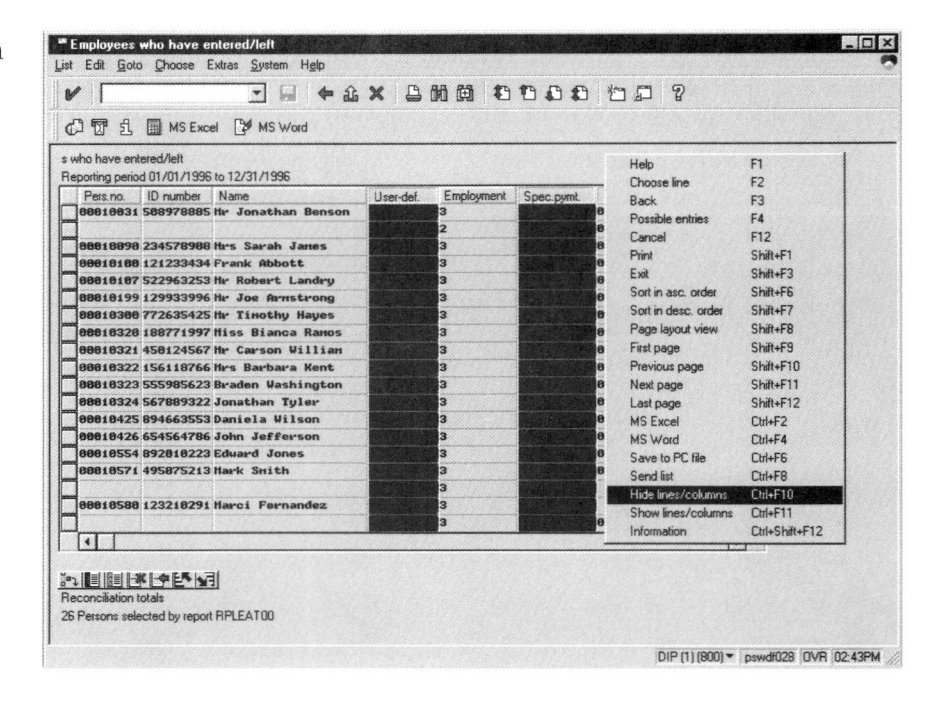

The resulting screen hides the undesired columns.

6. Choose *List → WEB display* to export report data to HTML.

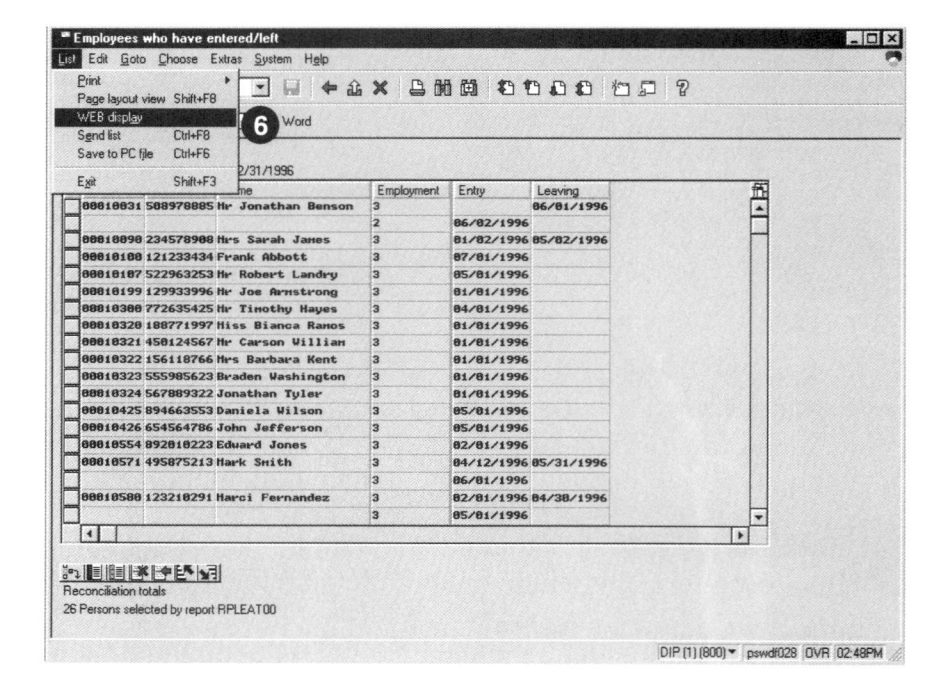

Section 8: Human Resources Reports

Entries and Withdrawals Report

An HTML version of the report (as it appears in a web browser) is shown here.

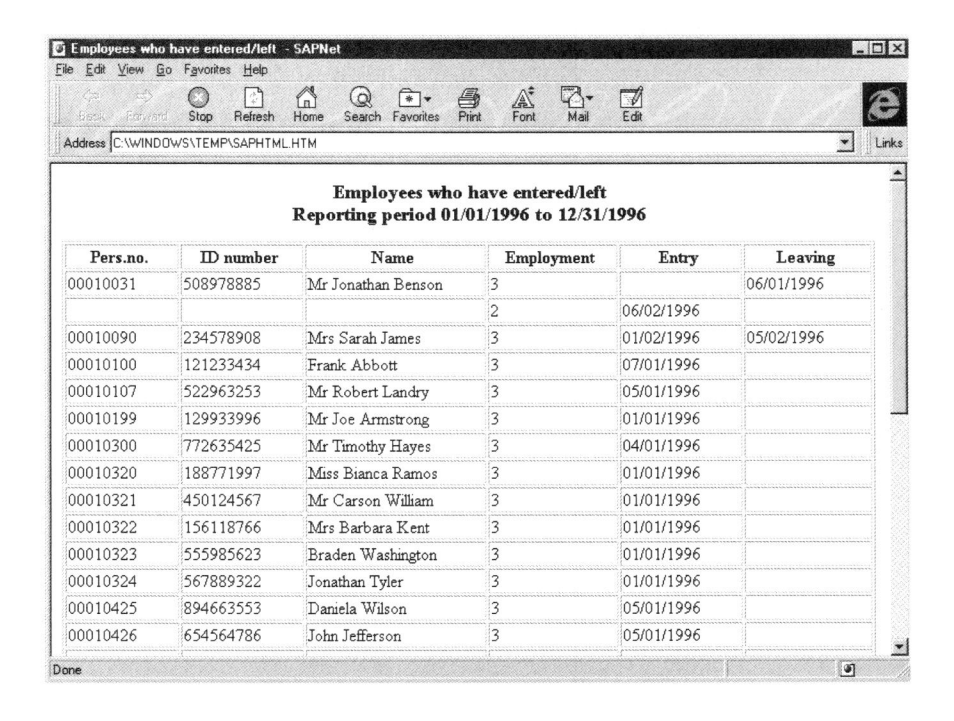

Employees who have entered/left
Reporting period 01/01/1996 to 12/31/1996

Pers.no.	ID number	Name	Employment	Entry	Leaving
00010031	508978885	Mr Jonathan Benson	3		06/01/1996
			2	06/02/1996	
00010090	234578908	Mrs Sarah James	3	01/02/1996	05/02/1996
00010100	121233434	Frank Abbott	3	07/01/1996	
00010107	522963253	Mr Robert Landry	3	05/01/1996	
00010199	129933996	Mr Joe Armstrong	3	01/01/1996	
00010300	772635425	Mr Timothy Hayes	3	04/01/1996	
00010320	188771997	Miss Bianca Ramos	3	01/01/1996	
00010321	450124567	Mr Carson William	3	01/01/1996	
00010322	156118766	Mrs Barbara Kent	3	01/01/1996	
00010323	555985623	Braden Washington	3	01/01/1996	
00010324	567889322	Jonathan Tyler	3	01/01/1996	
00010425	894663553	Daniela Wilson	3	05/01/1996	
00010426	654564786	John Jefferson	3	05/01/1996	

Commonly Used Reports: Illustrations and Perspectives

Section 8: Human Resources Reports
Entries and Withdrawals Report

Section 9: Sales and Distribution Reports

Contents

List of Sales Orders 9–2

Blocked Sales Orders 9–7

Backorders 9–13

Incoming Order Report (SIS Statistical Analysis) 9–22

Incoming Orders for Customers and Materials (Document or Statistical Analysis) 9–29

Incomplete Sales Documents 9–34

List of All or Open Billings (Document Analysis) 9–38

Invoiced Sales Report (Statistical Analysis) 9–43

List of All or Open Deliveries (Document Analysis) 9–50

Shipping Report (SIS Statistical Analysis) 9–56

Section 9: Sales and Distribution Reports
List of Sales Orders

List of Sales Orders

Quick Access   To run this report, use one of the following access options:

Option 1: Menu Path
Logistics → *Sales and distribution* → *Sales* → *Order* → *List*

Option 2: Transaction Code
In the *Command* field, enter transaction **VA05** and choose *Enter*.

Purpose   This report lists sales orders, grouped by sold-to party or material number.

Prerequisites   The following entries are required to run this report:
- Valid sold-to party or material master number
- Valid sales organization

Integration   You can branch to the SD document, document status, document flow, customer address, sold-to party and the material master.

Features   The selection screen of this report includes:
- Input sold-to party, material number, or a PO number
- Input SD organizational data
- Further selection criteria
  - Distribution
  - Division
  - Sales office
  - Sales group
  - Sales document type
  - Created by
  - SD document
- Date range
- Display variants (*0SAP*, *1SAP*, and *3SAP*)

Reporting Made Easy

Section 9: Sales and Distribution Reports
List of Sales Orders

- Output screen
  - Filter functions
  - Sort functions
  - Sum up (add values) function
  - Change the width of the column, and freeze or unfreeze columns.
  - Alternate between display variants
    (*Settings* → *Display variants* → *Choose*)
- Branch to the SD document, document status, document flow, and master data (customer address, partner (sold-to), and material)

Next Steps This report contains data from sales documents, which include materials and partners. It allows you to branch to the SD document for editing, but does not allow any other manipulation of the output.

Guided Tour

Example: List sales documents by sold-to party.

To access the first screen for this report, choose

Logistics → *Sales and distribution* → *Sales* → *Order* → *List*.

1. Enter a *Sold-to party* or *Material* number (for example, **1321**).

2. Enter the document date range (for example, **01.01.1998** to **12.31.1998**). This is based on the date the sales order was created.

3. Under *Selection criteria*, select *All sales orders*.

4. Choose *Enter*.

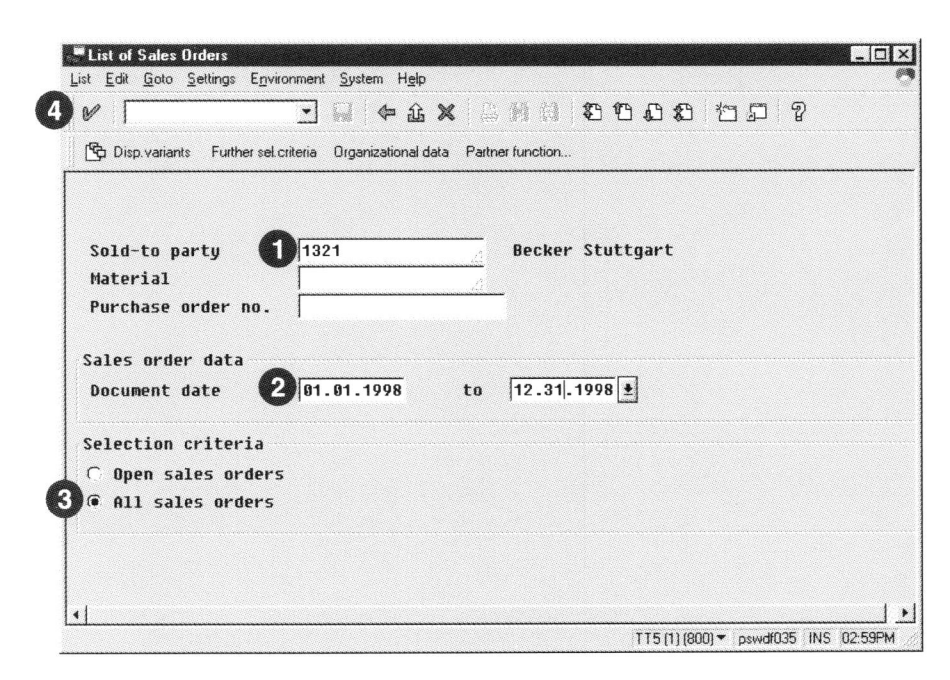

Commonly Used Reports: Illustrations and Perspectives

9–3

Section 9: Sales and Distribution Reports
List of Sales Orders

This screen shows the basic list of all sales orders without display variants.

5. Click on the *Doc. date* column.
6. Choose *Filter*.

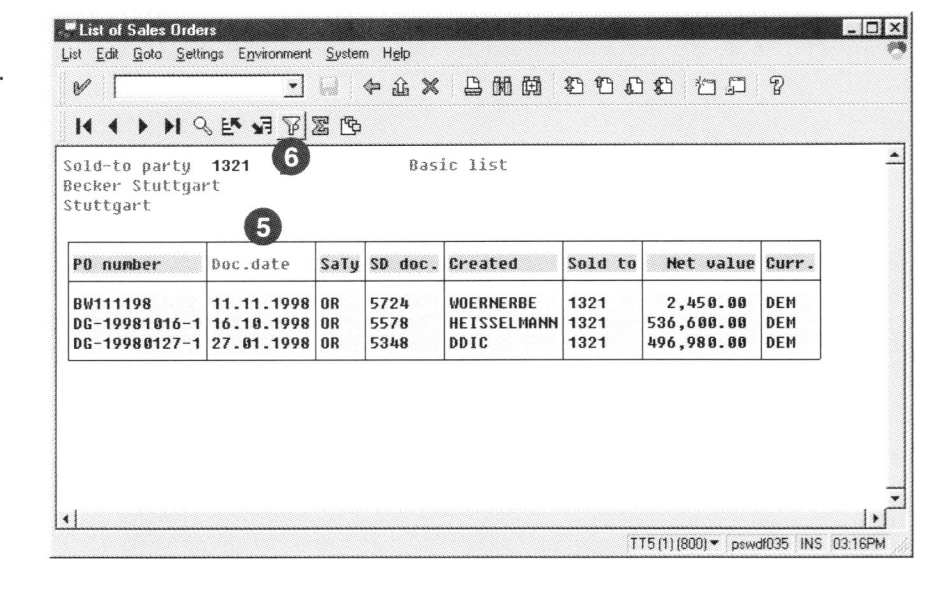

7. Enter the filter date range (for example, **10.16.1998** to **11.11.1998**) in *Document date*. Sales documents will be filtered only for this date range.
8. Choose *Copy*.

This screen shows the filtered output for sales orders that occurred in the above range.

9. Click on the *Net value* column.
10. Choose *Summation*.

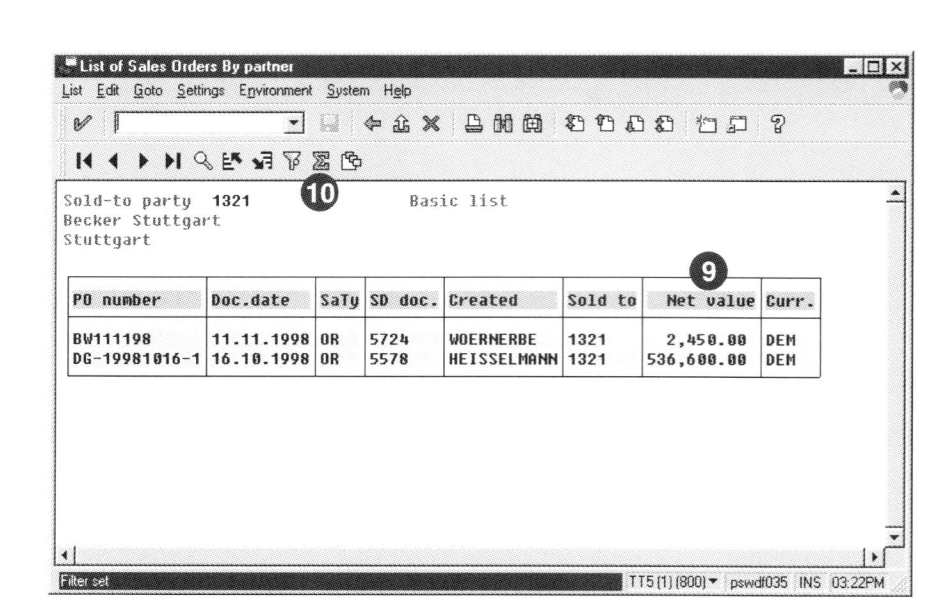

9–4   Reporting Made Easy

Section 9: Sales and Distribution Reports

List of Sales Orders

This screen shows the total net value.

11. To see an example of how display variants can be used, choose *Settings → Display variants → Choose*.

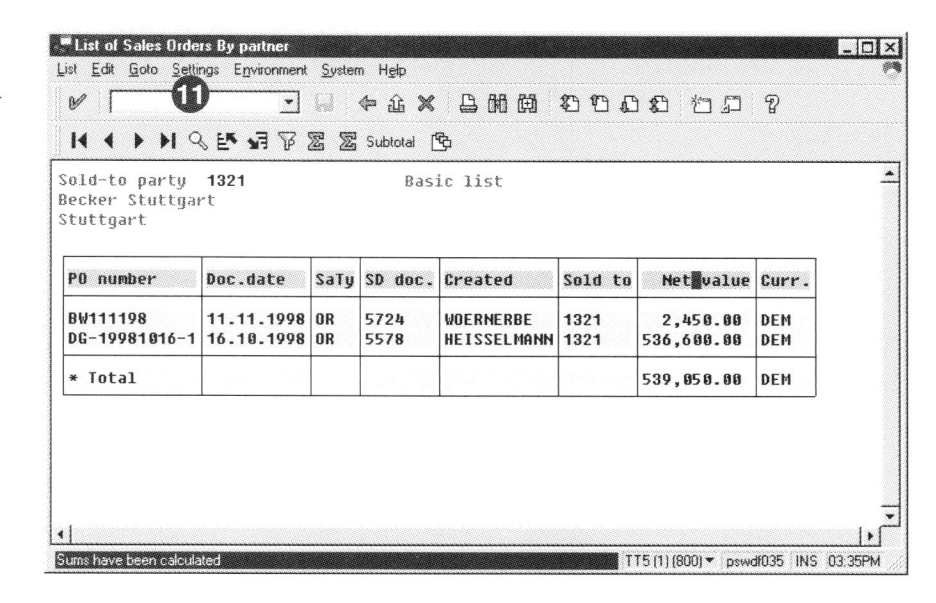

12. Select the variant *3SAP*.
13. Choose *Copy*.

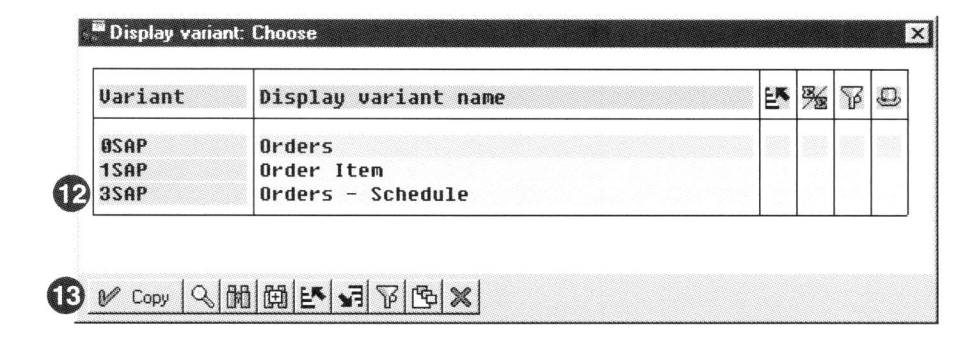

This screen shows output based on display variant *3SAP*.

14. Select *Standard order document 5348*.
15. Choose *Environment → Document flow* to view additional document information and master data.

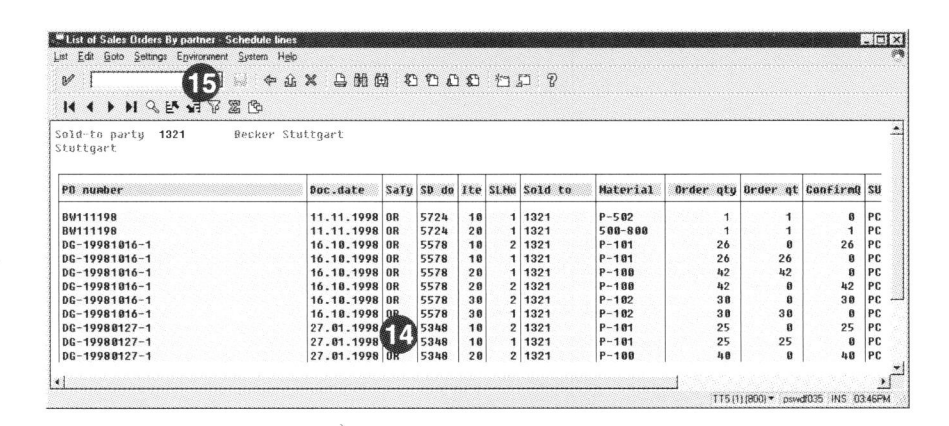

Commonly Used Reports: Illustrations and Perspectives

9–5

Section 9: Sales and Distribution Reports
List of Sales Orders

This screen shows document flow for *Standard order document 5348*.

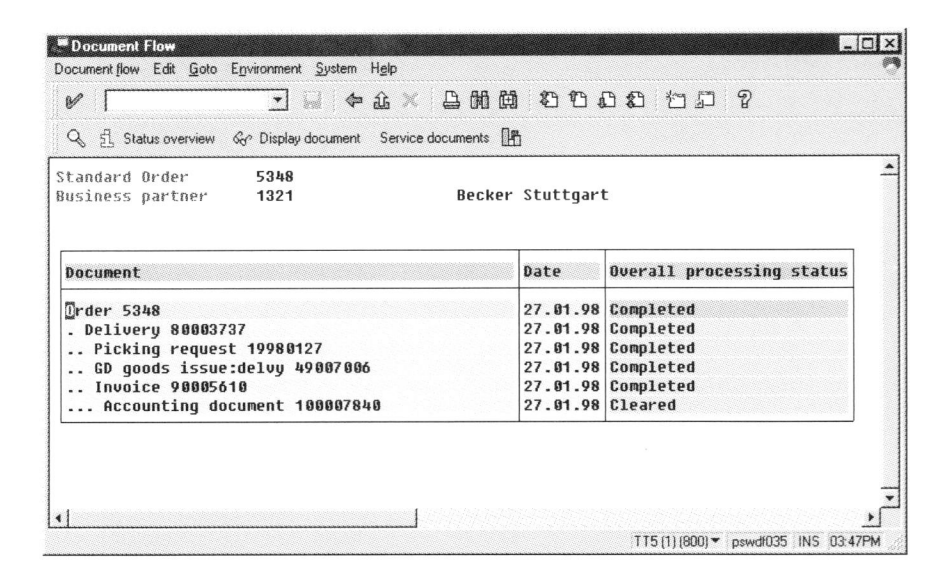

Document	Date	Overall processing status
Order 5348	27.01.98	Completed
. Delivery 80003737	27.01.98	Completed
.. Picking request 19980127	27.01.98	Completed
.. GD goods issue:delvy 49007006	27.01.98	Completed
.. Invoice 90005610	27.01.98	Completed
... Accounting document 100007840	27.01.98	Cleared

Standard Order 5348
Business partner 1321   Becker Stuttgart

Blocked Sales Orders

Quick Access   To run this report, use one of the following access options:

Option 1: Menu Path

Logistics → Sales and distribution → Sales → Environment → Document analysis → Blocked sales orders

Option 2: Transaction Code

In the *Command* field, enter transaction **V.14** and choose *Enter*.

Option 3: Program Name

Choose *System → Services → Reporting* and enter **RVSPERAU** in the *Program* field. Then, choose *Execute* to run the report.

Purpose   This report lists all orders blocked for shipping with corresponding order values derived from the confirmed quantities of the order items. You can modify this report to view and analyze related document data in a variety of ways.

A delivery block indicator can block the delivery of a sales order that has been entered in the system. Reasons for delivery block are typically customer related (for example, the customer postpones or changes the shipping date), product specific (for example, final QA check failed), or document/transaction related (for example, export papers are missing). Delivery block is an order header block, which means all open items are blocked. Blocked orders may block inventory or credits and should be released (unblocked) as soon as the blocking reason is no longer valid.

Prerequisites   No prerequisites are required to run this report. However, you should limit the selection criteria to reduce the run time (for example, by entering the delivery block, only blocked orders that are not product-related will list).

Integration   This report generates information that can be used to support order processing activities. For example, a customer service representative could find all blocked orders for delivery. A product manager could retrieve all blocked orders related to a particular product. An account manager could find out which orders are blocked for a particular customer.

Section 9: Sales and Distribution Reports
Blocked Sales Orders

Features

The selection screen of this report includes:

- Delivered standard variants: Select *Fast display/document overview* or one of the following list variants:
  - Display values for month
  - Customer
  - Material
  - Customer and material
- Output screen:
  - Fast display/document overview: Blocked orders list, sorted by the scheduled goods issue date. You can select any field for sorting. If you select one report line, the system displays the customer address. You can also branch to document processing (display or change the document).
  - Monthly overview: Confirmed and blocked order value shows in a monthly overview. The system uses the goods issue date to determine the month.
  - Customer view: Monthly total and blocked orders, and the customer (ship-to) lists.
  - Material view: Monthly total, blocked orders, and materials per order list. You can branch to document processing from the customer and material screens.
  - Material or customer view: Monthly total, blocked orders by ship-to, blocked orders by order number, and material lists.
  - Sorting capability by column for document, customer, and material views.
  - In all cases, the displayed list can be saved and reused (the date of *last data selection* lists).
- Background execution and printing

Next Steps

This report contains data obtained from order document data. As such, the data cannot be changed or manipulated from the report.

Section 9: Sales and Distribution Reports
Blocked Sales Orders

Guided Tour

Example 1: Display blocked sales orders in the *fast display/order overview* mode.

To access the first screen for this report, choose

Logistics → Sales and distribution → Sales → Environment → Document analysis → Blocked sales orders.

1. Under *List criteria*, select *Fast display/Document overview*.
2. Choose *Execute*.

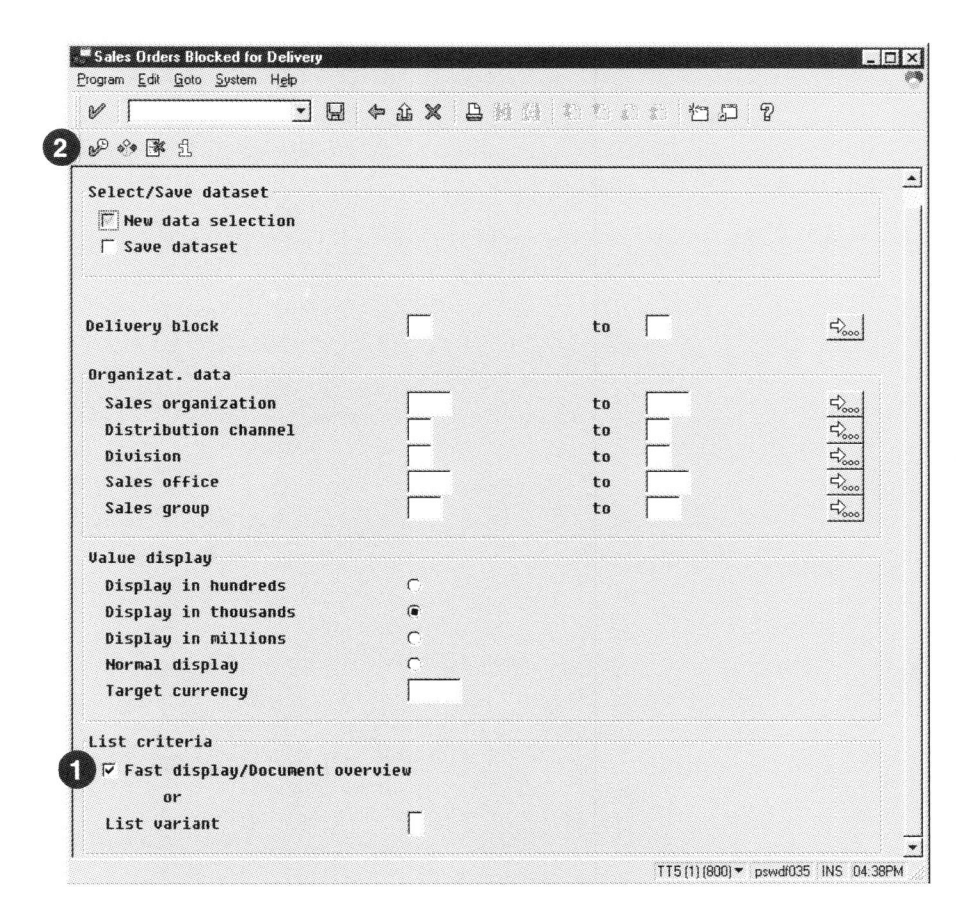

Section 9: Sales and Distribution Reports
Blocked Sales Orders

This screen shows all sales orders blocked by a delivery block.

3. Click on sales order *5664* to view detailed information

4. Choose *Environment→ SD document→ display/change* to branch into the document.

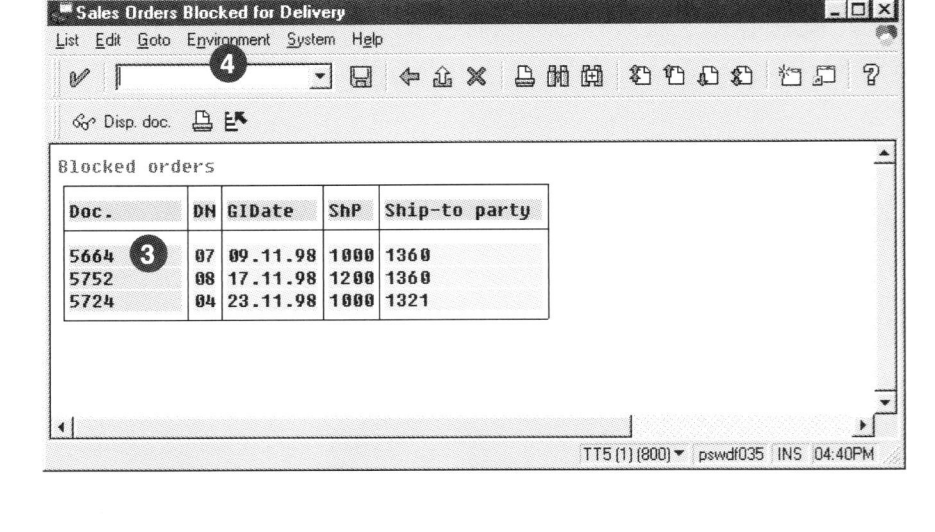

A This screen shows the standard function *display order* (transaction **VA03**). Sales order *5664* is blocked due to a quantity change.

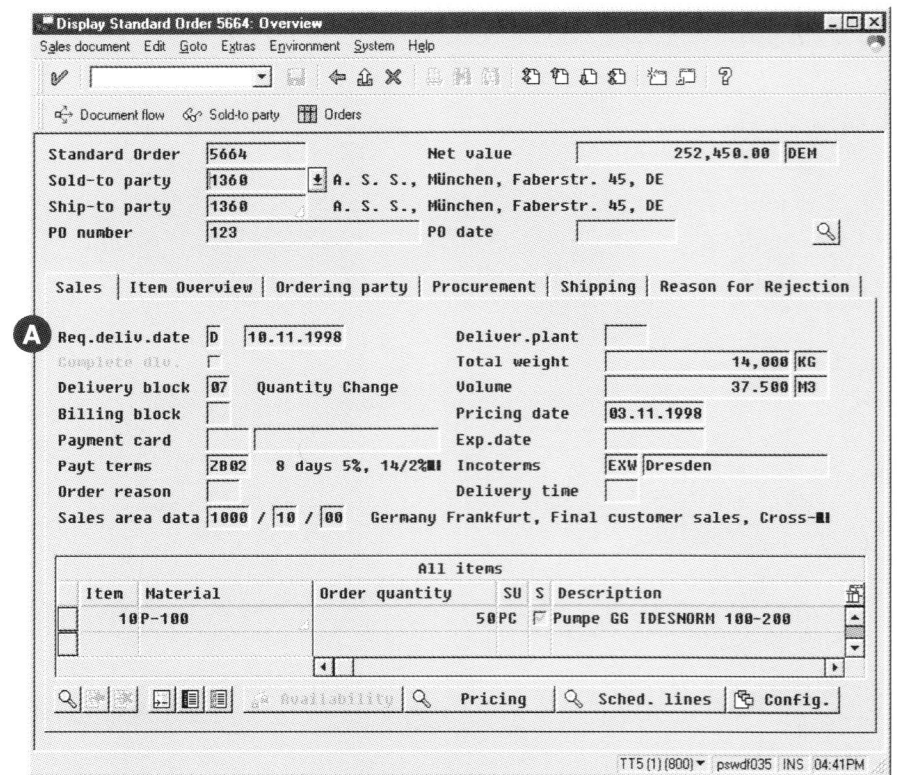

9–10 Reporting Made Easy

Section 9: Sales and Distribution Reports
Blocked Sales Orders

Example 2: Display blocked sales orders by customer and materials.

1. Under *List criteria*, enter **3** in *List variant*.
2. Choose *Execute*.

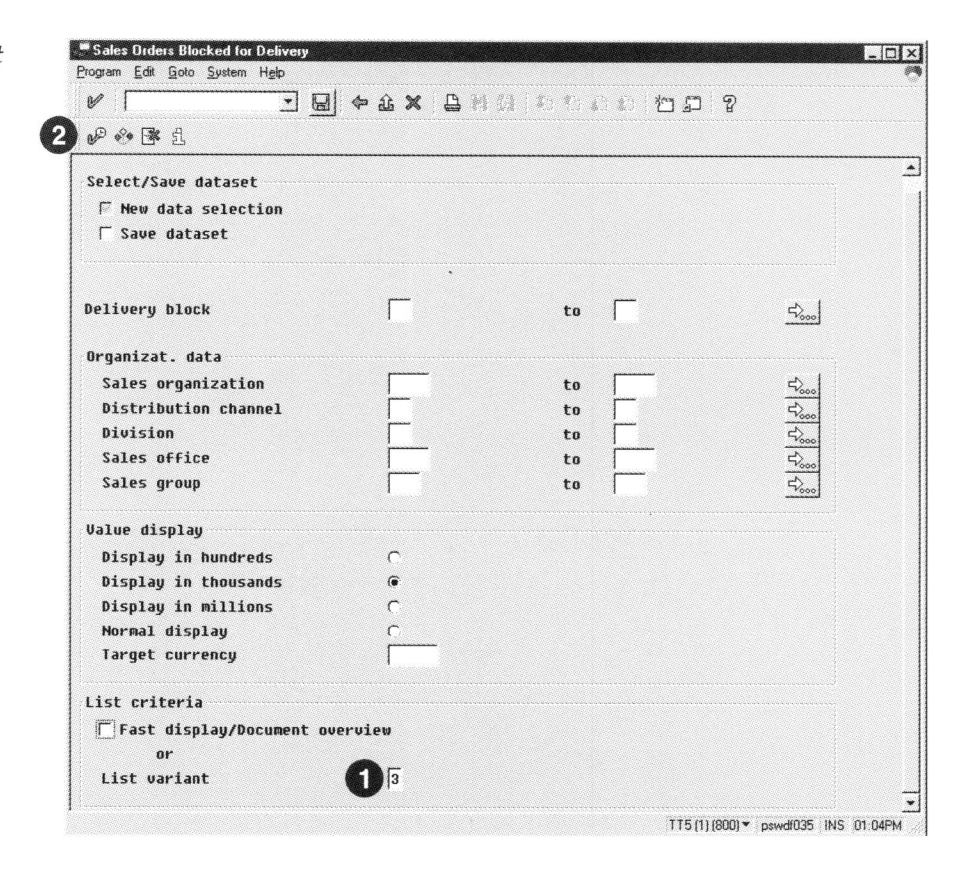

This screen shows all sales orders blocked by customer and materials.

3. Select *Customer and material* to view detailed information.
4. Choose *Enter*.

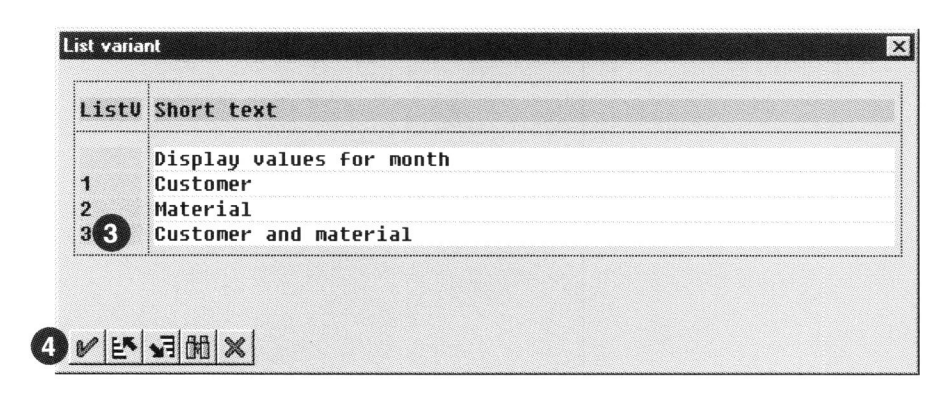

Commonly Used Reports: Illustrations and Perspectives

9–11

Section 9: Sales and Distribution Reports
Blocked Sales Orders

A   Blocked sales orders (by month)

B   Individual orders (by customer's name and blocked order value)

C   Blocking reason, order number, blocked materials, and blocked order value

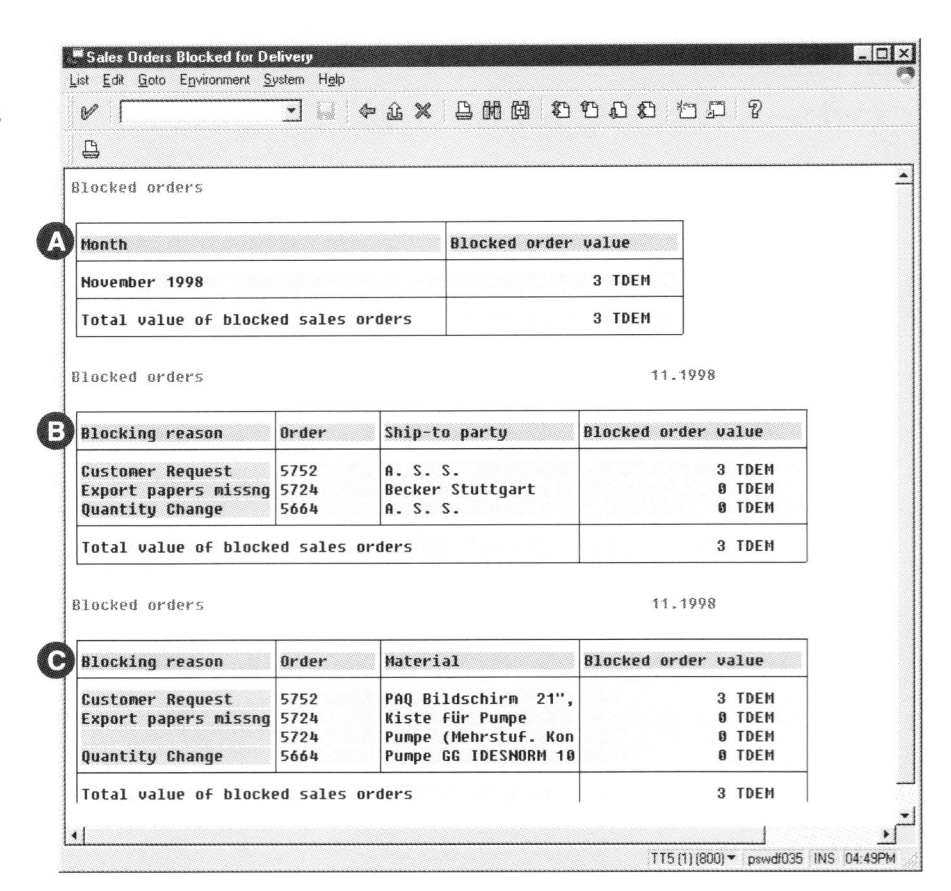

Backorders

Quick Access   To run this report, use one of the following access options:

Option 1: Menu Path

Logistics → Sales and distribution → Sales → Environment → Document analysis → Backorders

Option 2: Transaction Code

In the *Command* field, enter transaction **v.15** and choose *Enter*.

Option 3: Program Name

Choose *System → Services → Reporting* and enter **RVAUFRUE** in the *Program* field. Then, choose *Execute* to run the report.

Purpose   This report shows all orders still due to be shipped. Order values are determined from the confirmed quantities of the order items.

Prerequisites   No prerequisites are required to run this report. However, entering selection criteria is recommended.

Integration   From this report, you can branch out to the SD document, material master, or customer address.

Section 9: Sales and Distribution Reports
Backorders

Features

The selection screen of this report includes:

- Delivered standard variants: Select *Fast display/Document overview* or one of the following list variants:
  - Display values for month
  - Customer
  - Material
  - Customer and material
- Dynamic selection options
- User variables
- Output screen
  - Monthly overview: Confirmed order value in backlog lists. The system uses the goods-issue date to determine the month. You can branch out to customer and material views from the monthly view.
  - Customer view: Backorders and customer are specified.
  - Material view: Backorders and material are specified. You can branch out to document processing from the customer and material views.
  - Sort report data by document, customer, and material views.
- Background execution and printing.

Next Steps

This report contains data obtained from sales documents and includes material and customer data. From this report, you can branch out to view or edit the sales document.

TechTalk

> Note that users will only be able to edit sales documents if they are authorized to use transaction code VA02.

Section 9: Sales and Distribution Reports
Backorders

Guided Tour

Example 1: Display the backorders using *Fast Display/Document Overview*.

To access the first screen for this report, choose

Logistics → Sales and distribution → Sales → Environment → Document analysis → Backorders.

1. Under *Organizational data*, enter **0010** in *Sales organization*.
2. Under *List criteria*, select *Fast display/document overview*.
3. Choose *Execute*.

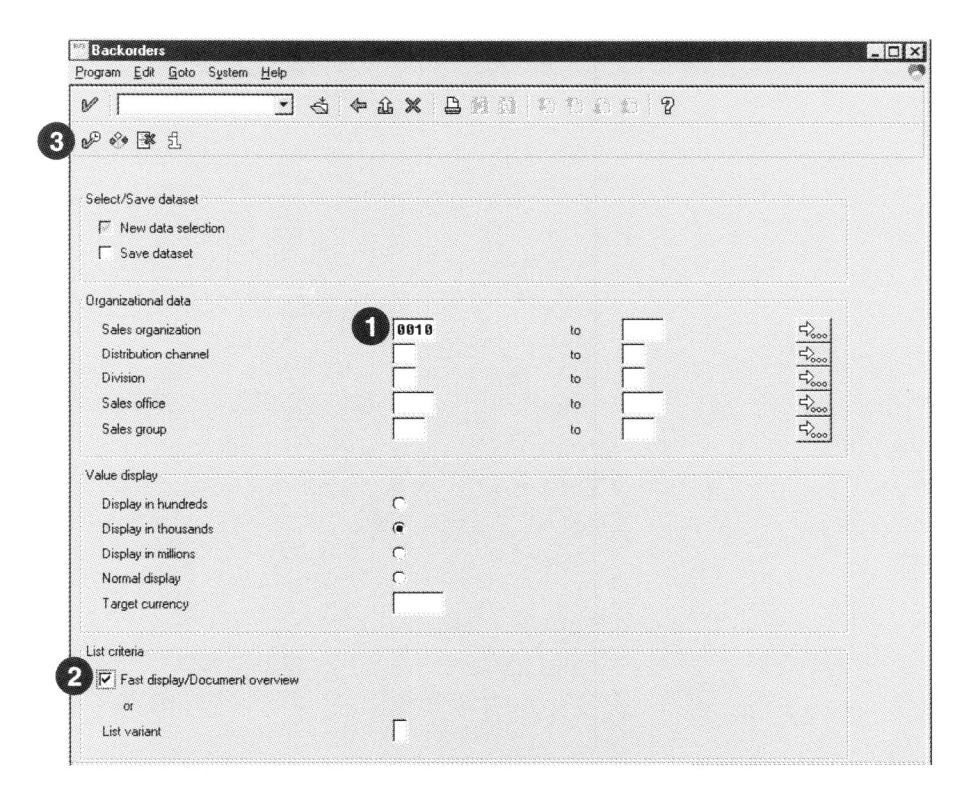

Commonly Used Reports: Illustrations and Perspectives

Section 9: Sales and Distribution Reports
Backorders

Backorder documents list by goods issue date (*GIDate*), shipping point (*ShP*), and ship-to party.

4. To drill down to an individual backorder document (for example, 9), click in the row for the document.

5. Choose *Display document*.

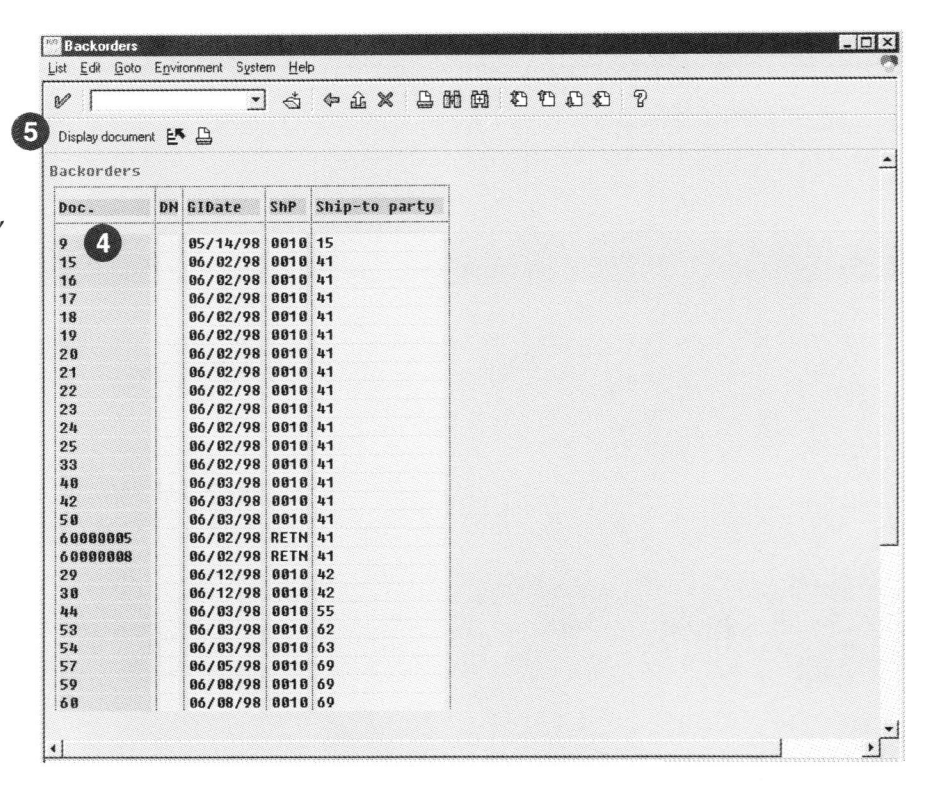

This screen shows an overview of standard order 9. From here, we can research the backorder. For example, we can:

A Review the document flow.

B View the details of any action that might have been taken in *Shipping*.

C Explore failures in quality inspection or other reasons for rejection.

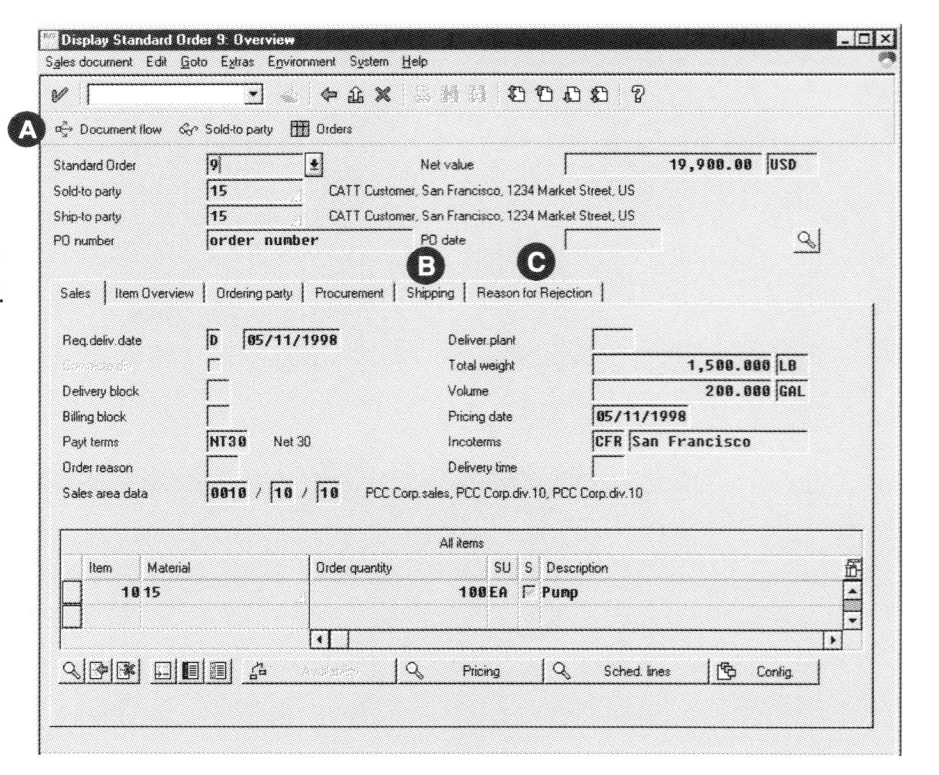

9–16

Reporting Made Easy

Example 2: Display the total value of the backorders for a particular month.

1. Under *Organizational data*, enter **0010** in *Sales organization*.
2. Make certain *Fast display/document overview* is deselected.
3. Leave the *list variant* blank. If you choose *possible entries* on the *List variant* field, possible list variants will appear.
4. Choose *Execute*.

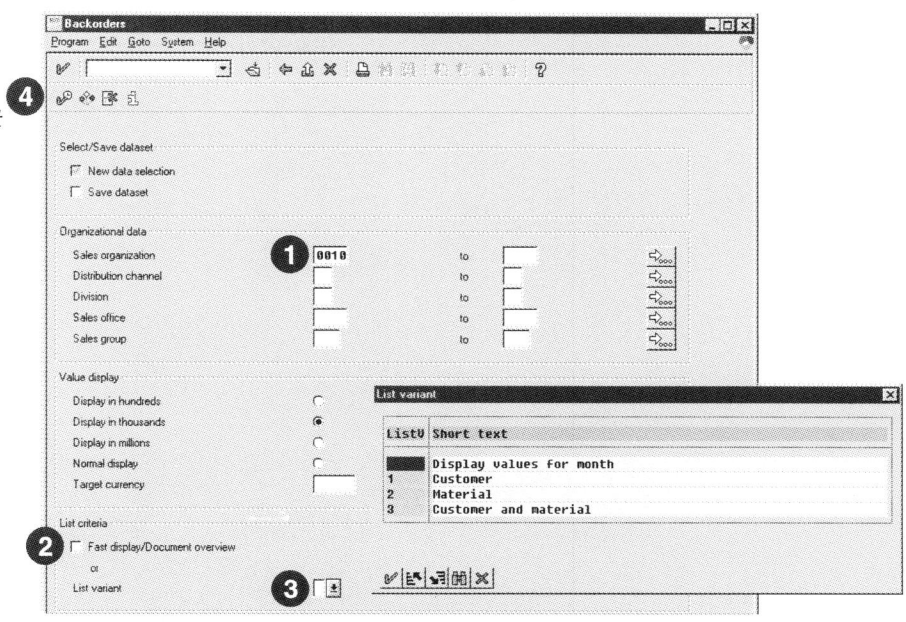

This screen shows the value of the backorders per month.

5. Choose *Customers*. This option produces a column listing by order number, customer, value, and GI date.

   If you choose *Material*, this option produces a column listing by order number, material, value, and GI date.

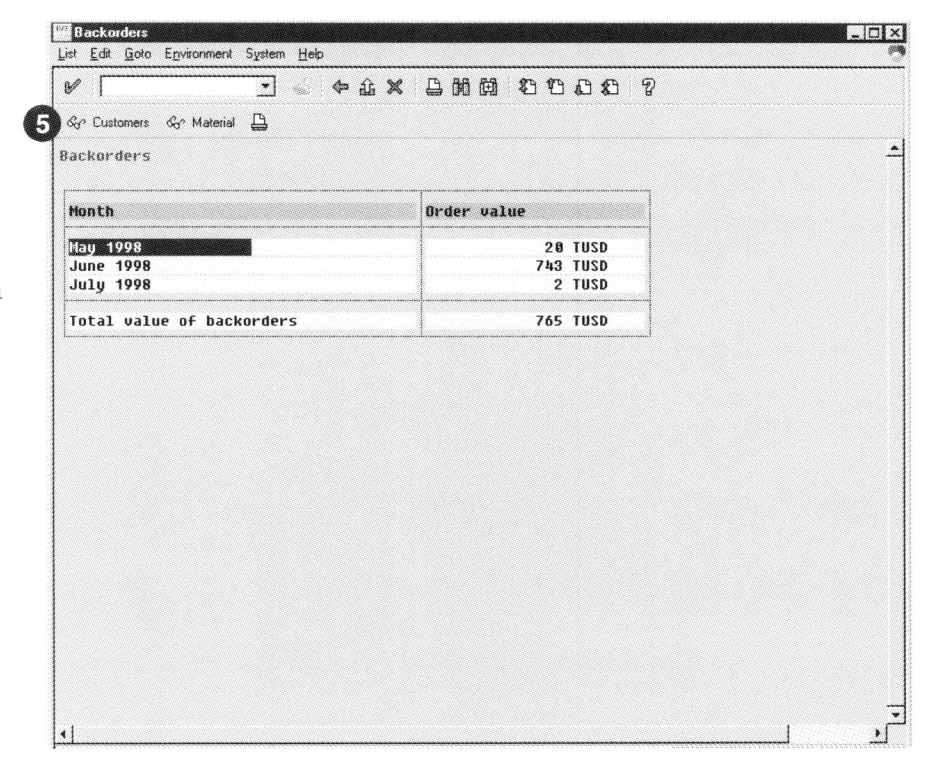

Section 9: Sales and Distribution Reports
Backorders

This screen shows backorders by *Customers*.

6. Choose *Display document* to view the details of the individual document.

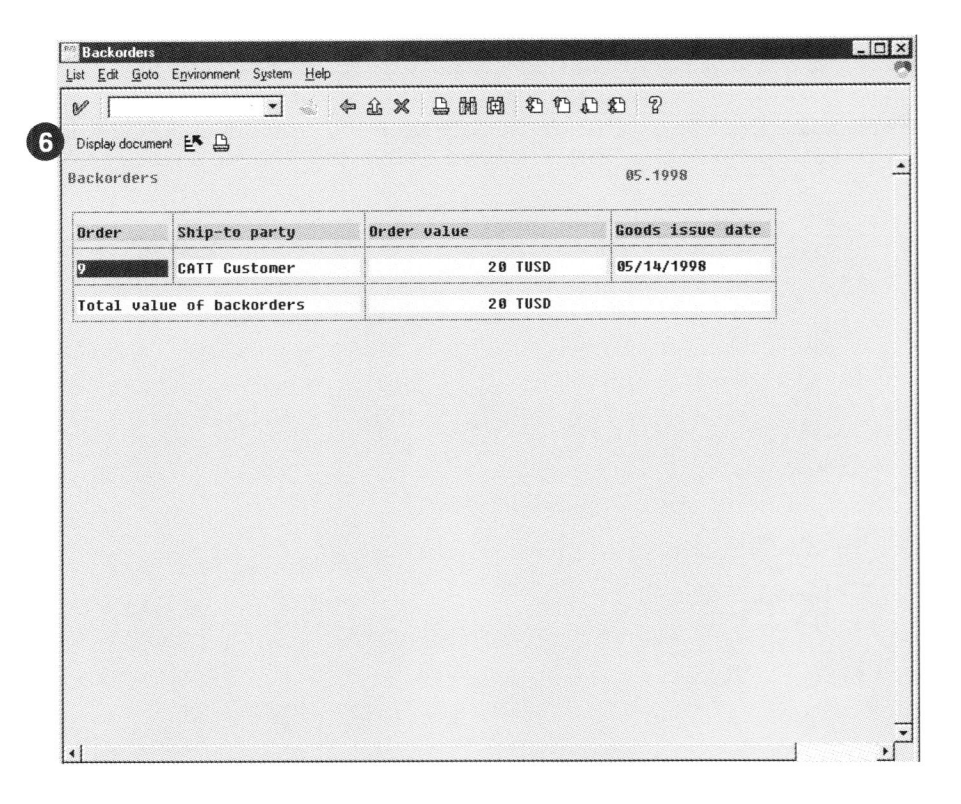

This screen shows backorders by *Material*.

7. Choose *Display document* to view the details of the individual document.

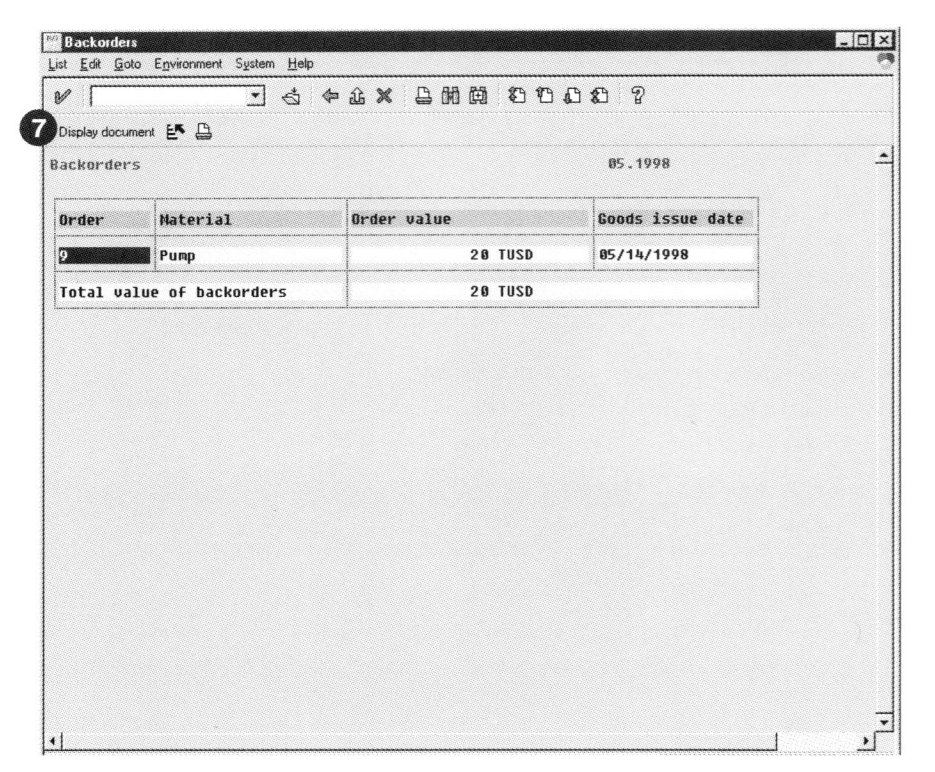

Example 3: Display the total value of backorders per month for customer and material.

1. Under *Organizational data*, enter **0010** in *Sales organization*.
2. Under *List criteria*, enter **3** in *List variant* to display customer and material information.
3. Choose *Execute*.

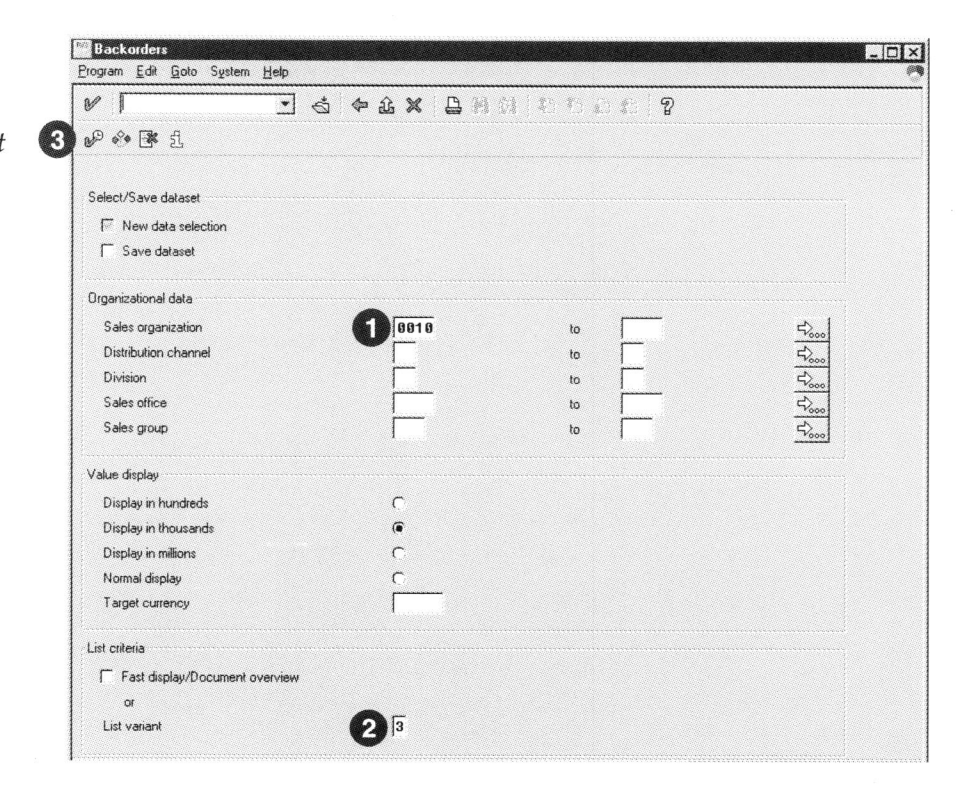

Section 9: Sales and Distribution Reports
Backorders

A   Backorder totals (by month)

B   Backorders (by customer)

C   Backorders (by month and material)

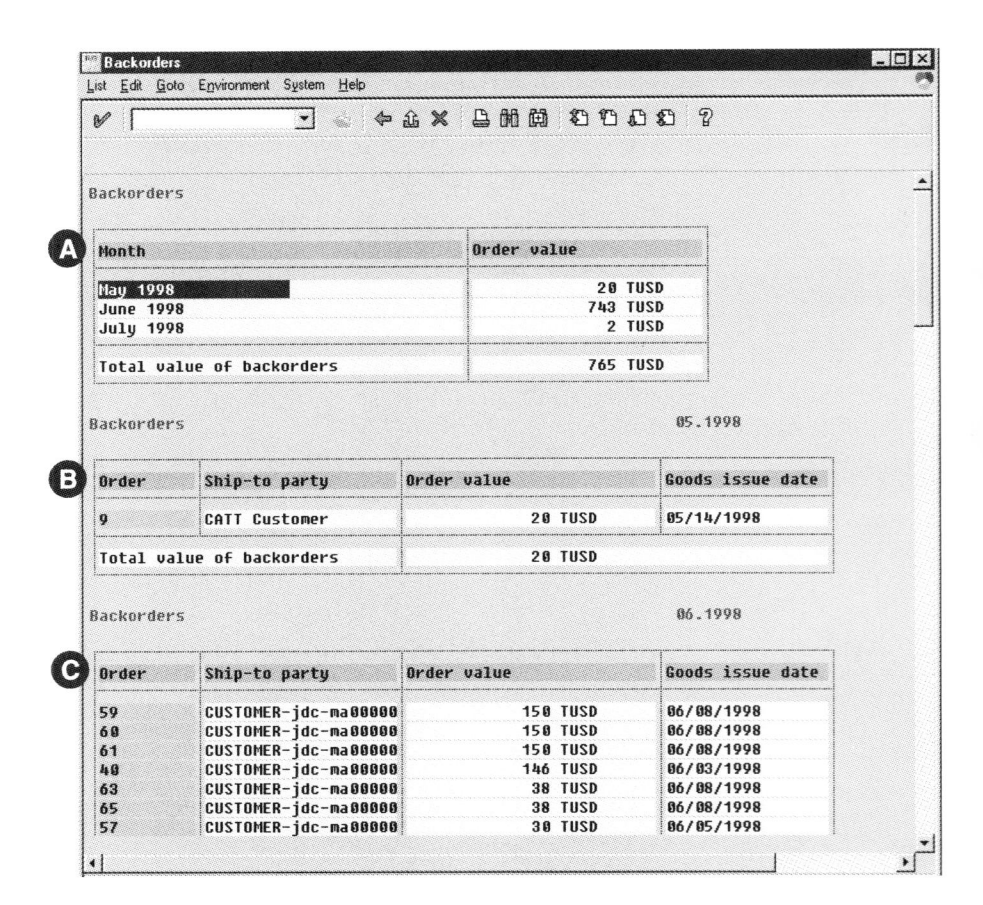

Backorders

A — Backorders

Month	Order value
May 1998	20 TUSD
June 1998	743 TUSD
July 1998	2 TUSD
Total value of backorders	765 TUSD

Backorders   05.1998

B —

Order	Ship-to party	Order value	Goods issue date
9	CATT Customer	20 TUSD	05/14/1998
Total value of backorders		20 TUSD	

Backorders   06.1998

C —

Order	Ship-to party	Order value	Goods issue date
59	CUSTOMER-jdc-ma00000	150 TUSD	06/08/1998
60	CUSTOMER-jdc-ma00000	150 TUSD	06/08/1998
61	CUSTOMER-jdc-ma00000	150 TUSD	06/08/1998
40	CUSTOMER-jdc-ma00000	146 TUSD	06/03/1998
63	CUSTOMER-jdc-ma00000	38 TUSD	06/08/1998
65	CUSTOMER-jdc-ma00000	38 TUSD	06/08/1998
57	CUSTOMER-jdc-ma00000	30 TUSD	06/05/1998

4. Scroll down the list to view additional backorder information by month and material.

5. You can access change/display functionality by selecting *Environment → SD Document → Change/Display*.

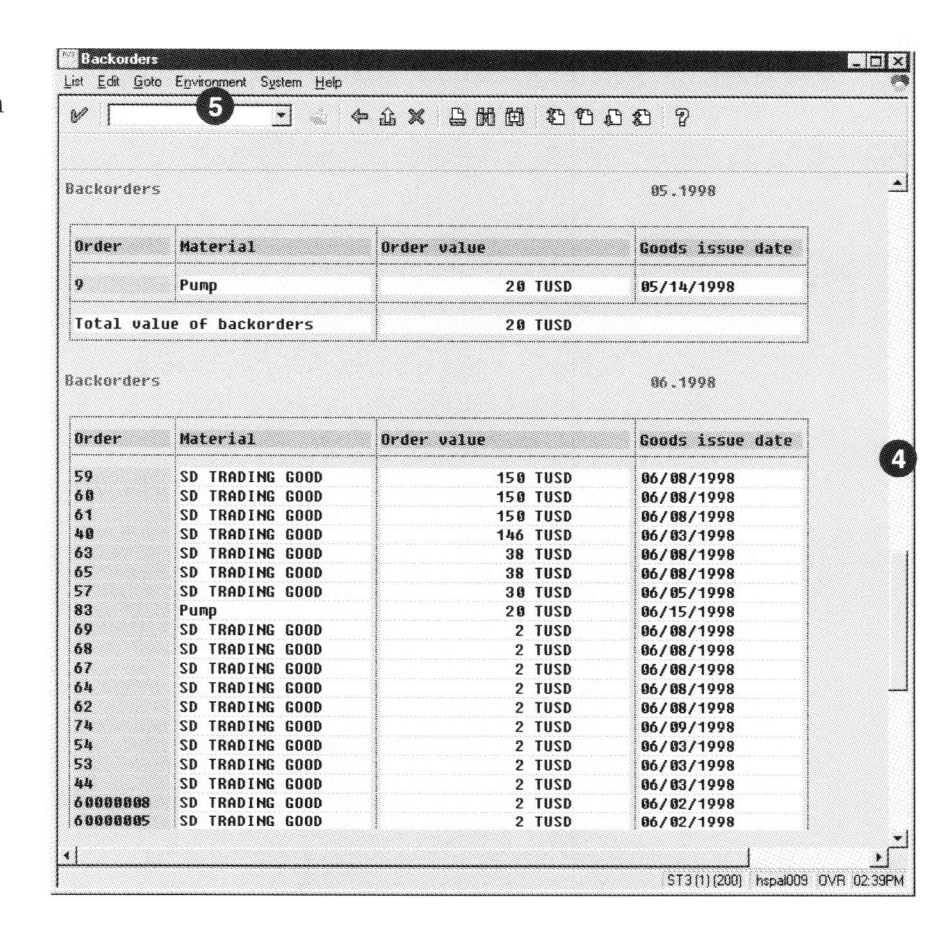

Backorders			05.1998
Order	Material	Order value	Goods issue date
9	Pump	20 TUSD	05/14/1998
Total value of backorders		20 TUSD	

Backorders			06.1998
Order	Material	Order value	Goods issue date
59	SD TRADING GOOD	150 TUSD	06/08/1998
60	SD TRADING GOOD	150 TUSD	06/08/1998
61	SD TRADING GOOD	150 TUSD	06/08/1998
40	SD TRADING GOOD	146 TUSD	06/03/1998
63	SD TRADING GOOD	38 TUSD	06/08/1998
65	SD TRADING GOOD	38 TUSD	06/08/1998
57	SD TRADING GOOD	30 TUSD	06/05/1998
83	Pump	20 TUSD	06/15/1998
69	SD TRADING GOOD	2 TUSD	06/08/1998
68	SD TRADING GOOD	2 TUSD	06/08/1998
67	SD TRADING GOOD	2 TUSD	06/08/1998
64	SD TRADING GOOD	2 TUSD	06/08/1998
62	SD TRADING GOOD	2 TUSD	06/08/1998
74	SD TRADING GOOD	2 TUSD	06/09/1998
54	SD TRADING GOOD	2 TUSD	06/03/1998
53	SD TRADING GOOD	2 TUSD	06/03/1998
44	SD TRADING GOOD	2 TUSD	06/03/1998
60000008	SD TRADING GOOD	2 TUSD	06/02/1998
60000005	SD TRADING GOOD	2 TUSD	06/02/1998

Incoming Order Report (SIS Statistical Analysis)

Quick Access

To run this report, use one of the following access options:

Option 1: Menu Path

Logistics → Sales and distribution → Sales information system → Standard analyses → Customer | Material | Sales organization | Sales employee | Sales office

Option 2: Transaction Code

In the *Command* field, enter transaction (see table below) and choose *Enter*. Choose one of the following options:

Transaction code	Standard analyses
MCTA	Customer
MCTC	Material
MCTE	Sales organization
MCTI	Sales employee
MCTG	Sales office

Option 3: Program Name

Choose *System* → *Services* → *Reporting* and enter `RMCV0100` in the *Program* field. Then, choose *Execute* to run the report.

Purpose

This report provides information on incoming orders. Not every manager within a company requires the same level of information on incoming orders. For example, a monthly summary of incoming orders (organized by sales office or customer) may be adequate for a senior executive, but a line manager may want to see a daily summary of the same data, perhaps listed by material. In this instance, the *Incoming Order Report* meets the unique information needs of both users.

Information systems reports, such as *Incoming orders*, are part of the *Logistics Information System*. The data reported is stored in special tables called information structures, which are separated from transaction levels. This allows much faster reporting and minimizes the impact on performance. The Sales Information System is part of the Logistics Information System. For more information on these tools, see books 1 and 2 of the *Reporting Made Easy* series.

Additionally, hundreds of end-user reporting functions in standard analyses and flexible analyses offer a range of options to analyze the information of incoming orders. The reporting data is updated at the information structures *S001-S004* and *S006* when an incoming order item is created or changed. Deleted orders are removed, but rejected orders are retained in the information structures.

Creating company specific information structures and update rules lets you specify different ways of collecting and reporting order data.

Section 9: Sales and Distribution Reports
Incoming Order Report (SIS Statistical Analysis)

Prerequisites You must use *Period to analyze* selection criteria to run this report.

You should limit the selection criteria to reduce the run time for the report.

Integration You can view other reports (such as open orders, returned orders, and invoiced sales) with the *SIS* end-user functions of standard or flexible analyses.

In standard analyses, a search/jump function lets you jump to the customer or material master records.

In flexible analyses, the report-to-report interface lets you jump to the customer or material master records.

Features The selection screen of this report includes:

- Variants
- Dynamic selection options
- User settings for report drilldown, default key figures, and other reporting parameters
- Execution

The output of this report includes:

- Listing order header, order item, and order schedule item data
- Selection of documents for individual display (double-click on one of the individual document line items)
- Dynamic filtering of output (by column) after the program has been executed (to narrow down the displayed results): Position the cursor on a column, then choose *Edit → Set filter* (Ctrl+Shift+F2)
- Sorting capability (by column): Select a column, then choose *Edit → Sort in ascending/descending order* (Ctrl+Shift+F5/F4)
- Summation by column: Select a column, then choose *Edit → Add up values* (Shift+F7)
- Column width optimization: Select a column, then choose *Settings → Columns → Optimize width*
- Data statistics for the output: Choose *Settings → List status* (Ctrl+F11)

Next Steps This report contains data that is statistically summarized. Based on your system's configuration, this data is updated online by sales events or periodically by batch programs. This data cannot be manipulated.

Section 9: Sales and Distribution Reports
Incoming Order Report (SIS Statistical Analysis)

Report Options

When running the report in *LIS/SIS* (standard analyses), choose

Logistics → *Sales and distribution* → *Sales information system* → *Standard analyses*.

Under *Standard analyses*, choose one of the following options:

Menu option	For reporting
Customer	Sold-to party, Material, Sales organization, Distribution channel, Division
Material	Material, Sales organization, Distribution channel
Sales organization	Distr. channel, Division, Material, Sales district, Sales organization, Sold-to party
Sales employee	Sales organization, Distr. channel, Division, Sales employee, Sold-to party, Material
Sales office	Sales organization, Sales group, Sales office, Distr. channel, Division

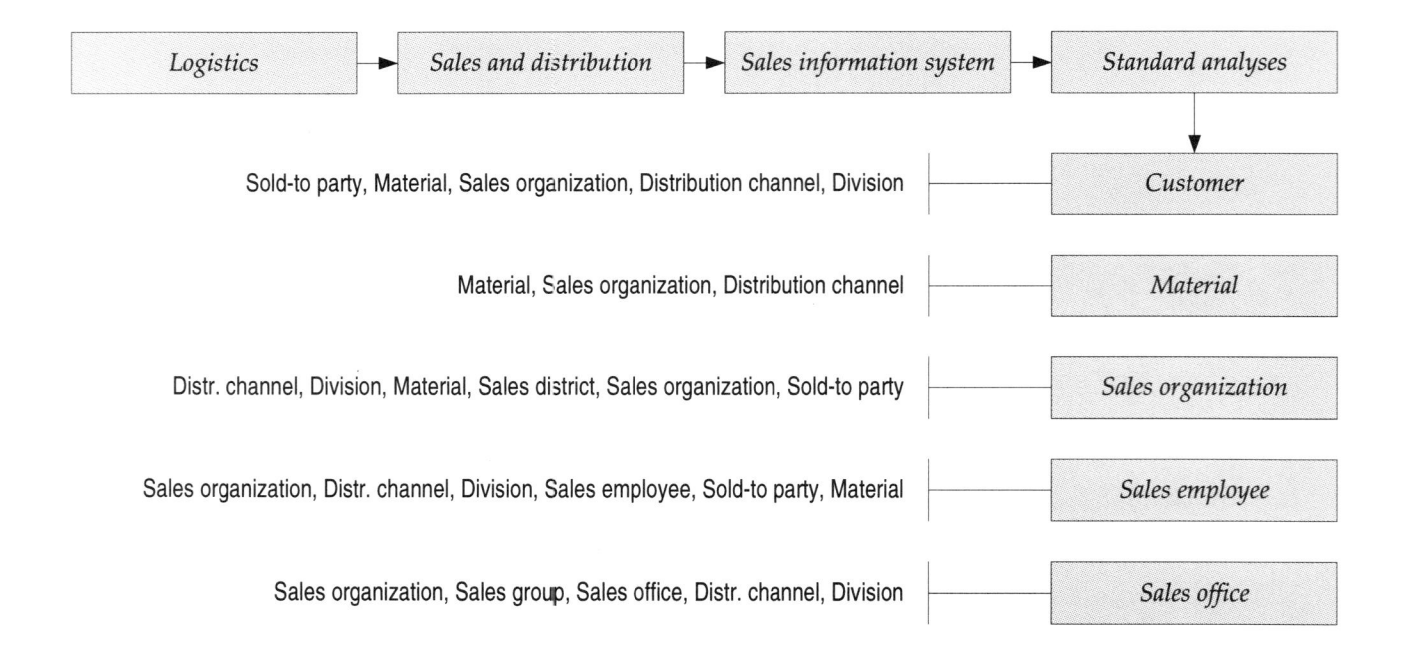

Guided Tour

Example: List and analyze the booked or incoming orders for a two-month period.

To access the first screen for this report, choose

Logistics → *Sales and distribution* → *Sales information system* → *Standard analyses* → *Customer.*

1. Under *Characteristics*, enter **1000** in *Sales organization*.

2. Under *Period to analyze*, enter a date range (for example, **06/1998** to **08/1998**) in *Month*.

   A period is determined by the date an ordered item is changed or deleted.

3. Choose *Execute*.

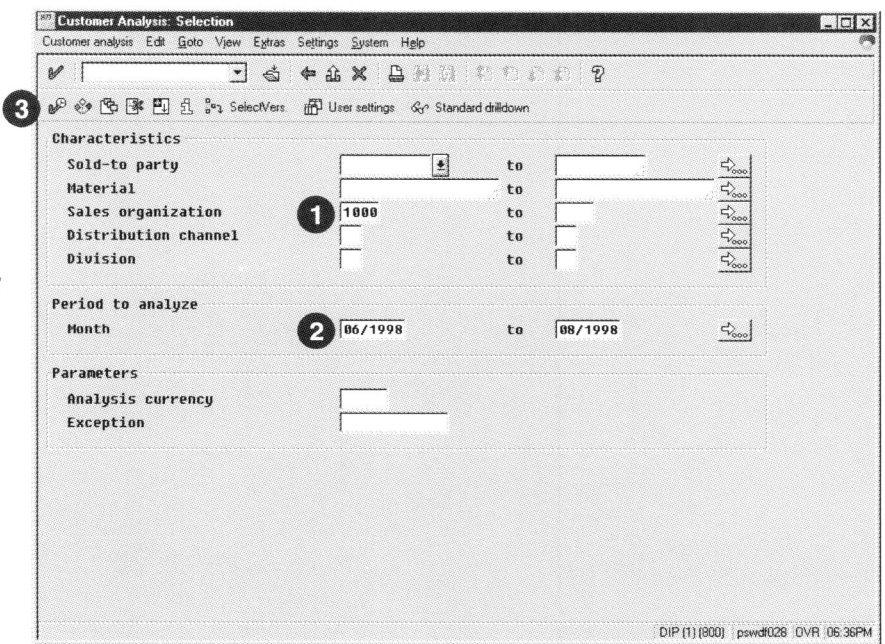

Section 9: Sales and Distribution Reports
Incoming Order Report (SIS Statistical Analysis)

This screen shows data based on the standard defaults for drilldown, key figures to be displayed, and other layout settings.

4. Choose *Edit → Choose Key figures*, to select additional key figures or to change their sequence.

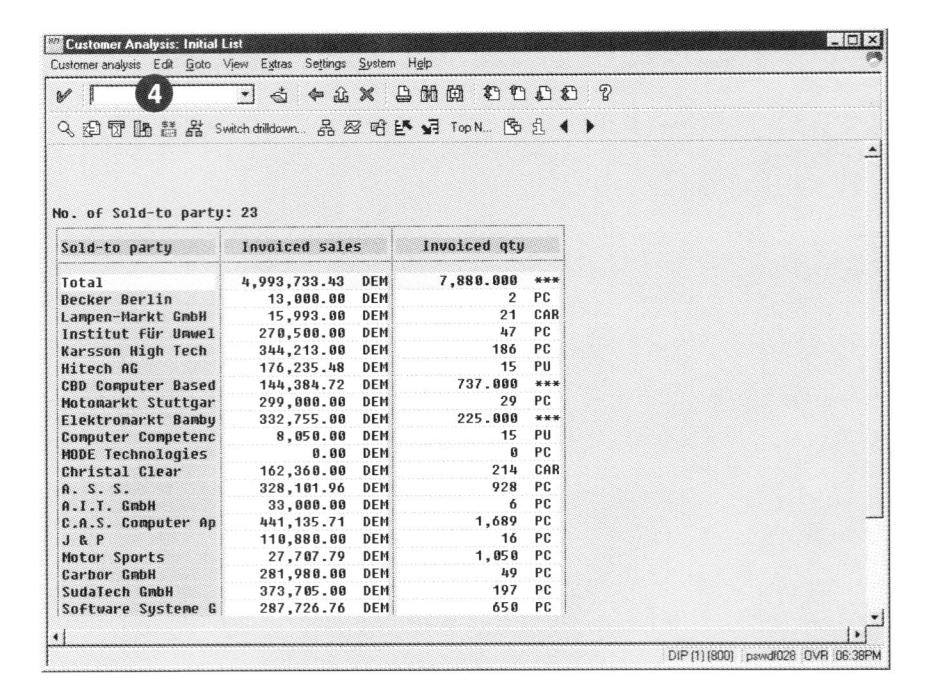

As shown to the right, the *Choose Key figures* screen has two columns:
- *Selected Key figures* lists the key figures which have been selected for display
- *All* lists all available key figures

5. Choose *Incoming orders qty.* from the column to the right.

6. Choose *Show key fields*.

This partial screen shows:
- Insertion of key figure *incoming order qty*
- Deletion of key figures *invoiced sales* and *credit memos*
- Number of decimal places set to 0

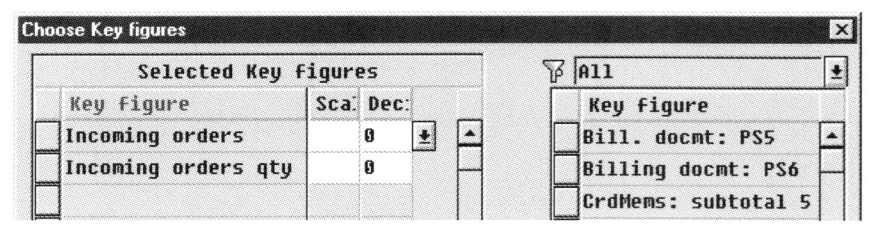

9–26　　　　　　　　　　　　　　　　　　　　　　　　　　　　Reporting Made Easy

Section 9: Sales and Distribution Reports
Incoming Order Report (SIS Statistical Analysis)

This screen shows data based on the standard defaults for drilldown, key figures to be displayed, and other layout settings. The columns in this table correspond to the key figures chosen in step 5.

7. Choose *Switch drilldown*.
8. Select *Distribution channel*.
9. Choose *Enter*.

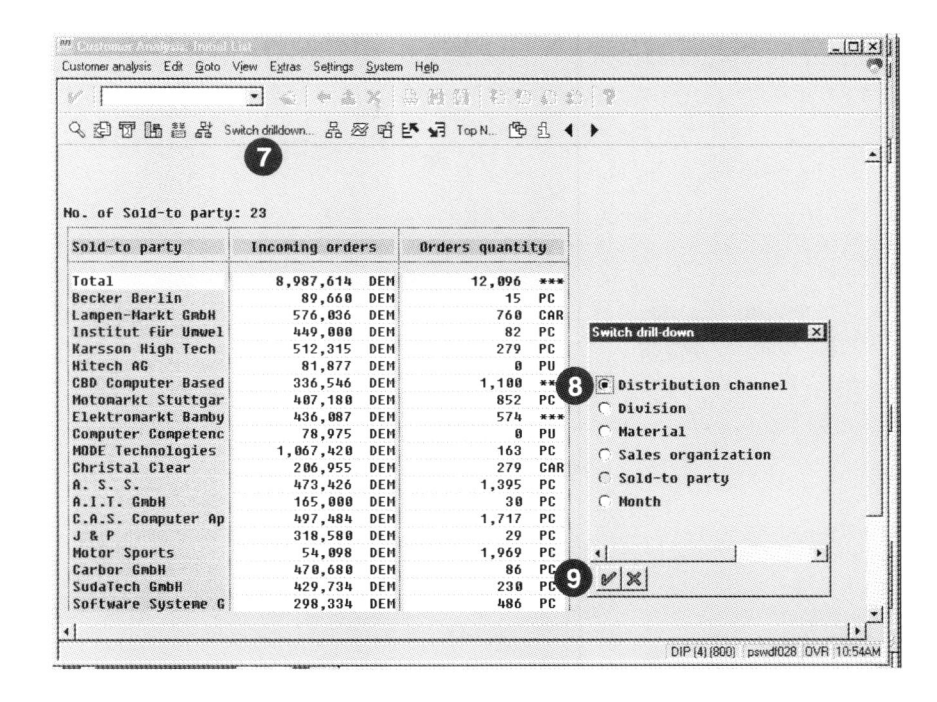

This screen shows data grouped by distribution channels.

The following functions (extract) are available on the toolbar to further analyze the shown data:

- Sorting (+ / -)
- Top N / Last N
- Time series (periods in columns)
- Graphics

The following functions are available from the *Edit* menu path:

- Comparing two key figures
- Comparing actual / plan
- Comparing current / last year ABC analysis
- Correlation / classification

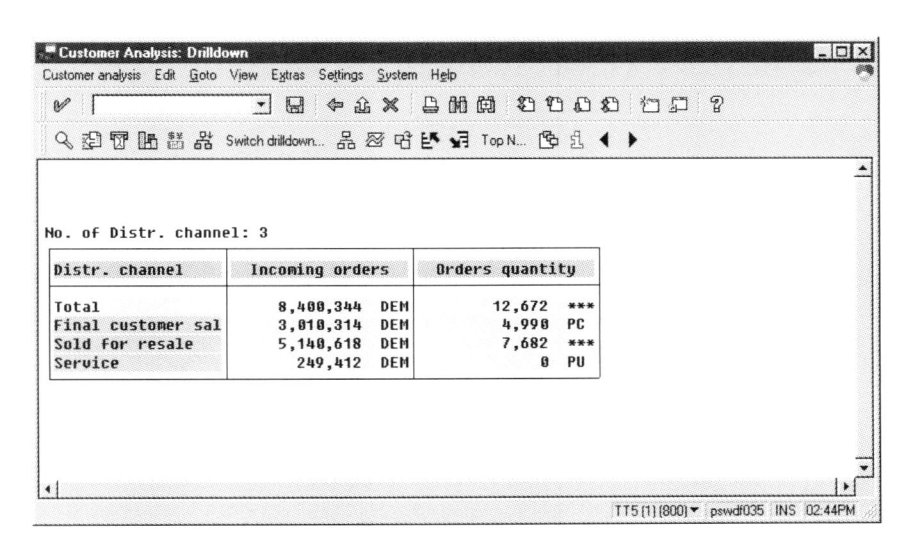

Commonly Used Reports: Illustrations and Perspectives

Section 9: Sales and Distribution Reports

Incoming Order Report (SIS Statistical Analysis)

To change the layout for:
- Display characteristics (Choose *Settings* → *Char. Display* → *Key description | Key*)
- Display key figures as value or percentage (Choose *Settings* → *Value display* → *Absolute | Percent*)
- Analysis currency (Choose *Settings* → *Currency* → *Analysis currency*)
- Column width (Choose *Settings* → *Column width* → *Characteristic | Key figure*)

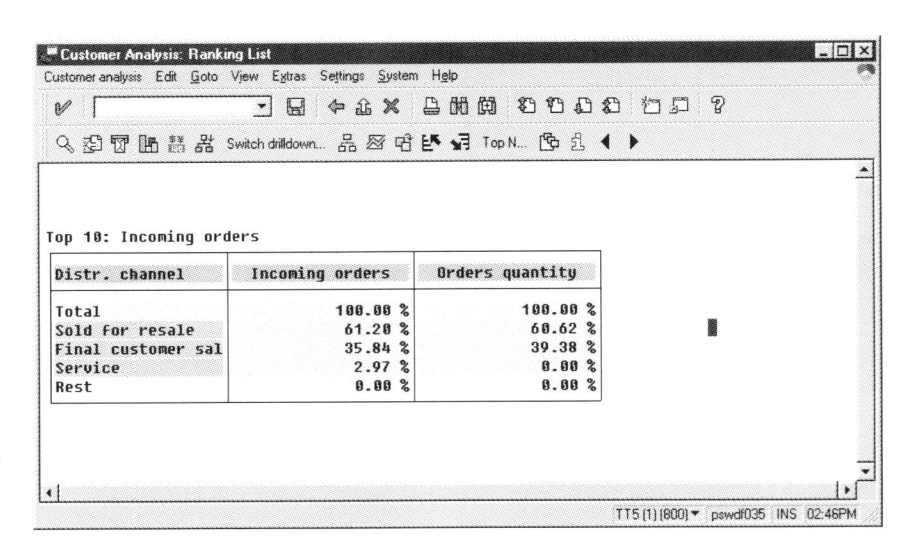

The output can be:
- Printed
- E-mailed
- Exported (to XXL or as a PC file)
- Saved (as selection version)

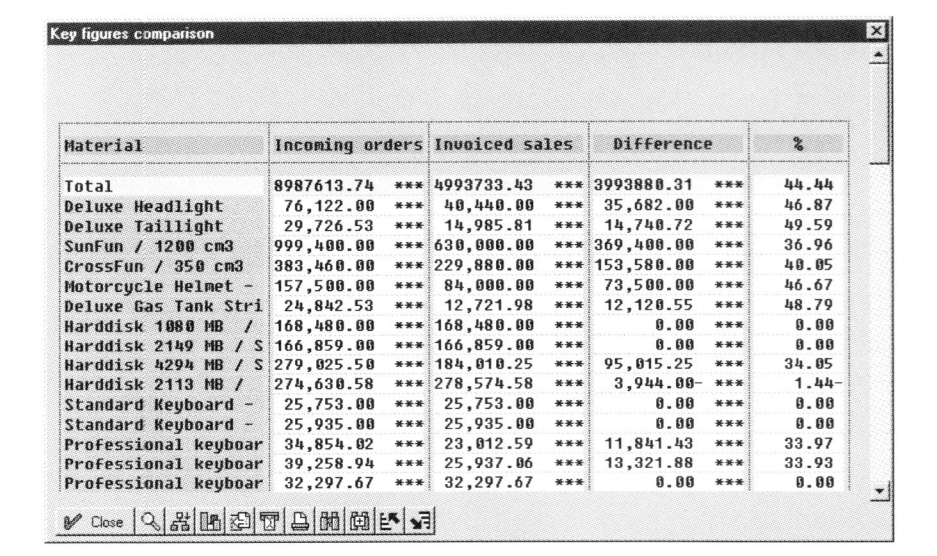

Incoming Orders for Customers and Materials (Document or Statistical Analysis)

Quick Access	To run this report, use one of the following access options:

Option 1: Transaction Code
In the *Command* field, enter transaction code **V.12** and choose *Enter*.

Option 2: Program Name
Choose *System → Services → Reporting* and enter **RVAUFEIN** in the *Program* field. Then, choose *Execute* to run the report.

Purpose	The purpose of this report is to provide document or statistical analysis of incoming orders. This report provides summarized order information with a minimal adverse impact on the system performance. This report displays orders for the selected top customers and materials. The system considers the order date when determining the time.

Prerequisites	No prerequisites are required to run this report. The compressed values for material and customer are read by the system from an intermediate file. These values are stored by month using report **RVMATRSL**. Depending on how current the desired data needs to be, you should normally run this report in the background.

Integration	From this report you can branch to the customer and material master.

Section 9: Sales and Distribution Reports
Incoming Orders for Customers and Materials (Document or Statistical Analysis)

Features

The selection screen of this report includes:
- Input time-period.
- Input SD organizational data (Sales organization is also required)
- Selection criteria
  - Distribution channel
  - Sales organization
  - Division (order header division)
  - Sales office
  - Sales group
- Date range
- Value display
- Display variants
  - Display values for month
  - 1   Customer
  - 2   Material
  - 3   Customer and material
- Output screen
  - Can change the width of the column, and freeze or unfreeze columns.
  - Can alternate between display variants if starting with variant
- Branch to the master data (sold-to and material) on some levels.

Next Steps

This report contains data that is statistically summarized. Based on your system's configuration, this data is updated online by sales events or periodically by batch programs. This data cannot be manipulated.

Section 9: Sales and Distribution Reports
Incoming Orders for Customers and Materials (Document or Statistical Analysis)

Guided Tour

Example: Display sales documents by sold-to party.

To access the first screen for this report, choose

System → Services → Reporting and enter **RVAUFEIN** in the *Program* field.

1. Under *Time period*, enter a date range (for example, **01 1998** to **08 1998**) in *Month*.

2. Under *List criteria*, enter **100** in *No. of top customers/materials*. You can also do this from the output screen.

3. Under *Value display*, select *Display in thousands*.

4. Choose *Execute*.

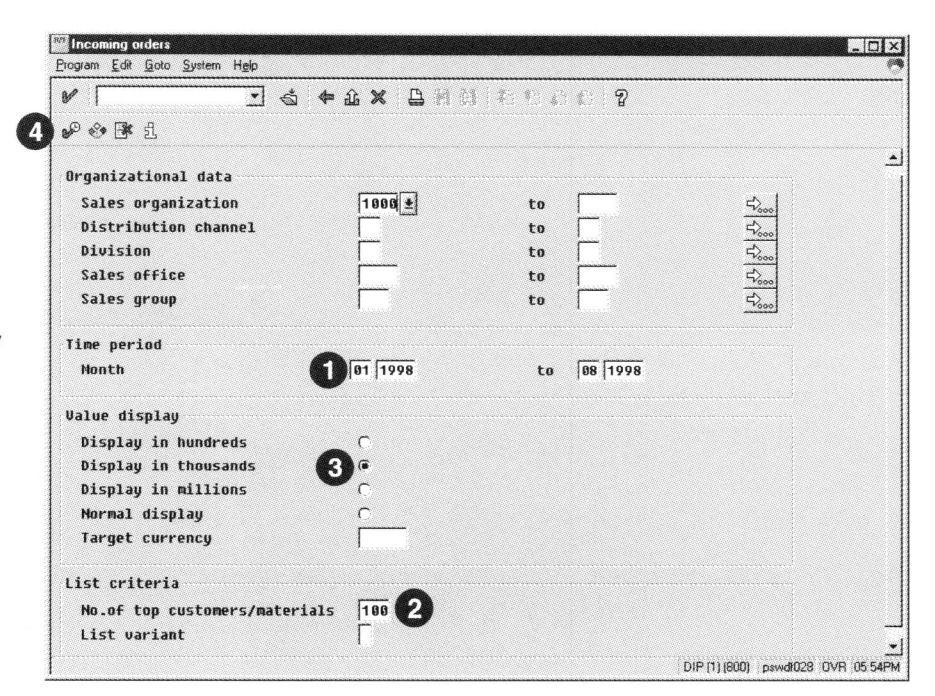

Commonly Used Reports: Illustrations and Perspectives

9–31

Section 9: Sales and Distribution Reports

Incoming Orders for Customers and Materials (Document or Statistical Analysis)

This screen shows output as a basic list with no display variant(s).

5. Choose *Customer* for further drilldown. The resulting output is shown on the following page.

6. Choose *Material* for further drilldown. The resulting output is shown on the following page.

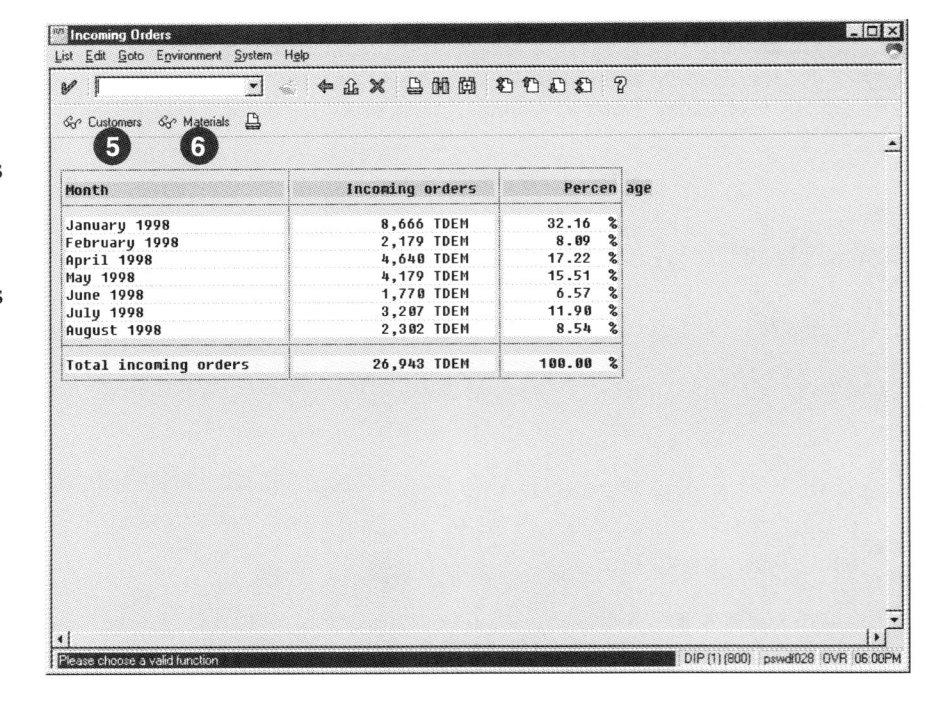

Month	Incoming orders	Percentage
January 1998	8,666 TDEM	32.16 %
February 1998	2,179 TDEM	8.09 %
April 1998	4,640 TDEM	17.22 %
May 1998	4,179 TDEM	15.51 %
June 1998	1,770 TDEM	6.57 %
July 1998	3,207 TDEM	11.90 %
August 1998	2,302 TDEM	8.54 %
Total incoming orders	26,943 TDEM	100.00 %

This screen shows incoming orders by *Customer* (sold-to) for the selected period, as well as the total value of the incoming orders.

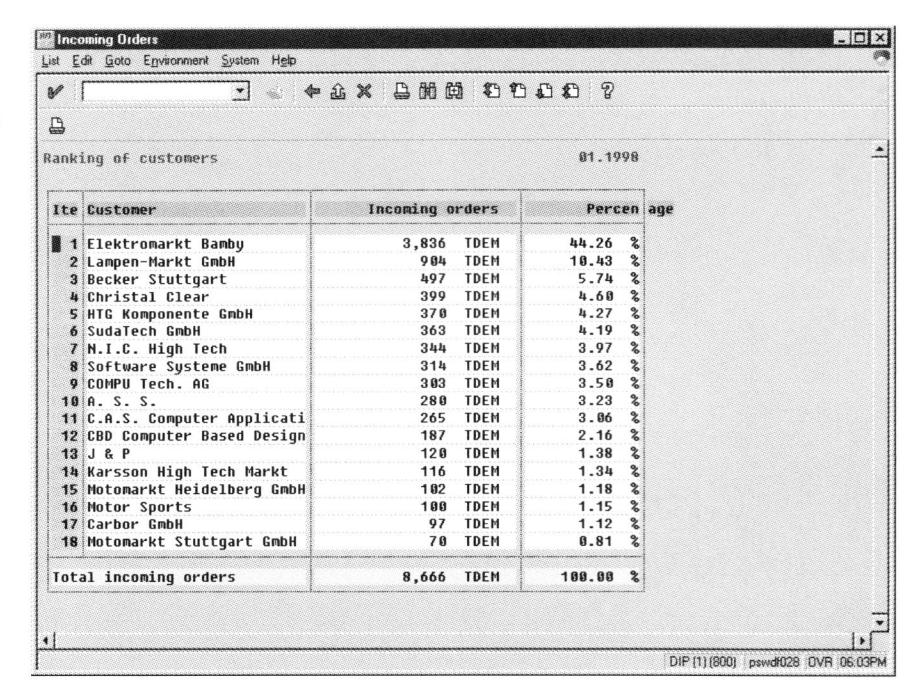

Ranking of customers — 01.1998

Ite	Customer	Incoming orders	Percentage
1	Elektromarkt Bamby	3,836 TDEM	44.26 %
2	Lampen-Markt GmbH	904 TDEM	10.43 %
3	Becker Stuttgart	497 TDEM	5.74 %
4	Christal Clear	399 TDEM	4.60 %
5	HTG Komponente GmbH	370 TDEM	4.27 %
6	SudaTech GmbH	363 TDEM	4.19 %
7	N.I.C. High Tech	344 TDEM	3.97 %
8	Software Systeme GmbH	314 TDEM	3.62 %
9	COMPU Tech. AG	303 TDEM	3.50 %
10	A. S. S.	280 TDEM	3.23 %
11	C.A.S. Computer Applicati	265 TDEM	3.06 %
12	CBD Computer Based Design	187 TDEM	2.16 %
13	J & P	120 TDEM	1.38 %
14	Karsson High Tech Markt	116 TDEM	1.34 %
15	Motomarkt Heidelberg GmbH	102 TDEM	1.18 %
16	Motor Sports	100 TDEM	1.15 %
17	Carbor GmbH	97 TDEM	1.12 %
18	Motomarkt Stuttgart GmbH	70 TDEM	0.81 %
	Total incoming orders	8,666 TDEM	100.00 %

9–32   **Reporting Made Easy**

Section 9: Sales and Distribution Reports
Incoming Orders for Customers and Materials (Document or Statistical Analysis)

This screen shows incoming orders by *Material*, for the selected period, as well as the total for the *top N* materials and remaining materials.

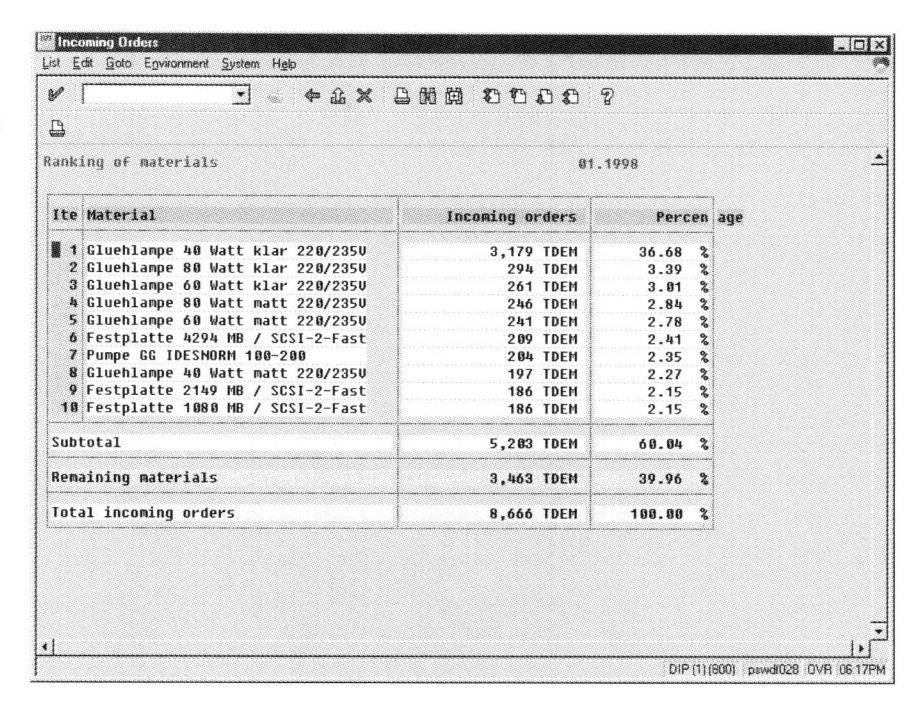

Ite	Material	Incoming orders		Percentage	
1	Gluehlampe 40 Watt klar 220/235U	3,179	TDEM	36.68	%
2	Gluehlampe 80 Watt klar 220/235U	294	TDEM	3.39	%
3	Gluehlampe 60 Watt klar 220/235U	261	TDEM	3.01	%
4	Gluehlampe 80 Watt matt 220/235U	246	TDEM	2.84	%
5	Gluehlampe 60 Watt matt 220/235U	241	TDEM	2.78	%
6	Festplatte 4294 MB / SCSI-2-Fast	209	TDEM	2.41	%
7	Pumpe GG IDESNORM 100-200	204	TDEM	2.35	%
8	Gluehlampe 40 Watt matt 220/235U	197	TDEM	2.27	%
9	Festplatte 2149 MB / SCSI-2-Fast	186	TDEM	2.15	%
10	Festplatte 1080 MB / SCSI-2-Fast	186	TDEM	2.15	%
	Subtotal	5,203	TDEM	60.04	%
	Remaining materials	3,463	TDEM	39.96	%
	Total incoming orders	8,666	TDEM	100.00	%

Ranking of materials — 01.1998

Section 9: Sales and Distribution Reports
Incomplete Sales Documents

Incomplete Sales Documents

Quick Access To run this report, use one of the following access options:

Option 1: Menu Path

Logistics → *Sales and distribution* → *Sales* → *Environment* → *Document analysis* → *Incomplete documents*

Option 2: Transaction Code

In the *Command* field, enter transaction **V.02** and choose *Enter*.

Option 3: Program Name

Choose *System* → *Services* → *Reporting* and enter **RVAUFERR** in the *Program* field. Then, choose *Execute* to run the report.

Purpose This report lists all incomplete sales documents based on specified selection criteria.

Prerequisites No prerequisites are required to run this report. However, entering selection criteria is recommended.

If you do not select the type of incomplete sales document you want to list, the list will be empty.

Integration From this report, you can branch out to the SD document and edit missing data from the report.

Section 9: Sales and Distribution Reports
Incomplete Sales Documents

Features

The selection screen of this report includes:
- Selecting incompleteness
  - General
  - Delivery
  - Billing
  - Price determination
  - Status group
- Document selection
- Dynamic selection options
- User variables
- Output screen
  - Type of incompleteness (shown on overview list)
- Background execution and printing

Next Steps

From this report, you can view missing data by marking a document and selecting the function *Details*. You can edit the selected document from this branch of the list. Position the cursor on a specific document to branch into that document and make your changes.

You can also process incomplete documents from the overview list by marking the documents to be changed and by selecting the function *Edit documents*. The list is not updated.

Section 9: Sales and Distribution Reports
Incomplete Sales Documents

Guided Tour

Example: Display all incomplete sales documents.

To access the first screen for this report, choose

Logistics → Sales and distribution → Sales → Environment → Document analysis → Incomplete documents.

1. Under *Incompleteness*, select all types of incompleteness.
2. Under *Organizational data*, enter `0010` in *Sales Organization*.
3. For this example, no SD transactions need to be entered. For a list of transactions, click on the *SD transaction* field to reveal a *possible entries* list.
4. Choose *Execute*.

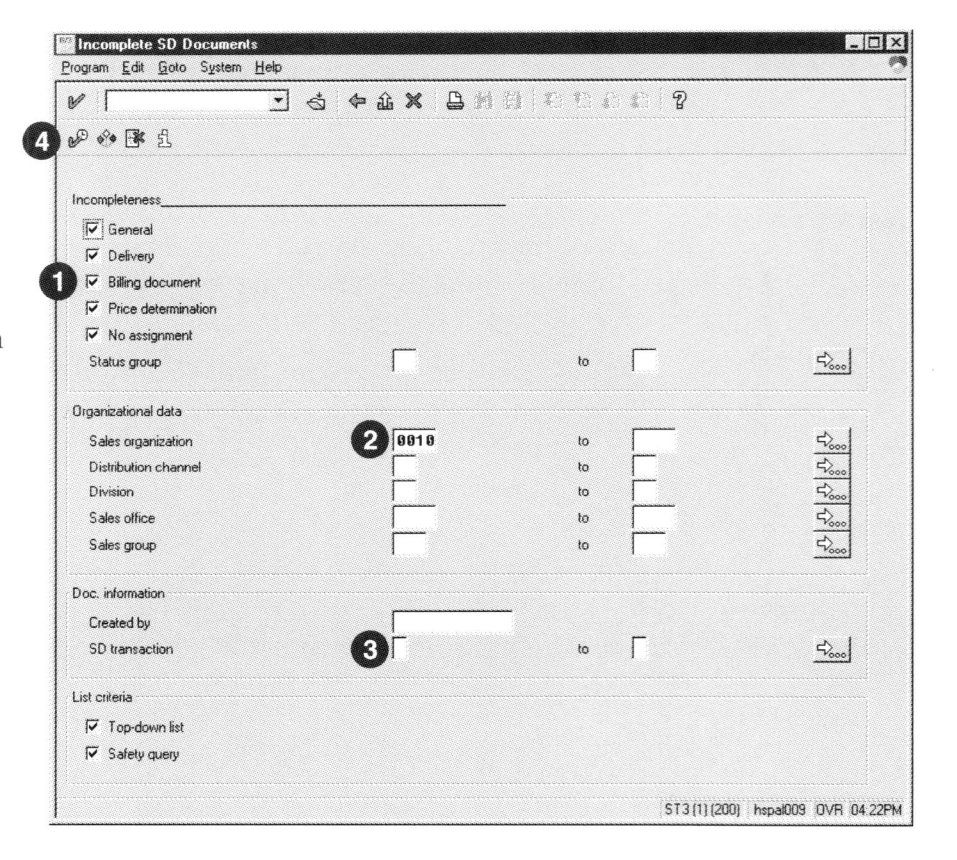

Section 9: Sales and Distribution Reports
Incomplete Sales Documents

This screen shows the list of incomplete sales documents. The matrix indicates the reasons for the incompleteness.

5. To edit a document, select the checkbox to the left of the desired SD document (for example, *Order 28*).

6. Choose *Edit documents*.

7. Choose Display to navigate to details of the incompleteness.

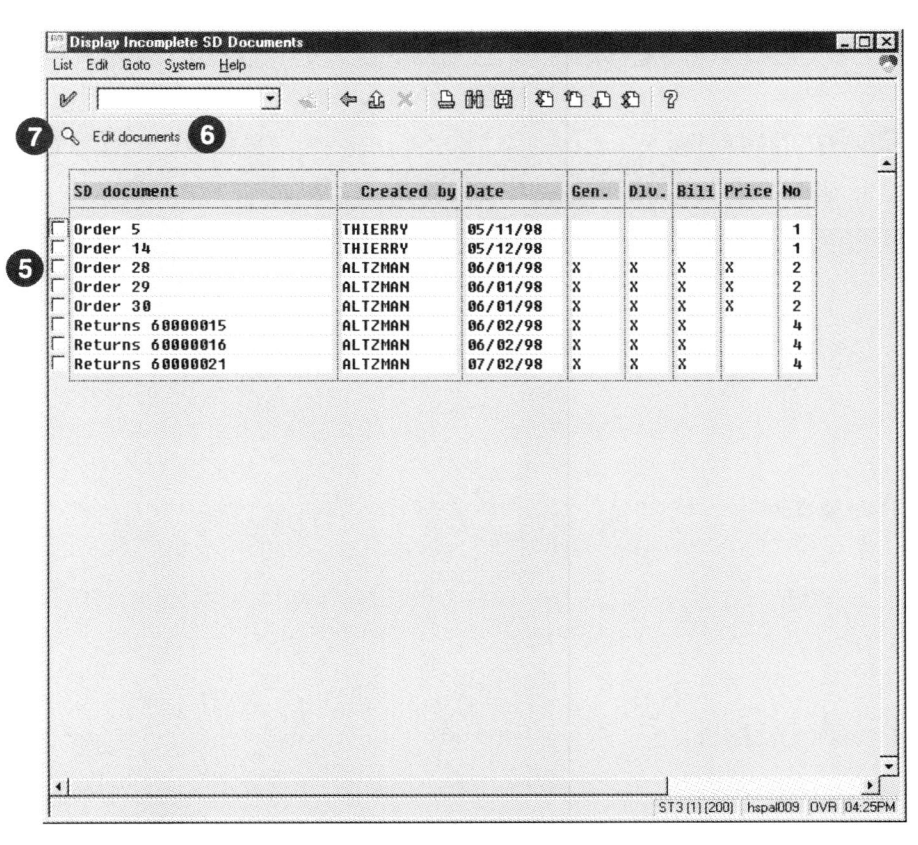

This screen shows the selected sales document and indicates missing data.

8. Choose *Edit documents*, to edit this sales document.

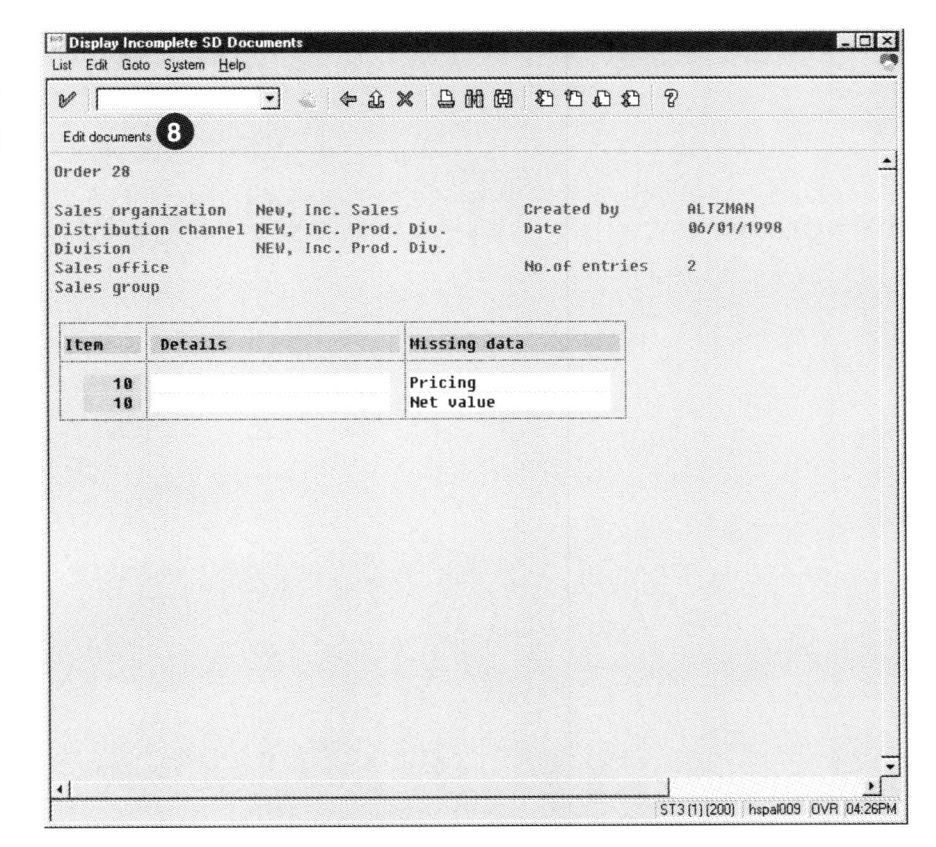

Commonly Used Reports: Illustrations and Perspectives

List of All or Open Billings (Document Analysis)

Quick Access To run this report, use one of the following access options:

Option 1: Menu Path

Logistics → Sales and distribution → Billing → Billing document → List billing documents

Option 2: Transaction Code

In the *Command* field, enter transaction **VF05** and choose *Enter*.

Purpose This report provides a list of billing documents by either pay-to party or material number.

Depending on the selection criteria you choose, you may view all billings or only those that remain open.

Prerequisites The following entries are required to run this report:
- Valid sold-to party or material master number
- Valid sales organization

This report shows all billing documents, regardless of whether or not they posted to accounting or cleared. The *Summarize* function may display incorrect totals. You might expect credit or returns to be subtracted, but the summary includes all documents.

Integration From this report, you can branch to the SD document, document status, document flow, customer address, pay-to party, and the material master.

Section 9: Sales and Distribution Reports
List of All or Open Billings (Document Analysis)

Features

The selection screen of this report includes:
- Input pay-to party and material number.
- Input SD organizational data (Sales organization is also required)
- Further selection criteria
  - Distribution channel
  - Billing category
  - Billing type
  - Created by
  - Billing date
  - Billing document
  - Document number
  - Fiscal year
- Date range
- Display variants
  - *0SAP*   Billing documents
  - *1SAP*   Billing items
- Output screen
  - Filter functions
  - Sort functions
  - Sum up function
  - Columnar display functions: Change the width of the column and freeze or unfreeze columns.
  - Variant display functions: Alternate between display variants (*Settings → Display variants → Choose*)
- Branch to the SD document, document status, document flow, and master data (customer address, partner [sold-to] and material).

Next Steps

This report contains data from SD documents which include materials and partners. From this report, you can branch to the SD document for editing. This data cannot be manipulated.

Section 9: Sales and Distribution Reports
List of All or Open Billings (Document Analysis)

Guided Tour

Example: Display a list of all billing documents by pay-to party.

To access the first screen for this report, choose

Logistics → *Sales and distribution* → *Billing* → *Billing document* → *List billing documents*.

1. Enter a valid pay-to party number in *Payer* (for example, **1172**).

2. Choose the document date range based on the billing date (for example, **05/01/1998** to **08/18/1998**).

3. Select *All billing docs*.

4. Optional: Choose *DisplayVariants* to change the variant. You can also do this from the output screen.

5. Optional: Choose *Further sel. criteria* to select additional selection criteria.

6. Choose *Enter*.

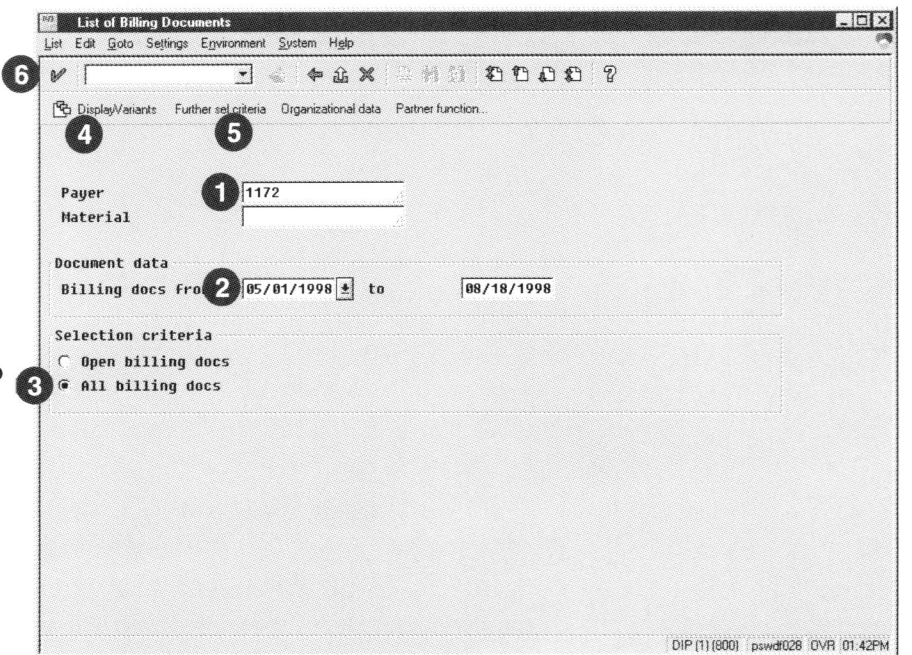

Reporting Made Easy

Section 9: Sales and Distribution Reports

List of All or Open Billings (Document Analysis)

This screen shows the *List of Billing Documents* for display variant *0SAP*.

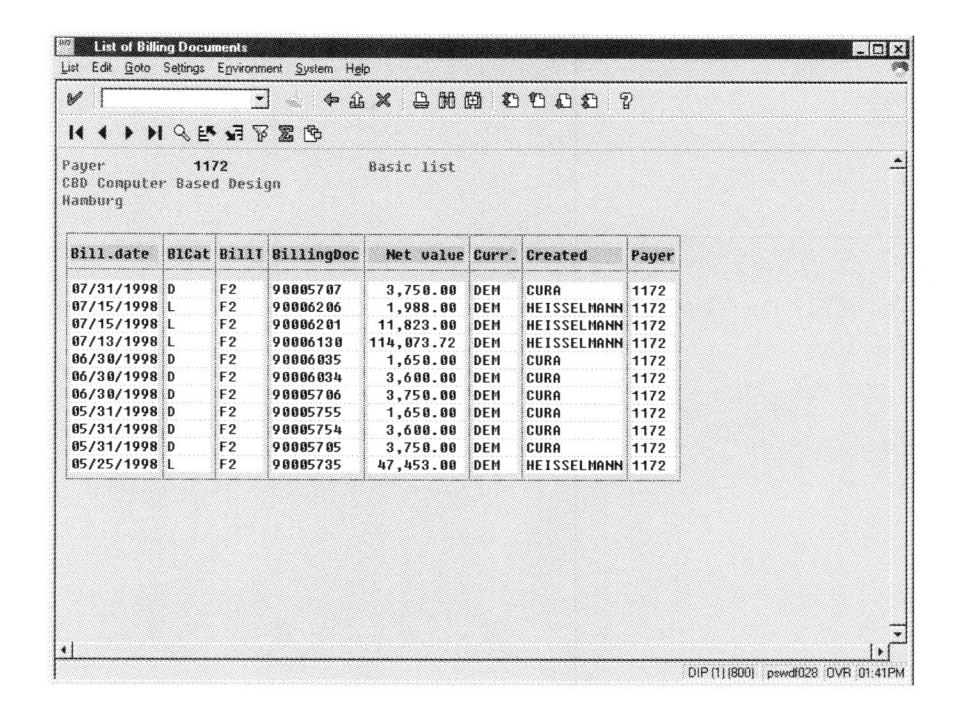

```
List of Billing Documents                                              _ □ ×
List  Edit  Goto  Settings  Environment  System  Help

Payer          1172              Basic list
CBD Computer Based Design
Hamburg

| Bill.date  | BlCat | BillT | BillingDoc | Net value  | Curr. | Created     | Payer |
| 07/31/1998 | D     | F2    | 90005707   |   3,750.00 | DEM   | CURA        | 1172  |
| 07/15/1998 | L     | F2    | 90006206   |   1,988.00 | DEM   | HEISSELMANN | 1172  |
| 07/15/1998 | L     | F2    | 90006201   |  11,823.00 | DEM   | HEISSELMANN | 1172  |
| 07/13/1998 | L     | F2    | 90006130   | 114,073.72 | DEM   | HEISSELMANN | 1172  |
| 06/30/1998 | D     | F2    | 90006035   |   1,650.00 | DEM   | CURA        | 1172  |
| 06/30/1998 | D     | F2    | 90006034   |   3,600.00 | DEM   | CURA        | 1172  |
| 06/30/1998 | D     | F2    | 90005706   |   3,750.00 | DEM   | CURA        | 1172  |
| 05/31/1998 | D     | F2    | 90005755   |   1,650.00 | DEM   | CURA        | 1172  |
| 05/31/1998 | D     | F2    | 90005754   |   3,600.00 | DEM   | CURA        | 1172  |
| 05/31/1998 | D     | F2    | 90005705   |   3,750.00 | DEM   | CURA        | 1172  |
| 05/25/1998 | L     | F2    | 90005735   |  47,453.00 | DEM   | HEISSELMANN | 1172  |
```

Section 9: Sales and Distribution Reports
List of All or Open Billings (Document Analysis)

This screen shows the *List of Billing Documents* for display variant *1SAP* (billing items).

You may select any line, choose *Environment*, and then branch out to the SD document information and master data.

From within the report, you may change the layout by choosing *Setting→ Display variant → Current*. The fields on the left side of the screen are those that are to be displayed. The fields on the right side are currently "hidden" but can be selected for display.

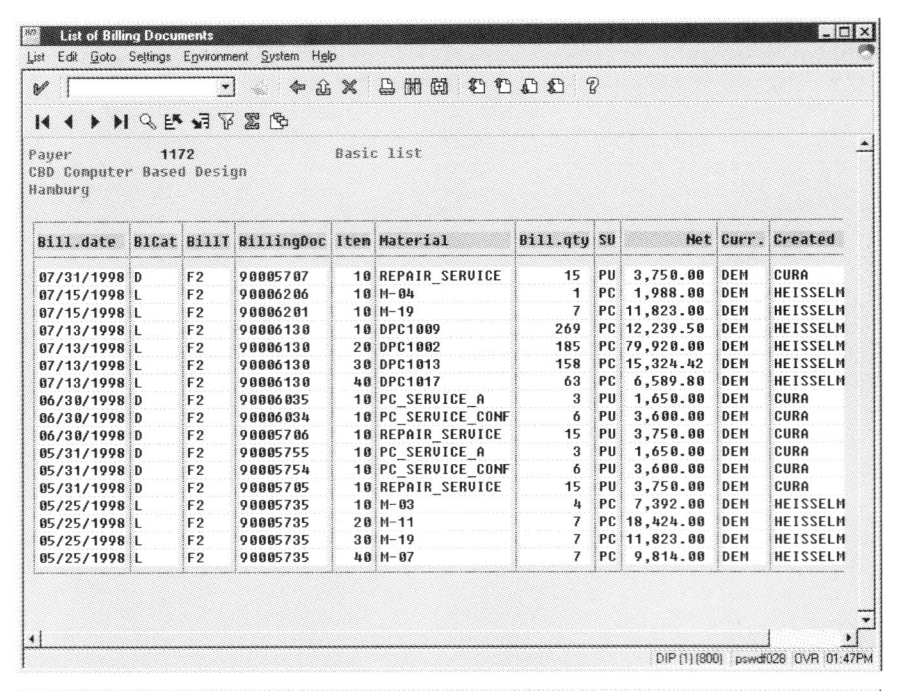

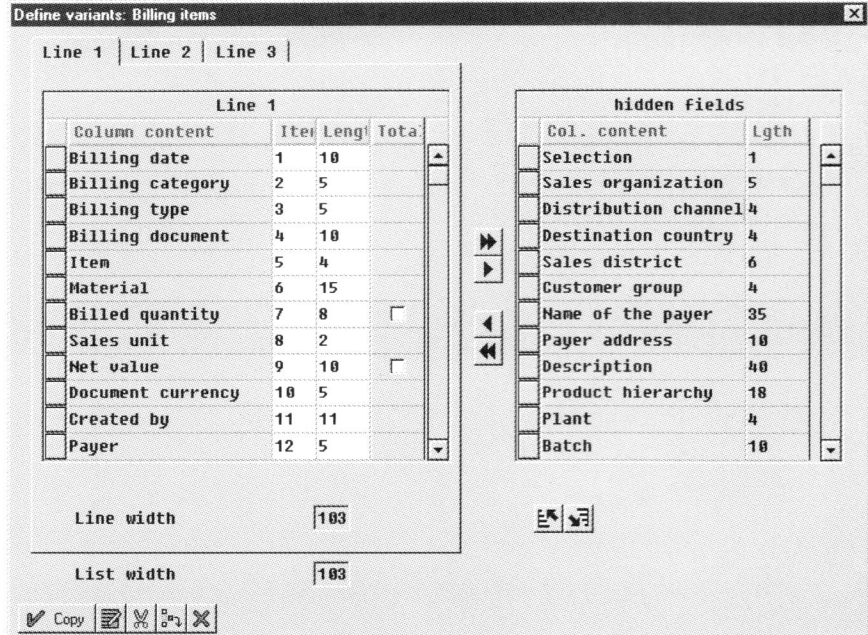

9–42

Reporting Made Easy

Invoiced Sales Report (Statistical Analysis)

Quick Access

To run this report, use one of the following access options:

Option 1: Menu Path

Logistics → Sales and distribution → Sales information system → Standard analyses →

Customer | Material | Sales organization | Sales employee | Sales office

Option 2: Transaction Code

In the *Command* field, enter transaction (see table below) and choose *Enter*. Choose one of the following options:

Transaction code	Standard analyses
MCTA	*Customer*
MCTC	*Material*
MCTE	*Sales organization*
MCTI	*Sales employee*
MCTG	*Sales office*

Option 3: Program Name

Choose *System* → *Services* → *Reporting* and enter `RMCV0100` in the *Program* field. Then, choose *Execute* to run the report.

Purpose

This report is used to analyze invoiced sales. An invoiced sale is the net value of the billing item stated in the document currency. With this report, you can use multiple selection and drilldown criteria to evaluate invoiced sales data. This report is updated in the information structures *S001-S004* and *S006* when billed. Since the accounting status (posted to accounting) is not a filter criteria, the report results may differ from a sales revenue report in FI accounting.

Not every manager within a company requires the same level of information on incoming orders. For example, a monthly summary of billing data (organized by sales office or customer) may be adequate for a senior executive but a line manager may want to see a daily summary of the same data. In this instance, the *Invoiced Sales report* meets the unique information needs of both users.

Information systems reports, such as *Invoiced Sales*, are a part of the *Logistics Information System*. The data reported is stored in special tables called information structures, which are separated from transaction levels. This allows much faster reporting and minimizes the impact on performance.

Additionally, hundreds of end-user reporting functions in standard analyses and flexible analyses offer a range of options to analyze the information of incoming orders. The reporting data is updated at the information structures *S001-S004* and *S006* when an incoming order item is created or changed. Deleted orders are removed, but rejected orders are retained in the information structures.

Section 9: Sales and Distribution Reports
Invoiced Sales Report (Statistical Analysis)

Creating company specific information structures and update rules lets you specify different ways of collecting and reporting order data.

Prerequisites

You must use *Period to analyze* selection criteria to run this report.

You should limit the selection criteria to reduce the run time for the report.

Integration

You can view other reports (such as incoming orders, credit memos, open orders, returned orders, invoice sales, etc.) with the *SIS* end-user functions of standard or flexible analyses.

In standard analyses, a search/jump function lets you jump to the customer or material master records.

In flexible analyses, the report/report interface lets you jump to the customer or material master records.

Features

The selection screen of this report includes:

- Variants
- Dynamic selection options
- User settings for report drilldown, default key figures, and other reporting parameters
- Execution

The output of this report includes :

- Listing order header, order item, and order schedule item data
- Selection of documents for individual display (double-click on one of the individual document line items)
- Dynamic filtering of output (by column) after the program has been executed (to narrow down the displayed results): Position the cursor on a column, then choose *Edit → Set filter* (Ctrl+Shift+F2)
- Sorting capability (by column): Select a column, then choose *Edit → Sort in ascending/descending order* (Ctrl+Shift+F5/F4)
- Column width optimization: Select a column, then choose *Settings → Columns → Optimize width*
- Data statistics for the output: Choose *Settings → List status* (Ctrl+F11)

Next Steps

This report contains data that is statistically summarized. Based on your system's configuration, this data is updated online by sales events or periodically by batch programs. This data cannot be manipulated.

Report Options

When running the report in *LIS/SIS* (standard analyses), choose *Logistics → Sales and distribution → Sales information system → Standard analyses*.

Under *Standard analyses*, choose one of the following options:

Menu option	For reporting
Customer	Sold-to party, Material, Sales organization, Distribution channel, Division
Material	Material, Sales organization, Distribution channel
Sales organization	Distr. channel, Division, Material, Sales district, Sales organization, Sold-to party
Sales employee	Sales organization, Distr. channel, Division, Sales employee, Sold-to party, Material
Sales office	Sales organization, Sales group, Sales office, Distr. channel, Division

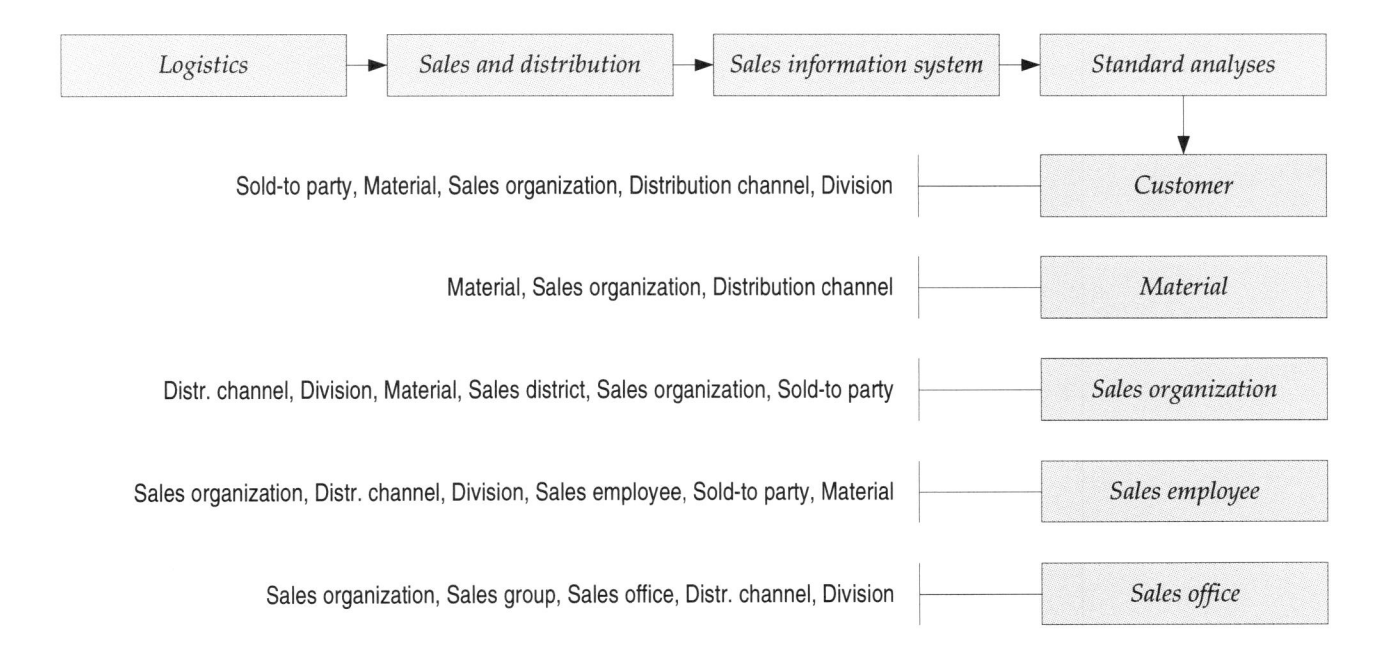

Section 9: Sales and Distribution Reports
Invoiced Sales Report (Statistical Analysis)

Guided Tour

Example: List and analyze the invoiced sales of last two months.

To access the first screen for this report, choose

Logistics → Sales and distribution → Sales Information System → Standard Analyses → Customer.

1. Enter **1000** in *Sales organization*.

2. Under *Period to analyze*, enter a date range (for example, **06 1998** to **08 1998**) in *Month*.

3. Choose *Selection* to view only billing related key figures.

   A period is determined by the date an ordered item is changed or deleted.

4. Choose *Execute*.

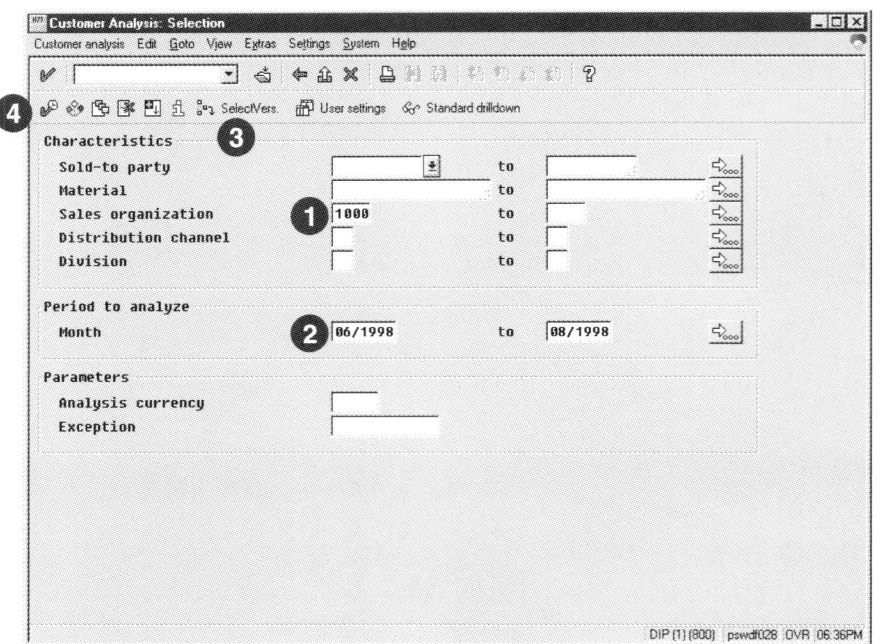

9–46 Reporting Made Easy

Section 9: Sales and Distribution Reports

Invoiced Sales Report (Statistical Analysis)

This screen shows data based on the standard defaults for drilldown, key figures to be displayed, and other layout settings.

5. Choose *Edit → Choose Key figures*, to select additional key figures or to change their sequence.

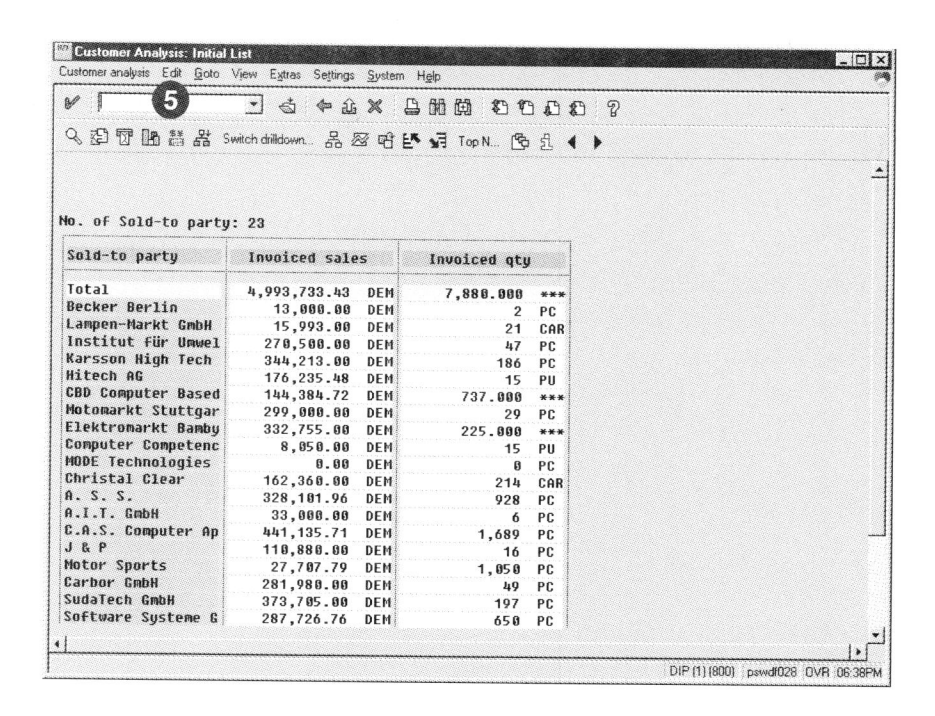

Sold-to party	Invoiced sales		Invoiced qty	
Total	4,993,733.43	DEM	7,880.000	***
Becker Berlin	13,000.00	DEM	2	PC
Lampen-Markt GmbH	15,993.00	DEM	21	CAR
Institut für Umwel	270,500.00	DEM	47	PC
Karsson High Tech	344,213.00	DEM	186	PC
Hitech AG	176,235.48	DEM	15	PU
CBD Computer Based	144,384.72	DEM	737.000	***
Motomarkt Stuttgar	299,000.00	DEM	29	PC
Elektromarkt Bamby	332,755.00	DEM	225.000	***
Computer Competenc	8,050.00	DEM	15	PU
MODE Technologies	0.00	DEM	0	PC
Christal Clear	162,360.00	DEM	214	CAR
A. S. S.	328,101.96	DEM	928	PC
A.I.T. GmbH	33,000.00	DEM	6	PC
C.A.S. Computer Ap	441,135.71	DEM	1,689	PC
J & P	110,880.00	DEM	16	PC
Motor Sports	27,707.79	DEM	1,050	PC
Carbor GmbH	281,980.00	DEM	49	PC
SudaTech GmbH	373,705.00	DEM	197	PC
Software Systeme G	287,726.76	DEM	650	PC

No. of Sold-to party: 23

Commonly Used Reports: Illustrations and Perspectives

9–47

Section 9: Sales and Distribution Reports
Invoiced Sales Report (Statistical Analysis)

In this example, the key figure *Credit Memos* is inserted and the number of decimal places is set to 0.

6. Choose *Show key fields* to transfer fields from the right side of the screen to the *Selected Key figures* column.

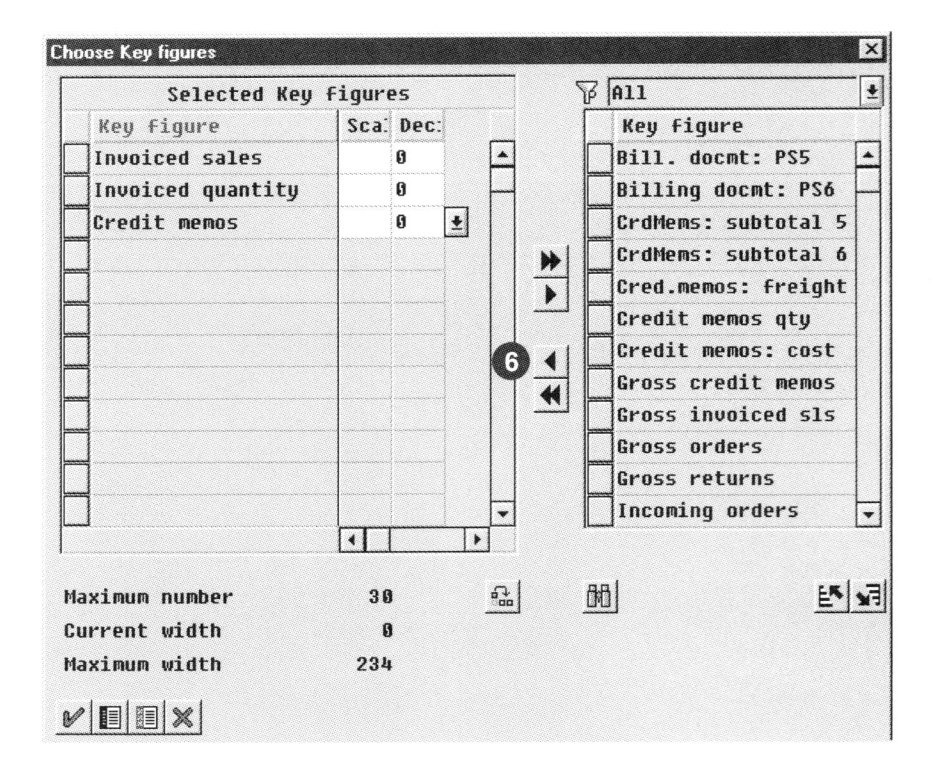

This screen shows how the (above) changes result in a different layout. From this screen, you can drill down further or switch to other characteristics.

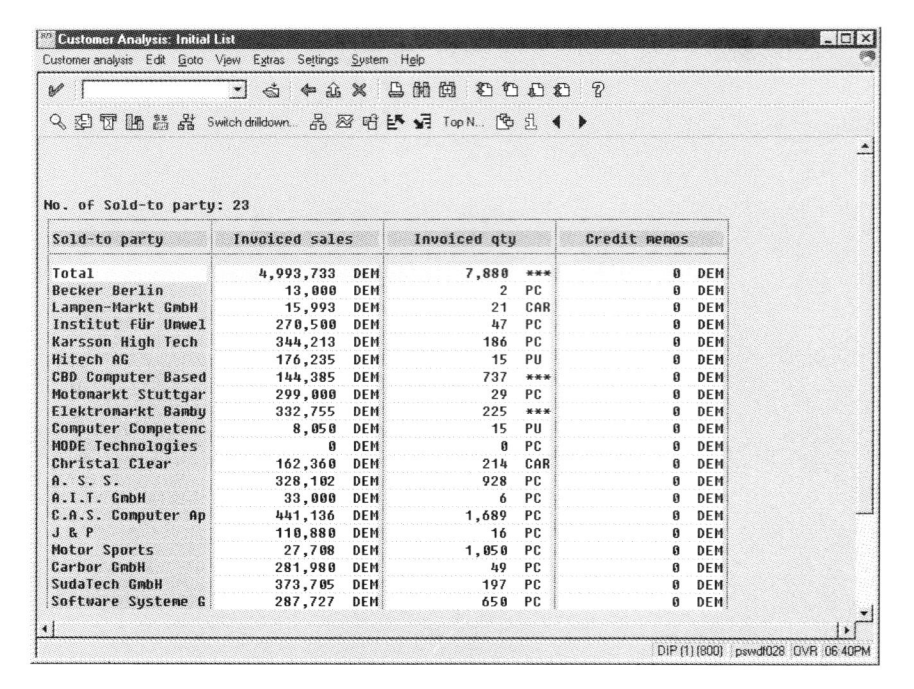

Section 9: Sales and Distribution Reports

Invoiced Sales Report (Statistical Analysis)

The following functions (extract) are available on the toolbar to further analyze the shown data:
- Sorting (+ / -)
- Top N/Last N
- Time series (periods in columns)
- Graphics

The following functions are available from the *Edit* menu path:
- Comparing two key figures
- Comparing actual/plan
- Comparing current/last year ABC analysis
- Correlation/classification

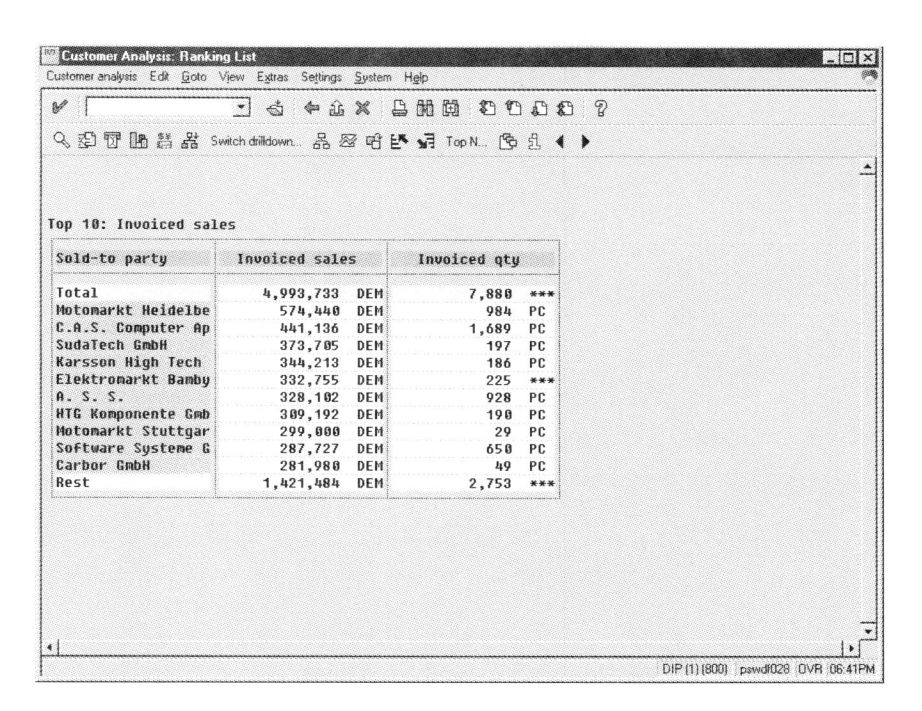

To change the layout for:
- Display characteristics (choose *Settings* → *Char. Display* → *Key description | Key*)
- Display key figures as value or percentage (choose *Settings* → *Value display* → *Absolute | Percent*)
- Analysis currency (choose *Settings* → *Currency* → *Analysis currency*)
- Column width (choose *Settings* → *Column width* → *Characteristic | Key figure*)

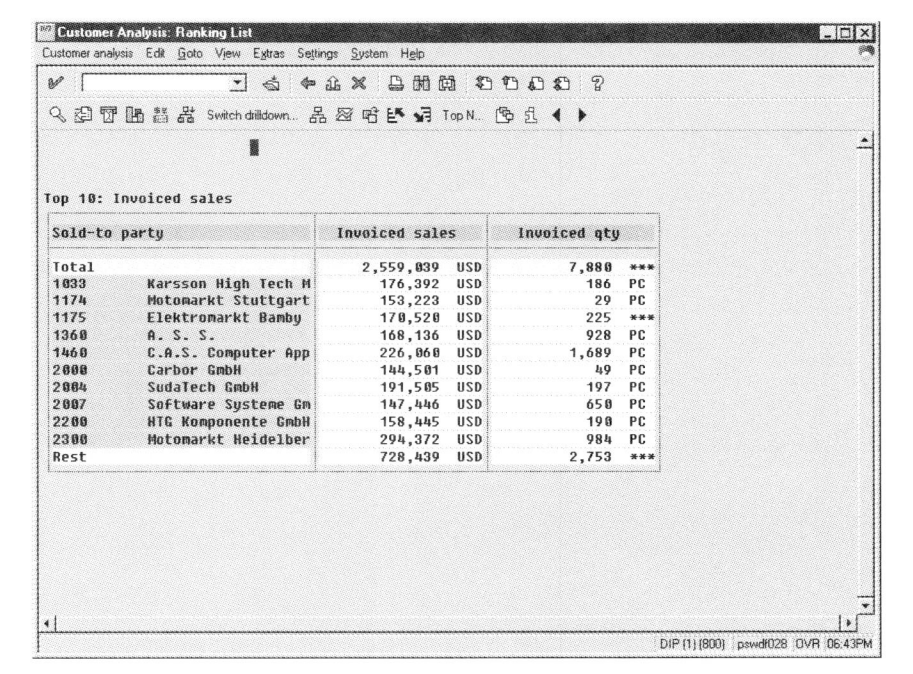

Commonly Used Reports: Illustrations and Perspectives

9–49

List of All or Open Deliveries (Document Analysis)

Quick Access To run this report, use one of the following access options:

Option 1: Menu Path

Logistics → Sales and distribution → Shipping → Delivery → List → Deliveries

Option 2: Transaction Code

In the *Command* field, enter transaction **VL05** and choose *Enter*.

Purpose This report lists deliveries by either ship-to party or material number.

You can either display all deliveries or only the open deliveries. Depending on your selection criteria, the system displays the desired report.

Prerequisites The following entries are required to run this report:
- Valid ship-to party or material master number
- Valid shipping point

Integration From this report, you can branch to the SD document, document status, document flow, ship-to party, and material master.

Section 9: Sales and Distribution Reports
List of All or Open Deliveries (Document Analysis)

Features

The selection screen of this report includes:
- Input ship-to party and material number.
- Input SD organizational data (Shipping point is also required)
- Other selection criteria
  - Delivery type
  - Delivery number
  - Created by
- Date range
- Display variants
  - *0CUS*   Delivery overview
  - *0LPK*   Delivery: Material/partner view
  - *0LZK*   Partner deliveries
  - *0LZM*   Deliveries by material
  - *0PZK*   Partner delivery items *1SAP*
- Output screen
  - Filter functions
  - Sort functions
  - Sum up function
  - Change the width of the column, and freeze or unfreeze columns.
  - Alternate between display variants
    (*Settings → Display variants → Choose*)
  - Branch to the SD document, document status, document flow, and master data (customer address, partner [sold-to] and material).

Next Steps

This report contains data from SD documents which include materials and partners. You can branch to the SD document for editing, but you cannot manipulate data from the output.

Section 9: Sales and Distribution Reports
List of All or Open Deliveries (Document Analysis)

Guided Tour

Example: Display all deliveries for a specific ship-to party.

To access the first screen for this report, choose

Logistics → Sales and distribution → Shipping → Delivery → List → Deliveries.

1. Enter **2300** in *Ship-to party*. Alternatively, you could enter a valid *Material* number.

2. Under *Document data*, enter a date range (for example, **07/19/1998** to **08/18/1998**) in *Delivery date*.

   The delivery due date is the date on which the delivery should be made.

3. Select *All deliveries* as your selection criteria.

4. Choose *Enter*.

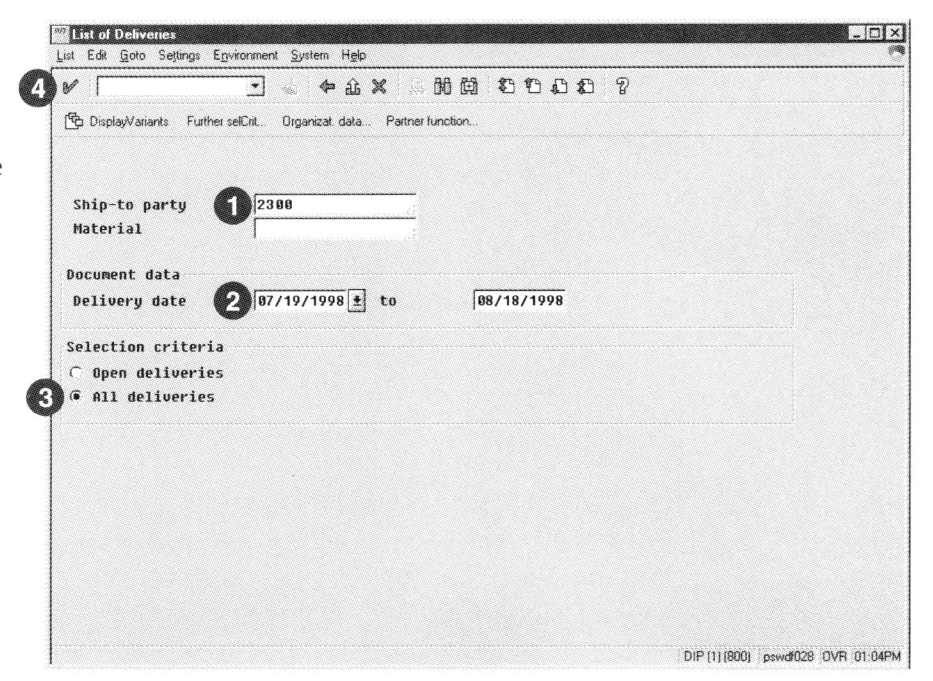

Reporting Made Easy

Section 9: Sales and Distribution Reports

List of All or Open Deliveries (Document Analysis)

This screen shows the output as a basic list with no display variant. It lists all open deliveries for ship-to party *2300*.

You may choose *Filter*, *Summation*, or *Display variant* to change the layout.

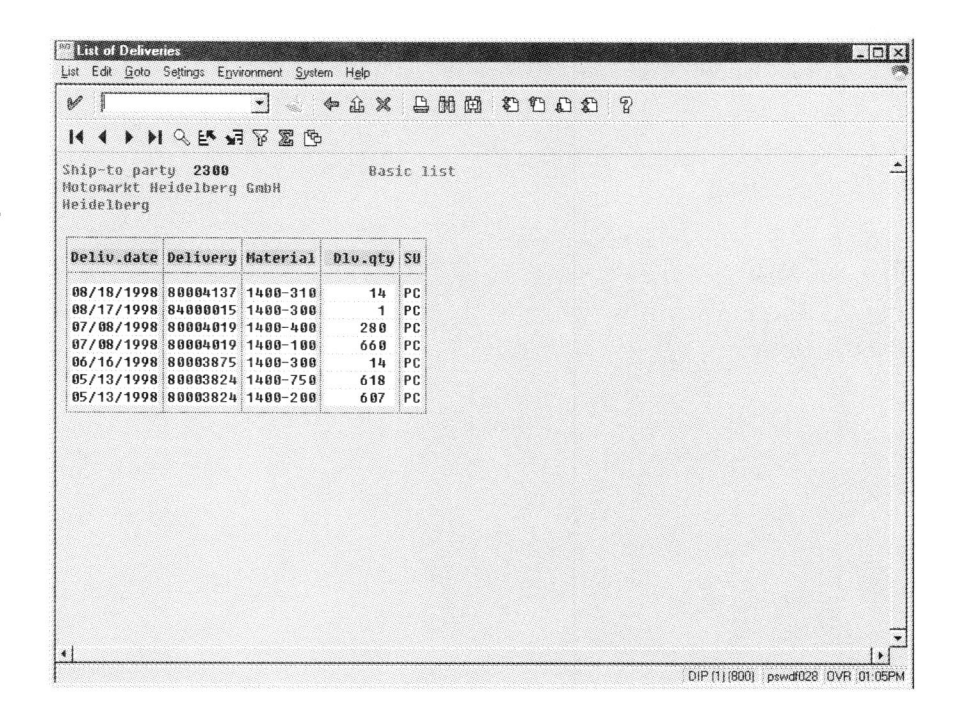

```
List of Deliveries
List Edit Goto Settings Environment System Help

Ship-to party  2300                    Basic list
Motomarkt Heidelberg GmbH
Heidelberg

| Deliv.date | Delivery | Material | Dlv.qty | SU |
| 08/18/1998 | 80004137 | 1400-310 |      14 | PC |
| 08/17/1998 | 84000015 | 1400-300 |       1 | PC |
| 07/08/1998 | 80004019 | 1400-400 |     280 | PC |
| 07/08/1998 | 80004019 | 1400-100 |     660 | PC |
| 06/16/1998 | 80003875 | 1400-300 |      14 | PC |
| 05/13/1998 | 80003824 | 1400-750 |     618 | PC |
| 05/13/1998 | 80003824 | 1400-200 |     607 | PC |
```

Section 9: Sales and Distribution Reports

List of All or Open Deliveries (Document Analysis)

This screen shows the *List of Deliveries By partner* for display variant *3SAP* (schedule lines).

You may select any line, choose *Environment*, and then branch out to the SD document information and master data.

You may change the layout by choosing *Setting → Display variant → Current*.

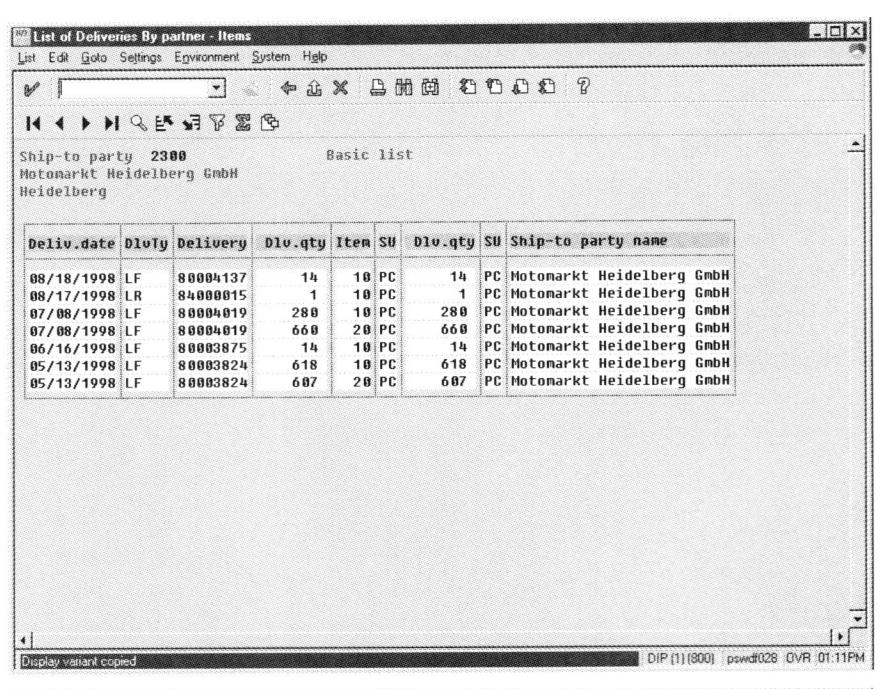

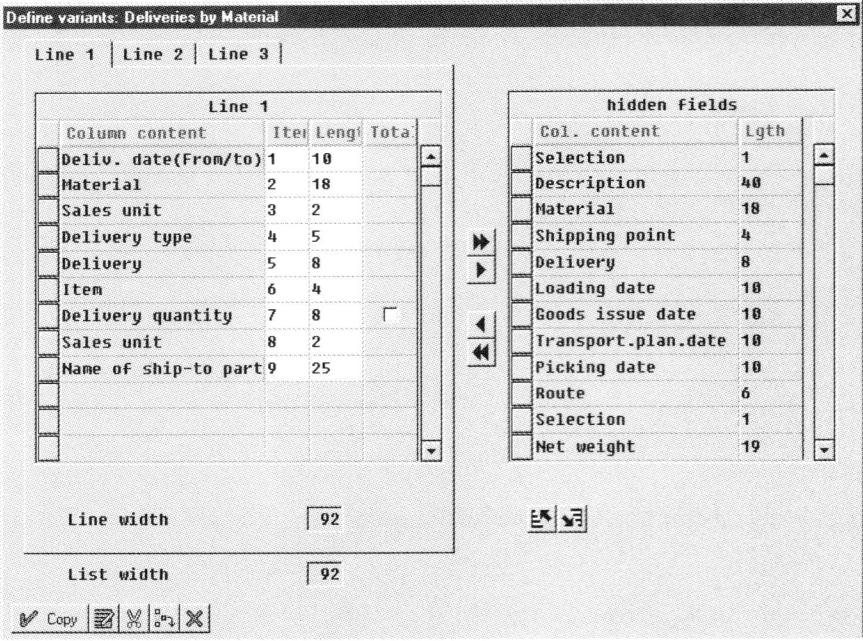

Section 9: Sales and Distribution Reports
List of All or Open Deliveries (Document Analysis)

You may use this same report to list open deliveries, as well as deliveries that have not yet processed to billing.

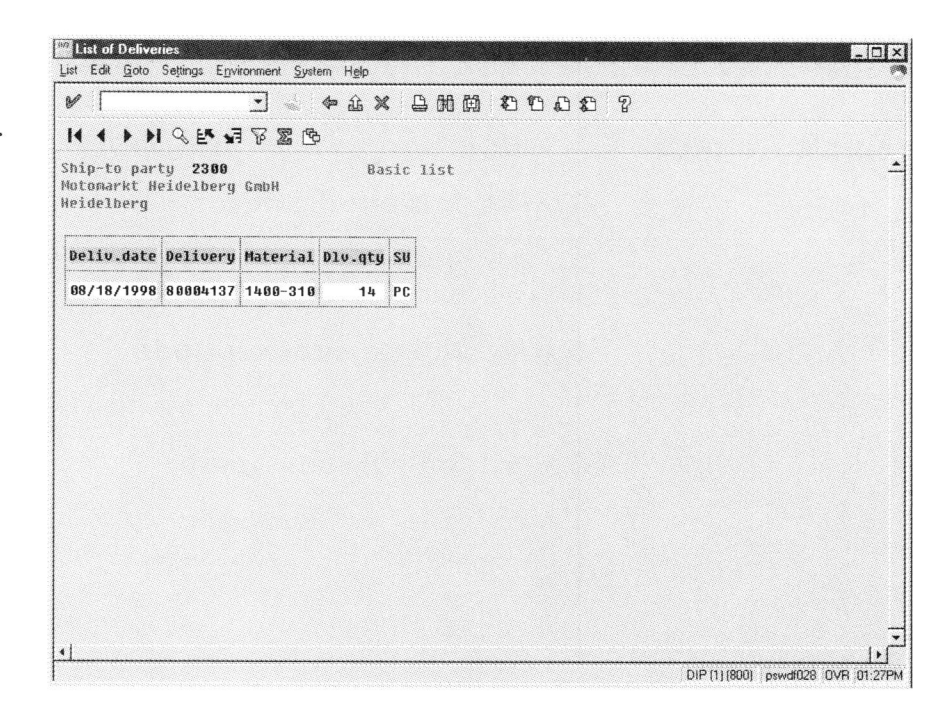

Shipping Report (SIS Statistical Analysis)

Quick Access To run this report, use one of the following access options:

Option 1: Menu Path

Logistics → *Sales and distribution* → *Sales information system* → *Standard analyses* → *Shipping point*

Option 2: Transaction Code

In the *Command* field, enter transaction **MCTK** and choose *Enter*.

Option 3: Program Name

Choose *System* → *Services* → *Reporting* and enter **RMCV0400** in the *Program* field. Then, choose *Execute* to run the report.

Purpose This report facilitates the shipping point analysis by shipping point, route, forwarding agent, and destination country. When processing deliveries, the shipping point is the principal criterion used to select deliveries. This report is updated in the information structure *S005* when a delivery has been made.

You can create company specific information structures and update rules to specify different means of collecting and reporting order data.

Prerequisites You must use *Period to analyze* selection criteria to run this report.

You should limit the selection criteria to reduce the run time for the report.

Section 9: Sales and Distribution Reports
Shipping Report (SIS Statistical Analysis)

Features

The selection screen of this report includes:

- Variants
- Dynamic selection options
- User settings for drilldown reports, default key figures, and other reporting parameters
- Execution

The output of this report includes:

- Dynamic filtering of output (by column) after the program has been executed to narrow down the displayed results: Position the cursor in a column and choose *Edit → Set filter* (Ctrl+Shift+F2)
- Sorting capability (by column): Select a column and choose *Edit → Sort in ascending/descending order* (Ctrl+Shift+F5/F4)
- Column width optimization: Select a column and choose *Settings → Columns → Optimize width*.

Next Steps

This report contains data that is statistically summarized. Based on your system's configuration, this data is updated online by sales events or periodically by batch programs. This data cannot be manipulated.

Section 9: Sales and Distribution Reports
Shipping Report (SIS Statistical Analysis)

Guided Tour

Example: List and analyze shipping activity for a 10-week period.

To access the first screen for this report, choose

Logistics → Sales and distribution → Sales information system → Standard analyses → Shipping point.

1. Enter the 10-week period you wish to analyze (for example, **24/1998** to **34/1998**) in *Period to analyze*.

   A period is determined by the date an order item is entered or changed.

2. Choose *Execute*.

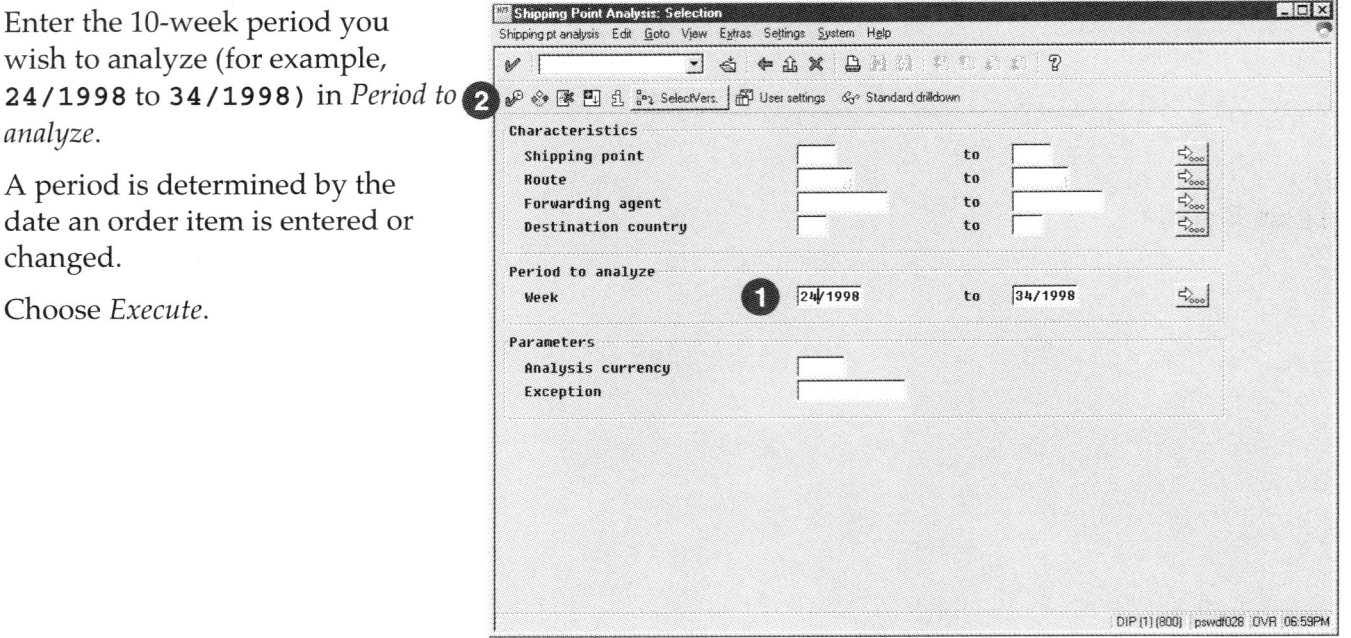

Section 9: Sales and Distribution Reports
Shipping Report (SIS Statistical Analysis)

This screen shows data based on the standard defaults for drilldown, key figures to be displayed, and other layout settings.

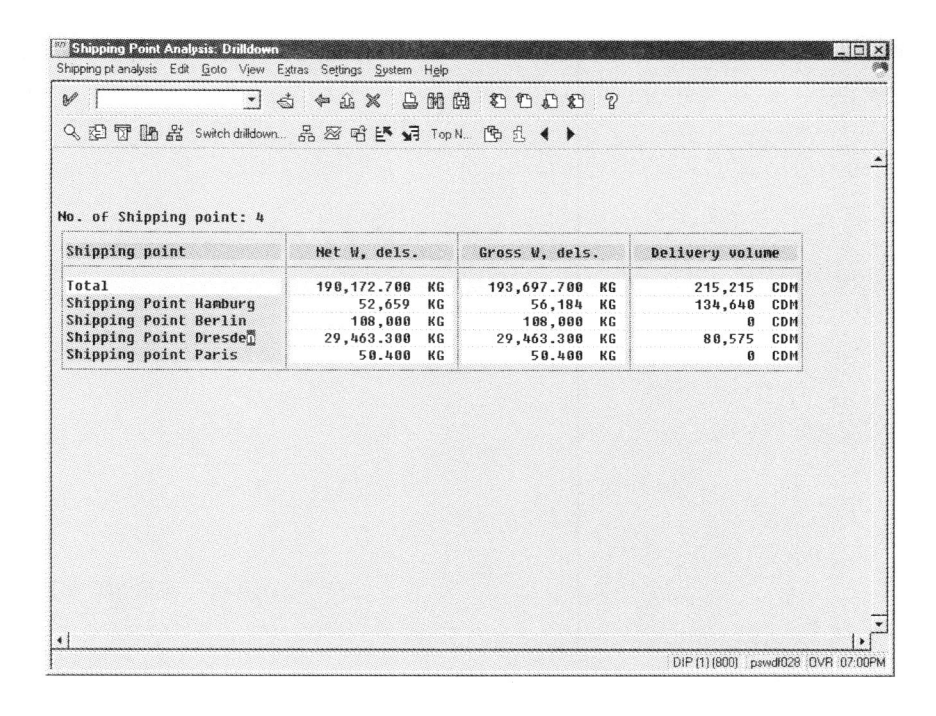

3. Double-click on a line item (for example, *Dresden*).

4. Choose *Edit → Choose key figures* to specify additional key figures or to change their sequence.

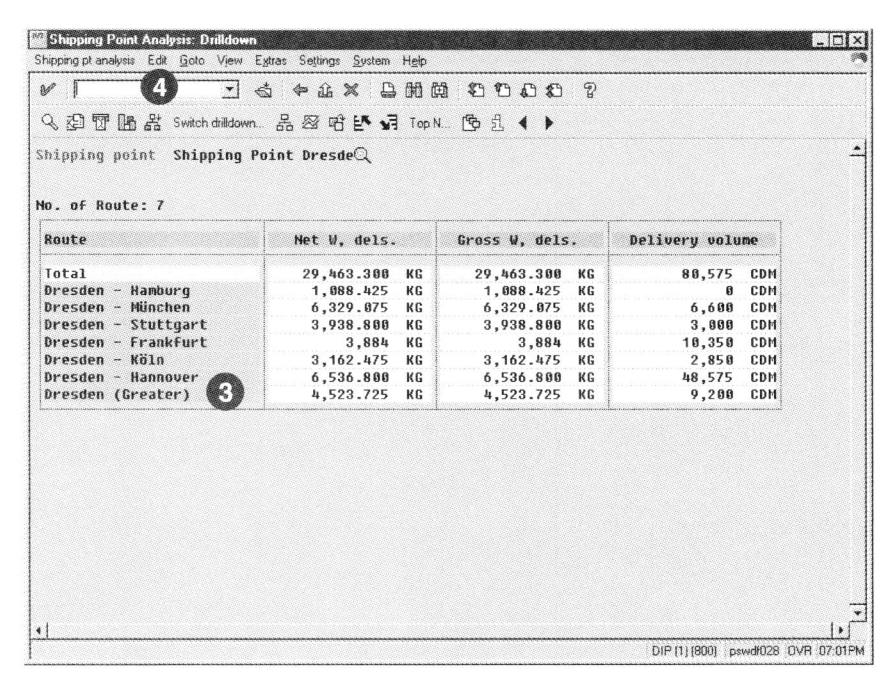

Commonly Used Reports: Illustrations and Perspectives

Section 9: Sales and Distribution Reports
Shipping Report (SIS Statistical Analysis)

The following functions (extract) are available to further analyze the displayed data:

- Sorting (+/-)
- Top N/Last N
- Time series (periods in columns)
- Comparing two key figures
- Comparing actual/plan
- Comparing current/last year
- ABC analysis
- Correlation/classification
- Graphics

This screen shows a comparison between previous year shipping and current shipping information from the Dresden shipping point.

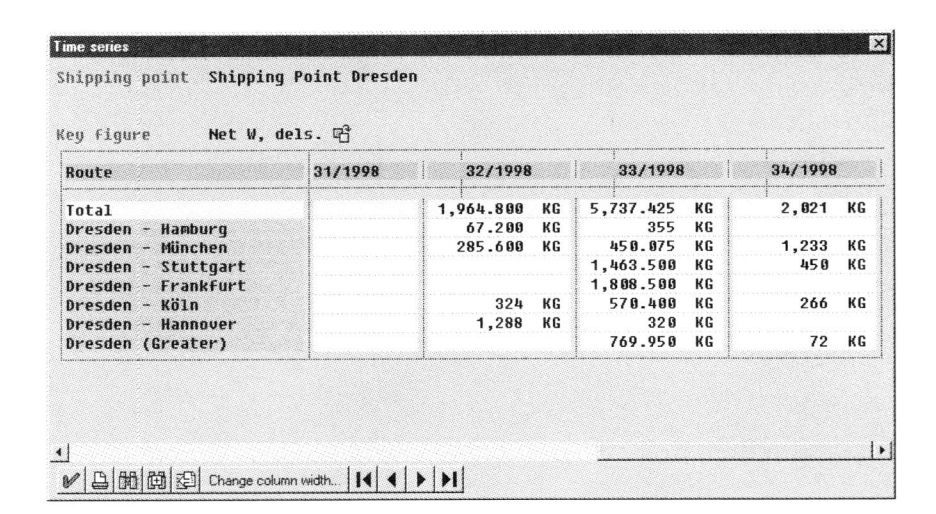

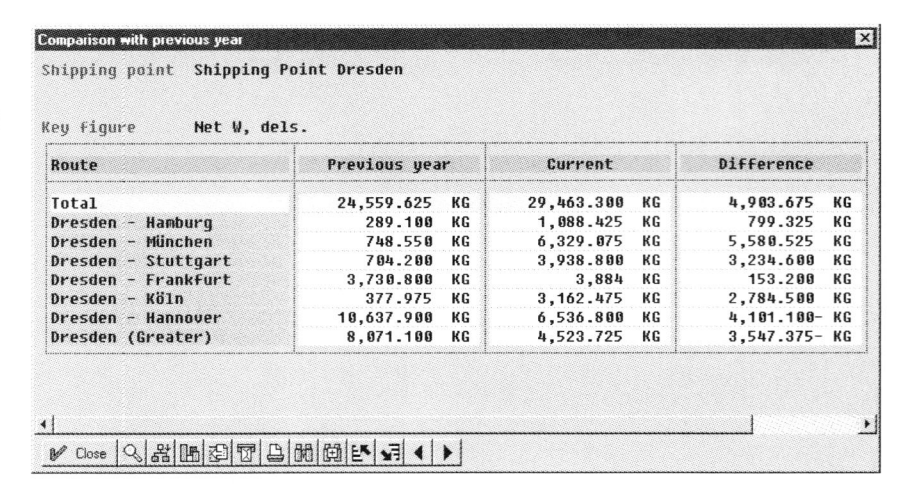

Section 9: Sales and Distribution Reports
Shipping Report (SIS Statistical Analysis)

This screen shows an optional graphical view of the year-to-year comparison.

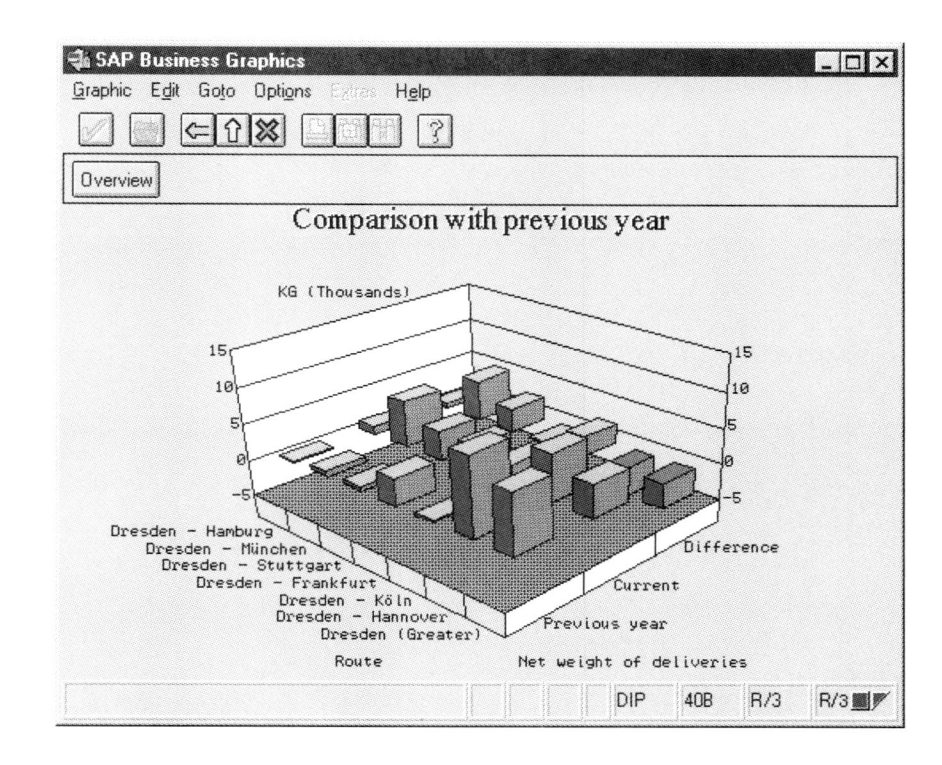

The output can be:
- Printed
- E-mailed (as shown in this example)
- Exported (to XXL or as a PC file)
- Saved (as selection version)

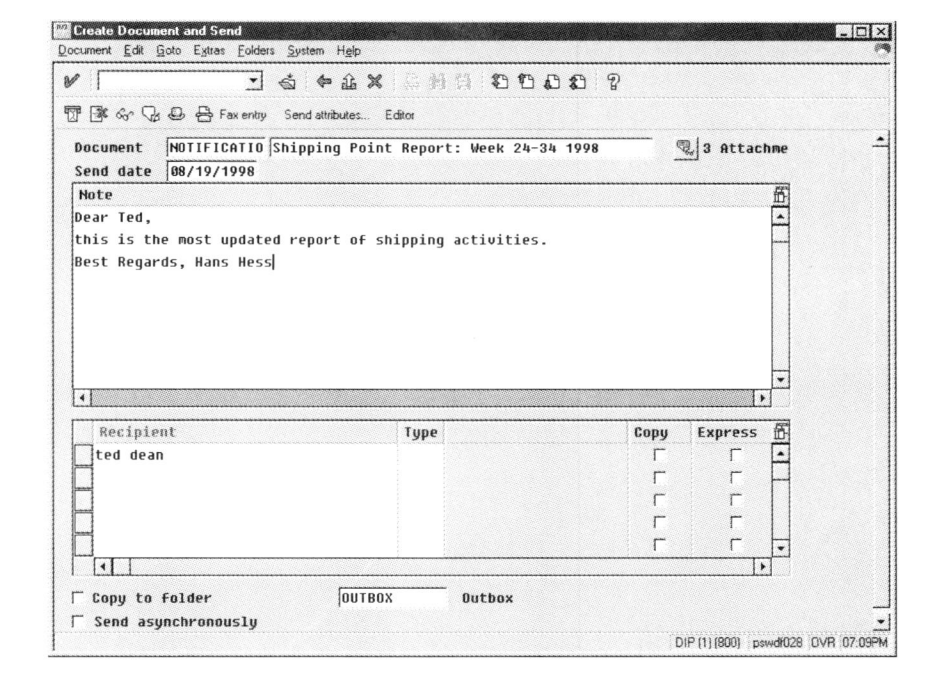

Commonly Used Reports: Illustrations and Perspectives

9–61

Section 9: Sales and Distribution Reports
Shipping Report (SIS Statistical Analysis)

Section 10: Materials Management Reports

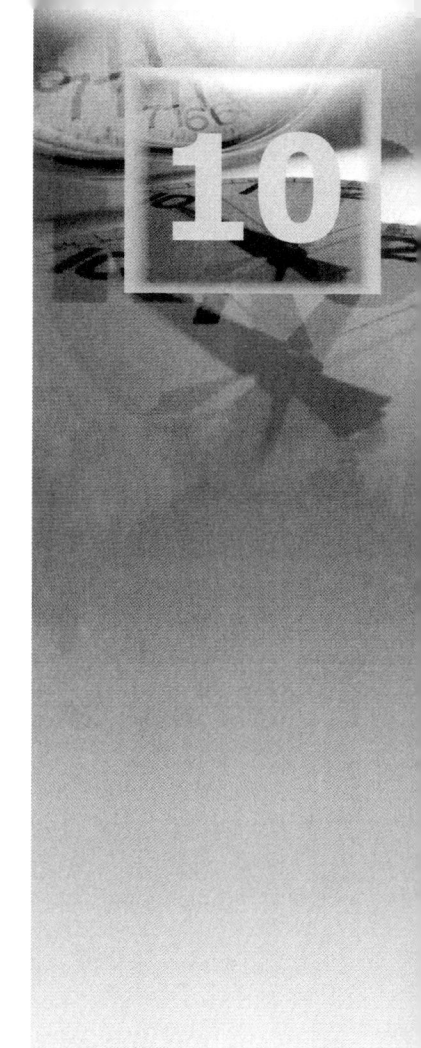

Contents

Stock Overview 10–2
List Displays of PO—Material or Vendor 10–6
Material Documents for Material 10–13
List Display of Purchase Requisitions...10–20

Stock Overview

Quick Access To run this report, use one of the following access options:

Option 1: Menu Path

Logistics → Materials management → Inventory management → Environment → Stock → Stock overview

Option 2: Program Name

Choose *System → Services → Reporting* and enter **RMMMBEST** in the *Program* field. Then, choose *Execute* to run the report.

Option 3: Transaction Code

In the *Command* field, enter transaction **MMBE** and choose *Enter*.

Purpose This report lets you view the stock of a material across all organizational levels.

Within a company, individuals at various levels use this report to assess the stock situation of a material. The stock overview can be displayed in two formats:

- The basic list gives you an overview of a material's stock at all existing organizational levels (depending on your selection criteria).
- The detail list gives you an overview of a material's stock at a specified—and the next lower—organizational level (depending on your selection criteria).

Depending on the stock type, a number of display versions exist for both lists. The system administrator normally determines which stocks appear in which columns, as well as the order in which these columns are displayed.

Prerequisites You must enter the material number before you run this report.

To narrow your search, we suggest using additional selection criteria.

Integration This report enables you to view the inventory breakdown for a material at all organizational levels:

- Client codes
- Company codes
- Plants
- Storage locations
- Batches

Section 10: Materials Management Reports
Stock Overview

Features The selection screen of this report includes:
- Variants
- Dynamic selection options
- User variables
- Execution (and print) in background

Next Steps This report does not allow manipulation of data.

Guided Tour

Example 1: Display a stock overview list for a material (100-103) across all organizational levels.

To access the first screen for this report, choose

Logistics → *Materials management* → *Inventory management* → *Environment* → *Stock* → *Stock overview.*

1. Enter **103-100** in *Material*.

   Accept all defaults on this screen. This will produce a stock overview report for the material across all plants and storage locations.

2. Choose *Execute*.

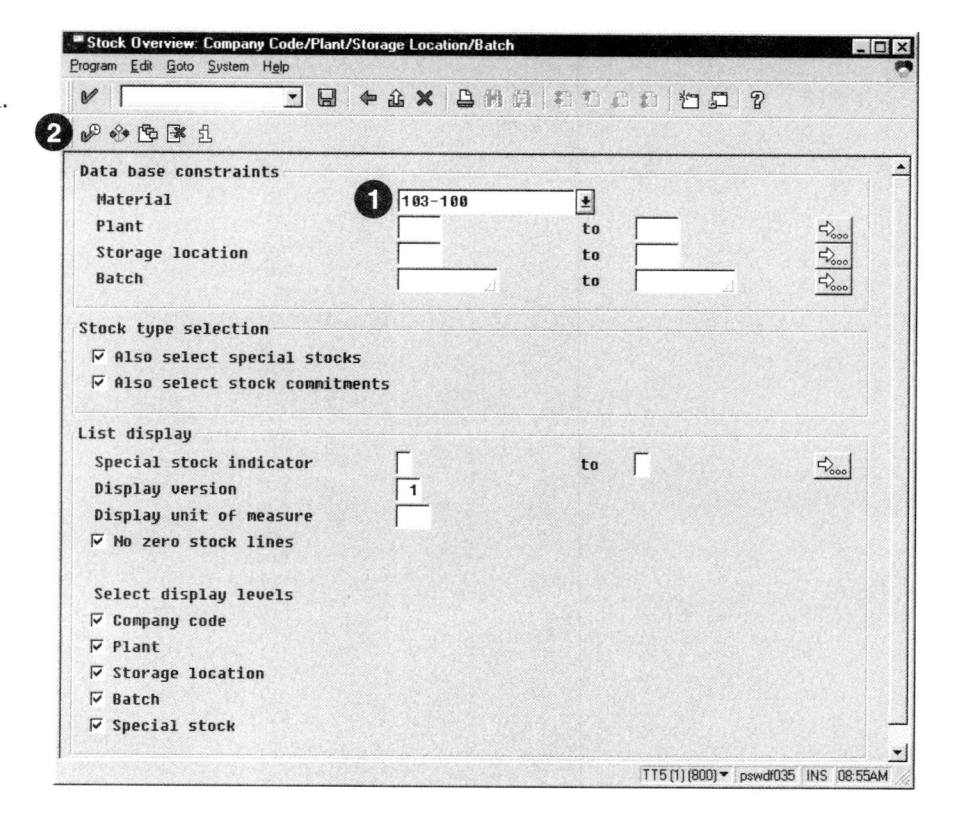

Section 10: Materials Management Reports
Stock Overview

This screen shows the entire inventory for material *103-100* across all plants, regardless of company code. In this example, the report includes both Germany (company code *1000*) and the United States (company code *3000*).

3. Double click on a specific line (for example, storage location *0088*) to drill down to a lower level of detail.

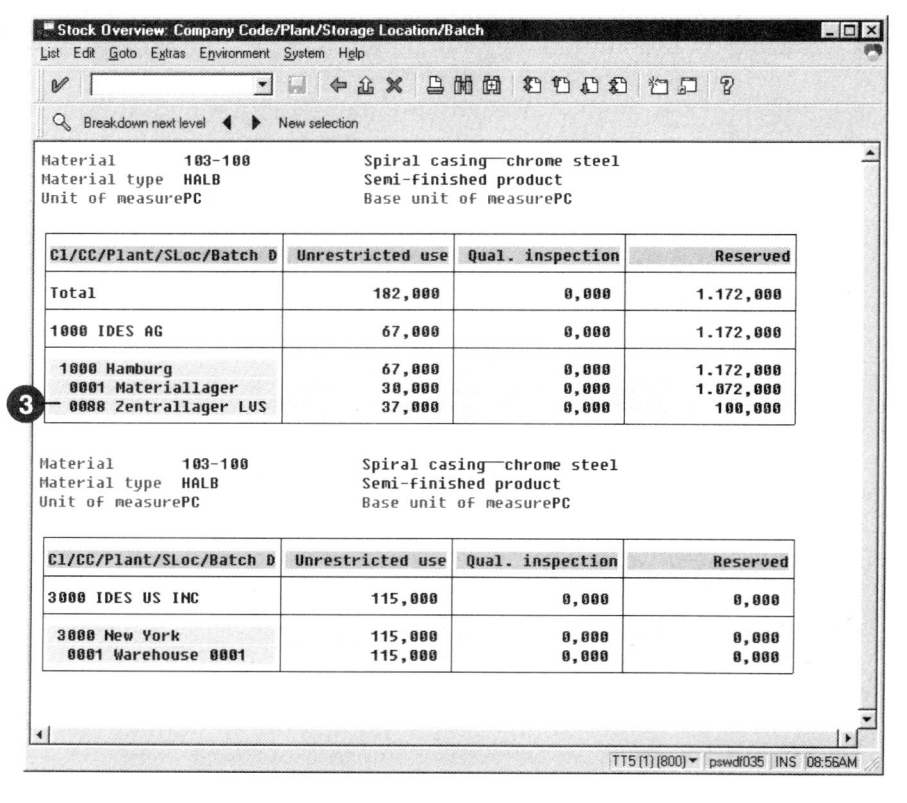

Stock Overview: Company Code/Plant/Storage Location/Batch			
Material 103-100	Spiral casing—chrome steel		
Material type HALB	Semi-finished product		
Unit of measure PC	Base unit of measure PC		

Cl/CC/Plant/SLoc/Batch D	Unrestricted use	Qual. inspection	Reserved
Total	182,000	0,000	1.172,000
1000 IDES AG	67,000	0,000	1.172,000
1000 Hamburg	67,000	0,000	1.172,000
0001 Materiallager	30,000	0,000	1.072,000
0088 Zentrallager LVS	37,000	0,000	100,000

Material 103-100	Spiral casing—chrome steel
Material type HALB	Semi-finished product
Unit of measure PC	Base unit of measure PC

Cl/CC/Plant/SLoc/Batch D	Unrestricted use	Qual. inspection	Reserved
3000 IDES US INC	115,000	0,000	0,000
3000 New York	115,000	0,000	0,000
0001 Warehouse 0001	115,000	0,000	0,000

This screen shows detailed information for storage location *0088*.

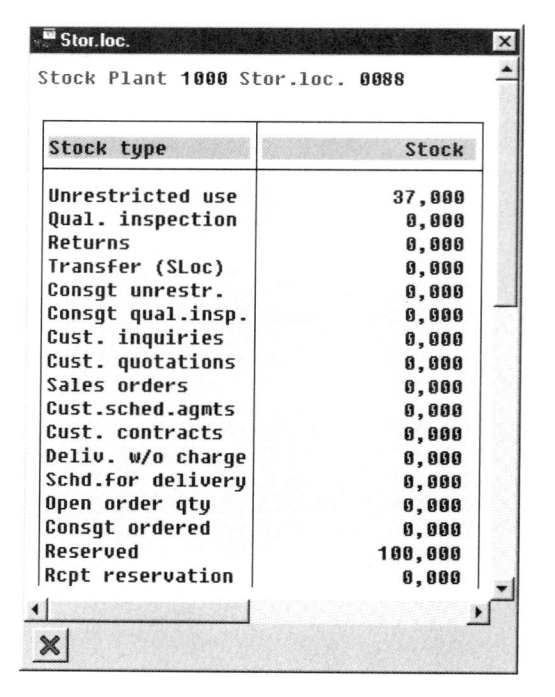

Stor.loc.

Stock Plant 1000 Stor.loc. 0088

Stock type	Stock
Unrestricted use	37,000
Qual. inspection	0,000
Returns	0,000
Transfer (SLoc)	0,000
Consgt unrestr.	0,000
Consgt qual.insp.	0,000
Cust. inquiries	0,000
Cust. quotations	0,000
Sales orders	0,000
Cust.sched.agmts	0,000
Cust. contracts	0,000
Deliv. w/o charge	0,000
Schd.for delivery	0,000
Open order qty	0,000
Consgt ordered	0,000
Reserved	100,000
Rcpt reservation	0,000

Section 10: Materials Management Reports
Stock Overview

Example 2: Display a stock overview list for a material (100-103) for a specific plant (3000) and all its storage locations.

1. Enter **103-100** in *Material*.
2. Enter **3000** in *Plant*.
3. Choose *Execute*.

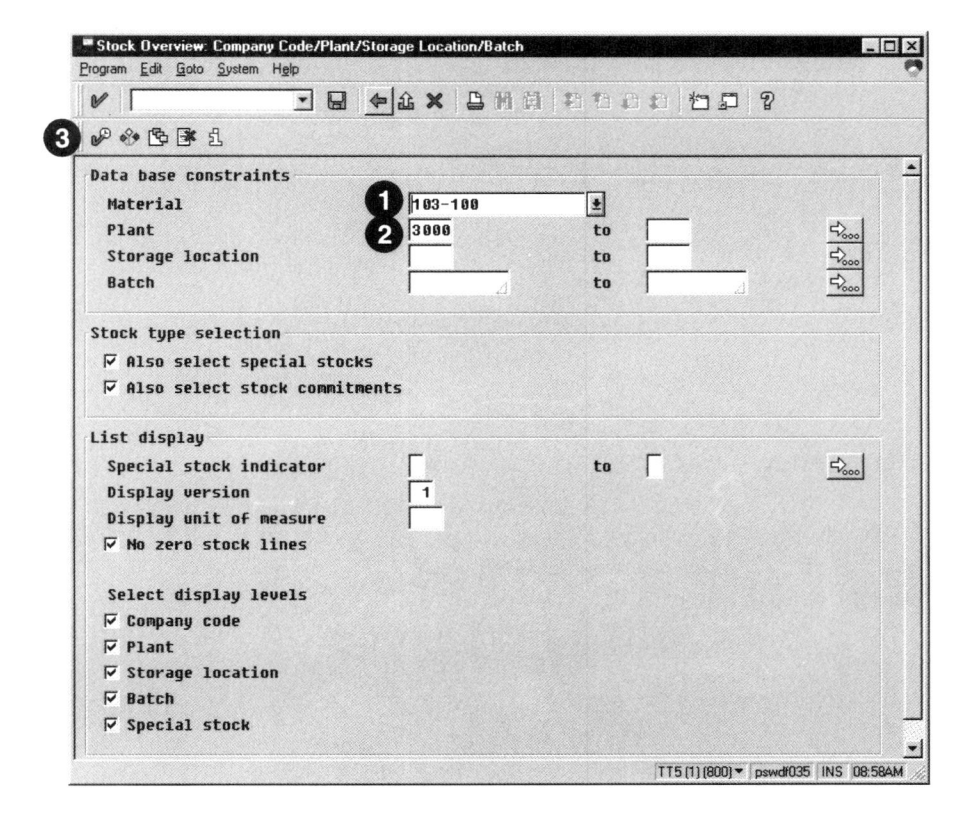

This screen shows the entire inventory for material *103-100* in plant *3000*.

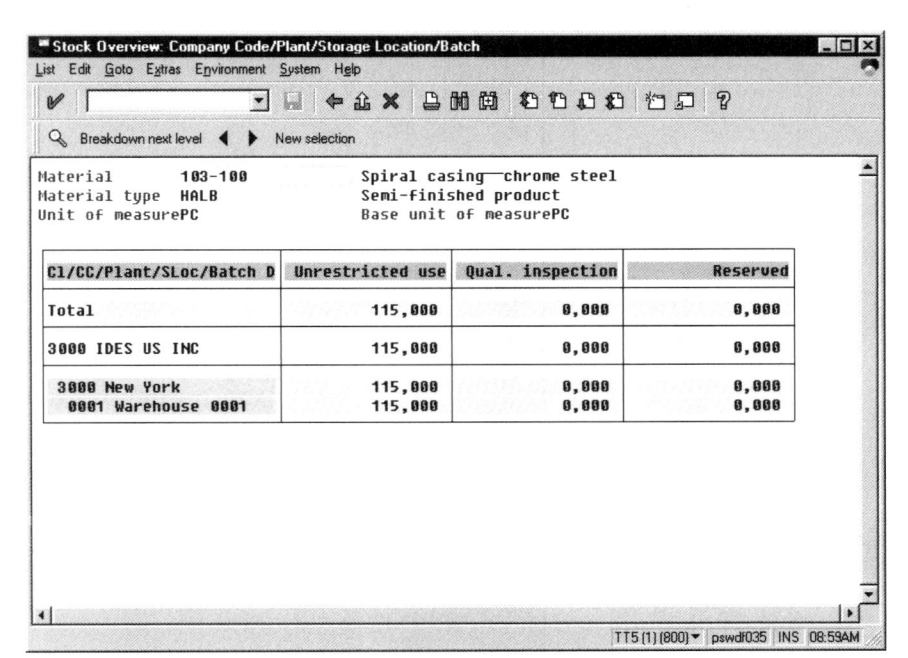

Commonly Used Reports: Illustrations and Perspectives

10–5

List Displays of PO—Material or Vendor

Quick Access To run this report, use one of the following access options:

Option 1: Menu Path

Logistics → *Materials management* → *Purchasing* → *Purchase order* → *List displays* → *By vendor | By material*

Option 2: Program Name

Choose *System* → *Services* → *Reporting* and enter **RM06EL00** in the *Program* field. Then, choose *Execute* to run the report.

Option 3: Transaction Code

In the *Command* field, enter transaction **ME2L** (by vendor) or **ME2M** (by material) and choose *Enter*.

Purpose You can customize this report to analyze purchase orders according to:

- **Account assignment** (Lists purchase orders for a given account assignment, for example, by cost center)
- **PO number** (Lists all purchase orders within a range of numbers)
- **Archived purchasing documents** (Lists POs that have been removed from the system and archived)
- **Requirement tracking number** (Lists all purchasing documents created with reference to a series of purchase requisitions having a certain requirement tracking number. The analysis shows the requisitions for which purchase orders have already been created.)
- **Vendor/material** (Lists purchase orders created for a particular vendor, material, or material group)

Prerequisites If you are in the program *Purchase orders by material*, you must enter the *Material*.

If you are in the program *Purchase orders by account assignment*, you must enter the *Account assignment*.

The selection options are based on the relevant purchasing document and the list can vary to some extent among documents. The more information the list contains, the more time it will take for the report to run. Larger reports should be reserved for background processing to save time.

Integration You can combine search criteria to find a specific purchase order (for example, you could search for a PO that was issued to a specific vendor for a specific cost center in July).

Features

The selection screen of this report includes:
- Variants
- Dynamic selection options
- User variables
- Execution (and print) in background

The output of this report includes :
- Listing purchase order, sorted by item number
- Selection of purchase orders for individual display (double-click on the individual purchase order)
- Selection of purchase order items for individual display (double-click on one of the purchase order line items, or click on it and choose *History → Changes → Delivery schedule*)

Next Steps

This report does not allow manipulation of data.

Section 10: Materials Management Reports
List Displays of PO—Material or Vendor

Guided Tour

Example 1: Display the list of purchase orders by vendor.

To access the first screen for this report, choose

Logistics → *Materials management* → *Purchasing* → *Purchase order* → *List displays* → *By vendor.*

1. Enter **1010** in *Vendor*.

   This will produce a report of all purchase orders for this vendor.

2. Choose *Execute*.

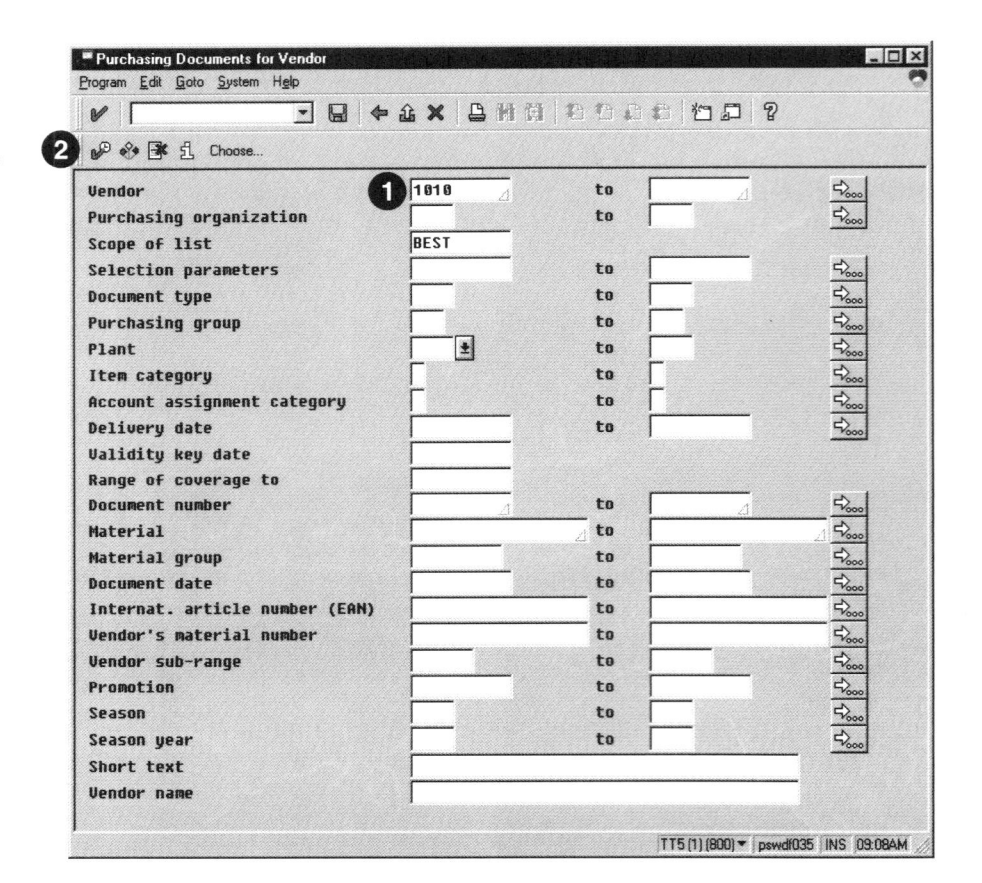

Reporting Made Easy

Section 10: Materials Management Reports

List Displays of PO—Material or Vendor

This report shows all the purchase orders for vendor *1010*.

From this screen, you can drill down to get more information.

3. Double-click on the PO header to access the purchase order (for example, *450005024*).

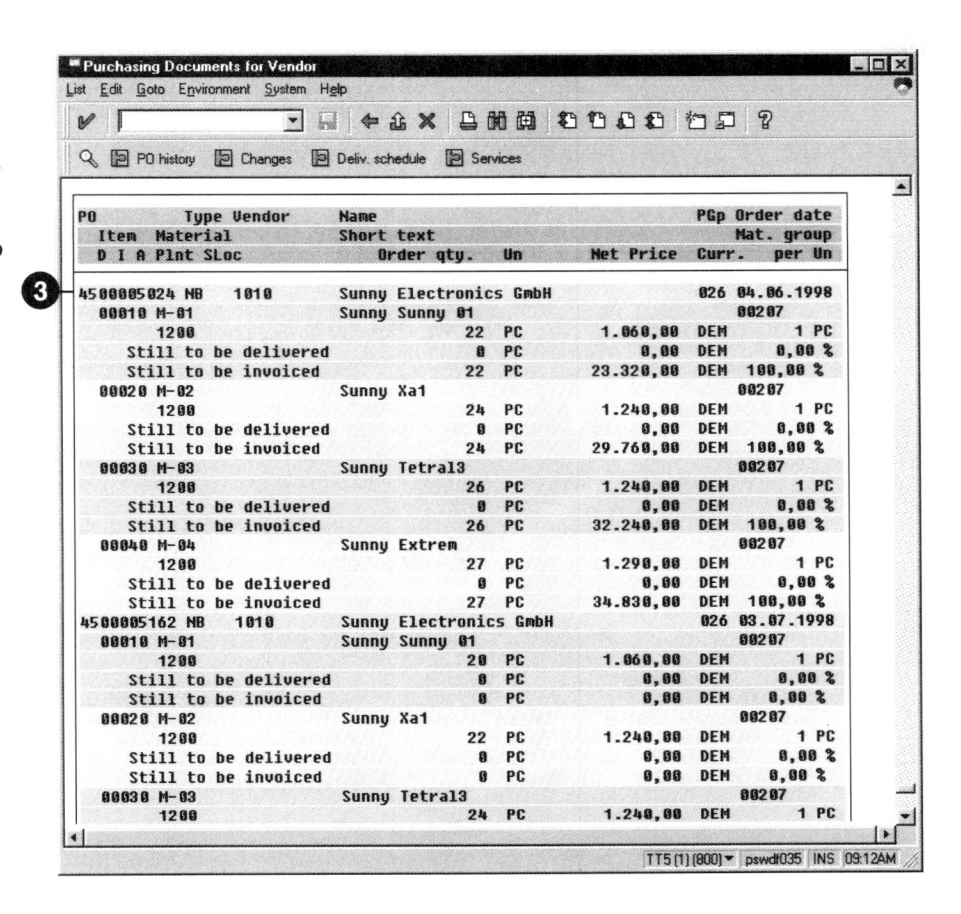

This screen shows the selected purchase order.

4. Choose *Back* ⬅ to return to the original report.

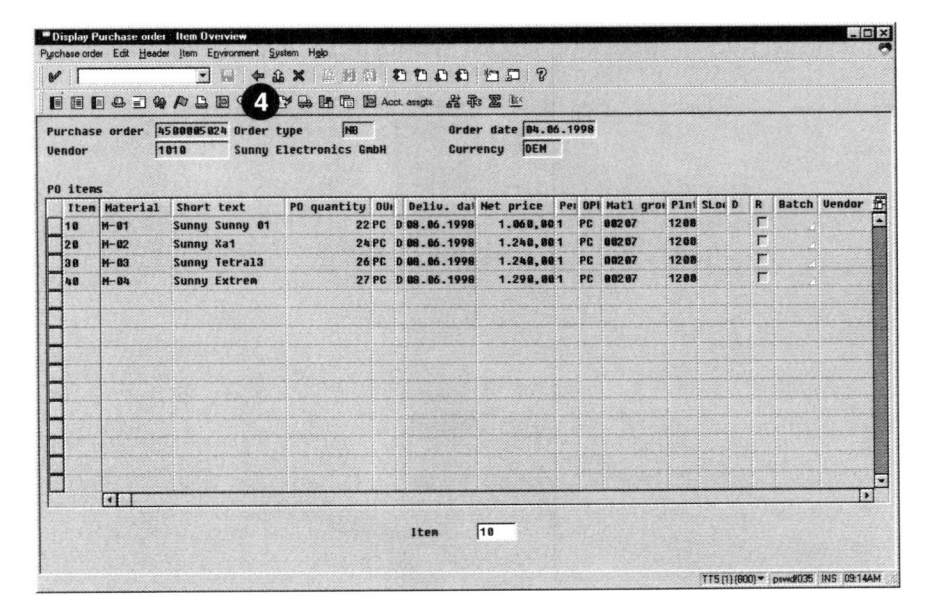

Commonly Used Reports: Illustrations and Perspectives

10–9

Section 10: Materials Management Reports

List Displays of PO—Material or Vendor

You are back in the original report.

An alternative way to drill down on a PO line item follows:

5. Double-click on the PO line item to access the purchase order (for example, *00010 M-01*).

6. Depending on your needs, you can drill down further using *Details*, *PO History*, *Changes*, *Delivery schedule*, or *Services* buttons.

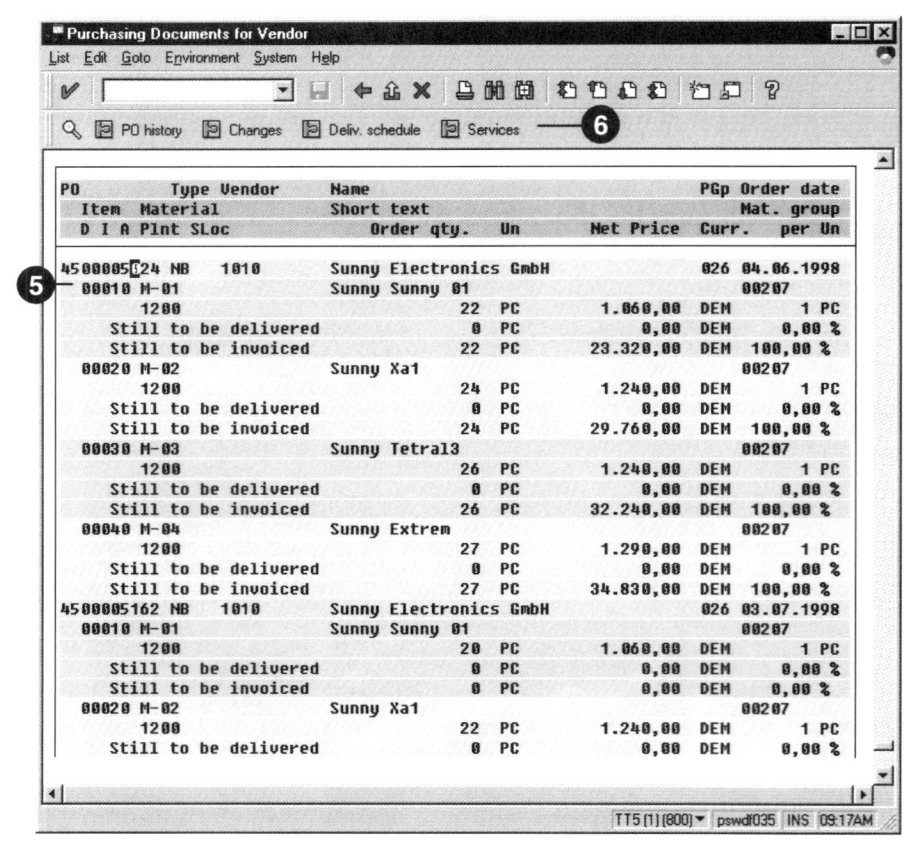

This screen shows the *Purchase Order* history. In this example, only one goods receipt has been processed.

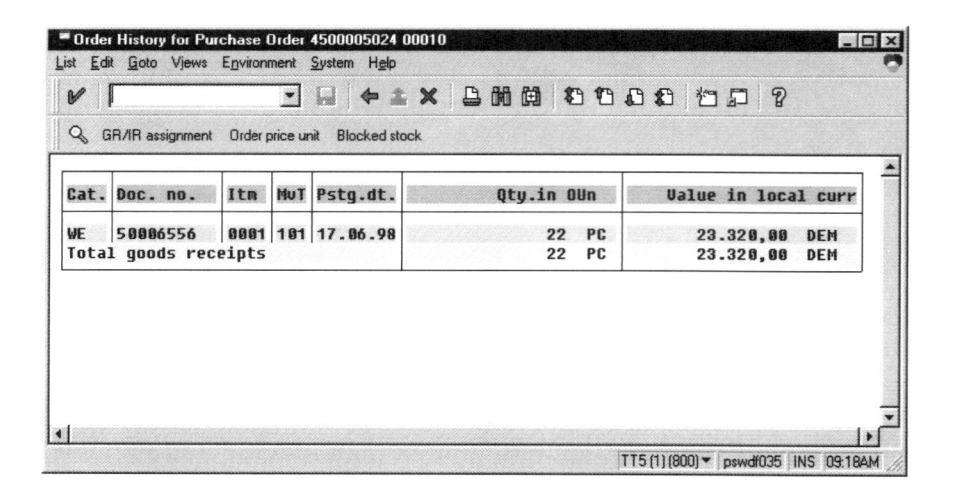

10–10 Reporting Made Easy

Section 10: Materials Management Reports
List Displays of PO—Material or Vendor

Example 2: Display a list of purchase orders by material.

1. Enter a range for the material (for example, **M-01** through **M-03**).
2. Choose *Execute*.

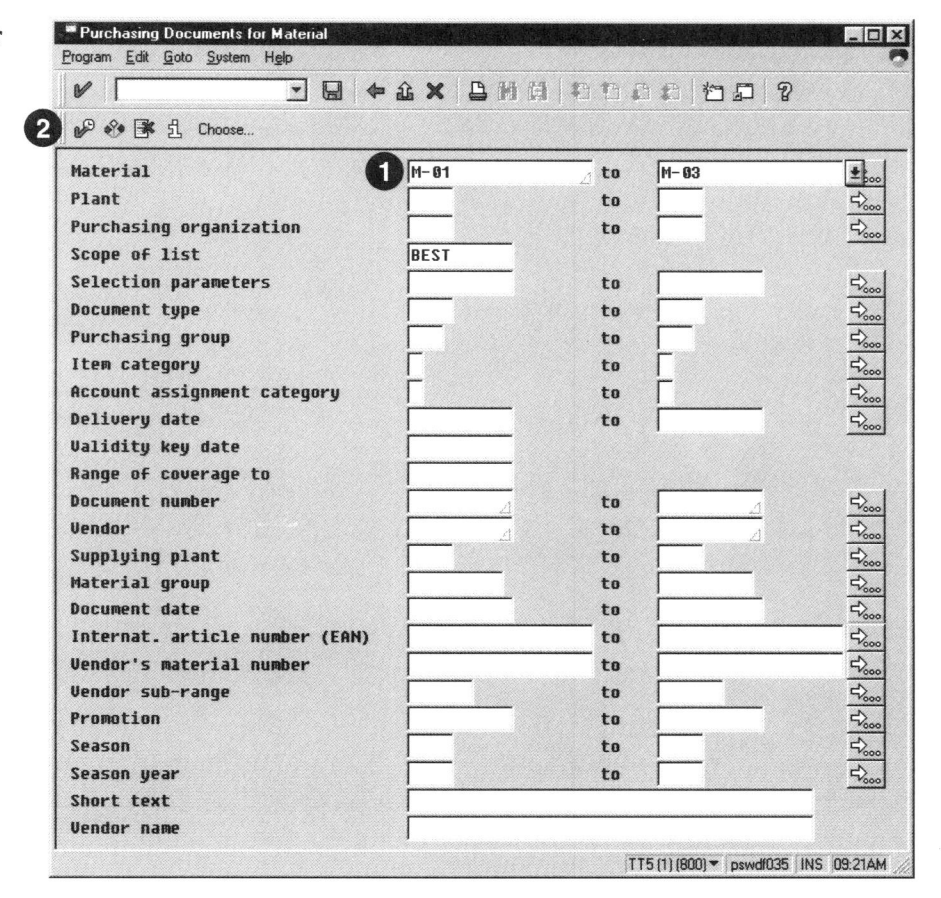

Commonly Used Reports: Illustrations and Perspectives

10–11

Section 10: Materials Management Reports
List Displays of PO—Material or Vendor

This screen shows all purchase orders created for materials *M-01* through *M-03*.

From this screen, you can drill-down for more information.

3. Select a purchase order line item (for example, *45000045*).

4. Choose *Display*.

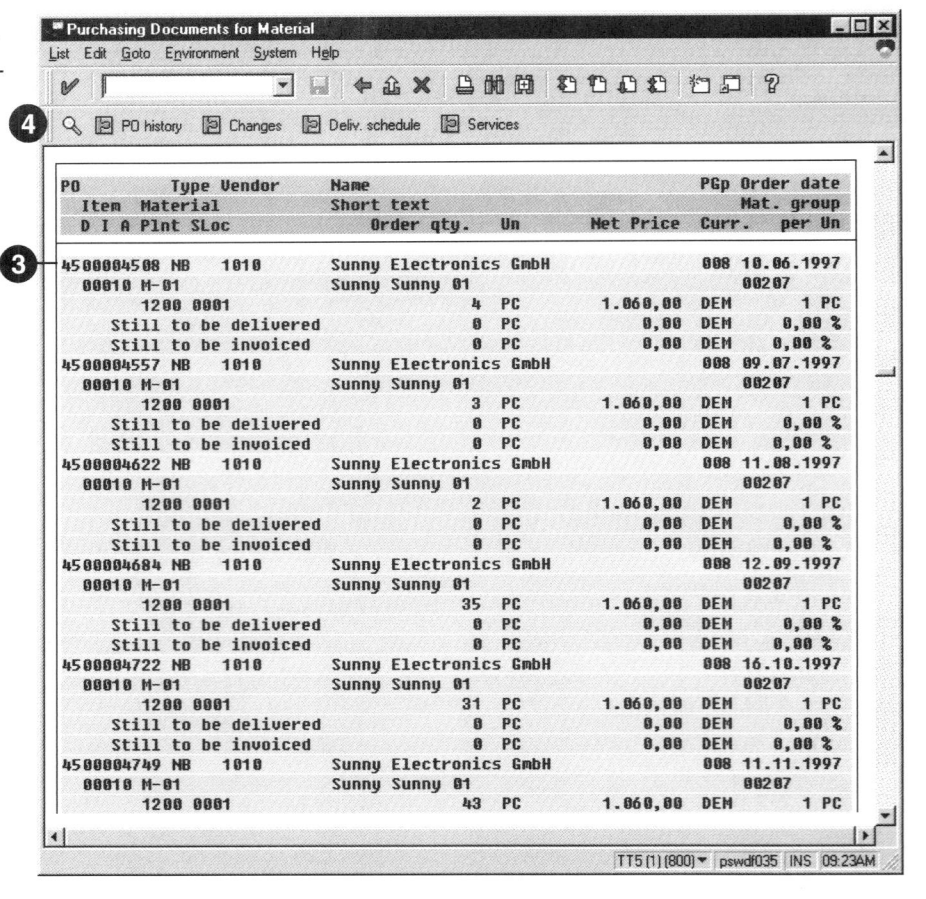

This is the purchase order detail screen for item *00010*.

5. Choose *Back* to return to the original report.

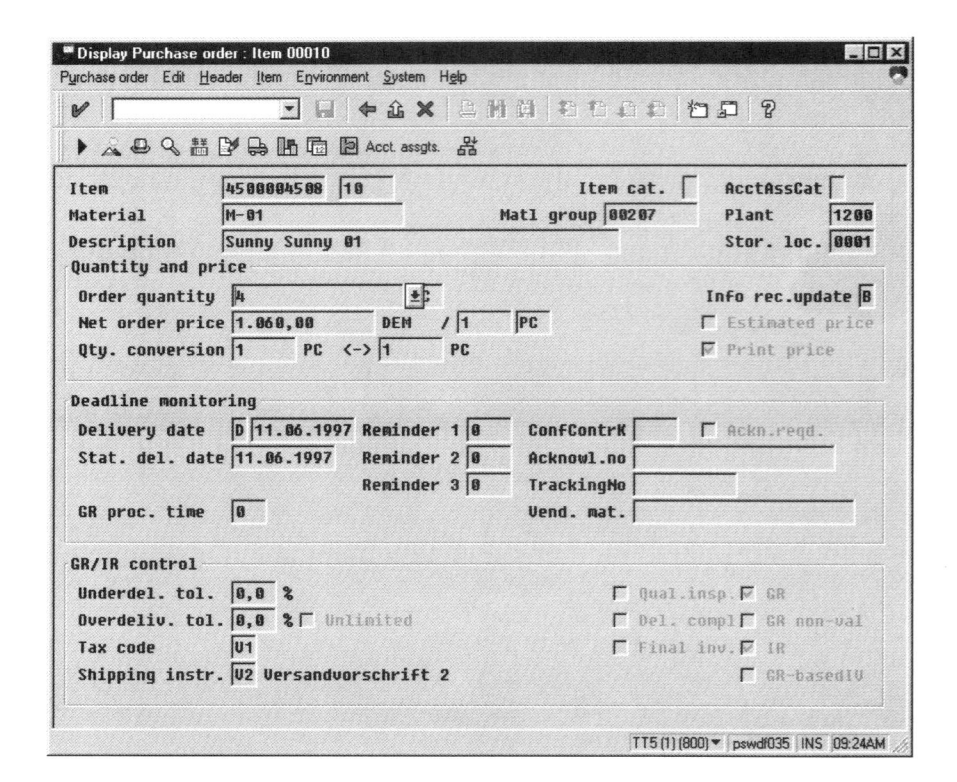

10–12

Reporting Made Easy

Material Documents for Material

Quick Access To run this report, use one of the following access options:

Option 1: Menu Path

Logistics → Materials management → Inventory management → Environment → List displays → Mat.doc.for material

Option 2: Program Name

Choose *System → Services → Reporting* and enter **RM07MMAT** in the *Program* field. Then, choose *Execute* to run the report.

Option 3: Transaction Code

In the *Command* field, enter transaction **MB51** and choose *Enter*.

Purpose This report lists the material documents that posted for one or more materials. The report's drilldown capacity allows you to view all supporting documents.

Material documents are posted with all goods movements, including those in which stock does not actually move (for example, a change in batch number for a material). Material documents are posted from transactions such as purchase order receipts, issuing components to production orders, and the "post goods issue" for a delivery on a sales order.

Prerequisites No prerequisites are required to run this report. However, you should limit the selection criteria to restrict the material document listing. The *Setting* checkboxes allow you to select different ways the output can be shown at the bottom of the selection screen (for example, you can list only those documents posted for given materials, in certain plants, and of certain movement types).

Integration This report generates information that can be used to find all the production order receipts for a set of materials in a given time period. For example, you can find all the movements of a particular material batch (lot) within a quarter. From the list, you can select (and view) any of the listed material documents. In addition to viewing a material, you can view the total stock quantities (stock overview) for the material.

Section 10: Materials Management Reports
Material Documents for Material

Features

The selection screen of this report includes:
- Variants
- Dynamic selection options
- User variables
- Execution (and print) in background

The output of this report includes:
- Listing of material documents (grouped by material)
- Selection of material documents for individual display (double-click on one of the individual material document line items)
- Dynamic filtering of output (by column) after the report runs (to narrow down the displayed results); this is done by positioning the cursor on a column, then choosing *Edit → Set filter* (Ctrl+Shift+F2)
- Sorting capability (by column): Select a column, then choose *Edit → Sort in ascending/descending order* (Ctrl+Shift+F5/F4)
- Summation by column: Select a column, then choose *Edit → Add up values* (Shift+F7)
- Column width optimization: Select a column, then choose *Settings → Columns → Optimize width*
- Data statistics for the output: Choose *Settings → List status* (Ctrl+F11)

Next Steps

This report contains data obtained from material documents and material information. As such, the data cannot be changed or manipulated from the report.

Guided Tour

Example 1: Display a simple listing of receipts to a plant in a year.

To access the first screen for this report, choose

Logistics → Materials management → Inventory management → Environment → List displays → Mat.doc.for material.

1. Enter **3000** in *Plant*.
2. Enter **101** in *Movement type*.
3. Enter a date range in *Posting date* (for example, **01/01/1997** to **12/31/1997**).
4. Choose *Execute*.

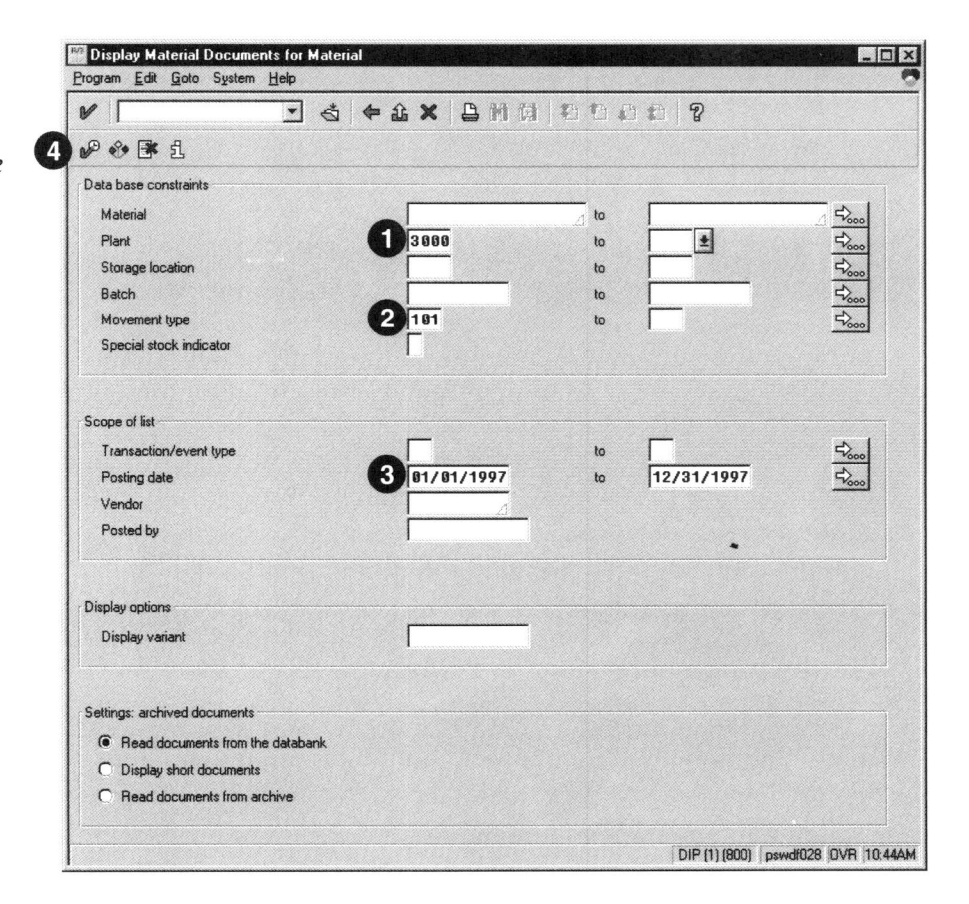

Section 10: Materials Management Reports
Material Documents for Material

This screen shows a listing of material document line items arranged by material. In this example, if you scroll down to material *P-100*, you find two receipts made on two separate documents.

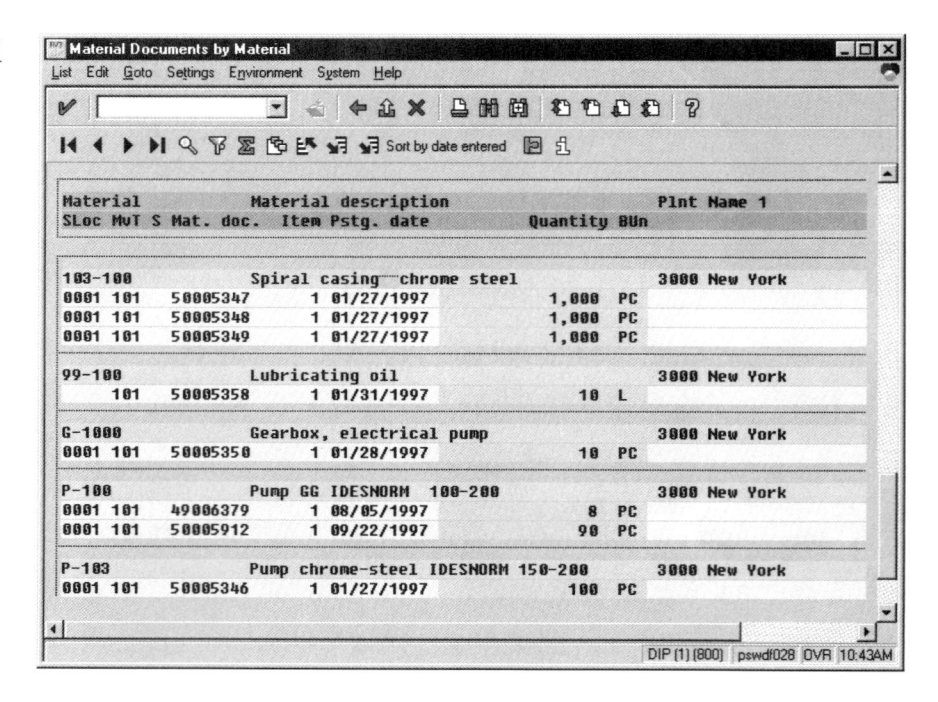

```
Material Documents by Material                                    _ □ ×
List  Edit  Goto  Settings  Environment  System  Help

 ✔  [         ▼]  ⇐ ⇧ ✕   🖨 🔍 📋   🔄 🔄 🔄 🔄   ?
 ◄◄ ◄ ► ►►  🔍 ▼ Σ 📋 📋 📋 📋  Sort by date entered  📋 📋

Material              Material description                 Plnt Name 1
SLoc MvT S Mat. doc.  Item Pstg. date         Quantity BUn

103-100               Spiral casing chrome steel           3000 New York
0001 101   50005347      1 01/27/1997          1,000 PC
0001 101   50005348      1 01/27/1997          1,000 PC
0001 101   50005349      1 01/27/1997          1,000 PC

99-100                Lubricating oil                      3000 New York
     101   50005358      1 01/31/1997             10 L

G-1000                Gearbox, electrical pump             3000 New York
0001 101   50005350      1 01/28/1997             10 PC

P-100                 Pump GG IDESNORM  100-200            3000 New York
0001 101   49006379      1 08/05/1997              8 PC
0001 101   50005912      1 09/22/1997             90 PC

P-103                 Pump chrome-steel IDESNORM 150-200   3000 New York
0001 101   50005346      1 01/27/1997            100 PC

                                              DIP (1) (800)  pswdf028  OVR  10:43AM
```

Example 2: Display the totals for material document postings.

1. Enter **DG-1000** in *Material*.
2. Enter **3000** in *Plant*.
3. Enter **261** in *Movement type*. This is the standard movement type for goods issued to production.
4. Choose *Execute*.

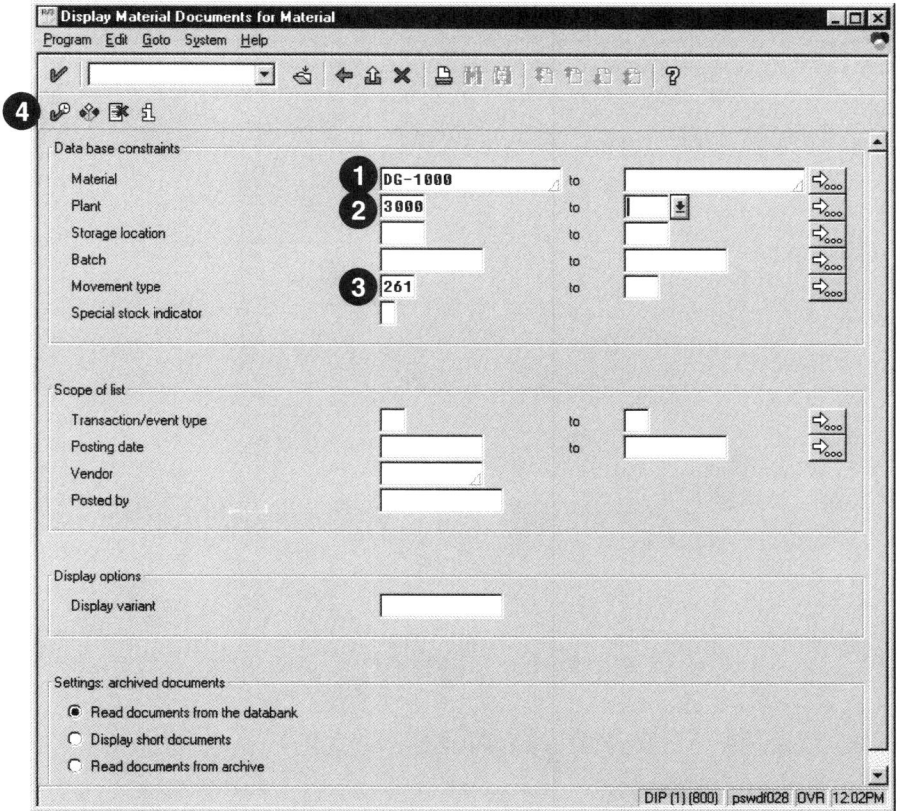

Section 10: Materials Management Reports

Material Documents for Material

This screen shows a listing of material document line items arranged by material.

5. Select the *Quantity* column.
6. Choose *Summation*.
7. The total number (*78* pieces) of items issued for this material appears.

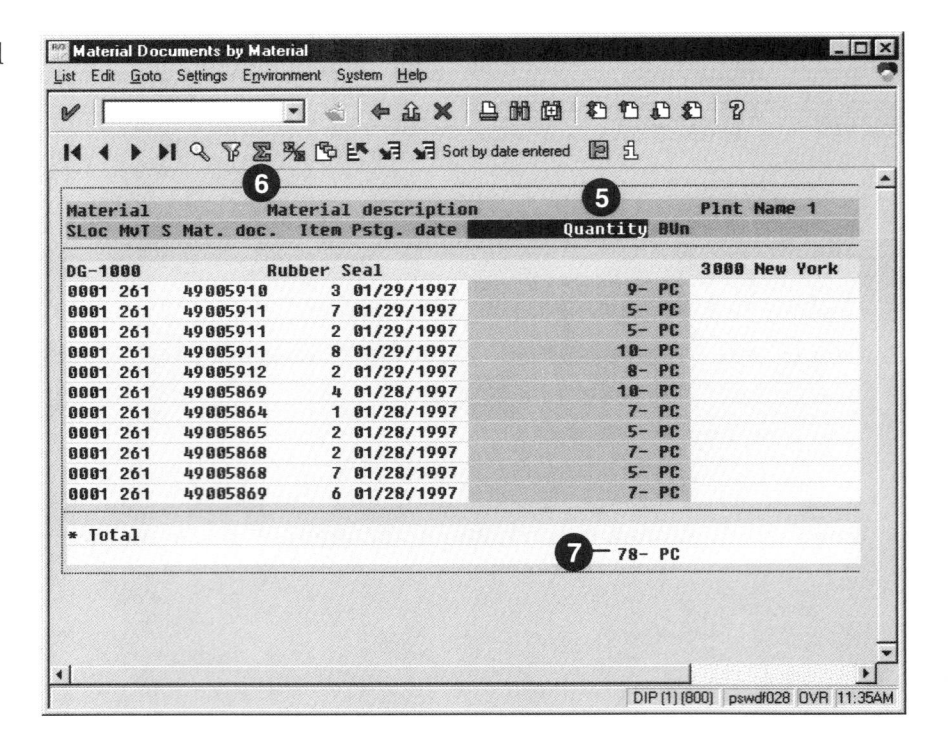

Section 10: Materials Management Reports
Material Documents for Material

Example 3: Display a specific batch (or lot) history.

1. Enter **103-SG** in *Material*.
2. Enter **3000** in *Plant*.
3. Enter **2KPG392** in *Batch*.
4. Choose *Execute*.

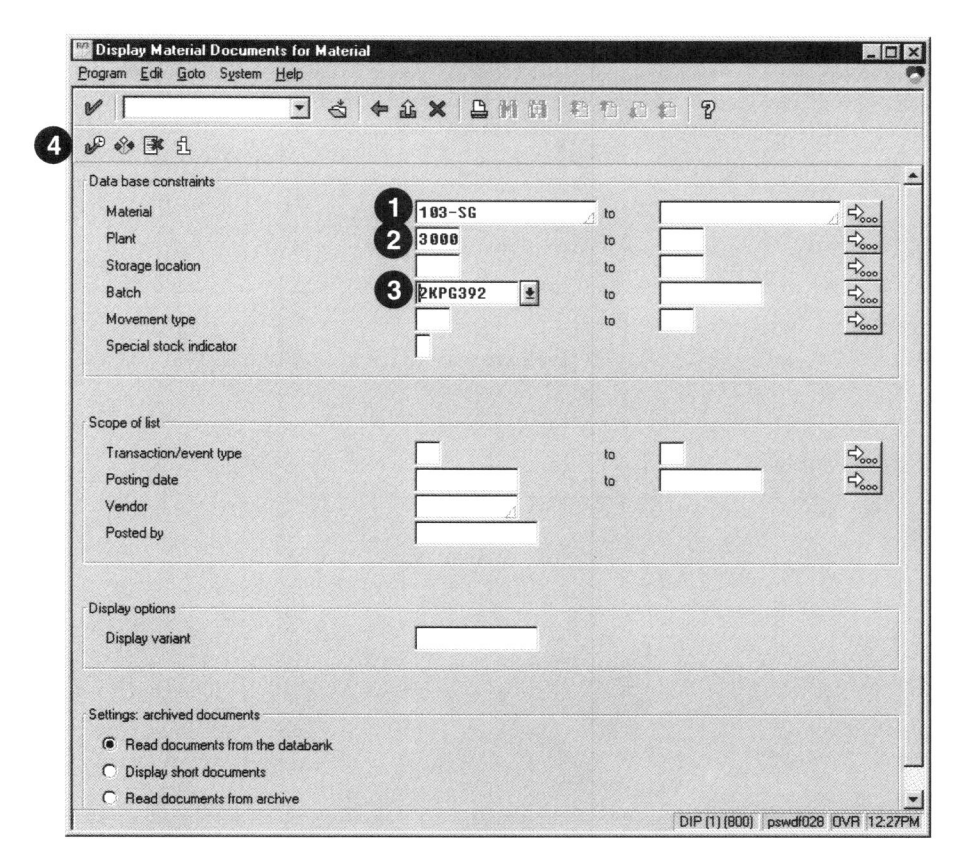

A A total of *785* pieces of material *103-SG* remains in plant *3000*.

B *1000* pieces were received in storage location *0001* with movement type *501*.

C 475 pieces were transferred from storage location *0001* to location *0002* with movement type *311*.

Note that line item *0001* is a withdrawal from storage location *0001*, and line item *0002* is a receipt into location *0002*.

D *215* pieces were issued to a cost center movement type *201*.

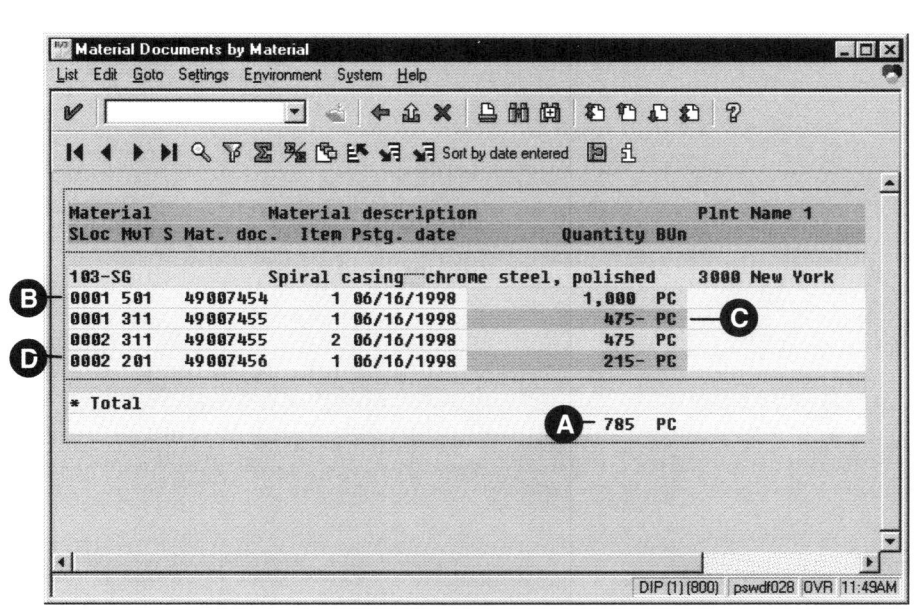

List Display of Purchase Requisitions

Quick Access   To run this report, use one of the following access options:

Option 1: Menu Path

Logistics → *Materials management* → *Purchasing* → *Requisition* → *List displays* → *General*

Option 2: Program Name

Choose *System* → *Services* → *Reporting* and enter **RM06BA00** in the *Program* field. Then, choose *Execute* to run the report.

Option 3: Transaction Code

In the *Command* field, enter transaction **ME5A** and choose *Enter*.

Purpose   This report displays a set of purchase requisitions according to selected criteria. You can control both the display of these requisitions and how they are sorted.

Frequently a "purchasing group" is set up as a set of buyers, or each group number is assigned to an individual buyer. Lists of created requisitions can be viewed according to the buyer who may process them or the requestor who entered them. Purchase requisitions also can be directed for certain plants and storage locations. Consequently, displaying requisitions by plant and storage location can provide a view beyond purchase orders.

Listing purchase requisitions is also useful for managers who are required to release requisitions begun by their employees.

Prerequisites   You must enter a *scope of list* to run this report. This identifies how the set of purchase requisitions will be displayed (for example, 2-line, 3-line, etc.) and a display sort indicator.

The output will only be meaningful if valid purchase requisitions have first been entered into the system.

Section 10: Materials Management Reports
List Display of Purchase Requisitions

Integration

From the output of this report, you can run many other reports including :
- Individual requisition display
- Individual material display
- Stock overview
- Stock/requirements list
- Outline agreement display
- Purchasing info record display
- Display of vendor evaluation

Features

We suggest you carefully choose selection criteria, as this report is capable of listing all requisitions across several plants and among several purchasing groups.

To assure a more meaningful report, you should know the items that will limit the display (for example, purchase group, material, plant, delivery date, processing status, etc.).

You can use the sort indicator to sort the report as desired, however you can also change the sorting once the report has run. Summary data can be displayed from the output.

This report also uses such features as dynamic selections, user variables, and selection variants.

Next Steps

This report contains data obtained from purchase requisitions, related materials, vendor information, and outline agreements. As such, the data cannot be changed or manipulated from the report.

Section 10: Materials Management Reports
List Display of Purchase Requisitions

Guided Tour

Example 1: Display a simple listing of purchase requisitions for a plant.

To access the first screen for this report, choose

Logistics → Materials management → Purchasing → Requisition → List displays → General.

1. Enter **A** in *Scope of list*. This creates a three-line display in the output.
2. Enter **3000** in *Plant*.
3. Enter **1** in *Sort indicator*. This creates sorting by purchase requisition number and item.
4. Make certain that *Closed requisitions* is deselected.
5. Choose *Execute*.

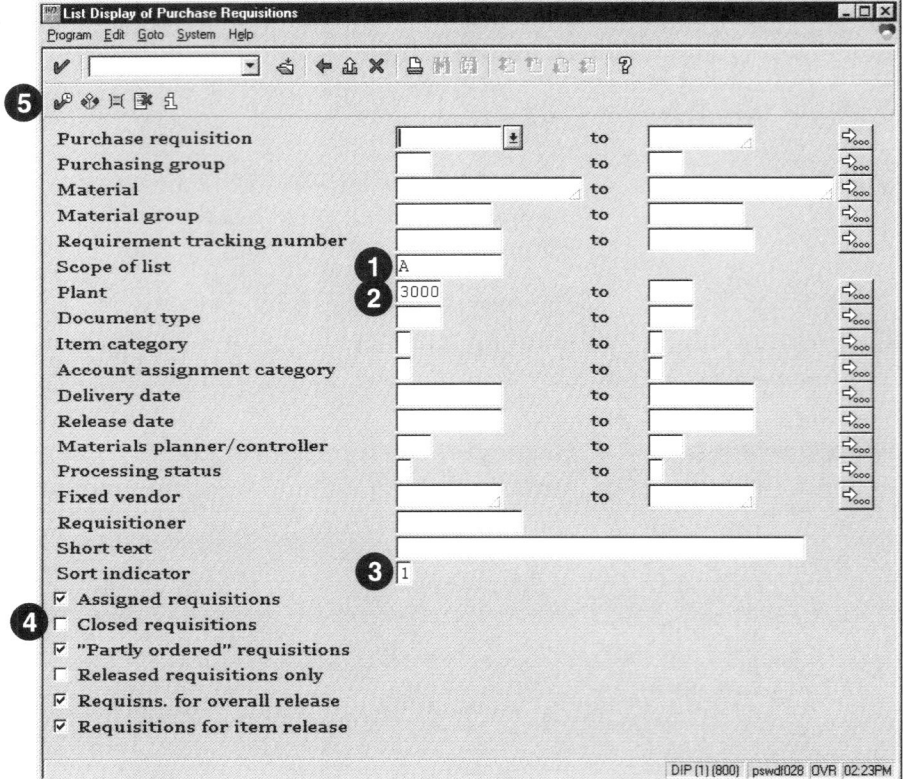

10–22

Reporting Made Easy

Section 10: Materials Management Reports
List Display of Purchase Requisitions

This display of purchase requisitions corresponds to the header lines defined according to selections for the *Scope of list*.

Requisitions are sequentially numbered, all with the same date, plant, material group, and requestor. Thus, it is likely that the requisitions came from the material planner *MEIER*.

6. Double-click on an individual line (for example, *10004956*) to view detailed information.

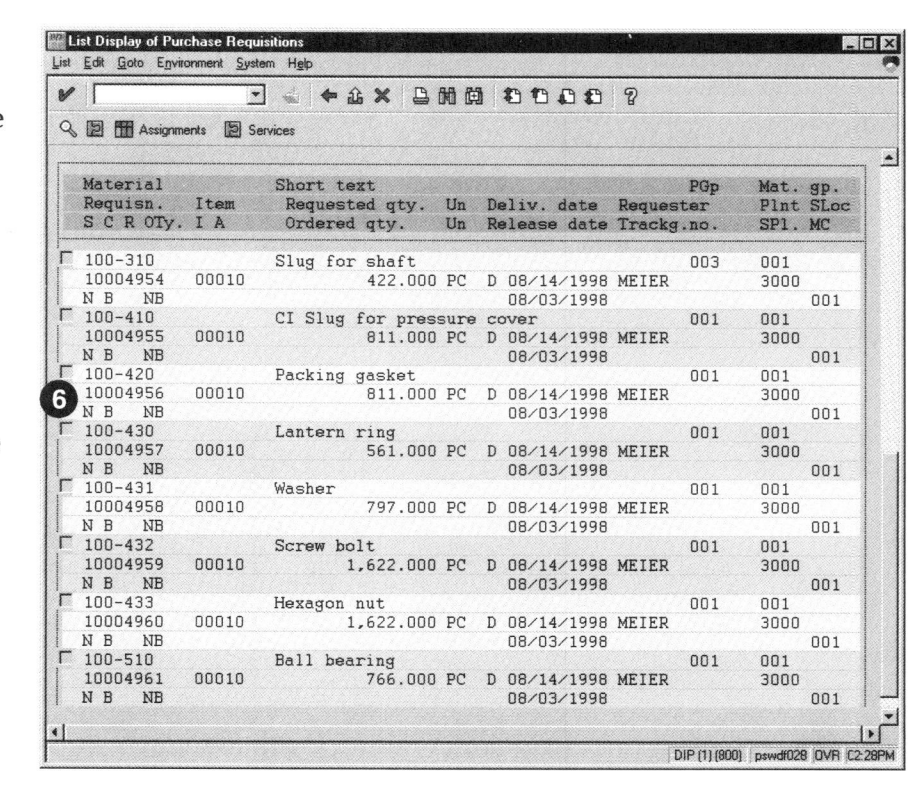

This screen shows detailed information for requisition number *10004956*.

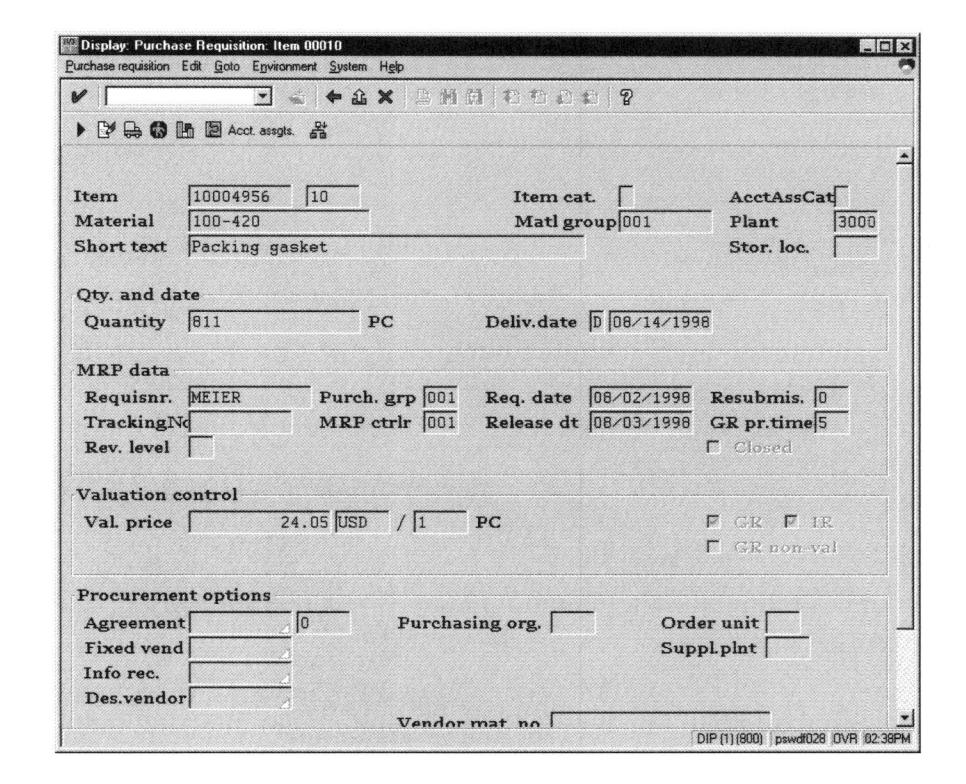

Commonly Used Reports: Illustrations and Perspectives

Section 10: Materials Management Reports
List Display of Purchase Requisitions

Example 2: Display a simple listing of purchase requisitions for a set of materials within a plant.

1. Enter **R-1000** to **R-1500** in *Material*.
2. Enter **3200** in *Plant*.
3. Enter **7** in *Sort indicator*. This creates sorting by material number.
4. Choose *Execute*.

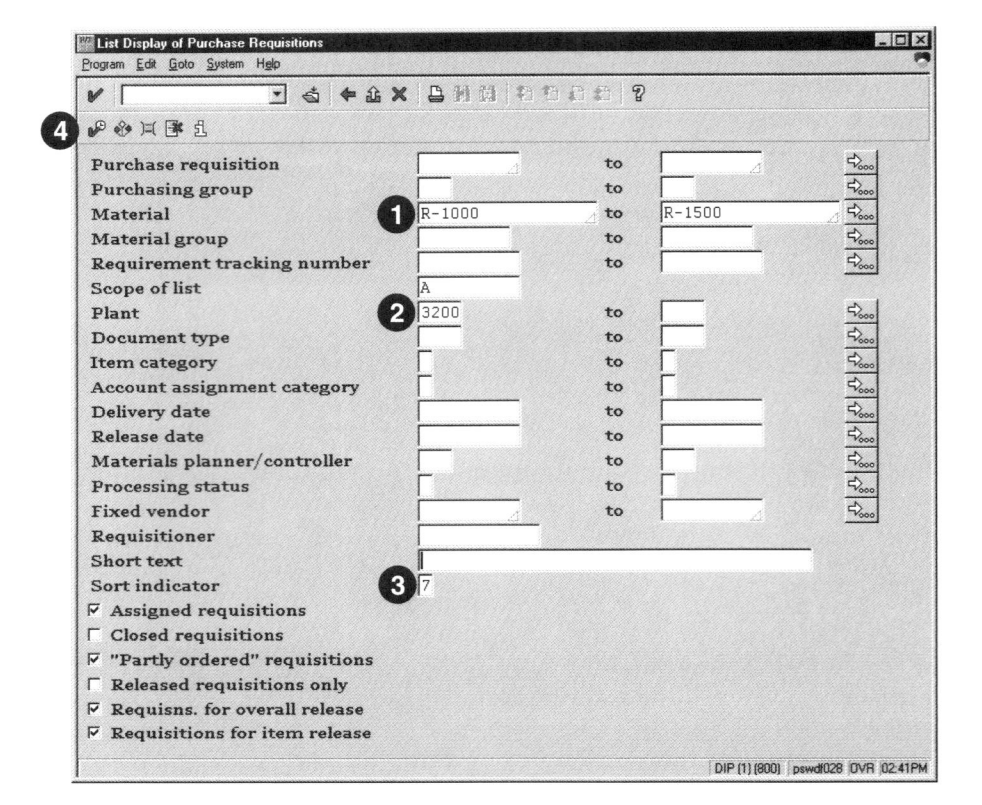

This screen shows six purchase requisition line items.

A Two of these line items are from the same requisition, but are not shown together because the display is sorted by material.

B Four of these requisitions are appropriated to cost centers (account assignment category is K).

C To view a stock/requirements list on a requisition item first select its checkbox and then, choose *Environment → stock rqmts./list*.

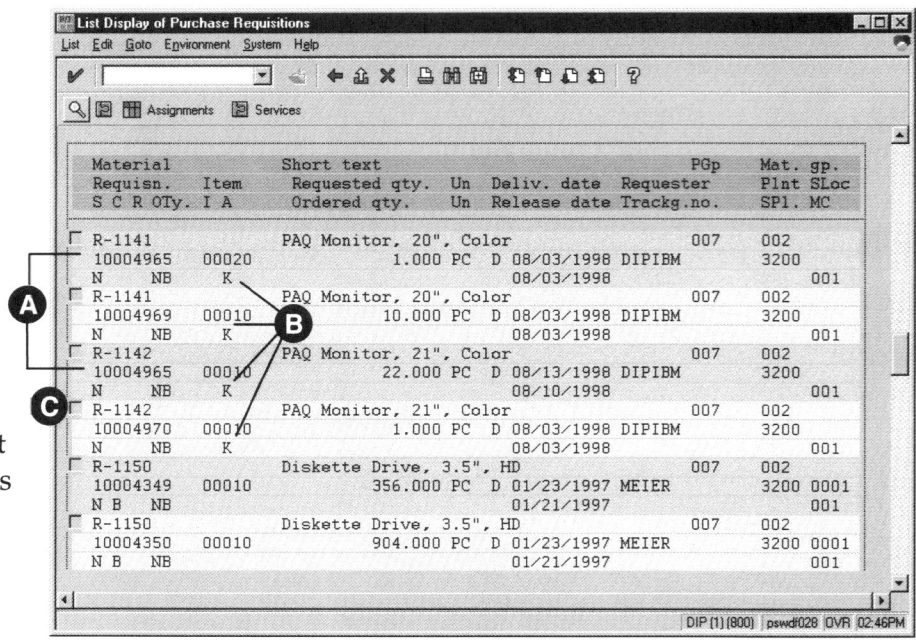

10–24   Reporting Made Easy

Section 10: Materials Management Reports
List Display of Purchase Requisitions

The stock/requirements list is shown for material R-1141.

D The incorporation of requisitions 10004965 and 10004969 (shown in the previous display) can be seen.

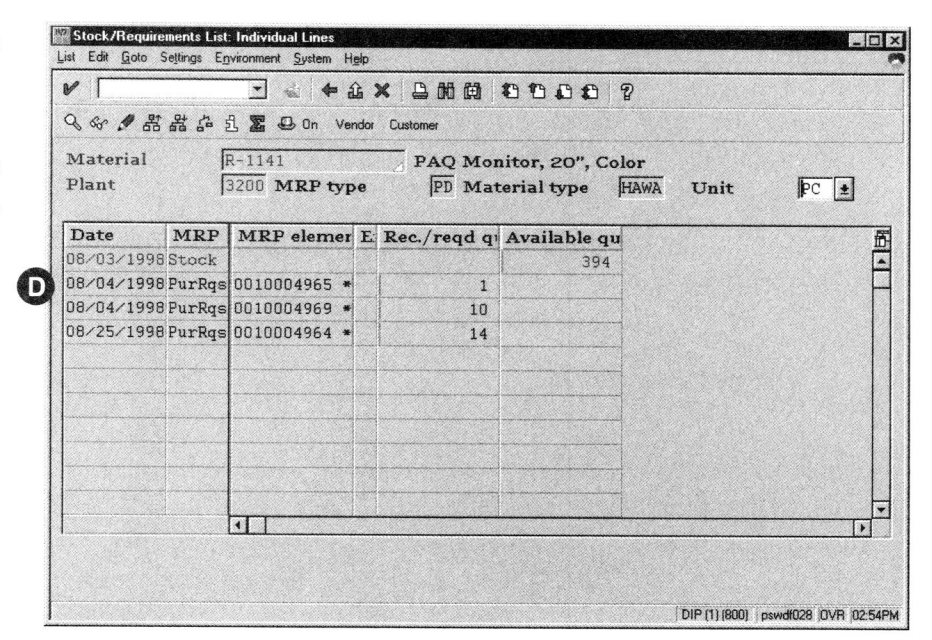

Date	MRP	MRP elemer	E	Rec./reqd q	Available qu
08/03/1998	Stock				394
08/04/1998	PurRqs	0010004965	*	1	
08/04/1998	PurRqs	0010004969	*	10	
08/25/1998	PurRqs	0010004964	*	14	

Commonly Used Reports: Illustrations and Perspectives

Section 11: Plant Maintenance Reports

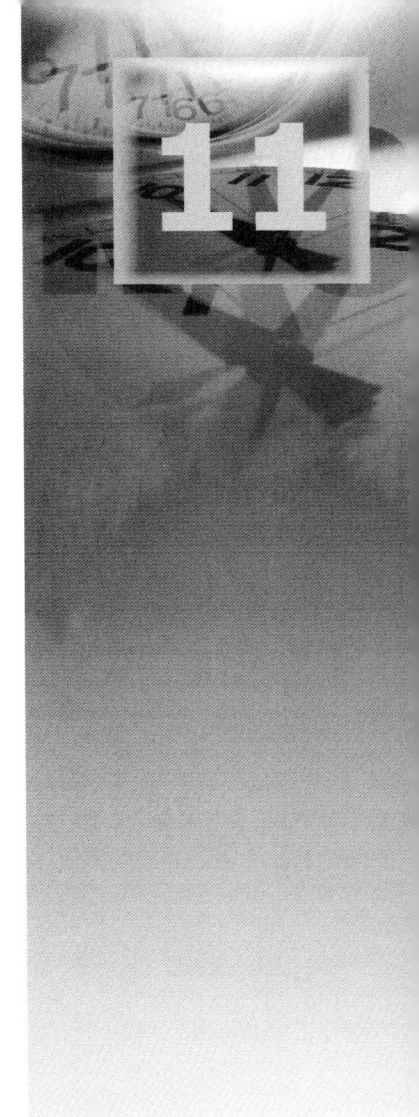

Contents

List of Notification Tasks 11–2
Order Cost Element Display 11–6

List of Notification Tasks

Quick Access   To run this report, use one of the following access options:

Option 1: Menu Path

Logistics → *Plant maintenance* → *Maintenance processing* → *Notifications*

List of tasks → *Change | Display*

Option 2: Program Name

Choose *System* → *Services* → *Reporting* and enter `RIQMEL30` in the *Program* field. Then, choose *Execute* to run the report.

Option 3: Transaction Code

In the *Command* field, enter transaction `IW66` (for change mode) or transaction `IW67` (for display mode) and choose *Enter*. You can toggle between the display and change mode from the list of notification tasks for both transactions.

Purpose   You can use this report to describe the condition of a technical object, or to report a malfunction in a technical object and request the damage to be repaired.

This report displays a list of tasks for selected maintenance notifications.

Prerequisites   No prerequisites are required to run this report.

If you run the report without entering any selection criteria, the system date is used as the notification date and all uncompleted tasks list for this date.

Integration   From this report, you can select and view (or edit) notifications and execute functions (for example, put in process, print, postpone, complete, and create an order for the notification).

If available, you can also branch to the following:

- Maintenance order linked to the notification
- Functional location
- Equipment
- Assembly defined in the notification header
- Multilevel list displays for notifications, orders, functional locations, and equipment

Section 11: Plant Maintenance Reports
List of Notification Tasks

Features

The selection screen of this report includes:
- Variants
- Execution (and print) in background

You can modify the layout of the selection screen and the list display format.

Next Steps

This report contains data obtained from maintenance notifications which have tasks assigned to them. Data can be manipulated by selecting and editing notifications, and by executing functions (such as postpone, complete, put in process, etc.).

Note: The system administrator can prevent users from editing notifications with transaction code IW67 by making the appropriate restrictions to the authorization profiles of the users.

Guided Tour

Example 1: Display all notification tasks to be completed for a given period.

To access the first screen for this report, choose

Logistics → *Plant maintenance* → *Maintenance processing* → *Notifications* and then, *List of tasks* → *Display*.

1. Enter the desired date range (for example, **16.08.1998** to **20.08.1998**) in *Notification date*.

2. Enter the task completion dates (for example, **23.08.1998** to **28.08.1998**) in *Planned end*.

3. Deselect *Only uncompleted tasks* to exclude tasks that have not been completed.

4. Choose *Execute*.

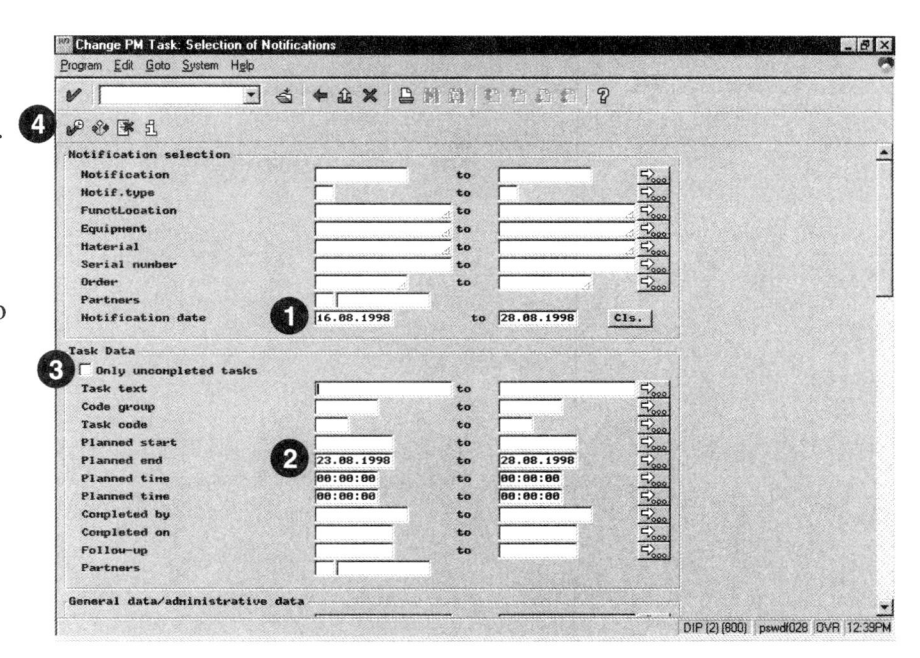

Commonly Used Reports: Illustrations and Perspectives

Section 11: Plant Maintenance Reports
List of Notification Tasks

This screen shows all notification tasks due to be completed in the given period.

5. To change the display format of this report, choose *Settings* → *Display variant* → *Current*.

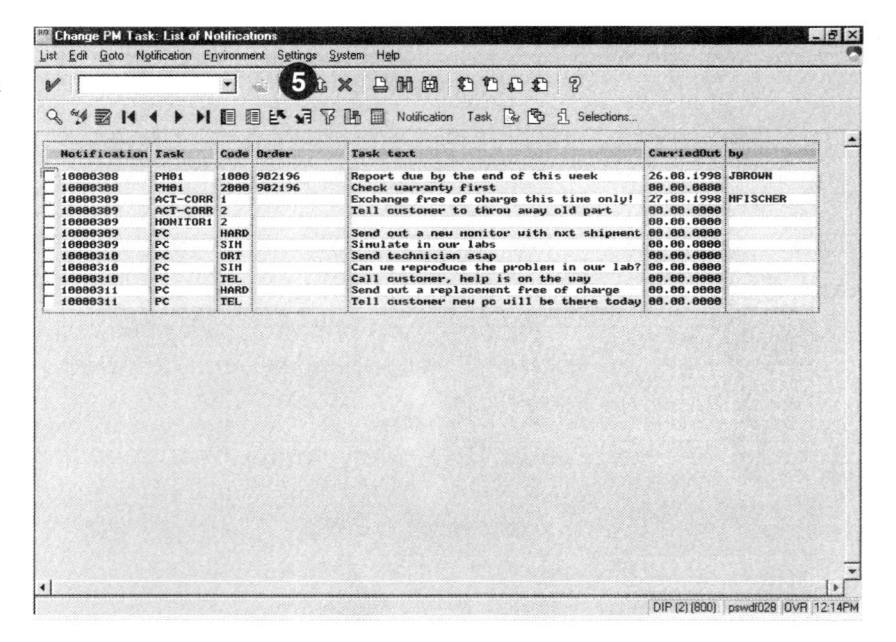

Section 11: Plant Maintenance Reports
List of Notification Tasks

Example 2: Display a notification list using the task list monitor.

1. Select a *Reference field for monitor* from *possible entries* to start the task list monitor.
   In this example, 1 means the monitor will reference the notification priority field.

2. Choose *Execute*.

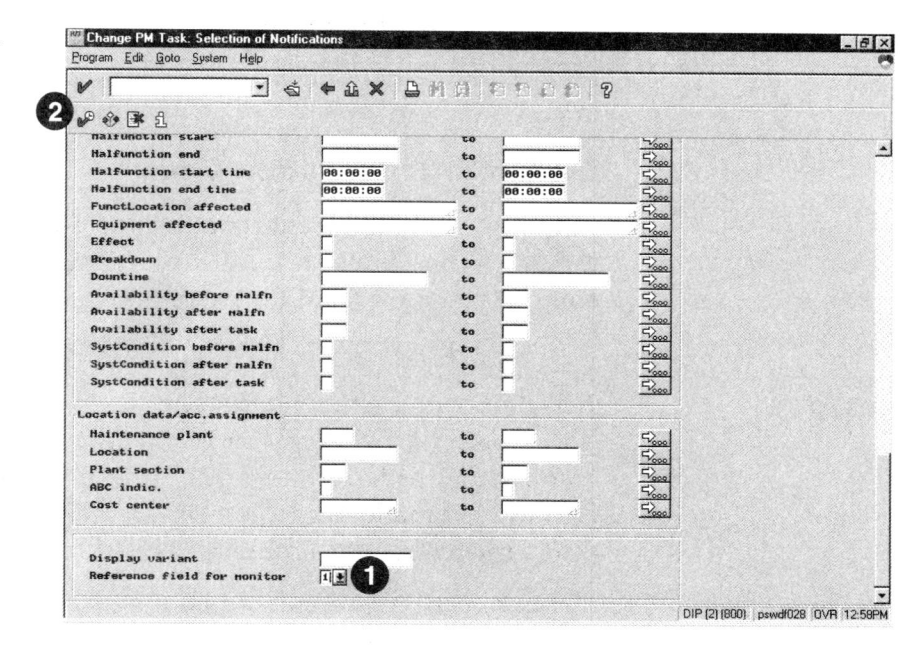

The task list monitor appears in the first column of the screen.

When viewing the monitor on screen, priorities list according to the following colors:

- Priority 1 (red)
- Priority 2 (yellow)
- Priority 3 (green)

If no priority is entered, no color is viewable.

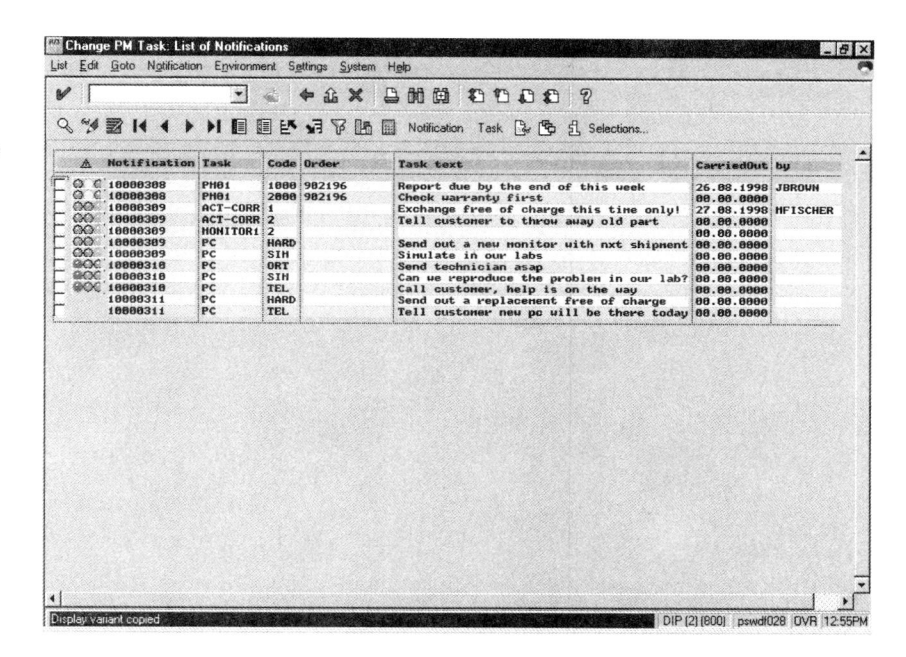

Commonly Used Reports: Illustrations and Perspectives

11–5

Order Cost Element Display

Quick Access

To run this report, use one of the following access options:

Option 1: Menu Path

Logistics → *Plant maintenance* → *Maintenance processing* → *Orders* → *Change | Display*

Option 2: Transaction Code

In the *Command* field, enter transaction **IW32** (for change mode) or transaction **IW33** (for display mode) and choose *Enter*. You can toggle between the display and change mode from the list of notification tasks for both transactions.

Purpose

This report summarizes costs by cost element and shows the current, planned, and actual costs, as well as planned and actual credits, debits, and quantities for a maintenance order. It shows the current status of the maintenance order as postings are made, regardless of when the accounting period closes. It also differentiates between settlement postings, and planned and actual costs.

Planned costs are a result of planning labor hours, materials (stock reservations and purchase requisitions), and external services for maintenance order operations.

Actual costs are a result of time postings (through HR or through the PM confirmation screen), material issues, service entry confirmations, and purchase order receipts. If the maintenance order has actual cost postings, you can drill down to the relevant documents for more information. This will give you detailed information about when and by whom the entries were made, which postings were made, what materials were issued, what overhead costs or cost allocations were included in the cost calculations, etc.

Section 11: Plant Maintenance Reports
Order Cost Element Display

Prerequisites For the cost overview report, you must define value categories in *Customizing*, and the cost elements for each value category. You must then assign the value categories to corresponding *PM key figures* for costs. This allows you to set up value categories which group together several cost-element accounts, and allocate one or more value categories to each PM key figure for costs.

For the order cost element report, you must define G/L accounts and cost elements, valuation and account determination (for materials configured), and valid prices (for activity types). You must then set up the configuration for maintenance order costs and maintenance work centers with appropriate cost calculation formulas.

When you run this report you will get a message saying *The order has no costs* if no planned or actual costs exist for the maintenance order. If there are planned costs, but no actual postings, the report displays these but you will not be able to drill down by line item.

If you feel that the cost display is showing incorrect costs, you may want to check the following:

- From the *Central Header* screen of the order, choose *Order → Functions → Determine Costs*. The costs are not recalculated with every change to the order, but only when you execute this function, save, and exit the order.

- Check that a costing variant has been defined for the order type in configuration. From the *Central Header* screen of the order, choose *Header → Usage data/parameters*. There should be a costing variant defined for both planned and actual costs. If this has not been configured properly, you will see no costs on the order.

- Check that the work center has been set up properly. The work center contains formulas that calculate the planned and actual labor rates. On the *Capacities* screen, check that a formula exists in the field *Other formulas* (for example, *SAP008*). On the *Cost centers* screen, check that a valid cost center is defined, a valid activity type entered for that cost center, and that a formula exists for the labor rate calculation (for example, *SAP008*).

- Check that a valid cost of labor has been defined for the cost center/activity type and posting period. From the main R/3 menu, choose *Accounting → Controlling → Cost Centers → Planning → Activities/prices → Display*

- Check to see if there are overhead charges included in the cost calculations. From the *Central Header* screen of the order, choose *Header → Usage data/parameters*. The costing sheet and the overhead key control the calculation of overhead for materials and orders.

- Check the material master to see what the cost of the material or service has been defined as. From the main R/3 menu, choose *Logistics → Materials Management → Material Master → Material → Display → Display current*. Enter the material number, select *Accounting 1*, and enter the plant and valuation type. You should see the standard or moving average price.

Commonly Used Reports: Illustrations and Perspectives

11–7

Order Cost Element Display

Integration

The following features are available with this report:
- Print
- Export (to spreadsheet, Microsoft Excel, word processing, HTML, dBase, WK1 format, local PC or application server)
- Graphics (to analyze order costs)
- Explode (to obtain greater detail)
- Drill down
- Threshold value (to filter report data)
- Sort (ascending and descending)

Features

You can use this report to obtain cost information while currently viewing a maintenance order. However, remember it is cost information as viewed from an accounting perspective. An alternate cost overview display allows you to configure the desired cost elements from a maintenance perspective.

The **cost buckets** (value categories) are defined in configuration and allow you to define which cost elements make up a value category to filter out unwanted cost elements or group together cost element accounts into one value category with a user-defined label. You can view this overview by choosing *Cost Overview*, or choosing *Goto → Cost Overview* from the central header screen of the order.

If you run this report from within the order, there is no selection screen. The system defaults to the controlling area and the order number. If you run this report with transaction *GR55*, report group *7K0Q*, you will need to enter this information.

Next Steps

This report contains data obtained from accounting and material documents. As such, you cannot manipulate the data.

Section 11: Plant Maintenance Reports
Order Cost Element Display

Guided Tour

Example 1: Display cost report.

To access the first screen for this report, choose

Logistics → Plant maintenance → Maintenance processing → Orders → Change.

Note: In both examples we show *change* transactions which are typically not regarded as reports. However, these transactions have been included for informational purposes only.

1. Enter `901913` in *Order*.
2. Choose *Enter*.

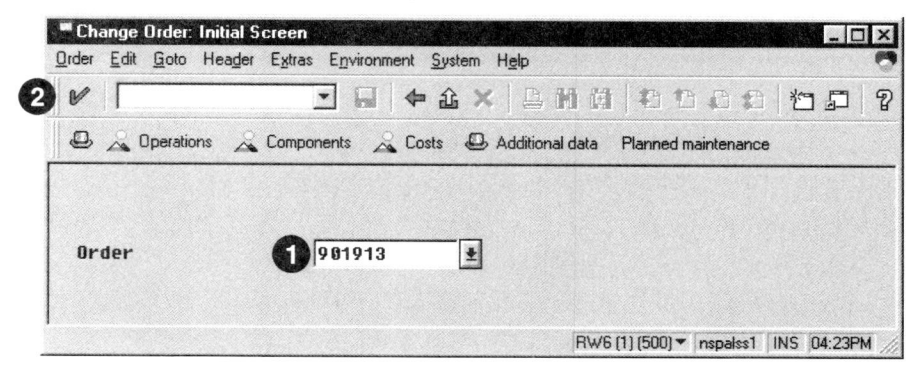

This screen shows the *Central Header* for the *Change Maintenance order*.

3. Choose *Extras → Cost Reports → Plan/act. Comparison*.

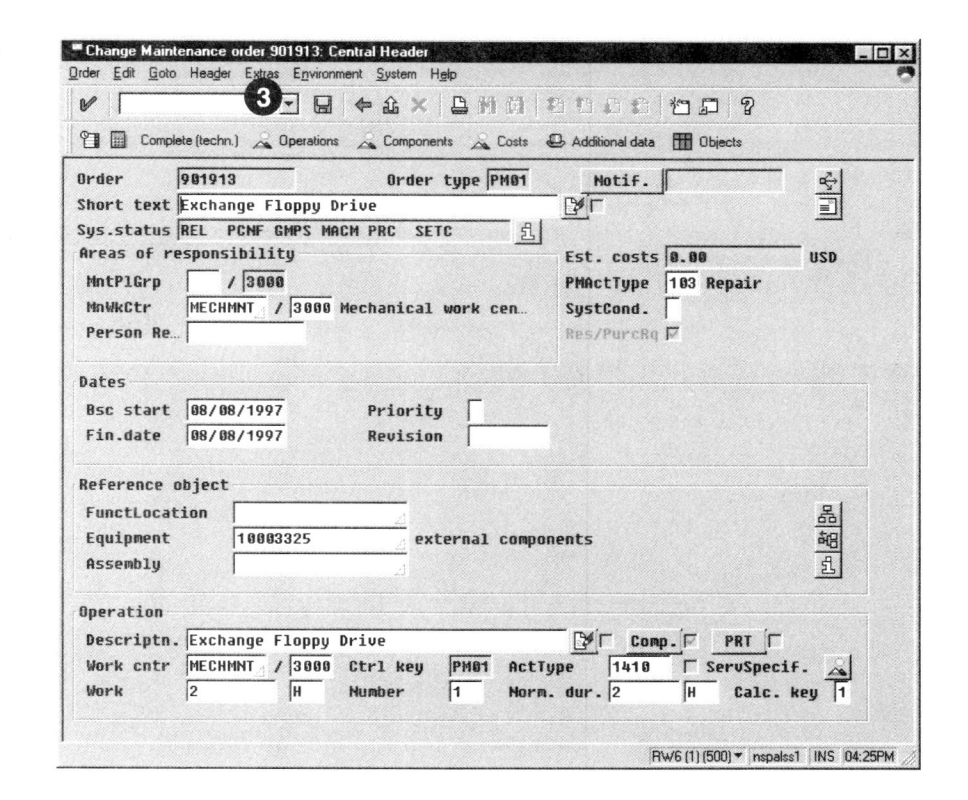

Commonly Used Reports: Illustrations and Perspectives

11-9

Section 11: Plant Maintenance Reports
Order Cost Element Display

Planned costs, actual costs, and quantities for the order summarize by cost element and group by debit or credit postings.

4. Double-click on the *Cost elements* column header to drill down to further information about the posting.

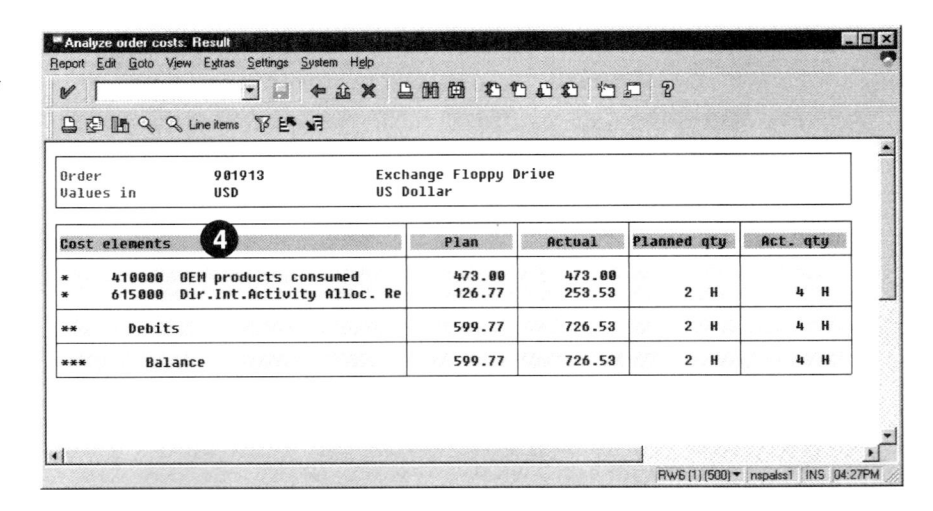

In this example, we see the cost center and activity type for the time posted to the maintenance order.

5. If actual costs were posted, choose *Line Items* to further drill down and view the actual documents.

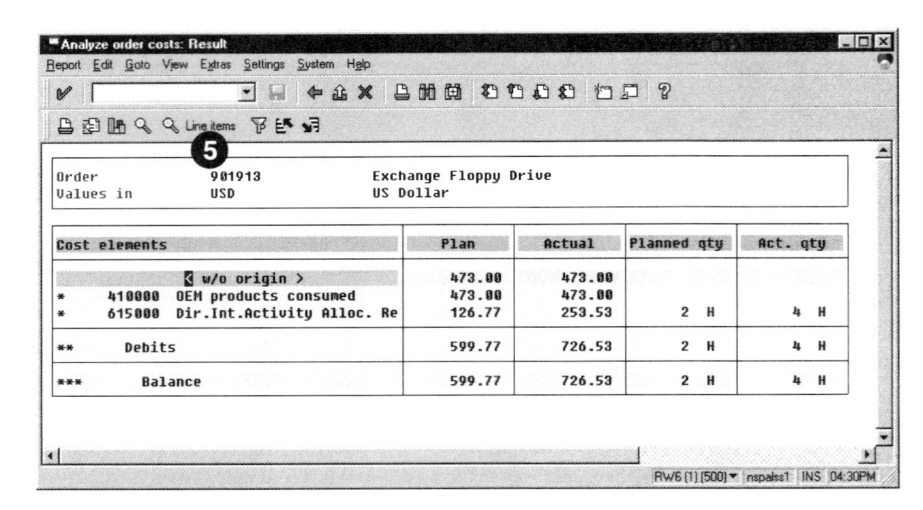

This screen shows the list of individual postings to the order.

Fields in this list can be configured by creating user-defined display variants.

6. To change the appearance of this display, choose *Settings → Display Variant → Current*.

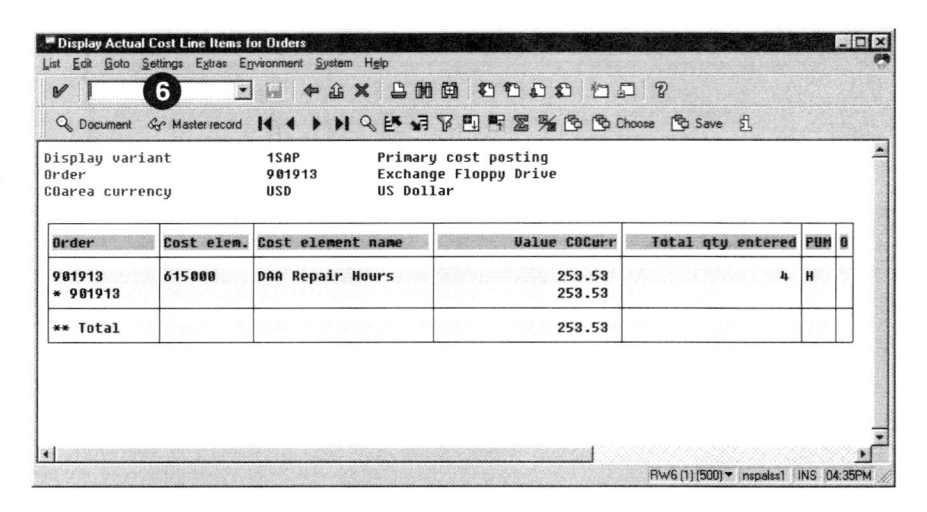

Reporting Made Easy

Section 11: Plant Maintenance Reports
Order Cost Element Display

This screen shows how the layout of the previous screen can be changed based on key figures selected in the previous step.

7. If you double-click on any of the line items, or position the cursor on a line item and choose *Display Document*, you can drill down even further to the actual document.

This screen shows that the actual document is the confirmation screen where time was posted.

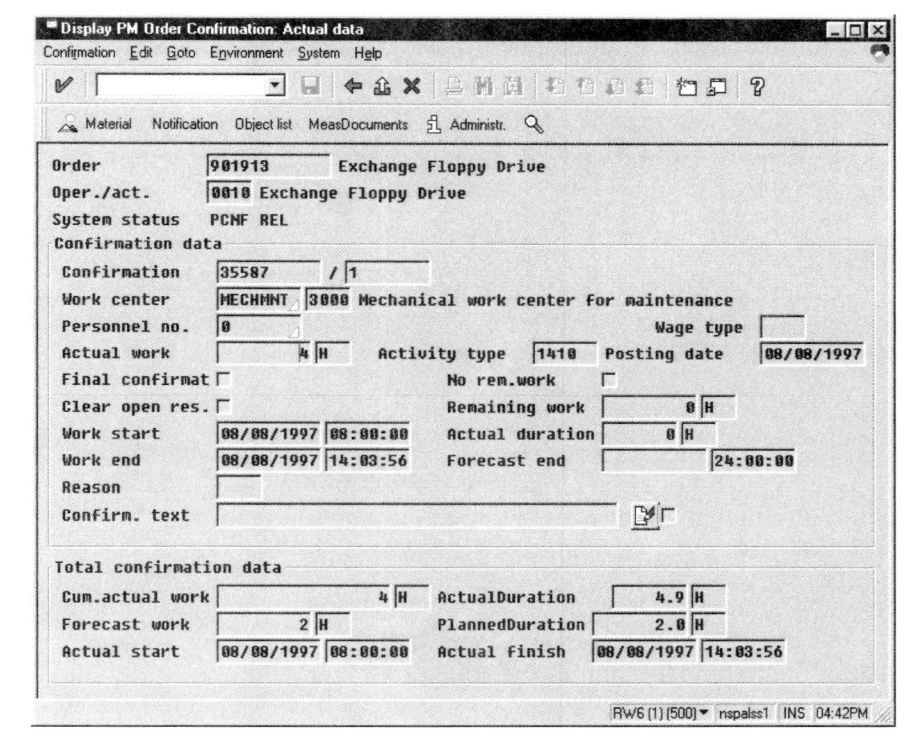

Commonly Used Reports: Illustrations and Perspectives

11–11

Section 11: Plant Maintenance Reports
Order Cost Element Display

Example 2: Display the cost overview of a maintenance order.

1. From the *Central Header* screen of the order, choose *Costs*.

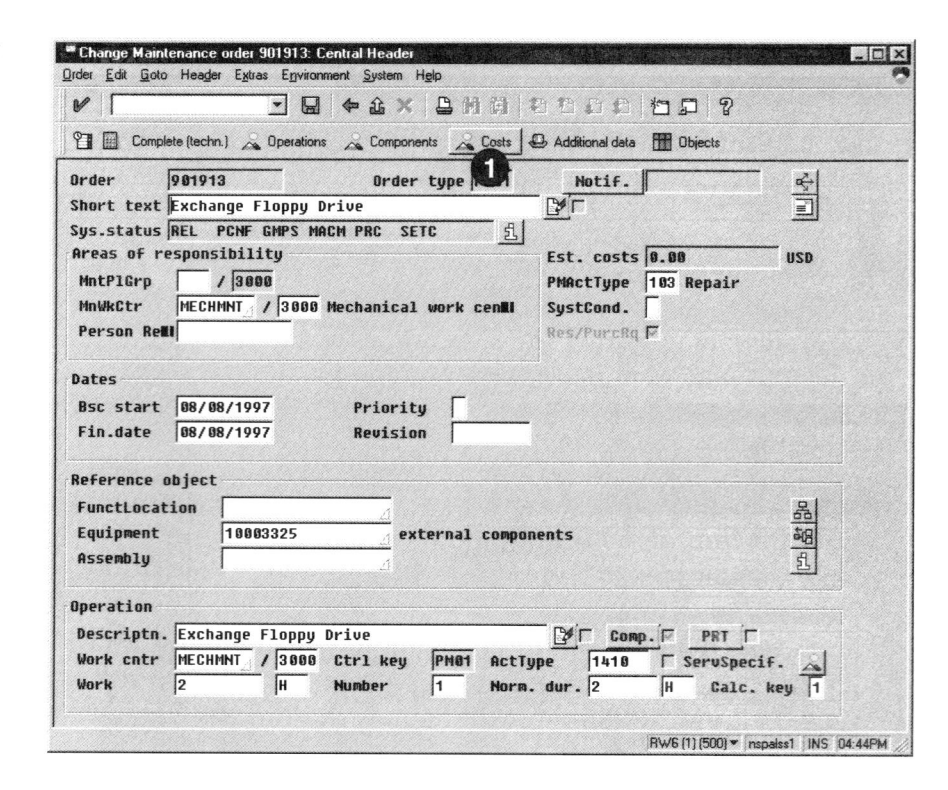

This screen shows an overview of costs.

You can also enter or change the order estimated costs on this screen.

This overview may show results that differ from the cost element display, depending on how the value categories have been configured.

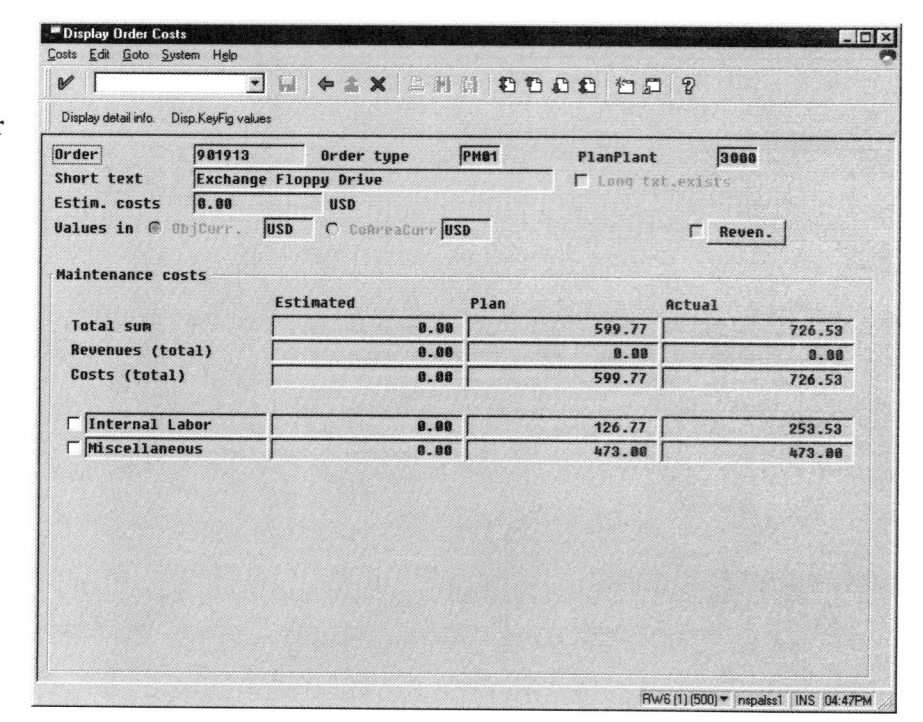

Section 12: Production Planning Reports

Contents

Stock/Requirements List 12–2
Production Order Overview 12–12
MRP List—Collective Display 12–22
Shop Floor Info System 12–27
Multi-Level BOMs 12–39
Missing Parts Info System 12–44
Backorder Processing 12–51
Capacity Planning—Evaluation 12–56

Section 12: Production Planning Reports
Stock/Requirements List

Stock/Requirements List

Quick Access   To run this report, use one of the following access options:

Option 1: Menu Path

The *Stock/Requirements List* is widely used in *Logistics* functions; you can access this report using any of the following menu paths:

Production Planning:

Logistics → Production → MRP → Evaluations → Stock/reqmts list

Materials Management:

Logistics → Materials management → Inventory management → Environment → Stock → Stock/rqmts. List

Sales and Distribution:

Logistics → Sales and distribution → Shipping → Environment → Lists → Stock/reqmts list

Option 2: Transaction Code

In the *Command* field, enter transaction **MD04** and choose *Enter*.

Purpose   This report provides a real-time display of the inventory on hand and the requirements for a specific material. All recommendations and exception messages from MPS/MRP are as current as the most recent planning-run.

Starting with the current date, this report displays the inventory on hand, followed by one line for each element of supply and demand, any related MPS/MRP exception messages, and the projected balance. The report offers drilldown capabilities for additional detail to enable a quick assessment of the inventory position.

Prerequisites   You must enter the *Material number* and *Plant* before running this report. If you want to review a product group instead of a specific material, you will need to enter the *Product group* on the first screen.

Section 12: Production Planning Reports
Stock/Requirements List

Integration

From the output of this report, you can:

- Immediately convert MPS/MRP planned orders into production orders
- Immediately convert purchase requisitions into purchase orders or scheduling agreements
- Start a pegging report for any element to determine the source of demand
- View lower-level dependent requirements and call up an order report
- Select various menu options to review detailed planning parameters
- Display available-to-promise calculations
- Invoke capacity planning functions from the menu
- Compare the last MRP report to assess changes in the planning situation

Note: As previously mentioned, this program can be used to convert orders and invoke capacity planning. Thus, the system administrator may want to limit user authorization to this program.

Features

The primary stock/requirements screen displays the following information in columns:

- Receipt or requirements date
- MRP element: A short description of the type of supply or demand
- Start date for production orders or the release date for purchase documents
- Opening date: A system-calculated date determined by subtracting the opening period from the start date
- Additional data for line, dependent on the type of supply/demand (for example, planned or production order number, purchase requisition, type of requirement, interplant transfer information, etc.)
- Rescheduling date (if applicable): Indicates that the requirements need to be rescheduled to meet the requirements date; it is shown only if the rescheduling function is executed from the menu.
- Exception message: The most significant exception message, if any, is generated by the last MPS/MRP planning run. Further detail is accessible by double-clicking anywhere on the line.
- The quantity required or to be received in the unit of measure shown in the upper right of the screen. This is typically the base unit of measure on the material master.
- Available quantity: This is the up-to-date running balance based on the receipts/requirements.
- Additional columns may be displayed based on the specific line and planning situation.
- Column width can be adjusted by dragging the column separator in either direction; the changed settings can be saved for future sessions.

Section 12: Production Planning Reports
Stock/Requirements List

Next Steps   From this report, you can select the following functions:

- Print the displayed stock/requirements results (*List → Print*).
- Invoke the rescheduling function (*List → Rescheduling*).
- Calculate ATP (*List → Calculate ATP*).
- Display additional detail:
  - Stock statistics such as receipts, issues, quantities in restricted stock, at vendors, in transit, QI, and returns (*Goto → Stock statistics*)
  - Sales statistics such as quantity of a material on sales orders, quotes, and contracts (*Goto → Sales statistics*)
  - Planning data drawn from the material master, such as the MRP controller, MRP group, MRP type, reorder point and lot sizing data, availability check, special procurement type, and a recap of all receipts and issue by source/type (*Goto → Material overview*)
- Branch to various capacity planning functions, such as display of utilization by period, review of available capacities, use of the graphical planning table, etc. (*Goto → Capacity planning*).
- Compare to the last MPS/MRP list (*Goto → Compare MRP list*).
- Expand the header-level information shown at the top of the display: This displays almost all parameters related to MPS/MRP planning runs drawn from the material master or other tables (*Settings → Detailed header*; icon also available).
- Toggle the display of various dates and groupings (*Settings* menu).
- Branch to material master in display or change mode (*Environment → Display/change material*).

Features that act on a specific MRP element (line) and require the cursor be positioned on the desired line include:

- Display MPS/MRP exception messages (*Edit → Display exception message*; an icon also available).
- Display additional data such as a second exception message, order dates, quantity, strategy (*Edit → Additional data*; an icon is also available or you can simply double-click). From the popup window, it is possible to convert the item or invoke pegging reports; this can also be done directly from various *Environment* menu options.

Section 12: Production Planning Reports
Stock/Requirements List

- Display or change the underlying object, such as the planned order, purchase requisition, independent requirement, etc. (*Environment → Display or change*).
- Convert the element from a planned order to a production order or purchase order, or a purchase requisition into a purchase order (*Environment → Convert*).
- Firm the planned order (*Environment → Set firming date*).
- Call up a pegging report to the demand source, or drill down to the lower level dependent requirements in detail (*Environment → Pegged requirements or Order report*; icons are also available for both functions).

Guided Tour

Example 1: Display the basic stock/requirements for a material.

To access the first screen for this report, choose

Logistics → Production → MRP → Evaluations → Stock/reqmts list.

1. Enter the material (for example, `100-100`) or product group in *Material*.
2. Enter the plant associated with the material (for example, `3000`) or product group in *Plant*.
3. If you entered a product group in step 1 above, select *Product group* (not shown).
4. Choose *Enter*.

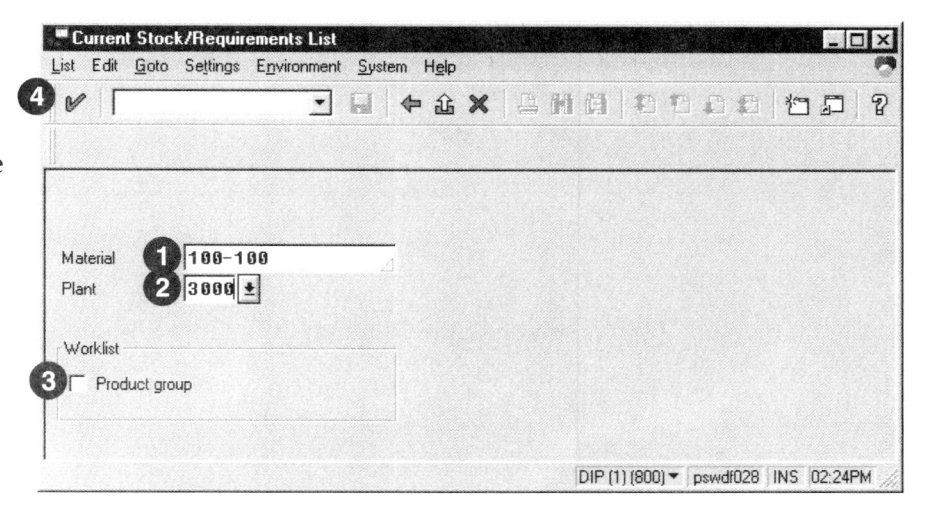

Section 12: Production Planning Reports
Stock/Requirements List

The system displays the following:

A Date of receipt/requirement and associated type of supply or demand
B Material number, order number, etc.
C MRP exception message
D Receipt or requirement quantity
E Available quantity

The width of columns may be adjusted by dragging the column divider.

5. To save the settings, choose *Save columns*.
6. Choose *Refresh* to view the changes.
7. The material and plant may also be overwritten to display another item.
8. Choose *Header* to drill down into various planning parameters from the material master and other files (as shown in example 2).

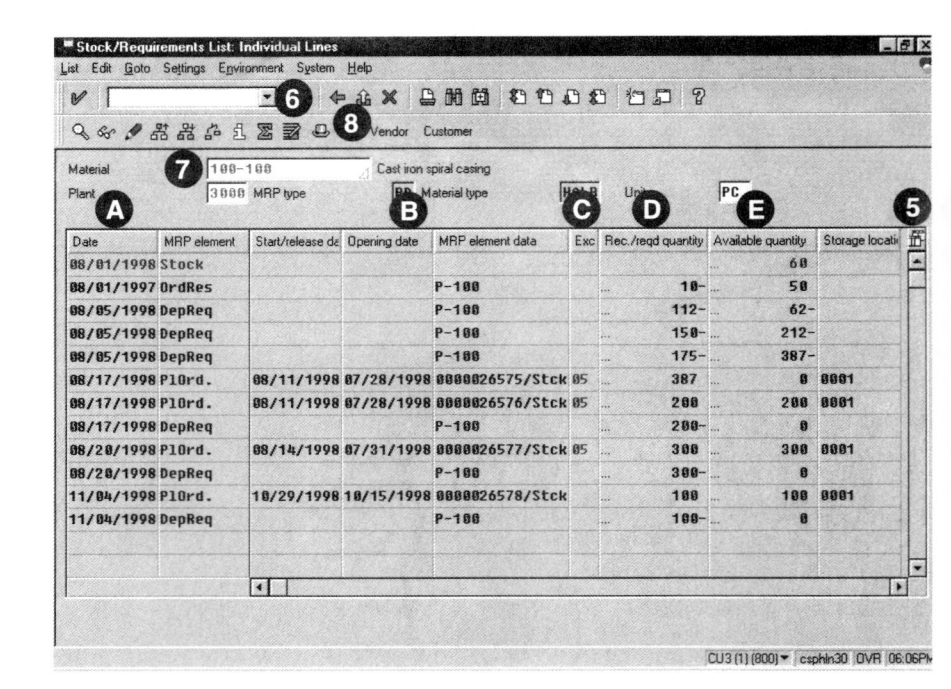

Section 12: Production Planning Reports
Stock/Requirements List

Example 2: Drill down into various planning parameters from the material master and other files.

Expanded header information is shown here. Included here are parameters from the material master and other records.

1. Choose *Header* to display additional data for the planned order (as shown in example 3).
2. Note the *Periods total* button. We will use this button in example 7.

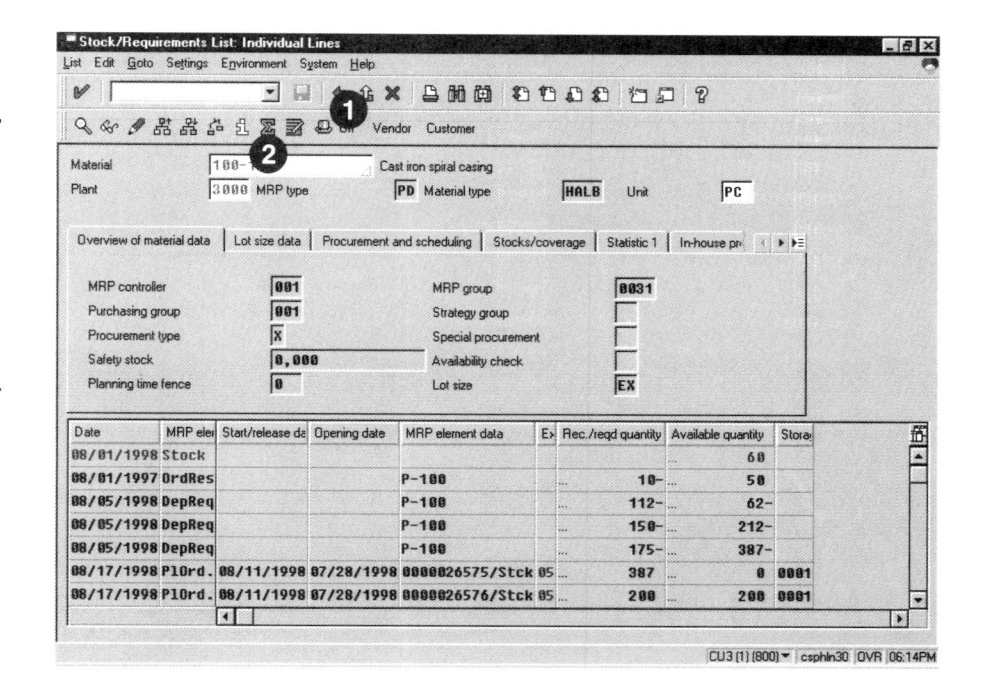

Commonly Used Reports: Illustrations and Perspectives

12–7

Section 12: Production Planning Reports
Stock/Requirements List

Example 3: Display additional data for the planned order for 08/17/1998.

1. Double-click on the planned order (for example, **08/17/1998**).

2. The popup window displays additional information for the *MRP element*. It also provides options to display or change the planned order, or to view the pegging report and convert it to a production order.

3. To display the underlying *MRP element* for the planned order, choose *Environment → Display element*.

This screen shows additional details for the planned order.

4. For the next example, choose *Back* to return to the *Stock/Requirements List: Individual Lines* screen.

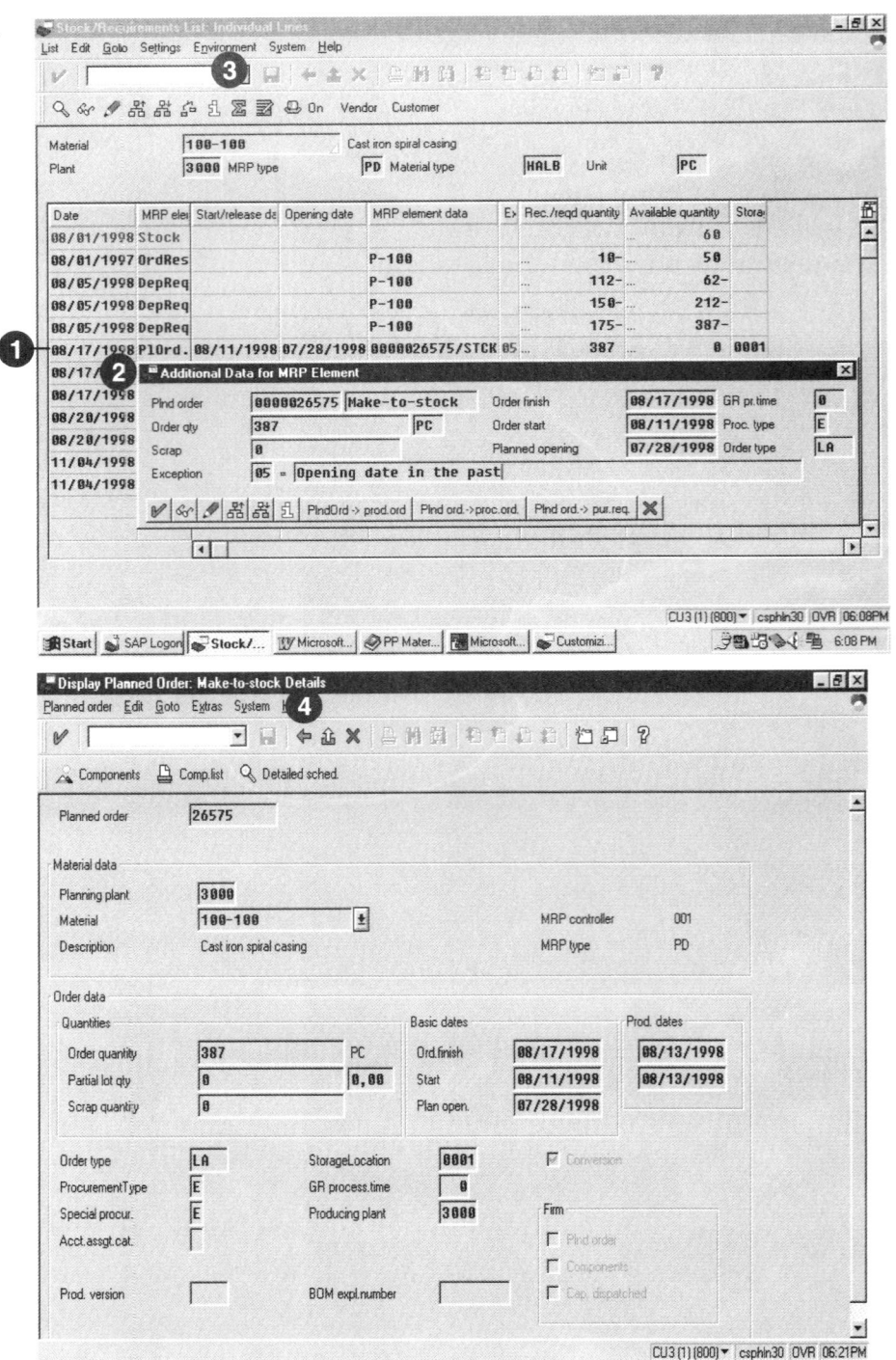

12–8 Reporting Made Easy

Section 12: Production Planning Reports
Stock/Requirements List

Example 4: Review the capacity planning situation.

To access the report from the *Stock Req. List:Indiv lines* screen, choose

Goto → *Capacity planning* → *Capacity situation (detailed).*

A   Available capacity for each period

B   Total requirements for all materials in this period

C   Requirements related to the material being viewed

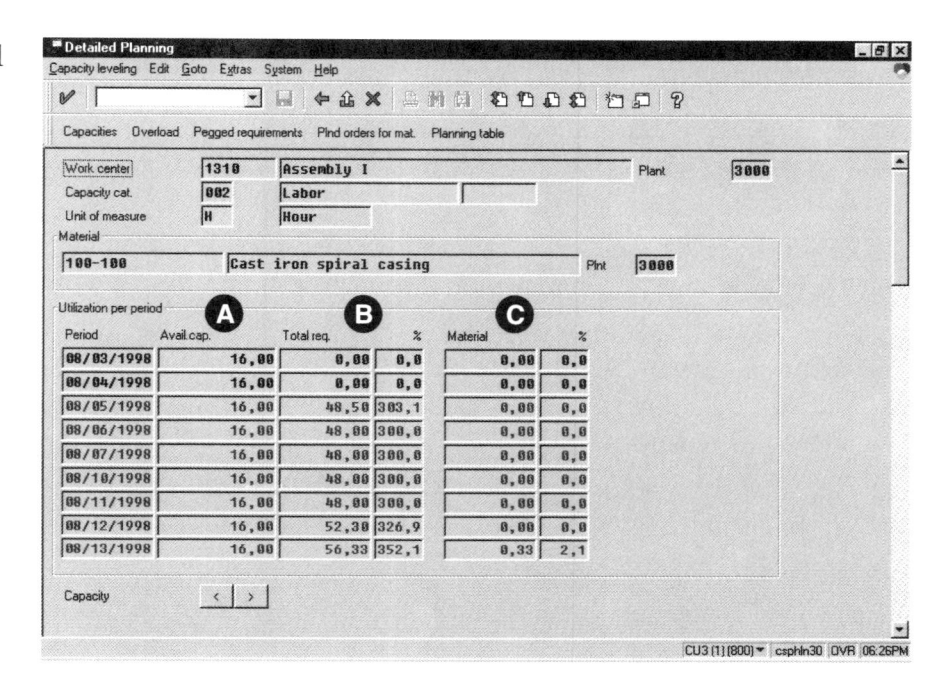

Commonly Used Reports: Illustrations and Perspectives

12–9

Section 12: Production Planning Reports
Stock/Requirements List

Example 5: Create a production order from a planned order.

1. To convert a planned order to a production order (in the item listing from the previous example) position the cursor on the planned order for *08/17/1998*.

2. Choose *Environment → Convert → Planned order → Production order → Total qty*

You can conduct a complete review of the proposed production order and make changes if required. All data is carried over from the planned order created by MPS/MRP.

Other tools within the production planning module support batch conversion of planned orders.

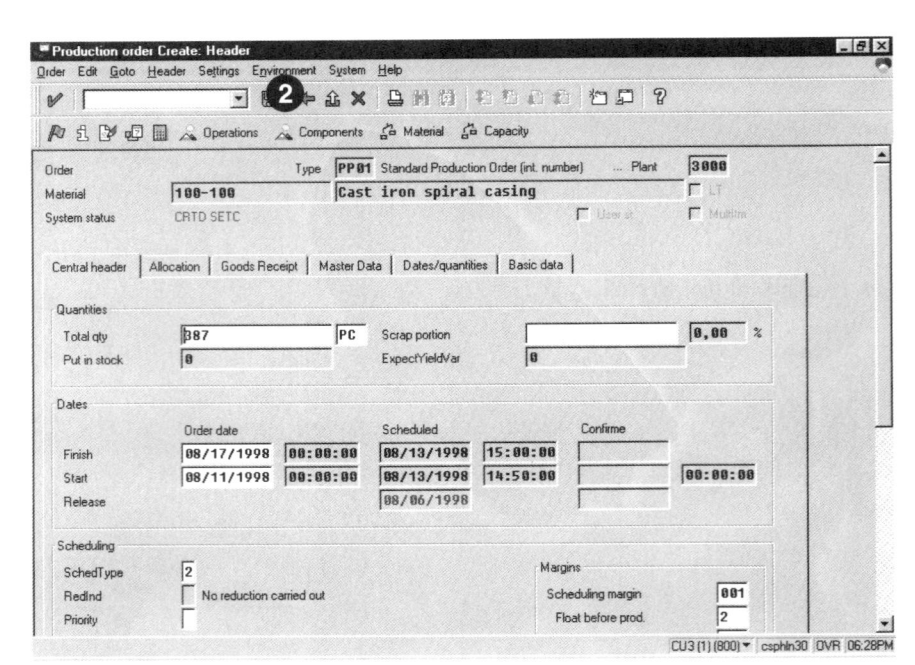

Example 6: Display a pegging report for the 08/17/1998 requirement.

From the previous screen, choose *Environment → Pegged requirements*.

A This column shows the total requirements quantity for the associated line on the stock/requirements display.

B This column shows the quantity required by upper-level demand.

   In this example, the quantity is the same. In other situations, there may be multiple sources.

C This column shows *Requirements* for the specific upper-level demand to which this requirement is pegged.

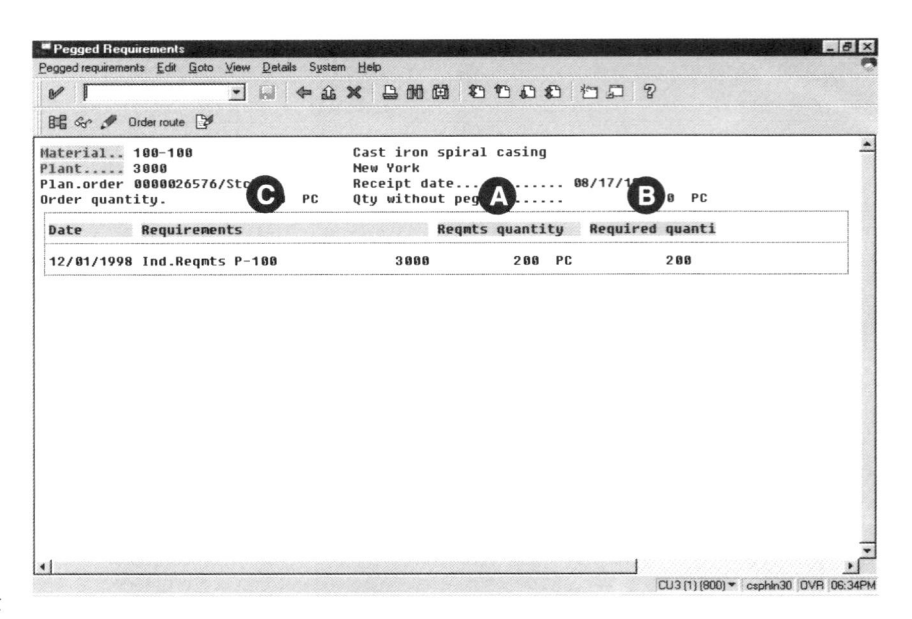

12–10 Reporting Made Easy

Section 12: Production Planning Reports

Stock/Requirements List

Example 7: Display the period totals for the stock/requirements list.

We now use the *Period totals* button highlighted in example 2.

The *Period display* reformats the data to show various quantities in a columnar format, including ATP calculations.

The ATP column reflects future demand and the resulting quantity available for commitment.

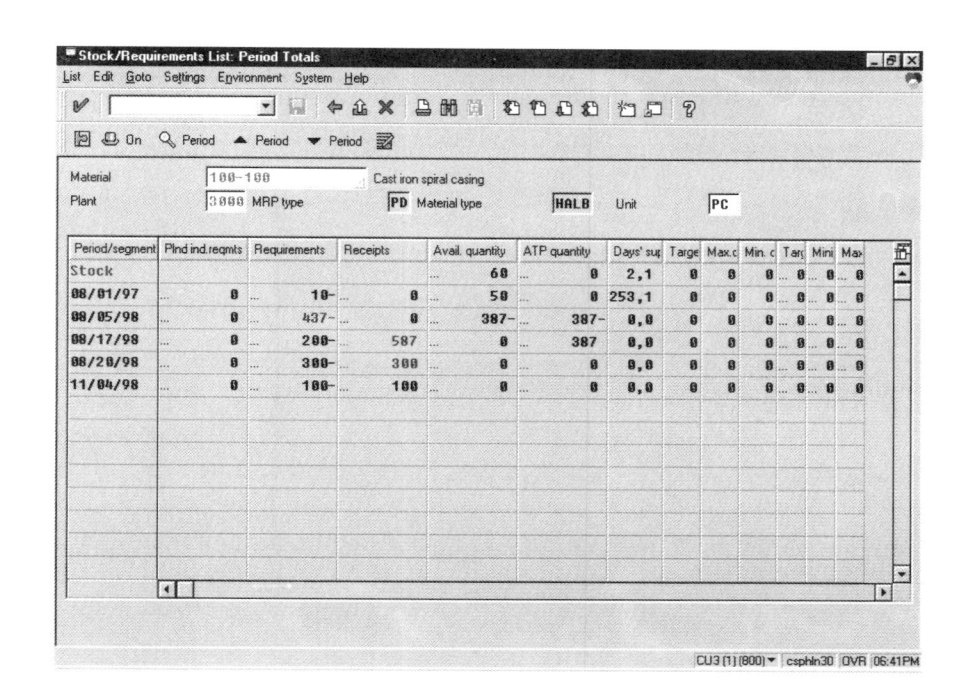

Period/segment	Plnd ind. reqmts	Requirements	Receipts	Avail. quantity	ATP quantity	Days' sup	Targe	Max.c	Min. c	Tar	Mini	Max
Stock				60	0	2,1	0	0	0	0	0	0
08/01/97	0	10-	0	50	0	253,1	0	0	0	0	0	0
08/05/98	0	437-	0	387-	387-	0,0	0	0	0	0	0	0
08/17/98	0	200-	587	0	387	0,0	0	0	0	0	0	0
08/20/98	0	300-	300	0	0	0,0	0	0	0	0	0	0
11/04/98	0	100-	100	0	0	0,0	0	0	0	0	0	0

Material: 100-100 Cast iron spiral casing
Plant: 3000 MRP type: PD Material type: HALB Unit: PC

Commonly Used Reports: Illustrations and Perspectives

Production Order Overview

Quick Access To run this report, use one of the following access options:

Option 1: Menu Path

Logistics → Production → Production control → Control → Information systems → Order Info system → Object overview

Option 2: Program Name

Choose System→ Services→ Reporting and enter **PPIOA000** in the Program field.

Option 3: Transaction Code

In the Command field, enter transaction **CO26** and choose Enter.

Purpose This report provides a summarized list of production orders based on user-specified criteria. It is a powerful tool for monitoring the progress of orders through the production process, both from a manufacturing and an accounting perspective.

Prerequisites No prerequisites are required to run this report.

You can add profiles for customized detail. The delivered profiles include a general use "standard profile," in addition to others for pick lists and goods movement transactions.

Integration From this report, you can drill down to the order in display or change mode. The report also lets you display the dependent demand for components and the pegging reports to the demand source. For a configured product, it lets you drill down to the details of the configuration.

Section 12: Production Planning Reports
Production Order Overview

Features   This report lets you select orders using the following criteria, all of which include the multiple selection feature for ranges, logical operators, pattern matches, include/exclude, and so on:

- Order number
- Material number
- Plant
- Order type
- MRP controller/Production scheduler
- Sales order (if linked)
- WBS element (project module)
- Sequence/priority number (user-defined)
- Order status
- Start/finish dates (basic, scheduled, and actual)

There are some additional flags such as component storage location, deletion indicator, and rework and collective order indicators which may further filter the selection. Since a production order database can be very large, it is advisable to use the filters provided in the first section to limit data selection and improve performance. All filters and settings may be saved for future use as a variant.

The report provides three basic views:

- Object overview (MRP controller, plant, order type, system status, basic dates)
- Order header overview (all header-level dates, last changed by, material description)
- Object detail list (based on objects chosen, displays/groups related fields; see below)

Use of the standard profile will list a predefined set of fields for each order, but these may be changed for the particular session, or a new profile may be created for the future.

You can view the types of objects which are related to the order, such as

- Components (default choice)
- Operations (default choice)
- Goods movements for the order (default choice)
- Trigger points
- Purchase documents
- PRTs
- Confirmations

Section 12: Production Planning Reports
Production Order Overview

Next Steps   This report contains data obtained from production orders. There are two cases in which data may be changed:

- An order brought up in change mode from the menu option (*Environment* → *Change order*; an icon is also provided).
- By choosing *Goto* → *Object detail list* → *Components* you are provided various branch points under the subsequent *Environment* menu, including the ability to change the order, create and process pick lists (goods issues) and invoke backorder processing.

Guided Tour

Example 1: Display a basic listing of the orders for a plant.

To access the first screen for this report, choose

Logistics → *Production* → *Production control* → *Control* → *Information systems* → *Order Info system* → *Object overview.*

Section 12: Production Planning Reports
Production Order Overview

1. Select the standard profile in *Overall profile*.
2. Enter **3000** in *Plant*.
3. Choose *List → Execute*.

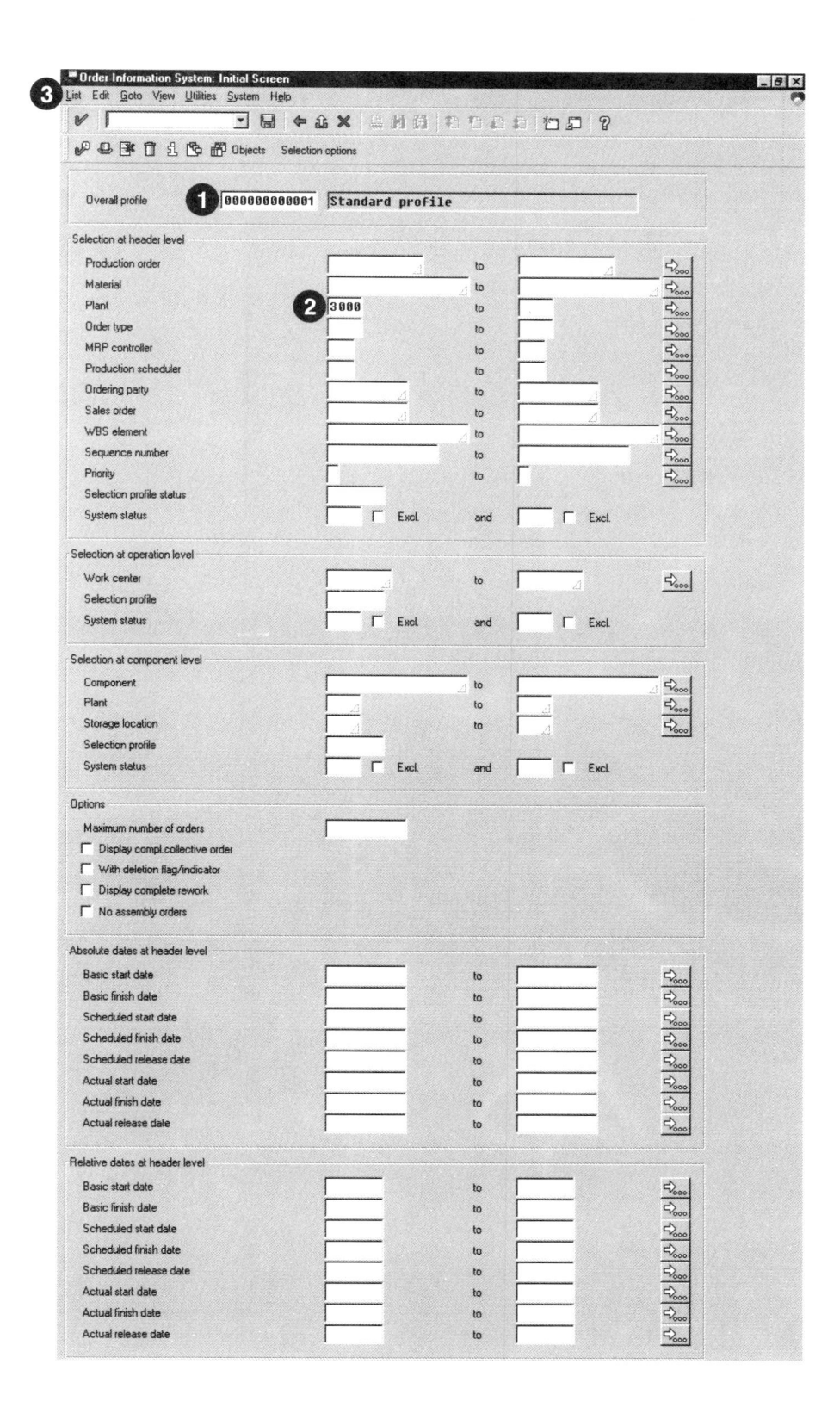

Section 12: Production Planning Reports
Production Order Overview

This screen shows the *Object Overview*. The orders are listed along with the various status codes from the order.

Click the node to expand the line entry.

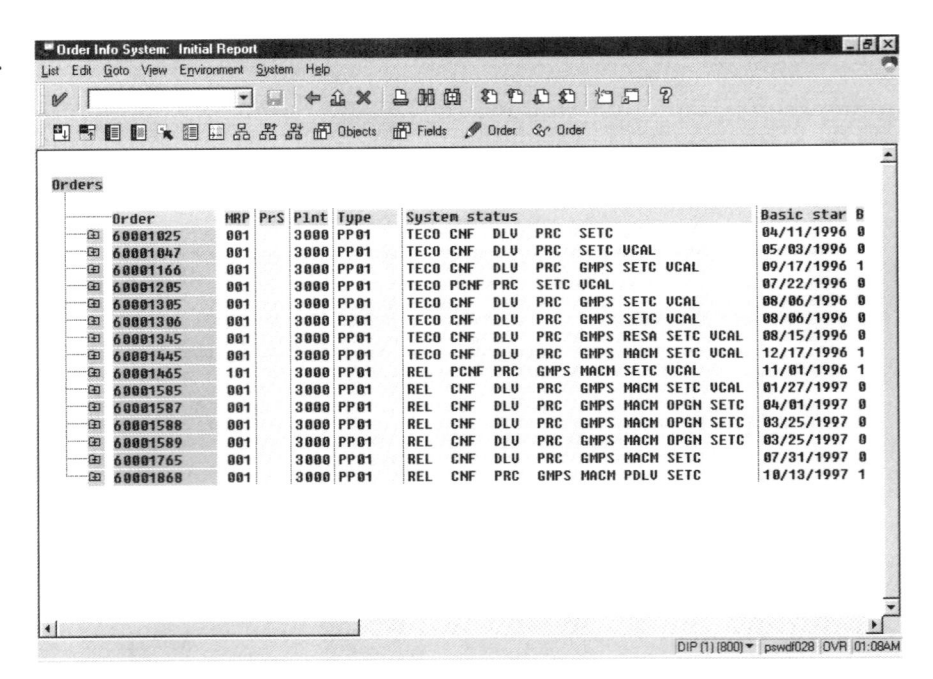

Section 12: Production Planning Reports
Production Order Overview

Example 2: Select additional filters to narrow your order selection to orders that remain open and were started more than 60 days ago.

1. Enter **DLV** in *System status* and then, select *Excl.* (exclude).

   This selection assures that the report will ignore orders that are "technically completed."

2. Under *Relative dates at header level* enter the number of days (plus or minus) from the current day.

   Combining the number of days (for example, **60**) with the selection option of less than (<) selects orders started more than 60 days ago.

3. Choose *Execute*.

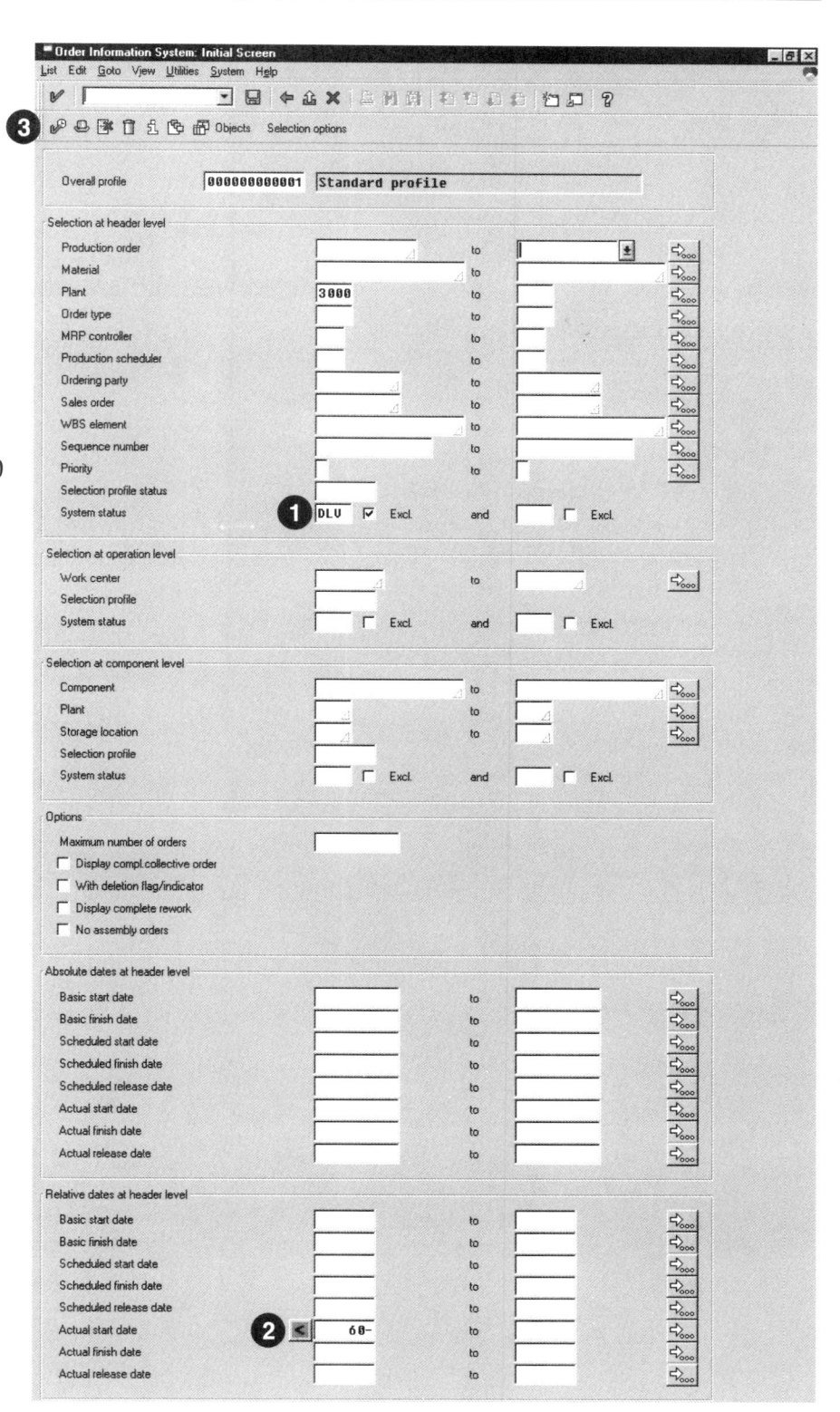

Commonly Used Reports: Illustrations and Perspectives

12–17

Section 12: Production Planning Reports
Production Order Overview

This screen shows the list restricted to orders that do not have the *DLV* status.

The actual start date for these orders is more than 60 days ago.

1. Click the node for the production order you want to expand on.

2. Select the *expand node* button to display a full listing for the order.

3. Each subordinate object can be expanded to reveal more detail.

4. Choose *Fields* to modify individual columns.

5. The individual order can be displayed or changed by selecting the appropriate menu choice or icon. The cursor is placed on the order to display or change, then the icon is selected. In this example, we choose *Display order*.

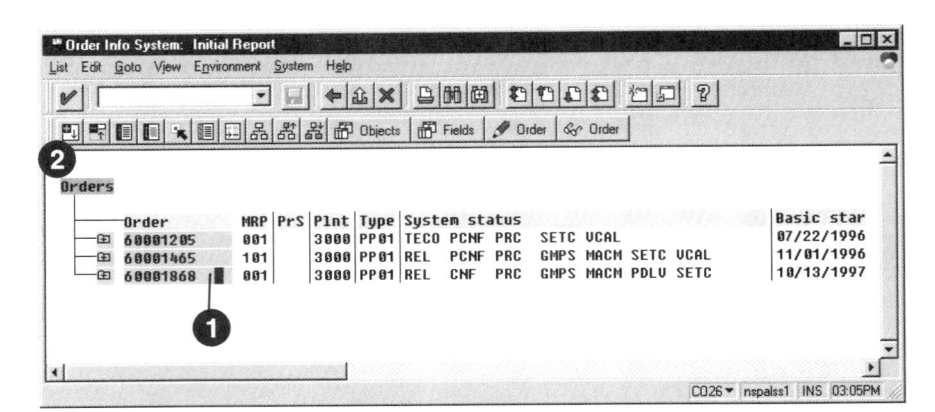

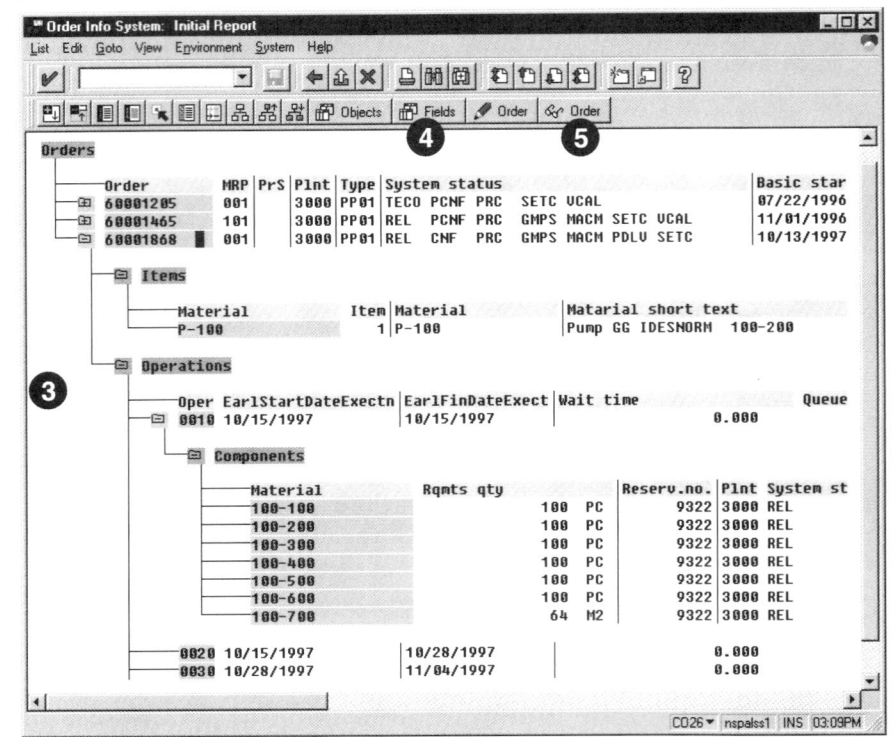

12–18

Reporting Made Easy

Section 12: Production Planning Reports
Production Order Overview

The individual order is then displayed or brought up in display mode.

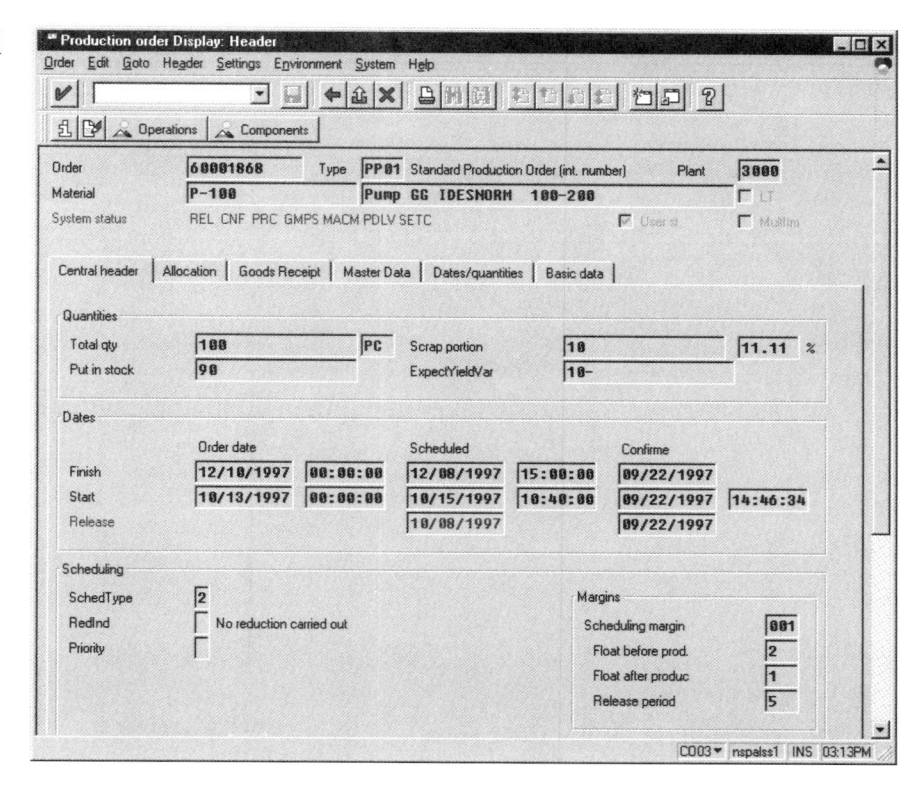

Example 3: Use the *Order headers* view to provide a slightly different set of data that allows for additional review and comparison.

1. Enter **3000** in *Plant*.
2. Choose *Header* to view the *Order headers*.

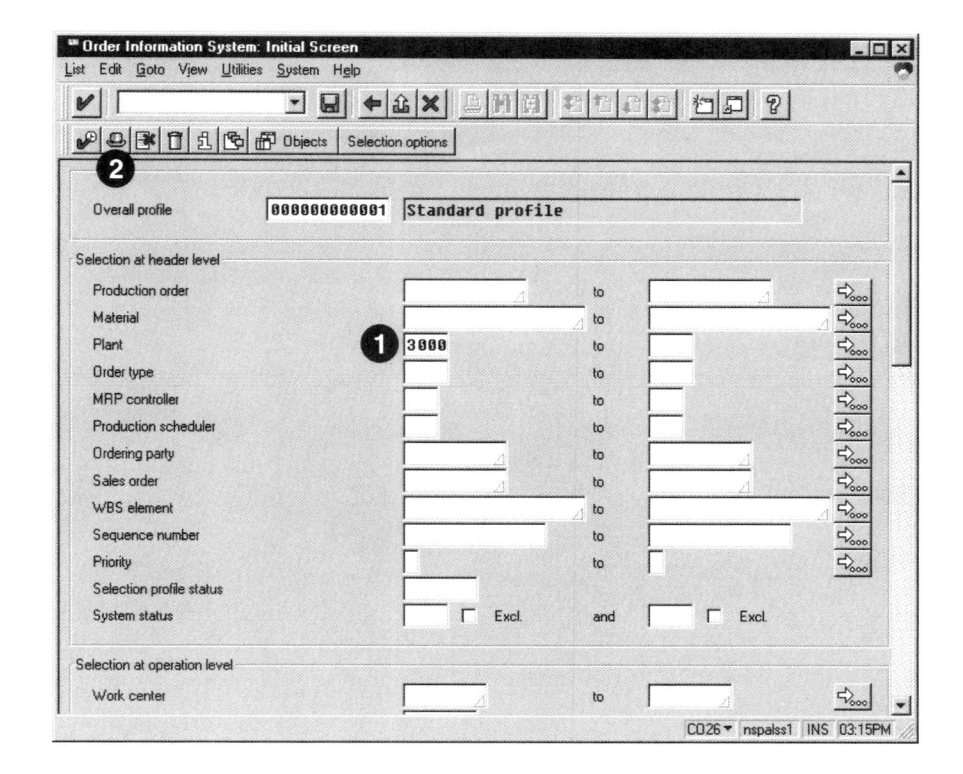

Commonly Used Reports: Illustrations and Perspectives

12–19

Section 12: Production Planning Reports
Production Order Overview

This screen shows all header date fields.

3. Position the cursor within the listing to compare that field to other fields.

4. Choose *Field Comparison* to select and compare fields.

5. You can decide which fields you want to compare. The text shows us this is a comparison to the *Basic start date*.

6. The *Actual start time* (date) is selected for comparison.

7. Choose *Enter* to continue.

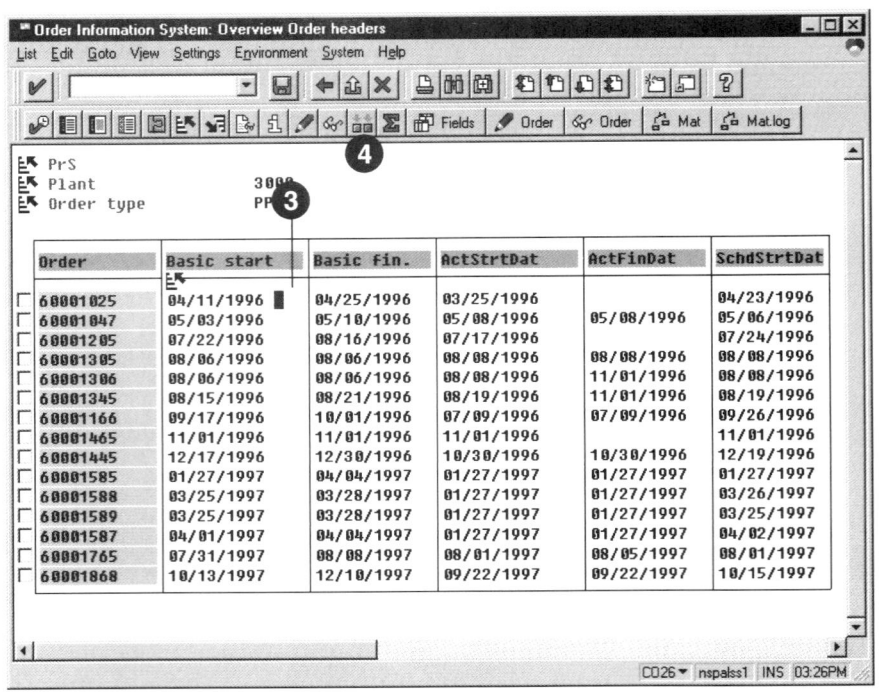

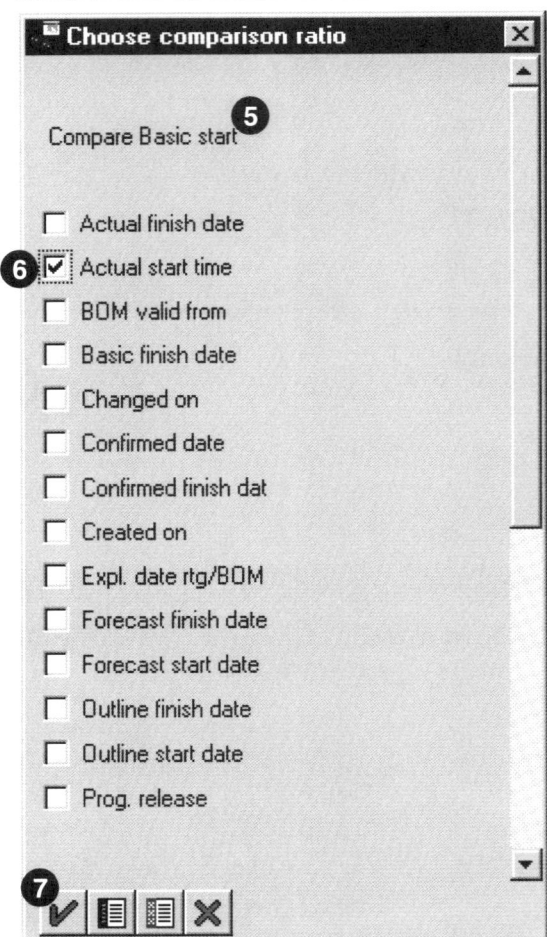

Reporting Made Easy

Section 12: Production Planning Reports
Production Order Overview

8. This screen shows the basic start date compared to the actual start.
9. The differences are also shown.

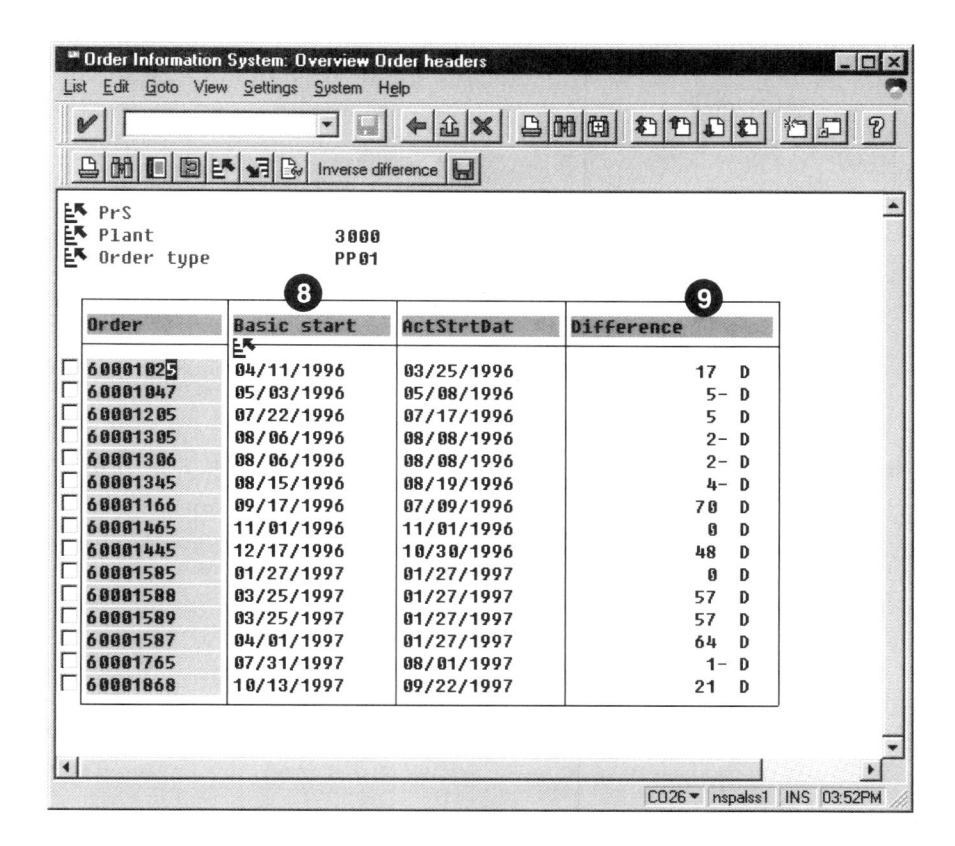

Order	Basic start	ActStrtDat	Difference
60001025	04/11/1996	03/25/1996	17 D
60001047	05/03/1996	05/08/1996	5- D
60001205	07/22/1996	07/17/1996	5 D
60001305	08/06/1996	08/08/1996	2- D
60001306	08/06/1996	08/08/1996	2- D
60001345	08/15/1996	08/19/1996	4- D
60001166	09/17/1996	07/09/1996	70 D
60001465	11/01/1996	11/01/1996	0 D
60001445	12/17/1996	10/30/1996	48 D
60001585	01/27/1997	01/27/1997	0 D
60001588	03/25/1997	01/27/1997	57 D
60001589	03/25/1997	01/27/1997	57 D
60001587	04/01/1997	01/27/1997	64 D
60001765	07/31/1997	08/01/1997	1- D
60001868	10/13/1997	09/22/1997	21 D

PrS
Plant   3000
Order type   PP01

Commonly Used Reports: Illustrations and Perspectives

12-21

MRP List—Collective Display

Quick Access To run this report, use one of the following access options:

Option 1: Menu Path

Logistics → *Production* → *MRP* → *Evaluations* → *MRP list – coll. display*

Option 2: Transaction Code

In the *Command* field, enter transaction **MD06** and choose *Enter*.

Purpose This report is a tool you can use to analyze and act on the recommendations from the last MRP/MPS run. Depending on user-defined filters, the report collectively displays all of the materials, exception messages, on-hand quantities, and other data used in the run.

A production planner or buyer would use this report to assess and prioritize procurement action or manufacturing runs.

Prerequisites No prerequisites are required to run this report.

However, this report does rely on the underlying settings for MRP. There is one key piece of master data required for reporting: the MRP controller on the MRP 1 view of the material master. Since the report reflects data current as of the last MRP run, its use should be coordinated with the timing and frequency of the run.

Integration From the summary, you can review the individual MRP list for a given material. Then, you can display additional material data, detailed review, or immediate conversion of MRP recommendations to procurement/manufacturing orders.

Features The following data for each material displays in columns:
- Material number and description
- Indicators as to whether the MRP list has been set by user, and whether the exception message is new since the last planning run
- Number of exception messages for the material (grouped by type)
- Days of coverage
- On-hand inventory (as of the date of the planning run)
- Unit of measure
- Material type (ROH, HALB, etc.)
- Procurement type (make or buy)
- MRP type
- Special procurement key
- Low-level code

Section 12: Production Planning Reports
MRP List—Collective Display

Next Steps   From the report, an individual MRP list may be selected and displayed by double-clicking on the line. Another option is to select several lines and sequentially page through these lines using *Edit → MRP list sequence.*

From the *Edit* menu, it is possible to search and sort on exceptions.

From the *Goto* menu you can branch to the current stock/requirements list, review the exception message codes and their grouping logic, and invoke interactive MRP planning. Interactive MRP planning can update the MRP database with new results, if saved. Once the individual MRP list is displayed, numerous options are provided for a detailed display of the underlying master data and the conversion action on planned orders and purchase requisitions. The capabilities are essentially the same as the stock/requirements list, and as such have the potential for updates to the database.

Guided Tour

Example 1: Generate a basic display of the collective list for a plant and MRP controller (planner).

To access the first screen for this report, choose

Logistics → Production → MRP → Evaluations → MRP list – coll.display.

1. You must enter the *Plant* and *MRP controller*.

   All other fields are optional filters that further limit the selection.

2. Choose *Enter*.

A The message in the status bar is a precaution to avoid wasted runtime on incomplete selections.

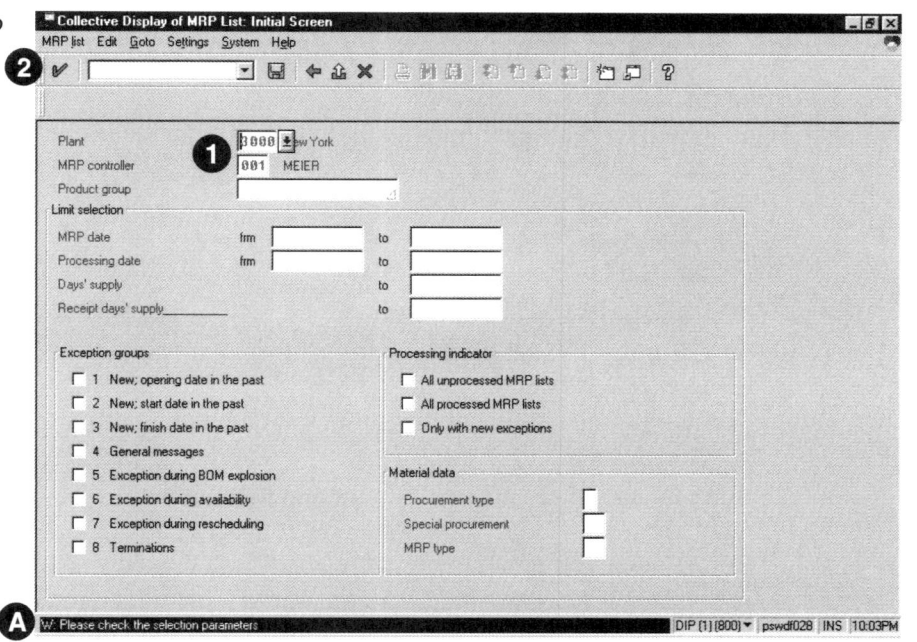

Commonly Used Reports: Illustrations and Perspectives

12–23

Section 12: Production Planning Reports

MRP List—Collective Display

The collective display reflects the following:

B Material number and description

C Processing and new exception indicators

D Number of exception messages and exception group for material (see icon for list)

E Additional information about the material

4. Double-click on a line to display the individual MRP list.

F The individual MRP list reflects the source of supply and demand by date.

G For further detail, choose *Goto* or *Environment* menus.

H The processing indicator may be manually set to flag the item. This indicator can also be set as a filter criteria on the first screen of this report.

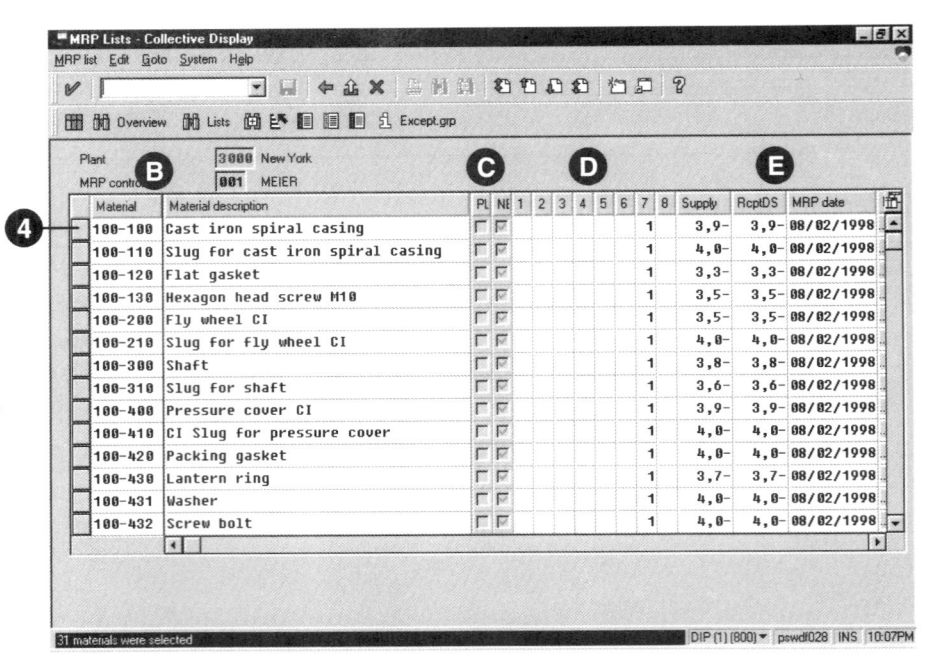

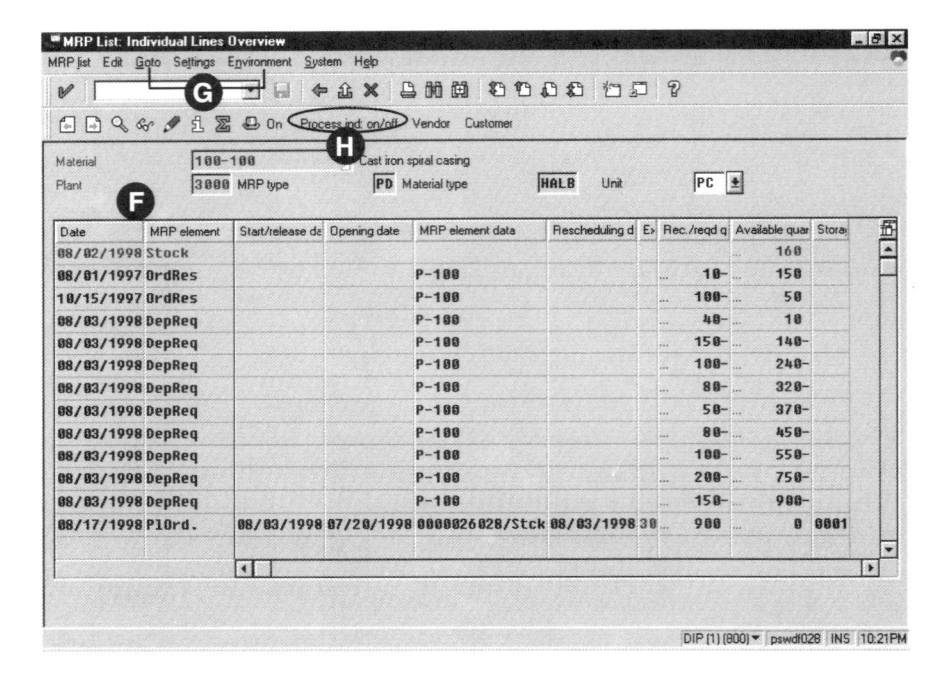

12–24

Reporting Made Easy

Section 12: Production Planning Reports

MRP List—Collective Display

I   The message in the status bar shows that the indicator was set.

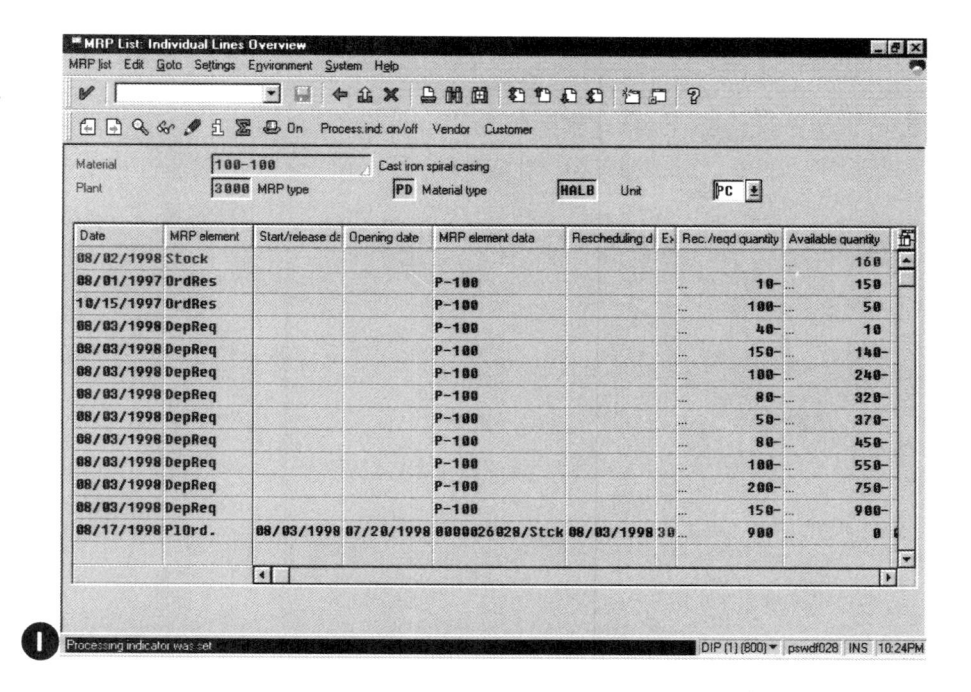

Section 12: Production Planning Reports
MRP List—Collective Display

Example 2: Using additional filters for the selection, generate a collective display of the MRP lists.

1. Select *All unprocessed MRP lists*.

   This action excludes previously reviewed items.

2. Enter **F** in *Procurement type*.

   This action further limits the list to materials that were externally procured.

3. Choose *Enter*.

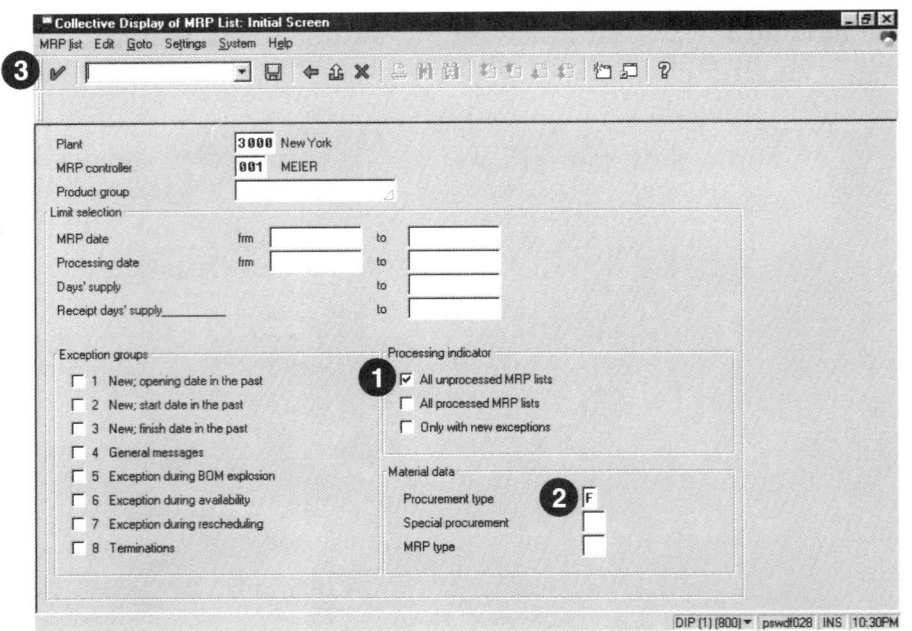

A This screen shows that the material from example 1 no longer appears.

B The record count is reduced.

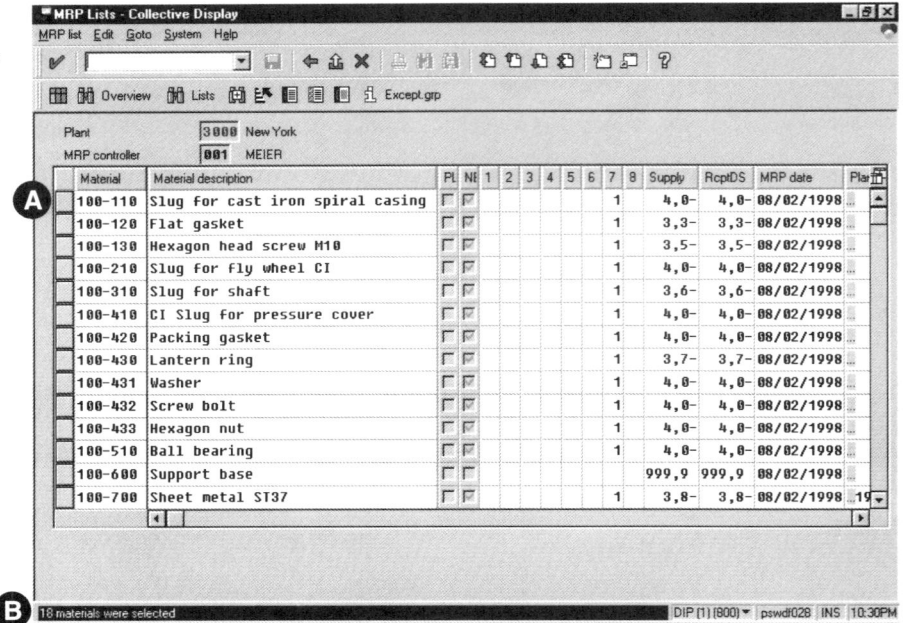

12–26

Reporting Made Easy

Section 12: Production Planning Reports
Shop Floor Info System

Shop Floor Info System

Quick Access   To run this report, use one of the following access options:

Option 1: Menu Path

Logistics → *Production* → *Production control* → *Control* → *Info. systems* → *Shop floor info sys.*

Option 2: Transaction Code

In the *Command* field, enter transaction **MCP0** and choose *Enter*.

Purpose   The *Shop Floor Info System* is a subset of the *LIS* and provides tools to summarize and analyze data generated on the shop floor. The techniques range from summarized reports of key figures (for example, actual lead time in a work center) to automatic notification when user-defined thresholds are exceeded. These tools allow rapid identification of problem areas that need corrective action.

Prerequisites   *Standard analyses* and some *flexible analyses* reports use predefined information structures which contain summarized data representing a particular measure of shop floor activity, such as quantities processed, run times, etc. *Flexible Analyses* allows you to use custom info structures, or combine existing structures with other data dictionary objects.

In addition, formulas may be defined in some cases. The *Early Warning System* (also known as *Exception Analysis*) requires advance creation of user-defined thresholds for exception reporting. Standard info system menus allow quick creation of such thresholds and periodic comparison jobs. Some analyses allow you to drill down by hierarchies and define additional hierarchies from info system menus.

Integration   The shop floor info system provides the following four basic methods to retrieve and analyze data:

- Standard analysis
- Flexible analysis
- Early Warning System
- Info library

Depending on the method you choose, additional analysis is possible from the report, including drill down, ranking, key figure comparison, and branching to master data files. Additionally, the info system menu provides listings of orders based on a variety of selection criteria, as well as a review of missing parts on manufacturing orders. Finally, the menu provides specialized functions related to sales and operations planning.

Section 12: Production Planning Reports
Shop Floor Info System

Features

Because of the extensive nature of the info system, the general features available will be identified within each of the basic methods noted in the previous section.

For *Standard* and *Flexible Analyses*, reporting and drilldown is available and is based on:

- Work centers (info structure *S024*)
- Operations (info structure *S022*)
- Materials (info structure *S023*)
- Production orders (info structure *S021*)
- Material usage (info structure *S026*)
- Product costs (info structure *S027*)
- Run schedule headers (info structure *S025*)
- Reporting point statistics (info structure *S028*)
- Kanban (info structure *S029*)
- User-defined evaluation structures

The individual fields which may be used for selection criteria vary by the underlying info structure. As delivered, a representative group of key figures will be displayed on the report, however these may be changed as desired.

For the *Early Warning System* (*Exception Analysis*), exceptions may be defined on any key figure in the info structures above. These exceptions take the form of:

- Plan versus actual
- Specific value
- Trend analysis

For the *Info Library*, predefined analysis of existing info structures may be selected by:

- Info sets (grouped by functional area or info structure)
- Text strings (string search of key figure description)
- Classification (based on classification of key figures, if used)

The *Environment* menu provides for branching to display of:

- Master files
  - Material master
  - Work center
  - Routings
- Listings of production orders selected by
  - Production order number
  - Material number
  - MRP controller
  - Production scheduler
  - PRT
- Missing parts review (this allows changes to production orders)

The *Planning* menu gives you specialized functions related to Sales and Operations planning; these options are intended to provide updates to the database for *flexible planning*.

Regardless of the method chosen, the resulting summary report may be saved, printed, or exported to a PC file. The format of the summary report varies depending on the method used and the object, characteristics, and key figures chosen. However, they will generally follow a row and column format, where rows represent characteristics and columns represent key figures. Note that exceptions defined in the *Early Warning System* may be applied on the first screen of most analyses.

Next Steps

Once the summary report is displayed, you can do the following:

- Sort by any key figure (*View* menu or sort icons)
- Ranking (for example, top 10; *Edit* menu or *Top N* icon)
- Add additional key figures to display (*Edit* menu or icon)
- Time series (breakout by period; *View* menu or *Trend* icon)
- Initiate drilldown by standard or user-defined hierarchy (*View* menu or *Hierarchy* icons)
- Charting (*Goto* menu or *Bar chart* icon)
- Switching to another info structure from this point (*Goto* menu or *Switch drilldown* icon)
- Statistical analysis: Cumulative curve, correlation, ABC ranking (*Edit* menu)
- Comparison between key figures (*Edit* menu)
- Branch to production order, material master (*Extras* or *Environment* menu)
- Recap of all key figures (*Extras* menu)
- Format changes to report (column widths, currency, etc.; *Settings* menu)
- Saving of settings per user or as variant (*Settings* menu)
- Saving of analysis to "freeze" data (Left-most menu or *Save* icon)
- Printing (Left-most menu or *Printer* icon)
- Export to PC file (Left-most menu or *Export* icon)

Section 12: Production Planning Reports
Shop Floor Info System

Guided Tour

Example 1: Display a standard analysis of work centers.

To access the first screen for this report, choose

Logistics → Production → Production control → Control → Info. systems → Shop floor info sys. → Standard analyses → Work center

1. Enter the plant number for analysis (for example, **1000**) in *Plant*.

2. Enter a date range (for example, **09/1997** to **12/1997**) in *Month*.

3. Choose *Execute*.

This screen shows summarized data for the plant. This simple display can be expanded.

4. Choose *Choose key figures* to display additional key figures.

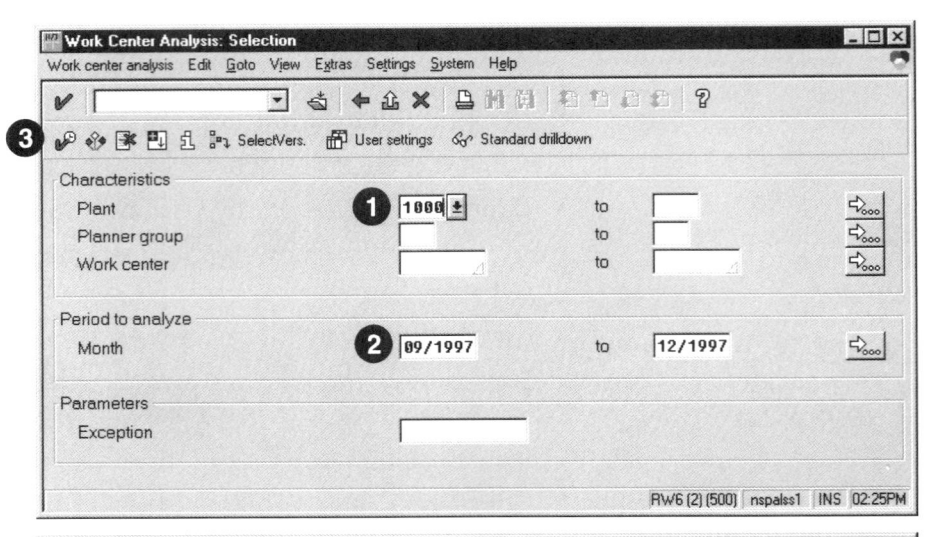

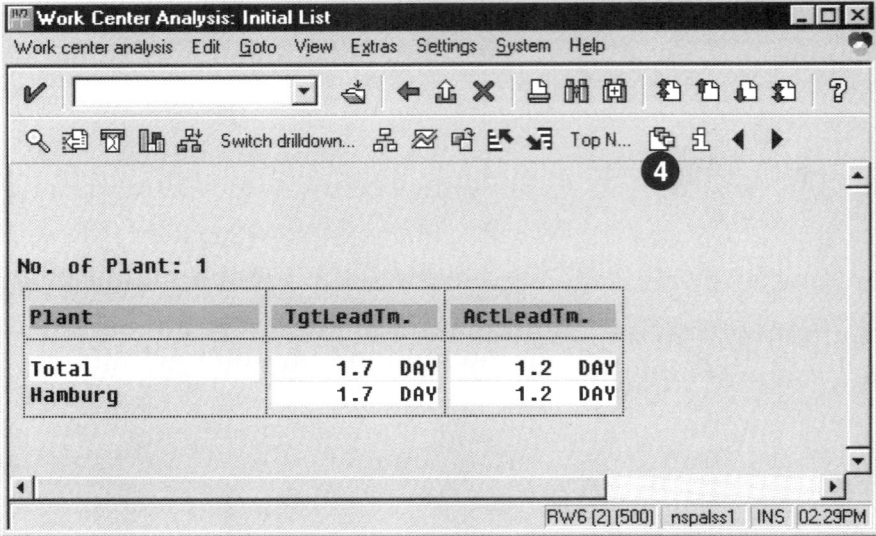

12–30 Reporting Made Easy

Section 12: Production Planning Reports
Shop Floor Info System

The popup window lists additional key figures.

5. To understand the impact on lead time, three related key figures were added.

6. Choose *Enter* to continue.

This screen shows additional key figures. Data is still at the total plant level.

7. Click the *Plant* column to select it.

8. Select the *Drill down by* button.

9. Select *Work center*.

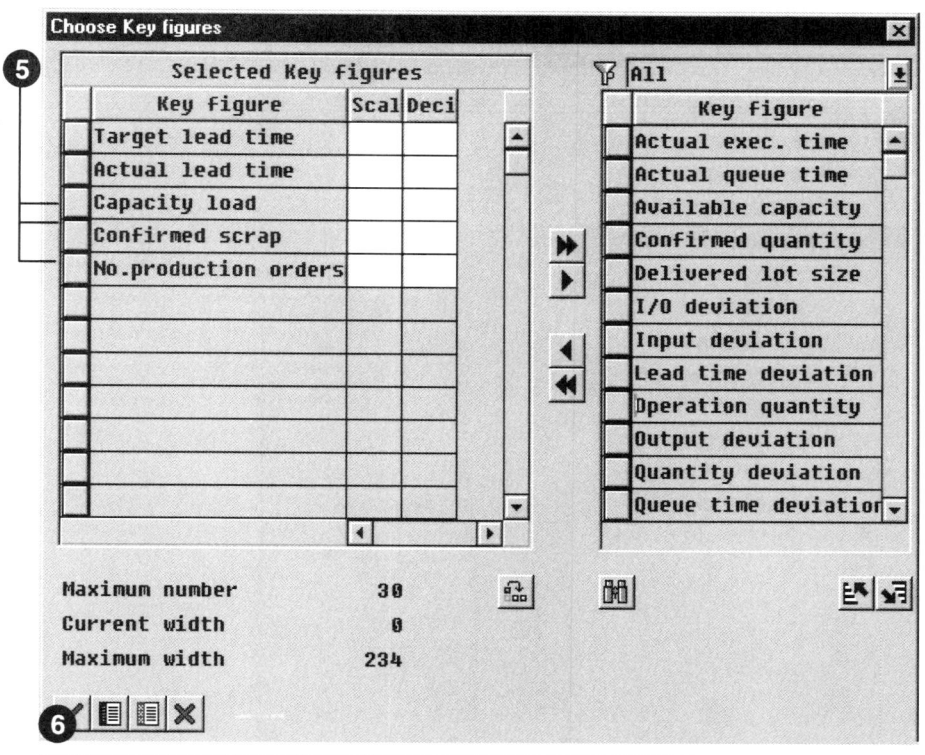

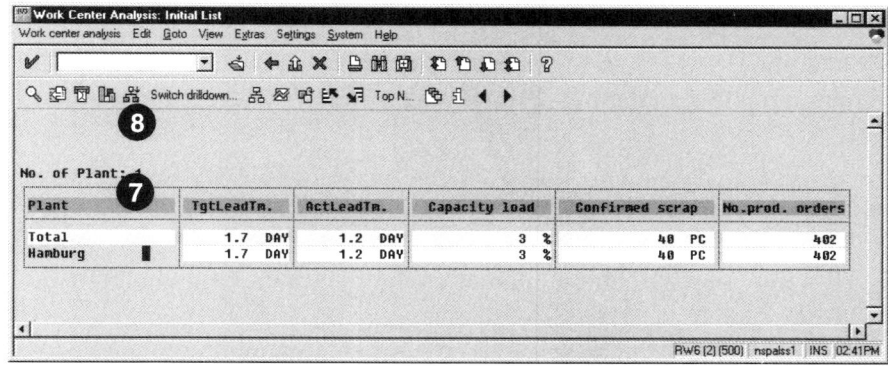

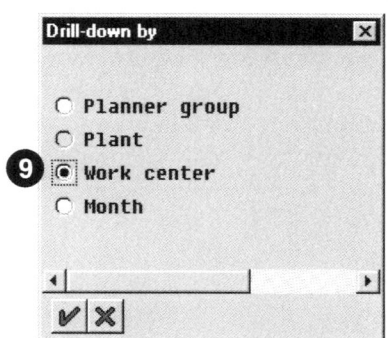

Commonly Used Reports: Illustrations and Perspectives

12–31

Section 12: Production Planning Reports
Shop Floor Info System

This screen shows data organized by work center to identify problem areas where you should take corrective action.

You can use several other features to refine your display, such as:

10. Column sorting:

11. Graphics display:

12. Column width adjustment (double-click on the heading of any column)

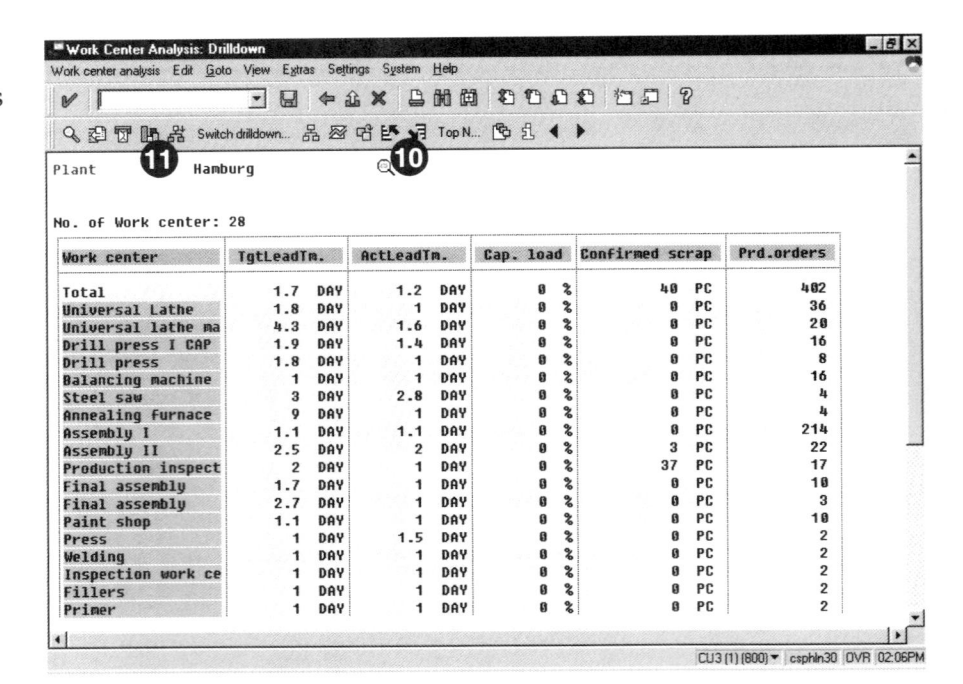

Reporting Made Easy

12–32

Section 12: Production Planning Reports
Shop Floor Info System

Example 2: Early Warning System (Exception Analysis) and orders with unplanned scrap.

To access the first screen for this report, choose

Logistics → Production → Production control → Control → Info. systems → Shop floor info sys. → Early Warning System → Exception analysis

1. Use the pull-down arrow to select from exception conditions.

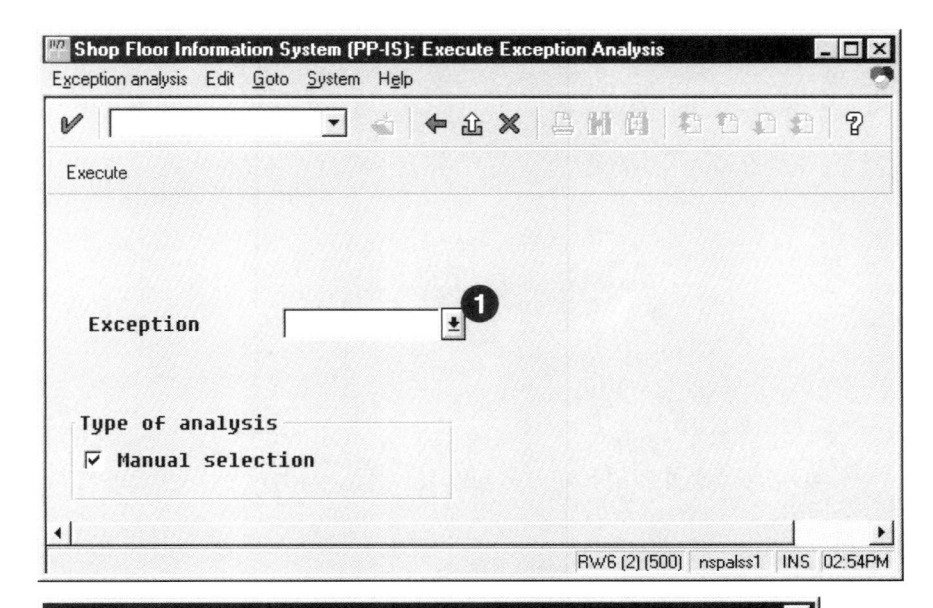

2. Click on a previously defined exception condition (for example, *PP02*). The selection should appear in the *Exception* field.

3. Choose *Enter* to continue.

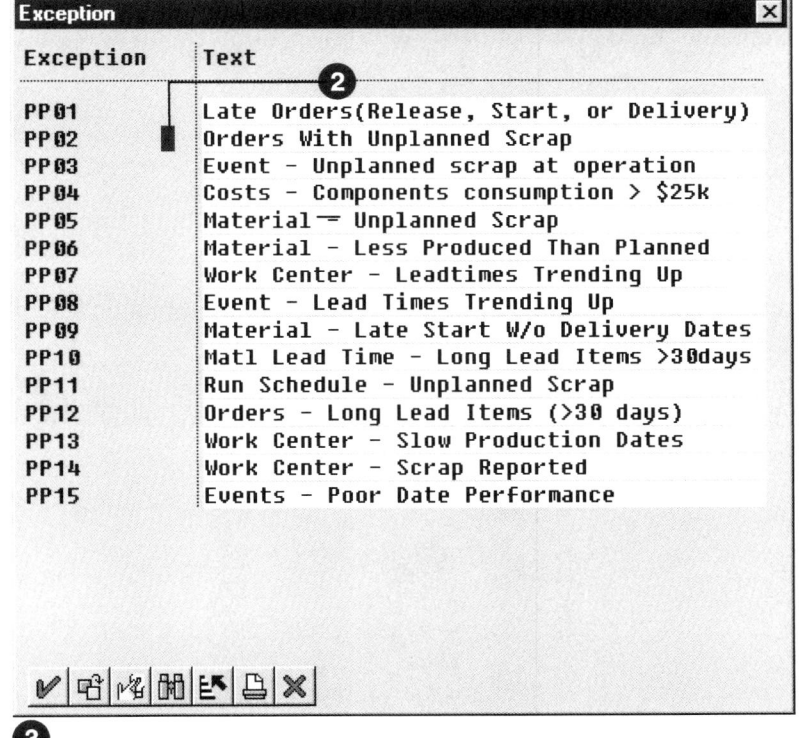

Exception	Text
PP 01	Late Orders(Release, Start, or Delivery)
PP 02	Orders With Unplanned Scrap
PP 03	Event – Unplanned scrap at operation
PP 04	Costs – Components consumption > $25k
PP 05	Material – Unplanned Scrap
PP 06	Material – Less Produced Than Planned
PP 07	Work Center – Leadtimes Trending Up
PP 08	Event – Lead Times Trending Up
PP 09	Material – Late Start W/o Delivery Dates
PP 10	Matl Lead Time – Long Lead Items >30days
PP 11	Run Schedule – Unplanned Scrap
PP 12	Orders – Long Lead Items (>30 days)
PP 13	Work Center – Slow Production Dates
PP 14	Work Center – Scrap Reported
PP 15	Events – Poor Date Performance

Commonly Used Reports: Illustrations and Perspectives

Section 12: Production Planning Reports
Shop Floor Info System

4. Choose *Execute*.

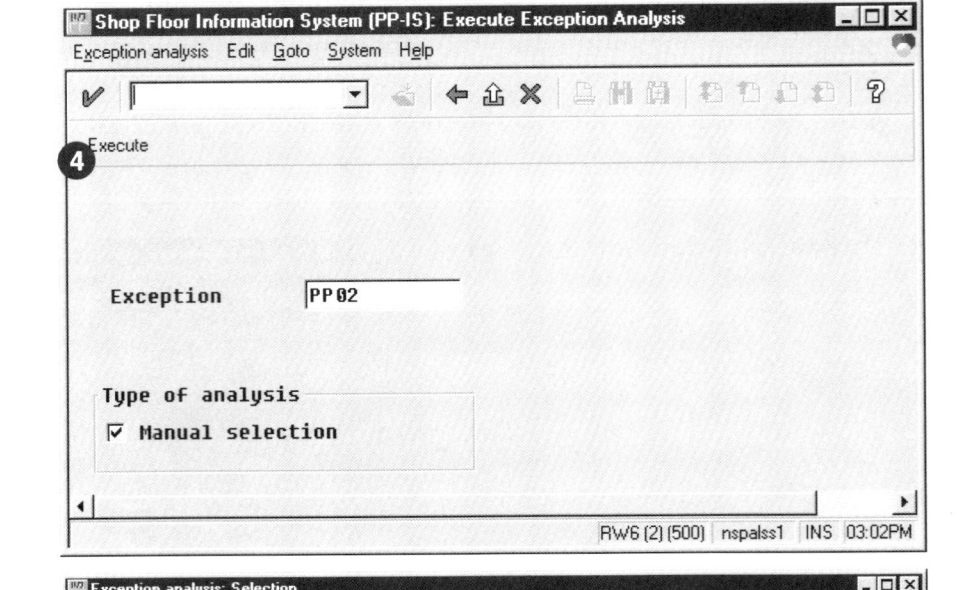

5. Enter a plant for analysis (for example, **1000**) in *Plant*.

   Leave *Material* and *Order* blank to examine all exceptions.

6. Enter a date range (for example, **07/01/1997** to **09/30/1997**) in *Day*.

7. Choose *Execute*.

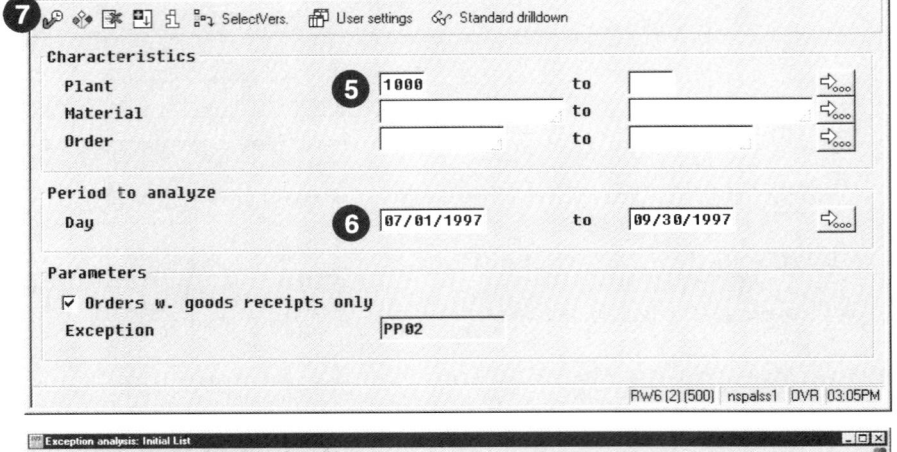

The screen shows exception data for the plant. As shown in the last example, we can drill down into some of the data. In this example, we will drill down to look at orders.

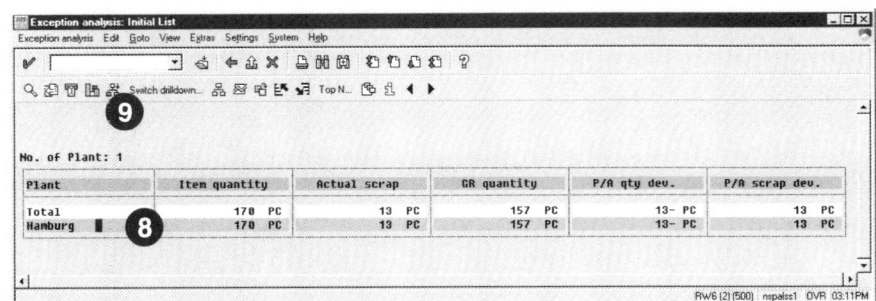

8. Select the plant row.

9. Select the *drill down by* button:

12-34

Reporting Made Easy

Section 12: Production Planning Reports
Shop Floor Info System

10. Select *Order*.

11. Choose *Enter* to continue.

The final list is arranged by *Order* number.

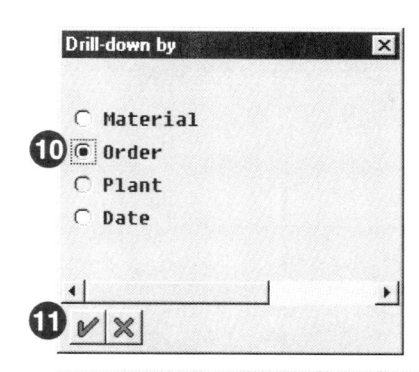

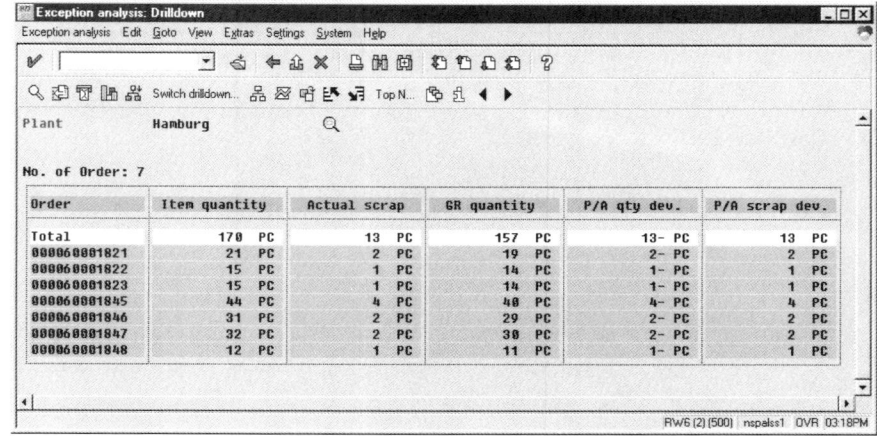

Commonly Used Reports: Illustrations and Perspectives

12–35

Section 12: Production Planning Reports
Shop Floor Info System

Example 3: Searching for a report using key figure retrieval.

To access the first screen for this report, choose

Logistics → Production → Production control → Control → Info. systems → Shop floor info sys. → Info library → Key figure retrieval → Using text strings

1. To find all reports, which may provide analysis for a given topic, enter the keyword (for example, a search is made for **scrap**).

2. Choose *Enter* to continue.

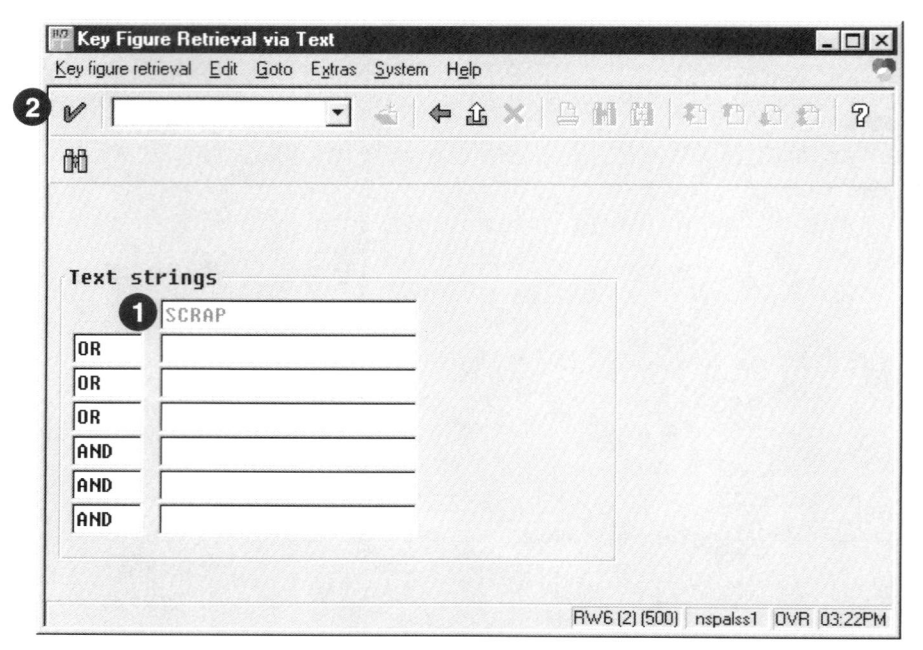

Section 12: Production Planning Reports
Shop Floor Info System

The resulting list reflects many possible reports.

3. Double-click on the *Confirmed scrap quantity for operation* line to analyze it.

4. Enter the plant for analysis (for example, **3000**) in *Plant*.

5. Enter the date range for the period (for example, **07/01/1997** to **09/30/1997**) in *Day*.

6. Choose *Execute*.

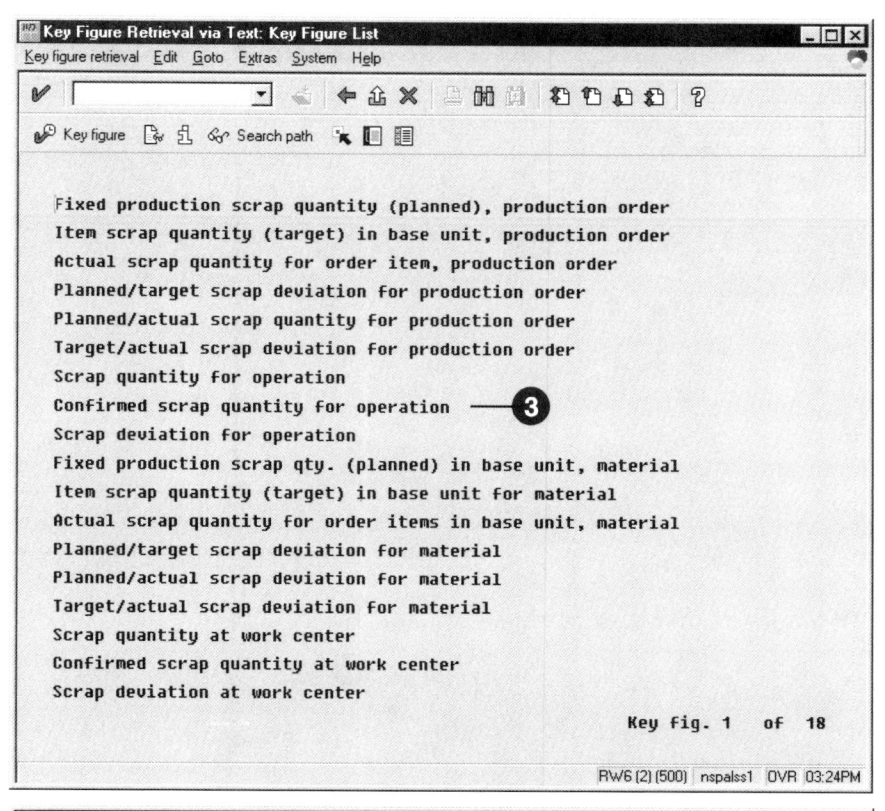

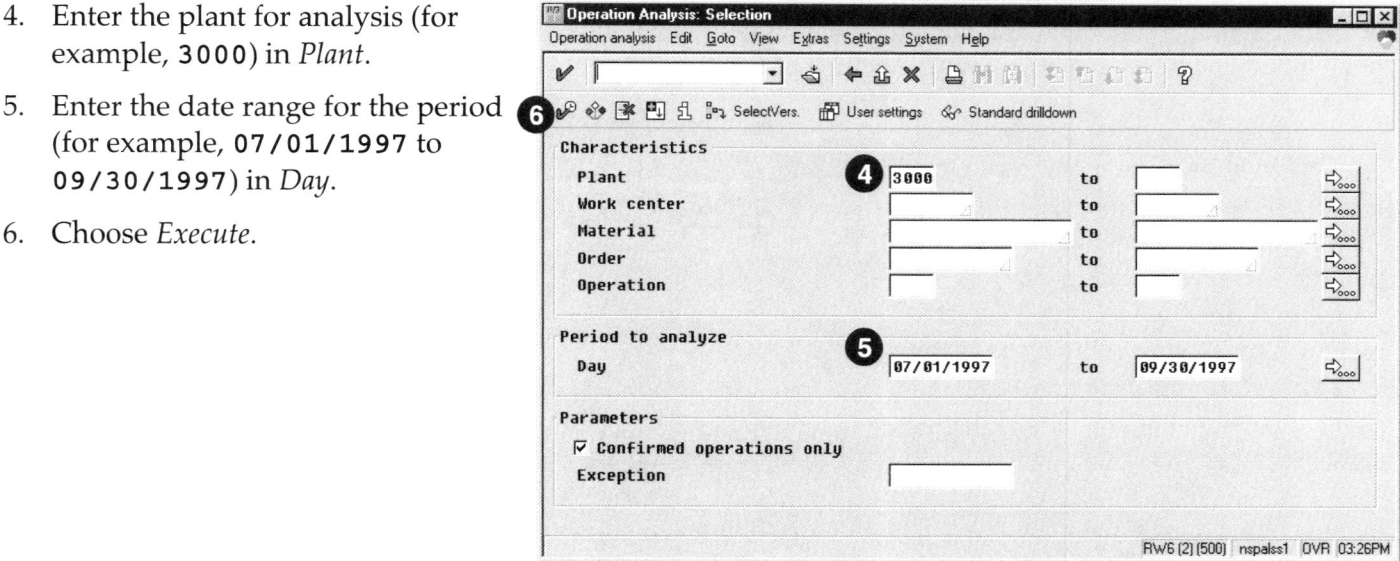

Commonly Used Reports: Illustrations and Perspectives

12–37

Section 12: Production Planning Reports
Shop Floor Info System

This is the first screen of the report.

7. Position the cursor on the row with the plant.
8. Select the *Drill down by* button.

9. Choose *Operation/activity*.
10. Choose *Enter* to continue.

This screen shows the same report after drilldown with the source of *SCRAP* listed by operation. The problem is traced to the operation where final production is delivered to stock. It indicates a problem may exist in the material handling process.

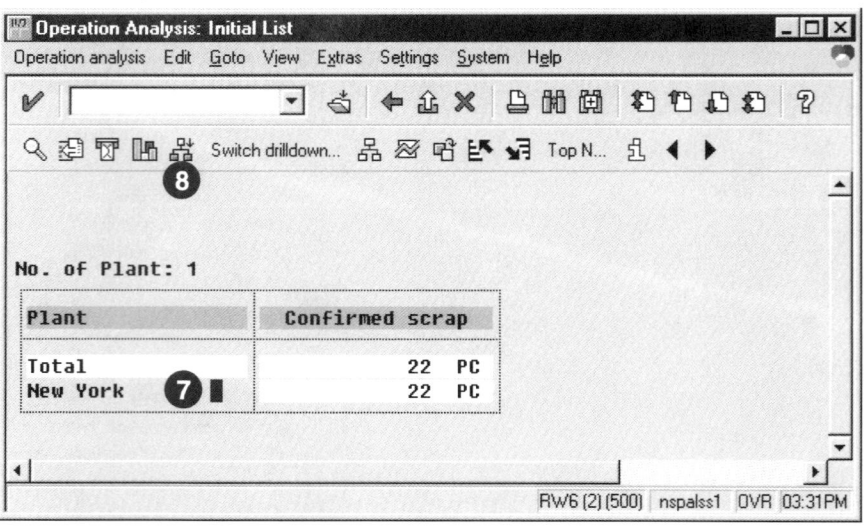

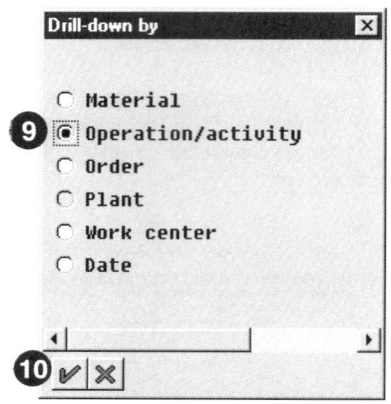

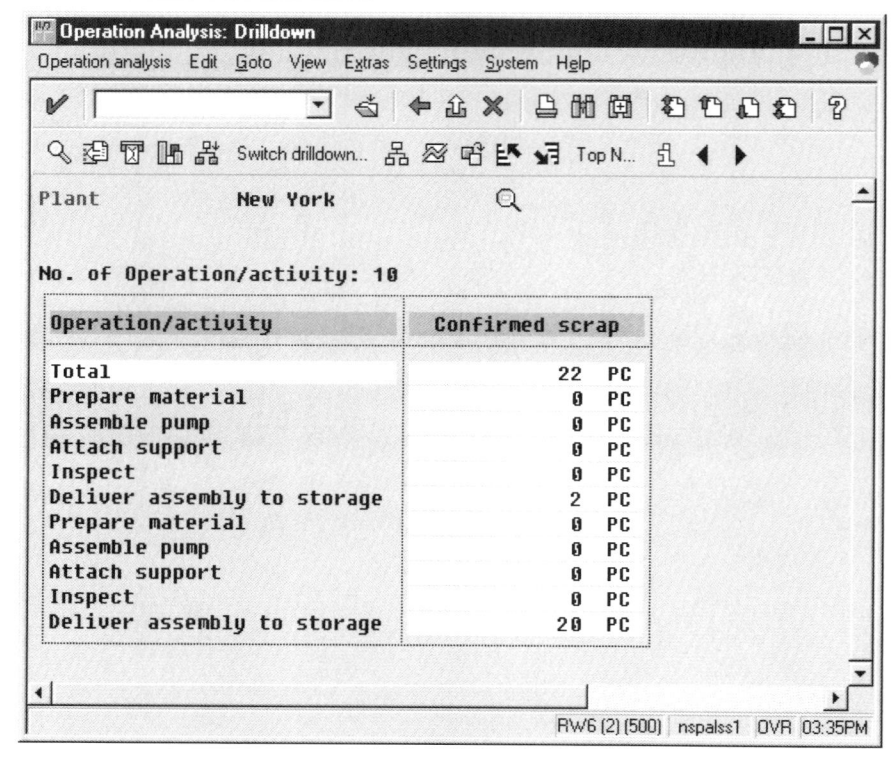

Multi-Level BOMs

Quick Access
To run this report, use one of the following access options:

Option 1: Menu Path

Logistics → Production → Master data → Bills of material → Reporting → BOM explosion → Multi-level BOM

Option 2: Transaction Code

In the *Command* field, enter transaction **CS12** and choose *Enter*.

Purpose
This report provides a list of all components in a bill of material (BOM). The BOM lists in an indented format to illustrate the hierarchical relationship among the assemblies and components. You can use this report to provide a quick display of the structure at any point to analyze a parent/child relationship and the potential impact of changes.

Prerequisites
No prerequisites are required to run this report.

The system provides several application codes (for example, transaction **OS30**) which are already configured to select and filter among any alternative BOMs for the material. It is possible to add to these codes, or to modify the settings, but it is generally not necessary.

You can choose selection criteria based on the functional purpose (for example, inventory management), costing, production, etc. For example, if you choose to use Engineering Change Management (ECM) and a specific Engineering Change Number (ECN) is involved, the display may optionally be restricted to a given ECN.

Integration
From the display, you can view additional information about the item on the BOM, including any scrap factors, co-product indicator, offset lead-time, component discontinuation data, and ECNs.

In addition, you can branch from the first screen of the report and apply additional filters such as the item category, item status, and material provision indicators, as well as scrap calculations. You can choose menu options to branch to the material master of the component, as well as to the display of a where-used list for the component.

Features

Assembly, plant, and application information is entered on the first screen of the report. If necessary, additional filters and settings may be applied from the menu *Edit → View* (or icon). These include:

- Inclusion of scrap specified on the BOM
- Limited explosion to first-level components only, to a specific subassembly, or for a specific alternate BOM
- Filters by item usage (engineering, production, etc.)
- Filters by material provision indicators, cost relevance, bulk material, or spare part indicator
- Inclusion of long texts
- Change of display or print format (by specifying different profiles)

The first screen then provides a listing of all components. If the component is a subassembly, its components will list in an indented format. Additional columns show the material number and description, the "quantity per," and the item category.

Next Steps

From the indented listing, you may print the results or view a graphical display of the BOM by choosing *Goto → Graphics*.

Additionally, a given component may be selected and the following functions invoked:

- Display of the general data view of BOM component, including scrap factors, co-product indicator, offset lead-time, component discontinuation and ECN (*Goto → Item data*). From this point it is possible to branch throughout the BOM display.
- Display of the material master for the component (*Environment → Detail*)
- Callup of a where-used list for the component (*Environment → Where-used list*)
- Display of the selection criteria used to perform the display (*Extras → Selection criteria*)

Section 12: Production Planning Reports
Multi-Level BOMs

Guided Tour

Example 1: Display a basic multi-level BOM, followed by a where-used list for one component.

To access the first screen for this report, choose

Logistics → Production → Master data → Bills of material → Reporting → BOM explosion → Multi-level BOM.

1. Enter a material (for example, **P-100**) in *Material*.

2. Enter a plant (for example, **3000**) in *Plant*.

3. Enter **BEST** in *BOM application*. BEST is the German abbreviation for inventory management.

4. If required, enter a past or future effective date. The *Valid from* field will default to the current date. Leave the other fields blank unless a specific ECN number or revision level is required.

5. If *Required quantity* is left blank, it defaults to *1*.

6. Choose *Execute*.

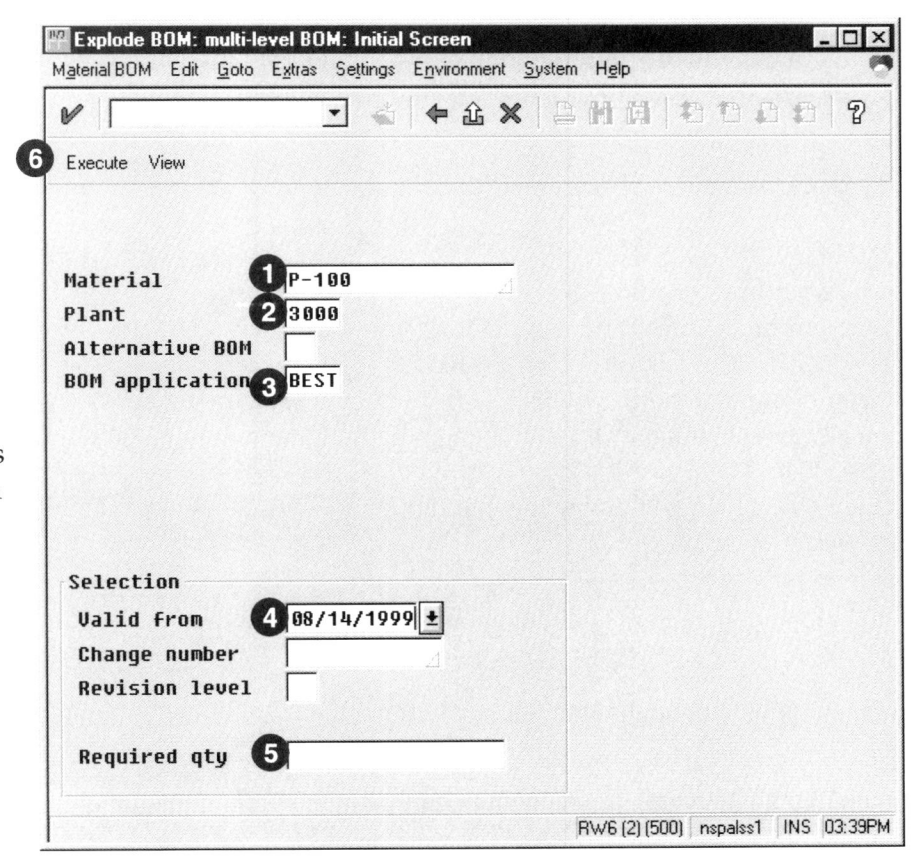

Commonly Used Reports: Illustrations and Perspectives

12–41

Section 12: Production Planning Reports
Multi-Level BOMs

This screen lists each component in the BOM. If it is a subassembly, the components making up the subassembly are shown:

A   Level number for the component within the BOM (numbering and indentation illustrate the parent/child relationship)

B   Component number and description.

C   Number of subassembly components needed to produce the desired components

D   Item category (for example, *L* = stock item, *D* = document)

7. To find out where a given component might be used, position the cursor on the desired line and choose *Environment* → *Where-used list*.

This screen shows the where-used list for material *100-120*.

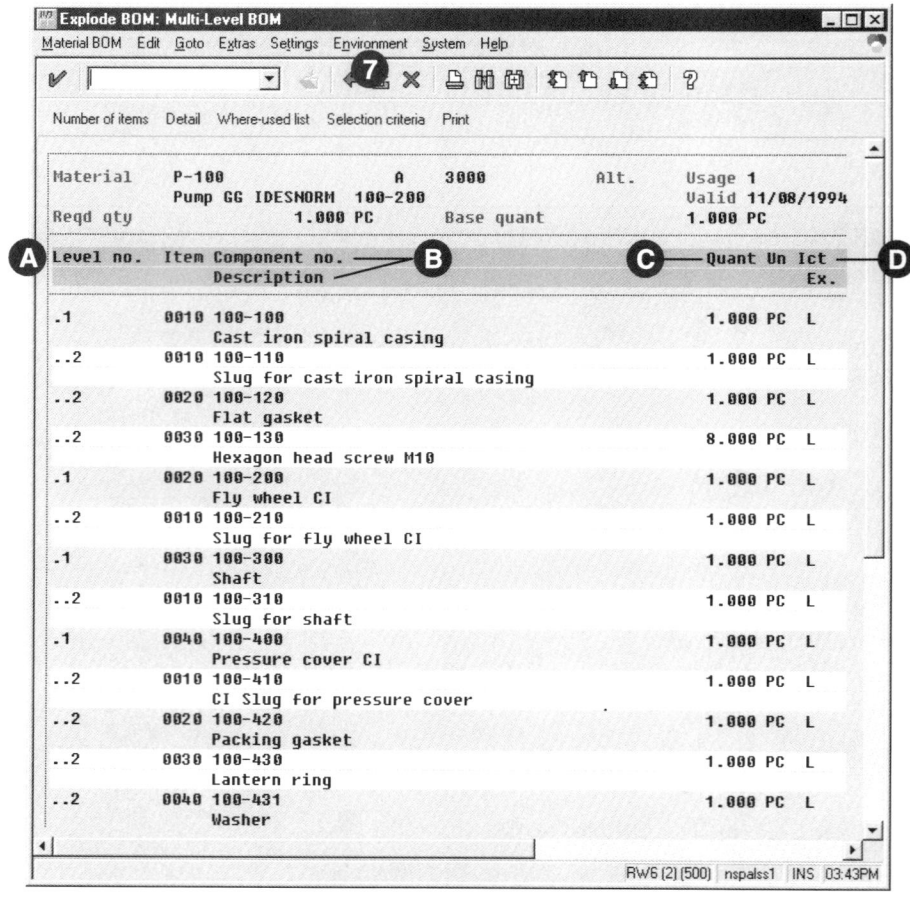

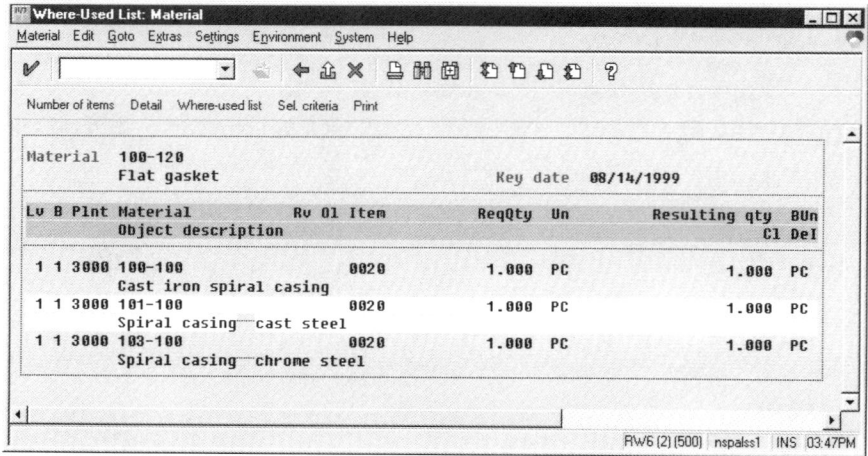

Explode BOM: Multi-Level BOM

Material	P-100	A	3000	Alt.	Usage 1
	Pump GG IDESNORM	100-200			Valid 11/08/1994
Reqd qty		1.000 PC	Base quant		1.000 PC

Level no.	Item	Component no. Description	Quant	Un	Ict Ex.
.1	0010	100-100 Cast iron spiral casing	1.000	PC	L
..2	0010	100-110 Slug for cast iron spiral casing	1.000	PC	L
..2	0020	100-120 Flat gasket	1.000	PC	L
..2	0030	100-130 Hexagon head screw M10	8.000	PC	L
.1	0020	100-200 Fly wheel CI	1.000	PC	L
..2	0010	100-210 Slug for fly wheel CI	1.000	PC	L
.1	0030	100-300 Shaft	1.000	PC	L
..2	0010	100-310 Slug for shaft	1.000	PC	L
.1	0040	100-400 Pressure cover CI	1.000	PC	L
..2	0010	100-410 CI Slug for pressure cover	1.000	PC	L
..2	0020	100-420 Packing gasket	1.000	PC	L
..2	0030	100-430 Lantern ring	1.000	PC	L
..2	0040	100-431 Washer	1.000	PC	L

Where-Used List: Material

Material	100-120					
	Flat gasket			Key date	08/14/1999	

Lv	B	Plnt	Material Object description	Rv Ol Item	ReqQty Un	Resulting qty Cl	BUn DeI
1	1	3000	100-100 Cast iron spiral casing	0020	1.000 PC	1.000	PC
1	1	3000	101-100 Spiral casing—cast steel	0020	1.000 PC	1.000	PC
1	1	3000	103-100 Spiral casing—chrome steel	0020	1.000 PC	1.000	PC

Section 12: Production Planning Reports
Multi-Level BOMs

Example 2: Display a BOM after choosing additional filter or selection criteria available from the first screen.

1. Choose *Edit → View* to select additional filters or change settings.

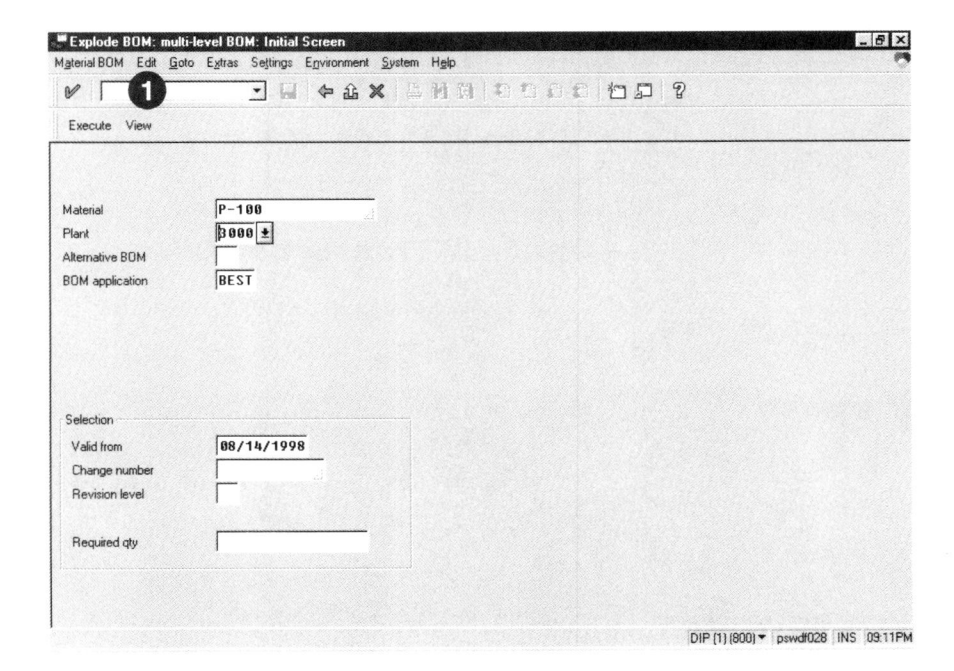

From this screen you can apply additional filters and restrictions before displaying the BOM.

2. Choose *Execute*.

This filter allows you to change the display of the previous example.

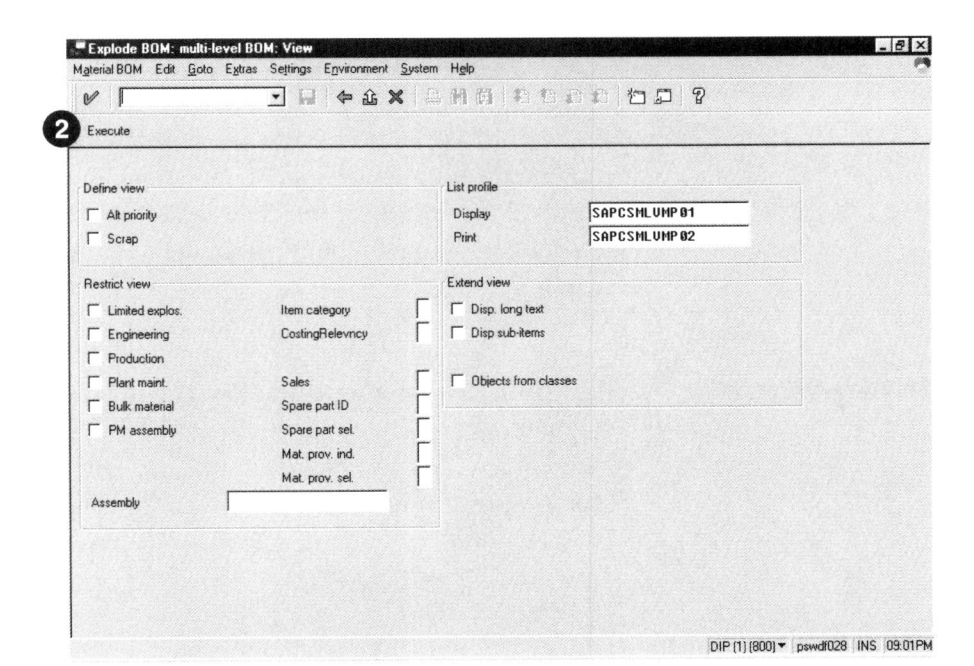

Commonly Used Reports: Illustrations and Perspectives

Section 12: Production Planning Reports
Missing Parts Info System

Missing Parts Info System

Quick Access To run this report, use one of the following access options:

Option 1: Menu Path

Logistics → Production → Production control → Control → Information system → Missing parts info system

Option 2: Program Name

Choose *System → Services → Reporting* and enter `PPCMP000` in the *Program* field.

Option 3: Transaction Code

In the *Command* field, enter transaction `CO24` and choose *Enter*.

Purpose This report provides a quick recap of material shortages based on reservations that were not fully committed on their requirements date during an availability check. As such, you can use this report to monitor critical components or orders, and to reallocate materials based on inventory availability.

Prerequisites You must check the availability before running this report, since it is based on the results of availability checking. These checks are typically made during order creation or release, but may also be invoked manually. If there is a shortage, the order header will carry the status *MSPT* and the shortage will be noted in the Missing Parts Info listing.

Availability checking parameters must be defined in configuration (PP or SD) and may be referenced on various levels including material, order type, and MRP group. Two standard *profiles* are delivered which provide the basic organization of the report (grouped by material or order). Additional profiles can be created where needed.

Integration Backorder processing is the key function which may be called up from the primary display of missing parts. It allows you to change the allocation of components. Menu options also provide for branching to the stock overview and stock/requirements list, as well as for display or change of an order.

Features

The first screen provides filters to limit the selection of missing parts from reservations or orders based on single values, ranges, or multiple selection functions for:

- Plant
- Material
- MRP controller
- Requirements date
- Sales order
- Production Order number
- Production scheduler (orders only)

At a minimum, the plant must be entered. In addition, the profile which specifies grouping either by material or order must be entered.

- The primary display lists the missing parts—grouped as specified by the profile—and provides the fields listed below (see Example 1). Additions and changes to these fields are possible from the *View* menu and include:
- Material and description
- Plant
- MRP controller
- Requirements date
- Requirements quantity
- Committed quantity
- Storage location
- Reservation number
- Order number (if grouped by order)

Section 12: Production Planning Reports
Missing Parts Info System

Next Steps From the first screen, you may:

- Refresh the screen. This may be necessary if allocations are changed in backorder handling (*List → Refresh;* icon also available. Backorder handling is invoked from the *Environment* menu).
- Print the list (*List → Print,* or printer icon)
- Save the list (*List → Save,* or save icon)
- Display additional details of the reservation (*Goto → All fields;* icon also available)
- Compare field values (*Goto → Field comparison;* icon also available)
- Graphically display statistical data related to the material (*Goto → Graphics*)
- Group and Sort (*View → Group/Sort;* icons also available)
- Apply additional filter based on object status (*View → Set/Delete filter*)
- Display or substitute additional fields (*View → Choose fields;* icon available)
- Edit layout (*Settings menu*)
- Branch to stock/requirements list (*Environment → Stock/requirements*)
- Branch to stock/overview (*Environment → Stock overview*)
- Display material master (*Environment → Material master*)
- Call backorder processing (*Environment → Backorder handling*)
- Display or change order (*Environment → Display / change order;* icons available)

Section 12: Production Planning Reports
Missing Parts Info System

Guided Tour

Example 1: Display the missing parts information, including grouping and field selection options.

To access the first screen for this report, choose

Logistics → Production → Production control → Control → Information system → Missing parts info system.

1. Enter **1000** in *Plant* and any other criteria to narrow the selection process.
2. Choose a profile to display the data by material or by manufacturing order.
3. Choose *Execute*.

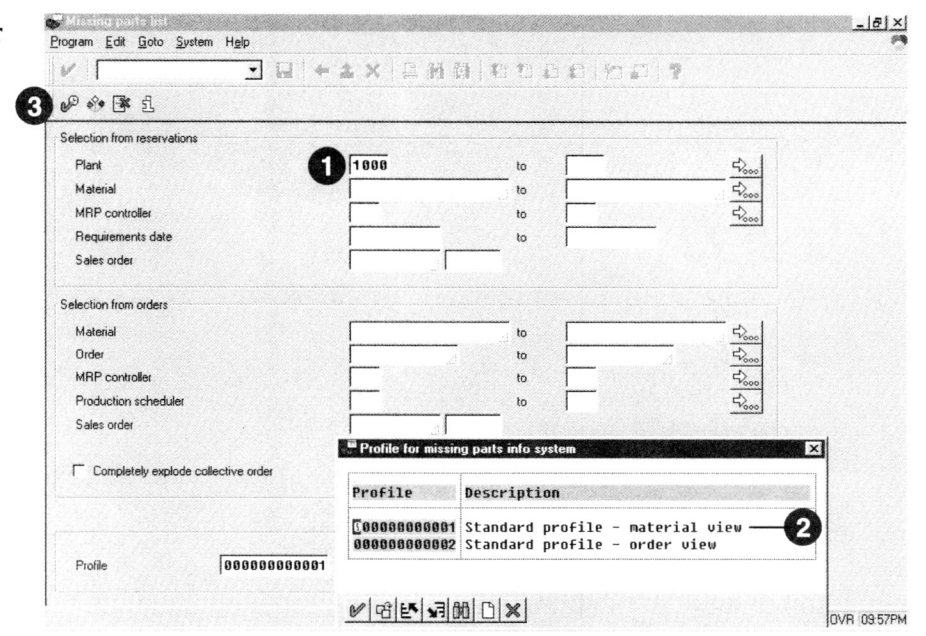

Commonly Used Reports: Illustrations and Perspectives

12–47

Section 12: Production Planning Reports
Missing Parts Info System

The first screen of the report shows data according to the display-by-material profile:

A Requirement date and quantity

B Quantity committed to date

C Reservation number

The first screen of the report can also show data according to the alternate profile, display-by-manufacturing order:

D From either profile, additional fields may be chosen or substituted using the *Fields* icon.

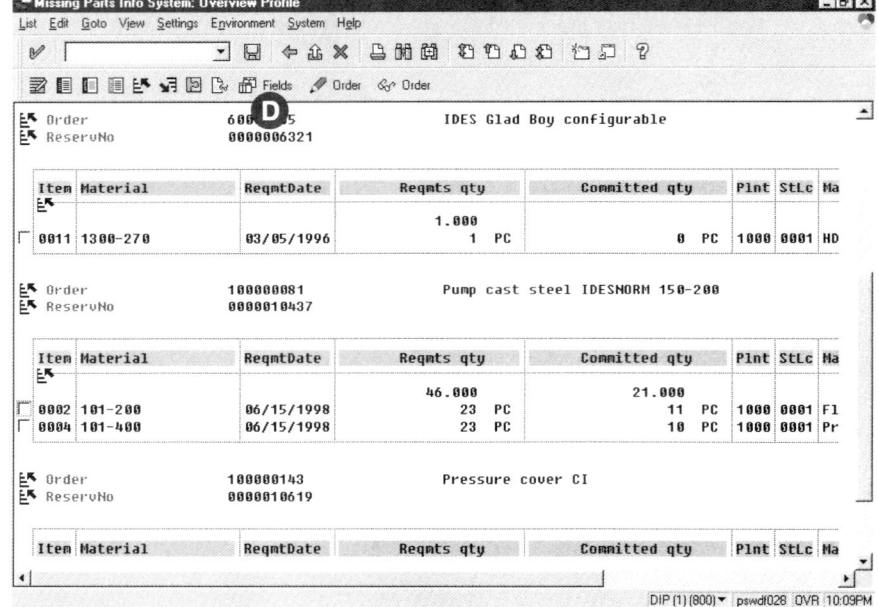

12–48

Reporting Made Easy

Section 12: Production Planning Reports

Missing Parts Info System

E   The resulting popup window lets you add or delete additional fields.

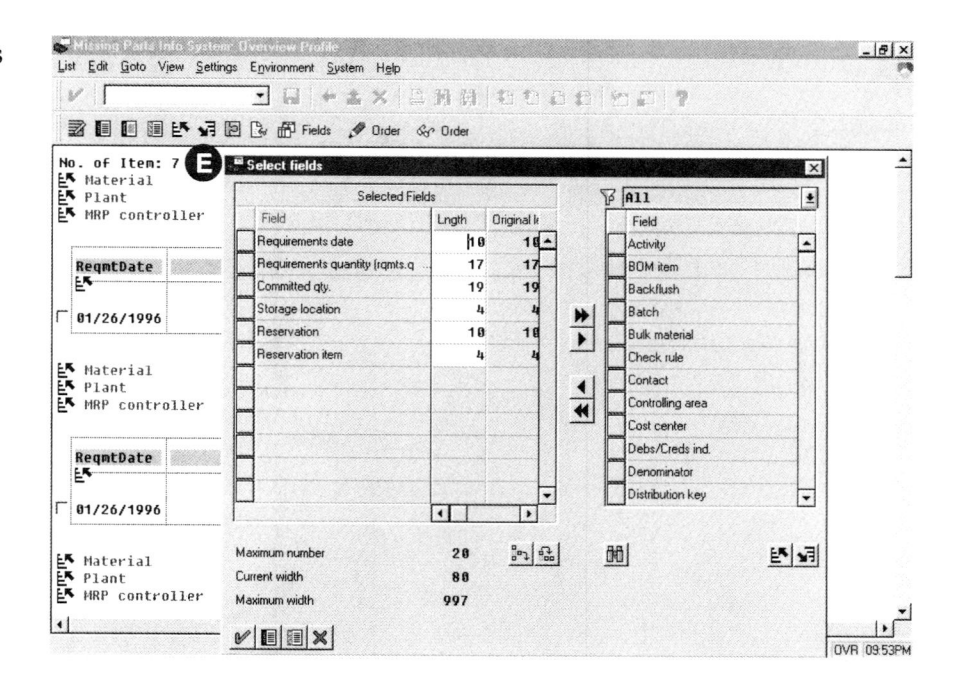

Commonly Used Reports: Illustrations and Perspectives

12–49

Section 12: Production Planning Reports
Missing Parts Info System

Example 2: Display a report that branches out to backorder handling screens.

1. From the first screen of the material or order profile, you can branch to backorder processing by choosing *Environment → Backorder handling*.

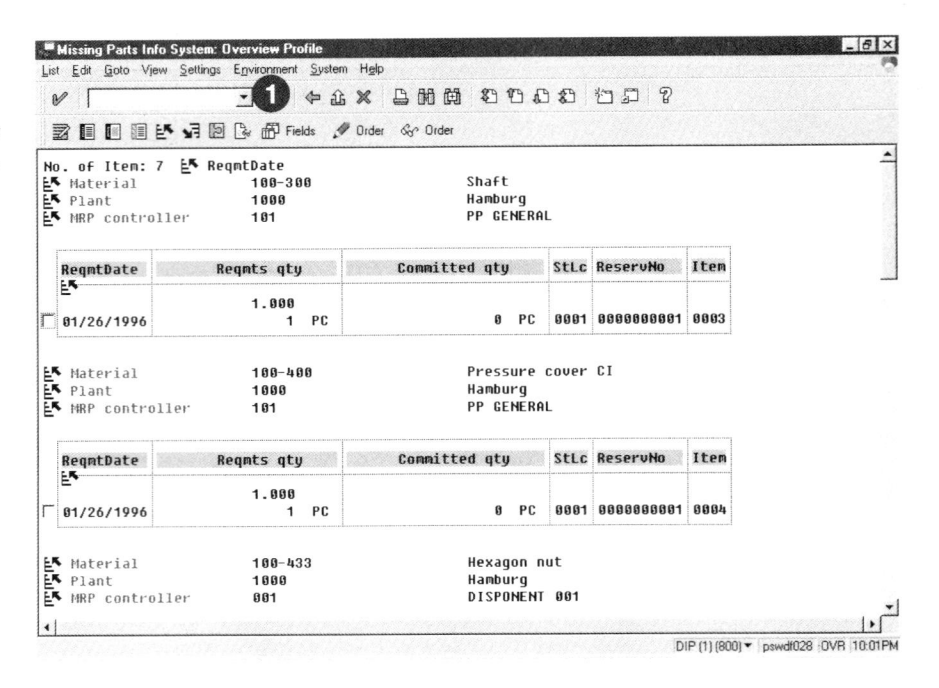

This is an example of backorder processing detail for *Material 100-300*.

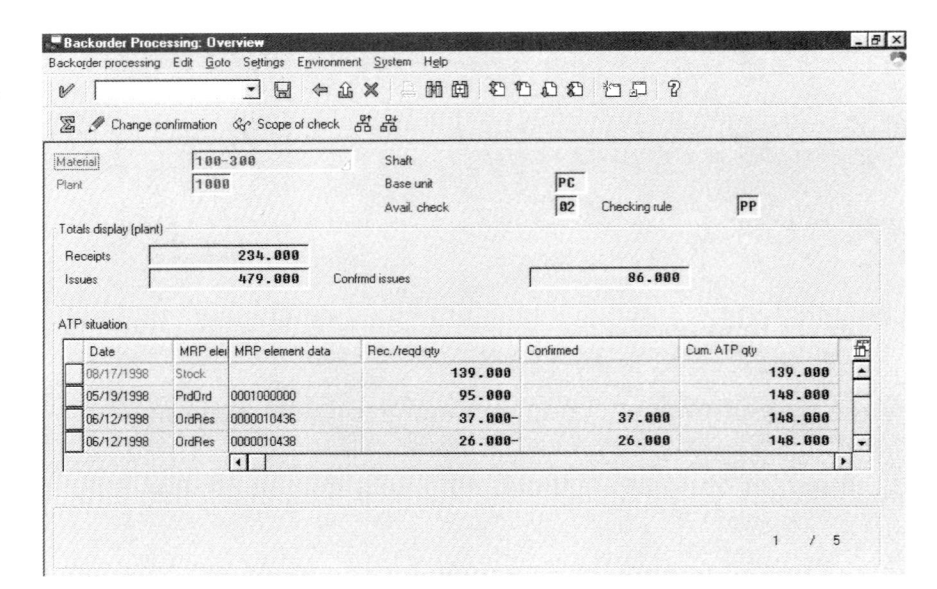

12–50

Reporting Made Easy

Backorder Processing

Quick Access To run this report, use one of the following access options:

Option 1: Menu Path

Logistics → Production → Production control → Control → Backorder processing → Material

Option 2: Transaction Code

In the *Command* field, enter transaction CO06 and choose *Enter*.

Purpose Related to the *Missing Parts Info System*, this report displays all requirements for a given material and allows you to change prior commitment quantities.

A planner would use this report to quickly assess demands and reallocate materials among manufacturing orders based on changing priorities and inventory availability.

Prerequisites The data displayed in backorder processing is based on commitments which are generally done automatically during order creation or release. Additional demand information will be reflected based on SD order allocations and the last MRP/MPS run. Consequently, backorder processing needs to consider this to ensure visibility of all potential demands. Backorder processing relies on the *availability checking rules* maintained in configuration and referenced on the MRP (and sales) view of the material master.

Integration You can run backorder processing from the *Missing Parts Info System*, or call it up directly from the menu.

You can change the commitment quantity from the first screen within backorder processing. The menu options let you:

- Branch to the stock overview
- Display the individual demand element from MRP
- Peg to upper-level demand
- Drill down to dependent requirements

Features The first screen prompts you for material, plant, and the availability checking rule to be used, typically PP in production planning. This screen provides a vertical listing of demands in date sequence, with columns displaying the required quantity, committed quantity, and the cumulative ATP balance.

Section 12: Production Planning Reports
Backorder Processing

Next Steps   From the first screen, you can change the commitment quantity for a given demand either by choosing *Change confirmation*, or by choosing *Edit → Change confirmation*.

Other actions which may be taken from the menus or icons are as follows:

- Save all changed commitment quantities (reallocations) (*Backorder processing → Save*).
- Display *Scope of Check* to verify sources of demand and supply being considered in the check (*Goto → Display scope of check*; icon also available).
- Filter the demands to show only SD requirements, reservations for production orders, or both (*Settings menu*).
- Switch to columns reflecting receipts, demands, etc. by period (*Settings → Period totals*; icon also available).
- Branch to the *Stock Overview* screen for the material (*Settings → Stock overview*).
- Display the individual demand element (MRP element) (*Environment → Disp MRP element*).
- Display pegging to upper-level demand or lower-level dependent requirements (*Environment → Pegging* or *Order report*; icons available).

Guided Tour

Example 1: Show demand and commitments in different ways.

To access the first screen for this report, choose

Logistics → Production → Production control → Control → Backorder processing → Material

1. Enter **100-100** in *Material*.
2. Enter **3000** in *Plant*.
3. Enter **PP** in *Checking rule*. Checking rule **PP** is typically used for manufacturing orders.
4. Choose *Enter*.

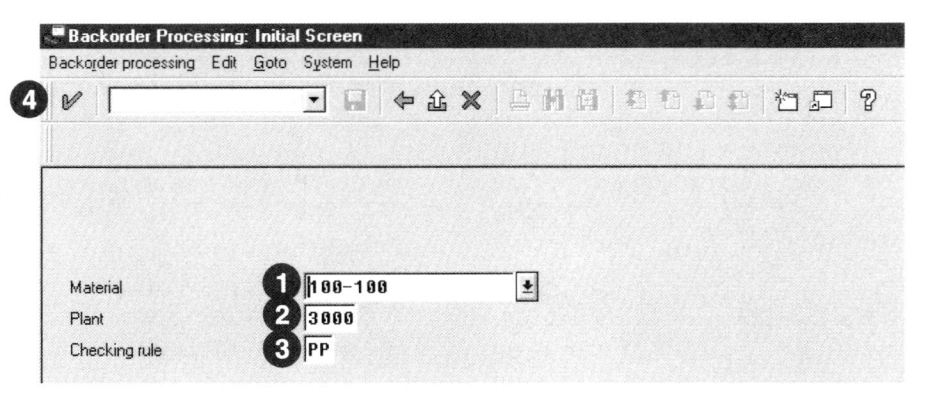

Section 12: Production Planning Reports
Backorder Processing

This screen shows a recap of the total receipts, issues, and confirmed issues:

A   Demand by date and source

B   Committed quantity

C   Cumulative ATP quantity

5. Choose *Period totals* to reformat the screen.

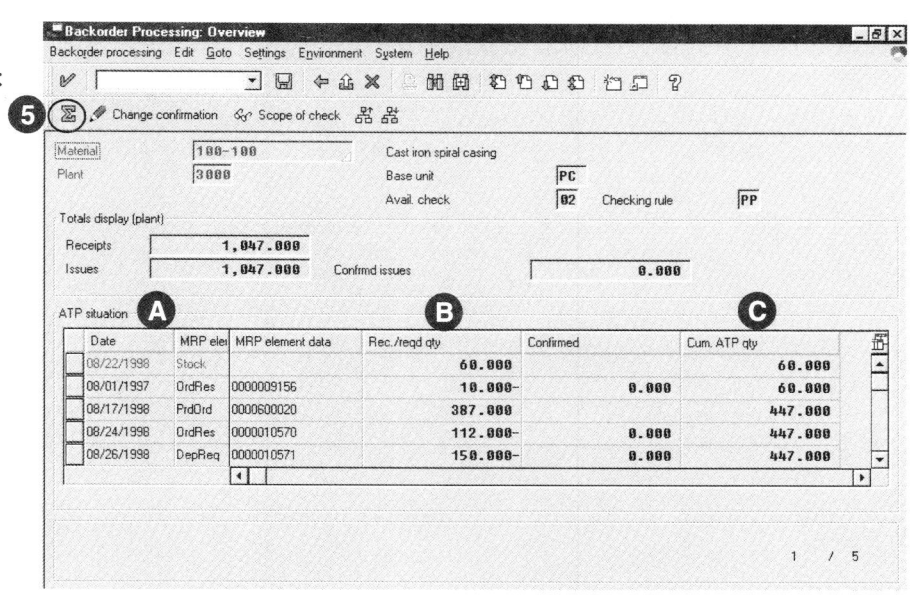

The screen is reformatted to bucket demand and supply by time periods.

Time buckets may be changed using the icons provided on the toolbar.

D   The *Scope of check* may be displayed using the icon.

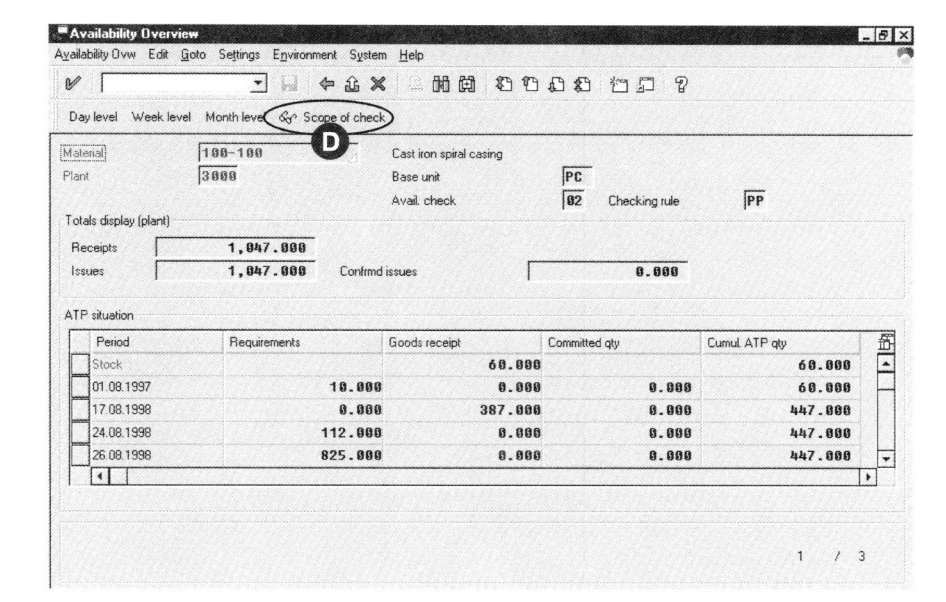

Commonly Used Reports: Illustrations and Perspectives

12–53

Section 12: Production Planning Reports

Backorder Processing

Parameters defined in configuration for the checking rule are displayed here.

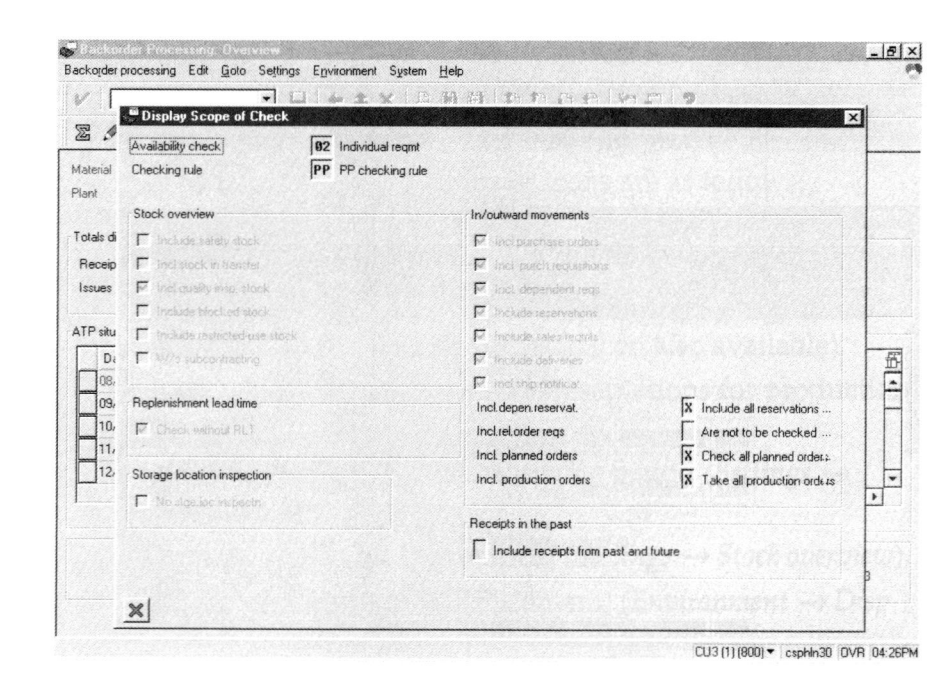

Note: This report is different from the *Backorders* report (found in Sales and Distribution) in that it focuses on production planning instead of sales and delivery.

Section 12: Production Planning Reports
Backorder Processing

Example 2: Display a report that shows how a commitment quantity is changed.

We now continue from the *Overview* screen of example 1.

1. Select the individual demand line by clicking on the cell to the left of the *Date* column.

2. Choose *Change confirmation*.

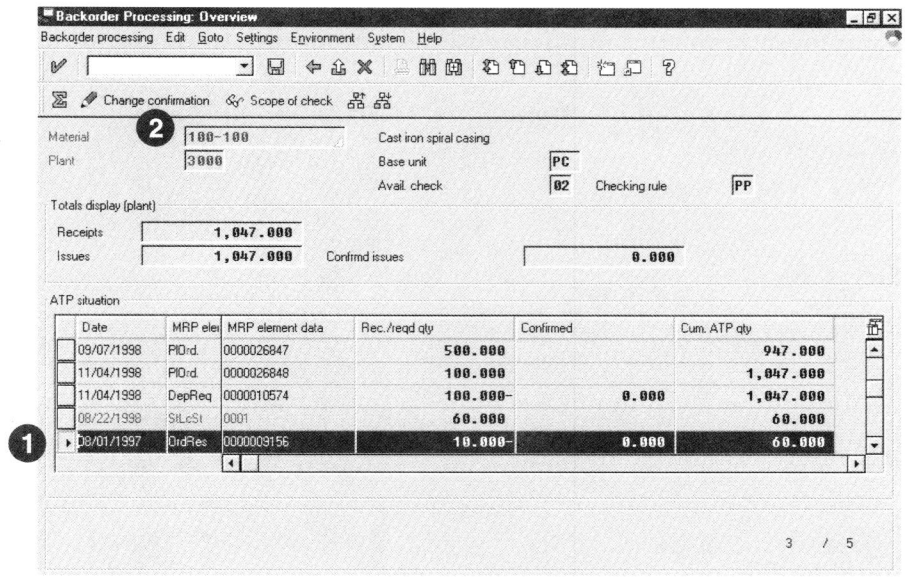

A panel appears at the bottom of the screen where you can enter or change the desired commitment quantity.

3. After you have made modifications, choose *Save*.

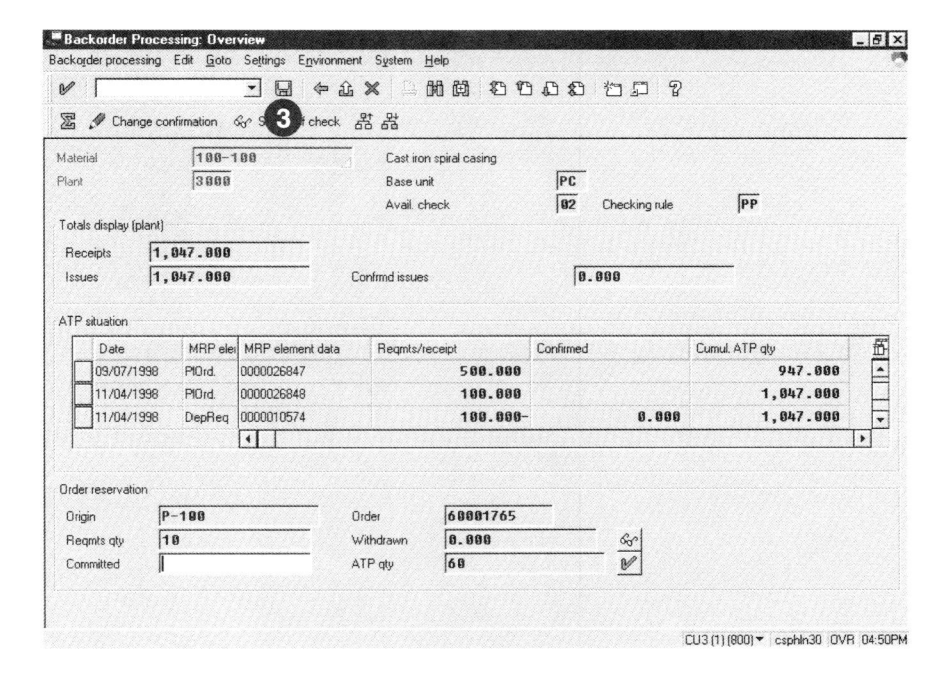

Commonly Used Reports: Illustrations and Perspectives

12–55

Capacity Planning—Evaluation

Quick Access To run this report, use one of the following access options:

Option 1: Menu Path

Logistics → Production → Capacity planning → Evaluation → Work center view → Load

Option 2: Transaction Code

In the *Command* field, enter transaction **CM01** and choose *Enter*.

Purpose This report provides both a summary and a detailed view of capacity requirements versus available capacity.

From the basic evaluation, a planner may identify current or impending work center overloads and take corrective action in order to meet required delivery dates.

Prerequisites No prerequisites are required to run this report.

From a capacity *availability* standpoint, evaluations are based on data from the work center capacity headers or standard capacities master data. MRP, MPS, and run generate capacity requirements only if the *Scheduling* parameter is set to 2 on the first screen of the MRP/MPS planning run. The screens are based on various *capacity planning profiles* defined during configuration. These are provided with the R/3 System and generally do not need further configuration.

Integration Capacity evaluation menus and screens provide extensive branching to related master data, stock/requirements listings, drill down to individual planned or production orders, and capacity leveling functions. Except for master data, the other three elements allow manipulation of data.

Section 12: Production Planning Reports
Capacity Planning—Evaluation

Features

The evaluation system offers several menu options for slightly different filters to limit the work centers, capacities, and requirements to be displayed. For purposes of this chapter, the chosen evaluation follows the menu path *Work Center view → Load*.

You should note that the first screen for evaluations is different from other first screens in the R/3 System. The input fields for selection parameters are present, but they may not be visible for some color settings of the workstation (for example, a white input field on a white background). Use of the tab key moves the cursor among the *From* and *to* selection fields. In addition, an *Operator* field appears to the right of each selection (for example, an equal to [=], greater than [>], etc.). This field may generally be left as is for the equal-to operator; other operators may be selected from the matchcode on the field (F4 key).

The first screen prompts you for any combination of work center, capacity planner group, and plant. The resulting *Standard Overview* is a summary of the capacity requirements and availability for each capacity category for the chosen selection parameters. The matrix displays requirements and availability data in columns, and time-periods in rows. Over-capacity periods are highlighted in red. From this display, you may select any specific time period for drilldown and a detailed capacity list will be generated that contains all orders consisting of the load on the given work center capacity. The fields shown in either display are governed by the various capacity planning profiles, but may be altered temporarily through menu options or icons.

Section 12: Production Planning Reports
Capacity Planning—Evaluation

Next Steps   The evaluation system provides extensive branching, drilldown, and editing of data. From the *Standard Overview* screen, you may:

- Print the results for any view (*Planning → Print*).
- Invoke a new selection of data based on work center, capacity category, etc. for background processing if the data is extensive (*Planning → Background processing*).
- Choose alternate versions of the planning profiles used for data selection and display during the session (*Planning → Change profiles*) Note: Planning profiles are defined in configuration and are extensive.
- Refresh the display if settings or underlying data have changed (*Edit → Refresh*, or icon).
- Graph various data elements (*Goto → Graphics*).
- Display the detailed capacity list (*Goto → Detailed view*).
- Change settings related to time intervals, work center hierarchy display, and versions of capacity (*Settings → General*).
- Change settings related to the graphical displays (*Settings → Graphics*).
- Set thresholds related to minimum or maximum capacity loads (*Settings → Evaluation*).
- Branch to related master data files for the work center and capacity headers (*Environment → WC* or *Capacity Header*).
- Export data Microsoft Excel in various formats (*Environment → Excel interface*; parameters chosen under *Settings → Excel interface*).

From the detailed capacity list, you may take additional actions. Actions that allow changes to data are shown below with an asterisk (*):

- Branch to the following (*Environment menu*):
  - Planned or production order*
  - Material master
  - Stock/requirements list
  - Pegging reports
  - Order confirmations*
  - Goods receipt processing*
  - Capacity *leveling* functions from tabular or graphical planning tables*
- Augment or change fields (*Settings → Choose fields*).
- Save a specific layout (*Settings → Save version*).
- Download data to a PC file (icon only).

Section 12: Production Planning Reports
Capacity Planning—Evaluation

Guided Tour

Example 1: Display the standard overview and detailed capacity list for one work center.

To access the first screen for this report, choose

Logistics → Production → Capacity planning → Evaluation → Work center view → Load.

1. Enter the work center (for example, `1111`) in *Work center*.
2. Enter the plant (for example, `3000`) in *Plant*.
3. Choose *Enter*.

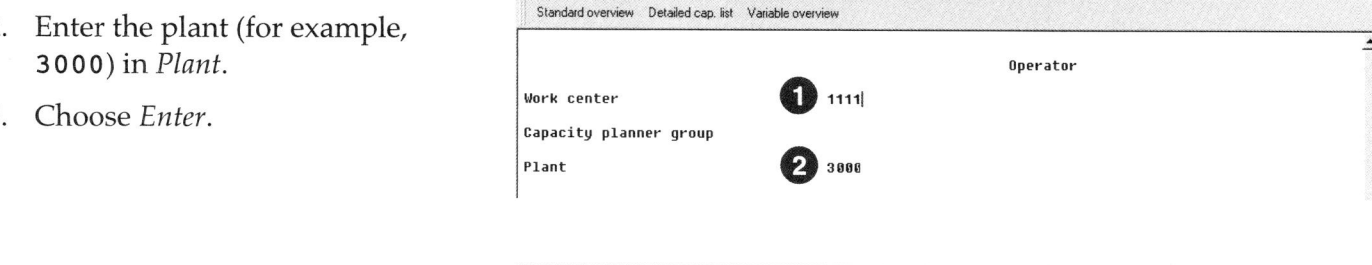

The standard overview shows each capacity category from the work center. Rows represent time periods (for example, weeks) and columns represent capacity requirements and availability.

Time periods with overload are highlighted in red.

4. Select the time period with the overload.
5. Choose *Cap. Details/period*.

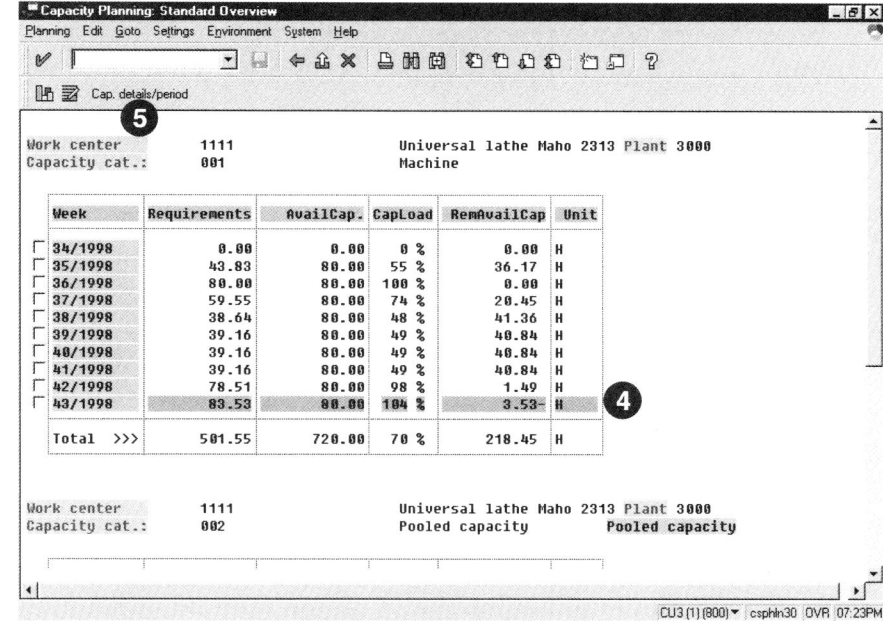

Commonly Used Reports: Illustrations and Perspectives

12–59

Section 12: Production Planning Reports
Capacity Planning—Evaluation

This screen shows a detailed capacity list of all orders comprising the total requirements for the period.

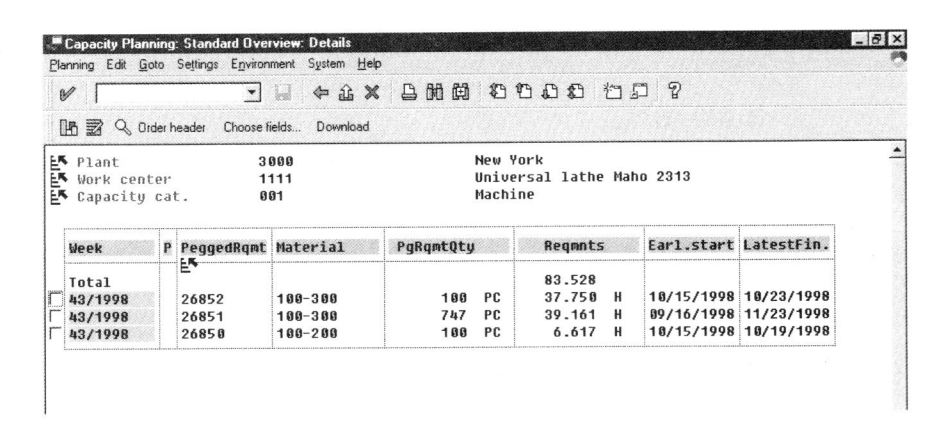

Example 2: From the detailed capacity list, branch to the order header to allow changes.

1. Select the individual demand line by clicking on the cell to the left of the *Work* column.

2. Choose *Environment → Order → Order header*.

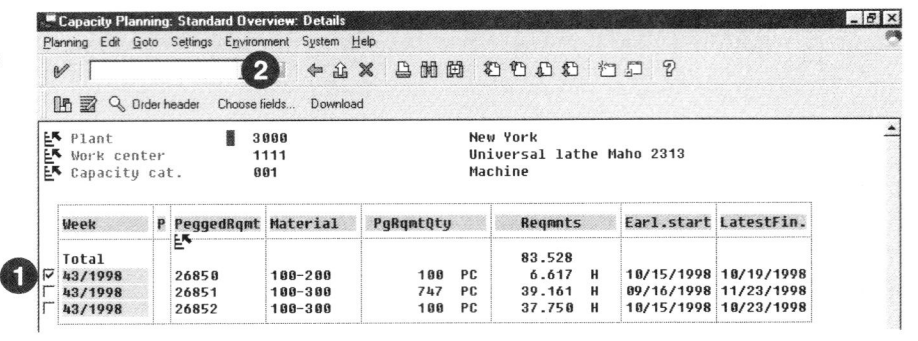

3. For planned orders, a popup window lets you branch to either the planned order (as shown in this example) or the routing order. We select the planned order.

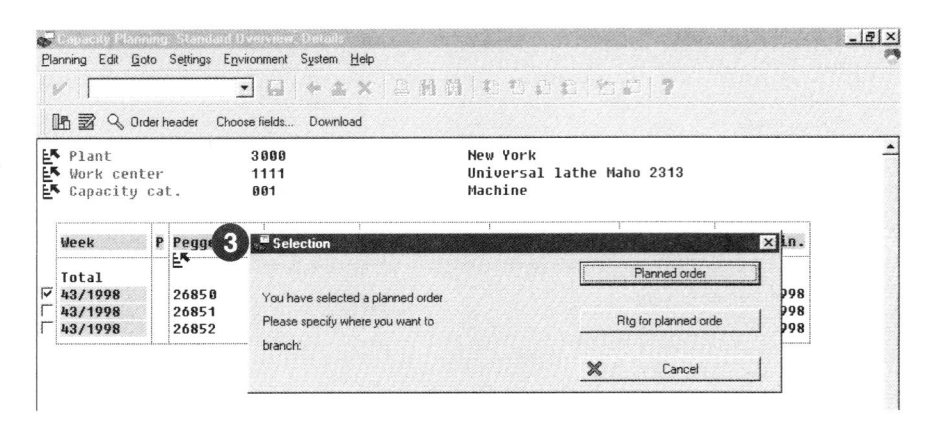

Reporting Made Easy

12–60

Section 12: Production Planning Reports
Capacity Planning—Evaluation

The underlying planned order is displayed in *Change* mode.

4. At this point, you can change the planned order dates.

5. Select *Plnd order* or *Components* to firm the order.

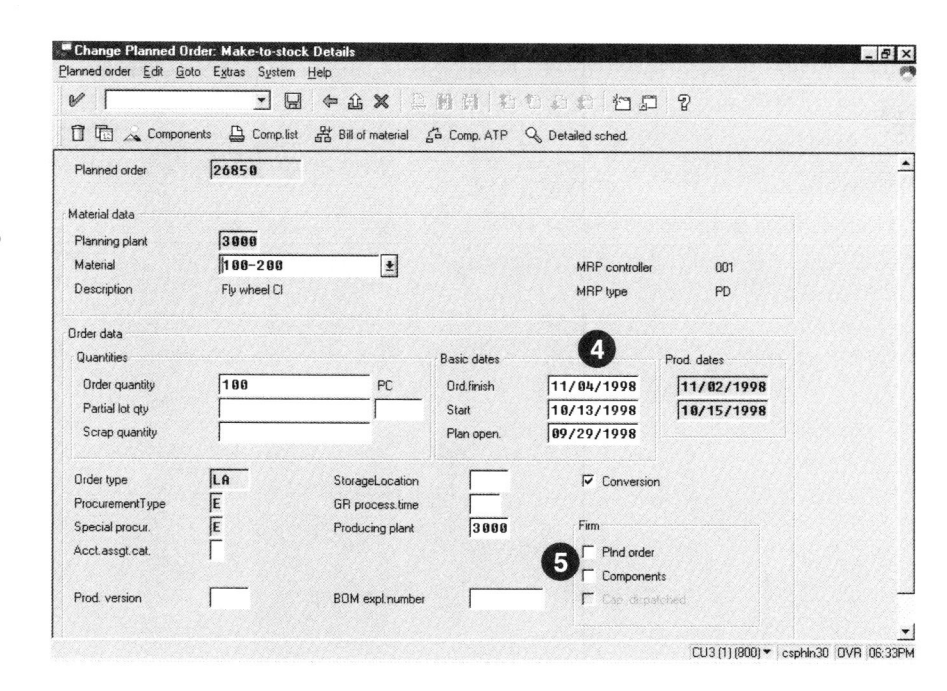

Example 3: Branch out from the detailed capacity list to the capacity-leveling functions in either tabular or graphical planning tables.

We are back at the capacity planning overview as described in the previous example.

1. Choose *Environment → Capacity leveling → Work center view → Tabular* (or graphical).

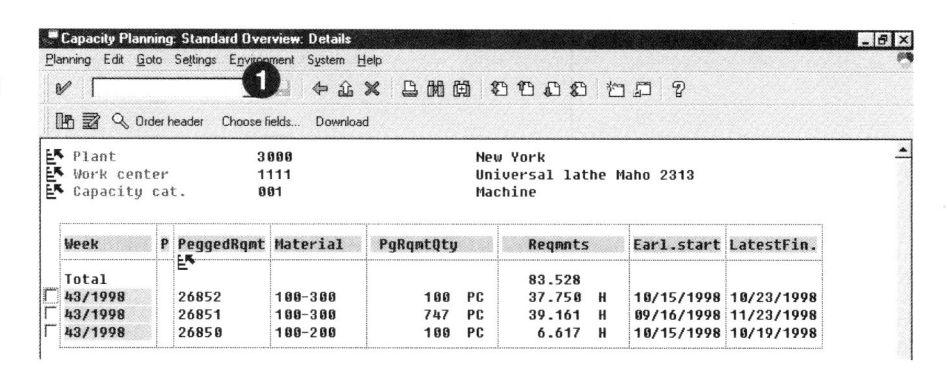

Commonly Used Reports: Illustrations and Perspectives

12–61

Section 12: Production Planning Reports
Capacity Planning—Evaluation

The tabular planning table is displayed for additional review or dispatching.

A. In this example, the *Change view* icon was selected to narrow the display to one capacity category at a time.

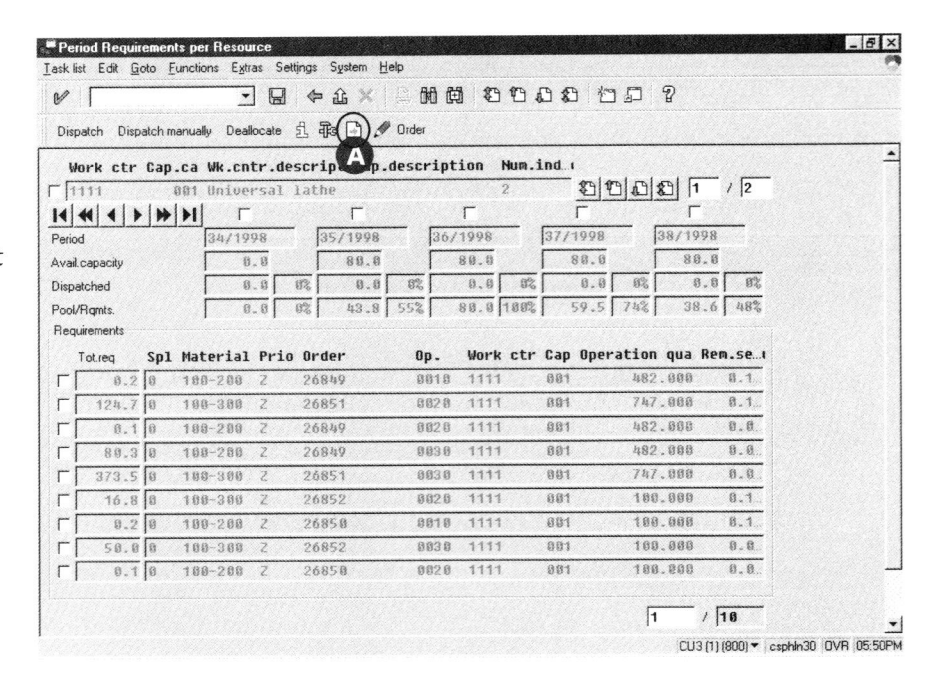

Alternatively, the graphical planning table is displayed for review or finite scheduling.

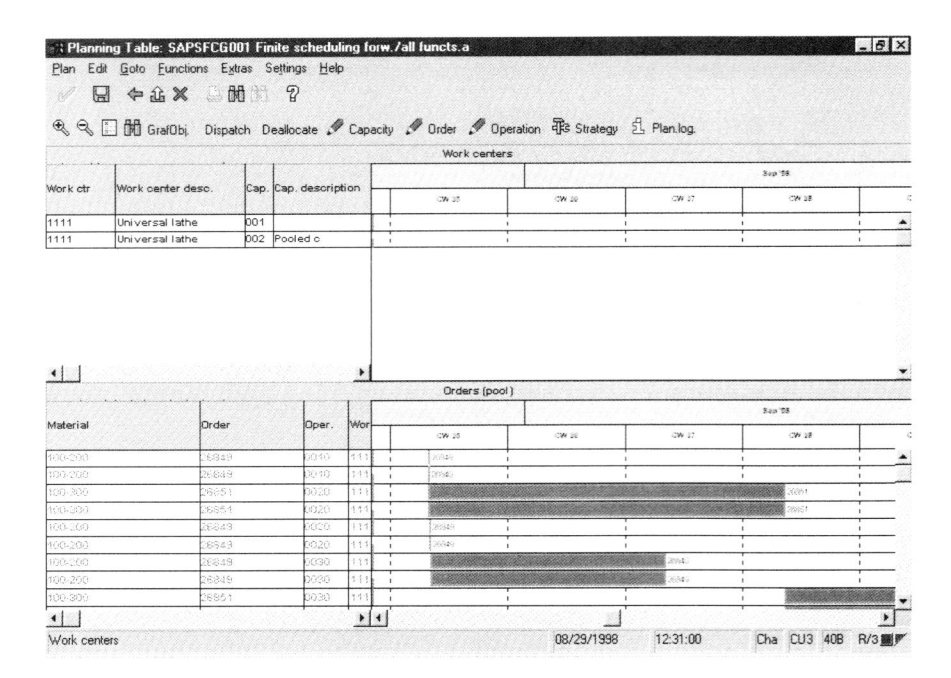

12–62

Reporting Made Easy

Section 13: Project System Reports

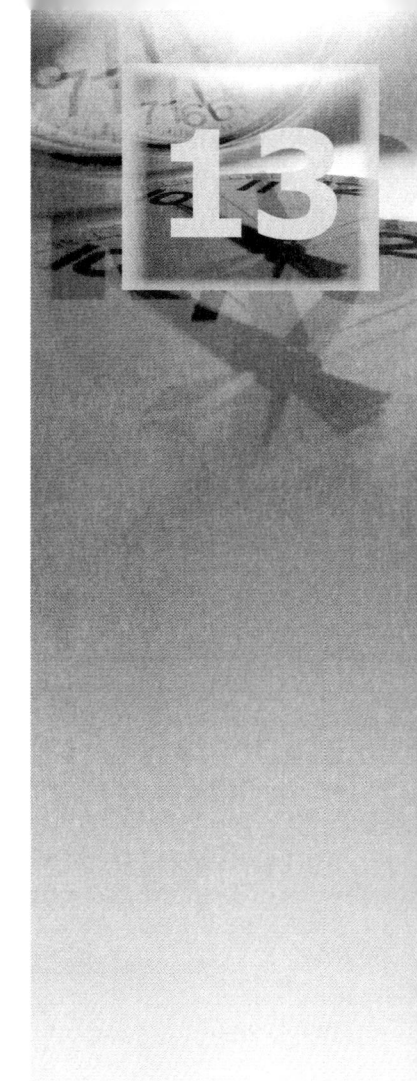

Contents

Project Cost Reporting—Planned/Actual/Variance 13–2

Cost Element Reporting—Plan vs. Actual..13–5

Budget Reporting—Budget vs. Plan/Actual/Commitments.............................13–9

Project Cost Reporting—Planned/Actual/Variance

Quick Access

To run this report, use one of the following access options:

Option 1: Menu Path

Logistics → Project management → Information system → Costs/rev/payments → Report selection, then *Costs:Planned/Actual/Variance*

From the reporting tree, choose the following report:

Costs:Planned/Actual/Variance

Option 2: Transaction Code

In the *Command* field, enter transaction **PS91** and choose *Enter*. Then, select the report listed as *Costs: Planned/Actual/Variance*.

Purpose

This report lists the planned and actual costs by project structure object. It also compares the variance and displays the variance amount in both absolute and percentage terms.

Prerequisites

You must enter a value for the *Controlling Area* the first time you run this report. You will need to change the *Controlling area* again only if it changes for subsequent reports. After you enter *Controlling area*, you see the *Database profile*. The *Database profile* determines what information from the Project System will be viewed.

Integration

In this report, you can use value categories to find all costs (planned or actual) based on the type of cost. Value categories are defined during configuration and consist of cost elements or cost element groups. Using value categories, you can list costs for a given project object, such as a *Work Breakdown Structure* element (WBS) and by the cost element groups instead of each cost element. Examples of cost element groups include:

- Labor costs
- Material costs
- Overhead costs
- Other costs

You can also list the cost by transaction currency instead of by project currency, delimit cost by year or period, and drill down to the transaction that created the cost.

Section 13: Project System Reports
Project Cost Reporting—Planned/Actual/Variance

Features The selection screen of this report includes:

- Variants
- Dynamic selection options
- Database profile
- Filters
- Version reporting
- Subproject reporting
- Reporting of planned costs using a version other than the default version

Next Steps This report includes data from cost planning and actual cost postings to WBS elements and network activities.

Guided Tour

Example: Display a list of costs by project.

To access the first screen for this report, choose

Logistics → Project management → Information system → Costs/rev/payments → Report selection, then, *Costs:Planned/Actual/Variance*.

Note: In this example we are using *Controlling area* 2000 and *Database profile* #1.

1. Under *Project information system*, enter C-1000 in *Project*.
2. Choose *Execute*.

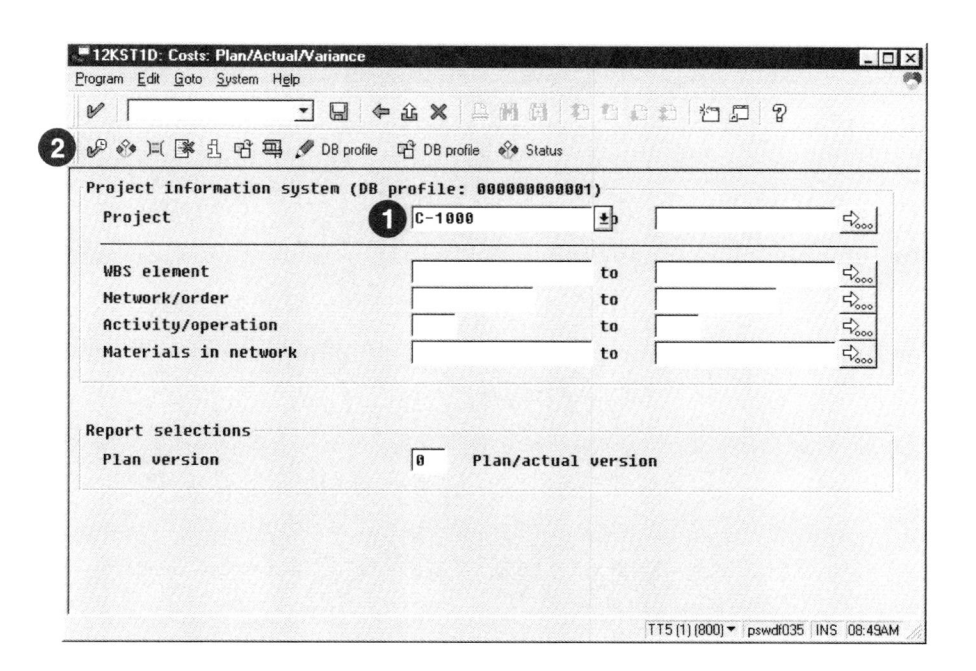

Commonly Used Reports: Illustrations and Perspectives

Section 13: Project System Reports

Project Cost Reporting—Planned/Actual/Variance

A This section of the screen shows possible navigation by:
- Value category
- Period/year
- Transaction currency
- Transaction

B This section of the screen shows a listing of project objects and their descriptions, as well as the planned and actual costs with associated variances.

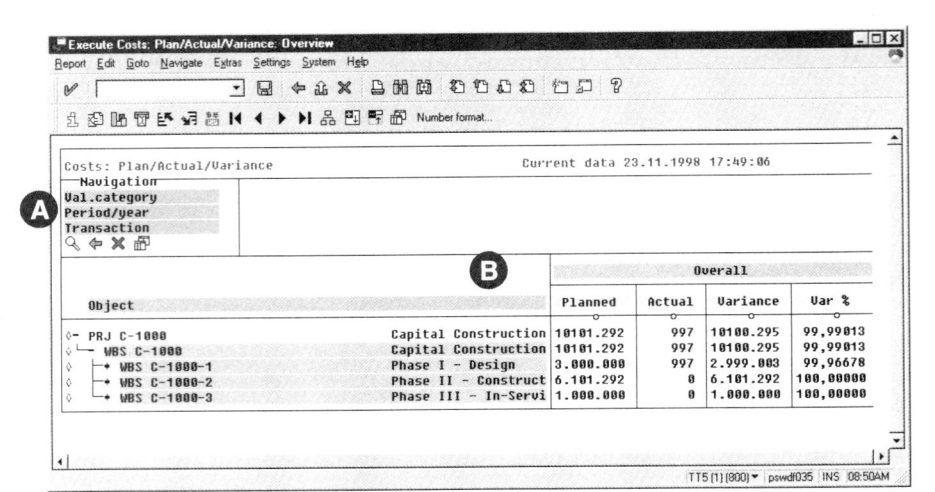

Cost Element Reporting—Plan vs. Actual

Quick Access To run this report, use one of the following access options:

Option 1: Menu Path
Logistics → Project management → Information system → Costs/rev/payments → Report selection
Costs → Plan-based → By cost elements → Act/plan/variance abs.% var

From the reporting tree, choose the following report:
Plan-based → By cost elements → Act/plan/variance abs.% var.

Option 2: Transaction Code
In the *Command* field, enter transaction **PS91** and choose Enter. Then, from the reporting tree, choose *Plan-based* → *By cost elements* → *Act/plan/variance abs.% var.*

Purpose This report lists the planned and actual costs (by project cost object) for each cost element. It also compares the variance and displays the variance amount in both absolute and percentage terms.

Prerequisites You must enter a value for the *Controlling Area* the first time you run this report. You will need to change the *Controlling area* again only if it changes for subsequent reports. After you enter *Controlling area*, you see the *Database profile*. The *Database profile* determines what information from the Project System will be viewed.

Integration This report only lists the cost for the object not the structure, as described in the previous report.

In this report, you can drill down to the line-item detail of a given cost element and find all costs for the project object entered in the selection screen. If the project is used in the selection screen, all costs listed are for the entire project by cost element.

Features The selection screen of this report includes:
- Execute
- Execute and Save
- Report parameters (that is, fiscal year, to/from period, and plan version)
- Dynamic selection options
- Database profile
- Version reporting
- Subproject reporting

Section 13: Project System Reports
Cost Element Reporting—Plan vs. Actual

Next Steps   This report includes data from cost planning and actual cost postings to WBS elements and network activities.

Guided Tour

Example: Display a simple listing of project costs by cost element.

To access the first screen for this report, choose

Logistics → Project management → Information system → Costs/rev/payments → Report selection

Costs → Plan-based → By cost elements → Act/plan/variance abs.% var.

Note: In this example we are using *Controlling area* 2000 and *Database profile* #1.

1. Under *Project information system*, enter **COSTING** in *Project*.
2. Choose *Execute*.

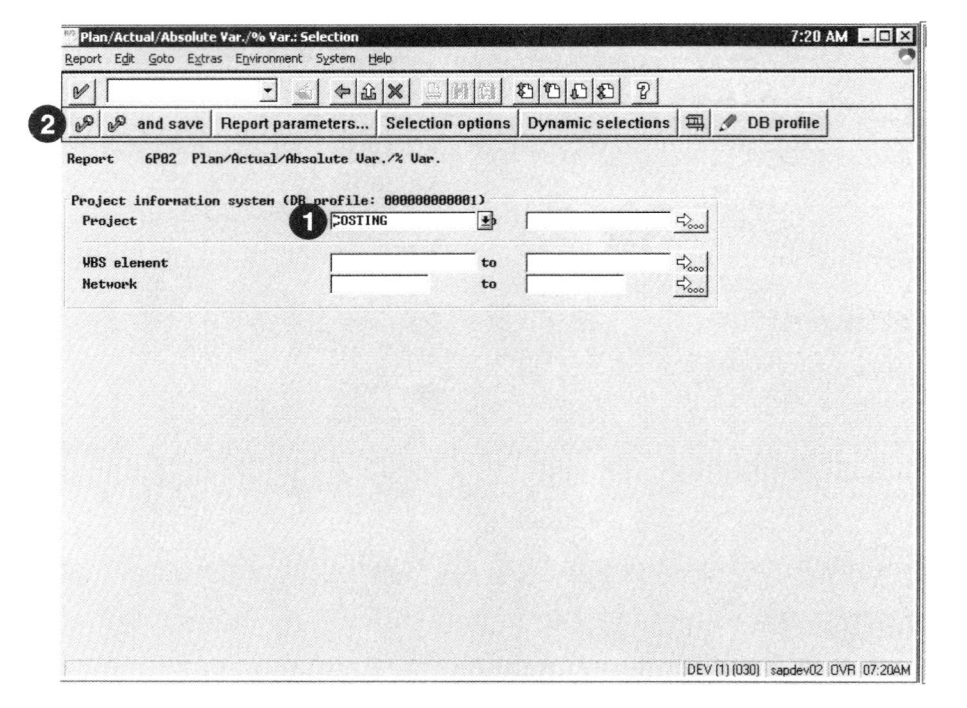

Section 13: Project System Reports
Cost Element Reporting—Plan vs. Actual

The first screen of the report shows all cost objects and includes:
- Fiscal year and period
- Cost elements and description
- Cost elements group
- Plan/Act – version

3. Choose *Next Columns*.

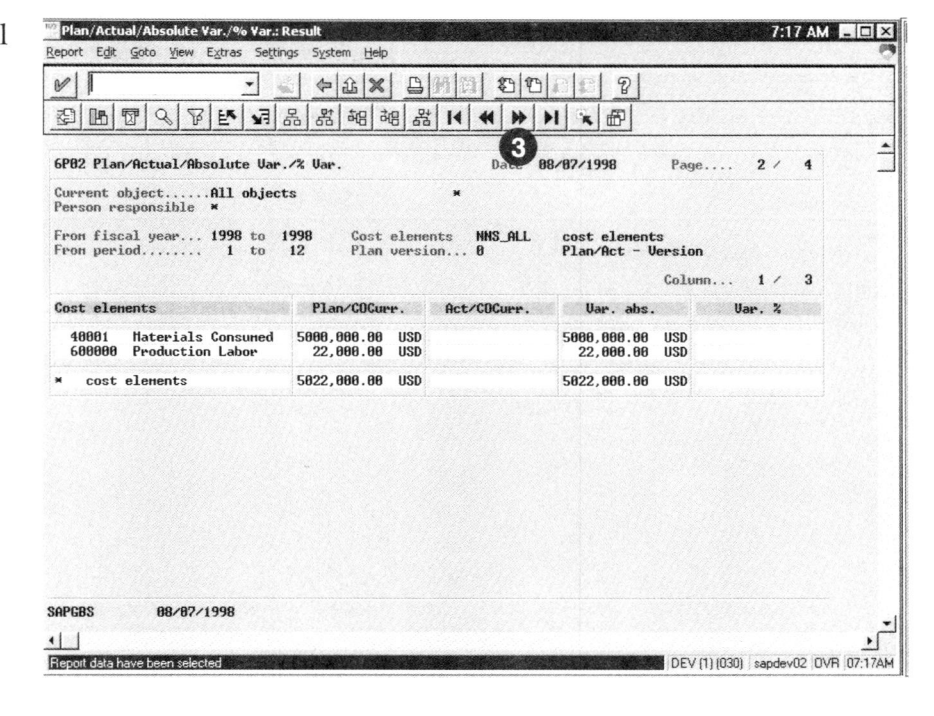

The report moves to the next set of columns which show:
- Project plan
- Appended order plan
- Apportioned order plan
- Actual costs

4. Choose *Next Columns*.

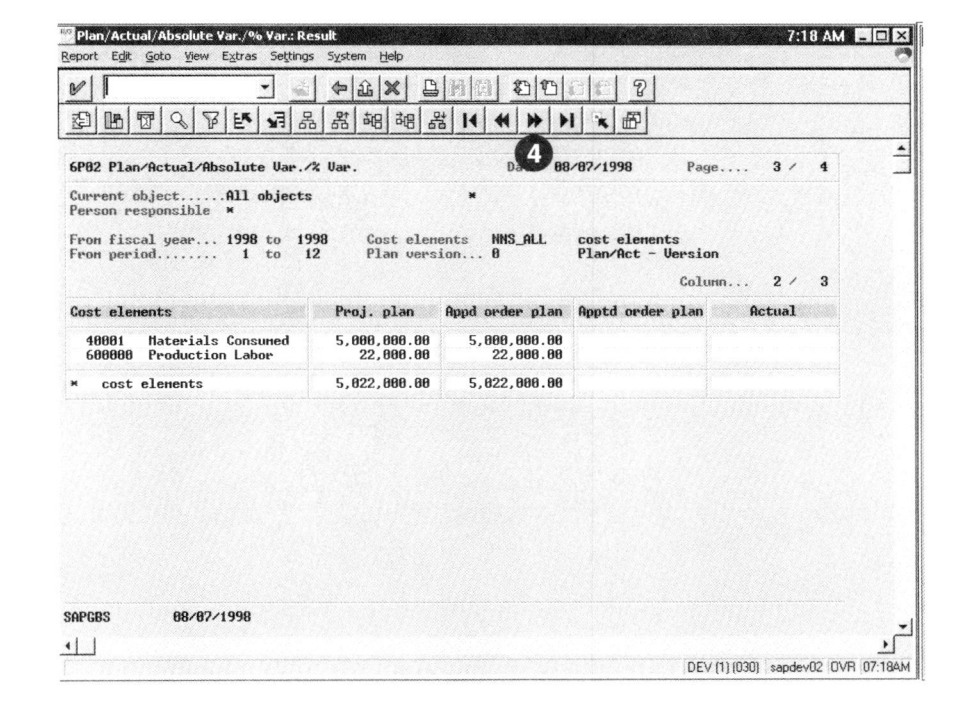

Commonly Used Reports: Illustrations and Perspectives

13–7

Section 13: Project System Reports

Cost Element Reporting—Plan vs. Actual

The report moves to the final set of columns which show:
- Planned quantity
- Actual quantity
- Absolute variance
- Percentage variance

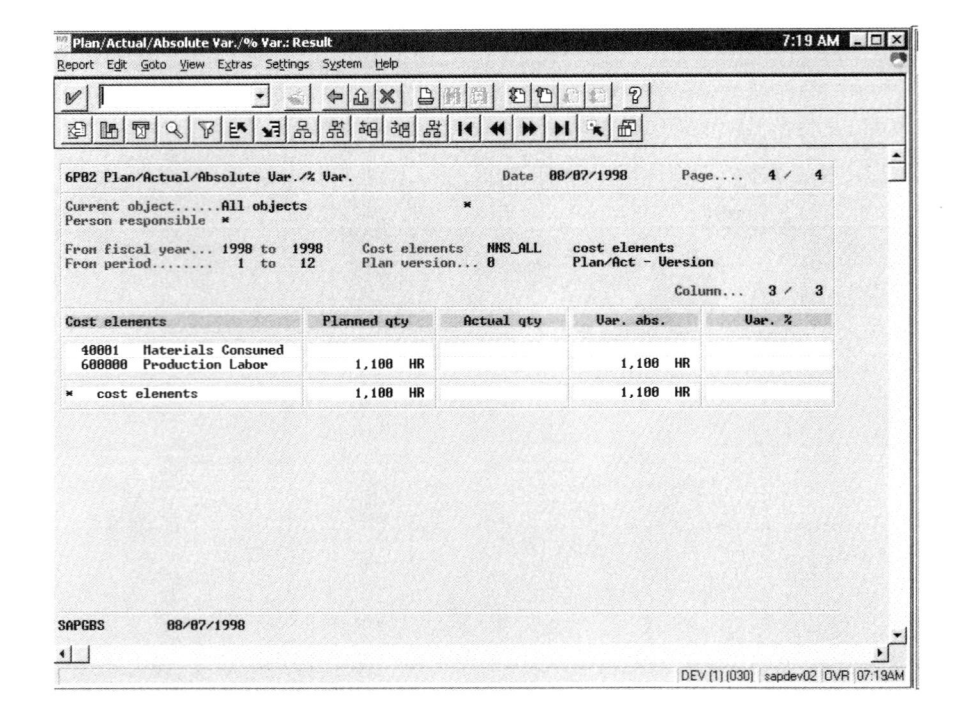

Budget Reporting—Budget vs. Plan/Actual/Commitments

Quick Access To run this report, use one of the following access options:

Option 1: Menu Path
Logistics → *Project management* → *Information system* → *Costs/rev/payments* → *Report selection*

Option 2: Program Name
Choose *System* → *Services* → *Reporting* and enter **RKP8928** in the *Program* field. Then, choose *Execute* to run the report.

Note: The report shown here is a custom report which was created with reference to other functions in the Project Systems module. It is included here for illustration purposes only.

Purpose This report lists project costs and compares them to the budget. It includes commitments and remaining order plan costs.

Prerequisites You must enter a value in the *Controlling Area* the first time you run this report. You will need to change the *Controlling area* again only if it changes for subsequent reports. After you enter *Controlling area*, you see the *Database profile*. The *Database profile* determines what information from the Project System will be viewed.

Integration In this report, you can use value categories to find all (planned or actual) costs based on the type of cost. Value categories are defined during configuration and consist of cost elements or cost element groups. Using value categories, you can list costs for a given project object, such as a *Work Breakdown Schedule* element (WBS), by the cost element groups instead of each cost element. Examples of cost element groups might include:

- Labor costs
- Material costs
- Overhead costs
- Other costs

You can also list the cost by transaction currency instead of by project currency, delimit cost by year or period, and drill down to the transaction that created the cost.

Section 13: Project System Reports
Budget Reporting—Budget vs. Plan/Actual/Commitments

Features

The selection screen of this report includes:

- Variants
- Dynamic selection options
- Filters
- Project
- WBS element
- Network
- Subproject
- Project version
- Cost plan version

Next Steps

This report includes data from cost planning and actual cost postings to WBS elements and network activities.

Guided Tour

Example: Display a simple listing of costs, commitments, and budget for a project.

Note: In this example we are using *Controlling area* 2000 and *Database profile* #1.

1. Under *Project information system*, enter **0681N** in *Project*.
2. Choose *Execute*.

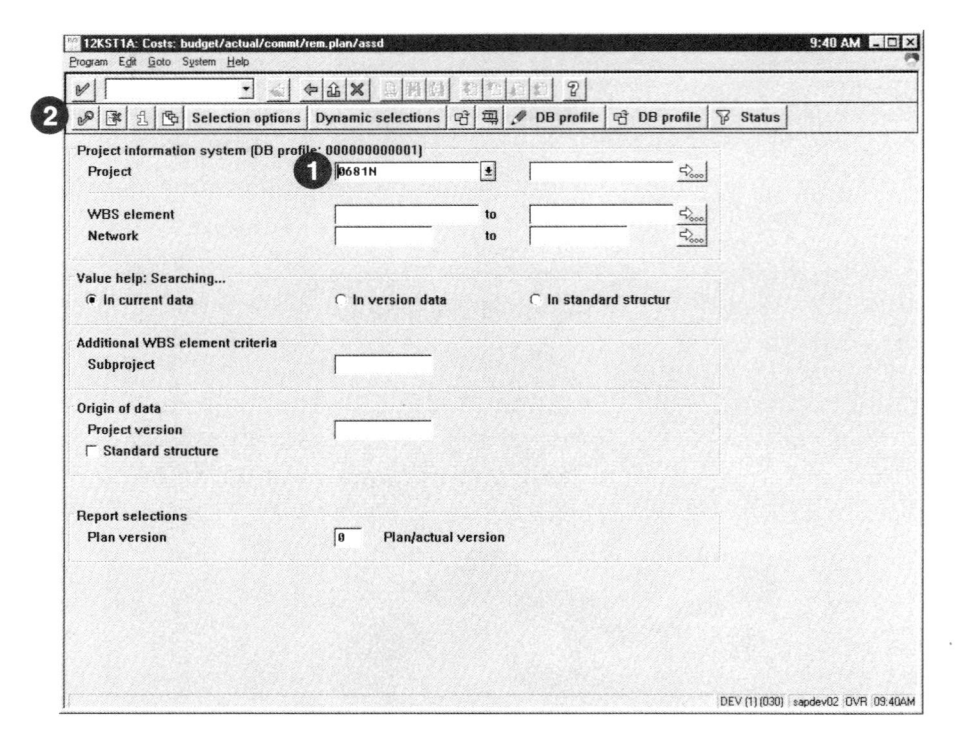

13–10 Reporting Made Easy

Section 13: Project System Reports
Budget Reporting—Budget vs. Plan/Actual/Commitments

A   This section of the screen shows possible navigation by:
    - Value category
    - Period/year
    - Transaction currency
    - Transaction

B   This section of the screen shows listings of project objects and their descriptions as well as the overall:
    - Project budget
    - Actual costs
    - Open Commitments
    - Remaining order plan
    - Assigned costs (sum of actual and open commitments)

3. Choose *Next Columns*.

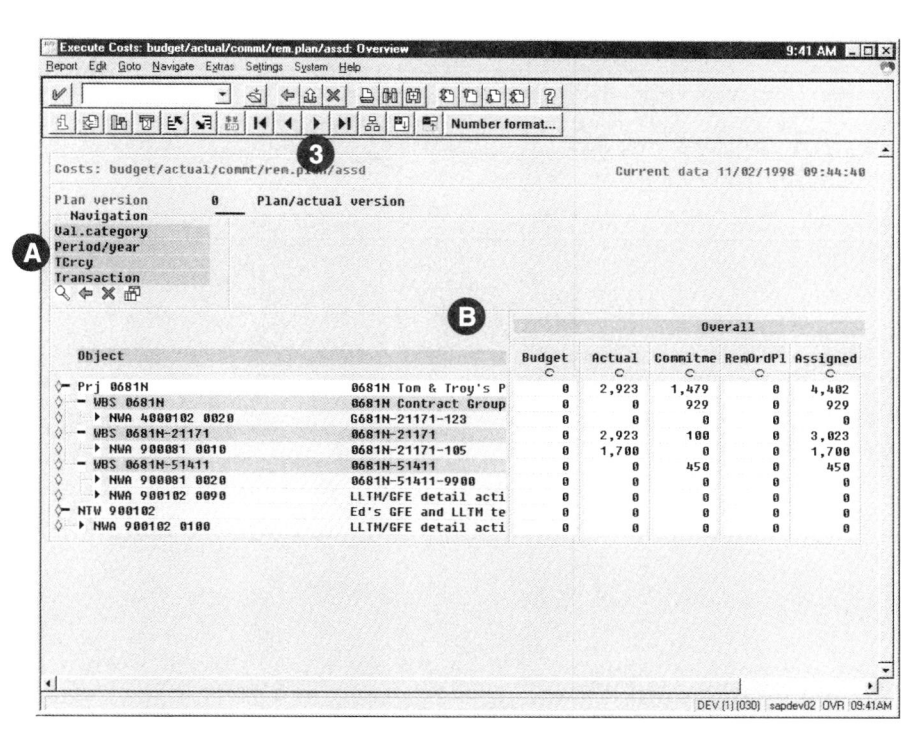

The report moves to the next section to show detail for previous project years.

4. Choose *Next Columns*.

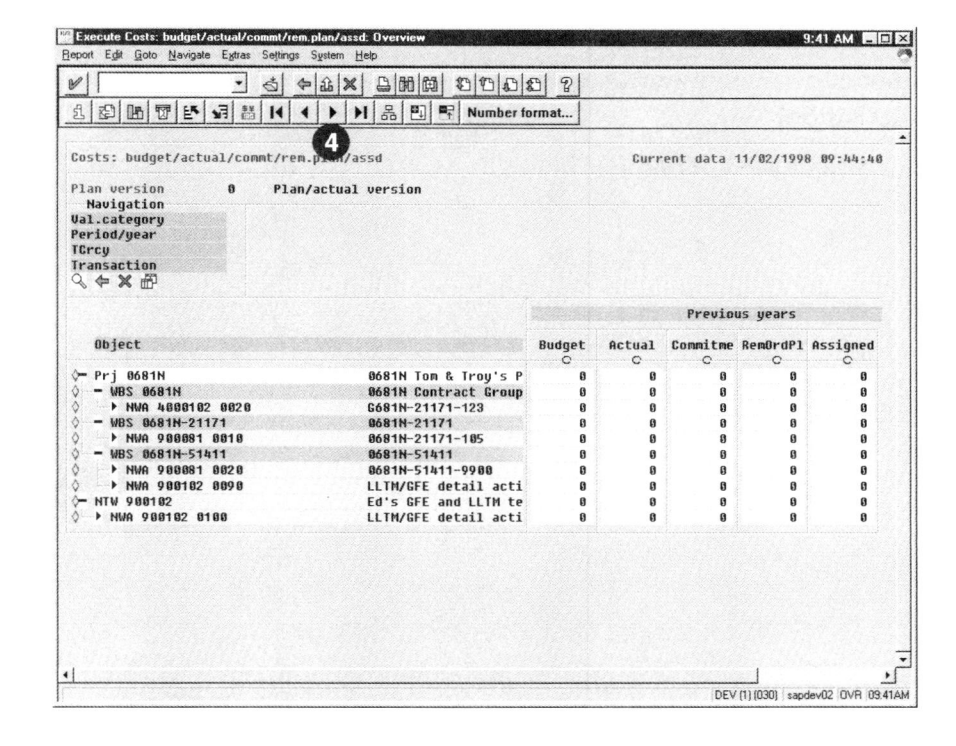

Commonly Used Reports: Illustrations and Perspectives

Section 13: Project System Reports
Budget Reporting—Budget vs. Plan/Actual/Commitments

The report moves to the next section to show annual views of the project.

5. Click on the *Val. Category* navigation bar to select it.

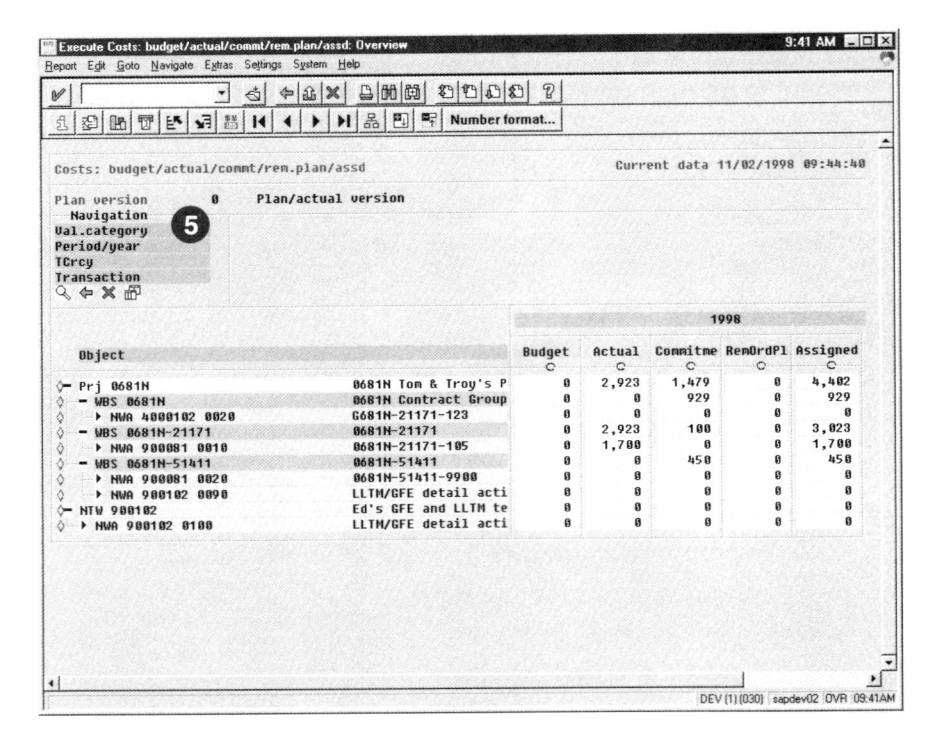

The diamond and navigation bars change color to indicate hot-spot activation.

6. Select *WBS 0681N-21171*.

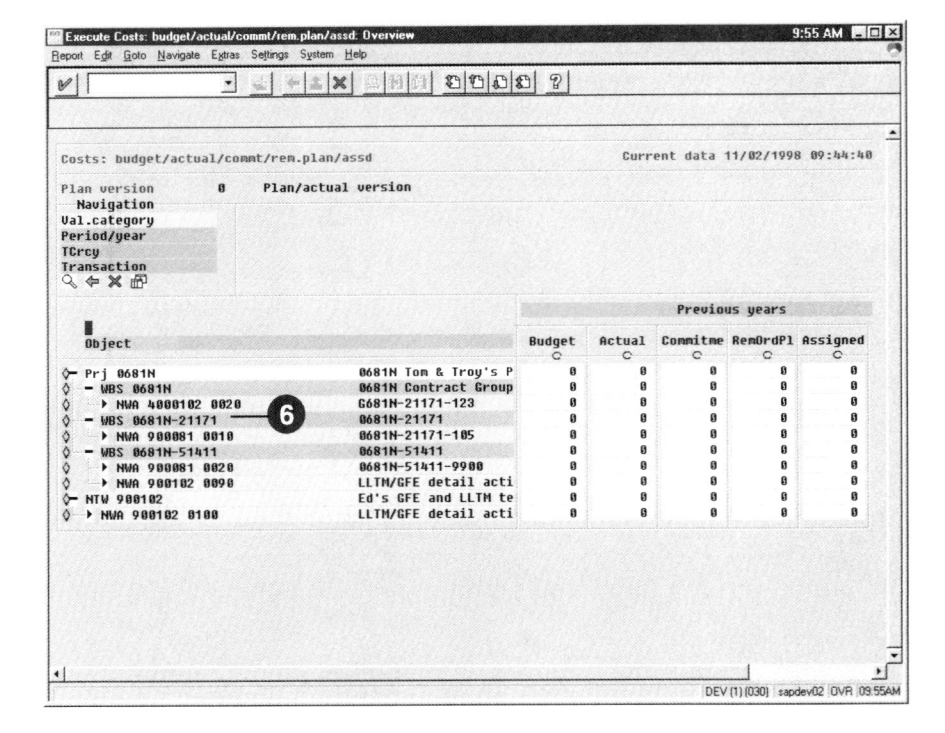

Section 13: Project System Reports
Budget Reporting—Budget vs. Plan/Actual/Commitments

The report moves to the final set of columns that show the costs by value category for the overall project.

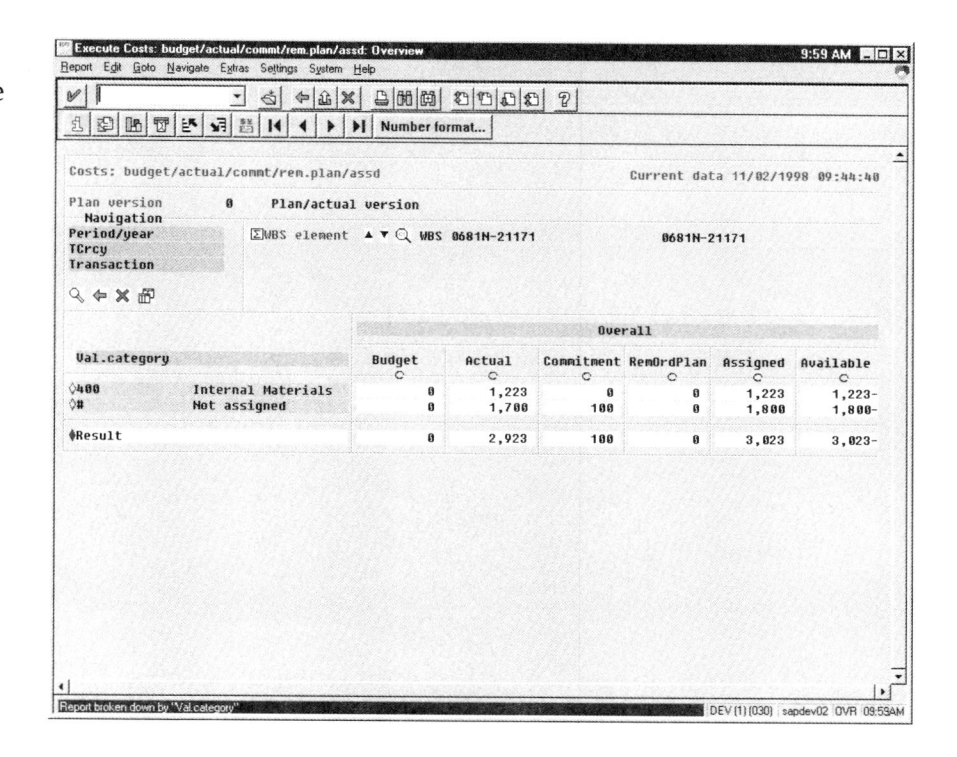

```
Costs: budget/actual/commt/rem.plan/assd          Current data 11/02/1998 09:44:40

Plan version        0      Plan/actual version
  Navigation
Period/year               ΣWBS element  ▲ ▼ Q  WBS 0681N-21171        0681N-21171
TCrcy
Transaction
```

		Overall					
Val.category		Budget	Actual	Commitment	RemOrdPlan	Assigned	Available
◇400	Internal Materials	0	1,223	0	0	1,223	1,223-
◇#	Not assigned	0	1,700	100	0	1,800	1,800-
♦Result		0	2,923	100	0	3,023	3,023-

Commonly Used Reports: Illustrations and Perspectives

Section 14: Quality Management Reports

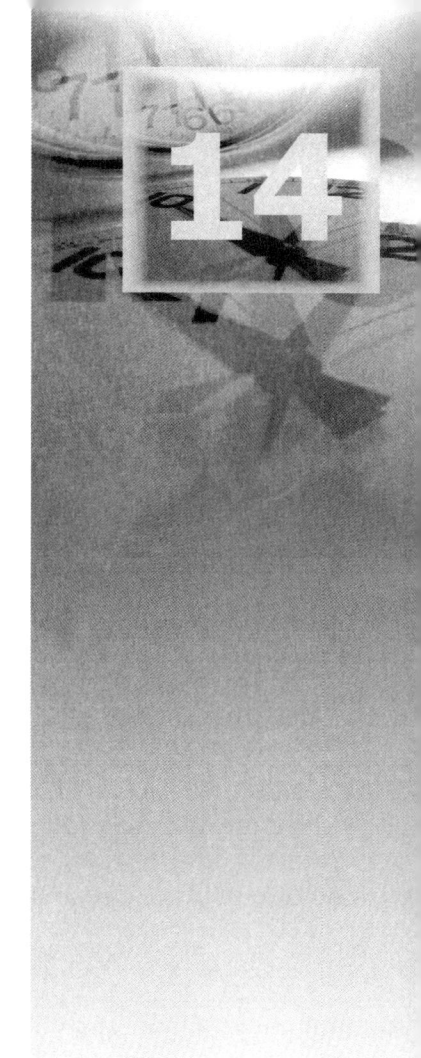

Contents

Inspection Lots Without Completion 14–2
Inspection Lots Without Usage Decision 14–6
Inspection Lot Selection 14–9

Section 14: Quality Management Reports
Inspection Lots Without Completion

Inspection Lots Without Completion

Quick Access To run this report, use one of the following access options:

Option 1: Menu Path

Logistics → *Quality management* → *Quality inspection* → *Worklist* → *Inspection lot completion* → *Inspection completion*

Option 2: Program Name

Choose *System* → *Services* → *Reporting* and enter **RQEVAM10** in the *Program* field. Then, choose *Execute* to run the report.

Option 3: Transaction Code

In the *Command* field, enter transaction **QVM1** and choose *Enter*.

Purpose This report provides a list of inspection lots having incomplete status.

Quality inspectors would use this report to view inspection lots, change inspection data, or record a usage decision for a specified inspection lot.

Prerequisites Inspection lots having incomplete status must exist before you to run this report. In addition, you may choose to use additional selection criteria to produce a more meaningful report.

Integration From this report, you can display an individual inspection lot, or the inspection lot's inspection results. You can also process an inspection lot to complete the inspection. Each inspection lot includes:
- Inspection lot number
- Plant responsible for the lot
- Dates related to inspection
- Status of the lot

Since this report allows users to change data, proper user authorizations need to be carefully considered.

Section 14: Quality Management Reports
Inspection Lots Without Completion

Features

The selection screen for this report contains parameters that affect the output. You can use display variants (for example, *1STANDARD*), user variants, and dynamic selections to change the way the output is viewed.

The output of this report also has such features as :

- Variants
- Execution (and print) in background
- Dynamic filtering of output (by column): To narrow the displayed results, place the cursor on a column, then *Edit → Set filter* (Ctrl-Shift+F2)
- Sorting capability (by column): Select a column, then *Edit → Sort in ascending/descending order* (Ctrl+Shift+F5/F4)
- Column width optimization: Select a column, then *Settings → Columns → Optimize width*
- Data statistics for the output: *Settings → List status* (Ctrl+F11)
- Per inspection lot
- Inspection lot number
- Plant which owns each inspection lot
- Material for inspection
- Number of open inspection characteristics

Next Steps

- List incomplete inspection lots
- Display inspection results
- Display inspection lots
- Complete inspection lots

Section 14: Quality Management Reports
Inspection Lots Without Completion

Guided Tour

Example: Display a list of all "incomplete" inspection lots in a plant for a given year.

To access the first screen for this report, choose

Logistics → Quality management → Quality inspection → Worklist → Inspection lot completion → Inspection completion.

1. Enter **1000** in *Plant*.

2. Enter **1STANDARD** in *Display variant* to select a smaller set of fields than the program would otherwise show.

3. Enter **3** in *Monitor control* to show a format which highlights the status of inspection lots.

4. Choose *Execute*.

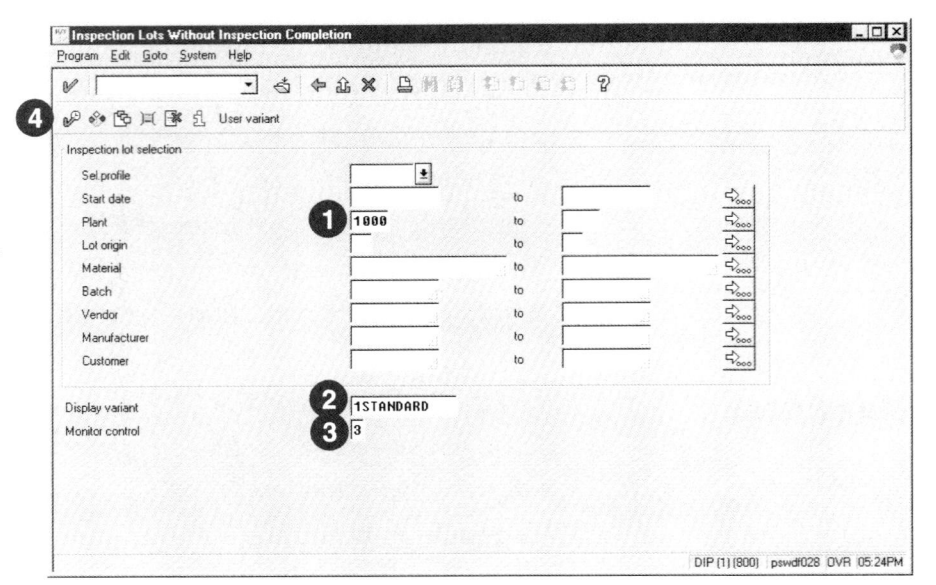

14–4

Reporting Made Easy

Section 14: Quality Management Reports
Inspection Lots Without Completion

This screen shows each inspection lot listing.

The first column shows the status of each inspection lot:

- A red light indicates that no inspection has taken place and the start date has passed.
- A yellow light indicates that the inspection has begun, but has not yet been completed.
- A green light indicates that the start date has not yet been reached.

The last column shows the system status for each lot (which is within each inspection lot):

- *REL* indicates that an inspection lot has been released.
- *CALC* indicates that sample sizes have been calculated.

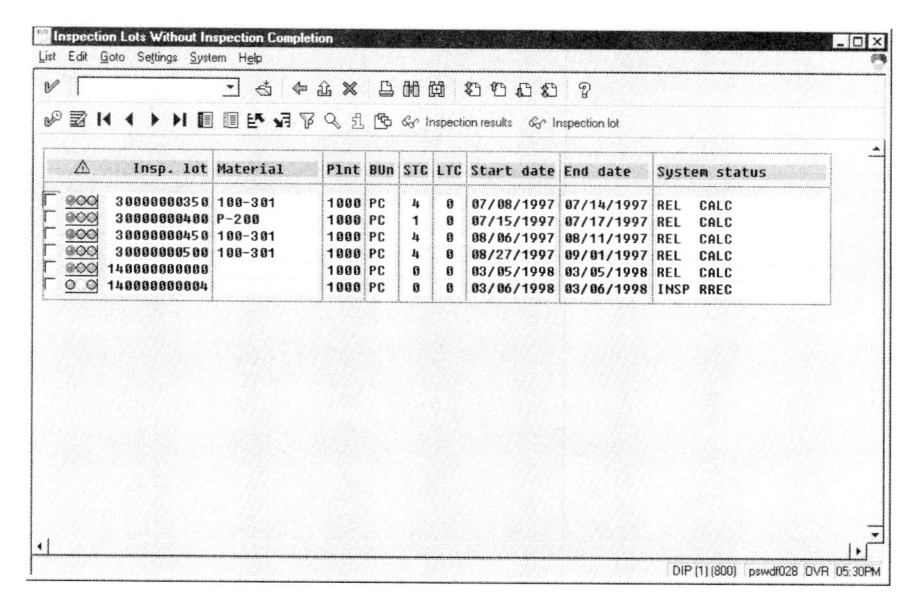

Section 14: Quality Management Reports
Inspection Lots Without Usage Decision

Inspection Lots Without Usage Decision

Quick Access   To run this report, use one of the following access options:

Option 1: Menu Path

Logistics → Quality management → Quality inspection → Worklist → Inspection lot completion → Usage decision

Option 2: Program Name

Choose *System→ Services→ Reporting* and enter **RQEVAM30** in the *Program* field. Then, choose *Execute* to run the report.

Option 3: Transaction Code

In the *Command* field, enter transaction **QVM3** and choose *Enter*.

Purpose   This report shows a list of inspection lots for which a usage decision has not been completed. Usage decisions, usually made after the results of QM inspection are recorded, involve deciding what to do with the inspection lot (for example, use, scrap, additional sampling, etc.).

This report should be used with caution because it is more than a "display report"; it allows users to change inspection lot data. Therefore, authorizations should be used to limit user access to the inspection lot data.

Prerequisites   Inspection lots for which a usage decision is pending need to exist before you run this report.

You should also limit the selection criteria to restrict the inspection lot listing.

Integration   This report lets you view a list of inspection lots for which usage decisions are required. You can display an individual inspection lot or the results of an inspection lot, as well as process an inspection lot to complete an inspection.

For each inspection lot, the following information is shown:
- Inspection lot number
- Plant responsible for the lot
- Dates related to inspection
- Status of the lot

This report allows you to change data. Therefore, carefully consider your choice of user authorizations.

Section 14: Quality Management Reports
Inspection Lots Without Usage Decision

Features

The selection screen for this report contains parameters that affect the output. You can use display variants (for example, *1STANDARD*), user variants, and dynamic selections to change the way the output is viewed.

The output of this report includes:

- Variants
- Execution (and print) in background
- Dynamic filtering of output (by column): To narrow the displayed results, position the cursor on a column, then choose *Edit → Set filter* (Ctrl+Shift+F2).
- Sorting capability (by column): Select a column, then choose *Edit → Sort in ascending/descending order* (Ctrl+Shift+F5/F4).
- Column width optimization: Select a column, then choose *Settings → Columns → Optimize width*.
- Data statistics for the output: *Settings → List status* (Ctrl+F11)
- Per inspection lot
- Inspection lot number
- Plant which owns each inspection lot
- Material for inspection
- Number of open inspection characteristics

Next Steps

This report is more than a display report because you can record a usage decision for an inspection lot and change data.

From this report you can:

- List incomplete inspection lots
- Display inspection results
- Display inspection lots
- Complete inspection lots
- Enter usage decisions

Section 14: Quality Management Reports
Inspection Lots Without Usage Decision

Guided Tour

Example: Display a list of all incomplete inspection lots for which a usage decision has not been made.

To access the first screen for this report, choose

Logistics → Quality management → Quality inspection → Worklist → Inspection lot completion → Usage decision.

To narrow your search, you can specify various selection criteria on this screen.

1. Enter **1STANDARD** in *Display variant*.
2. Enter **5** in *Monitor control* to display a format that highlights the status of inspection lots.
3. Choose *Execute*.

This screen shows each inspection lot listing.

The first column shows the status of each inspection lot:

- A red light indicates that no inspection has taken place and the start date has passed.
- A yellow light indicates that the inspection has begun, but has not yet been completed.
- A green light indicates that the start date has not yet been reached.

The last column shows the system status for each lot (which is within each inspection lot):

- *REL* indicates that an inspection lot has been released.
- *CALC* indicates that sample sizes have been calculated.

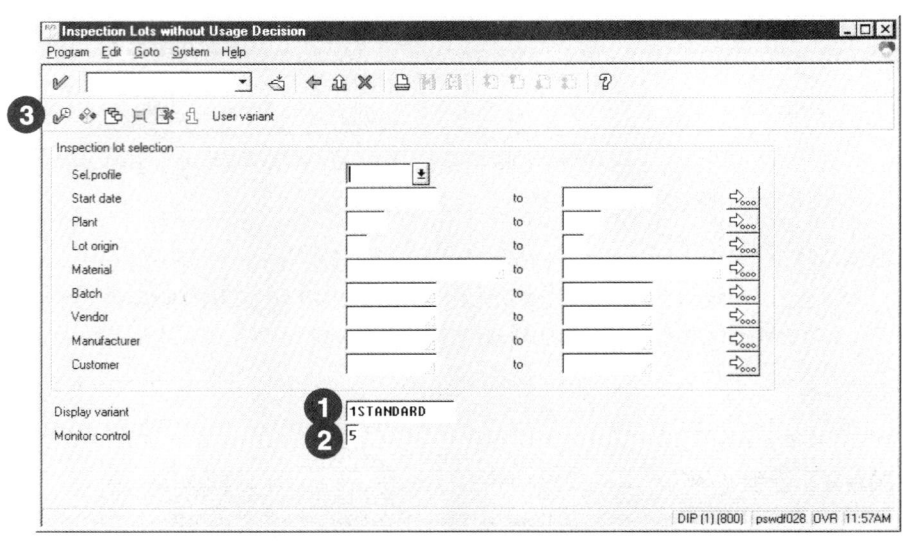

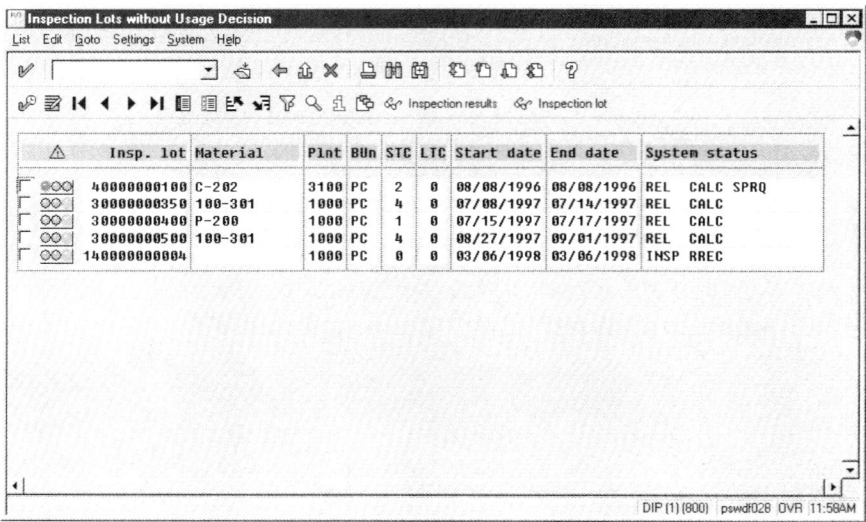

14–8

Reporting Made Easy

Inspection Lot Selection

Quick Access To run this report, use one of the following access options:

Option 1: Menu Path

Logistics → *Quality management* → *Quality inspection* → *Worklist* → *Inspection* → *Display data*

Option 2: Program Name

Choose *System* → *Services* → *Reporting* and enter `RQEEAL10` in the *Program* field. Then, choose *Execute* to run the report.

Option 3: Transaction Code

In the *Command* field, enter transaction `QA33` and choose *Enter*.

Purpose This report shows the inspection lots of different statuses across several business units.

This report should be used with caution because it is more than a "display report"; it allows users to change inspection lot data. Therefore, authorizations should be used to limit user access to the inspection lot data.

Prerequisites Inspection lots having incomplete status must exist before you to run this report and you must enter a date-range (for when the inspection lots were created) in the selection criteria.

Integration From this report, you can:

- Display or maintain an inspection lot
- Display or maintain recorded inspection lot results
- Display or maintain inspection defect data
- Display or maintain inspection lot usage decisions

Inspection Lot Selection

Features

The selection screen for this report contains parameters that affect the output. You can use display variants (for example, *1STANDARD*), user variants, and dynamic selections to change the way the output is viewed.

The output of this report includes:

- Execution (and print) in background
- Dynamic filtering of output (by column) after the program has been executed: Position the cursor on a column, then choose *Edit → Set filter* (Ctrl+Shift+F2).
- Sorting capability (by column): Select a column, then choose *Edit → Sort in ascending/descending order* (Ctrl+Shift+F5 / F4).
- Column width optimization: Select a column, then choose *Settings → Columns → Optimize width.*
- Graphics (for each column)
- Refresh display
- Spreadsheet downloads to Microsoft Excel
- Per inspection lot:
  - Inspection lot number
  - Plant which owns each inspection lot
- Material for inspection
- Number of open inspection characteristics

Next Steps

All features of an inspection lot are provided in a list by double-clicking on an inspection lot line. This generates a more compact list than selecting *Display inspection lot*.

Section 14: Quality Management Reports
Inspection Lot Selection

Guided Tour

Example: Display a listing of inspection lots for a given date range.

To access the first screen for this report, choose

Logistics → Quality management → Quality inspection → Worklist → Inspection → Display data.

1. Enter a date range (for example, **04/01/1997** to **08/31/1997**) in *Lot created*.

2. Enter a material (for example, **100-301**) in *Material* and select **CH_1302** using the multiple selection icon.

3. Enter **1STANDARD** in *Display variant*.

4. Enter **4** in *Monitor control* to show a format which highlights the status of inspection lots.

5. Choose *Execute*.

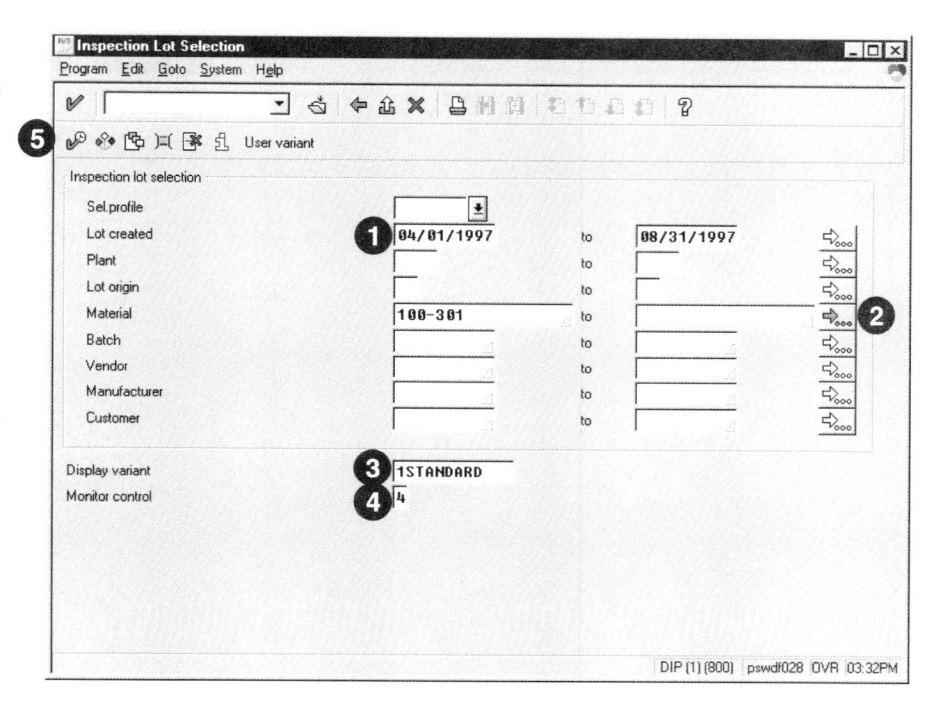

This screen shows a list of each inspection lot, including:

- Lot number
- Material number
- Plant
- Open inspection characteristics
- Other

6. To view a histogram of the breakdown of lot distribution, select a column heading.

7. Choose *Graphics*.

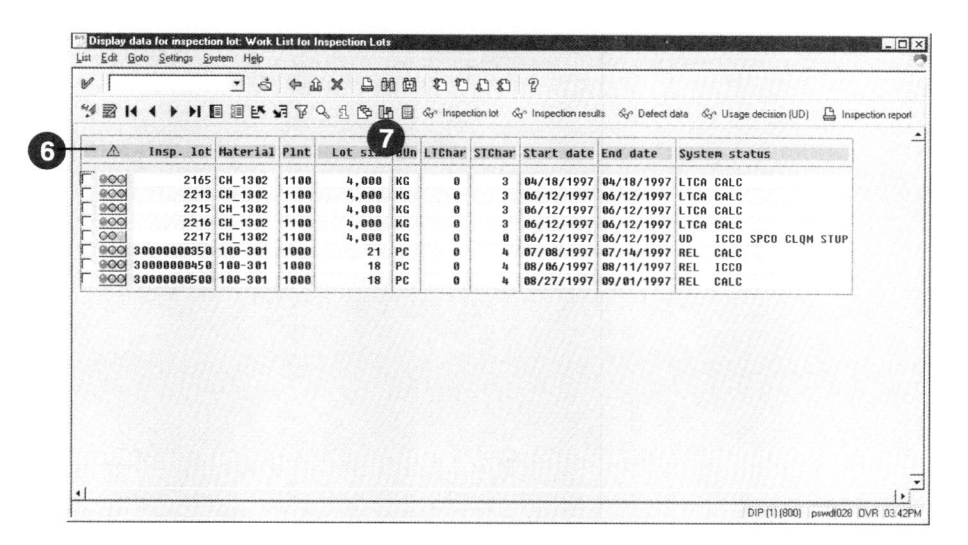

Commonly Used Reports: Illustrations and Perspectives

14–11

Section 14: Quality Management Reports
Inspection Lot Selection

This screen shows the histogram with a breakdown of the number of inspection lots listed per material.

For illustration purposes, only two materials are shown in this example. For plants with a large list of materials open for inspection, the histogram could show which materials have the most outstanding inspections.

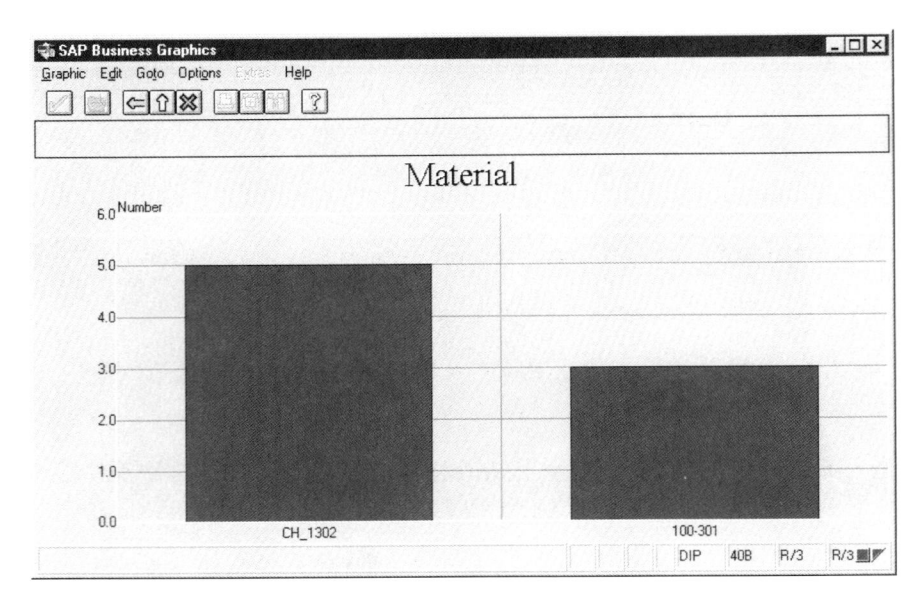

Section 15: Warehouse Management Reports

Contents

Stock Overview 15–2

Material Stock List 15–7

List of Posting Change Notices 15–11

Empty Storage Bins 15–18

Stock Overview

Quick Access To run this report, use one of the following access options:

Option 1: Menu Path

Logistics → *Materials management* → *Warehouse management* → *Master data* → *Material* → *Stock* → *Stock overview*

Option 2: Program Name

Choose *System* → *Services* → *Reporting* and enter **RLLS2600** in the *Program* field. Then, choose *Execute* to run the report.

Option 3: Transaction Code

In the *Command* field, enter transaction **LS26** and choose *Enter*.

Purpose This report shows the total stock for a material in a warehouse.

The general stock overview report in Materials Management differs from this report in that it shows general stock figures across many business units (company codes, plants and storage locations). However, you can access each of these reports from the other.

Warehouse staff would use this report to find material stock at locations down to each physical bin.

Prerequisites A warehouse and material number must exist before you to run this report.

In addition, you may choose to use additional selection criteria to produce a more meaningful report.

Integration This report allows access to other reports, including:
- Bin stock report
- Single bin display report
- Materials management stock overview report
- Stock reports for other materials

Features

This report is different from many other standard R/3 reports in that it does not use any variants. The entry screen requires only a warehouse and material number. You can minimize the output by entering additional selection criteria such as a plant, storage location, and storage type.

Entering a plant, storage location and storage type is an important consideration because:

- A material might be "owned" by several plants, but held in just one warehouse. Therefore, it is important to distinguish which material belongs to which plant.
- A material can be "held" in several storage types. A storage type may be a distinct storage area (for example, a QA inspection area), a goods receipt dock or a high-rack storage. However, stock can be on a shipping dock (another storage type), and you should consider whether or not stock is available (regardless of configuration status) before allocating it.

Next Steps

This report shows stock levels for a material in a warehouse. The display is separated according to the storage types where the material is contained—plants and storage locations. Since this report is tightly integrated with many other reports, you can select further data for review.

The output of this report includes :

- Material stock data listed by storage type, plant, and storage location
- Summary material stock information
- Basic material information

This report does not allow changes to the database.

Section 15: Warehouse Management Reports
Stock Overview

Guided Tour

Example 1: Display a list of a material in stock in a warehouse.

To access the first screen for this report, choose

Logistics → Materials management → Warehouse management → Master data → Material → Stock → Stock overview.

The selection screen for the report is shown.

1. Enter a warehouse number (for example, 001) in *Warehouse number*.

2. Enter a material (for example, 100-700) in *Material*.

3. Choose *Enter*.

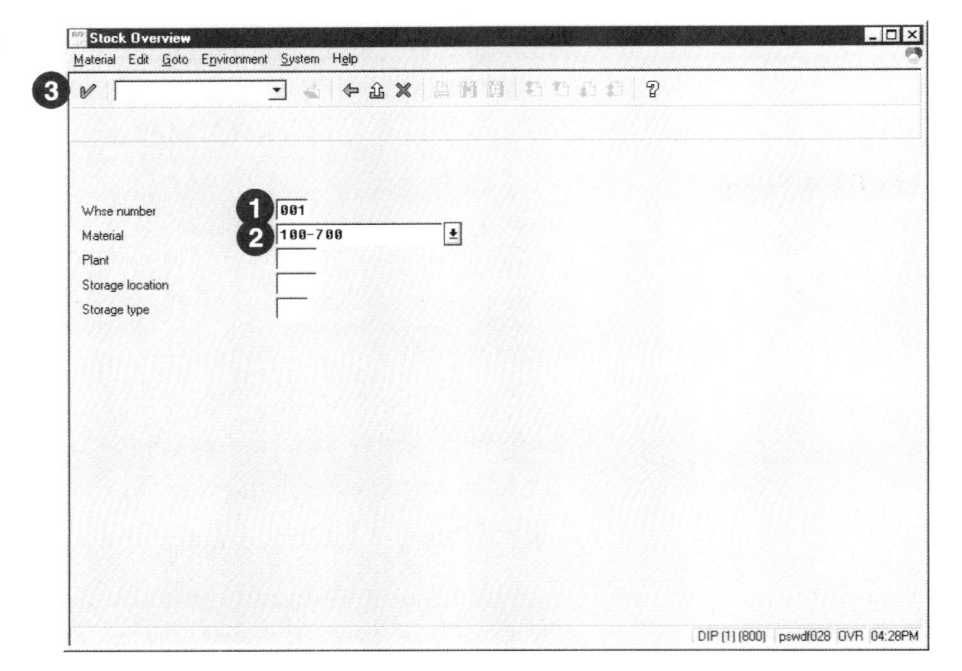

This screen shows general information about the warehouse and material.

In this example, there is a total stock quantity of: 57.6 square meters of the material in high-rack storage (storage type 001), 1.28 in production supply (storage type 100), and 2 in the good receiving area (storage type 902).

The listing also shows data listed as *For stock placement* or *For stock removal*. This means that stock will be shown in this report if it is in transit to bins, but has not yet reached the bins.

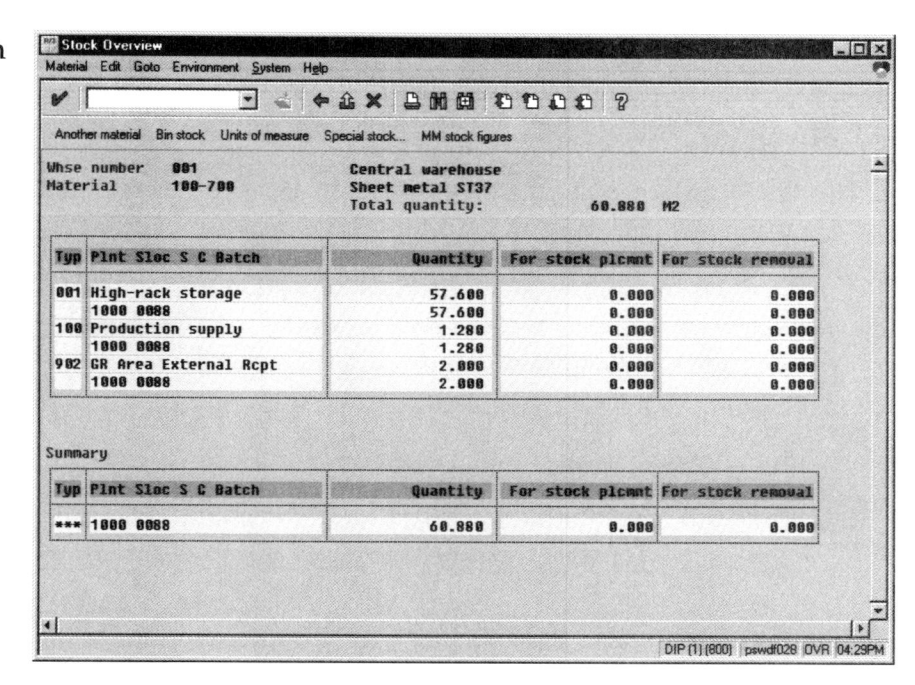

Example 2: Display a list of a material whose stock is being transferred.

Repeat steps 1 through 3 shown in Example 1 using material number **100-300**.

A display of a different material (for example, **100-300**) for the same plant shows a different situation. This time there is stock in transit from the goods receipt area to a bin in high-rack storage.

The stock shows 10 pieces are earmarked *For stock removal* from the goods receipt area and 10 pieces *For stock placement* into high-rack storage.

Note that the stock transfer also appears in the summary data.

1. Select the *High-rack storage* bins.
2. Choose *Bin stock* to view more information about these bins.

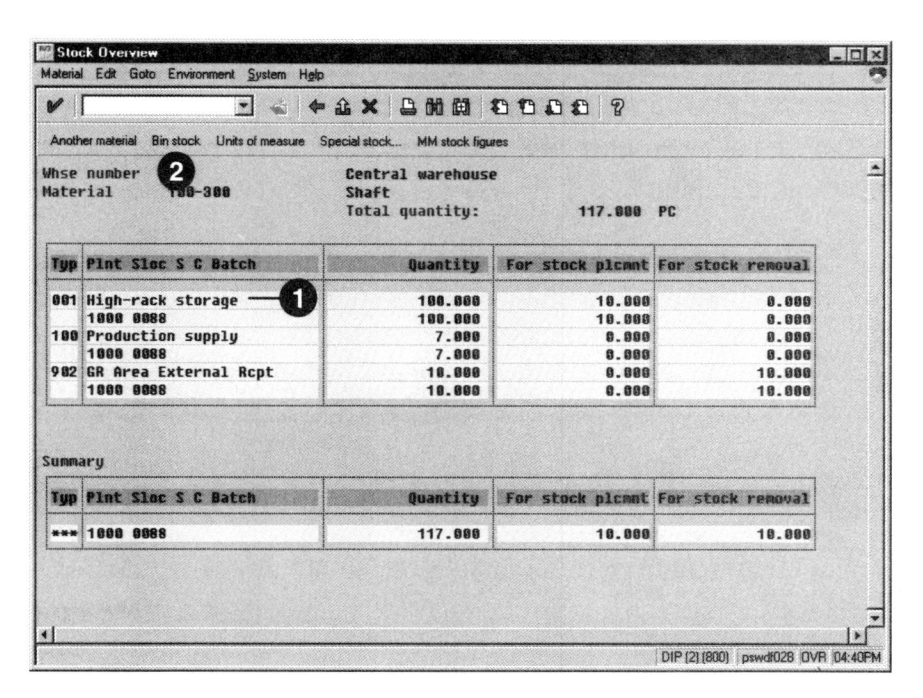

Section 15: Warehouse Management Reports
Stock Overview

This screen shows the bin stock. Twenty pieces of stock are in each of the first five bins (along with the date the stock was originally received). The last line shows that 10 pieces of the stock are due for placement into bin *03-02-01*.

3. Double-click bin *01-01-08* to view more information about it.

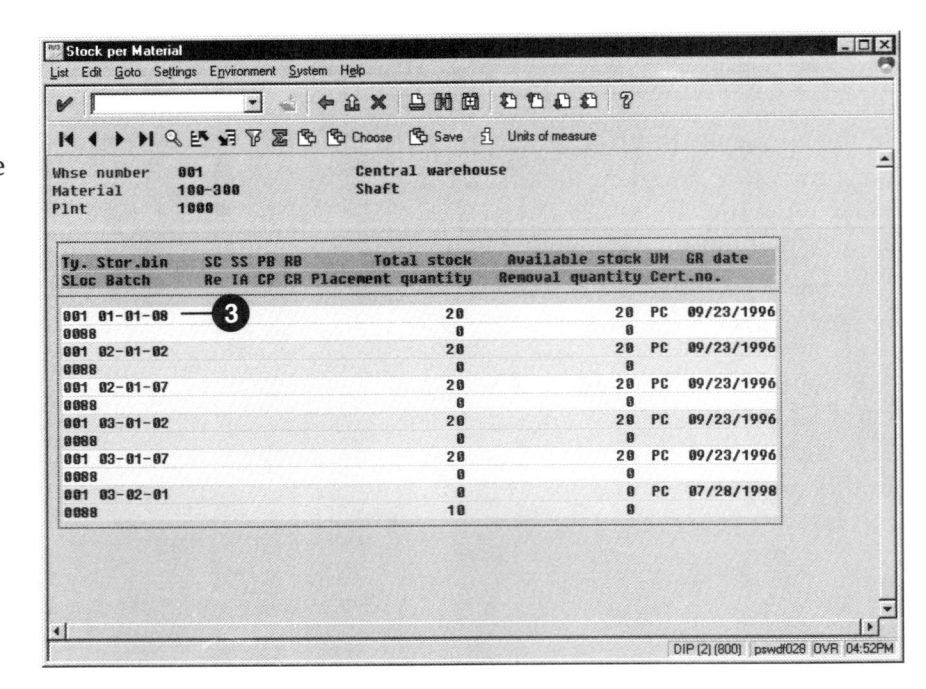

This screen shows more information about bin *01-01-08*.

General data for the bin includes:
- Bin type
- Capacity
- Blocking indicators

The rest of the bin's stock could also be found from this screen.

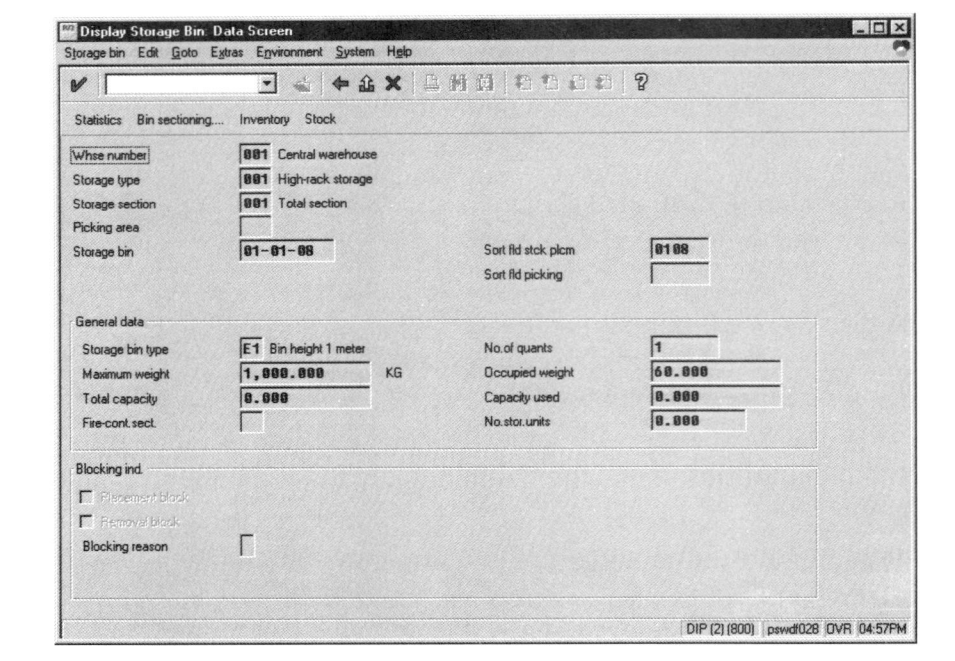

15–6

Reporting Made Easy

Material Stock List

Quick Access — To run this report, use one of the following access options:

Option 1: Menu Path

Logistics → Materials management → Warehouse management → Master data → Material → Evaluations → Stock list

Option 2: Program Name

Choose *System → Services → Reporting* and enter `RLS10020` in the *Program* field. Then, choose *Execute* to run the report.

Option 3: Transaction Code

In the *Command* field, enter transaction `LX02` and choose *Enter*.

Purpose — This report shows a list of all material stock contained in a warehouse. The display can include stock from various storage types and plants, and the list of material stock quantities can be sorted according to various sort criteria.

This report may be useful for tasks such as :
- Reporting on-hand stock listings
- Checking during physical inventories
- Record-keeping for end-of-month closings

Prerequisites — At a minimum, you must select a warehouse in the selection criteria before running this report. The report will only show stock data if stock exists in the warehouse.

Integration — This report allows access to other reports, including:
- Bin stock reports
- Material-bin stock reporting

Section 15: Warehouse Management Reports
Material Stock List

Features

This report is different from many other standard R/3 reports in that it does not use any variants. The entry screen requires only a warehouse and material number. You can minimize the output by entering additional selection criteria such as a plant, storage location, and storage type.

Entering a plant, storage location and storage type is an important consideration because:

- A material might be "owned" by several plants, but held in just one warehouse. Therefore, it is important to distinguish which material belongs to which plant.
- A material can be "held" in several storage types. A storage type may be a distinct storage area (for example, a QA inspection area), a goods receipt dock or a high-rack storage. However, stock can be on a shipping dock (another storage type), and you should consider whether or not stock is available (regardless of configuration status) before allocating it.

Next Steps

This report shows stock levels for a material in a warehouse. The display is separated according to the storage types where the material is contained—plants and storage locations. Since this report is tightly integrated with many other reports, you can select further data for review.

The output of this report includes :

- Material stock data listed by storage type, plant, and storage location
- Summary material stock information
- Basic material information

This report does not allow changes to the database.

Section 15: Warehouse Management Reports
Material Stock List

Guided Tour

Example: Display a stock list for a warehouse, sorted by the goods-receipt date.

To access the first screen for this report, choose

Logistics → Materials management → Warehouse management → Master data → Material → Evaluations → Stock list.

The selection screen is shown for the warehouse material stock list report.

1. Enter a warehouse number (for example, 001) in *Warehouse number*.
2. Enter 2 in *Sort indicator* to sort the output according to warehouse, plant, and goods receipt date.
3. Choose *Execute*.

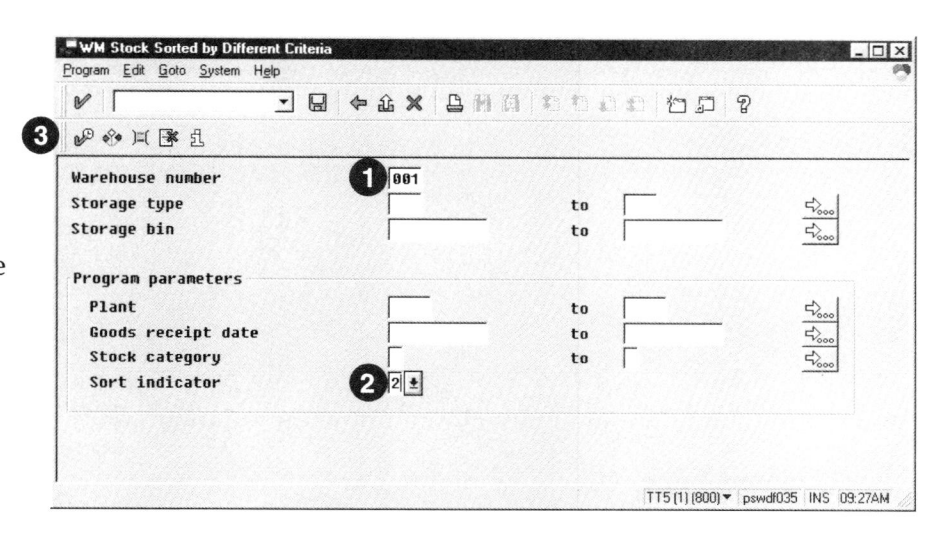

This screen shows materials data listed for materials within storage bins.

The storage bins containing the stock are listed in the last column.

To display the full report, you may need to move the horizontal scroll bar to the right to see the rest of the data.

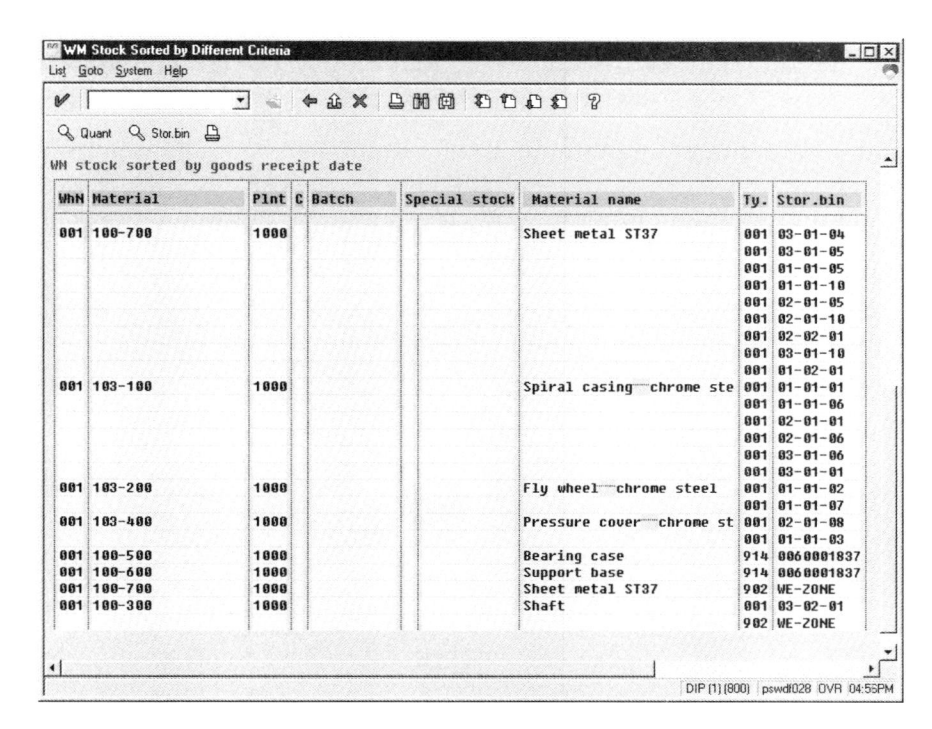

Section 15: Warehouse Management Reports
Material Stock List

This screen shows the far right side of the previous screen which includes:
- Available stock information
- Goods receipt dates of the material quantities.

You can change the sorting in this display using sort indicator selections on the initial screen.

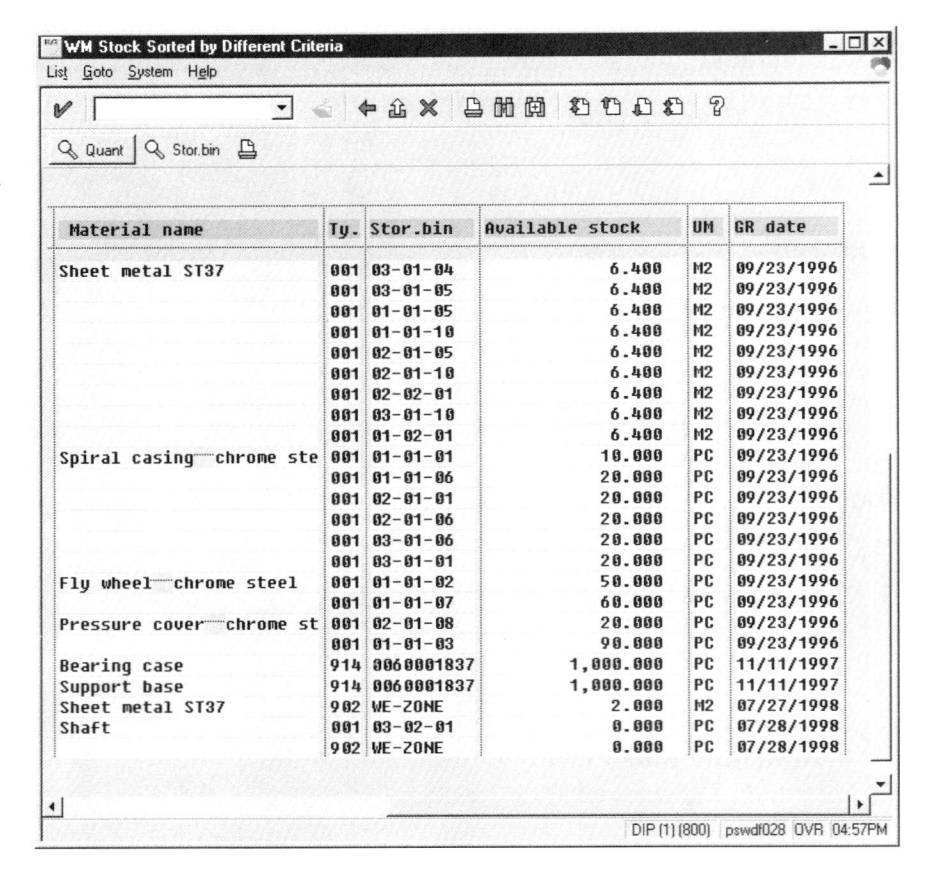

Material name	Ty.	Stor.bin	Available stock	UM	GR date
Sheet metal ST37	001	03-01-04	6.400	M2	09/23/1996
	001	03-01-05	6.400	M2	09/23/1996
	001	01-01-05	6.400	M2	09/23/1996
	001	01-01-10	6.400	M2	09/23/1996
	001	02-01-05	6.400	M2	09/23/1996
	001	02-01-10	6.400	M2	09/23/1996
	001	02-02-01	6.400	M2	09/23/1996
	001	03-01-10	6.400	M2	09/23/1996
	001	01-02-01	6.400	M2	09/23/1996
Spiral casing chrome ste	001	01-01-01	10.000	PC	09/23/1996
	001	01-01-06	20.000	PC	09/23/1996
	001	02-01-01	20.000	PC	09/23/1996
	001	02-01-06	20.000	PC	09/23/1996
	001	03-01-06	20.000	PC	09/23/1996
	001	03-01-01	20.000	PC	09/23/1996
Fly wheel chrome steel	001	01-01-02	50.000	PC	09/23/1996
	001	01-01-07	60.000	PC	09/23/1996
Pressure cover chrome st	001	02-01-08	20.000	PC	09/23/1996
	001	01-01-03	90.000	PC	09/23/1996
Bearing case	914	0060001837	1,000.000	PC	11/11/1997
Support base	914	0060001837	1,000.000	PC	11/11/1997
Sheet metal ST37	902	WE-ZONE	2.000	M2	07/27/1998
Shaft	001	03-02-01	0.000	PC	07/28/1998
	902	WE-ZONE	0.000	PC	07/28/1998

Section 15: Warehouse Management Reports
List of Posting Change Notices

List of Posting Change Notices

Quick Access — To run this report, use one of the following access options:

Option 1: Menu Path

Logistics → *Materials management* → *Warehouse management* → *PostChange* → *Display* → *List*

Option 2: Transaction Code

In the *Command* field, enter transaction **LU04** and choose *Enter*.

Purpose — This report lists the posting change notices (for simplicity, referred to as the posting change in this document) according to the selection criteria specified on the initial selection screen.

From this report, you can branch out to display detailed information about a particular posting change. In addition, you can convert any of the open posting changes into a transfer order in foreground processing mode. A posting change could be started from the Inventory Management module as a Transfer Posting, or from within Warehouse Management. Please see the online documentation for more information on this functionality.

Note: This report can be used to carry out data changes, such as the creation of a transfer order. Thus, system administrators may want to implement authorization control to limit users from taking advantage of such functionality.

Prerequisites — You must enter the warehouse number before running this report.

The report can be run with no further selection criteria entered, however, you may want to limit the selection by material number, plant, storage location, stock category, batch, or base it on a specific GR material document number or QM inspection lot number. For example, you can list only those posting changes posted for a given material, in a certain plant, of a certain stock.

Integration — From this report, double-click or choose *Details* to view more information about a particular posting change. From this level, you can get further information about the originating Transfer Posting material document, user ID, time and date, and movement type.

Section 15: Warehouse Management Reports
List of Posting Change Notices

Features

This report does not have any of the standard functionality found in many other R/3 reports. It only provides the report listing format in either a single-line (system default) or double-line format.

The output of this report includes:

- Listing posting changes by warehouse number in creation date sequence
- Selection of posting change documents for individual display (double-click or choose *Details* from one of the posting changes document)

Next Steps

Data presented in this report is from the posting change document. This report provides a function for users to convert a selected posting change document with an open status into a transfer order in a foreground processing mode.

Guided Tour

Example: Display all open posting changes in a warehouse. Then, convert them to transfer orders.

To access the first screen for this report, choose

Logistics → Materials management → Warehouse management → PostChange → Display → List.

1. Enter a warehouse number (for example, 001) in *Whse number*.
2. Make certain the system defaults to *Status: open*.
3. Choose *Enter*.

Optionally, you could further limit the report selection by entering a material number, plant, storage location, stock category, batch, and any specific GR material document number or QM inspection lot number.

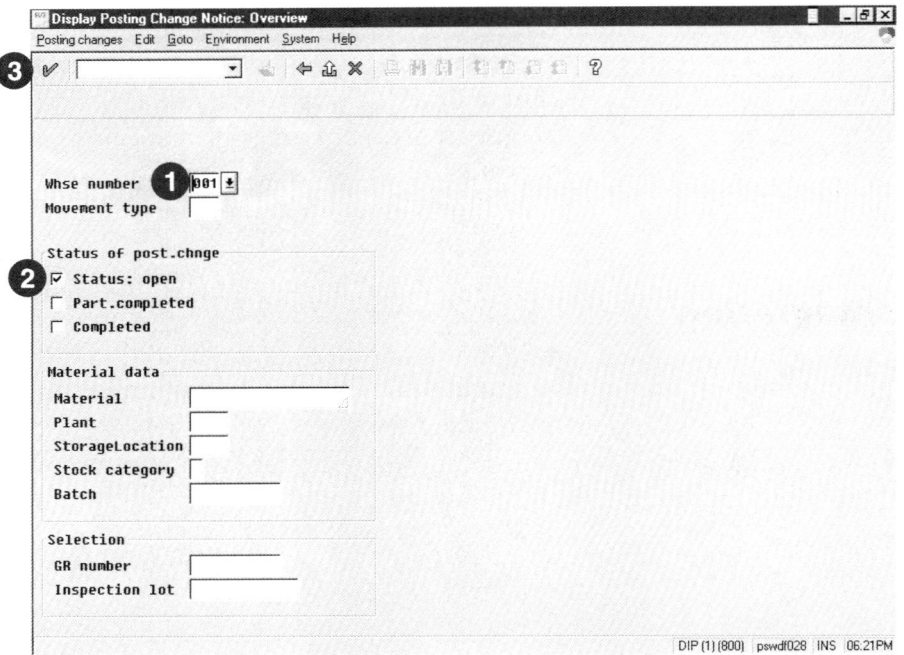

Section 15: Warehouse Management Reports
List of Posting Change Notices

This screen shows all the open posting changes by warehouse number.

The system default for the display is a single-line format.

4. Choose *Double-line* to change to a double-line format and show both sides of the *Posting change* document.

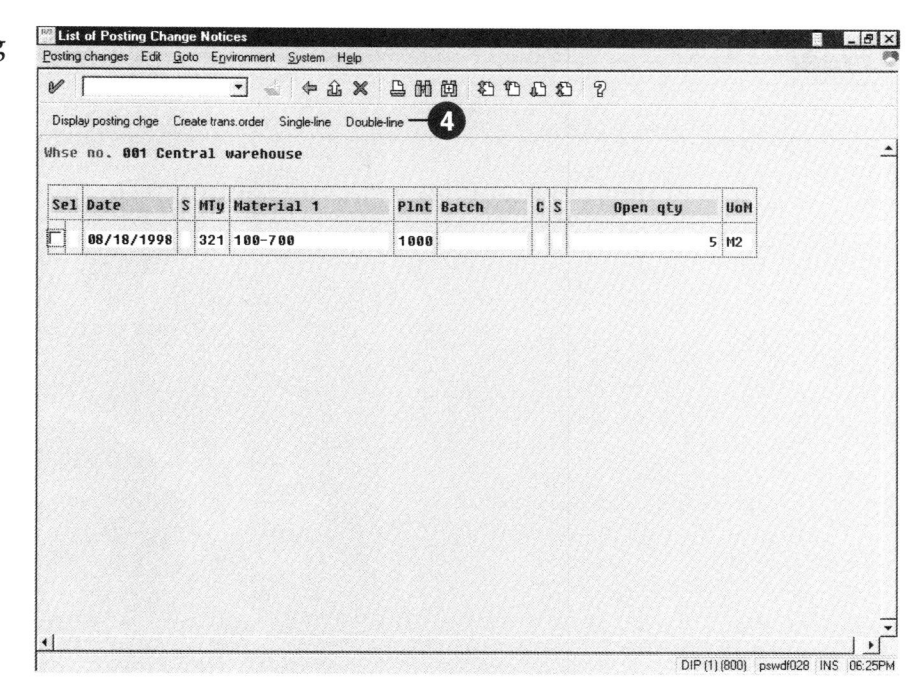

5. Select the posting change item by clicking on the checkbox to the left of the item.

6. Choose *Display posting chge*.

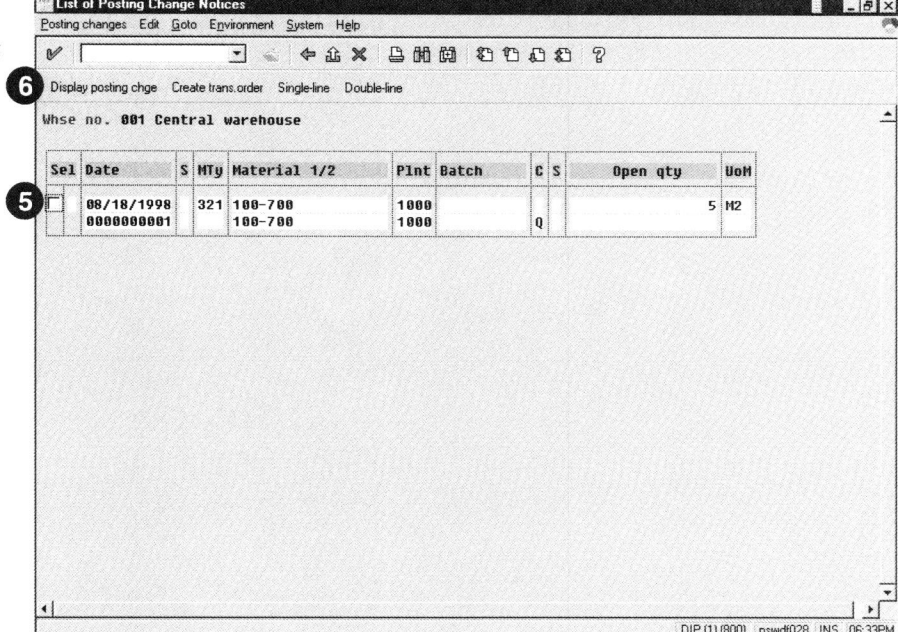

Commonly Used Reports: Illustrations and Perspectives

Section 15: Warehouse Management Reports

List of Posting Change Notices

The display branches out into a detailed information screen for that particular posting change.

7. Choose *Processing status*.

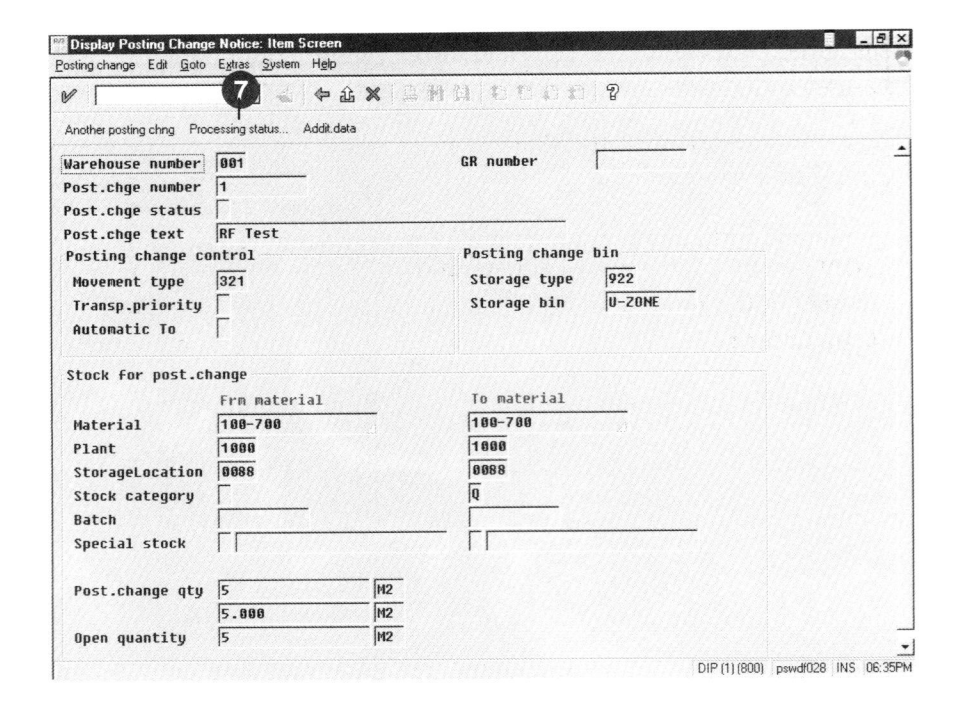

The popup window shows some information about the last transfer order (TO) data, user-ID, and creation date and time.

8. Choose *Continue*.
9. Choose *Addit.data*.

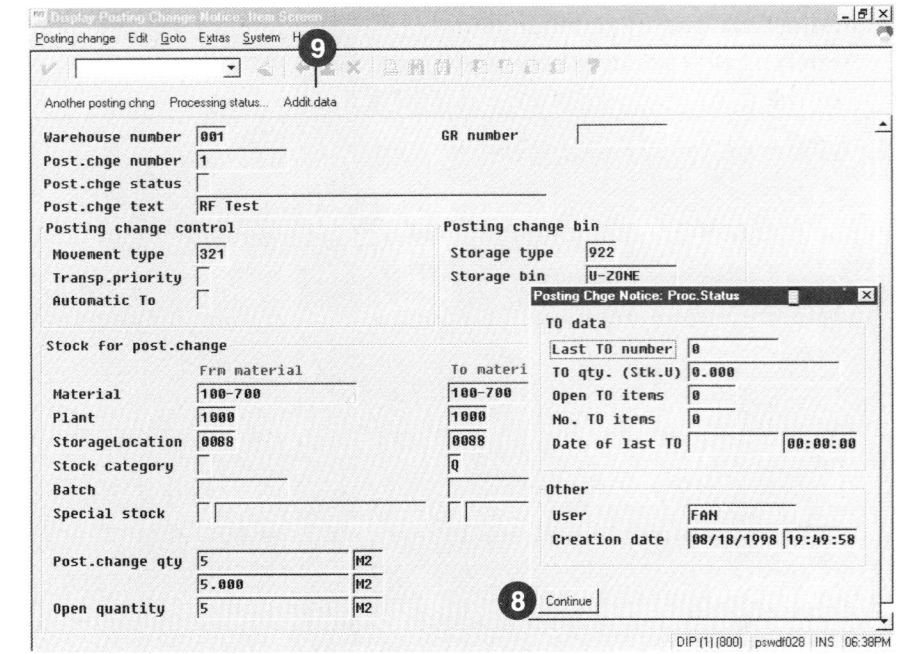

15–14 Reporting Made Easy

Section 15: Warehouse Management Reports
List of Posting Change Notices

The popup window shows the originating Transfer Posting transaction (if any) from Inventory Management.

10. Choose *Continue*.

11. Choose *Another posting chng*.

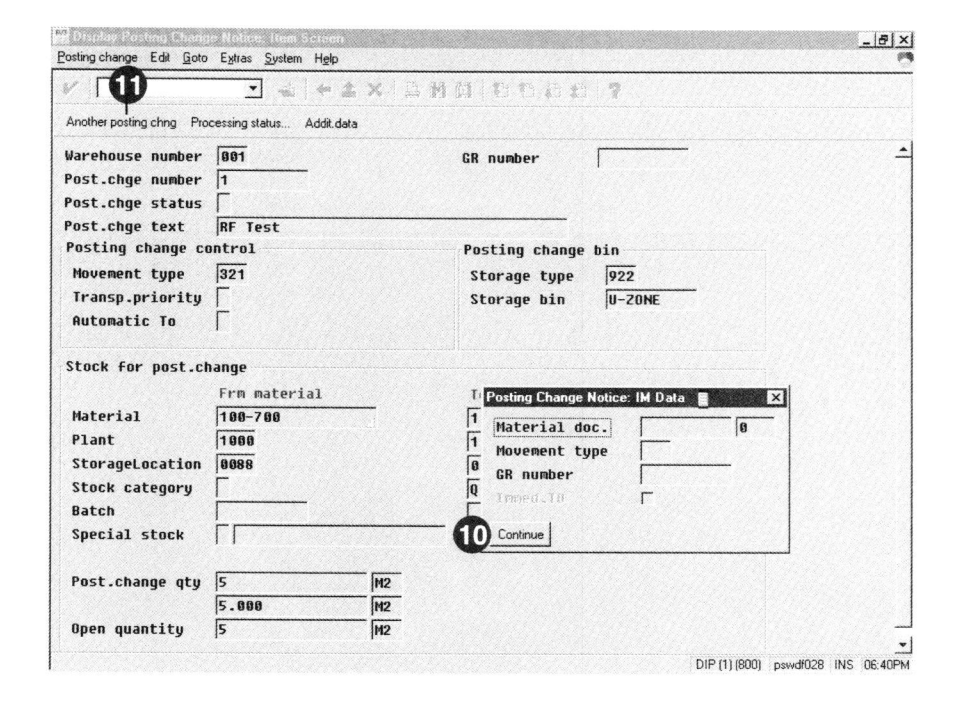

By choosing *Another posting chng*, the report branches to detailed information of the next posting change, if any.

In this example, there is no other posting change, therefore, the system returns to the first overview screen.

12. Select the posting change item.

13. Choose *Create trans. order* to convert the posting change into a transfer order.

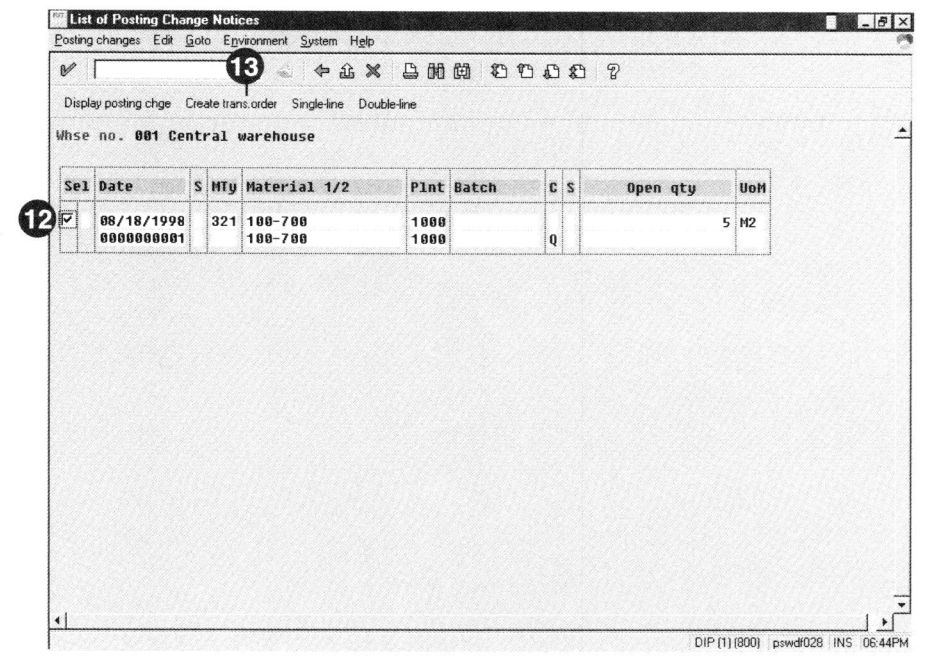

Commonly Used Reports: Illustrations and Perspectives

15–15

Section 15: Warehouse Management Reports
List of Posting Change Notices

The first screen (stock overview screen) lets you choose the quantity for the posting change.

14. Select the appropriate stock line.

15. Choose *Quant list*.

16. Enter **2.8** on the first quantity and **2.2** for the second quantity.

17. Select *P* for each quantity to indicate that both are to be changed into QI stock category and placed in the same bin.

18. Choose *Process in background* to automatically create the transfer order in the background.

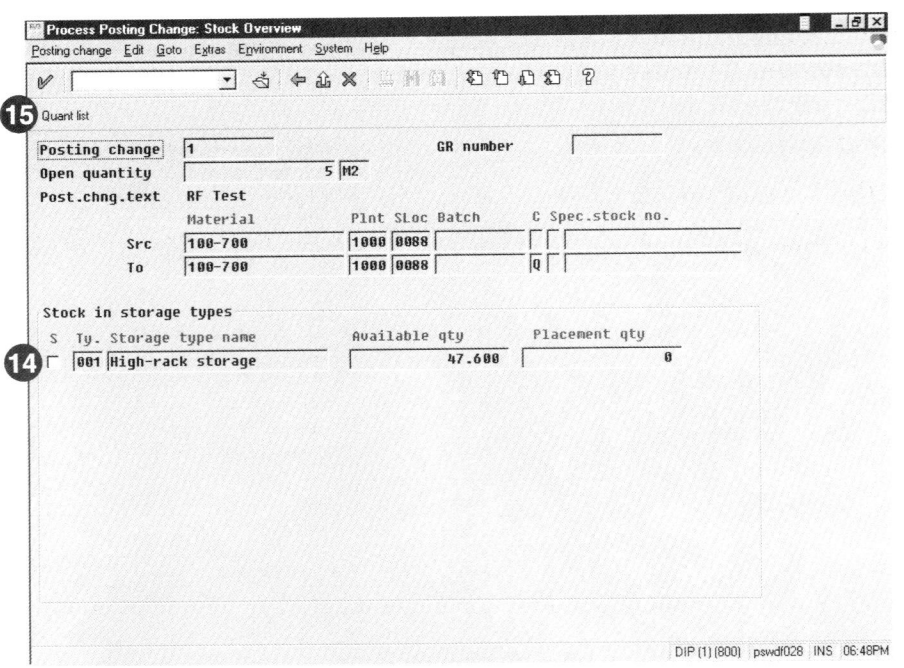

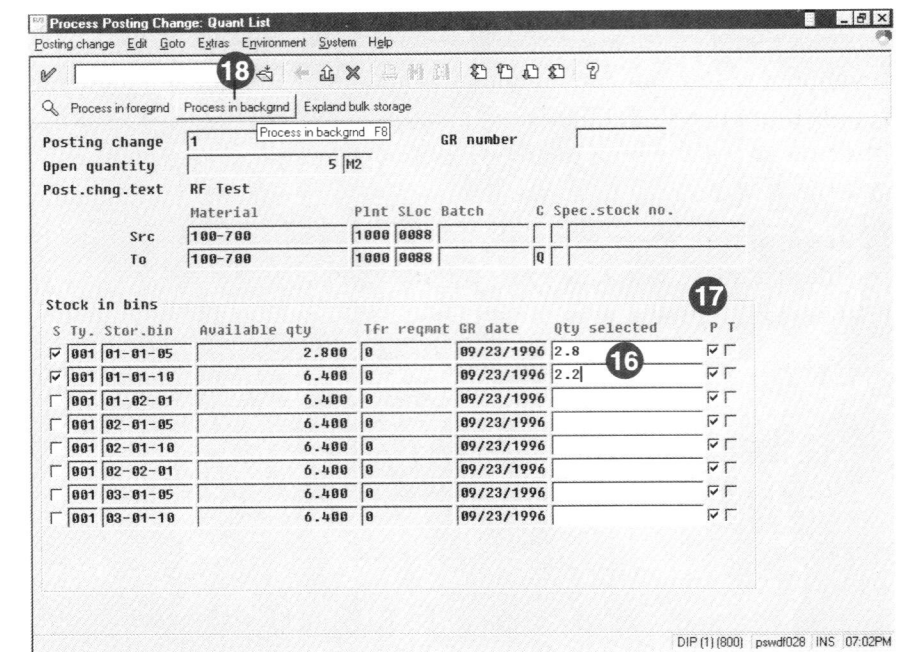

15–16

Reporting Made Easy

Section 15: Warehouse Management Reports

List of Posting Change Notices

Note that at this stage, you could elect to process the transfer order either in foreground or background mode.

In this example, background processing was selected.

19. Choose *Save* to save the transfer order.

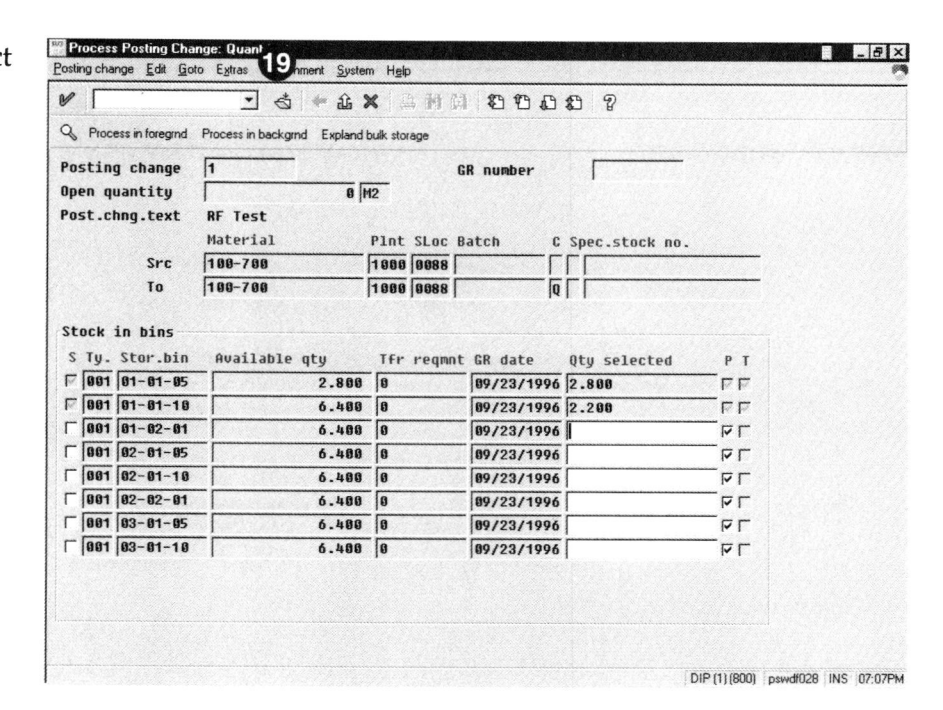

Commonly Used Reports: Illustrations and Perspectives

Empty Storage Bins

Quick Access To run this report, use one of the following access options:

Option 1: Menu Path

Logistics → Materials management → Warehouse management → Master data → Storage bin → Display → Empty storage bins

Option 2: Program Name

Choose *System → Services → Reporting* and enter `RLLS0400` in the *Program* field. Then, choose *Execute* to run the report.

Option 3: Transaction Code

In the *Command* field, enter transaction `LS04` and choose *Enter*.

Purpose This report provides a list (by storage type and section) of all the empty storage bins in a specified warehouse.

From the report, you can branch out to view detailed information about a particular storage bin. Empty storage bins list by warehouse number and storage type, and blocking/unblocking indicators.

Three business purposes for using this report include:

- To quickly locate an empty storage bin for assignment to a material master
- To assign a destination bin to a transfer order
- To find out specific details about a storage bin (for example, blocking indicator, maximum weight, capacity assigned, etc.)

Prerequisites You must enter the warehouse number and the storage type before running this report.

You can limit this report by entering additional selection criteria (for example, you could choose to list only blocked storage bins).

Integration

By drilling down on a storage bin line in this report, you will display the general data and blocking indicators about the storage bin. From that screen, you can select the following criteria to further detail you report:

- *Statistics* (Last Good Movement dates, transfer order number, and Last Changed information)
- *Bin Sectioning* (Bin sectioning within the bin, provided the storage bin is designated as bin sectioning allowed)
- *Inventory* (Physical inventory document information)
- *Stock* (Quantity information residing in the bin)

Features

There are no general report features like selection options, variants, user settings, sorting, totaling, optimizing column widths, etc. which are normally found in other SAP reports.

Next Steps

Data presented in this report is from the storage bin information. As such, it does not allow manipulation of data.

Section 15: Warehouse Management Reports
Empty Storage Bins

Guided Tour

Example 1: Display a simple listing of all empty storage bins for warehouse number *001* and storage type *001*.

To access the first screen for this report, choose

Logistics → Warehouse management → Master data → Storage bin → Evaluations → Empty storage bins.

1. Enter **001** in *Whse number*.
2. Enter **001** in *Storage type*.

Other selection criteria can be entered to limit the report to one specific storage bin, or certain bin type, or just to limit the number of storage bins to be displayed. The default is 32 but you can override it.

In this example, no further selection criterion is entered and the default of 32 bins is used.

3. Choose *Enter*.

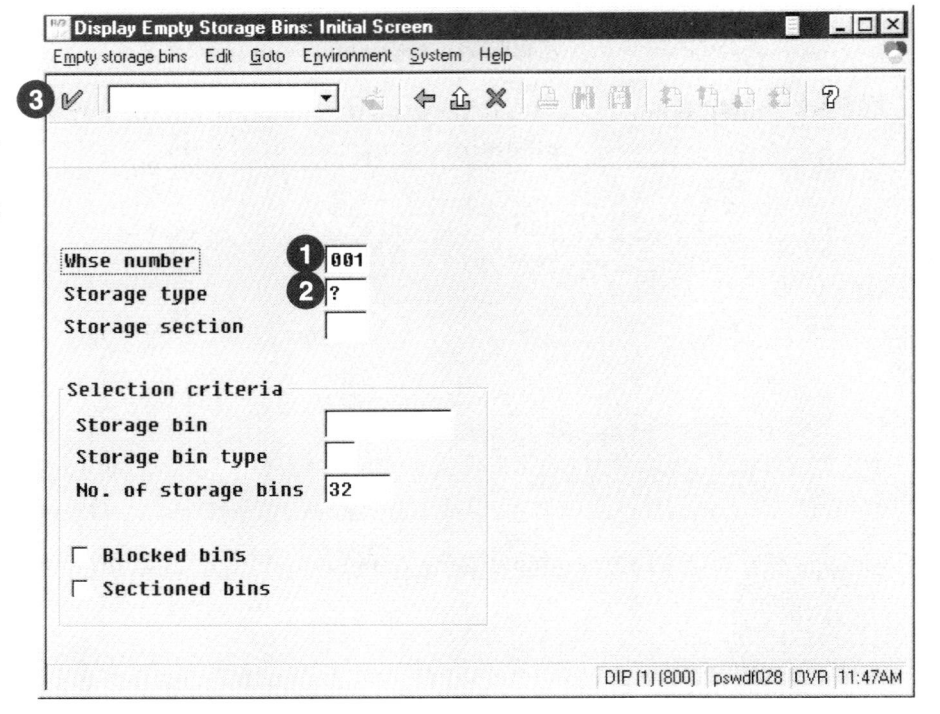

Section 15: Warehouse Management Reports
Empty Storage Bins

A Warehouse number and storage type which were entered in the first selection screen

B Listing of empty storage bins sorted in the storage section and storage bin number sequence

In a typical business scenario, you would then note down the bin number and assign to a material master as a fixed bin assignment or assign to a transfer order as the destination bin.

C Selecting a storage bin and choosing *Details* will branch into the bin details screen.

The *Storage Bin Data Screen* provides more general information on the bin and on the blocking indicators.

In addition, there are four buttons which branch to more specific information on the storage bin:

- *Statistics*
- *Bin sectioning*
- *Inventory*
- *Stock*

4. Choose *Statistics*.

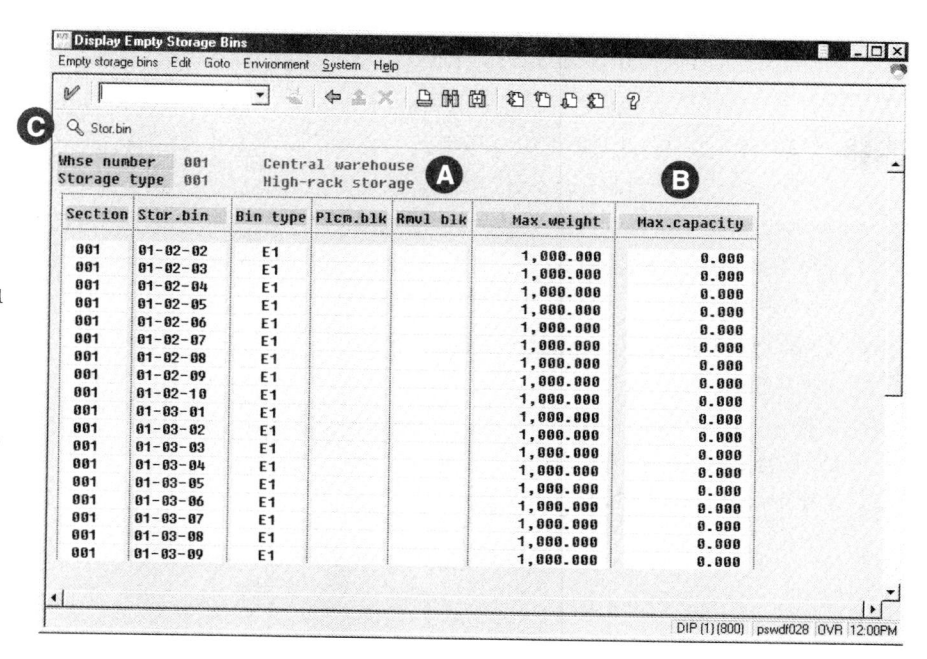

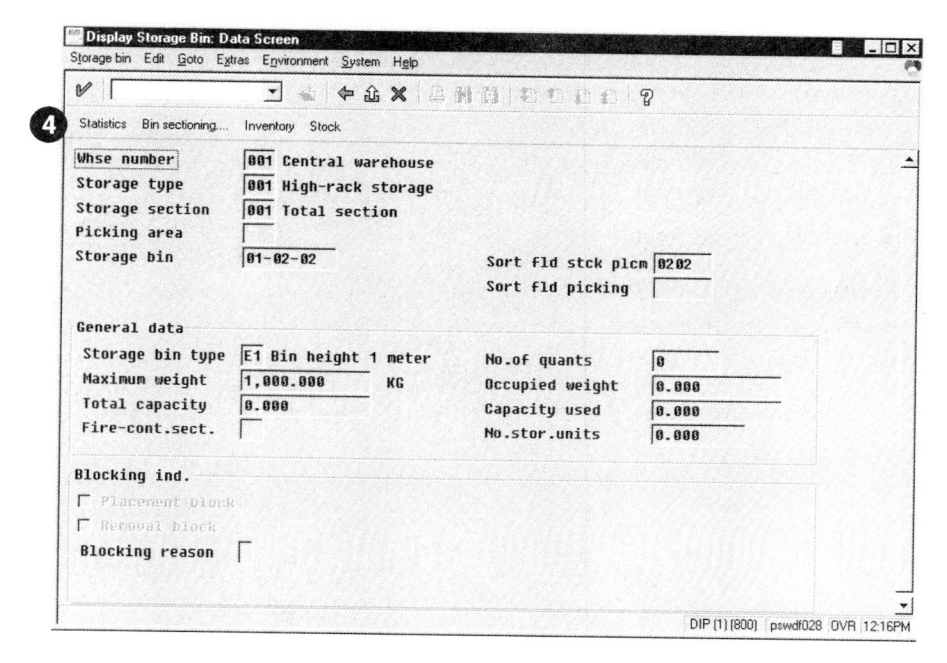

Commonly Used Reports: Illustrations and Perspectives

15–21

Section 15: Warehouse Management Reports
Empty Storage Bins

A popup window appears with the following information:

- Date and time of last movement
- Date and time the bin was last emptied
- Date when physical inventory was last done
- Last transfer order number accessing this bin
- Change details (For example, date of last maintenance and user ID of the person who last changed it.)

5. Choose *Bin sectioning*.

A popup window appears with detailed information on bin sectioning—provided there is bin sectioning defined for that storage type and storage bin.

In this example, no such definition exists, so an information message shows instead.

6. Choose *Enter*.
7. Choose *Inventory*.

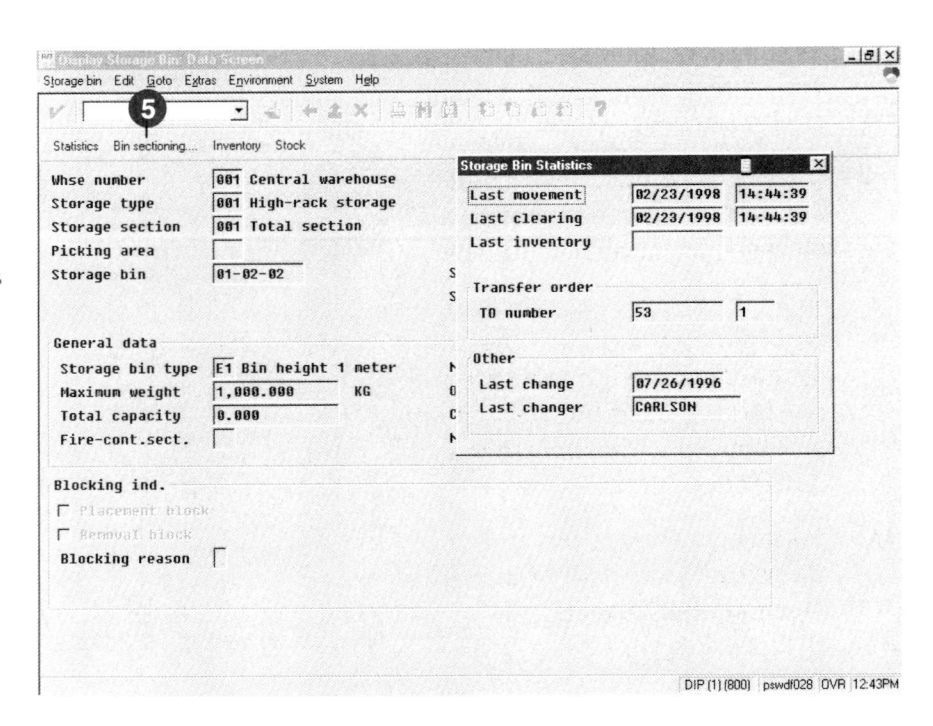

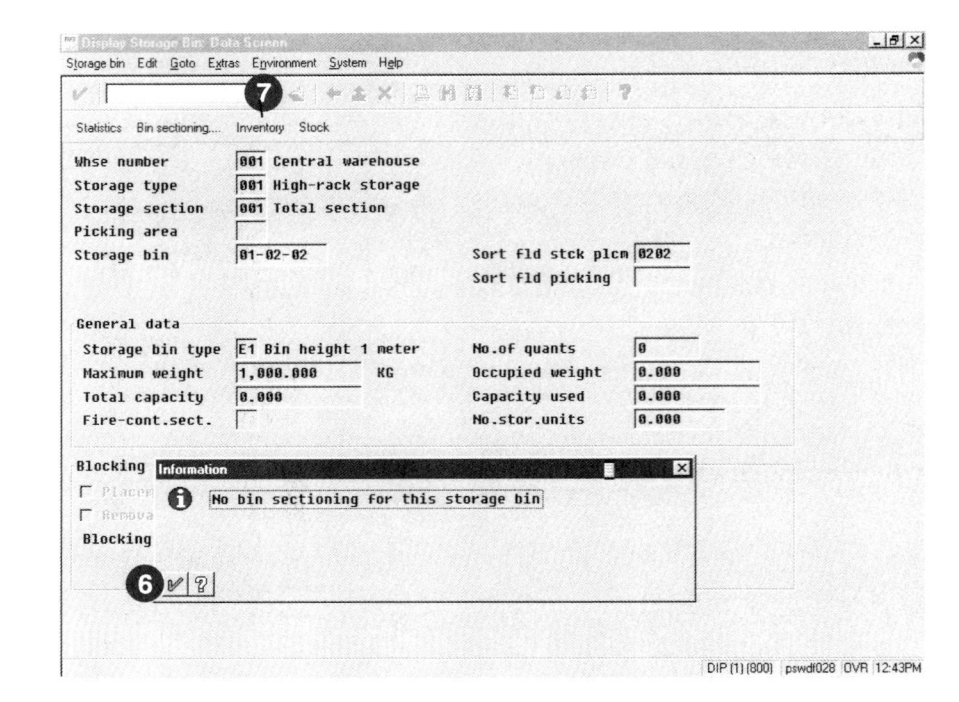

15–22

Reporting Made Easy

Section 15: Warehouse Management Reports
Empty Storage Bins

This screen shows a list of all physical inventory documents in this bin. From this screen, you can drill down into the details of each physical inventory document for more information.

8. Choose *Storage Bin*.

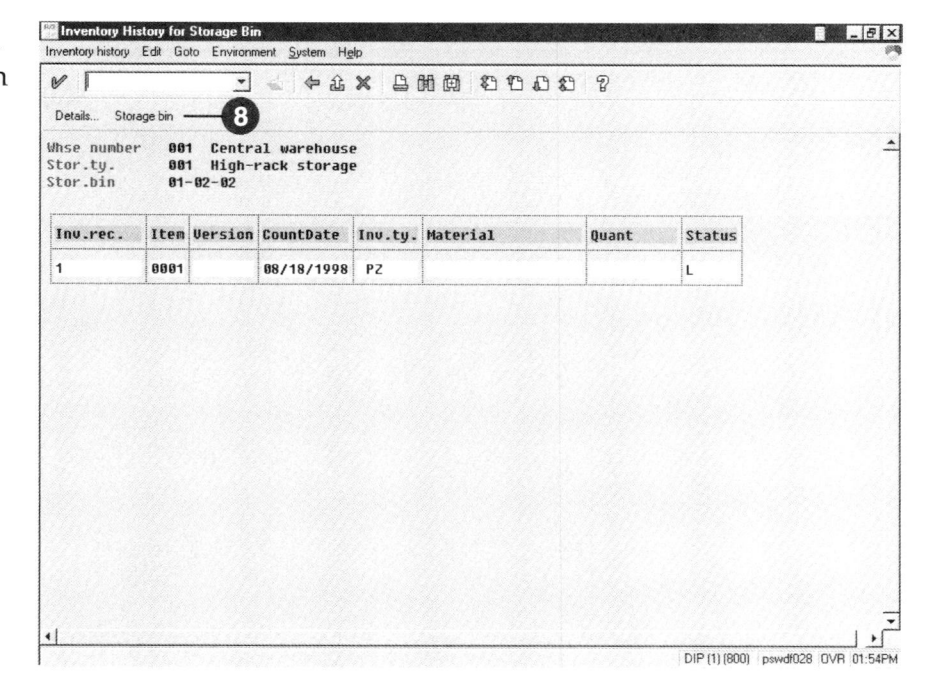

9. Choose *Stock*.

   A popup window appears and lists the existing quantity residing in that bin. Since this example involves an empty bin report, we receive a message stating that no quantity exists for that bin.

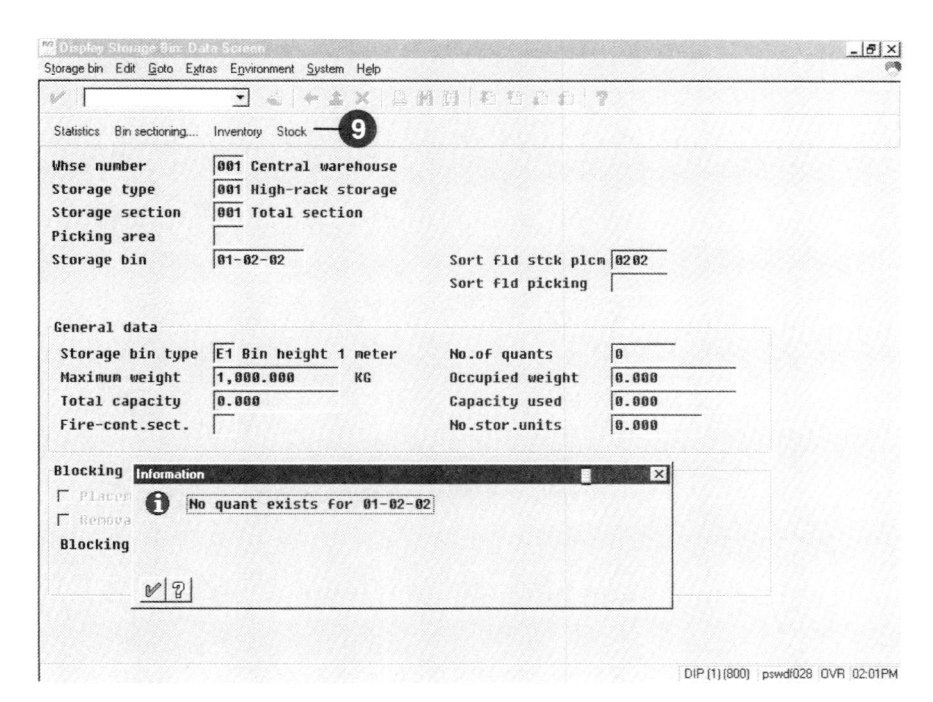

Commonly Used Reports: Illustrations and Perspectives

Section 15: Warehouse Management Reports
Empty Storage Bins

Appendix A: Report Documentation Template

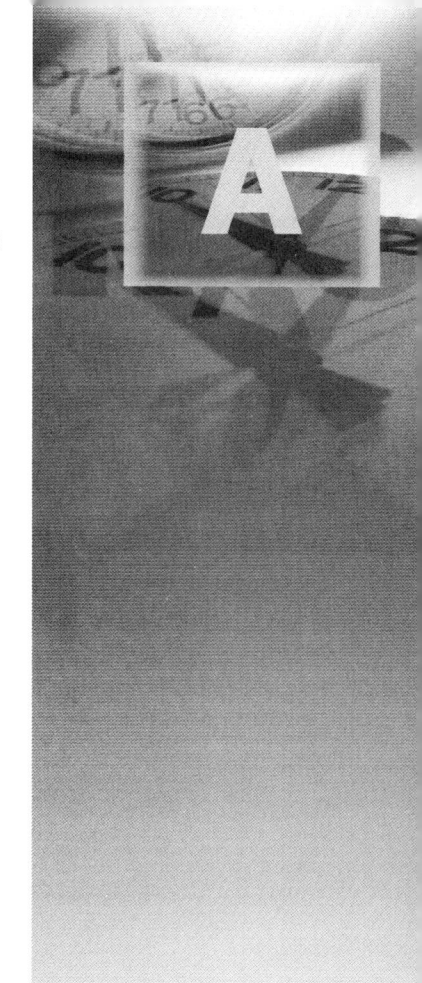

Contents

Why Use a Template? A–2
How to Use this Template A–2
Application Area: Report Title A–3

Why Use a Template?

Implementation and reporting teams in an enterprise are often faced with the task of creating report documentation for their end-users.

The template described in this appendix is intended to jumpstart the report documentation effort in your company.

Here are some of the reasons you should consider using a template to document the reports:
- Standard structure ensures that important information regarding a report is not overlooked.
- Similar look-and-feel makes it easier to use, learn, and understand reports.
- Saves time and effort spent in producing report documentation.
- Helps standardize documentation across business units/areas in a company.

How to Use this Template

Follow these three simple steps to get started with this template:

Step 1: Copy the template file to your PC

The companion CD supplied with this guidebook contains a Microsoft Word 97 file named `Report_Docu_Template.dot`. If you do not have a copy of the diskette, you may download it from *www.saplabs.com/rme*.

Copy this file into the *Templates* folder on your PC. Generally, you will find this folder in the following location on your PC: *Program Files/Microsoft Office/Templates*.

Step 2: Read the template instructions

Start by familiarizing yourself with the information blocks that make up the report documentation. Pay close attention to the questions that each report block is intended to answer.

Step 3: Use the template

Share this template with people involved with documenting R/3 reports in your company. The reports featured in this guide were documented using the same template. Report documentation in future releases of the R/3 System will be based on the same information blocks. Feel free to modify the template to suit your needs.

> **Tips & Tricks**
>
> **Capturing screenshots:**
>
> For best results, use *ALT+PrintScreen* to save the screen image to your clipboard. Then, choose *Edit → Paste Special*. Make sure to deselect the *Float over text* box.

Application Area: Report Title

Quick Access   *This section should provide direction for accessing the report.*
- What is a commonly used menu path for accessing this report?
- What is the technical (program) name of the report?

Example:

To run this report, use one of the following access options:

Option 1: Menu Path

Information systems → Accounting → Financial accounting

General ledger → Select report

Information systems → Account information → Line items → G/L line items

Option 2: Program Name

Choose *System → Services → Reporting* and enter `RFSOPO00` in the *Program* field. Then, choose *Execute* to run the report.

Purpose   *This section should briefly outline the purpose of the report. A short description of a typical business decision made with this report can be useful.*
- What does this report do, in general?
- What does this report do from a business point of view?
- What business decisions might be considered with this report?
- How is this report useful?

Prerequisites   *Several reports require IMG configuration. Many reports will not run if certain data does not exist. This should be explained here.*
- Which prerequisites have to be fulfilled to execute the report?
- Which system settings have to be made to execute the report?

Appendix A: Report Documentation Template
Application Area: Report Title

Integration

This section should describe how this report, within this module, relates to other modules and R/3 functionality. Users could decide here if the report is right for their role in their company.

- Who would typically use this report? Where would this report be used?
- Which other reports can I call up from this report?
- Which integrated functions can I use from this report? (for example, from other modules)
- Which other reports or functions do I need to be able to use this report?

Features

Describe any significant features the user might need to make for processing this report easier. For example: sorting, summations, refining the lists, etc.

- Describe any important features of the:
  - Selection screen
  - Output screen
- Delivered standard variants

Next Steps

This section does not describe the displayed list; this is described under purpose, features and the business example. Typically 'reports', in our definition, do not allow manipulation of data. However, this section can explain how the business decision(s) to be made can be carried out – within the report or outside of it.

- Can any data be manipulated on the database within this 'report'? If so, what?
- How is this report often used to implement a business decision?

Appendix A: Report Documentation Template

Application Area: Report Title

Example: Include a business scenario for the sample report.

Guided Tour

---

1. Include the steps needed to run this report.
2. Include a screenshot, where applicable.
3. Use numbered circles ❶ to provide visual cues to the users. To position the circled-numbers, simply click the number and drag it to the desired position.

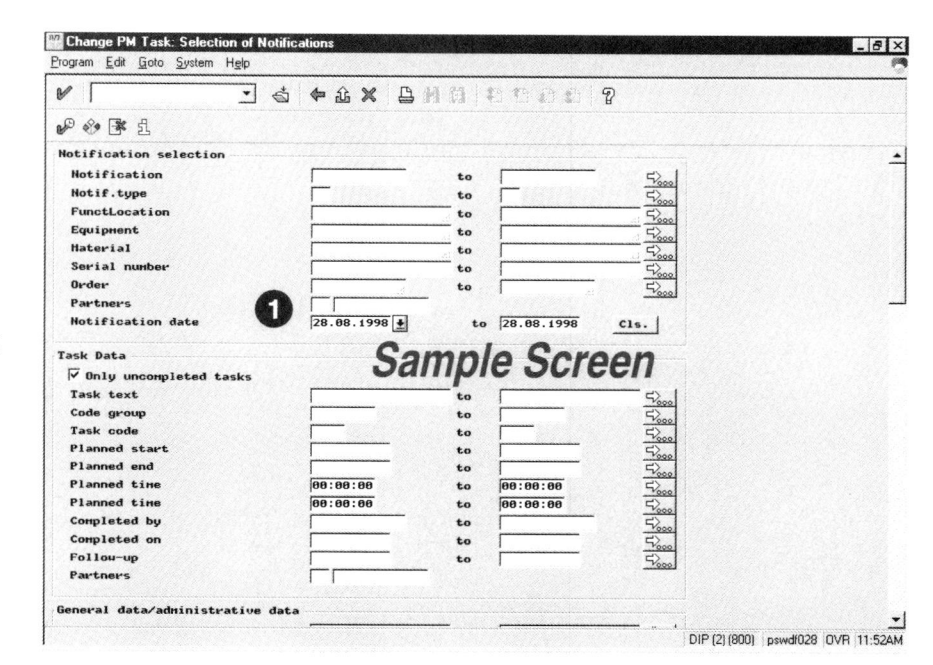

Sample Screen: Change PM Task: Selection of Notifications

Commonly Used Reports: Illustrations and Perspectives

Appendix A: Report Documentation Template
Application Area: Report Title

Appendix B: List of Sample Reports in this Guide

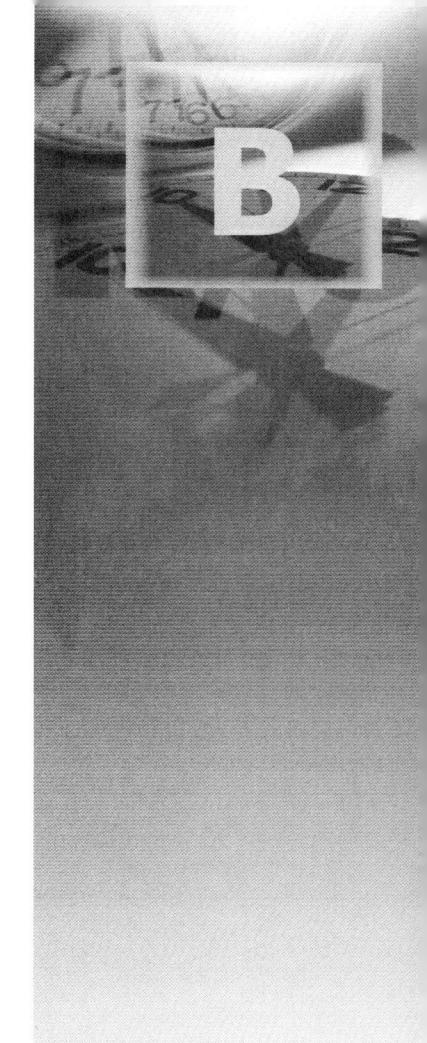

Contents

Sample Reports Organized by Application Area B–2

Sample Reports Organized by Application Area

Application	Report Title	Program Name	Transaction code	Page Number
CO	CO/FI Reconciliation in Group Currency	J5AF2TQX		7-13
CO	Cost Center Summary: Plan/Actual Costs by Period and Year-to-Date	J1SISTQX		4-31
CO	Cost Center Summary: Planned Costs, Actual Costs, and Variances	J1SIPTEX		4-2
CO	Cost Center Summary: Target Costs, Actual Costs, and Variances	J1SISTQX		4-37
CO	Cross-Company Code Reconciliation	J5AB1TQX		7-27
CO	Display Actual Line Items for Cost Centers	None	KSB1	4-18
CO	Display Actual Line Items for Internal Orders	None	KOB1	5-17
CO	FI/CO Reconciliation in Company Code Currency	J5AF1TQX		7-2
CO	Internal Order List: Balance Displays	J6L00TQX		5-33
CO	Internal Order Summary: Planned Costs, Actual Costs, and Variances	J6O00TQX		5-2
CO	Profitability Analysis: Plan/Actual Comparison	None		6-2
CO	Profitability Analysis: Sales Plan/Contribution Margin	None		6-27
CO	Profitability Analysis: SBU/Product/Customer Analysis	None		6-14
FI/AP	List of Vendor Open Items	RFKOPO00	F.41	3-2
FI/AP	Vendor Balances in Local Currency	RFKSLD00	F.42	3-6
FI/AR	Accounts Receivable Information System	RFDRRANZ		2-8
FI/AR	Customer Balances in Local Currency	RFDSLD00		2-19
FI/AR	Customer Open Item Analysis (A/R Aging)	RFDOPR10		2-2
FI/AR	List of Customer Open Items	RFDOPO00	F.21	2-14
FI/GL	General Ledger Account Balances	RFSSLD00	F.08	1-12
FI/GL	General Ledger Accounts List	RFXKVZ00		1-2
FI/GL	General Ledger Balance Sheet / P+L	RFBILA00	F.01	1-16
FI/GL	General Ledger Line Items	RFSOPO00		1-7
HR	EEO-1 Report	RPSEEOU1	4.5	8-16
HR	Entries and Withdrawals Report	RPLEAT00		8-21
HR	New Hire Report	RPLNHRU0	4.5	8-11
HR	Payroll Journal	None	PC1U	8-6
HR	Staffing Level Development Report (or Headcount Report)	RPSDEV00		8-2
MM	List Display of Purchase Requisitions	RM06BA00	ME5A	10-20
MM	List Displays of PO—Material or Vendor	RM06EL00	ME2M, ME2L	10-6
MM	Material Documents for Material	RM07MMAT	MB51	10-13
MM	Stock Overview	RMMMBEST	MMBE	10-2

Appendix B: List of Sample Reports in this Guide
Sample Reports Organized by Application Area

Application	Report Title	Program Name	Transaction code	Page Number
PM	List of Notification Tasks	RIQMEL30	IW66 or IW67	11-2
PM	Order Cost Element Display	None	IW32 or IW33	11-6
PP	Backorder Processing	None	CO06	12-51
PP	Capacity Planning—Evaluation	None	CM01	12-56
PP	Missing Parts Info System	PPCMP000	CO24	12-44
PP	MRP List—Collective Display	None	MD06	12-22
PP	Multi-Level BOM	None	CS12	12-39
PP	Production Order Overview	PPIOA000	CO26	12-12
PP	Shop Floor Info System	None	MCP0	12-27
PP	Stock Requirements List	None	MD04	12-2
PS	Cost Element Reporting—Plan vs. Actual	None		13-5
PS	Project Cost Reporting—Planned/Actual/Variance	None		13-2
QM	Inspection Lot Selection	RQEEAL10	QA33	14-9
QM	Inspection Lots Without Completion	RQEVAM10	QVM1	14-2
QM	Inspection Lots Without Usage Decision	RQEVAM30	QVM3	14-6
SD	Backorders	RVAUFRUE	V.15	9-13
SD	Blocked Sales Orders	RVSPERAU	V.14	9-7
SD	Incoming Order Report (SIS Statistical Analysis)	RMCV0100	MCT0	9-22
SD	Incoming Orders for Customers and Materials (Document or Statistical Analysis)	RVAUFEIN	V.12	9-29
SD	Incomplete Sales Documents	RVAUFERR	V.02 or V.01	9-34
SD	Invoiced Sales Report (Statistical Analysis)	RMCV0100	MCTA, C, E, I, G	9-43
SD	List of All or Open Billings (Document Analysis)	None	VF05	9-38
SD	List of All or Open Deliveries (Document Analysis)	None	VL05	9-50
SD	List of Sales Orders	None	VA05	9-2
SD	Shipping Report (SIS Statistical Analysis)	RMCV0400	MCTK	9-56
WM	Empty Storage Bins	RLLS0400	LS04	15-18
WM	List of Posting Change Notices	None	LU04	15-11
WM	Material Stock List	RLS10020	LX02	15-7
WM	Stock Overview	RLLS2600	LS26	15-2

Appendix B: List of Sample Reports in this Guide
Sample Reports Organized by Application Area

Appendix C: Glossary

Appendix C: Glossary

Note: Terms related to the SAP Business Information Warehouse are indicated by the ⓘ symbol.

ABAP	Advanced Business Application Programming. ABAP is a fourth-generation programming language developed by SAP for application development purposes.
ABAP Query	ABAP Workbench tool that allows users who have little or no knowledge of ABAP, tables, or field names, to define and execute their own reports.

To determine the structure of reports in ABAP Query, users enter text, then select fields and options. Fields are selected from functional areas and can be sequenced numerically.

There are three types of reports available:

- Basic lists
- Statistics
- Ranked lists

You can also define a combination of these.

To define a report, enter individual text, such as titles, then select the fields and options which determine the report layout. The system generates each query in the form of an ABAP program.

ABC analysis	Procedure that determines the importance of an object. An ABC analysis classifies objects according to specific criteria or performance measures. Each object is assigned one of the following three indicators:

- A: most important
- B: moderately important
- C: less important

An object can be material, a vendor, or a plant. ABC analyses are used in areas such as Materials Management, Plant Maintenance, Logistics Information System, and ABAP Query.

Activate update	In this IMG activity, you create settings for updating the information structures in the Logistics Information System. Data analysis in information systems is based on statistical data, which is updated from the operative application to information structures. Updating is triggered by an event in a logistics application (e.g. purchase order, sales order). An event is a point in time when information is created that needs to be recorded.

The following settings determine updates:

- Period unit of the update: Time level on which statistical data is to be collected (daily, weekly, monthly, posting period).
- Type of updating: When the information structures are updated. Here, you have the following options:
    - Synchronous update (V1 update)

Appendix C: Glossary

	- Asynchronous update (V2 update) - No update, i.e. the update is deactivated
Activation	Turning on Business Information Warehouse (BW) objects. BW objects such as transfer rules and aggregates can be created so that they are initially inactive. After activation, these objects are used by the system and can be transported.
Administrator Workbench	Controls how data from source systems reaches the InfoCubes of the Business Information Warehouse. The parts of the Administrator Workbench that are needed for requesting and managing of data include: Source system, InfoSource, InfoCube, InfoObject, Scheduler, and Monitor.
Aggregate	Saves the dataset of an InfoCube in a summarized form. The original fact table of the InfoCube in an aggregate table no longer contains some of the characteristics that are summarized across attributes, characteristic values, or hierarchy levels.
ALE	Application Link Enabling. ALE refers to the creation and operation of distributed applications to guarantee a distributed, but integrated, R/3 installation. This process involves business-controlled message exchange with consistent data across loosely linked SAP applications. Application integration is achieved not via a central database, but via synchronous and asynchronous communication. ALE consists of the three layers: Application services, distribution services, and communication services.
Audit Information System	Customized program developed to cover many kinds of audits a company may be involved with (for example, tax, personnel, inventory, and so on). The AIS uses a tree structure and can be downloaded from the Online Support Service (OSS).
Authorization Profile	Profile that gives users access to the system. Composite profiles contain other profiles. A composite profile assigns a user with all of the single and composite profiles it contains.
Background Job	Processing that does not take place on screen. You can process data in the background while performing other functions in parallel.
BAPI	Business Application Programming Interface (also called Business API).
Base Tables	Normalized data structures maintained in the target warehousing database. Also known as detail data.
Basic Lists	Original lists resulting from the execution of a report. Modify basic lists by navigating in the dataset and using a range of interactive processing functions to produce other list formats (e.g. ranked lists).
Business Explorer (BEx)	The SAP Business Information Warehouse frontend reporting tool. In the Business Explorer Analyzer (BEx Analyzer) you define queries based on a selected characteristics and key figures (InfoObjects) or the predefined query templates of an InfoCube. Analyze the selected InfoCube data by navigating in the query to generate different views of the data. Save queries in workbooks that can be assigned to one or more channels. Use the Business Explorer Browser (BEx Browser) to access workbooks that are assigned to you in channels.

Appendix C: Glossary

BW	SAP Business Information Warehouse, a data warehousing product.
Calculated Key Figure	Value found using formulas or calculation rules within a query. Calculated key figures are not stored in database tables.
CCMS	Computing Center Management System. Monitors, controls and configures the R/3 System. The CCMS supports round-the-clock system administration functions from the R/3 System. You can analyze and distribute the system load, as well as monitor the resource consumption of different system components.
Channels	Supply of workbooks of the Business Information Warehouse arranged according to topic areas. Using the channels of the Business Explorer, you access workbooks that are assigned to you.
Characteristic	Criterion (such as plant, material, company code, order, region, customer group) used to select data. Each characteristic has a number of characteristic values. Characteristics are also often referred to as "dimensions."
CO	Controlling instrument that supports management's decision-making processes. The various phases of controlling (e.g., planning, monitoring, reporting, consulting, and informing) cover internal financial transactions within a company. Controlling functions include: financial controlling, investment controlling, cost and profitability controlling for all business functions (procurement, production, sales, etc.).
Data Mart	Decision support environment that addresses the common decision support needs of a specific group within the organization (typically a department or geographic area). In BW, data marts can be created by queries on a specific aggregate.
Data Mining	Technique geared for the user who does not know exactly what he or she is searching for but is looking for particular patterns or trends. It is an automated or manual process of sifting through large amounts of data to produce data content correlation.
Data Warehouse	Database that contains summarized data from transactional data found in OLTP systems, legacy systems, or other sources. The data store is designed for efficient retrieval of data and decision support reporting. Data is organized by subject area and is time dependent. The data store contains figured quantities and dimensional data.
Delta Update and Full Update	Two types of update operations. A delta update refreshes only data changed since the last extraction. A full update replaces all data. Synonyms: Delta Change and Full Refresh/Update
Denormalization	Combining (and sometimes replicating) data to facilitate easy and effective access to relational data. For example, if an organization requires the customer name and address each time a query is processed against a customer, the data may be denormalized. See also Normalization.

Appendix C: Glossary

Dimension	▸ **Business Definition:** Combining evaluation groups (characteristics) that belong together from a contents point of view, under one joint evaluation group. If the dimension contains a characteristic whose value uniquely determines the values of all other values from a business perspective, then the dimension is named after this characteristic. The customer dimension could, for example, consist of the customer number, the customer group and the levels of the customer hierarchy. The sales dimension could contain the characteristics sales person, sales group and sales office. The time dimension could be produced from the characteristics day (in the form dd.mm.yyyy), week (in the form ww.yyyy), month (in the form mm.yyyy), year (in the form yyyy) and period (in the form ppp.yyyy). ▸ **Star Schema Definition:** Accompanies InfoCube definition. Characteristics are summarized into dimensions, in order to store them in a table of the star schema (dimension table). A grouping mentioned above, for example customer dimension, can form the foundation . The dimensions are connected to a key field of the fact table with the help of a simple foreign key relationship. From a technical point of view, a mapping takes place of a couple of characteristic values to an abstract dimension key, to which the values in the fact table refer. Characteristic values assigned to this key can be changed later, without reorganizating the fact table data. For example, the table in the InfoCube, that includes some (but not necessarily all) characteristics from the customer dimension, is the customer dimension of the InfoCubes. ▸ **Implementation:** The characteristics selected for an InfoCube are distributed to InfoCube-specific dimensions when the InfoCube is created.
Dimension Table	Table in a star schema with a single part primary key (e.g., customer key, product key, time key). See also Dimension and InfoCube.
Drilldown List	There are two types of lists in drilldown reporting: drilldown lists and detail lists. The drilldown list displays the selected key figures for a number of different report objects. For example, you can drill down on customer 001 and product 0815 to display all regions. In basic reports, the characteristics always appear in the rows of the drilldown list, while the key figures appear in the columns. In form reports, the characteristics also appear in the rows, but the column is structured according to the rows and columns defined in the form.
Drilldown Reporting	Evaluates data of an application according to its characteristics and key figures. Drilldown reporting allows you to generate simple data-driven lists (adhoc reports) as well as complex formatted reports (using forms). Using hierarchies, variables, formulas, cells and key figures, you can generate reports that satisfy all user requests. Available functions include database navigation and interactive list processing (sorting, ranked lists, ABC analyses, exceptions, etc.). Drilldown reporting is also linked to SAP Graphics, SAP Mail and the XXL.
EC	Enterprise Controlling

Commonly Used Reports: Illustrations and Perspectives

Appendix C: Glossary

Evaluation Structures
Evaluation structures form the interface to Report Writer, which is the underlying engine of the Report Painter. Evaluation structures are made up of characteristics and key figures. You can use evaluation structures to help you define your own evaluation by using the pickup technique to choose the characteristics and key figures you require.

An evaluation structure exists for each respective information structure in the standard R/3 System. An information structure and its corresponding evaluation structure always have the same name. Each time you define an information structure, a corresponding evaluation structure is generated. Since an evaluation structure is generated for each information structure, it is very easy to evaluate the information structures using flexible analyses of the LIS.

Executive Information Systems (EIS)
System used to collect and evaluate information from different areas of a business and its environment. Sources of information come from several areas including sales and distribution, and profit center accounting. The backbone of the EIS is the drilldown reporting tool. The information provides multiple levels of detail to meet the needs of a variety of users.

Extract Structure
Located in the source system and deposited by the application (application component). An extract structure always refers to one application. The data goes from the database to the extract structure using an API (Application Programming Interface). An API can fill several extract structures. In this structure, data from the applications is prepared for the InfoSource of the source system.

Fact Table
Located in the center of the star schema of an InfoCube. The data contains all key figures (also called "facts") of the InfoCube and the key is formed by links to the dimensions of the InfoCube.

FI
Financial accounting application area.

Field Catalogs
Logical grouping of relevant fields from LIS applications. All fields that refer to the sales organization (distribution channel, sales district, product hierarchy, etc.) can be combined into one field catalog. It is not necessary for the user to know whether these fields are used at document header, document item, or schedule line level.

Flexible Analyses
Part of the LIS, flexible analyses enable you to represent characteristics in self-defined, multilevel hierarchies and bring together the corresponding key figures. It is also possible to combine key figures from different information structures in the same application. With flexible analyses, you can easily create Report Writer reports for displaying data by using evaluation structures with the option of varying the layouts for these reports.

GUI
Graphical User Interface. Allows users to exchange information with the computer. On the user interface, you can choose commands, start programs, display files, and perform other functions by selecting menu options, function keys or pushbuttons, or pointing to icons with the mouse.

Appendix C: Glossary

Hierarchical Structure	Structure arranged in successive levels, where the individual elements in the different levels are interdependent.
	There are different types of hierarchical structures used; for example, organizational structures, business event structures, and reporting structures.
	Hierarchical structures contain parent-child relationships. This structure usually has multiple children aggregating up to one parent, for example, cost centers and profit centers can have parent-child relationships.
IMG	SAP's online Implementation Guide.
Info Set	Contains key figures that bear some logical relation to each other . For example, info sets relate to specific functions or are required by a single user. An info set can be single-level or multi-level. The members of a single-level info set are key figures. The members of a multilevel info set are one or more subordinate info sets—meaning that many different hierarchical levels are possible.
InfoCatalog	Tree-like structure in the Administrator Workbench that displays Business Information Warehouse queries. The various InfoCatalog trees contain SAP delivered workbooks that can be used by user groups, individual users, and as favorite queries (user favorites). The structure of the subtrees can be freely defined by the administrator. A user accesses InfoCatalog queries using the Business Explorer Browser.
InfoCube	Central data container for queries and evaluations. InfoCubes contain two types of data, namely key figures and characteristics.
	An InfoCube is a number of relational tables, put together according to the star schema: a large fact table in the center, surrounded by several dimension tables. The fact table is set up in order to save all key figures on the lowest level of detail while the dimension tables are used to save the characteristics that are required both in reporting and in the evaluations of these key figures. Dimension tables are independent of one another. Only the fact table connects the dimensions with the key figures; therefore all of the data is stored multi-dimensionally in the InfoCubes.
InfoObject	Generic term in the Business Information Warehouse for characteristics and key figures. InfoObjects are used in InfoCubes when referring to structures relevant to the data request (extract structure, transfer structure and communication structure). InfoObjects can only be named once. A distinction is made between time and unit characteristics. Examples of characteristics include evaluation groups such as cost centers or product groups.
	Key figures are currency, quantity or number fields such as sales revenue, or number of employees. Key figures usually refer to unit InfoObjects.
InfoPackage	Describes which data in an InfoSource should be requested from a source system so that data can be precisely selected using selection parameters (for example, only controlling area 001 in period 10.1997). An InfoPackage can request transaction data, attributes, or hierarchies for master data.

Appendix C: Glossary

InfoPackage Group

InfoPackages that logically belong together are summarized in an InfoPackage group. The InfoPackages of an InfoPackage group can be requested at the same time.

For example, an InfoPackage group could contain the following three InfoPackages:

- InfoPackage 1: Cost centers: Costs and allocations (transaction data)
- InfoPackage 2: Cost centers: Statistical key figures (transaction data)
- InfoPackage 3: Text on cost centers (text)

Information Structure

Structure in which data is collected in the Logistics Information System. An information structure defines a group of fields. It is used for the collection and reduction of data from an operative application (for example, sales or purchasing). Data relating to events in the operative applications (such as purchase orders or sales orders) is updated periodically in the information structures. Information structures form the basis for analyses and evaluations.

An information structure consists of:

- Characteristics: Dimensions of your business for which you collect data (also the aggregation or subtotal levels. Examples include sales organization, purchasing organization, plant, sold-to party, and vendor.
- A period unit: Used for aggregating data stored in the information structure. The period unit can be daily, weekly, monthly, or by fiscal period.
- Key figures: Measure of the business data you are collecting. Examples include invoiced sales value, PO order quantity, and goods receipt quantity.

InfoSource

The InfoSource represents a provider structure. Data (that logically belongs together from a business point of view) that can be transported from the source system into the SAP Business Information Warehouse, is grouped in one InfoSource. Each InfoSource is assigned to one R/3 application component or one external system. Transfer structures and communication structures are generated from the InfoSource.

Interactive Reporting

Screen-based evaluation technique. You can create reports ranging from highly aggregated to very detailed forms by using menus. In addition, you can access data across applications.

Key Figure

A value which you can report on. There are two types of key figures:

- The simplest form is a numerical value field stored in a database table. This type is called a basic key figure.
- You can also calculate key figures within a report using formulas or rules for computing other values. This type is called a calculated key figure.

Legacy System

Typically refers to a mainframe system that has been in place in an organization for a significant period of time. The term is also used to mean any computer system existing in an organization for any period of time, which is scheduled to be a source system for a Data Warehouse.

Appendix C: Glossary

Logistics Information Library	In the Logistics Information Library (LIL), all key figures available in the Logistics Information System (LIS) are systematically cataloged and organized in accordance with application-specific criteria.
Logistics Information System	The Logistics Information System is made up of the following information systems: ▸ Sales Information System ▸ Purchasing Information System ▸ Inventory Controlling ▸ Shop Floor Information System ▸ Plant Maintenance Information System ▸ Quality Management Information System ▸ Warehouse Management Information System ▸ Retail Information System ▸ Service Management Information System The information systems in LIS can be used to plan, control, and monitor business events at different stages in the decision-making process. They are flexible tools for collecting, aggregating and analyzing data from the operative applications. The level of detail in which information is displayed is freely definable. Informative key figures enable you to continually control target criteria and react in time to exceptional situations. Data can be analyzed using either standard analyses or flexible analyses. Flexible planning, the Early Warning System, and the Logistics Information Library are also integrated in the information systems. Tools are available in Customizing which enable you to create a self-defined information system and tailor it to specific requirements.
Matchcode	Comparison key. Allows you to locate the key of a particular database record (e.g. the account number) by entering information contained in the record. The system then displays a list of records matching the specifications.
Meta Data	Data about data. Meta data describes the origin, history, and other aspects of the data. The information stored in the SAP Business Information Warehouse can be effectively used for reporting and analysis via the meta data. There are two different classes of meta data: technical and business-oriented.
Meta Data Repository	Contains the various classes of meta data. Saving and presenting the data in this way results in a consistent and homogenous data model across all source systems.
MM	Materials Management.
MOLAP	Multi-Dimensional On-Line Analytical Processing (OLAP).
NFS	Network File System. Allows files of another computer to be accessed and enables communication between programs on different computers.

Appendix C: Glossary

Normalization of data	Process of reducing a complex data structure into its simplest, most stable structure. In general, the process entails the removal of redundant attributes, keys, and relationships from a conceptual data model.
ODS	See Operational Data Store.
OLAP	On-Line Anaytical Processing (OLAP) software is used to analyze summarized On-Line Transaction Processing (OLTP) data. Allows multidimensional views and analysis of that data for decision support processes.
OLTP	On-Line Transaction Processing (OLTP) is used for operational data, for example, data in the R/3 software.
Open Information Warehouse	Unifies the various information systems of the R/3 System into a single system. You can use the OIW to gain an overview of the various information units ("info objects") in the R/3 System and to combine particularly relevant information units into queries.
	The OIW obtains answers to queries without requiring you to understand the access paths involved in the R/3 System. To use the OIW for data retrieval, you do not need any knowledge of the tables, programs, reports or information systems, etc., which are held in the system. These structures only show up as meta data (i.e. data about data) in the OIW Catalog.
Operational Data Store	An integrated database that contains a copy of extracted data from source systems.
PA	Profitability Analysis.
PM	Plant Maintenance.
PP	Production Planning.
Primary Key	Key field or group of fields which form the unique identification of a record (a line) in a table.
QM	Quality Management.
Query Template	Components of a query (normally structures) that are saved for reuse in the InfoCube.
	You define a query template if you wish to use certain selection criteria in various queries. As a rule you define the structures as query templates. Structures are freely definable evaluations that consist of combinations of characteristics and basic key figures (for example, as calculated or restricted key figures) of the InfoCubes. A structure can, for example, be a plan / actual comparison or a contribution margin.
RDBMS	Relational Database Management System.

Report	An executable program that reads and evaluates data in the database, and then displays the results of the evaluation. Typically, a report will not allow manipulation of data.
	You can either display the output of a report on the screen or send it to a printer. You can also save it and display it as often as you like giving greater flexibility and minimizing the time spent reading large volumes of data.
Report Group	Group of reports which use the same library. Reports that read the same data can be grouped together in report groups to optimize processing times.
Report Painter	Tool for creating reports that meet specific business and reporting requirements. Report Painter enables the user to report on data from multiple applications. Report Painter uses a graphical report structure, forming the basis for report definition which also corresponds to the final structure of the report.
	The R/3 System is delivered with several row and column models that can be used as 'building blocks' to help the user create reports quickly and simply. The backbone of the Report Painter is the Report Writer tool.
Report Selection	Hierarchical structure of reports. Users create their own "views" of their report selection.
Report / Report Interface	Allows you to call a receiver report from a sender report in the information system. When you select the desired data in the sender report, corresponding characteristic values are sent to the receiver report via this interface and included in the data selection. The report/report interface is commonly used in the Report Painter/Report Writer and drilldown reporting tools.
Report Variant	Set of criteria that determine the content of a report. A report variant lets you determine which rows, texts, and columns the system displays when you call up a report.
Report Writer	Tool for creating reports that meet specific business and reporting requirements. The graphical user interface created for the Report Writer is the Report Painter. Report Writer enables the user to report on data from multiple applications. Using functions such as sets, variables, formulas, cells and key figures, the user can create complex reports that meet specific reporting requirements. When working with Report Writer, the user can use the following functions that are not supported by Report Painter:
	▸ Multidimensional column structures
	▸ User-defined definition of inactive row/column combinations
	▸ Enhanced functionality for using cells in column formulas
RFC	Remote Function Call. RFC is an SAP interface protocol. Based on CPI-C, it simplifies the programming of communication processes between systems. RFCs enable you to call and execute predefined functions in a remote system—or even in the same system. RFCs manage communication processes, parameter transfer and error handling.

Appendix C: Glossary

Scheduler ♦	Connection between source systems and InfoCubes. With the Scheduler you determine which data is to be requested from the source system and at which point in time. The Scheduler relies on the functionality of R/3 background processing. The data request can either be started at once, as a background job, or automatically at a later date.
SD	Sales and Distribution.
Selection criteria	Fields used to define the type and amount of information to be processed by a report. Each report list is generated using the report's own specific group of selection criteria.
SM	Service Management.
Star Schema ♦	Data structure that combines fact tables and dimension tables in a way that provides easy and efficient access to data.
Structured Query Language (SQL)	Query language developed by IBM to facilitate access to relational databases. SQL has two types of statements: DDL (data definition language) statements and DML (data manipulation language) statements.
Table	Array of data in matrix form. Consists of columns (data values of the same type) and rows (data records). Each record can be identified uniquely by one or several fields.
TCP/IP	Transmission Control Protocol/Internet Protocol. Software protocol developed for communication between computers.
Transaction	Logical process in the R/3 System. From the user's point of view, a transaction is a self-contained unit (e.g., generate a list of customers, change the address of a customer, book a flight reservation for a customer, and execute a program). In terms of dialog programming, it is a complex object consisting of a module pool and screens, and is called with a transaction code.
	After logon, there are three distinct levels—the main menu level, the application level, and the task level. A transaction is a task performed at the task level. To execute a transaction from the main menu level, navigate through the menus by choosing the appropriate menu options or specify the appropriate transaction code in the command field and go directly to the task level. Example: Suppose you want to maintain or execute a program in the ABAP/4 Development Workbench. To access the first screen of the task from the main menu level, proceed through the menus by selecting *Tools → ABAP/4 Workbench → ABAP/4 Editor*, or enter the transaction code *SE38* in the command field.
Transfer Structure ♦	Data from an InfoSource is transported into a Business Information Warehouse system and passed on to the communication structure using transfer rules.
	Technically (i.e., with respect to length and type) fields of the transfer structure correspond to the InfoSource fields of the Business Information Warehouse.

Appendix C: Glossary

Update rules	Help to define updating in detail depending upon the information structure and update group. Update rules consist of the source field, the event that will trigger (i.e., creation of a sales document) the update, requirements and formulas (if needed). Once you have defined the update rules, the corresponding update programs are automatically generated.
Once defined, activate the update in a separate step.
The creation of update rules, the generation of the update programs, and the eventual activation of the update are separate steps for security reasons.
User Exits	Points in the R/3 System where a customer's own program can be called. In contrast to customer exits, user exits allow developers to access program components and data objects in the standard system. On upgrade, each user exit must be checked to ensure that it conforms to the standard system.
There are two types of user exit:
- User exits that use includes. These are customer enhancements that are called from the program.
- User exits that use tables. These are used and managed directly via Customizing.
Variant	A group of selection criteria values that have been saved. Variants allow users to "recall" predefined selection criteria without having to reenter all the values each time a report is run. A report can have several different variants, with each variant retrieving different types of information. For example, a vendor report might have one variant to retrieve information on U.S. vendors and another variant for Asian vendors.
WM	Warehouse Management.
Web Reporting	Web RFC application that allows Internet users to access business information in the R/3 System. By clicking on URLs in web pages, Internet users can execute R/3 System reports or custom reports, display pregenerated lists, and browse report trees. Web Reporting has interactive capabilities.

Index

A

Account balances, general ledger, 1–12
Accounts list, general ledger, 1–2
Accounts payable reports
    vendor balances in local currency, 3–6
    vendor open items lists, 3–2
Accounts receivable reports
    customer balances in local currency, 2–19
    customer open item analysis, 2–2
    customer open items lists, 2–14
    information system, 2–8
Actual comparison, profitability analysis, 6–2
Actual costs
    cost center summaries, 4–2, 4–37
    cost center summaries by period and year-to-date, 4–31
    cost element reporting, 13–5
    internal order summaries, 5–2
Aging, accounts receivable. *See* Open items, analysis

B

Backorders
    processing, 12–51
    sales and distribution, 9–13
Balance displays
    internal order lists, 5–33
Balance sheets
    general ledger, 1–16
Bill of materials (BOMs)
    multi-level, 12–39
Billings
    listing all or open, 9–38
Budget reporting
    budget vs. plan/actual/commitments, 13–9

C

Capacity planning evaluation, 12–56
CO/FI reconciliation
    group currency, 7–13
Collective display, MRP list, 12–22
Company codes
    cross-company code reconciliation, 7–27
    FI/CO reconciliation, 7–2
Cost center reports
    displaying line items, 4–18
    planned and actual costs by period and year-to-date, 4–31
    summarizing planned costs, actual costs, and variances, 4–2
    summarizing target costs, actual costs, and variances, 4–37
Cost element reporting
    displaying order cost elements, 11–6
    planned vs. actual, 13–5
Cross-company code reconciliation, 7–27
Customer analysis, 6–14
Customers
    balances in local currency, 2–19
    open item analysis, 2–2
    open items lists, 2–14

D

Deliveries
    listing all or open, 9–50
Document analysis
    billings, 9–38
    listing deliveries, 9–50
    sales orders, 9–29

E

Empty storage bins, 15–18
Entries reports, 8–21
Equal employment opportunity report (EEO-1), 8–16

F

FI/CO reconciliation
    company codes, 7–2

G

General ledger reports
    account balances, 1–12
    accounts list, 1–2
    balance sheet/P+L, 1–16
    line items, 1–7
Group currency
    CO/FI reconciliation, 7–13

H

Headcount report, 8–2
Human resources reports
    entries reports, 8–21
    equal employment opportunity report (EEO-1), 8–16

Index

new hire report, 8–11
payroll journal, 8–6
staffing level development report, 8–2
withdrawals reports, 8–21

I

Incomplete sales documents, 9–34
Information systems
    accounts receivable, 2–8
    missing parts, 12–44
    shop floor, 12–27
Inspection lots
    selection, 14–9
    without completion, 14–2
    without usage decision, 14–6
Internal order reports
    balance displays, 5–33
    displaying actual line items, 5–17
    summarizing planned costs, actual cost,
        and variances, 5–2
Invoiced sales report, 9–43

L

Line items
    displaying actual, 5–17
    displaying for cost centers, 4–18
    general ledger, 1–7
Local currency
    customer balances, 2–19
    vendor balances, 3–6

M

Materials
    displaying purchase order lists, 10–6
    material documents, 10–14
    stock list, 15–7
Materials management reports
    displaying purchase order lists, material or vendor, 10–6
    displaying purchase requisitions list, 10–21
    material documents for material, 10–14
    stock overview, 10–2
Missing parts info system, 12–44
MRP list, collective display, 12–22

N

New hire reports, 8–11
Notification tasks lists, 11–2

O

Open items
    analysis, customers, 2–2
    list of customers, 2–14

    list of vendors, 3–2
Order cost element, displaying, 11–6
Orders
    incoming sales order report, 9–22
    incoming sales orders for customers and materials, 9–29

P

P+L
    general ledger, 1–16
Payroll journals, 8–6
Plan comparison, profitability analysis, 6–2
Planned costs
    cost center summaries, 4–2
    cost center summaries by period and year-to-date, 4–31
    cost element reporting, 13–5
    project cost reporting, 13–2
Plant maintenance reports
    notification tasks lists, 11–2
    order cost element Display, 11–6
Posting change notices, 15–11
Product analysis, 6–14
Production order overview, 12–12
Production planning reports
    backorder processing, 12–51
    capacity planning evaluation, 12–56
    missing parts info system, 12–44
    MRP list, collective display, 12–22
    multi-level BOMs, 12–39
    production order overview, 12–12
    shop floor info system, 12–27
    stock/requirements list, 12–2
Profitability analysis reports
    plan/actual comparison, 6–2
    sales plan/contribution margin, 6–27
    SBU/Product/Customer Analysis, 6–14
Project cost reporting
    planned/actual/variance, 13–2
Project system reports
    budget reporting, 13–9
    cost element reporting, planned vs. actual, 13–5
    project cost reporting, planned/actual/variance, 13–2
Purchase orders
    displaying lists of material or vendor, 10–6
Purchase requisitions
    displaying list, 10–21

Q

Quality management reports
    inspection lot selection, 14–9
    inspection lots without completion, 14–2
    inspection lots without usage decision, 14–6

R

Reconciliation reports

Index

company code currency, 7–2
cross-company code, 7–27
group currency, 7–13

S

Sales and distribution reports
   backorders, 9–13
   blocked sales orders, 9–7
   incoming order report, 9–22
   incoming orders for customers and materials, 9–29
   incomplete sales documents, 9–34
   invoiced sales report, 9–43
   listing billings, 9–38
   listing deliveries, 9–50
   sales orders lists, 9–2
   shipping report, 9–56
Sales contribution margin, 6–27
Sales documents
   incomplete, 9–34
Sales orders
   blocked, 9–7
   incoming for customers and materials, 9–29
   incoming order report, 9–22
   lists, 9–2
Sales plan margin, 6–27
Sales reports
   invoiced, 9–43
SBU analysis, 6–14
Shipping reports, 9–56
Shop floor info system, 12–27
SIS Statistical Analysis
   incoming order reports, 9–22
   shipping reports, 9–56
Staffing level development report, 8–2

Statistical analysis
   invoiced sales reports, 9–43
   sales orders, 9–29
Stock list, materials, 15–7
Stock overview
   materials management, 10–2
   warehouse management, 15–2
Stock/requirements list, 12–2
Storage bins, empty, 15–18

T

Target costs
   cost center summaries, 4–37

V

Variances
   cost center summaries, 4–2, 4–37
   internal order summaries, 5–2
Vendors
   balances in local currency, 3–6
   displaying purchase order lists, 10–6
   open items lists, 3–2

W

Warehouse management reports
   empty storage bins, 15–18
   list of posting change notices, 15–11
   material stock list, 15–7
   stock overview, 15–2
Withdrawals reports, 8–21

… fatbrain.com {*}

SAP R/3 Made Easy Guidebook™ Order Form

For a faster turnaround, visit **www.amazon.com** or **www.fatbrain.com/sap** and order online!
If you do not have access to the Internet, you can order the SAP R/3 Made Easy Guidebooks by completing and faxing this form to fatbrain.com

- Fax: +1 408.752.9919 (U.S. Number)
- Phone: 800.789.8590 or +1.408.752.9910 (U.S. Number)
- E-mail: orders@fatbrain.com

Ship To Information (* indicates required information)

Company*: _____ Phone*: _____
Contact Name*: _____ Fax: _____
Address*: _____ E-Mail: _____
_____

Order Information

Item	Release	ISBN	Price	Qty.	Total
Authorizations Made Easy	☐ 4.5A/B	1-893570-23-1	$46.00 each	x _____	= $ _____
	☐ 4.0B	1-893570-22-3	$46.00 each	x _____	= $ _____
	☐ 3.1G/H	1-893570-21-5	$46.00 each	x _____	= $ _____
Data Transfer Made Easy (English)	☐ 4.0B/4.5x	1-893570-04-5	$32.00 each	x _____	= $ _____
	☐ 3.1G/H	1-893570-02-9	$45.00 each	x _____	= $ _____
	☐ 3.0F	1-893570-01-0	$41.00 each	x _____	= $ _____
Data Transfer Made Easy (German)	☐ 4.0B/4.5x	1-893570-05-3	$32.00 each	x _____	= $ _____
MRP Strategies Made Easy	☐ 3.0D–3.1I	1-893570-81-9	$36.00 each	x _____	= $ _____
The Preconfigured Client Guide (U.S.) (two-volume set)	☐ 4.5B	1-893570-32-0	$88.00 per set	x _____	= $ _____
	☐ 4.0B	1-893570-31-2	$71.00 per set	x _____	= $ _____
SAPscript Made Easy (formerly *Printout Design Made Easy*)	☐ 4.0B	1-893570-13-4	$45.00 each	x _____	= $ _____
	☐ 3.1H	1-893570-12-6	$45.00 each	x _____	= $ _____
	☐ 3.0F	1-893570-11-8	$41.00 each	x _____	= $ _____
Product Costing Made Easy	☐ 3.x–4.x	1-893570-82-7	$30.00 each	x _____	= $ _____
System Administration Made Easy (1 book for 4.0B; two-volume set for 3.1H)	☐ 4.0B	1-893570-42-8	$51.00 each	x _____	= $ _____
	☐ 3.1H	1-893570-41-X	$84.00 per set	x _____	= $ _____
Reporting Made Easy (three-volume set)	☐ 4.0B	1-893570-65-7	$99.00 per set	x _____	= $ _____

Prices and availability are subject to change without notice.

Shipping Information

	First Item	Each Add'l Item	Total
Shipping in the **Continental United States**			
☐ Expedited (normally 2-3 business days)	$3.00	$1.95	= $
☐ Second Day Air (2 business days)	$6.00	$1.95	= $
☐ Overnight (1 business day)	$7.00	$2.95	= $
☐ Overnight for Saturday delivery	$16.00	$3.95	= $
☐ Standard (normally 3-7 business days)	$3.00	$0.95	= $_____

For all other locations, please call, email, or check www.fatbrain.com/shipping.html for shipping prices
(International Taxes, VAT and Tariffs NOT included) $

Sales Tax – California (8.25%) and Kentucky (6.0%) residents **only** $

TOTAL in US $ $_____

Shipping prices are subject to change without notice.

Payment Information (Please select one)

☐ Visa ☐ MasterCard ☐ American Express ☐ Discover Card ☐ Diner's Club

Card # _____ Exp. Date _____ Signature _____

amazon.com   fatbrain.com

SAP R/3 Made Easy Guidebooks™

Have you been looking for SAP documentation that explains complex topics in an easy-to-understand manner with step-by-step procedures and plenty of screenshots? If so, then the R/3 Made Easy guidebook series is for you. Discover what over 27,000 other guidebook readers have discovered—the R/3 Made Easy guidebooks, the perfect accessories to simplify SAP installations.

To order the R/3 Made Easy guidebooks, visit www.amazon.com or www.fatbrain.com/sap and order online, or use the form on the back of this brochure if you don't have access to the Internet.

Authorizations Made Easy

Written for SAP consultants and customers, this guidebook helps you set up the authorization concept in the R/3 System. Using step-by-step instructions, it shows how to use the Profile Generator during and after the implementation.

Release 4.5A/B $46.00
         4.0B $46.00
         3.1G/H $46.00

Data Transfer Made Easy

When performing data transfer from legacy systems to the R/3 System, this guidebook is particularly useful. The most common data transfer programs are covered with step-by-step details about how to use them.

Release 4.0B/4.5x $32.00
available in English and German
         3.1G/H $45.00
         3.0F $41.00

SAPscript Made Easy

This guidebook helps reduce consulting time in development and modification of SAPscript forms. It explains in an intuitive manner how to adapt forms quicker and more efficiently by using the new graphical WYSIWYG-based tools Form Painter and PC Editor.

Release 4.0B $45.00
         3.1H $45.00
         3.0F $41.00

Reporting Made Easy

The *R/3 Reporting Made Easy* guidebook series explains the nuts-and-bolts of R/3 reporting concepts and development tools. Book 1 introduces the basics of reporting, book 2 helps you understand the report development tools, and book 3 offers examples of commonly used reports.

Release 4.0B $99.00
(Three-volume set)

System Administration Made Easy

The most commonly performed system administration tasks are explained step-by-step in this guidebook. Eighty percent of the book is operation system or database-independent; the rest covers Oracle on Unix and Windows NT.

Release 4.0B (1 vol) $51.00
         3.1H (2 vol) $84.00

The Preconfigured Client Guide

The Preconfigured Client (PCC) gives customers a head start at configuration by providing a U.S.-oriented environment in which business processes run "out of the box." This two-book set describes the PCC and the Computer-aided test tools (CATTs) Procedures.

Release 4.5B $88.00
         4.0B $71.00

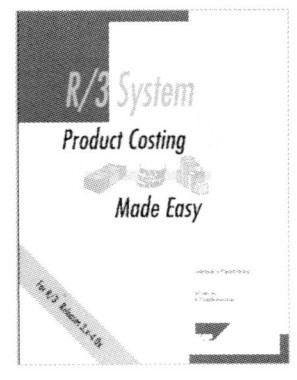

Product Costing Made Easy

This consultant's guide describes cost flows through various R/3 manufacturing processes. Graphical overviews precede the step-by-step analysis of each scenario.

Release 3.x–4.x $30.00

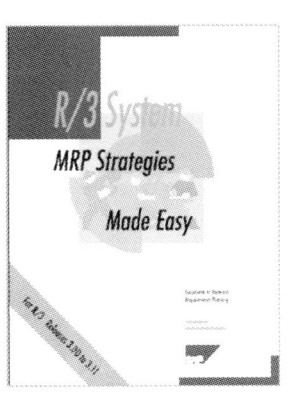

MRP Strategies Made Easy

This guidebook serves as a consultant's guide to using various strategy groups in R/3's PP module. Topics covered include strategies for make-to-stock and make-to order production, planning components, and production with variant configuration.

Release 3.0D–3.1I $36.00

Electronic guidebook files are also included in AcceleratedSAP. For additional information on other R/3 implementation accelerators, visit www.saplabs.com/simple

SAP